Withdrawn

01

FULLMETAL EDITION

FULLMETAL ALCHEMIST

by HIROMU ARAKAWA

01

FULLMETAL EDITION

FULLMETAL ALCHEMIST

by HIROMU ARAKAWA

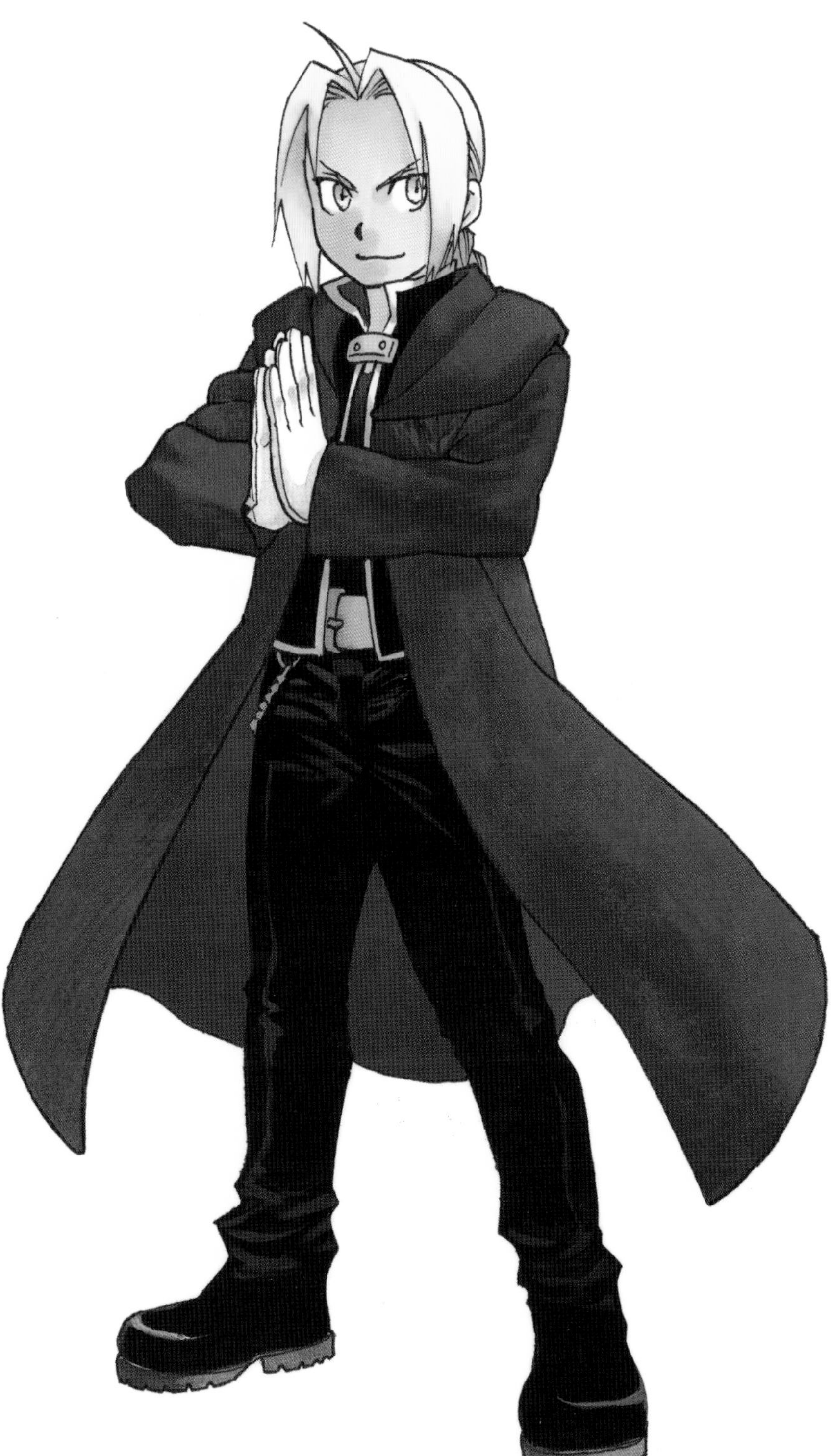

FULLMETAL EDITION

FULLMETAL ALCHEMIST

01
CONTENTS

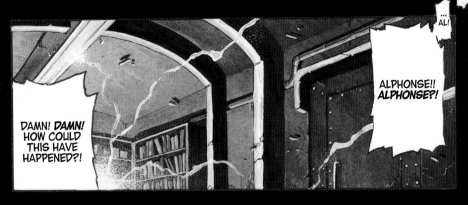

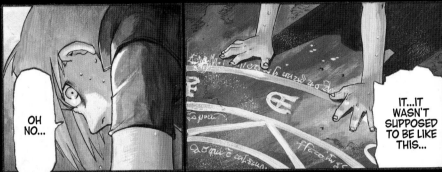

...
... AL!
ALPHONSE!! ALPHONSE?!
DAMN! DAMN! HOW COULD THIS HAVE HAPPENED?!
IT...IT WASN'T SUPPOSED TO BE LIKE THIS...
OH NO...
Teachings that do not speak of pain have no meaning...
HE'S GONE ...!!
...because humankind cannot gain something without first giving something in return.

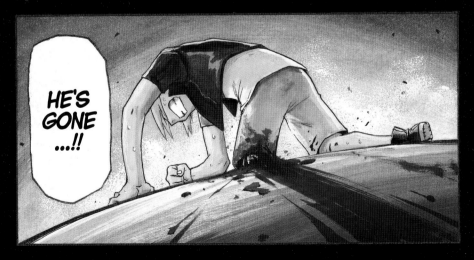

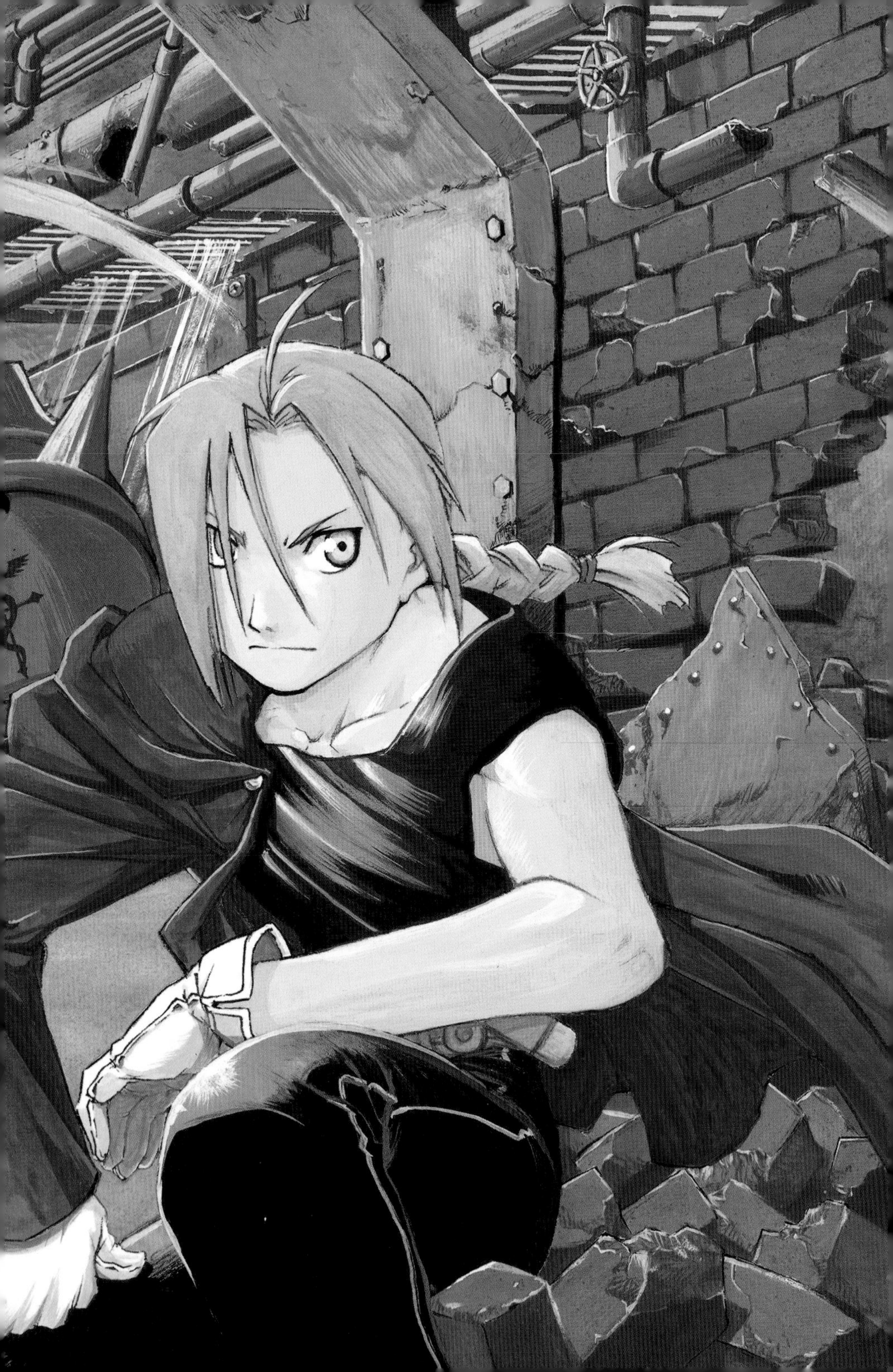

CHAPTER 1
THE TWO ALCHEMISTS

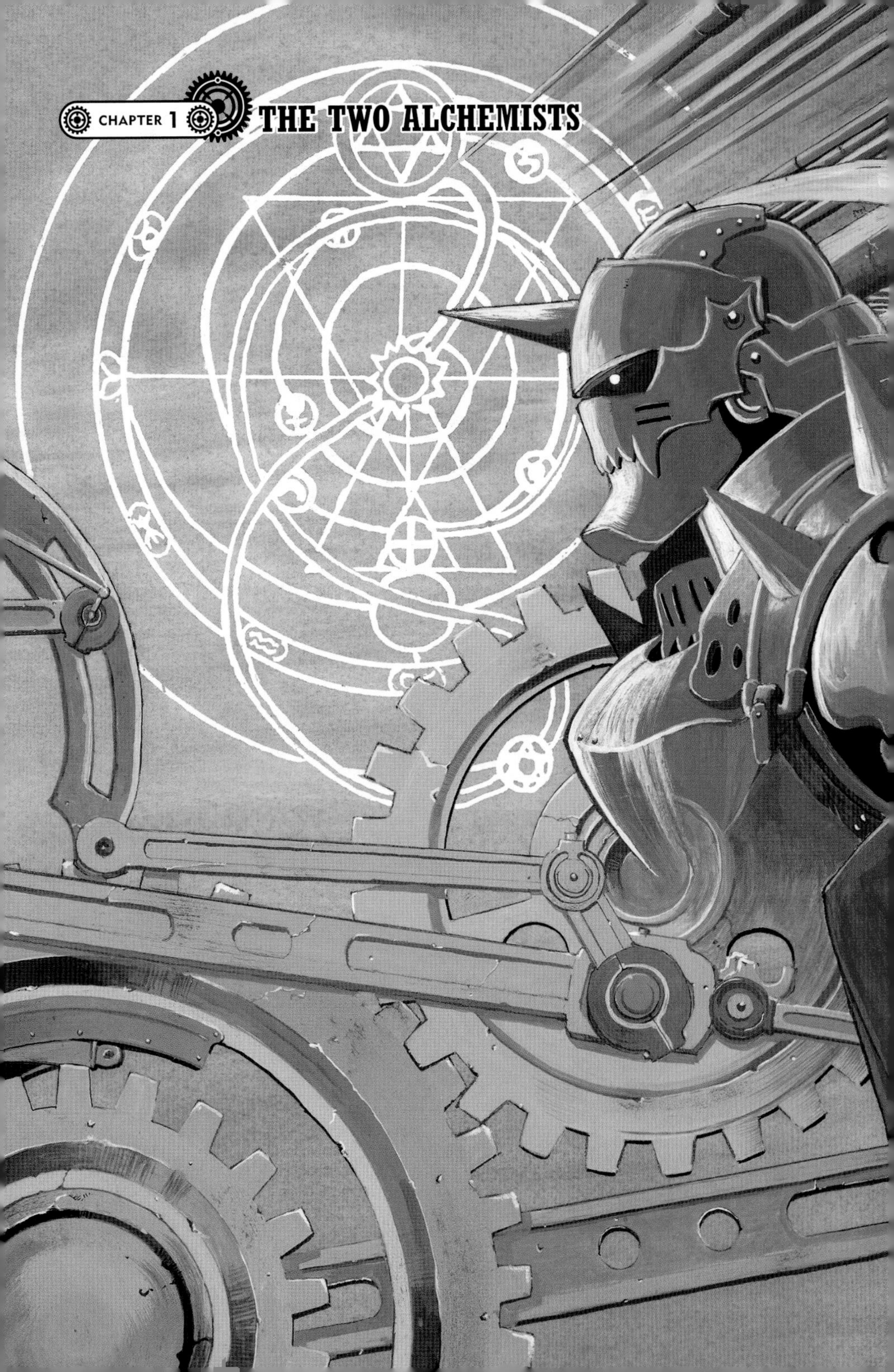

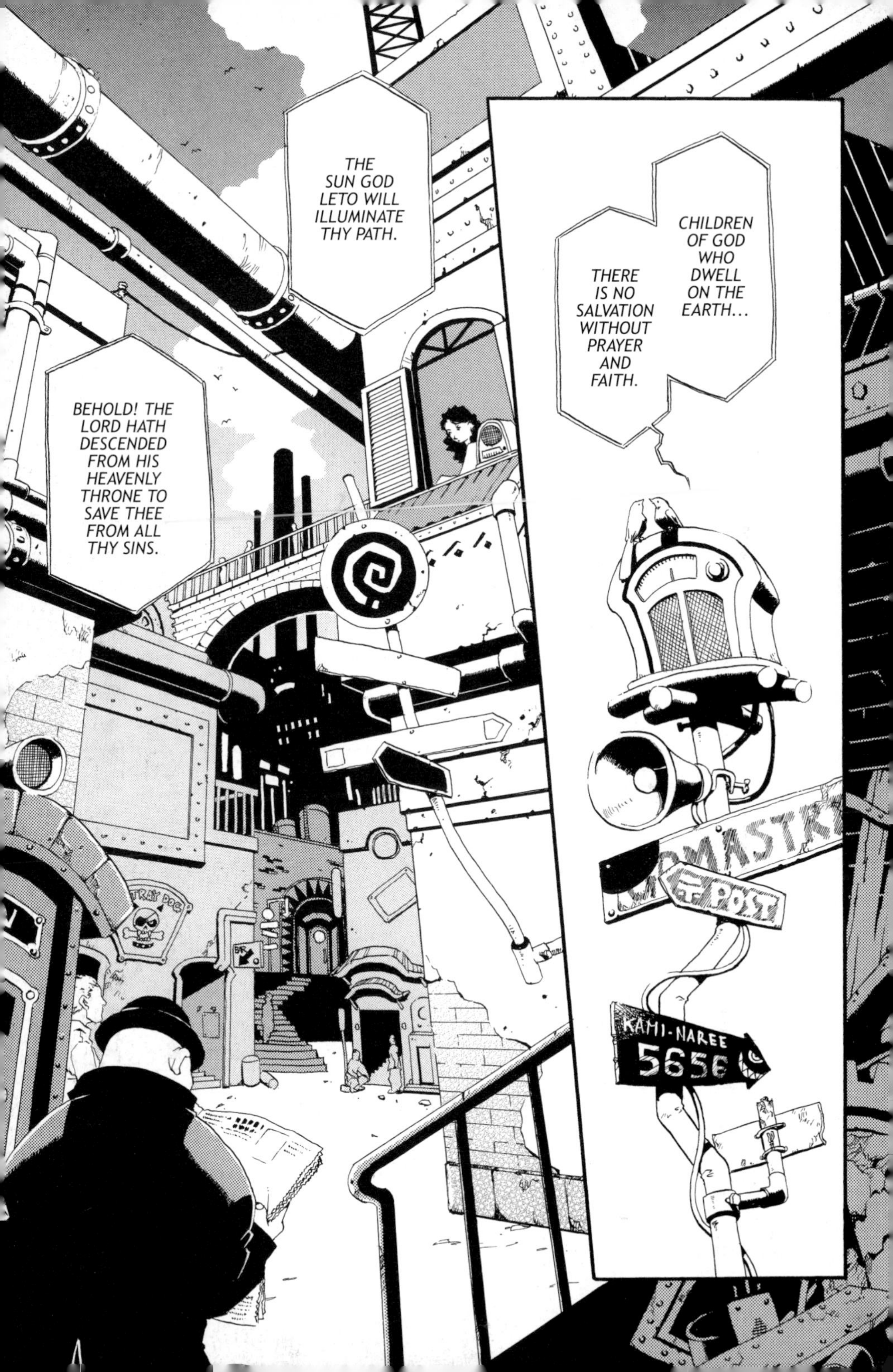
CHILDREN OF GOD WHO DWELL ON THE EARTH...
THERE IS NO SALVATION WITHOUT PRAYER AND FAITH.
KAMI-NAREE
5656
POST
THE SUN GOD LETO WILL ILLUMINATE THY PATH.
BEHOLD! THE LORD HATH DESCENDED FROM HIS HEAVENLY THRONE TO SAVE THEE FROM ALL THY SINS.
BAR

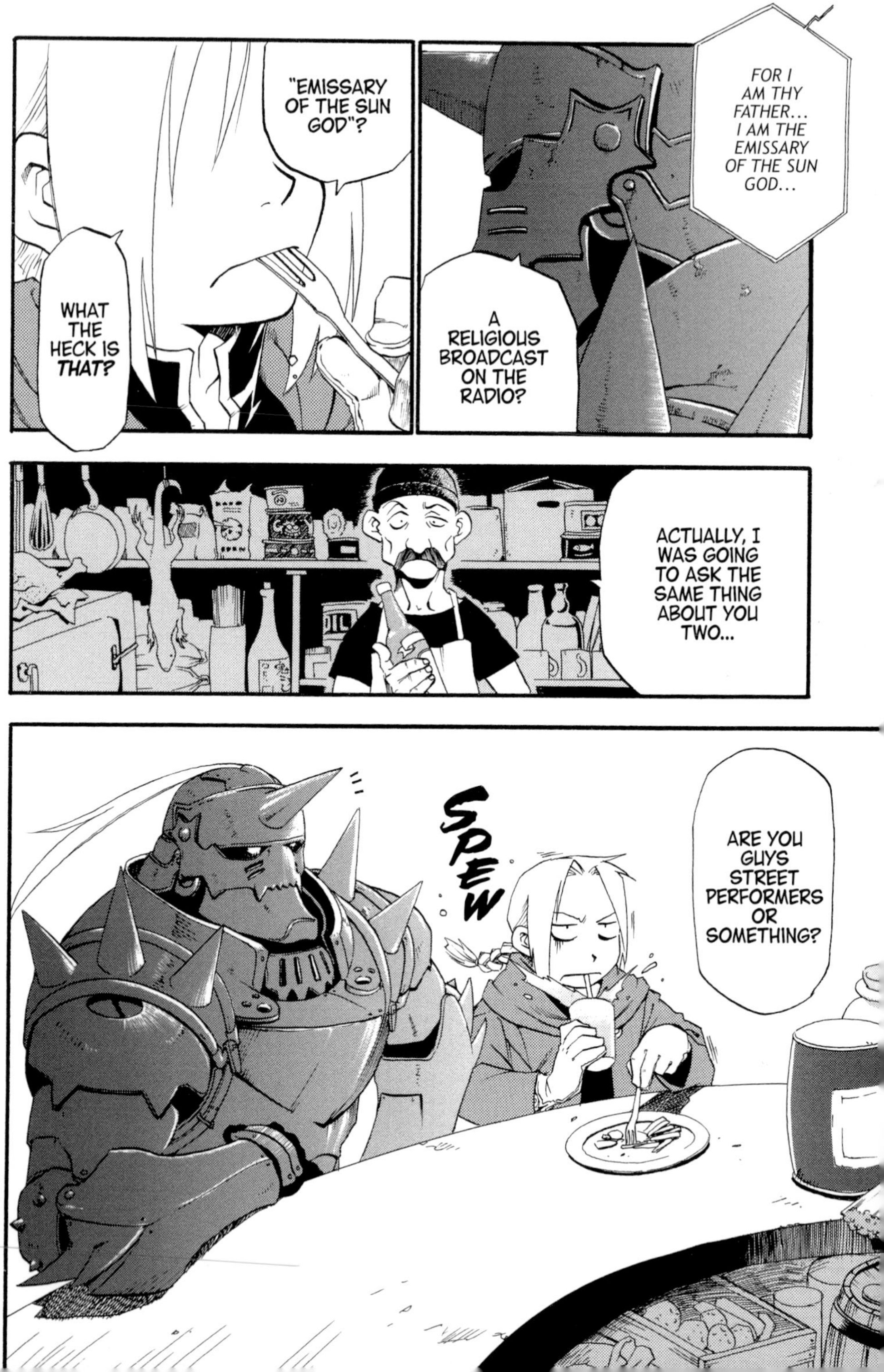
FOR I AM THY FATHER… I AM THE EMISSARY OF THE SUN GOD…
A RELIGIOUS BROADCAST ON THE RADIO?
"EMISSARY OF THE SUN GOD"?
WHAT THE HECK IS *THAT?*
ACTUALLY, I WAS GOING TO ASK THE SAME THING ABOUT YOU TWO...
ARE YOU GUYS STREET PERFORMERS OR SOMETHING?
SPEW

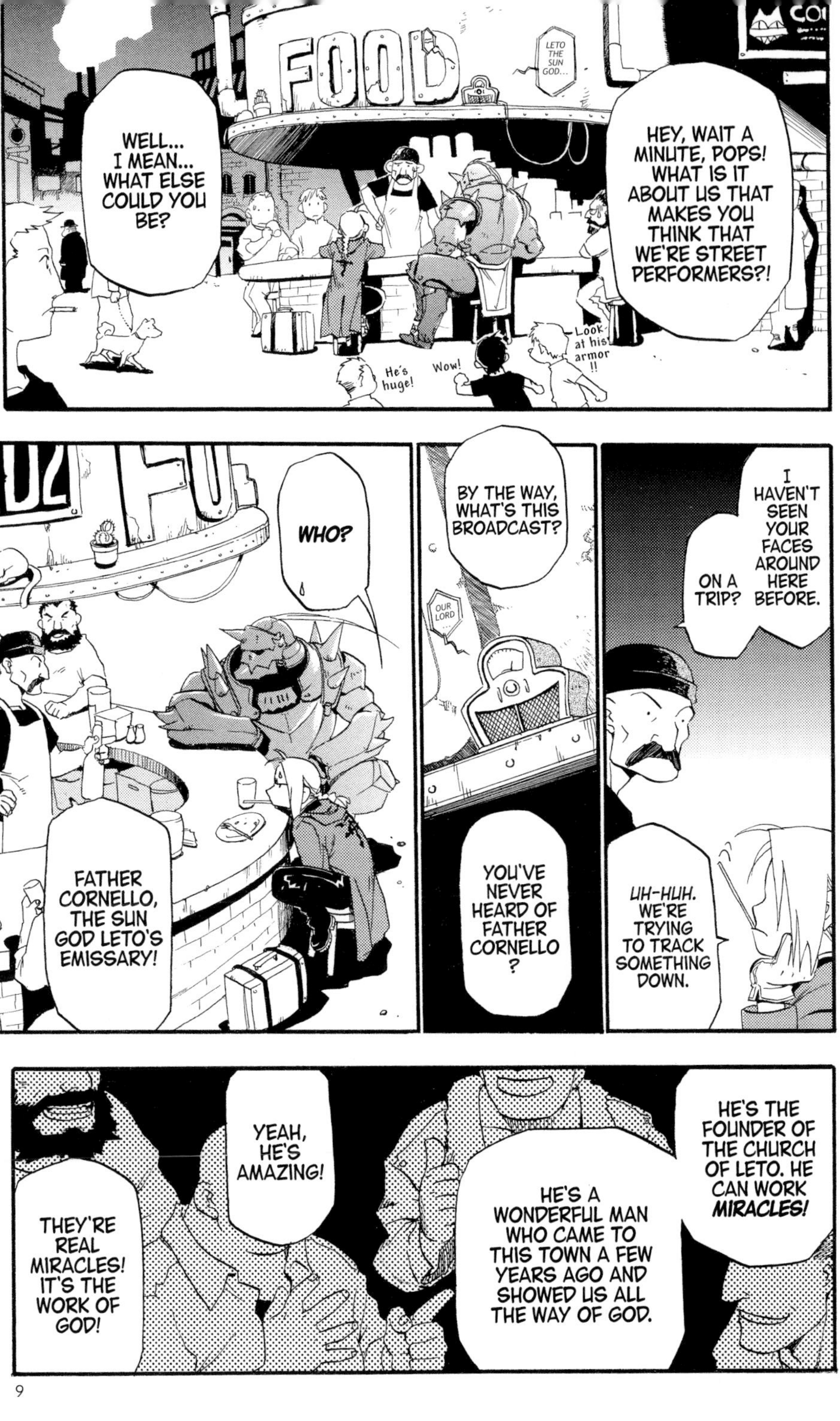
HEY, WAIT A MINUTE, POPS! WHAT IS IT ABOUT US THAT MAKES YOU THINK THAT WE'RE STREET PERFORMERS?!
LETO THE SUN GOD...
FOOD
WELL... I MEAN... WHAT ELSE COULD YOU BE?
Look at his armor !!
Wow!
He's huge!
I HAVEN'T SEEN YOUR FACES AROUND HERE BEFORE.
ON A TRIP?
UH-HUH. WE'RE TRYING TO TRACK SOMETHING DOWN.
BY THE WAY, WHAT'S THIS BROADCAST?
OUR LORD ...
YOU'VE NEVER HEARD OF FATHER CORNELLO?
WHO?
FATHER CORNELLO, THE SUN GOD LETO'S EMISSARY!
HE'S THE FOUNDER OF THE CHURCH OF LETO. HE CAN WORK MIRACLES!
HE'S A WONDERFUL MAN WHO CAME TO THIS TOWN A FEW YEARS AGO AND SHOWED US ALL THE WAY OF GOD.
YEAH, HE'S AMAZING!
THEY'RE REAL MIRACLES! IT'S THE WORK OF GOD!

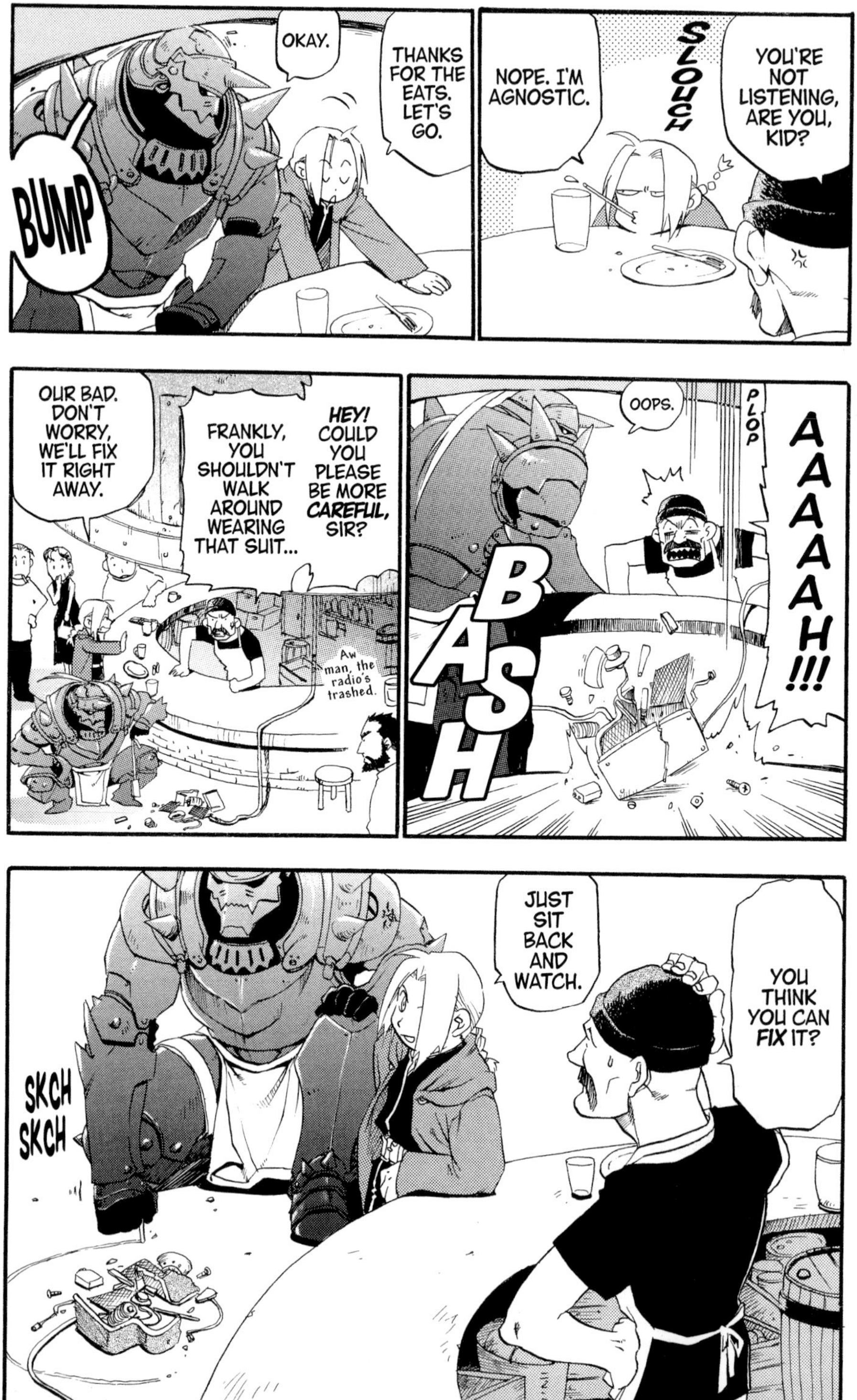
YOU'RE NOT LISTENING, ARE YOU, KID?
SLOUCH
NOPE. I'M AGNOSTIC.
THANKS FOR THE EATS. LET'S GO.
OKAY.
BUMP
AAAAAAH!!!
PLOP
OOPS.
BASH
HEY! COULD YOU PLEASE BE MORE CAREFUL, SIR?
FRANKLY, YOU SHOULDN'T WALK AROUND WEARING THAT SUIT...
OUR BAD. DON'T WORRY, WE'LL FIX IT RIGHT AWAY.
Aw man, the radio's trashed.
YOU THINK YOU CAN FIX IT?
JUST SIT BACK AND WATCH.
SKCH SKCH

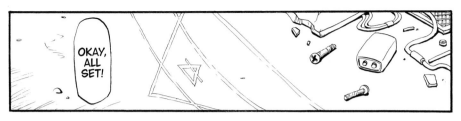

OKAY, ALL SET!

?

HERE WE GO...

WHA...?

AAGH?!

BOOM!!

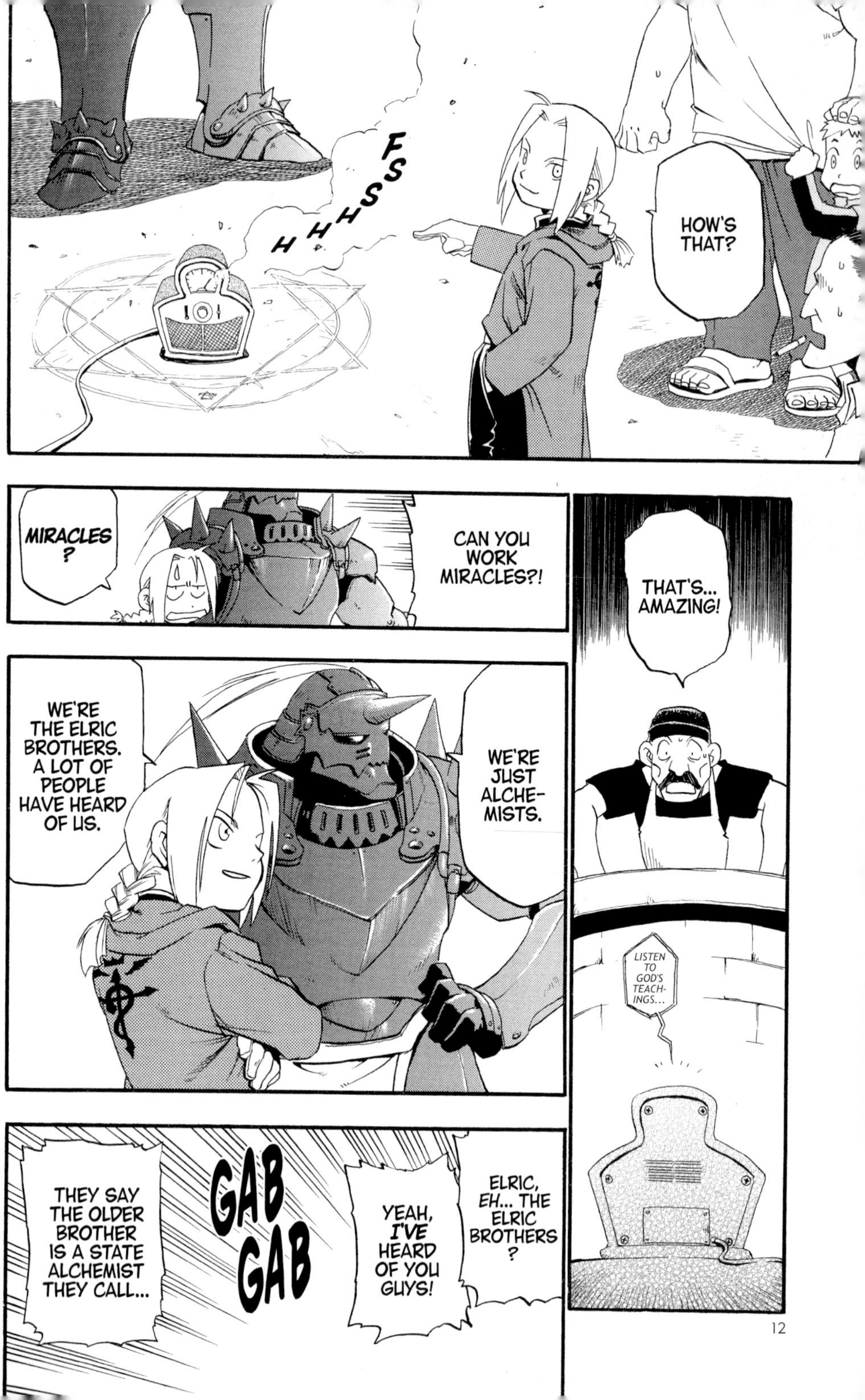
HOW'S THAT?
FSSHHHH
THAT'S... AMAZING!
LISTEN TO GOD'S TEACHINGS...
CAN YOU WORK MIRACLES?!
MIRACLES?
WE'RE JUST ALCHEMISTS.
WE'RE THE ELRIC BROTHERS. A LOT OF PEOPLE HAVE HEARD OF US.
ELRIC, EH... THE ELRIC BROTHERS?
YEAH, *I'VE* HEARD OF YOU GUYS!
GAB GAB
THEY SAY THE OLDER BROTHER IS A STATE ALCHEMIST THEY CALL...

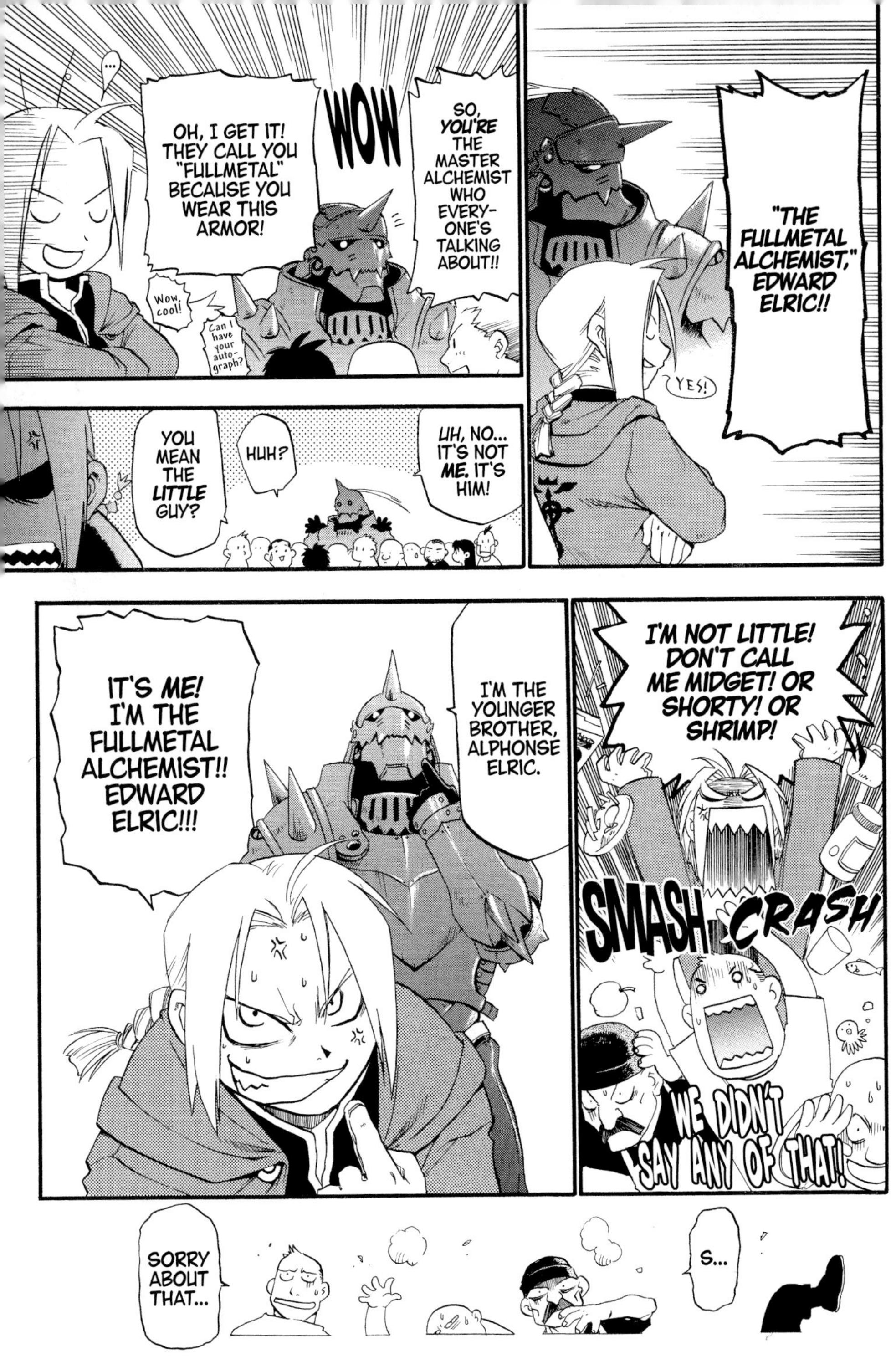
"THE FULLMETAL ALCHEMIST," EDWARD ELRIC!!
YES!
SO, YOU'RE THE MASTER ALCHEMIST WHO EVERY-ONE'S TALKING ABOUT!!
WOW
OH, I GET IT! THEY CALL YOU "FULLMETAL" BECAUSE YOU WEAR THIS ARMOR!
...
Wow, cool!
Can I have your auto-graph?
UH, NO... IT'S NOT ME. IT'S HIM!
HUH?
YOU MEAN THE LITTLE GUY?
I'M NOT LITTLE! DON'T CALL ME MIDGET! OR SHORTY! OR SHRIMP!
SMASH
CRASH
WE DIDN'T SAY ANY OF THAT!!
I'M THE YOUNGER BROTHER, ALPHONSE ELRIC.
IT'S ME! I'M THE FULLMETAL ALCHEMIST!! EDWARD ELRIC!!!
S...
SORRY ABOUT THAT...

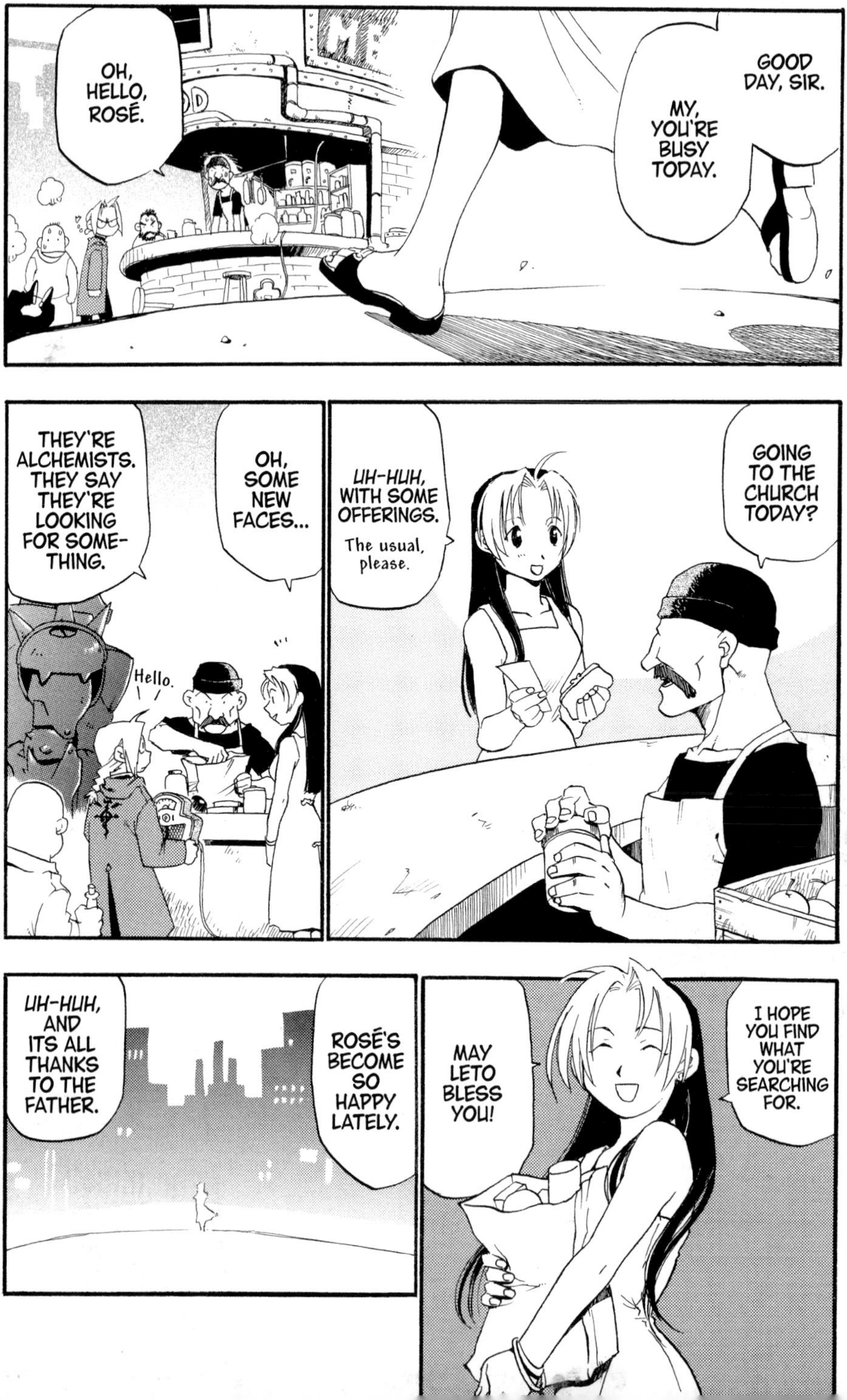
GOOD DAY, SIR.
MY, YOU'RE BUSY TODAY.
OH, HELLO, ROSÉ.
GOING TO THE CHURCH TODAY?
UH-HUH, WITH SOME OFFERINGS.
The usual, please.
OH, SOME NEW FACES...
THEY'RE ALCHEMISTS. THEY SAY THEY'RE LOOKING FOR SOME-THING.
Hello.
I HOPE YOU FIND WHAT YOU'RE SEARCHING FOR.
MAY LETO BLESS YOU!
ROSÉ'S BECOME SO HAPPY LATELY.
UH-HUH, AND ITS ALL THANKS TO THE FATHER.

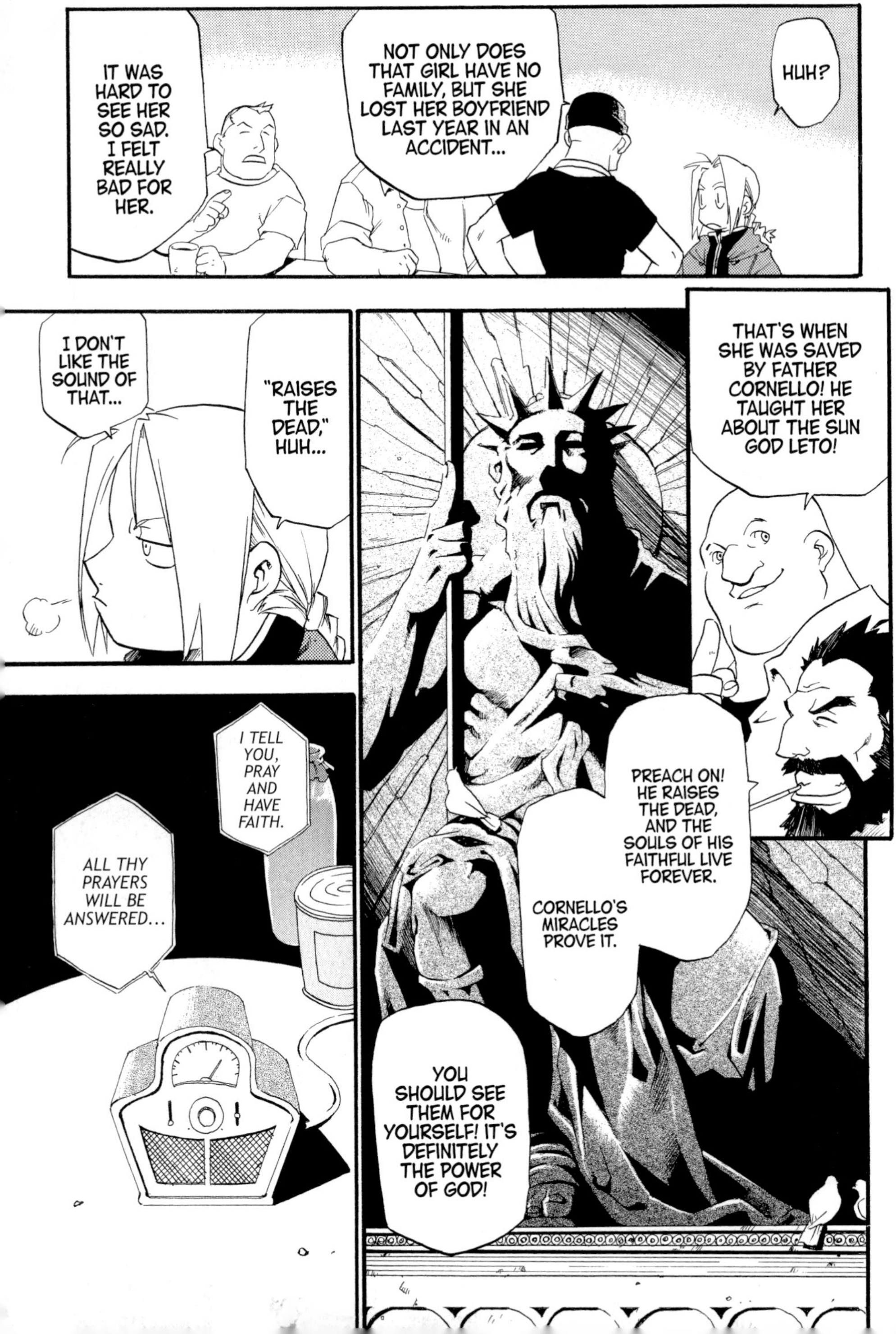
HUH?
NOT ONLY DOES THAT GIRL HAVE NO FAMILY, BUT SHE LOST HER BOYFRIEND LAST YEAR IN AN ACCIDENT...
IT WAS HARD TO SEE HER SO SAD. I FELT REALLY BAD FOR HER.
THAT'S WHEN SHE WAS SAVED BY FATHER CORNELLO! HE TAUGHT HER ABOUT THE SUN GOD LETO!
PREACH ON! HE RAISES THE DEAD, AND THE SOULS OF HIS FAITHFUL LIVE FOREVER.
CORNELLO'S MIRACLES PROVE IT.
YOU SHOULD SEE THEM FOR YOURSELF! IT'S DEFINITELY THE POWER OF GOD!
"RAISES THE DEAD," HUH...
I DON'T LIKE THE SOUND OF THAT...
I TELL YOU, PRAY AND HAVE FAITH.
ALL THY PRAYERS WILL BE ANSWERED...

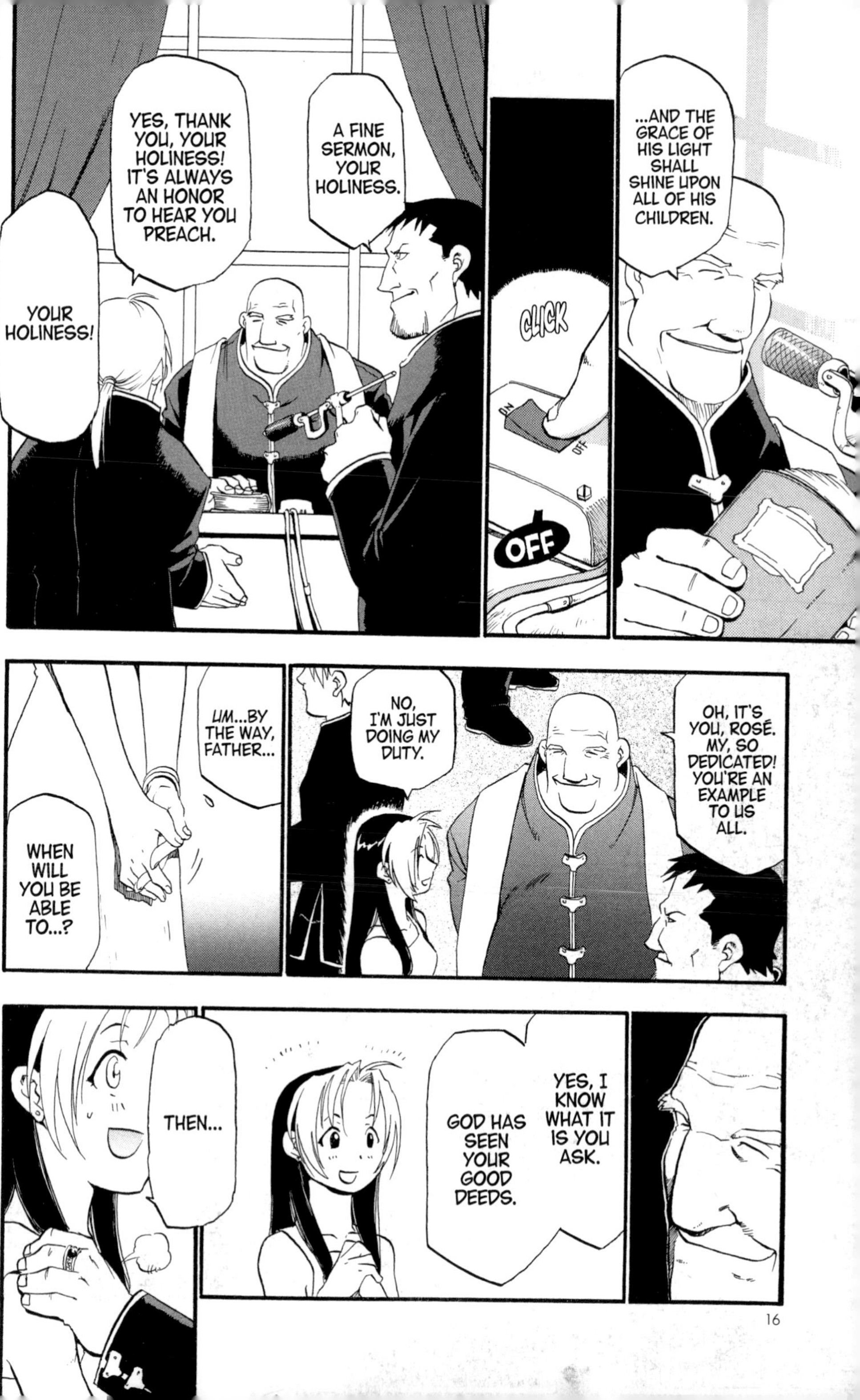
...AND THE GRACE OF HIS LIGHT SHALL SHINE UPON ALL OF HIS CHILDREN.
CLICK
OFF
A FINE SERMON, YOUR HOLINESS.
YES, THANK YOU, YOUR HOLINESS! IT'S ALWAYS AN HONOR TO HEAR YOU PREACH.
YOUR HOLINESS!
OH, IT'S YOU, ROSÉ. MY, SO DEDICATED! YOU'RE AN EXAMPLE TO US ALL.
NO, I'M JUST DOING MY DUTY.
UM...BY THE WAY, FATHER...
WHEN WILL YOU BE ABLE TO...?
YES, I KNOW WHAT IT IS YOU ASK.
GOD HAS SEEN YOUR GOOD DEEDS.
THEN...

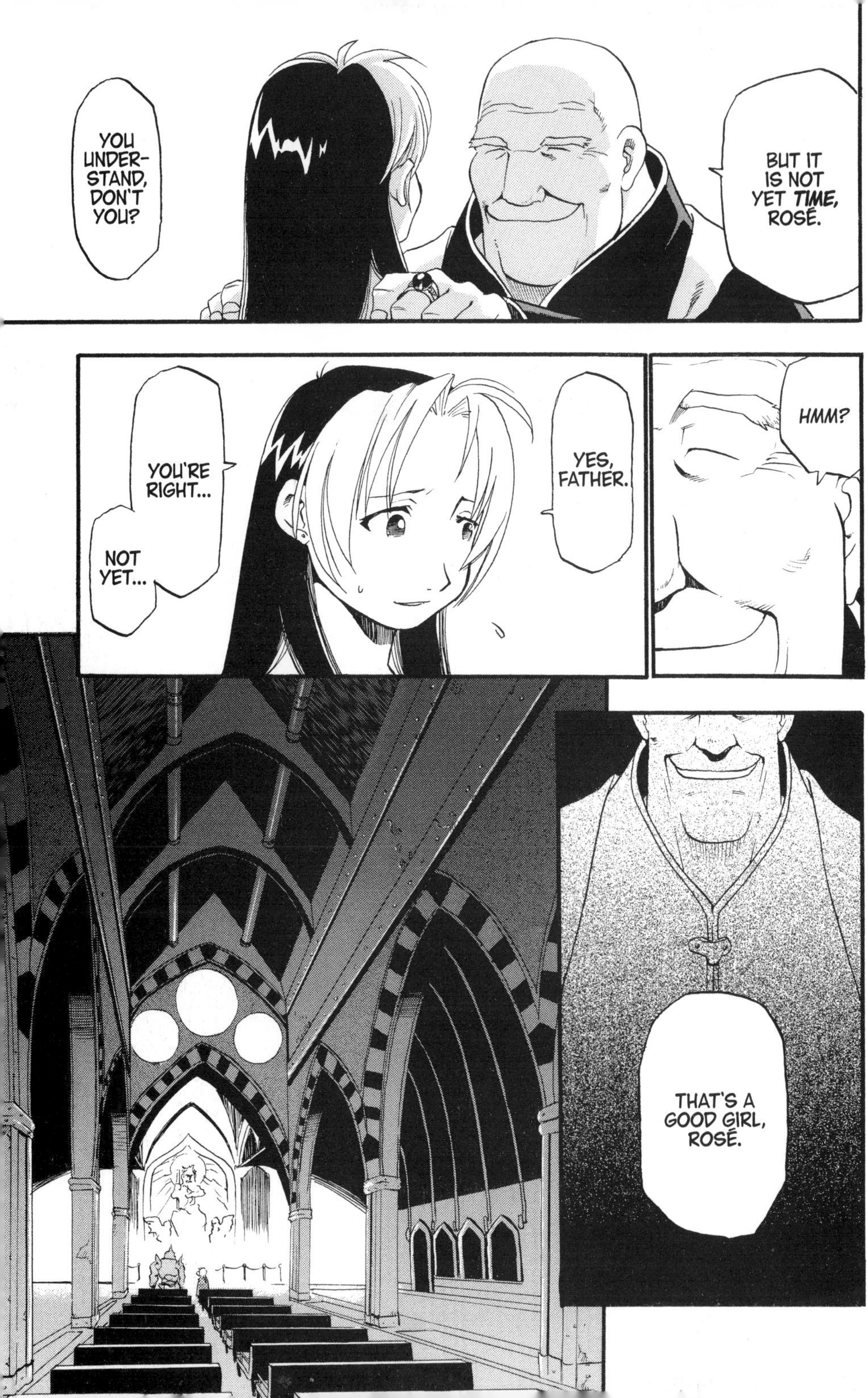
BUT IT IS NOT YET *TIME*, ROSÉ.
YOU UNDER-STAND, DON'T YOU?
HMM?
YES, FATHER.
YOU'RE RIGHT...
NOT YET...
THAT'S A GOOD GIRL, ROSÉ.

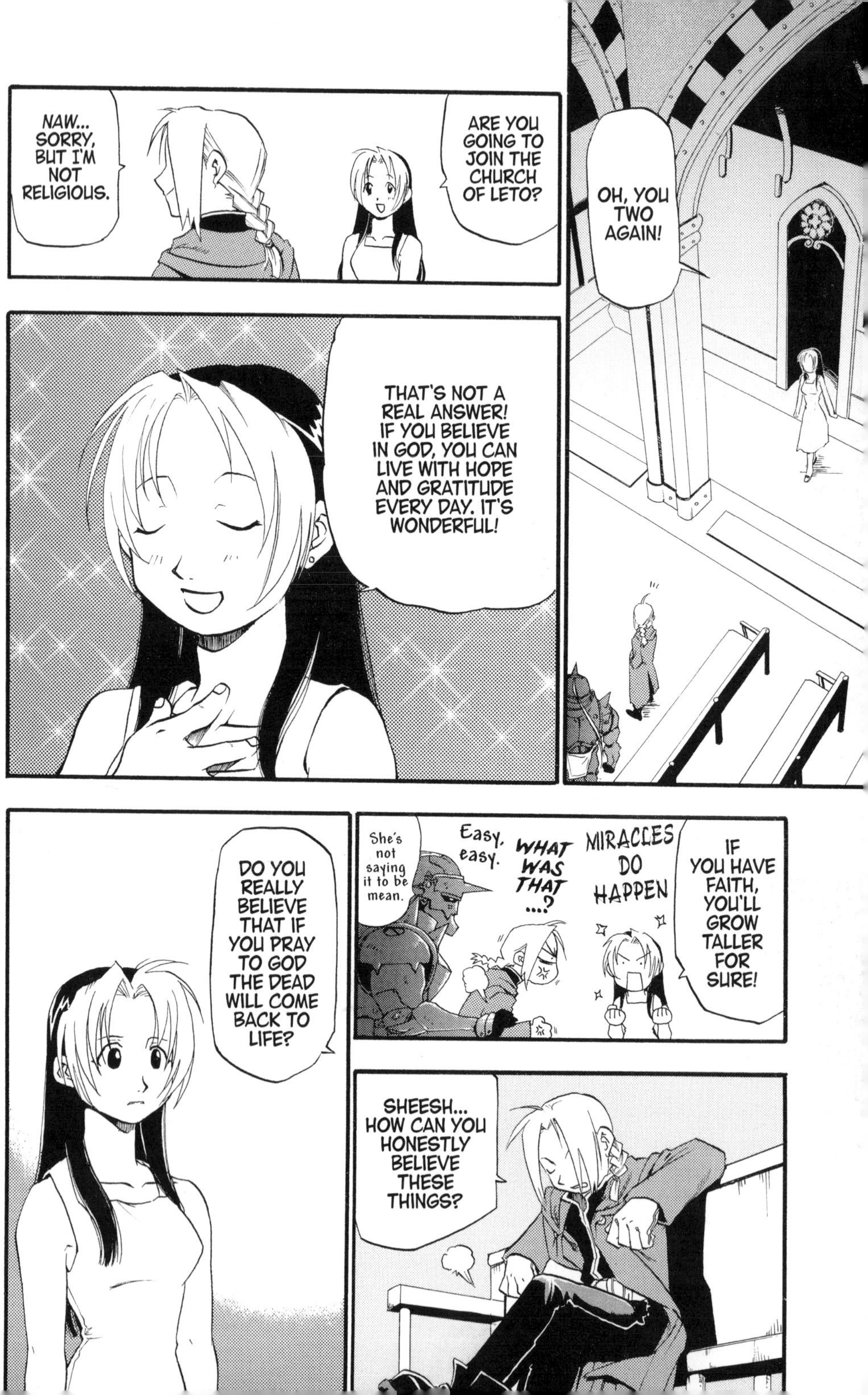
OH, YOU TWO AGAIN!
ARE YOU GOING TO JOIN THE CHURCH OF LETO?
NAW... SORRY, BUT I'M NOT RELIGIOUS.
THAT'S NOT A REAL ANSWER! IF YOU BELIEVE IN GOD, YOU CAN LIVE WITH HOPE AND GRATITUDE EVERY DAY. IT'S WONDERFUL!
IF YOU HAVE FAITH, YOU'LL GROW TALLER FOR SURE!
MIRACLES DO HAPPEN
WHAT WAS THAT ...?
Easy, easy.
She's not saying it to be mean.
SHEESH... HOW CAN YOU HONESTLY BELIEVE THESE THINGS?
DO YOU REALLY BELIEVE THAT IF YOU PRAY TO GOD THE DEAD WILL COME BACK TO LIFE?

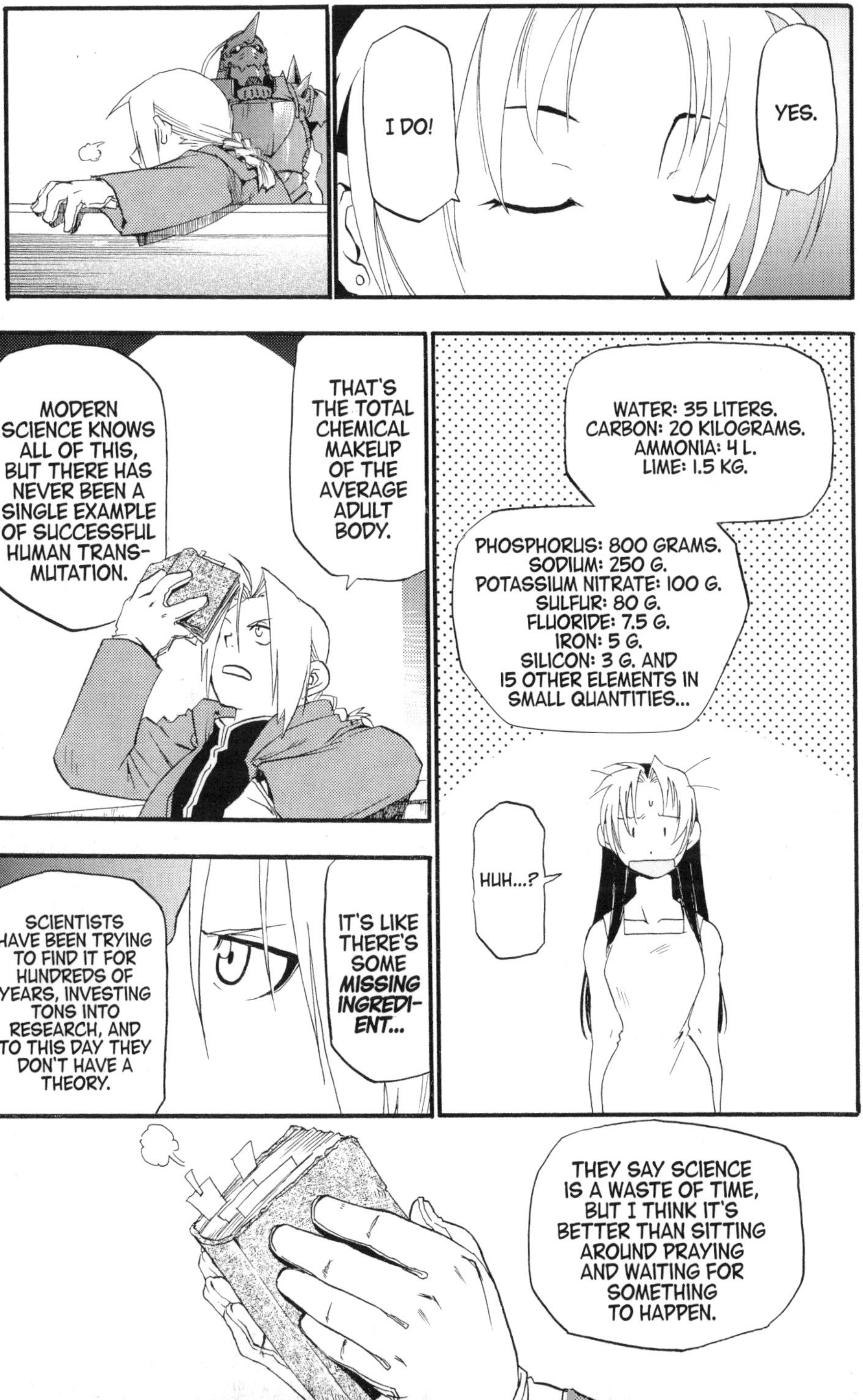
YES.
I DO!
WATER: 35 LITERS. CARBON: 20 KILOGRAMS. AMMONIA: 4 L. LIME: 1.5 KG.
PHOSPHORUS: 800 GRAMS. SODIUM: 250 G. POTASSIUM NITRATE: 100 G. SULFUR: 80 G. FLUORIDE: 7.5 G. IRON: 5 G. SILICON: 3 G. AND 15 OTHER ELEMENTS IN SMALL QUANTITIES...
HUH...?
THAT'S THE TOTAL CHEMICAL MAKEUP OF THE AVERAGE ADULT BODY.
MODERN SCIENCE KNOWS ALL OF THIS, BUT THERE HAS NEVER BEEN A SINGLE EXAMPLE OF SUCCESSFUL HUMAN TRANS-MUTATION.
IT'S LIKE THERE'S SOME *MISSING INGREDIENT*...
SCIENTISTS HAVE BEEN TRYING TO FIND IT FOR HUNDREDS OF YEARS, INVESTING TONS INTO RESEARCH, AND TO THIS DAY THEY DON'T HAVE A THEORY.
THEY SAY SCIENCE IS A WASTE OF TIME, BUT I THINK IT'S BETTER THAN SITTING AROUND PRAYING AND WAITING FOR SOMETHING TO HAPPEN.

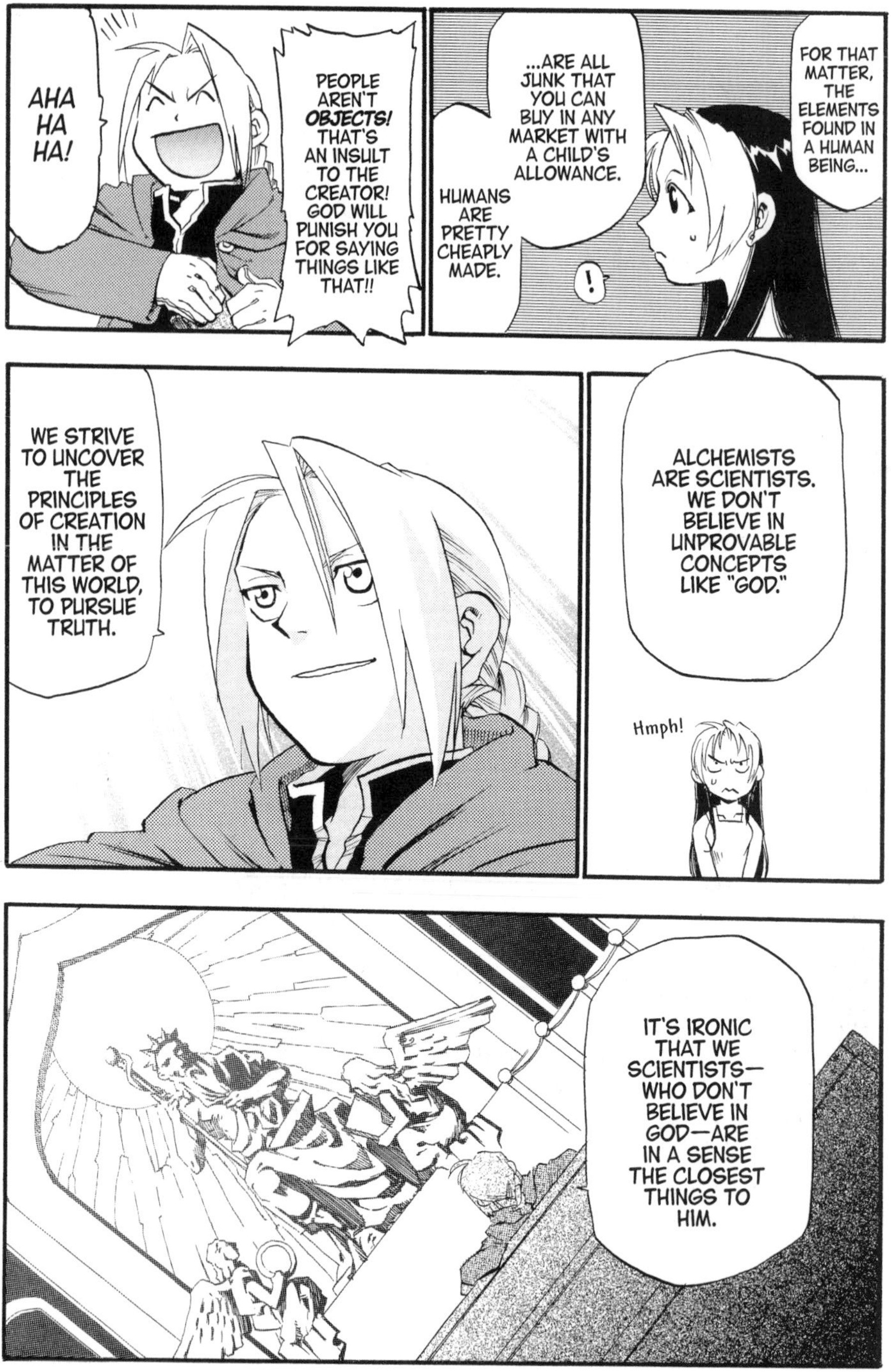
FOR THAT MATTER, THE ELEMENTS FOUND IN A HUMAN BEING...
...ARE ALL JUNK THAT YOU CAN BUY IN ANY MARKET WITH A CHILD'S ALLOWANCE.
HUMANS ARE PRETTY CHEAPLY MADE.
!
PEOPLE AREN'T *OBJECTS!* THAT'S AN INSULT TO THE CREATOR! GOD WILL PUNISH YOU FOR SAYING THINGS LIKE THAT!!
AHA HA HA!
ALCHEMISTS ARE SCIENTISTS. WE DON'T BELIEVE IN UNPROVABLE CONCEPTS LIKE "GOD."
Hmph!
WE STRIVE TO UNCOVER THE PRINCIPLES OF CREATION IN THE MATTER OF THIS WORLD, TO PURSUE TRUTH.
IT'S IRONIC THAT WE SCIENTISTS—WHO DON'T BELIEVE IN GOD—ARE IN A SENSE THE CLOSEST THINGS TO HIM.

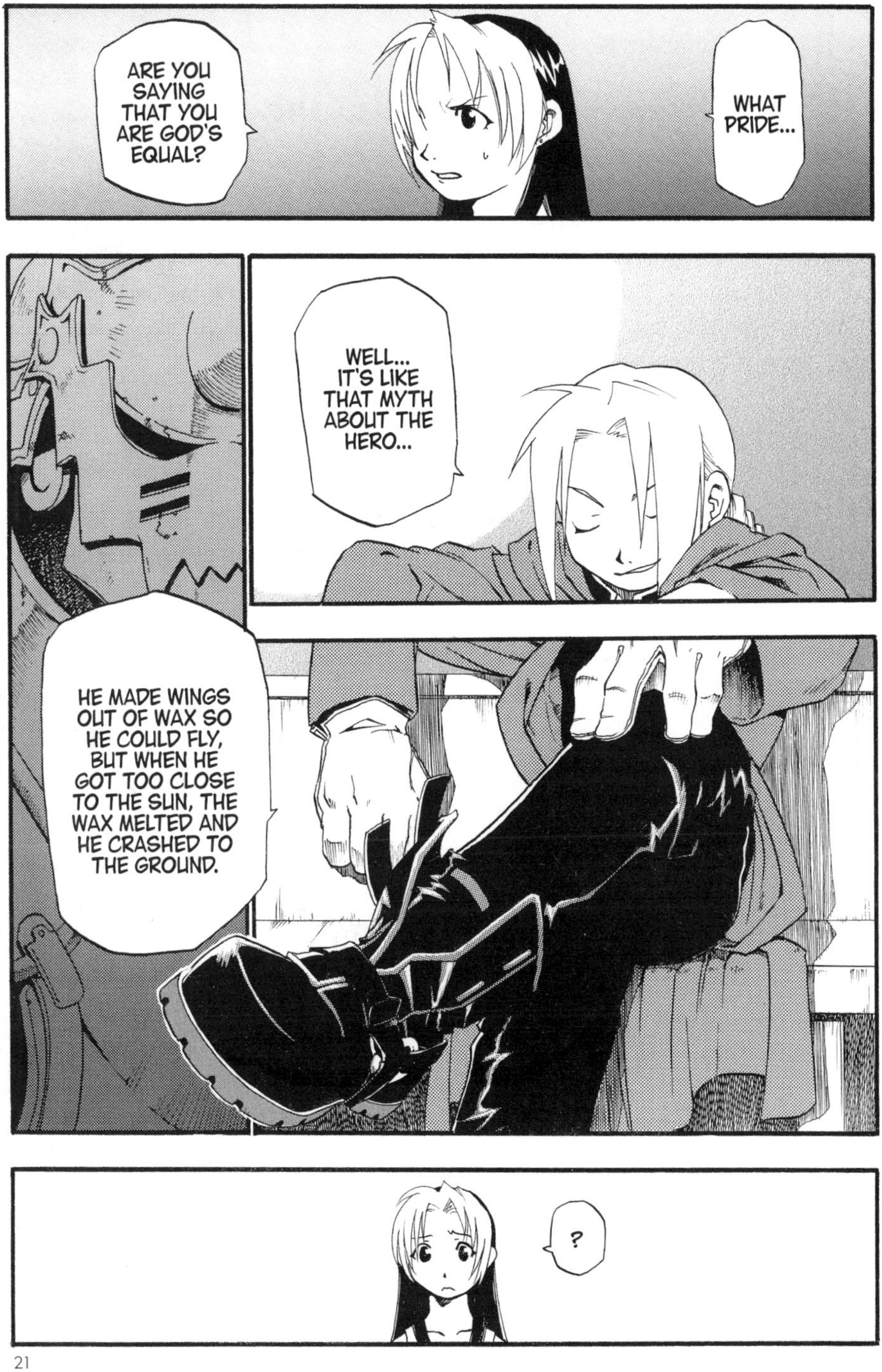
WHAT PRIDE...
ARE YOU SAYING THAT YOU ARE GOD'S EQUAL?
WELL... IT'S LIKE THAT MYTH ABOUT THE HERO...
HE MADE WINGS OUT OF WAX SO HE COULD FLY, BUT WHEN HE GOT TOO CLOSE TO THE SUN, THE WAX MELTED AND HE CRASHED TO THE GROUND.
?

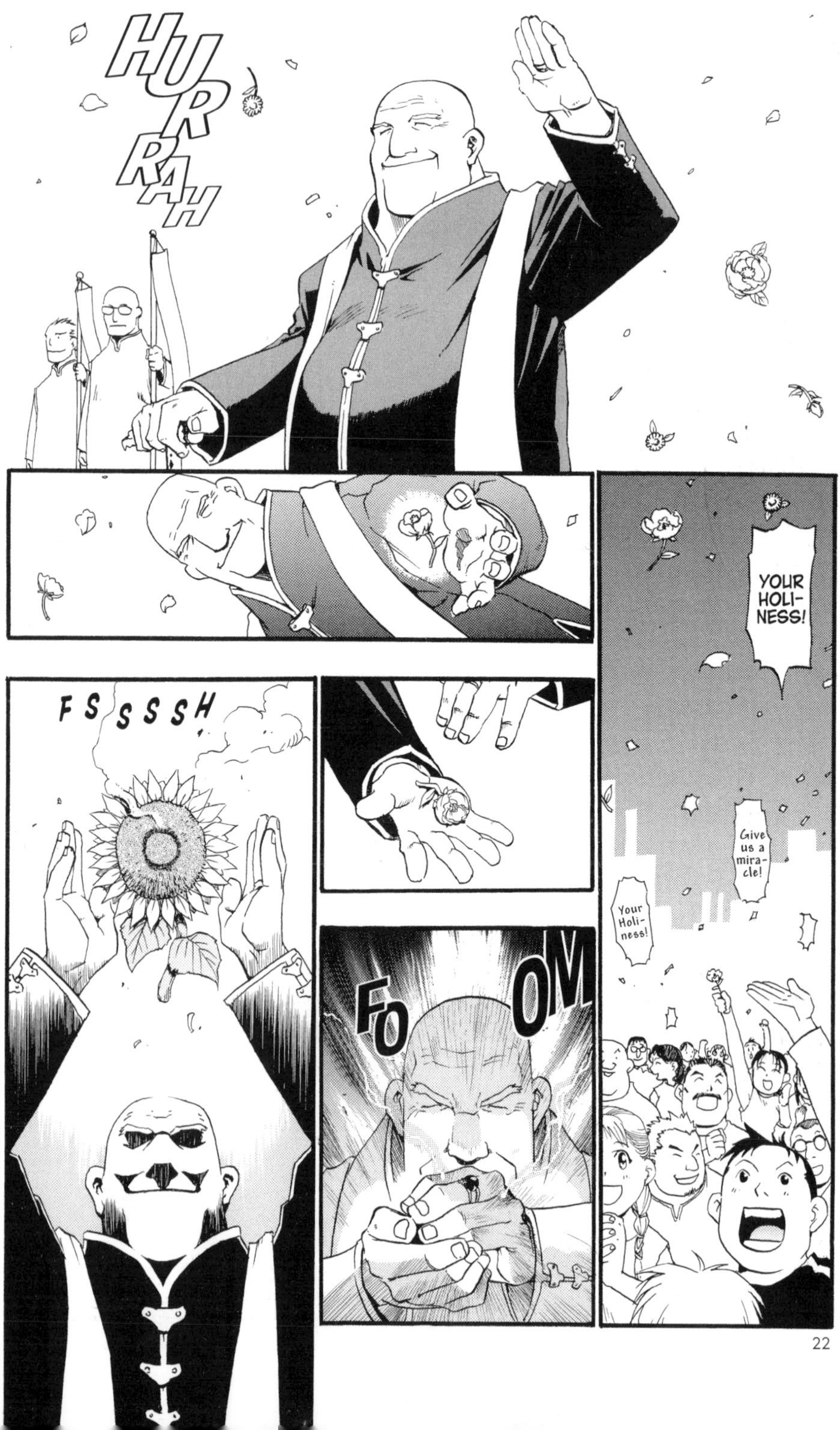
HURRAH
YOUR HOLINESS!
Give us a miracle!
Your Holiness!
FOOM
FSSSSH

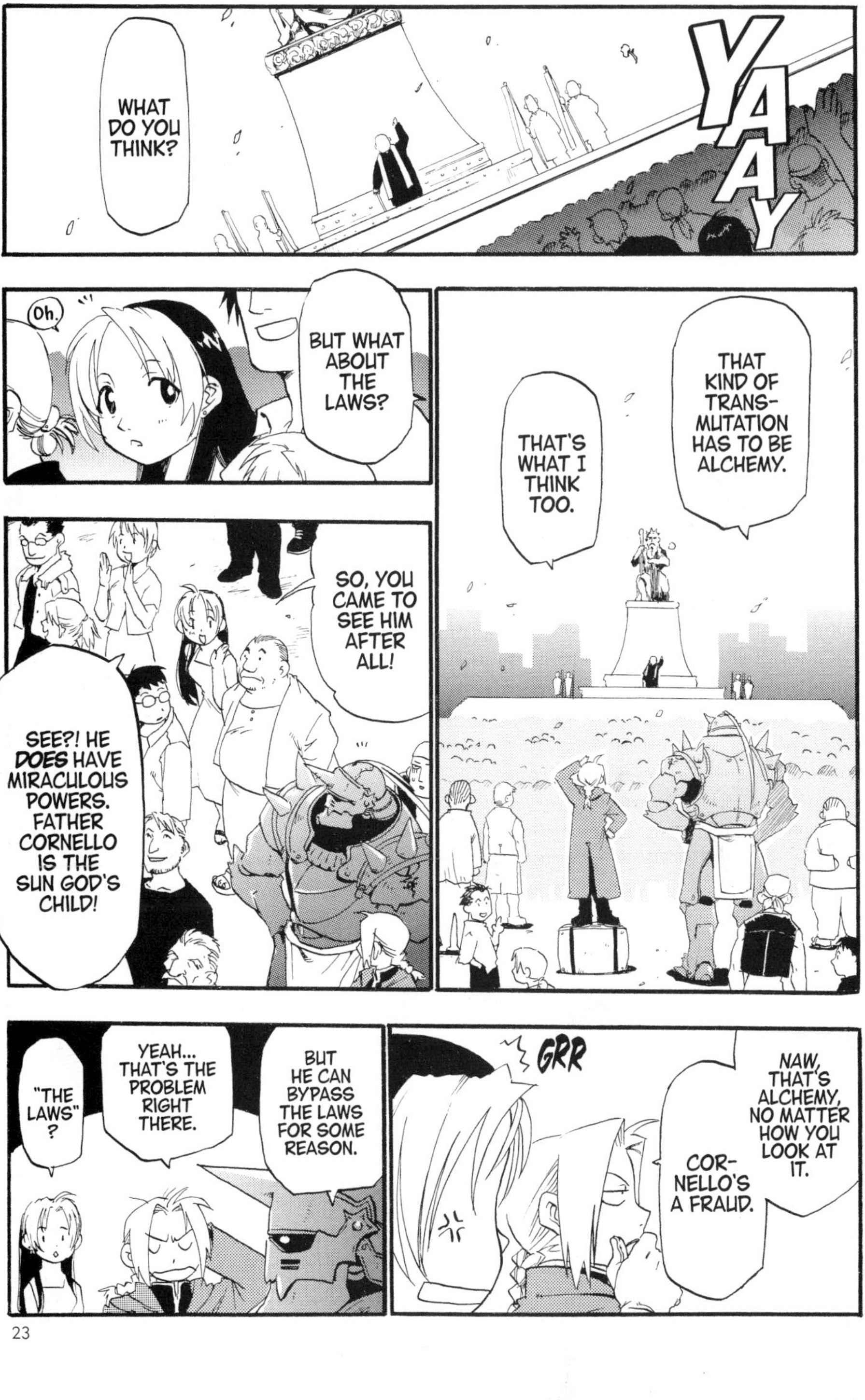
YAAY
WHAT DO YOU THINK?
THAT KIND OF TRANS-MUTATION HAS TO BE ALCHEMY.
THAT'S WHAT I THINK TOO.
BUT WHAT ABOUT THE LAWS?
Oh.
SO, YOU CAME TO SEE HIM AFTER ALL!
SEE?! HE **DOES** HAVE MIRACULOUS POWERS. FATHER CORNELLO IS THE SUN GOD'S CHILD!
GRR
NAW, THAT'S ALCHEMY, NO MATTER HOW YOU LOOK AT IT.
COR-NELLO'S A FRAUD.
BUT HE CAN BYPASS THE LAWS FOR SOME REASON.
YEAH... THAT'S THE PROBLEM RIGHT THERE.
"THE LAWS"?

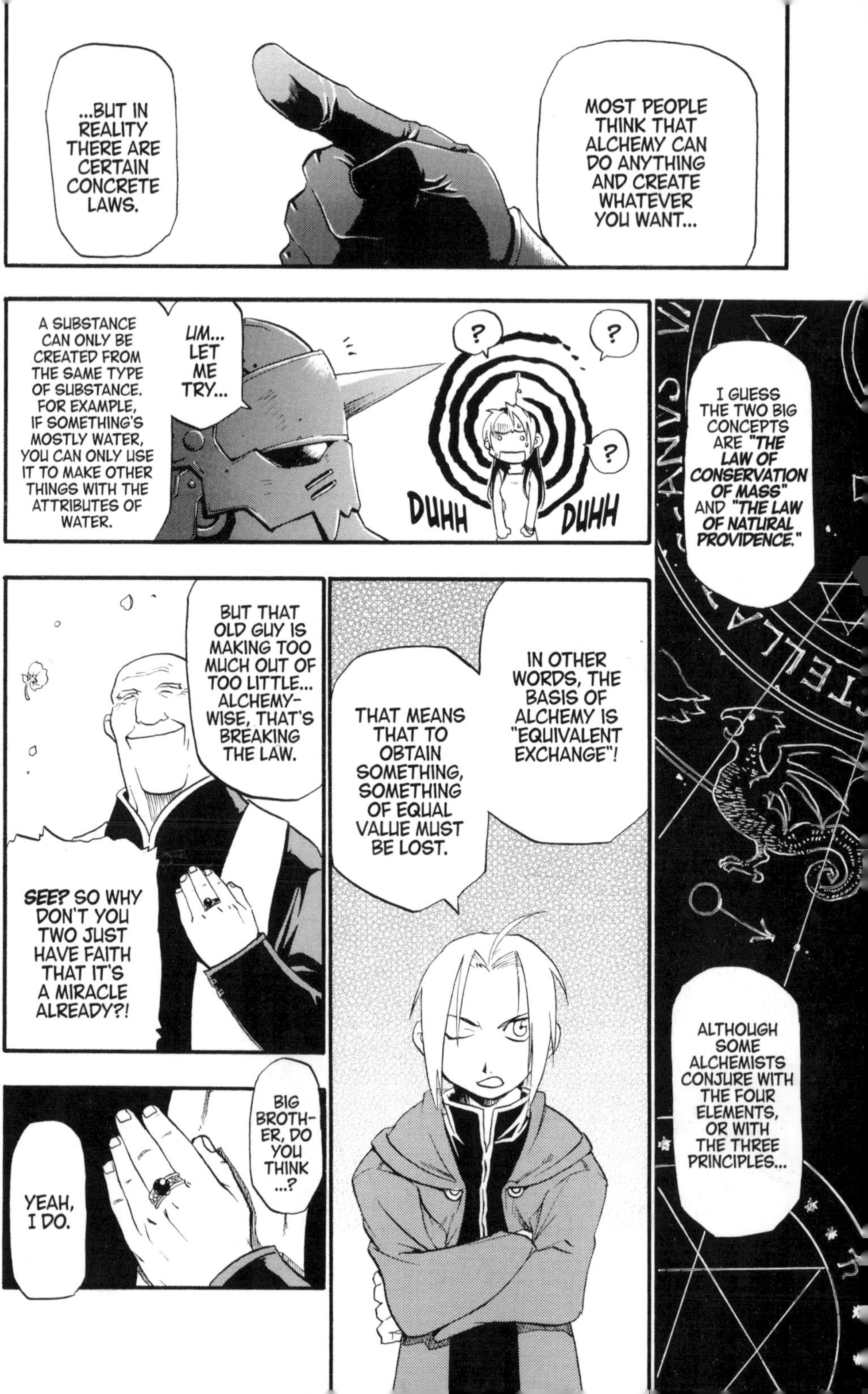
MOST PEOPLE THINK THAT ALCHEMY CAN DO ANYTHING AND CREATE WHATEVER YOU WANT...
...BUT IN REALITY THERE ARE CERTAIN CONCRETE LAWS.
I GUESS THE TWO BIG CONCEPTS ARE "THE LAW OF CONSERVATION OF MASS" AND "THE LAW OF NATURAL PROVIDENCE."
ALTHOUGH SOME ALCHEMISTS CONJURE WITH THE FOUR ELEMENTS, OR WITH THE THREE PRINCIPLES...
?
?
?
DUHH
DUHH
UM... LET ME TRY...
A SUBSTANCE CAN ONLY BE CREATED FROM THE SAME TYPE OF SUBSTANCE. FOR EXAMPLE, IF SOMETHING'S MOSTLY WATER, YOU CAN ONLY USE IT TO MAKE OTHER THINGS WITH THE ATTRIBUTES OF WATER.
IN OTHER WORDS, THE BASIS OF ALCHEMY IS "EQUIVALENT EXCHANGE"!
THAT MEANS THAT TO OBTAIN SOMETHING, SOMETHING OF EQUAL VALUE MUST BE LOST.
BUT THAT OLD GUY IS MAKING TOO MUCH OUT OF TOO LITTLE... ALCHEMY-WISE, THAT'S BREAKING THE LAW.
SEE? SO WHY DON'T YOU TWO JUST HAVE FAITH THAT IT'S A MIRACLE ALREADY?!
BIG BROTHER, DO YOU THINK ...?
YEAH, I DO.

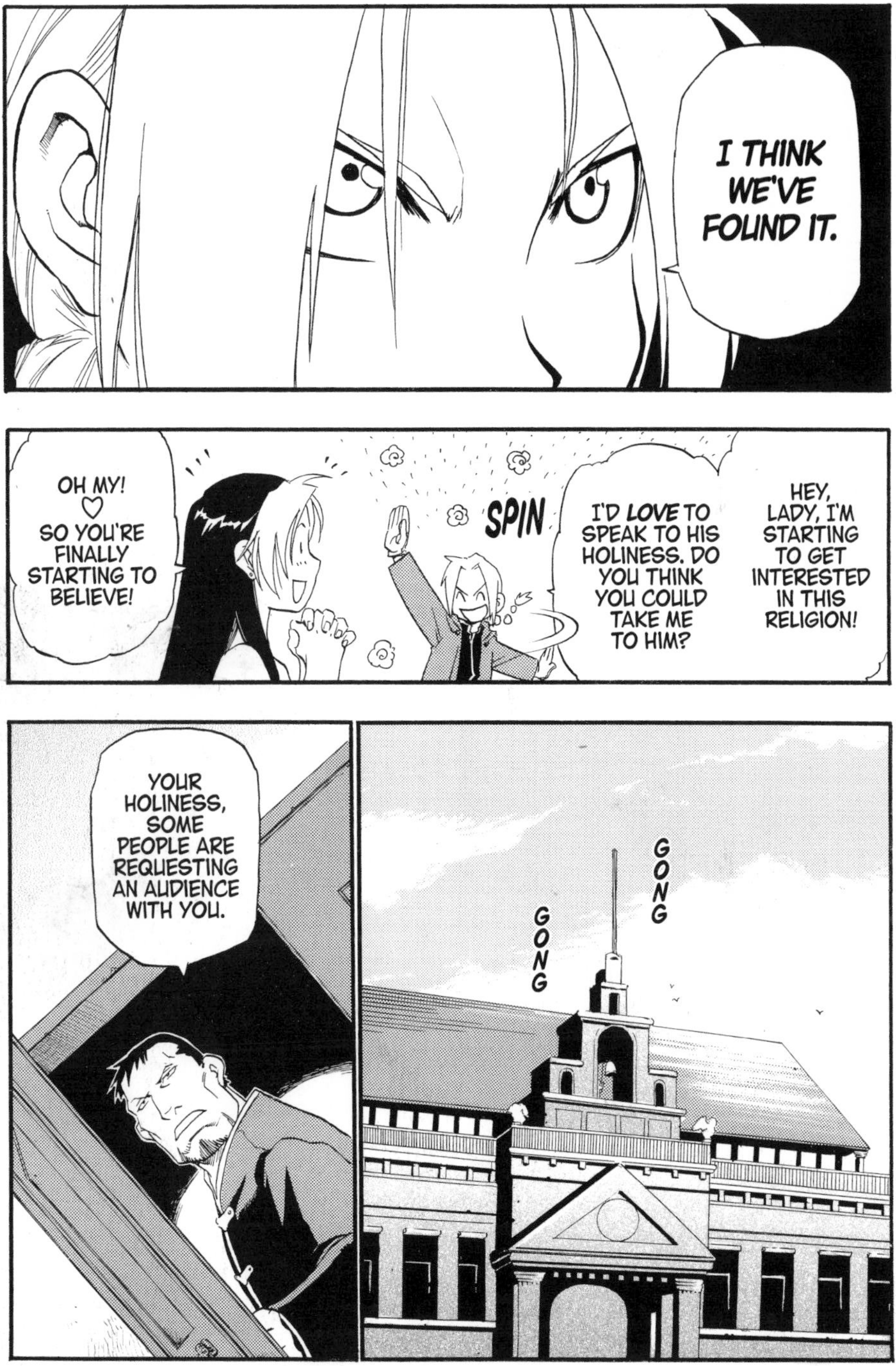
I THINK WE'VE FOUND IT.
HEY, LADY, I'M STARTING TO GET INTERESTED IN THIS RELIGION!
I'D LOVE TO SPEAK TO HIS HOLINESS. DO YOU THINK YOU COULD TAKE ME TO HIM?
SPIN
OH MY! ♡ SO YOU'RE FINALLY STARTING TO BELIEVE!
GONG
GONG
YOUR HOLINESS, SOME PEOPLE ARE REQUESTING AN AUDIENCE WITH YOU.

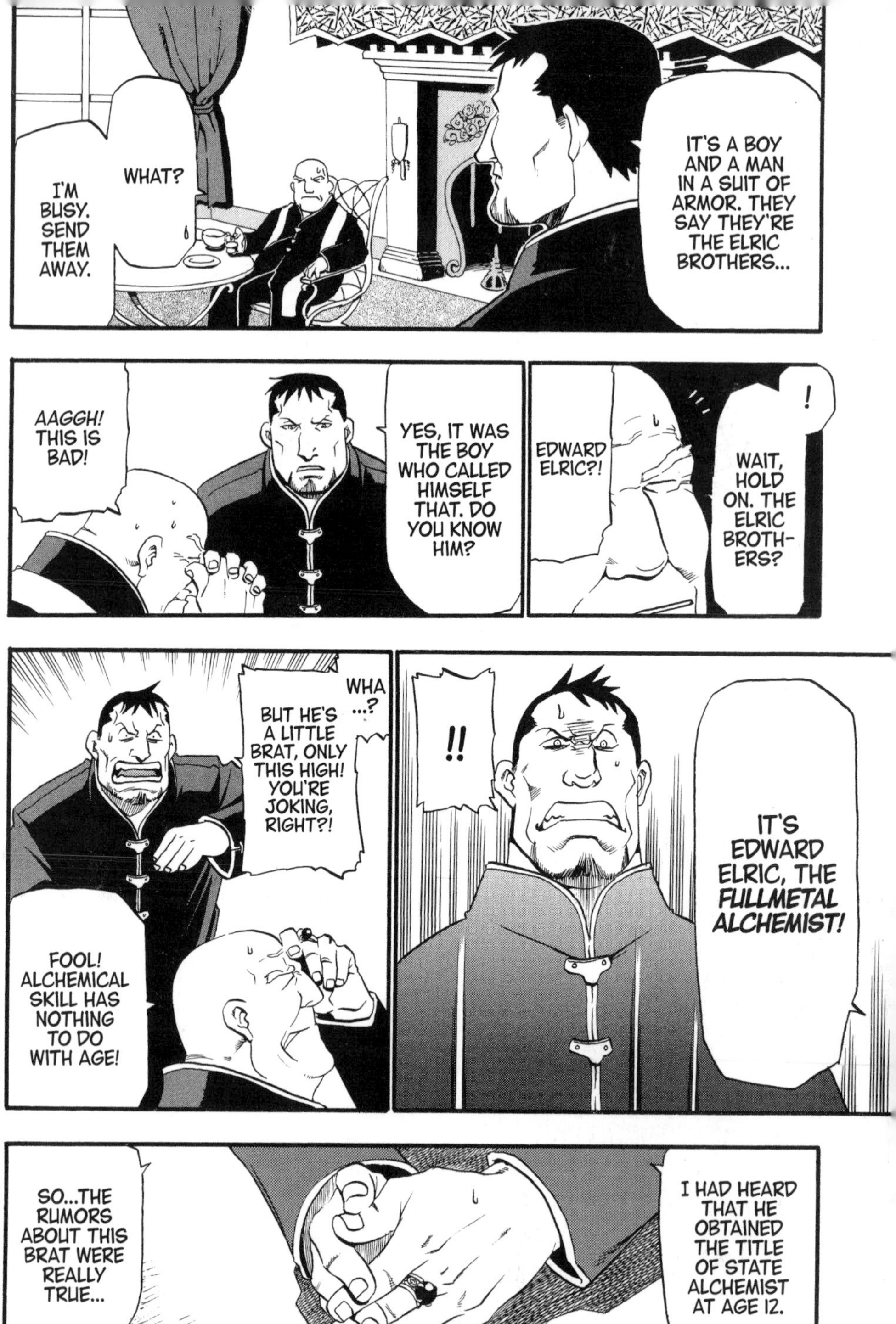
IT'S A BOY AND A MAN IN A SUIT OF ARMOR. THEY SAY THEY'RE THE ELRIC BROTHERS...
WHAT?
I'M BUSY. SEND THEM AWAY.
!
WAIT, HOLD ON. THE ELRIC BROTHERS?
EDWARD ELRIC?!
YES, IT WAS THE BOY WHO CALLED HIMSELF THAT. DO YOU KNOW HIM?
AAGGH! THIS IS BAD!
IT'S EDWARD ELRIC, THE FULLMETAL ALCHEMIST!
!!
WHA ...?
BUT HE'S A LITTLE BRAT, ONLY THIS HIGH! YOU'RE JOKING, RIGHT?!
FOOL! ALCHEMICAL SKILL HAS NOTHING TO DO WITH AGE!
I HAD HEARD THAT HE OBTAINED THE TITLE OF STATE ALCHEMIST AT AGE 12.
SO...THE RUMORS ABOUT THIS BRAT WERE REALLY TRUE...

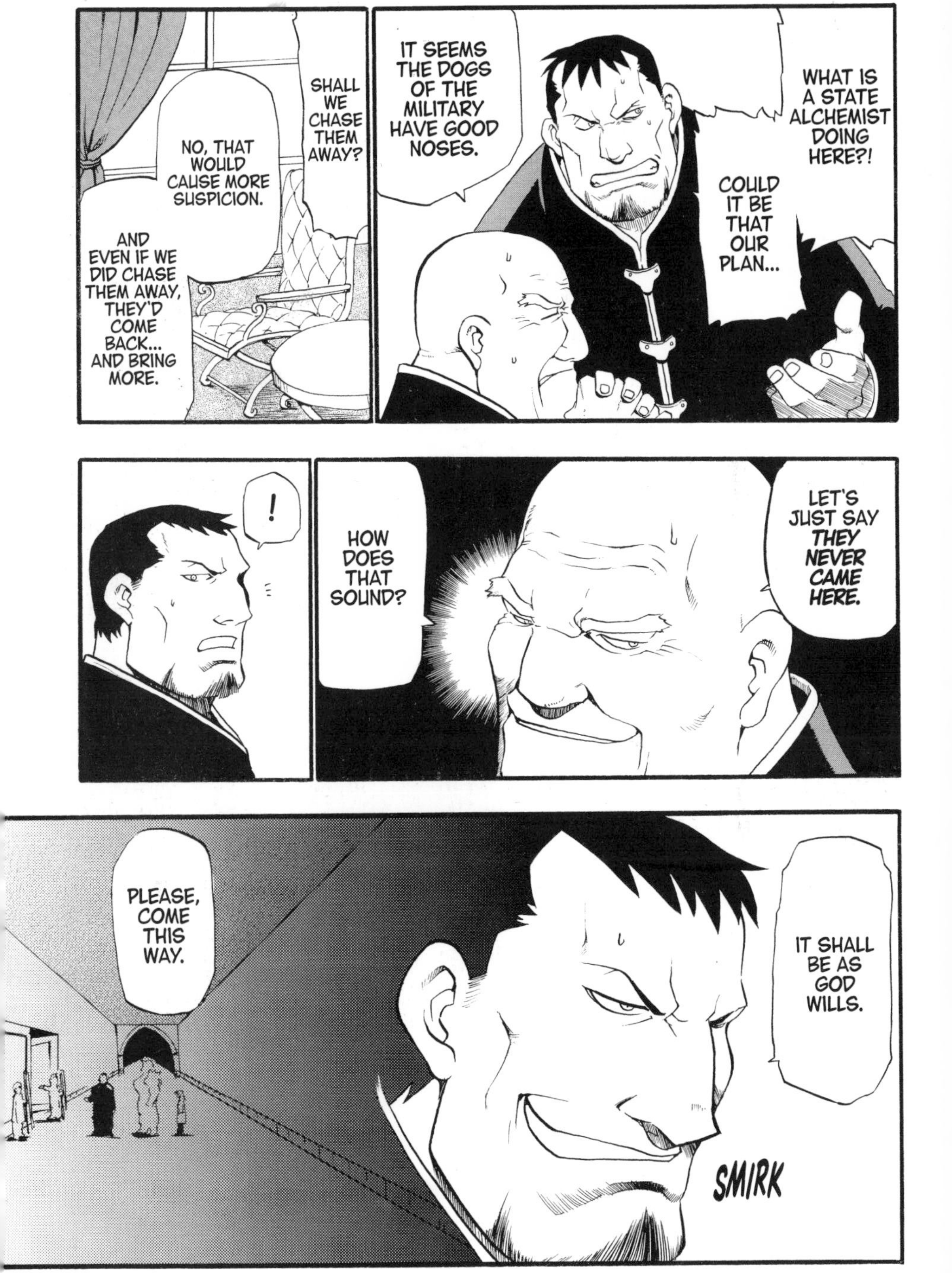
WHAT IS A STATE ALCHEMIST DOING HERE?!
COULD IT BE THAT OUR PLAN...
IT SEEMS THE DOGS OF THE MILITARY HAVE GOOD NOSES.
SHALL WE CHASE THEM AWAY?
NO, THAT WOULD CAUSE MORE SUSPICION.
AND EVEN IF WE DID CHASE THEM AWAY, THEY'D COME BACK... AND BRING MORE.
LET'S JUST SAY *THEY NEVER CAME HERE.*
HOW DOES THAT SOUND?
!
IT SHALL BE AS GOD WILLS.
SMIRK
PLEASE, COME THIS WAY.

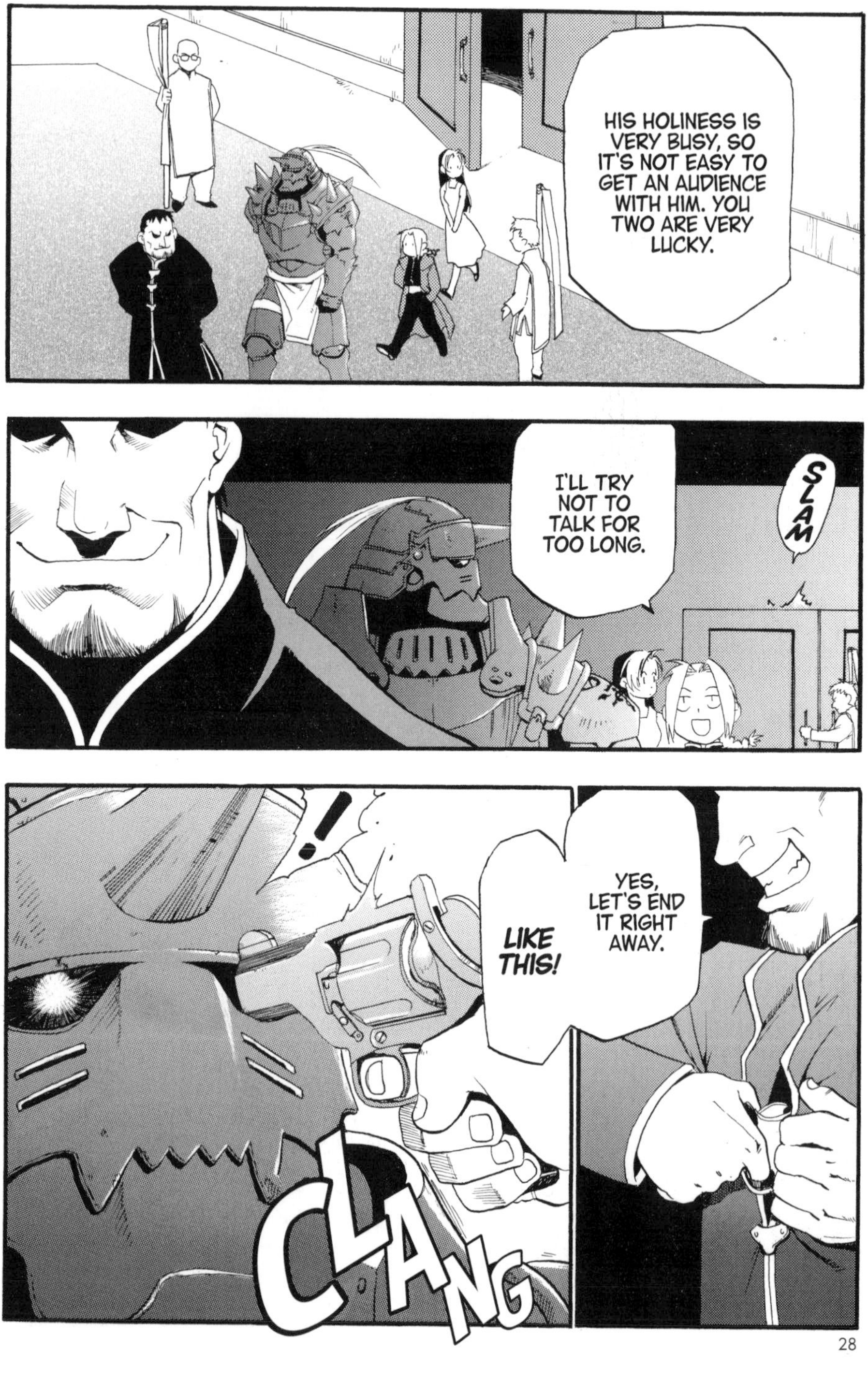
HIS HOLINESS IS VERY BUSY, SO IT'S NOT EASY TO GET AN AUDIENCE WITH HIM. YOU TWO ARE VERY LUCKY.
SLAM
I'LL TRY NOT TO TALK FOR TOO LONG.
YES, LET'S END IT RIGHT AWAY.
LIKE THIS!
!
CLANG

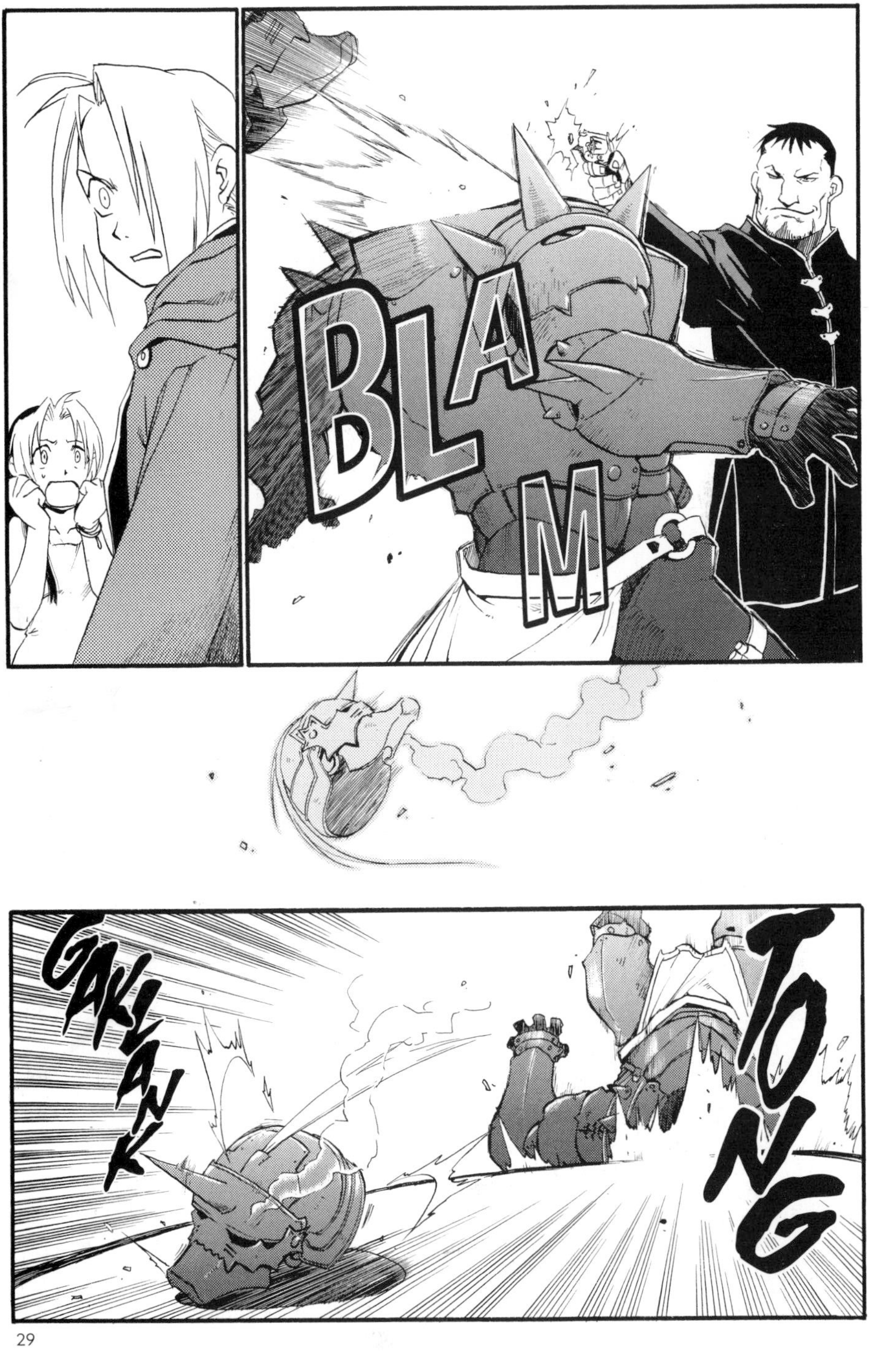
BLAM
TONG
GAKLANK

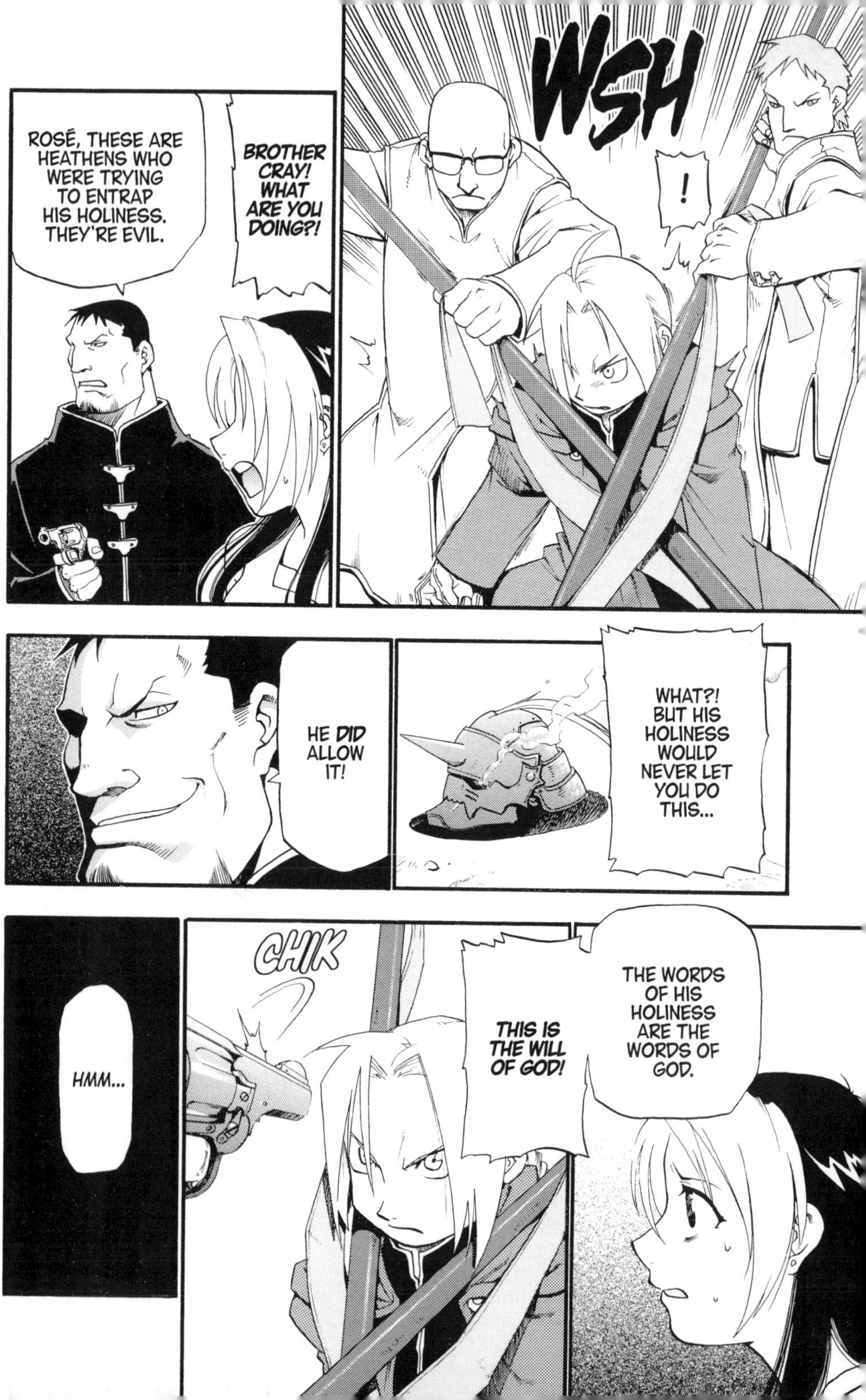
WSH
!
BROTHER CRAY! WHAT ARE YOU DOING?!
ROSÉ, THESE ARE HEATHENS WHO WERE TRYING TO ENTRAP HIS HOLINESS. THEY'RE EVIL.
WHAT?! BUT HIS HOLINESS WOULD NEVER LET YOU DO THIS...
HE **DID** ALLOW IT!
THE WORDS OF HIS HOLINESS ARE THE WORDS OF GOD.
THIS IS THE WILL OF GOD!
CHIK
HMM...

GUESS THERE'RE SOME REALLY BAD GODS OUT THERE.
GRIP
WHA ...?
SWIFF
GRAB

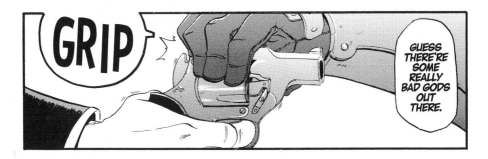

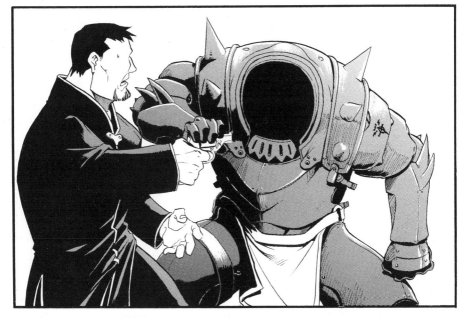

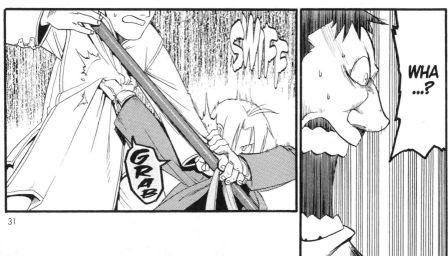

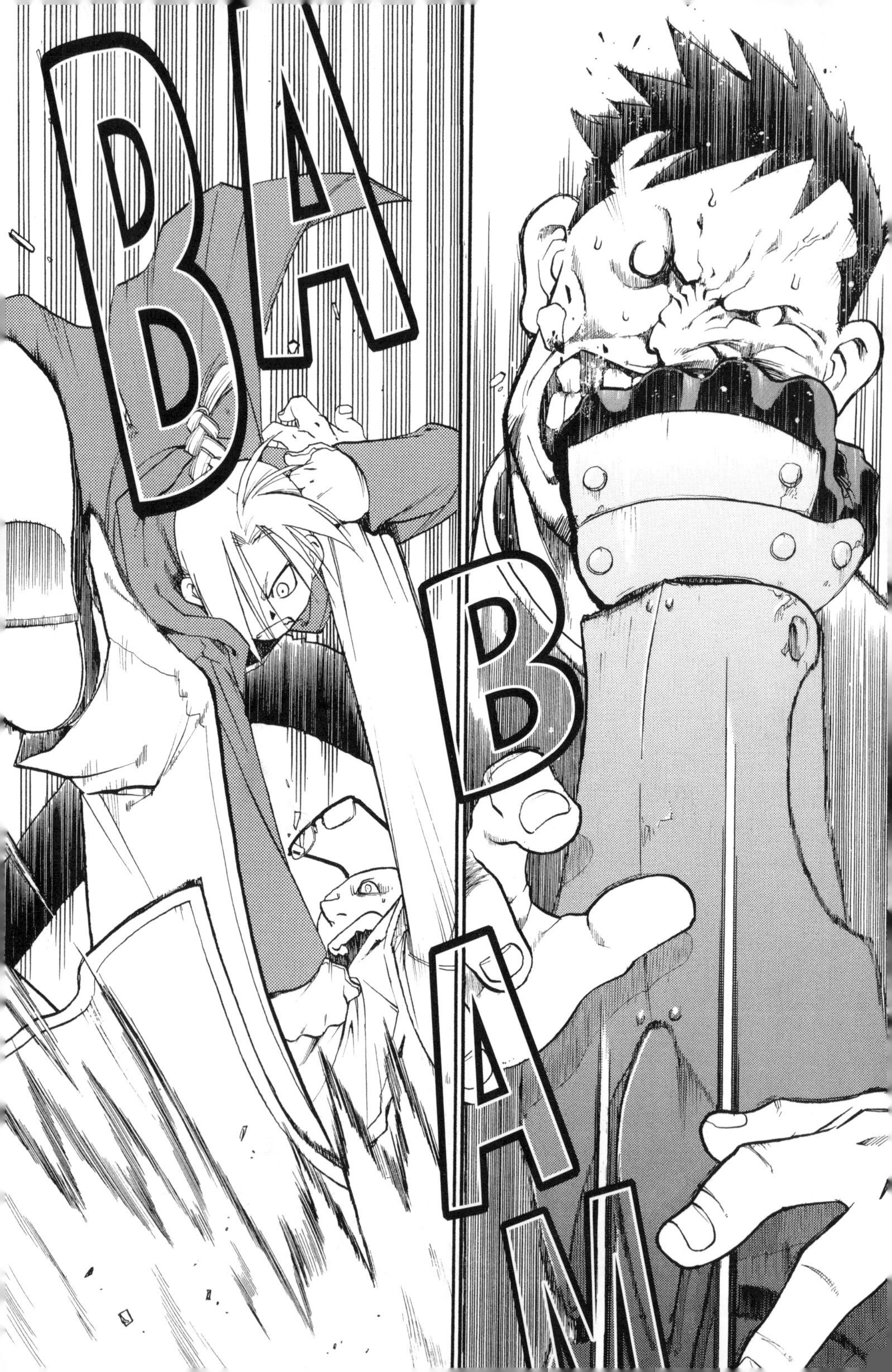
DA
BAM

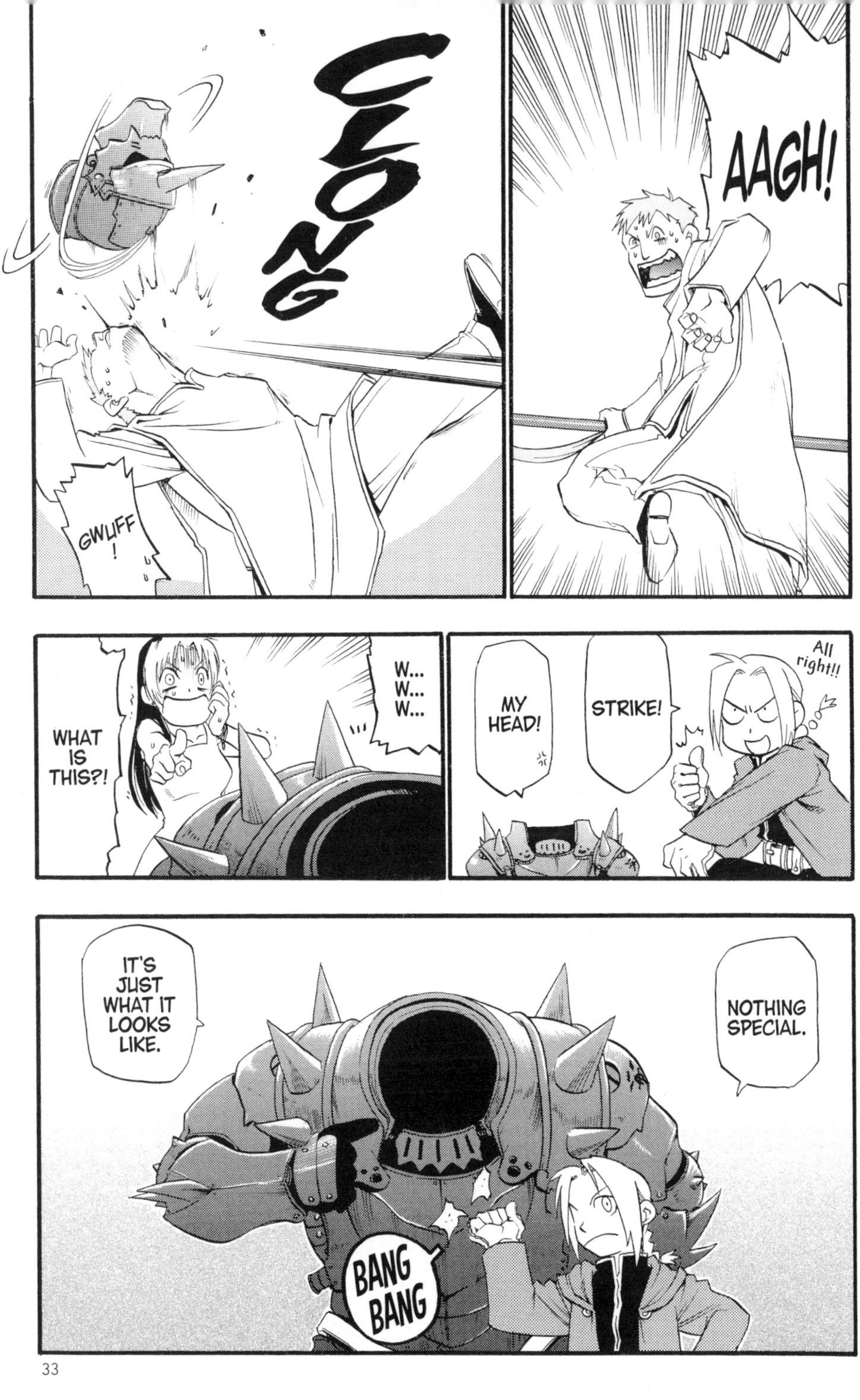
AAGH!
CLONG
GWUFF!
All right!!
STRIKE!
MY HEAD!
W... W... W...
WHAT IS THIS?!
NOTHING SPECIAL.
IT'S JUST WHAT IT LOOKS LIKE.
BANG BANG

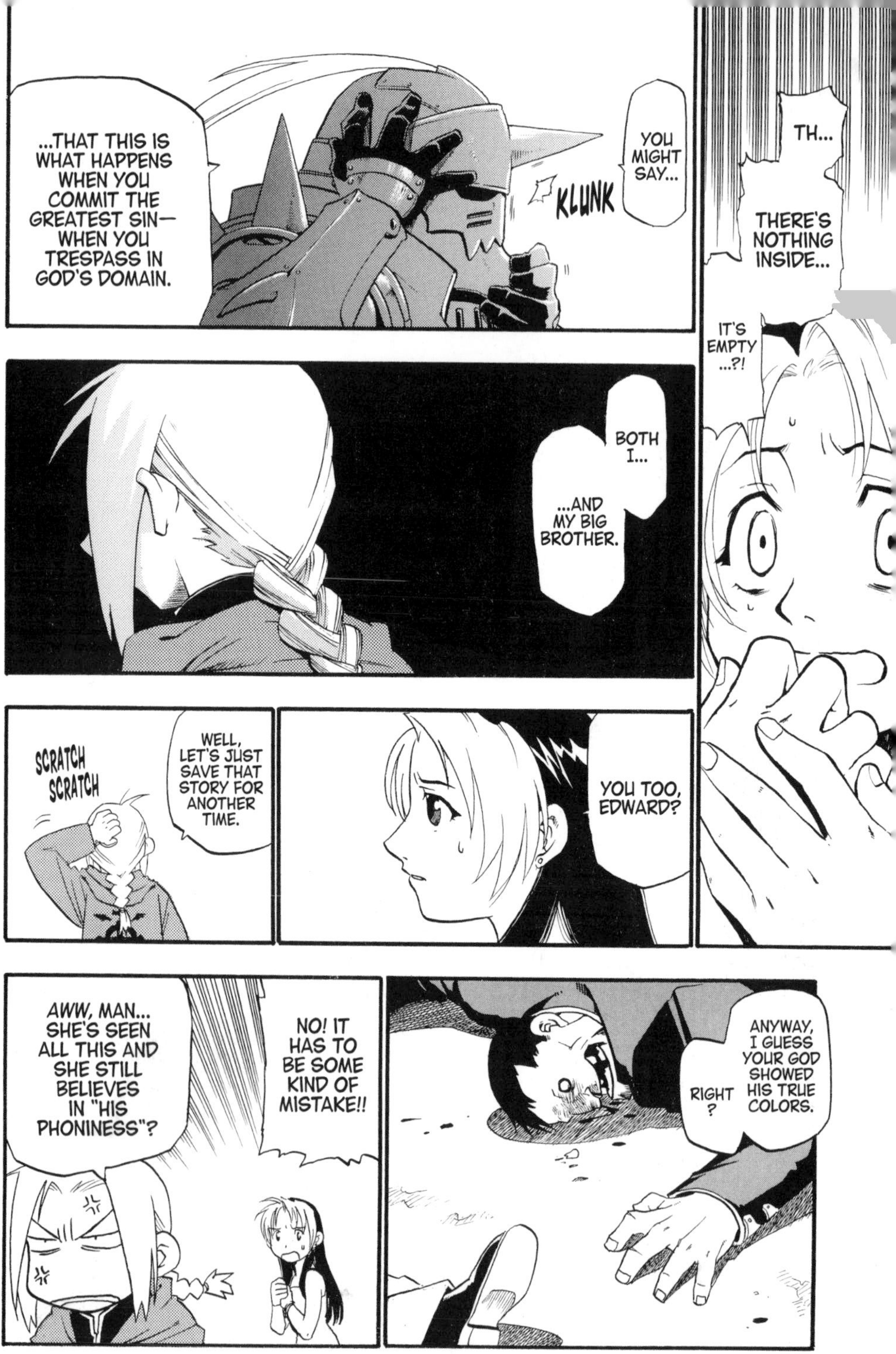
TH...
THERE'S NOTHING INSIDE...
IT'S EMPTY ...?!
YOU MIGHT SAY...
KLUNK
...THAT THIS IS WHAT HAPPENS WHEN YOU COMMIT THE GREATEST SIN— WHEN YOU TRESPASS IN GOD'S DOMAIN.
BOTH I...
...AND MY BIG BROTHER.
YOU TOO, EDWARD?
WELL, LET'S JUST SAVE THAT STORY FOR ANOTHER TIME.
SCRATCH SCRATCH
ANYWAY, I GUESS YOUR GOD SHOWED HIS TRUE COLORS.
RIGHT?
NO! IT HAS TO BE SOME KIND OF MISTAKE!!
AWW, MAN... SHE'S SEEN ALL THIS AND SHE STILL BELIEVES IN "HIS PHONINESS"?

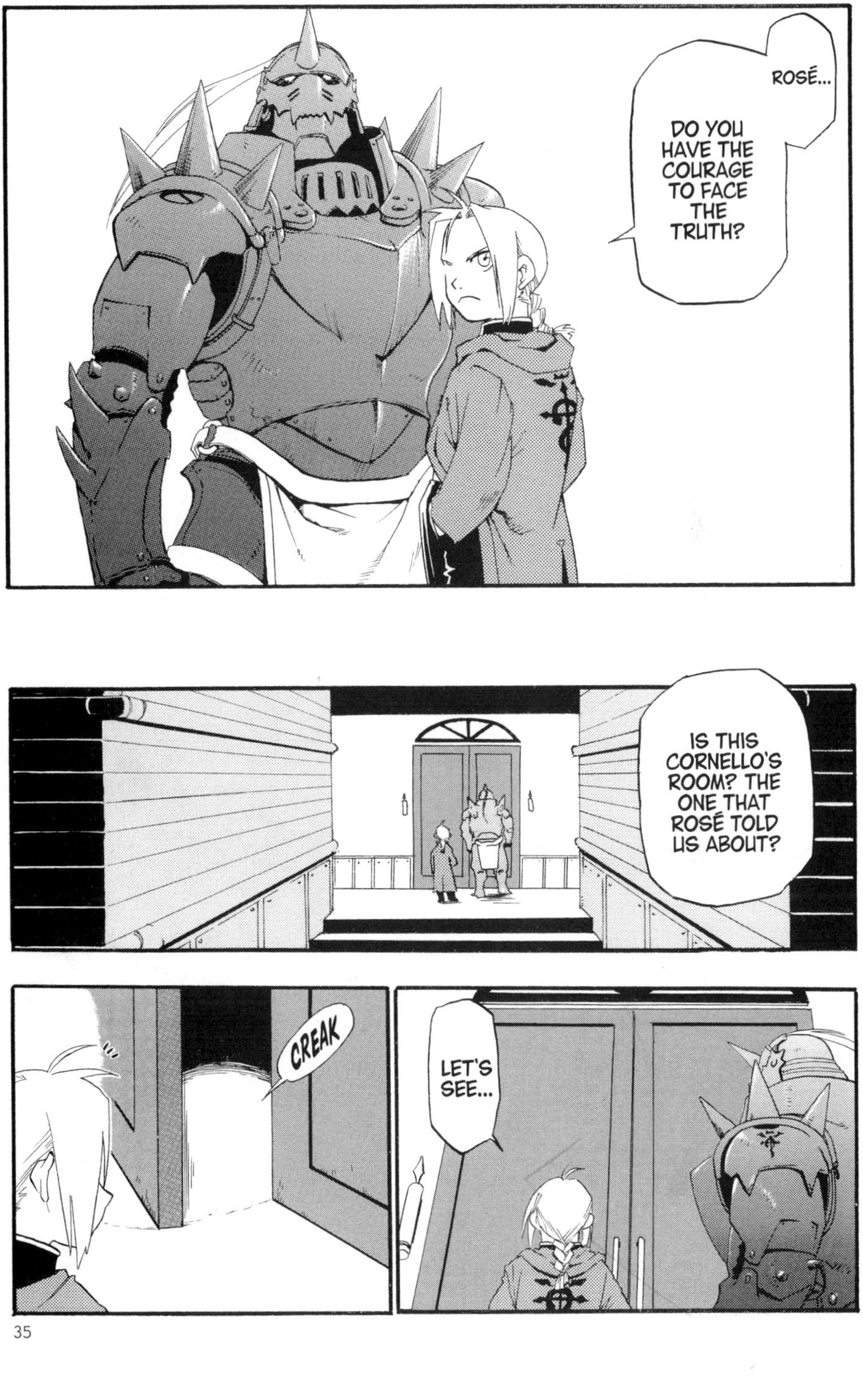
ROSÉ...
DO YOU HAVE THE COURAGE TO FACE THE TRUTH?
IS THIS CORNELLO'S ROOM? THE ONE THAT ROSÉ TOLD US ABOUT?
LET'S SEE...
CREAK

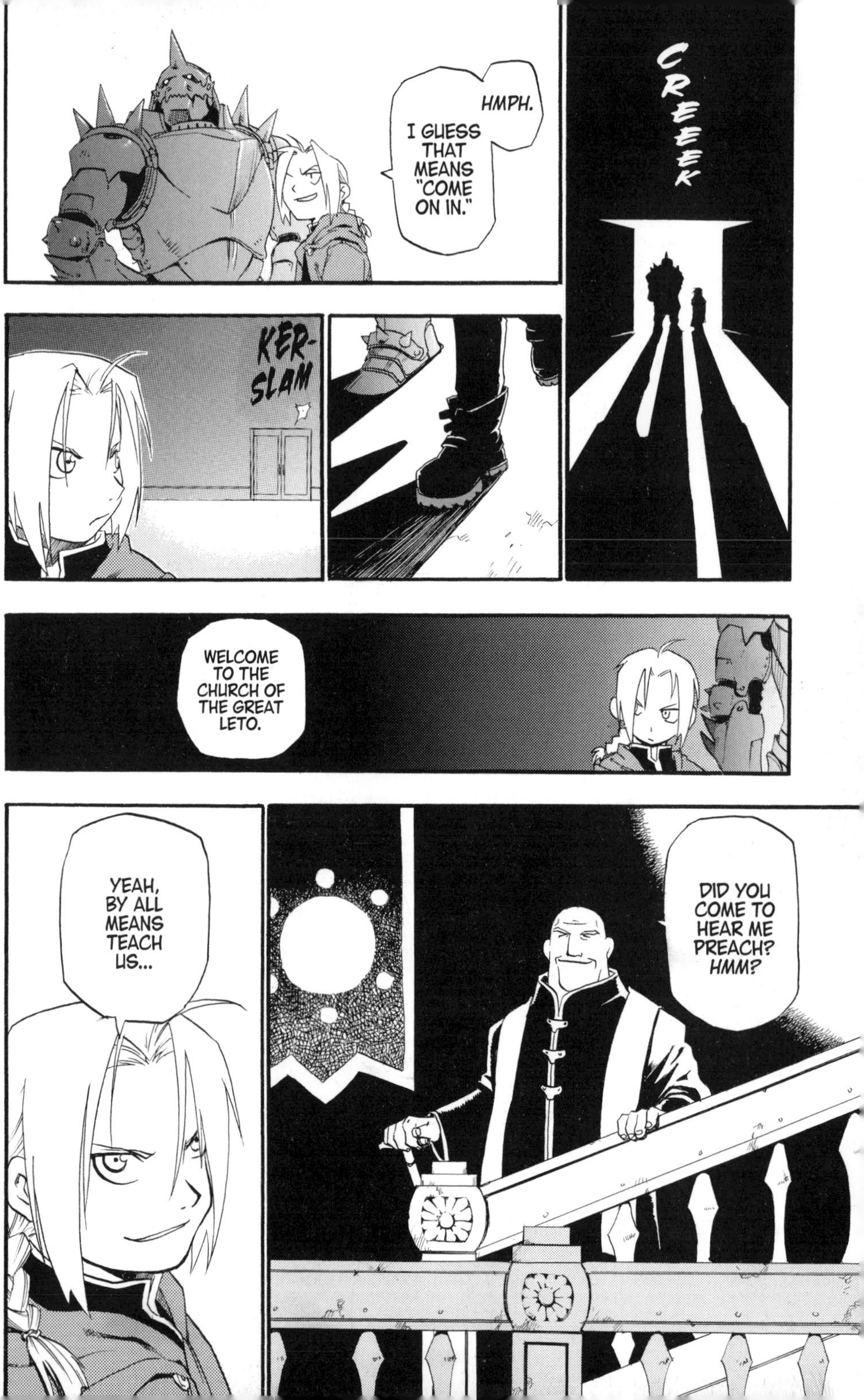
CREEEK
HMPH.
I GUESS THAT MEANS "COME ON IN."
KER-SLAM
WELCOME TO THE CHURCH OF THE GREAT LETO.
DID YOU COME TO HEAR ME PREACH? HMM?
YEAH, BY ALL MEANS TEACH US...

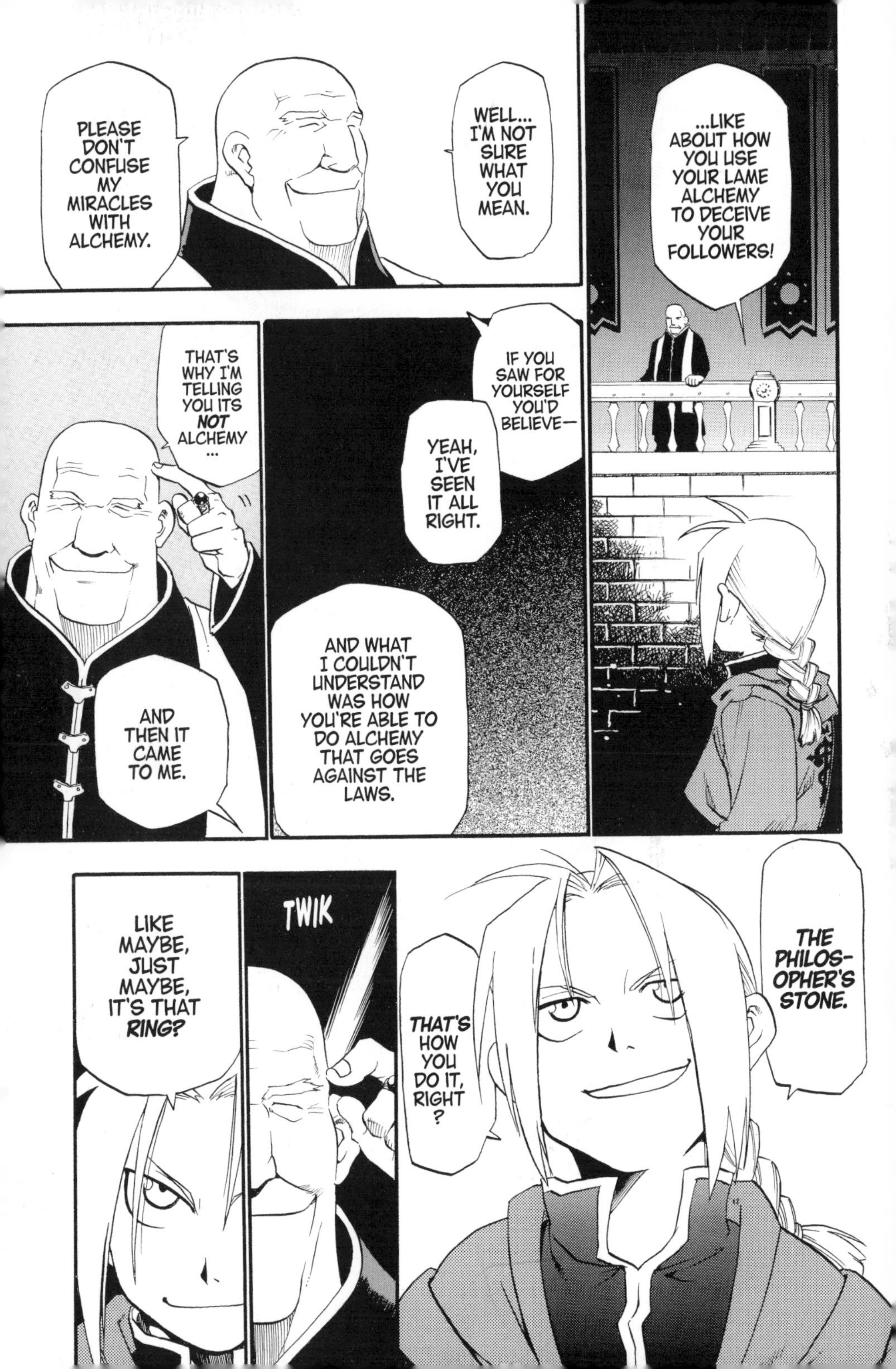

...LIKE ABOUT HOW YOU USE YOUR LAME ALCHEMY TO DECEIVE YOUR FOLLOWERS!
WELL... I'M NOT SURE WHAT YOU MEAN.
PLEASE DON'T CONFUSE MY MIRACLES WITH ALCHEMY.
IF YOU SAW FOR YOURSELF YOU'D BELIEVE—
YEAH, I'VE SEEN IT ALL RIGHT.
AND WHAT I COULDN'T UNDERSTAND WAS HOW YOU'RE ABLE TO DO ALCHEMY THAT GOES AGAINST THE LAWS.
THAT'S WHY I'M TELLING YOU ITS ***NOT*** ALCHEMY ...
AND THEN IT CAME TO ME.
THE PHILOS-OPHER'S STONE.
THAT'S HOW YOU DO IT, RIGHT?
TWIK
LIKE MAYBE, JUST MAYBE, IT'S THAT ***RING?***

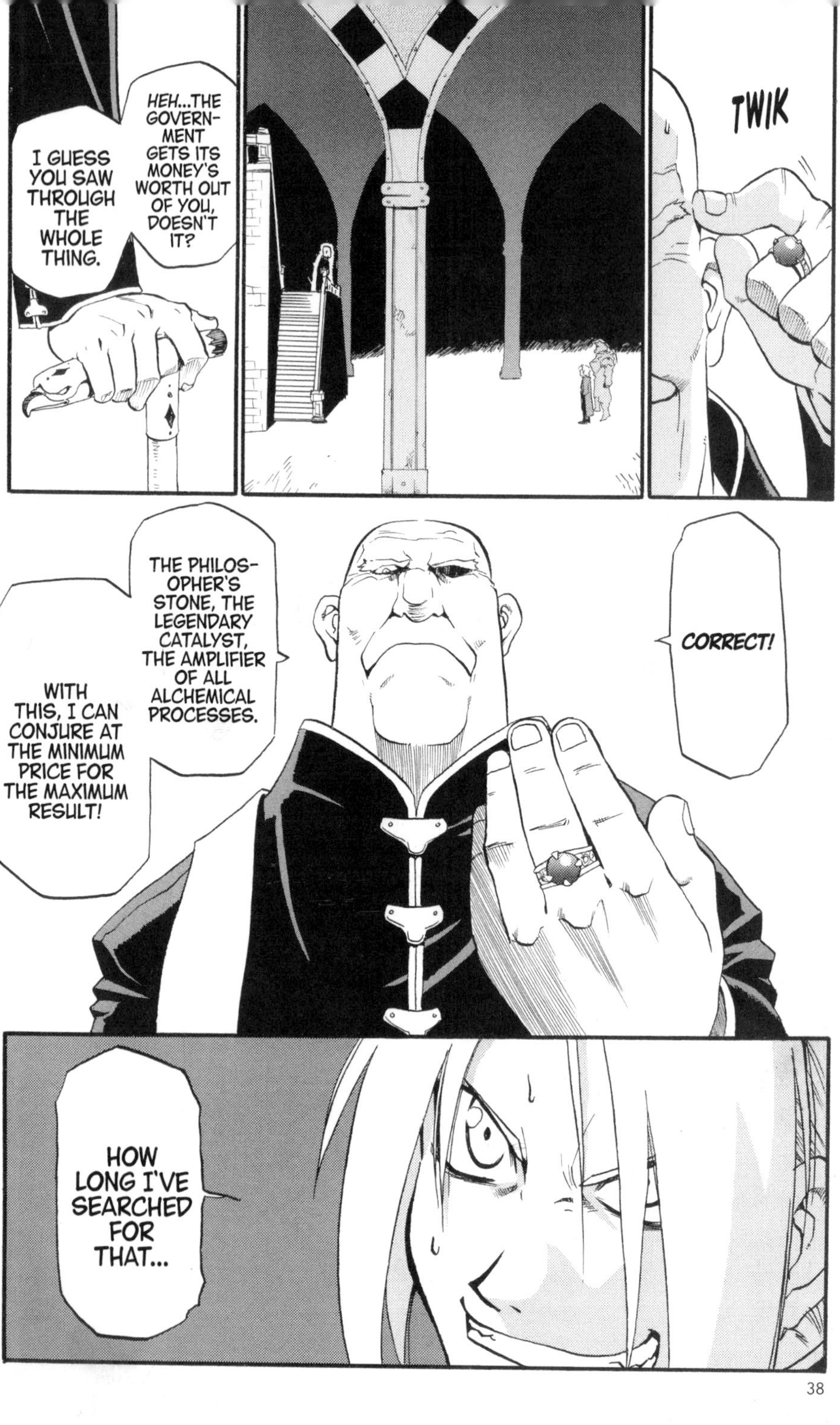
TWIK
HEH...THE GOVERNMENT GETS ITS MONEY'S WORTH OUT OF YOU, DOESN'T IT?
I GUESS YOU SAW THROUGH THE WHOLE THING.
CORRECT!
THE PHILOSOPHER'S STONE, THE LEGENDARY CATALYST, THE AMPLIFIER OF ALL ALCHEMICAL PROCESSES.
WITH THIS, I CAN CONJURE AT THE MINIMUM PRICE FOR THE MAXIMUM RESULT!
HOW LONG I'VE SEARCHED FOR THAT...

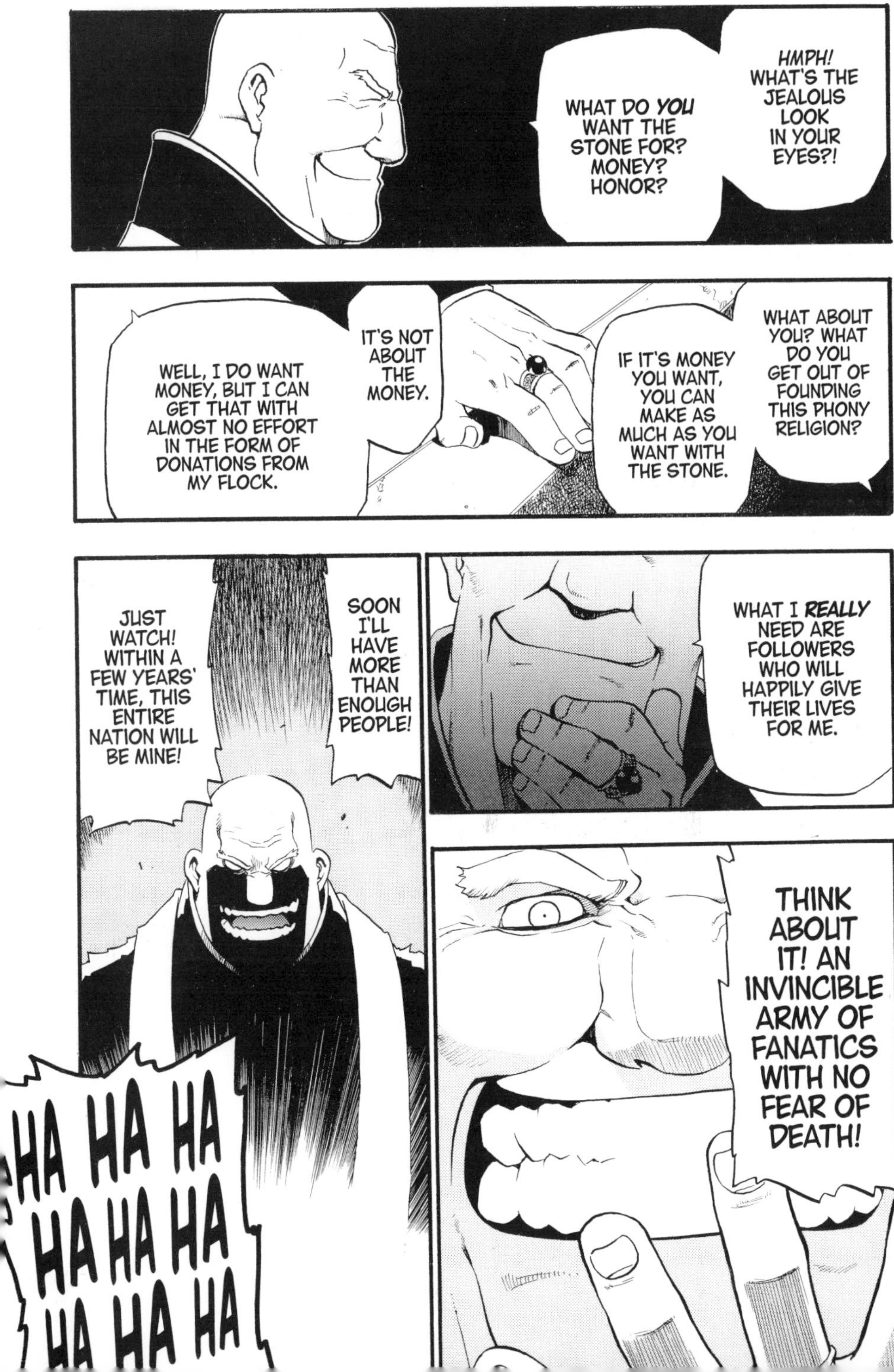
HMPH! WHAT'S THE JEALOUS LOOK IN YOUR EYES?!
WHAT DO *YOU* WANT THE STONE FOR? MONEY? HONOR?
WHAT ABOUT YOU? WHAT DO YOU GET OUT OF FOUNDING THIS PHONY RELIGION?
IF IT'S MONEY YOU WANT, YOU CAN MAKE AS MUCH AS YOU WANT WITH THE STONE.
IT'S NOT ABOUT THE MONEY.
WELL, I DO WANT MONEY, BUT I CAN GET THAT WITH ALMOST NO EFFORT IN THE FORM OF DONATIONS FROM MY FLOCK.
WHAT I *REALLY* NEED ARE FOLLOWERS WHO WILL HAPPILY GIVE THEIR LIVES FOR ME.
THINK ABOUT IT! AN INVINCIBLE ARMY OF FANATICS WITH NO FEAR OF DEATH!
SOON I'LL HAVE MORE THAN ENOUGH PEOPLE!
JUST WATCH! WITHIN A FEW YEARS' TIME, THIS ENTIRE NATION WILL BE MINE!
HA HA HA HA HA HA HA HA HA HA

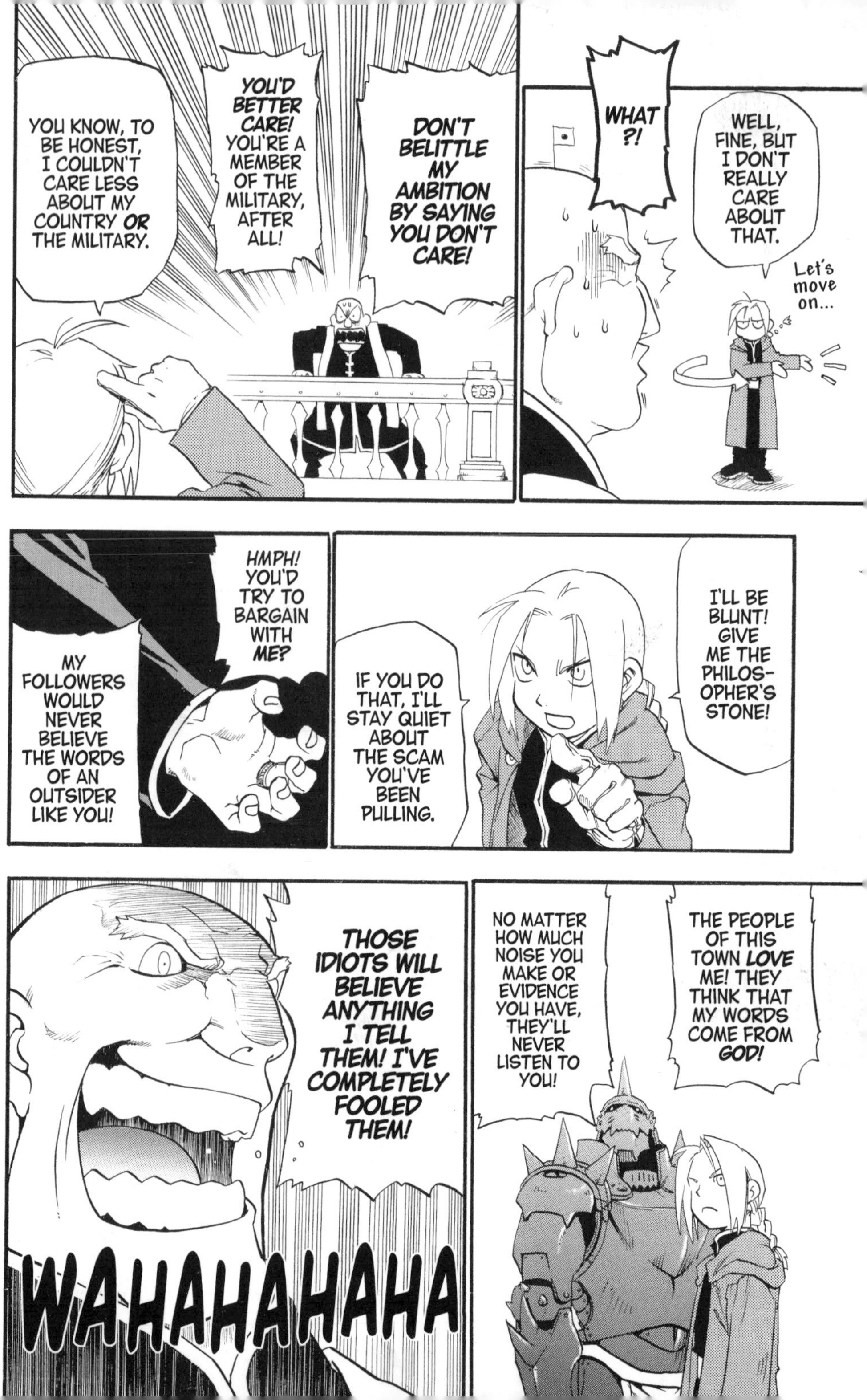
WELL, FINE, BUT I DON'T REALLY CARE ABOUT THAT.
Let's move on...
WHAT ?!
DON'T BELITTLE MY AMBITION BY SAYING YOU DON'T CARE!
YOU'D BETTER CARE! YOU'RE A MEMBER OF THE MILITARY, AFTER ALL!
YOU KNOW, TO BE HONEST, I COULDN'T CARE LESS ABOUT MY COUNTRY OR THE MILITARY.
I'LL BE BLUNT! GIVE ME THE PHILOS-OPHER'S STONE!
IF YOU DO THAT, I'LL STAY QUIET ABOUT THE SCAM YOU'VE BEEN PULLING.
HMPH! YOU'D TRY TO BARGAIN WITH ME?
MY FOLLOWERS WOULD NEVER BELIEVE THE WORDS OF AN OUTSIDER LIKE YOU!
THE PEOPLE OF THIS TOWN LOVE ME! THEY THINK THAT MY WORDS COME FROM GOD!
NO MATTER HOW MUCH NOISE YOU MAKE OR EVIDENCE YOU HAVE, THEY'LL NEVER LISTEN TO YOU!
THOSE IDIOTS WILL BELIEVE ANYTHING I TELL THEM! I'VE COMPLETELY FOOLED THEM!
WAHAHAHAHAHA

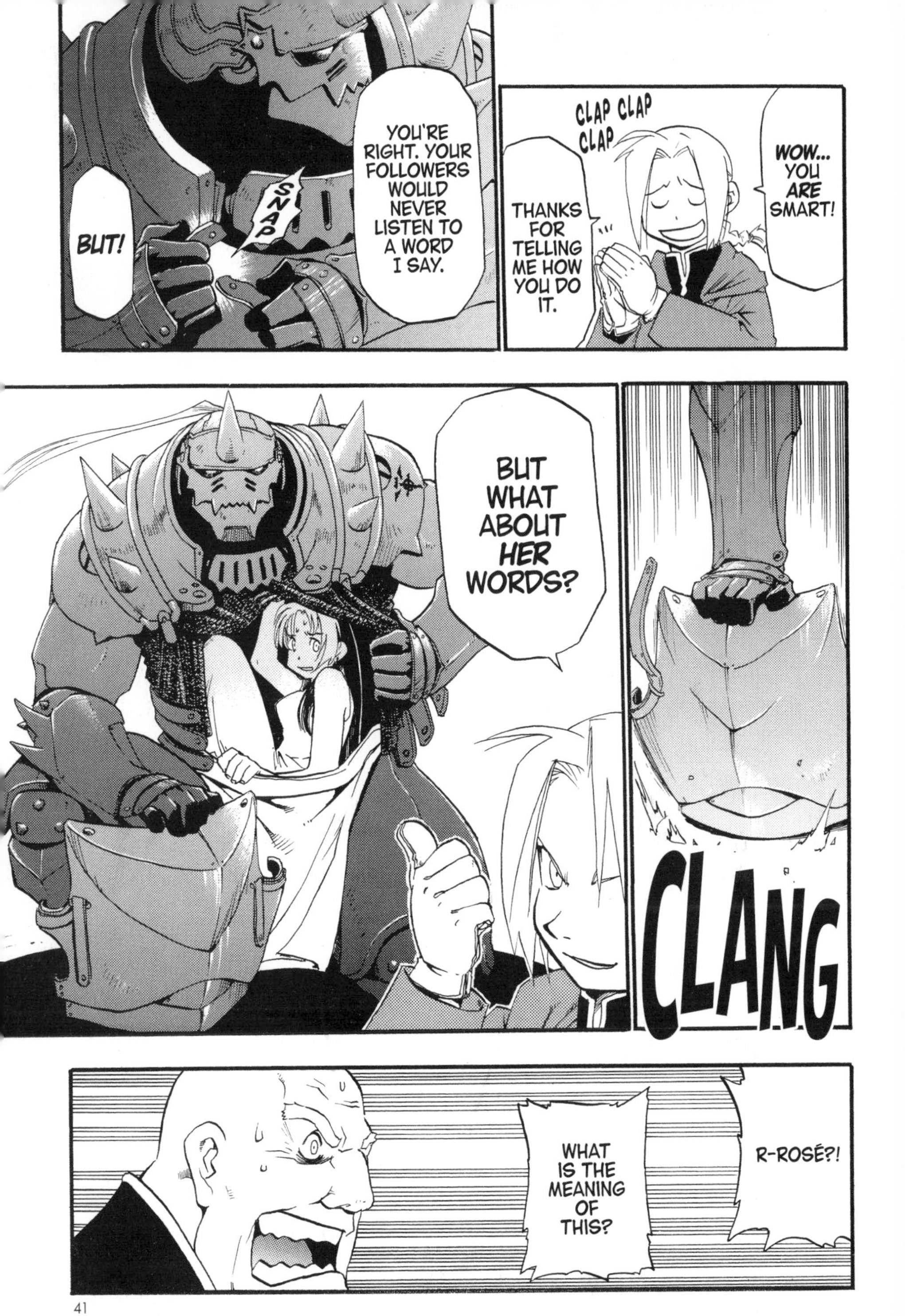
WOW... YOU ARE SMART!
CLAP CLAP CLAP
THANKS FOR TELLING ME HOW YOU DO IT.
YOU'RE RIGHT. YOUR FOLLOWERS WOULD NEVER LISTEN TO A WORD I SAY.
SNAP
BUT!
CLANG
BUT WHAT ABOUT HER WORDS?
R-ROSÉ?!
WHAT IS THE MEANING OF THIS?

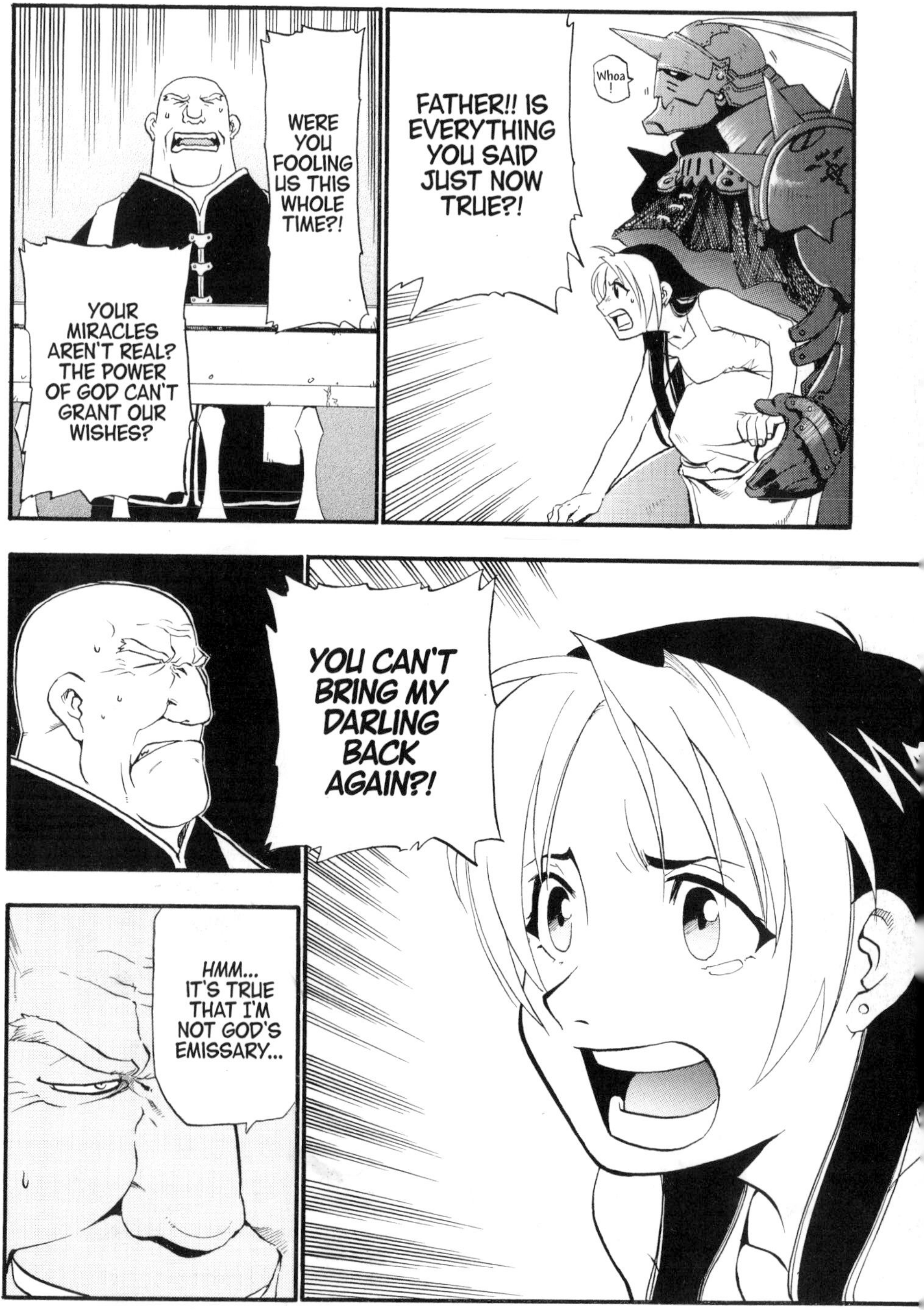
Whoa!
FATHER!! IS EVERYTHING YOU SAID JUST NOW TRUE?!
WERE YOU FOOLING US THIS WHOLE TIME?!
YOUR MIRACLES AREN'T REAL? THE POWER OF GOD CAN'T GRANT OUR WISHES?
YOU CAN'T BRING MY DARLING BACK AGAIN?!
HMM... IT'S TRUE THAT I'M NOT GOD'S EMISSARY...

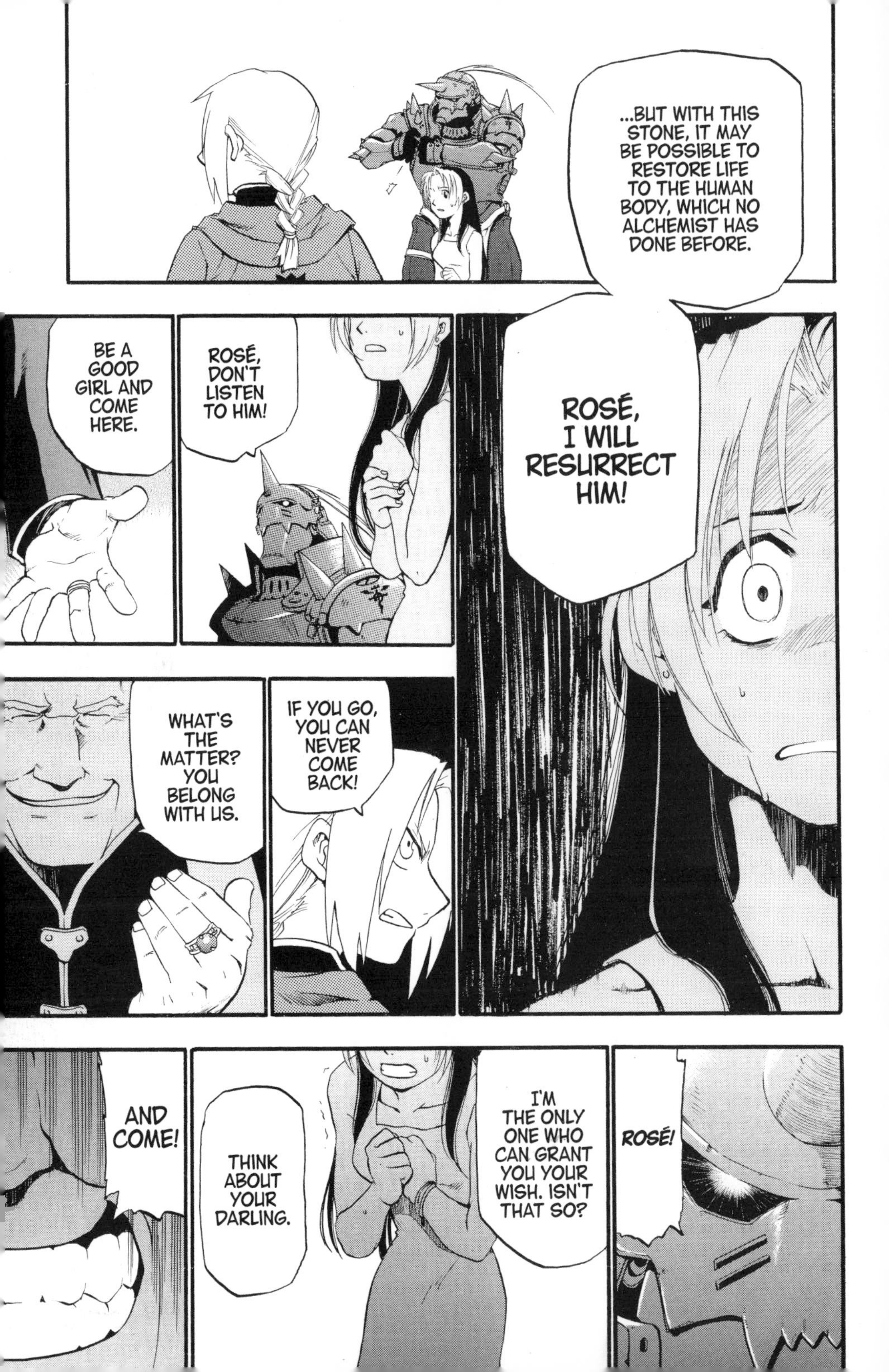
...BUT WITH THIS STONE, IT MAY BE POSSIBLE TO RESTORE LIFE TO THE HUMAN BODY, WHICH NO ALCHEMIST HAS DONE BEFORE.
ROSÉ, I WILL RESURRECT HIM!
ROSÉ, DON'T LISTEN TO HIM!
BE A GOOD GIRL AND COME HERE.
IF YOU GO, YOU CAN NEVER COME BACK!
WHAT'S THE MATTER? YOU BELONG WITH US.
ROSÉ!
I'M THE ONLY ONE WHO CAN GRANT YOU YOUR WISH. ISN'T THAT SO?
THINK ABOUT YOUR DARLING.
AND COME!

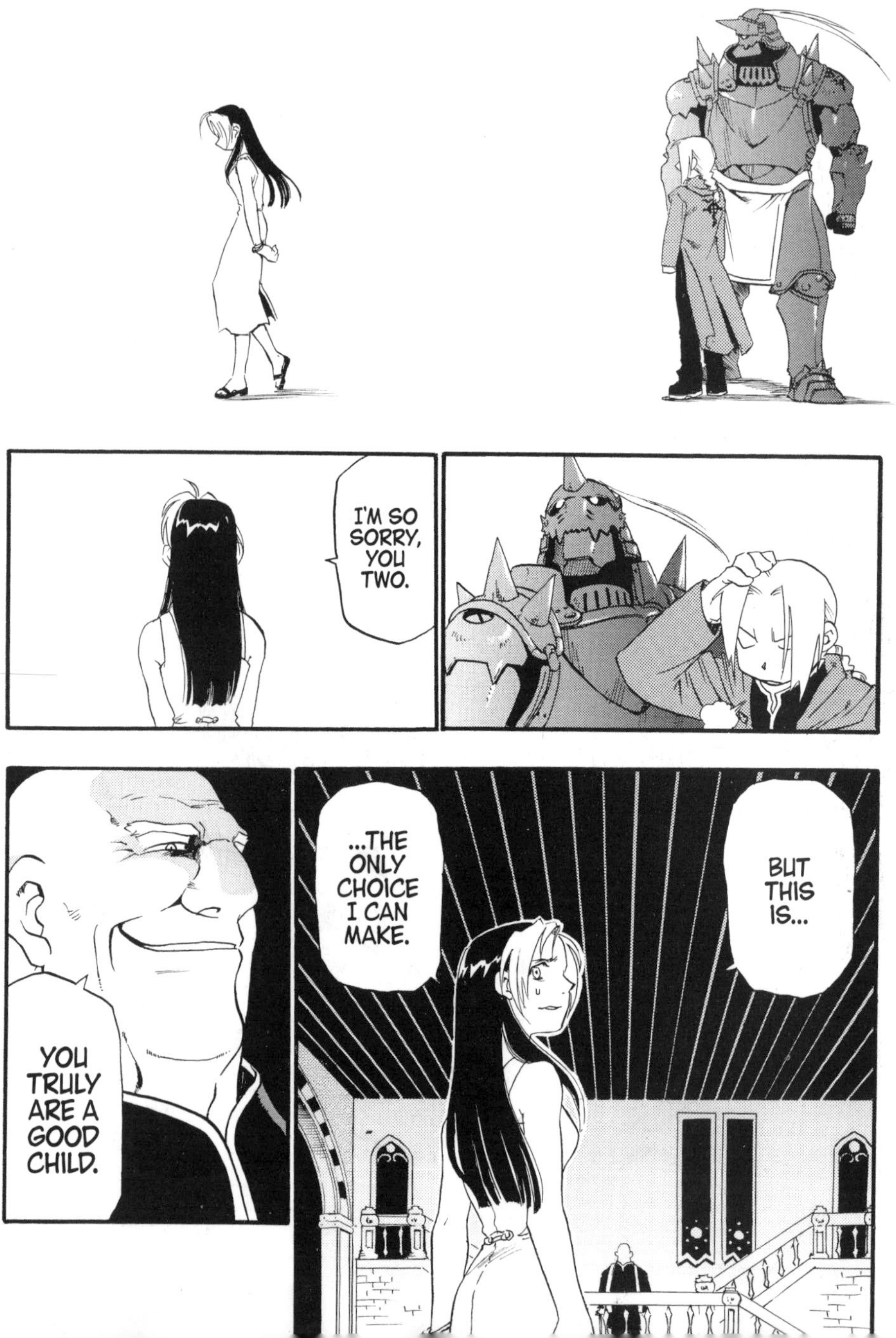
I'M SO SORRY, YOU TWO.
BUT THIS IS...
...THE ONLY CHOICE I CAN MAKE.
YOU TRULY ARE A GOOD CHILD.

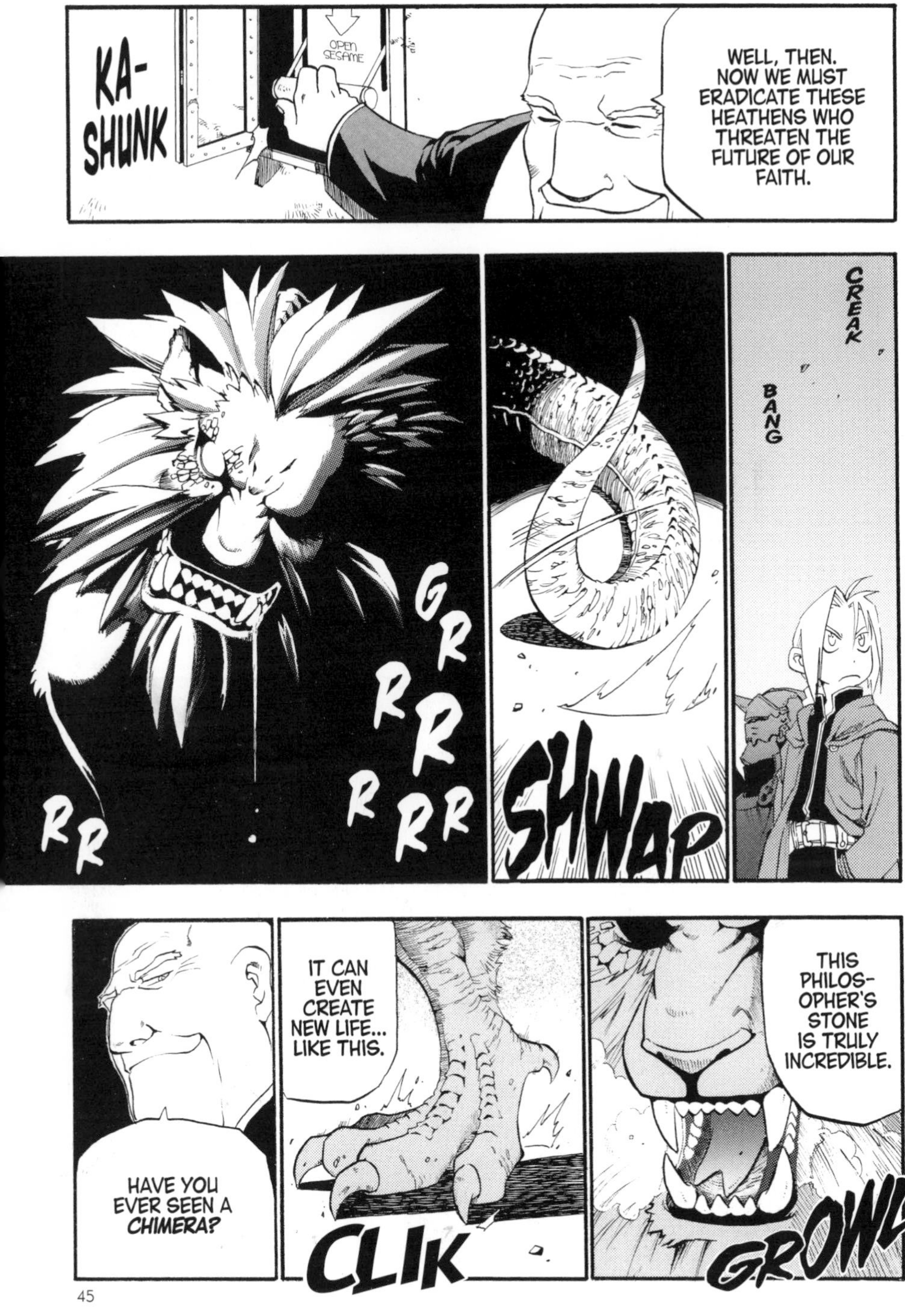
WELL, THEN. NOW WE MUST ERADICATE THESE HEATHENS WHO THREATEN THE FUTURE OF OUR FAITH.
OPEN SESAME
KA-SHUNK
CREAK
BANG
SHWAP
GRRRRRRR
RR
THIS PHILOSOPHER'S STONE IS TRULY INCREDIBLE.
GROWL
IT CAN EVEN CREATE NEW LIFE... LIKE THIS.
CLIK
HAVE YOU EVER SEEN A CHIMERA?

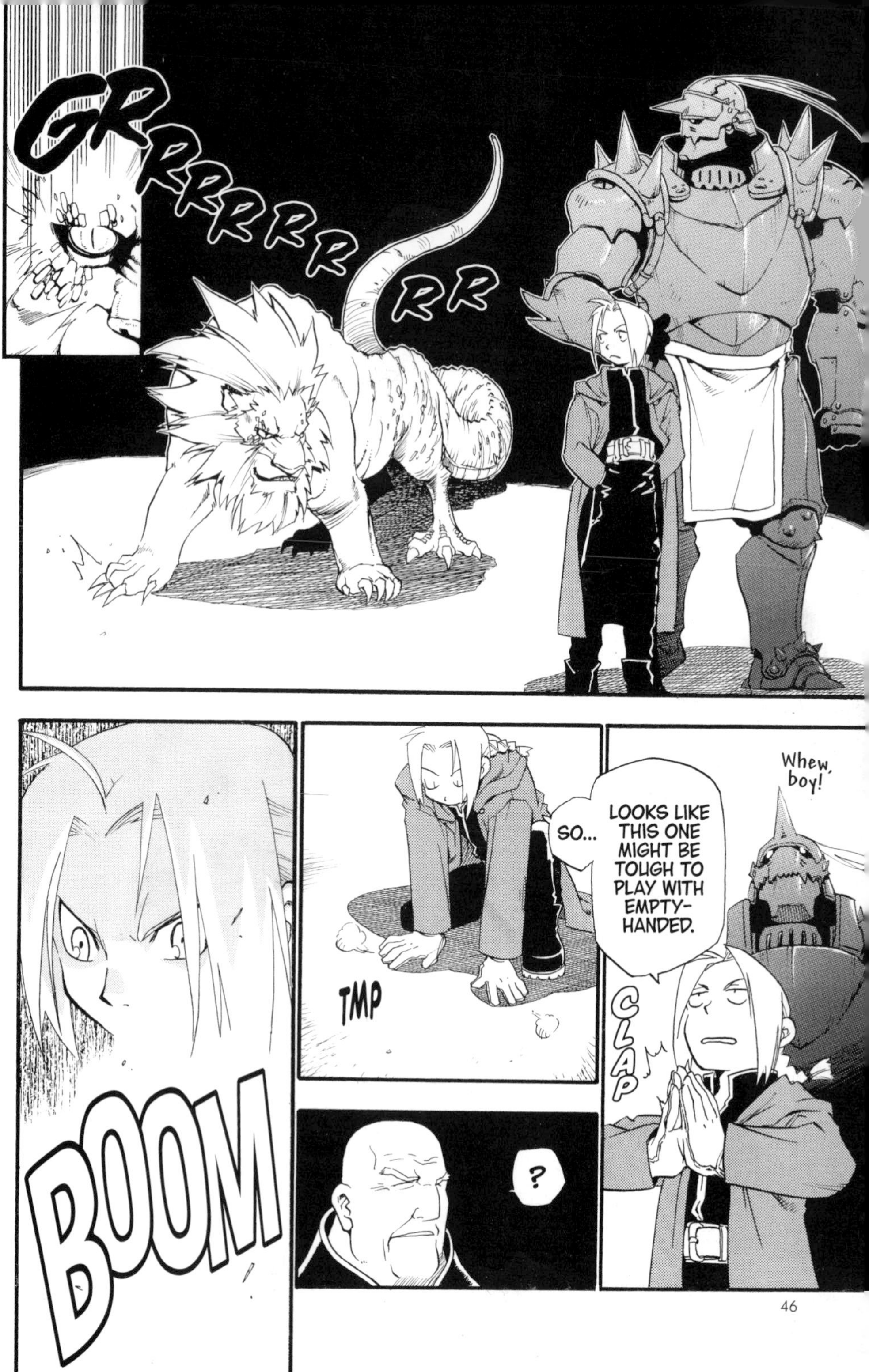
GRRRRRRRR
Whew, boy!
SO...
LOOKS LIKE THIS ONE MIGHT BE TOUGH TO PLAY WITH EMPTY-HANDED.
CLAP
TMP
?
BOOM

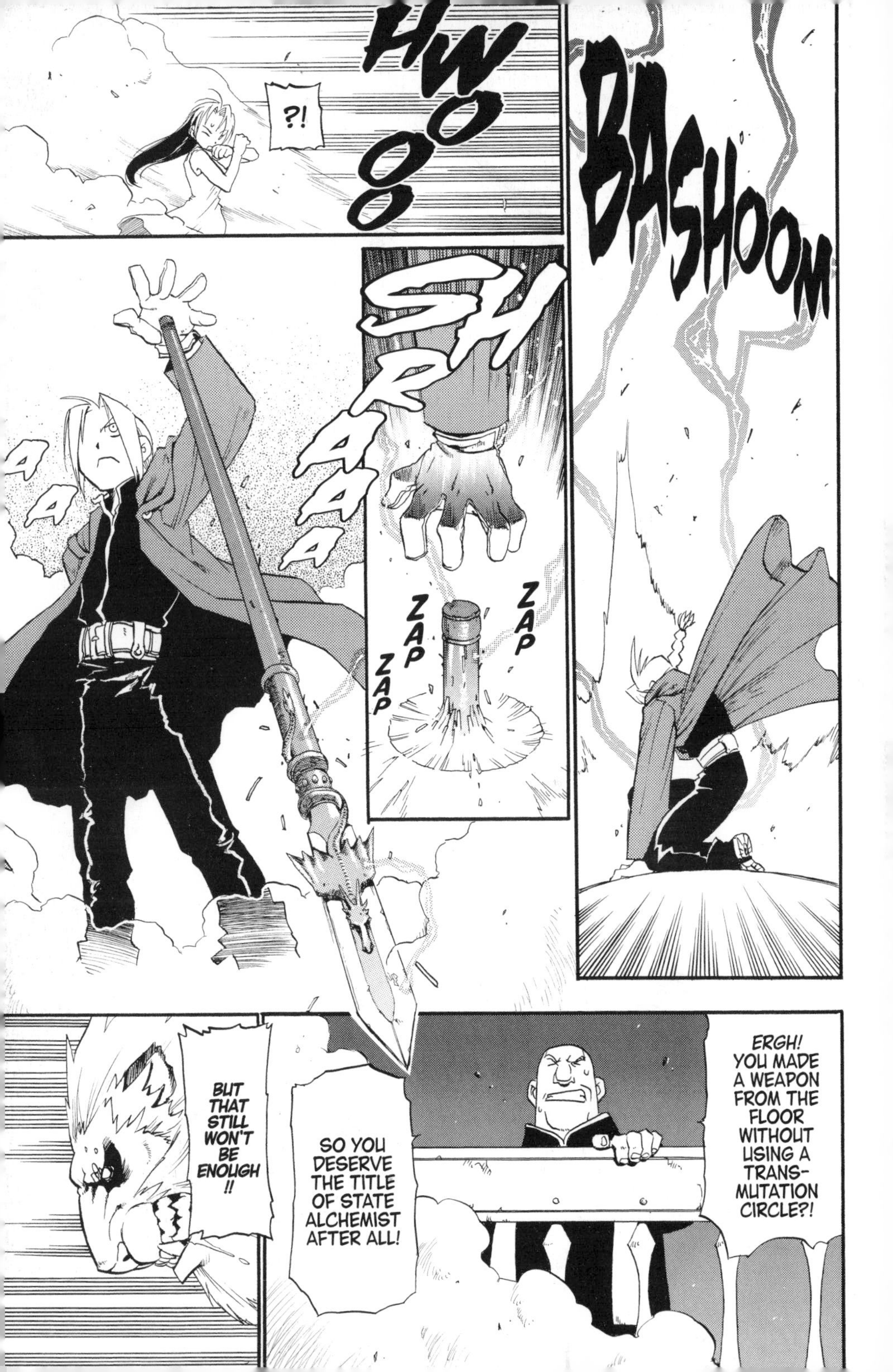
BASHOOM
HWOOO
?!
SHRAAAAAA
ZAP
ZAP
ZAP
ERGH! YOU MADE A WEAPON FROM THE FLOOR WITHOUT USING A TRANS-MUTATION CIRCLE?!
SO YOU DESERVE THE TITLE OF STATE ALCHEMIST AFTER ALL!
BUT THAT STILL WON'T BE ENOUGH!!

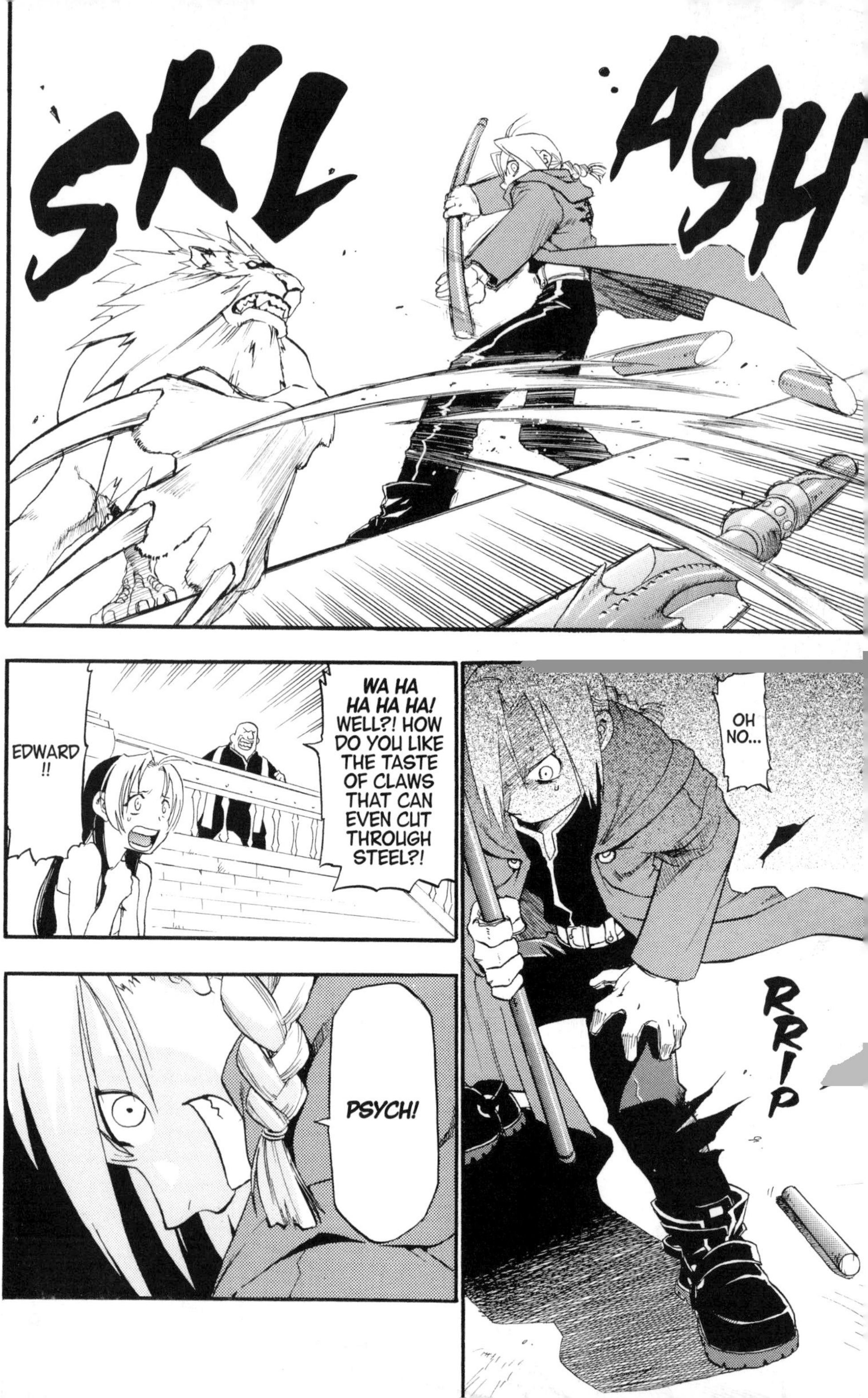
SKL
ASH
OH NO...
RRIP
WA HA HA HA HA! WELL?! HOW DO YOU LIKE THE TASTE OF CLAWS THAT CAN EVEN CUT THROUGH STEEL?!
EDWARD !!
PSYCH!

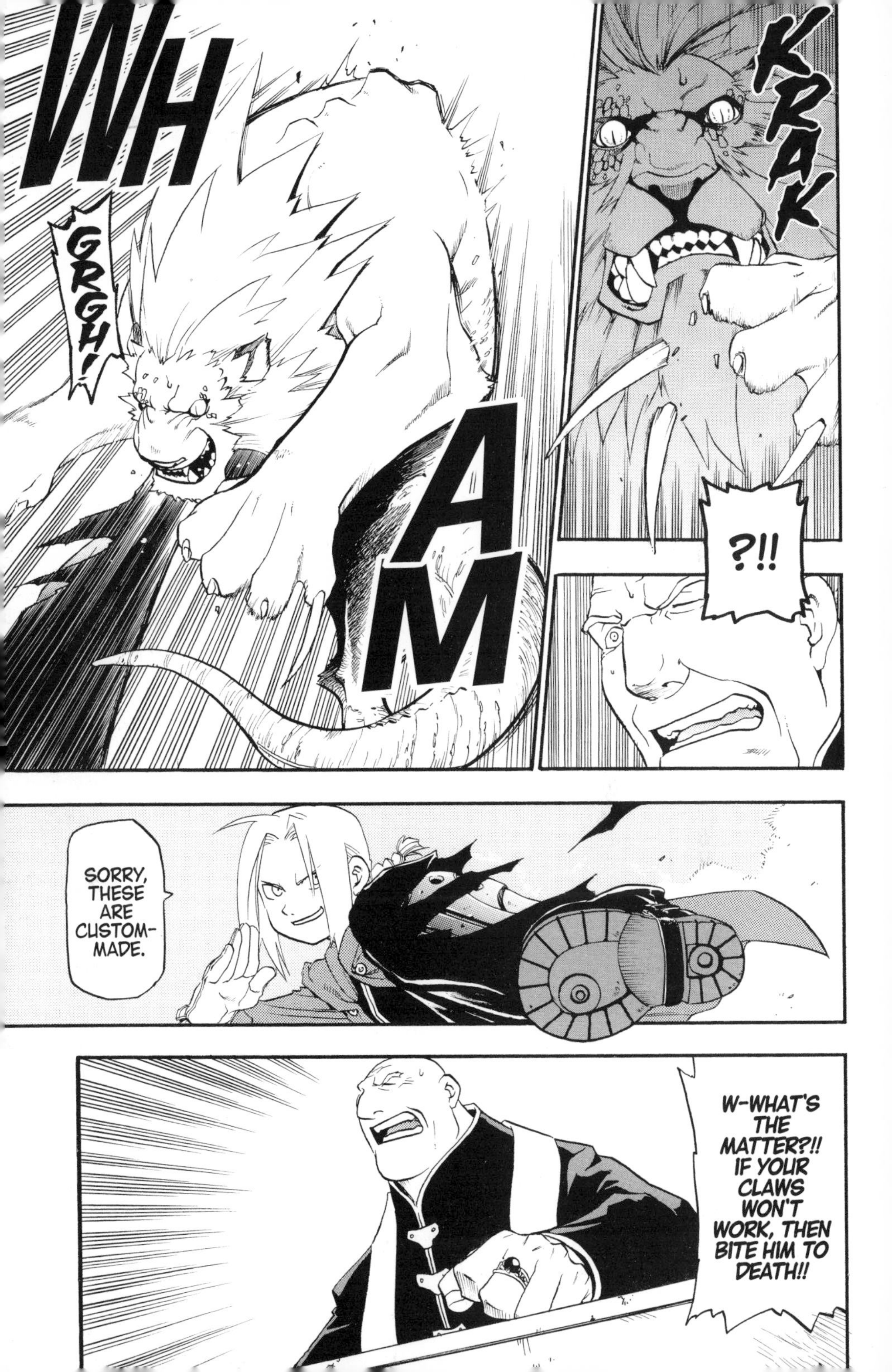
KRAK
?!!
WHAM
GRGH!
SORRY, THESE ARE CUSTOM-MADE.
W-WHAT'S THE MATTER?!! IF YOUR CLAWS WON'T WORK, THEN BITE HIM TO DEATH!!

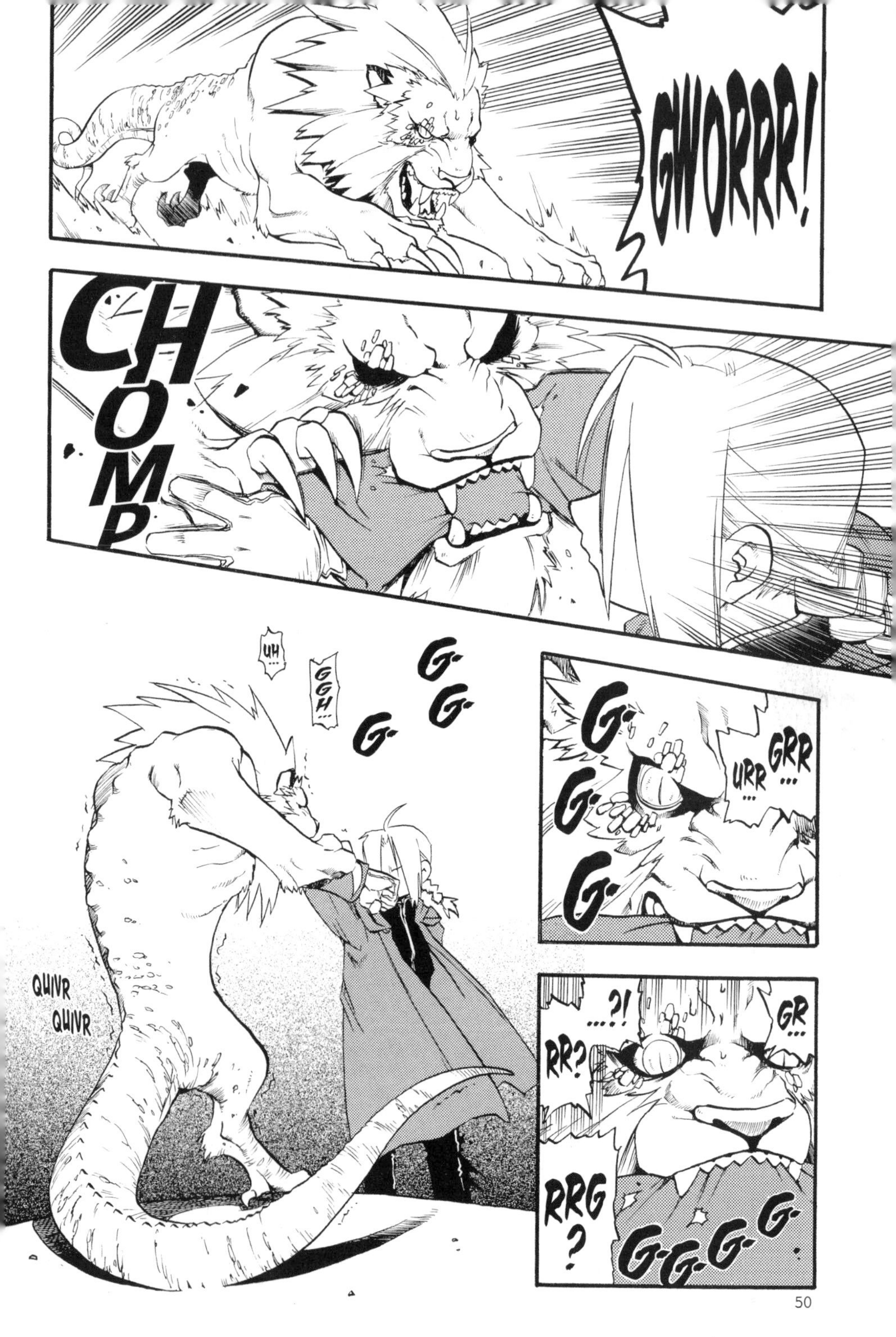
GWORRR!
CHOMP
G- G- G-
URR...
GRR...
...?!
GR...
RR?
RRG?
G-G-G-G-
UH...
GGH...
G- G- G-
QUIVR QUIVR

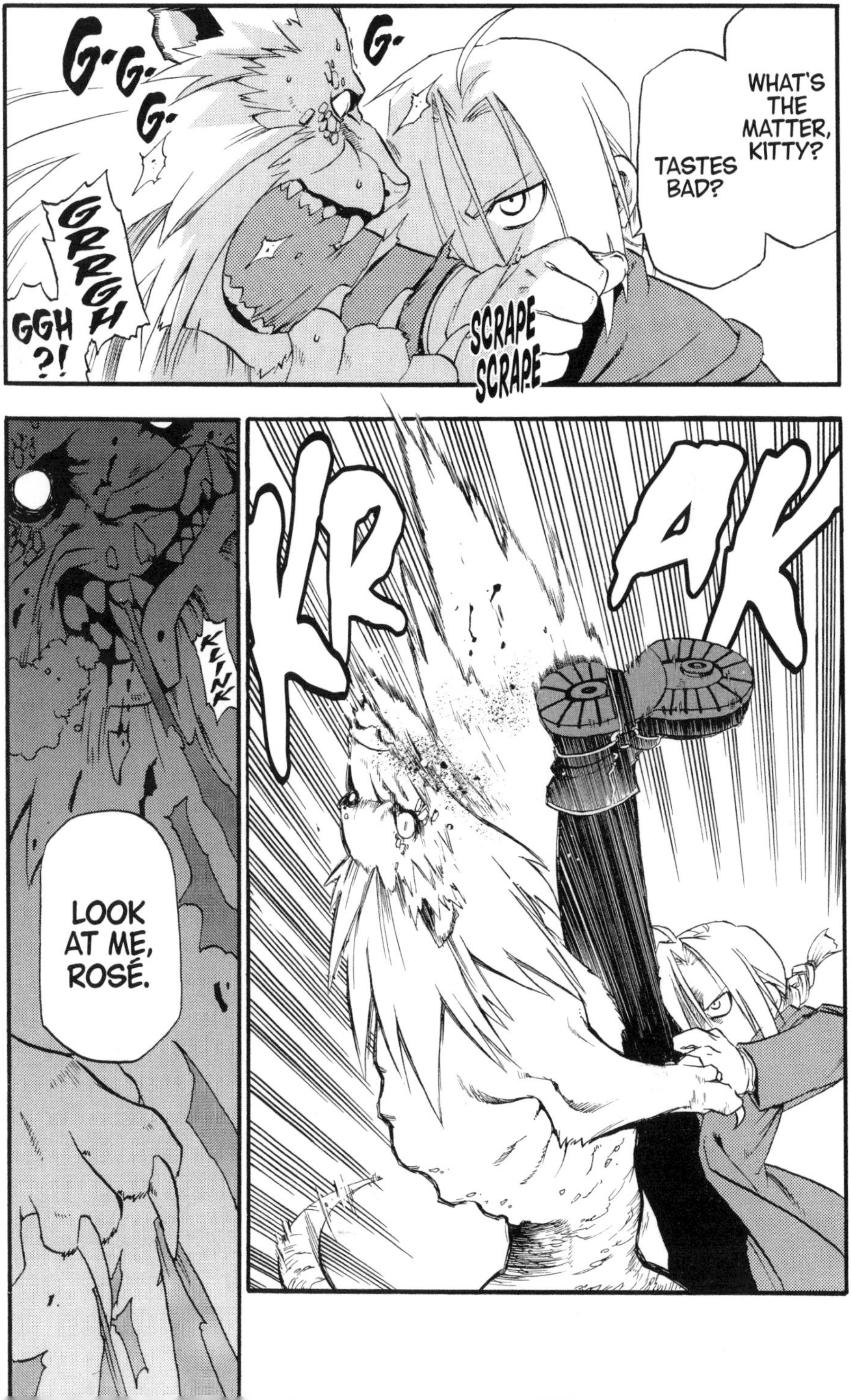
WHAT'S THE MATTER, KITTY?
TASTES BAD?
G-
G-G-G-
SCRAPE SCRAPE
GRRRGH
GGH?!
KRAK
KLINK
LOOK AT ME, ROSÉ.

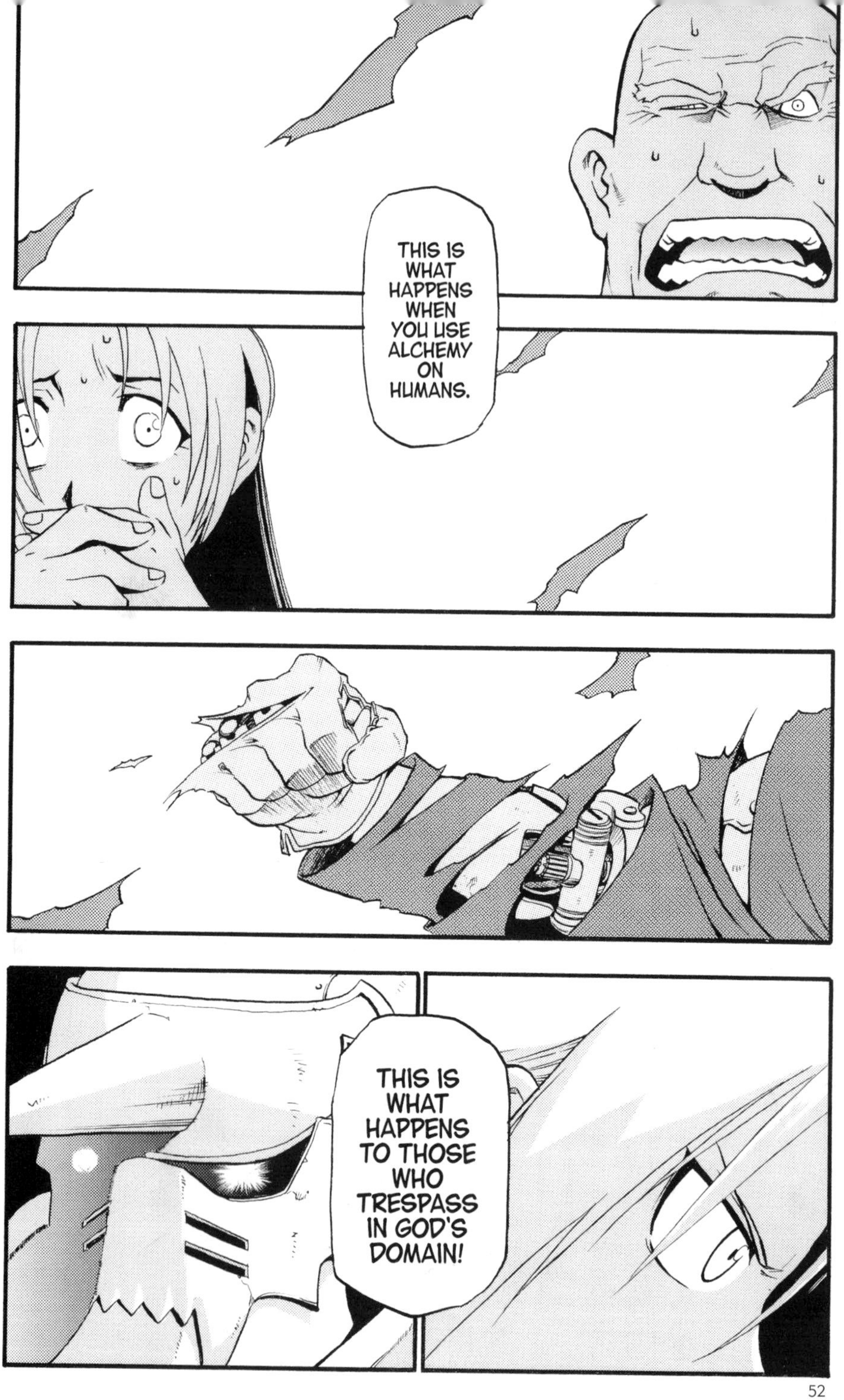
THIS IS WHAT HAPPENS WHEN YOU USE ALCHEMY ON HUMANS.
THIS IS WHAT HAPPENS TO THOSE WHO TRESPASS IN GOD'S DOMAIN!

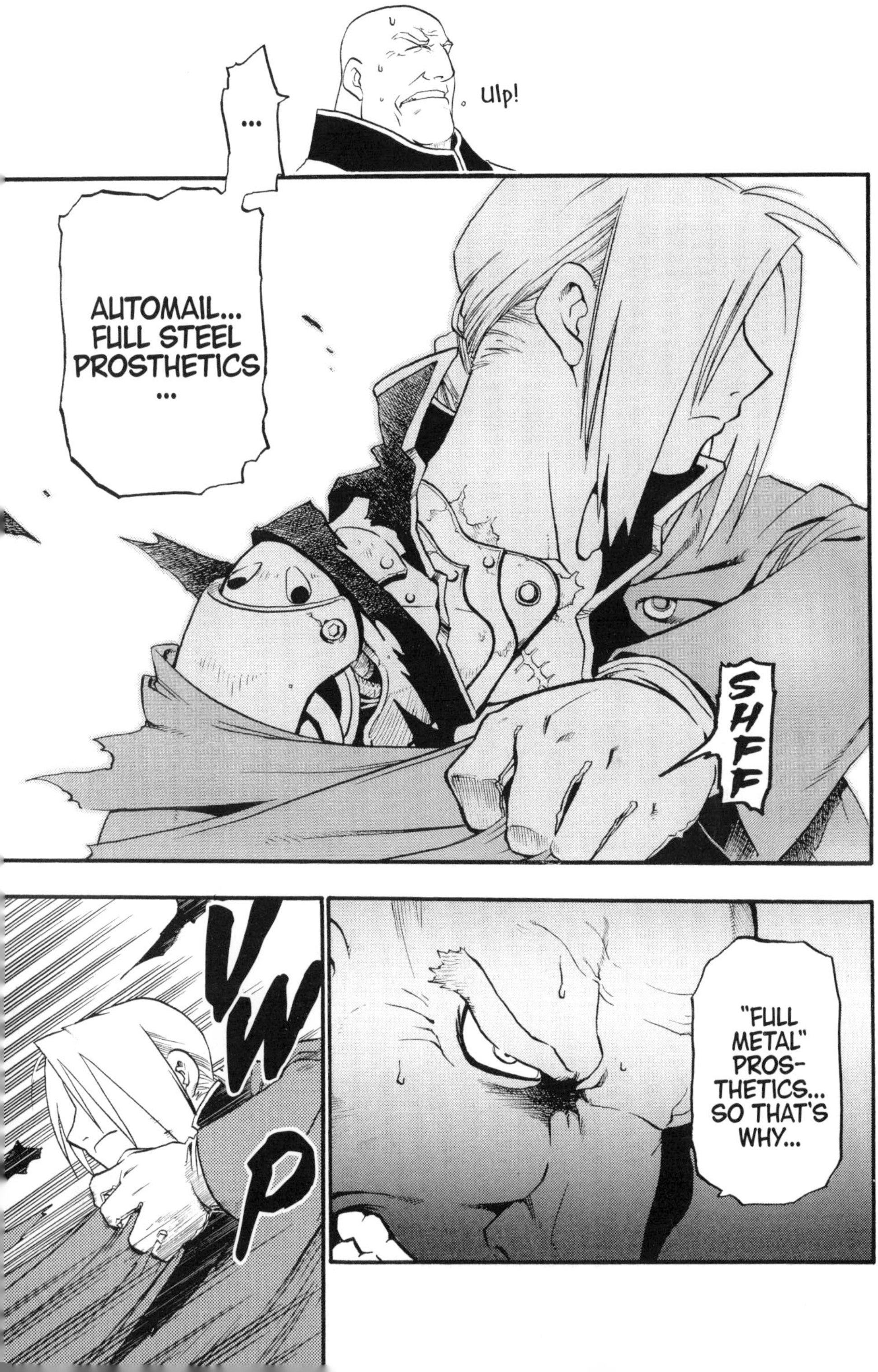
Ulp!
...
AUTOMAIL... FULL STEEL PROSTHETICS ...
SHFF
"FULL METAL" PROS-THETICS... SO THAT'S WHY...

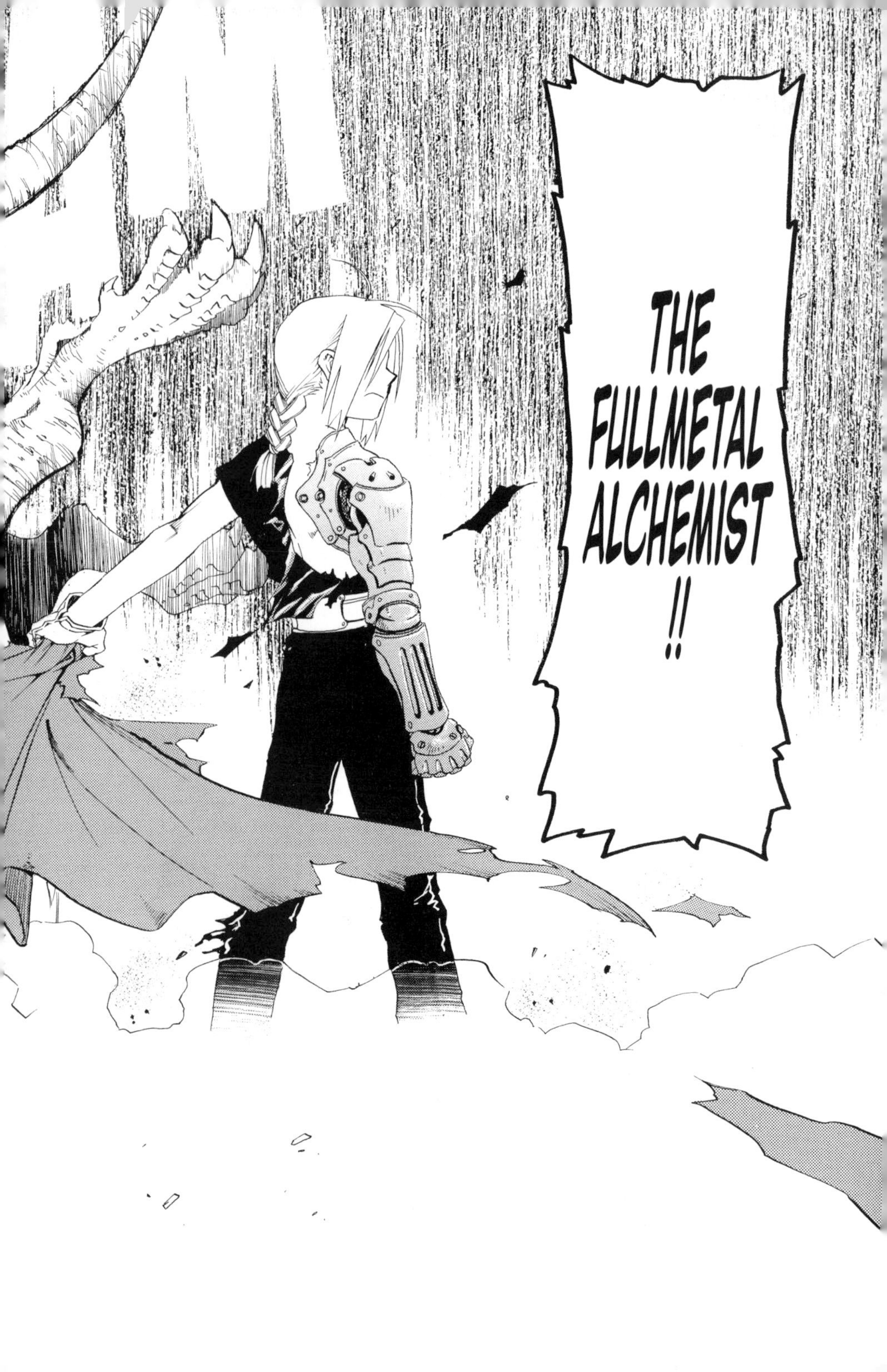
THE FULLMETAL ALCHEMIST !!

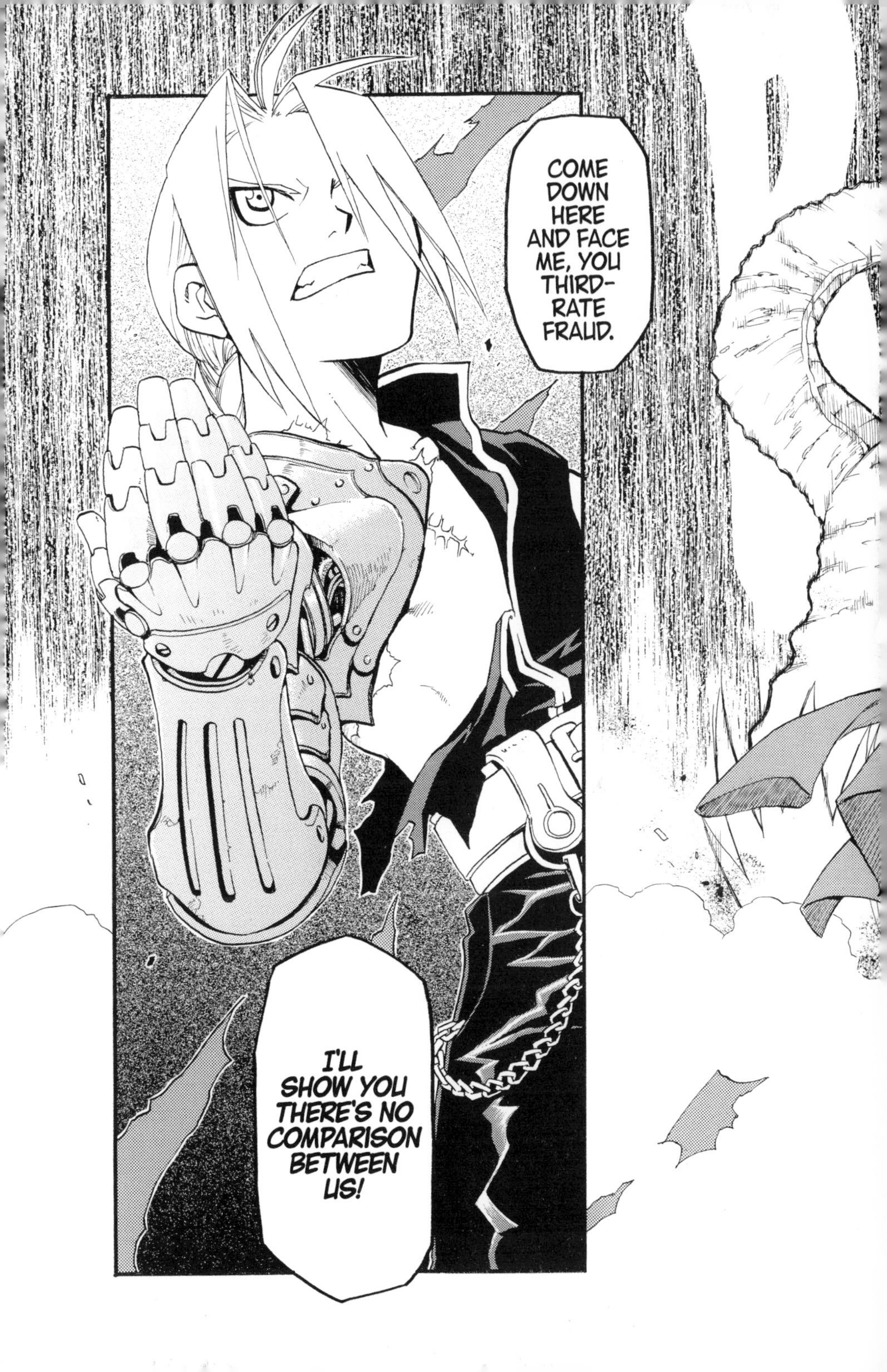
COME DOWN HERE AND FACE ME, YOU THIRD-RATE FRAUD.
I'LL SHOW YOU THERE'S NO COMPARISON BETWEEN US!

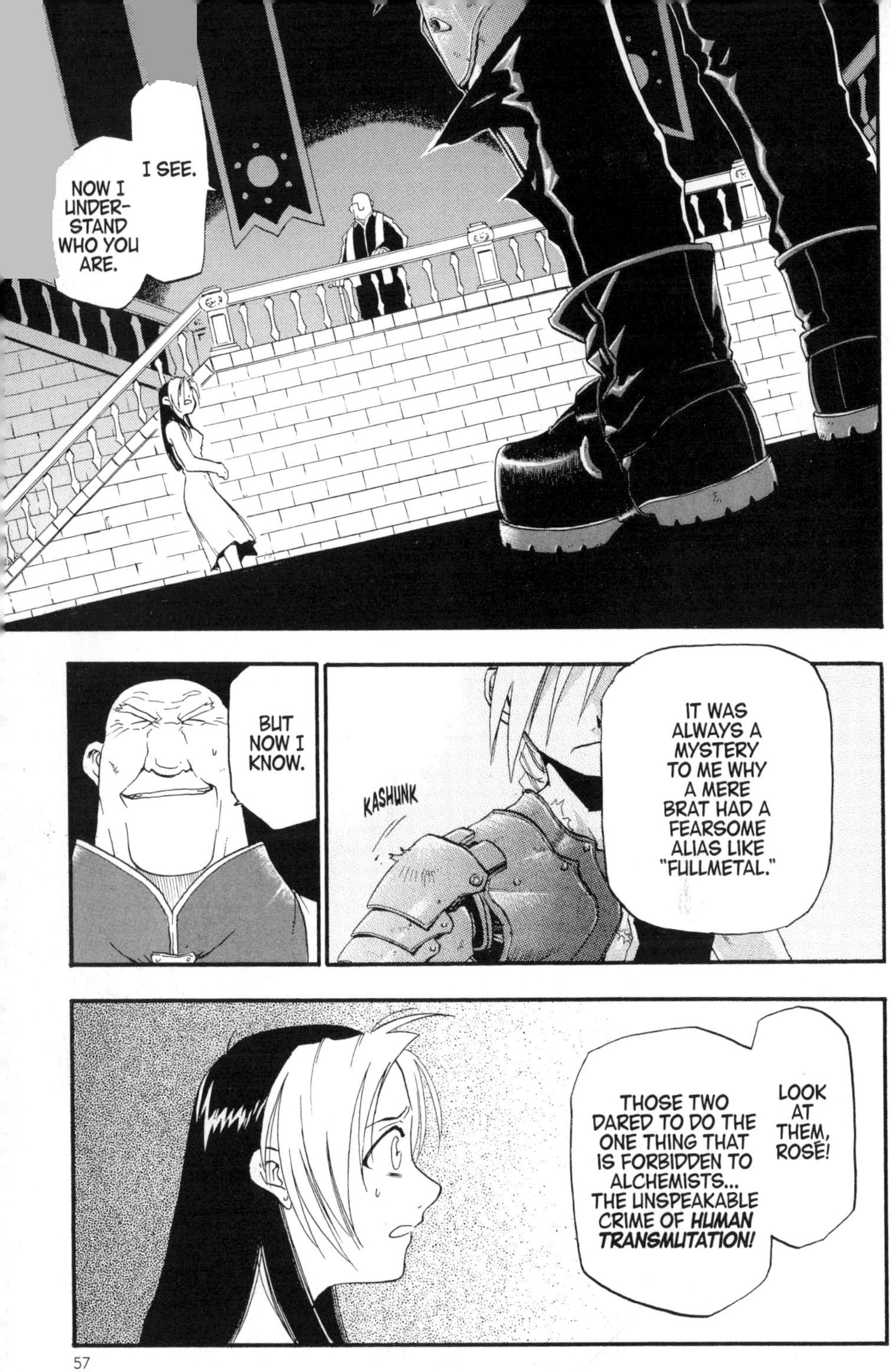
I SEE.
NOW I UNDER-STAND WHO YOU ARE.
IT WAS ALWAYS A MYSTERY TO ME WHY A MERE BRAT HAD A FEARSOME ALIAS LIKE "FULLMETAL."
KASHUNK
BUT NOW I KNOW.
LOOK AT THEM, ROSÉ!
THOSE TWO DARED TO DO THE ONE THING THAT IS FORBIDDEN TO ALCHEMISTS... THE UNSPEAKABLE CRIME OF *HUMAN TRANSMUTATION!*

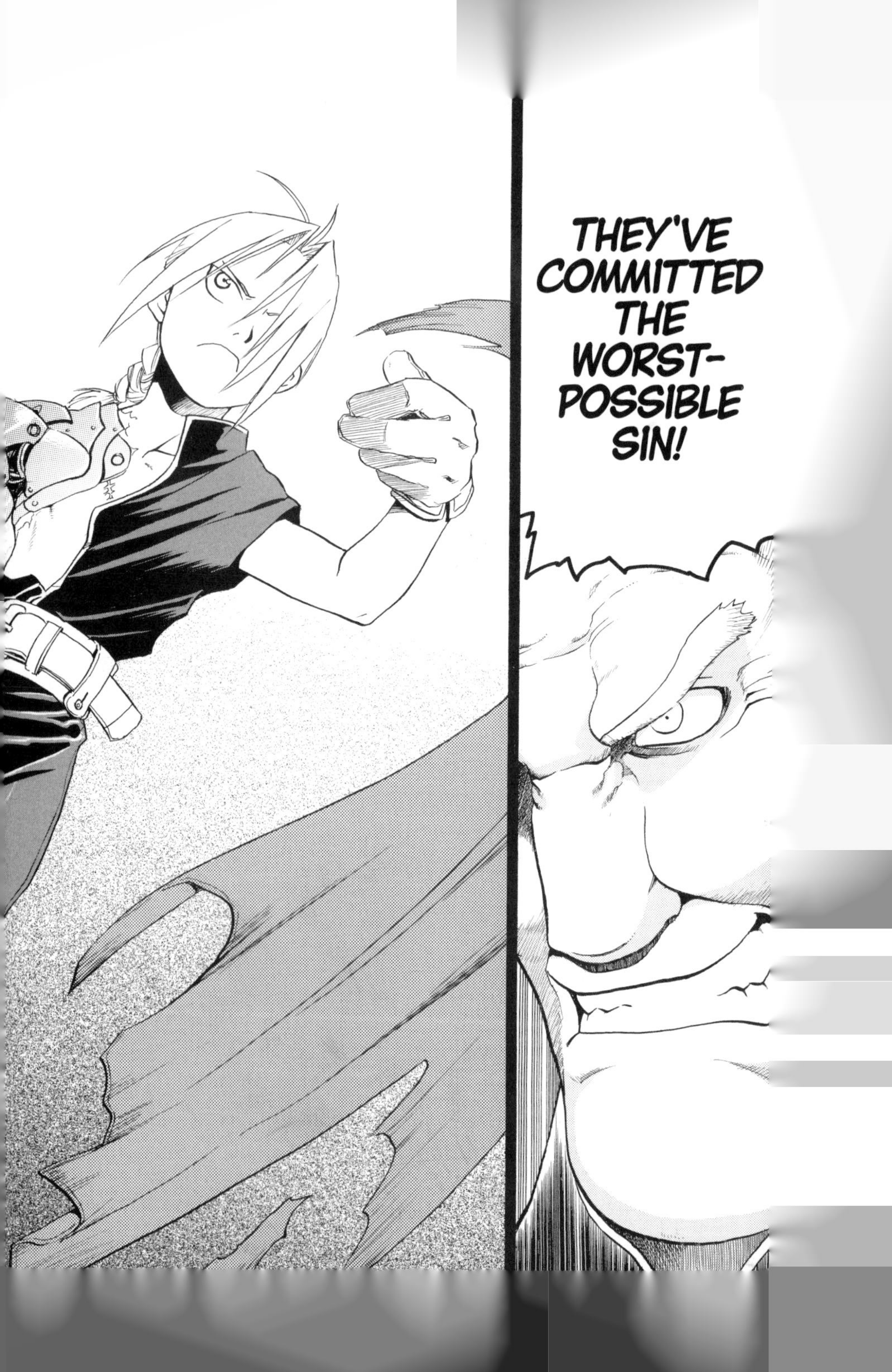
THEY'VE COMMITTED THE WORST-POSSIBLE SIN!

!

CHAPTER 2

THE PRICE OF LIFE

"HE MADE
WINGS OUT
OF WAX SO HE
COULD FLY,
BUT WHEN
HE GOT TOO
CLOSE TO THE
SUN, THE WAX
MELTED AND
HE CRASHED
TO THE
GROUND..."

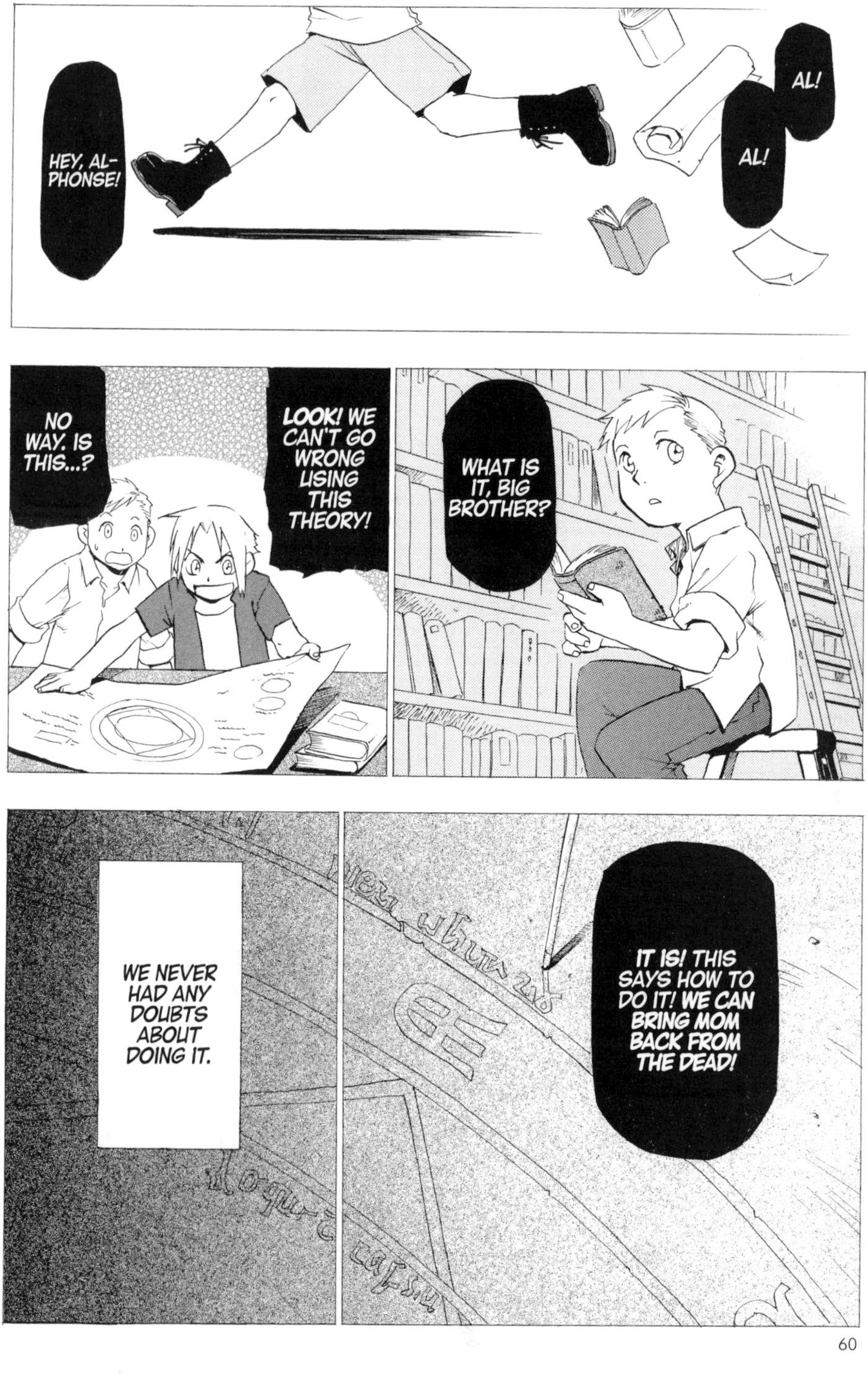
AL!
AL!
HEY, ALPHONSE!
WHAT IS IT, BIG BROTHER?
LOOK! WE CAN'T GO WRONG USING THIS THEORY!
NO WAY. IS THIS...?
IT IS! THIS SAYS HOW TO DO IT! WE CAN BRING MOM BACK FROM THE DEAD!
WE NEVER HAD ANY DOUBTS ABOUT DOING IT.

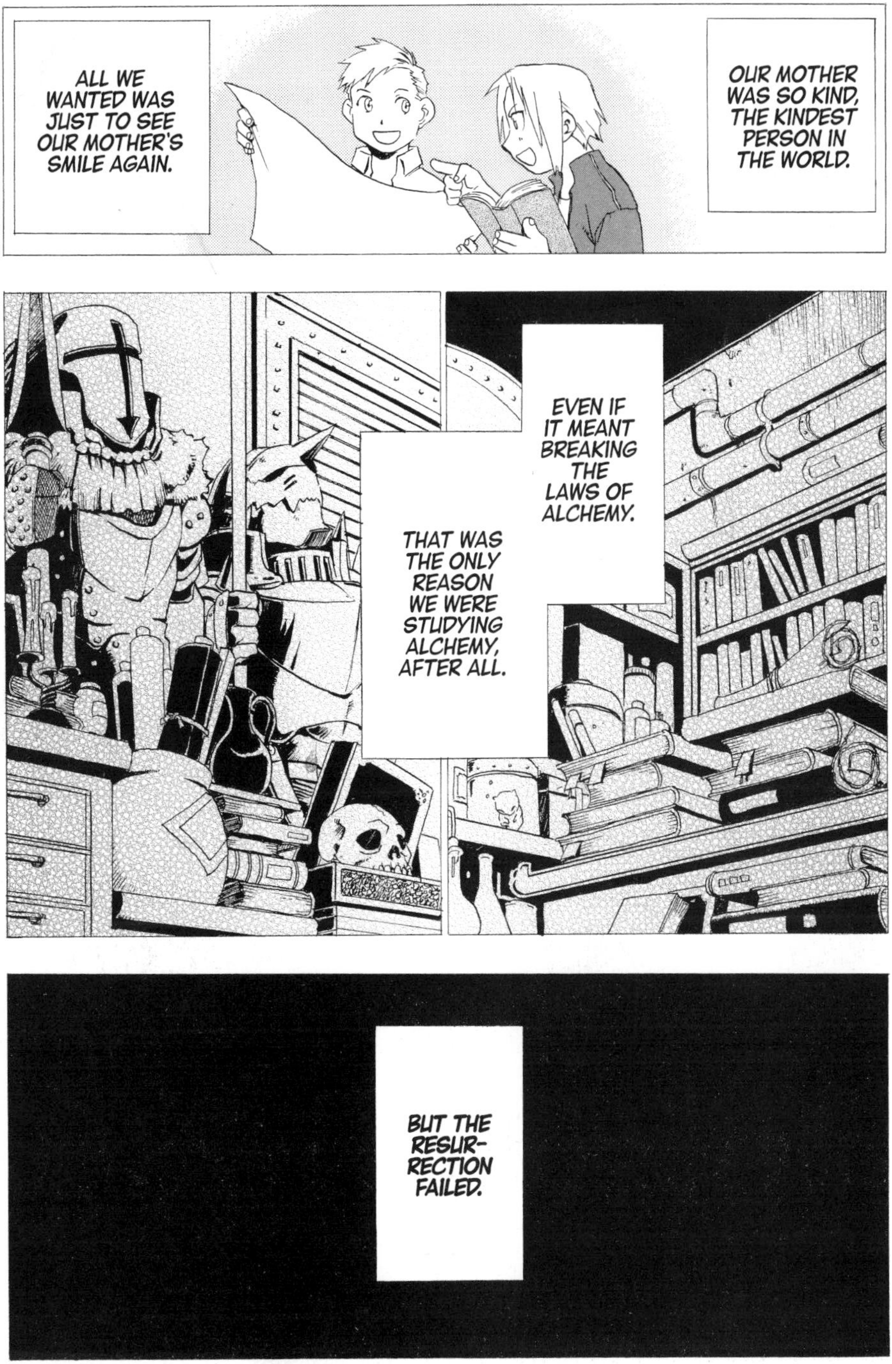
OUR MOTHER WAS SO KIND, THE KINDEST PERSON IN THE WORLD.
ALL WE WANTED WAS JUST TO SEE OUR MOTHER'S SMILE AGAIN.
EVEN IF IT MEANT BREAKING THE LAWS OF ALCHEMY.
THAT WAS THE ONLY REASON WE WERE STUDYING ALCHEMY, AFTER ALL.
BUT THE RESUR-RECTION FAILED.

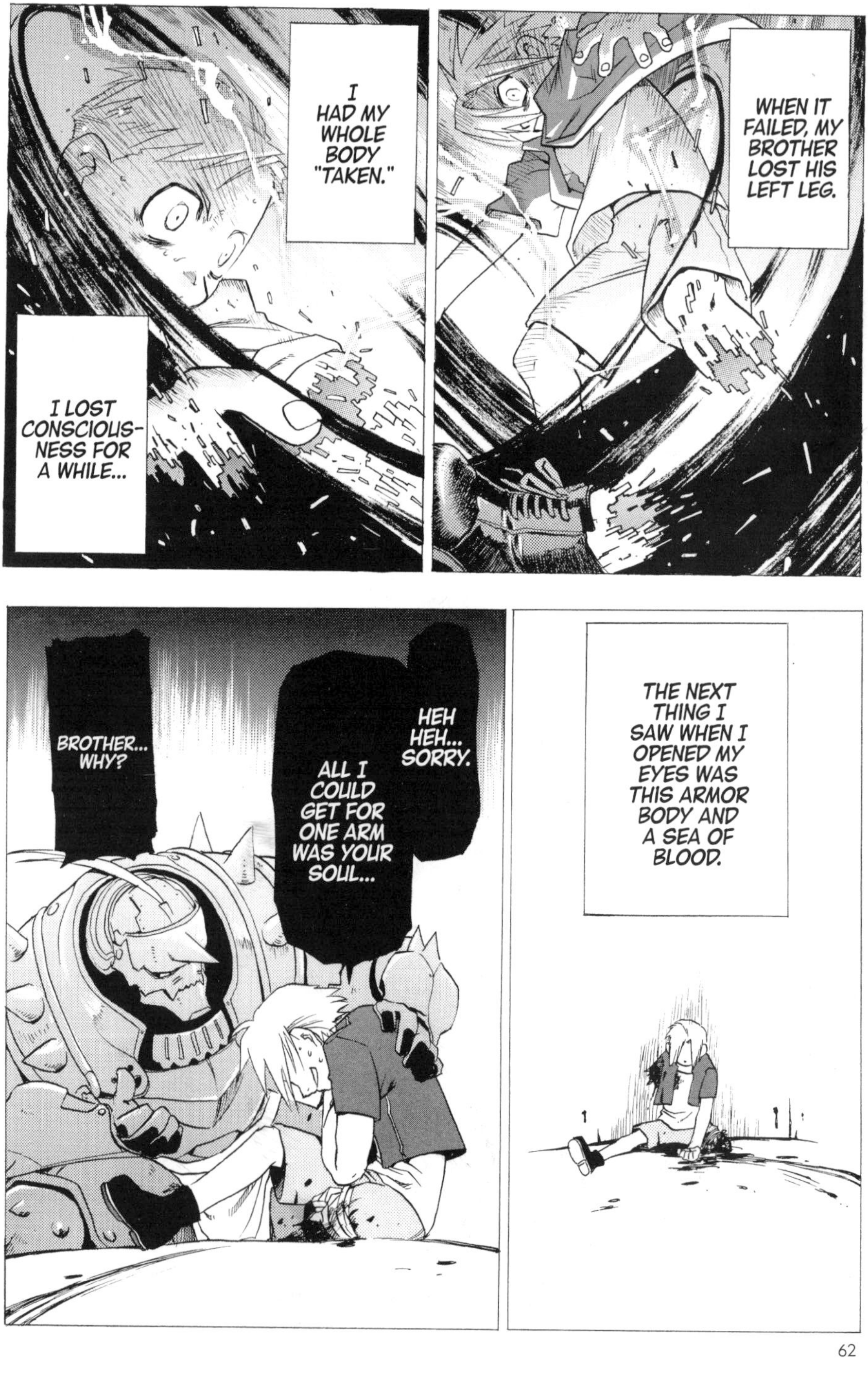
WHEN IT FAILED, MY BROTHER LOST HIS LEFT LEG.
I HAD MY WHOLE BODY "TAKEN."
I LOST CONSCIOUS-NESS FOR A WHILE...
THE NEXT THING I SAW WHEN I OPENED MY EYES WAS THIS ARMOR BODY AND A SEA OF BLOOD.
HEH HEH... SORRY.
ALL I COULD GET FOR ONE ARM WAS YOUR SOUL...
BROTHER... WHY?

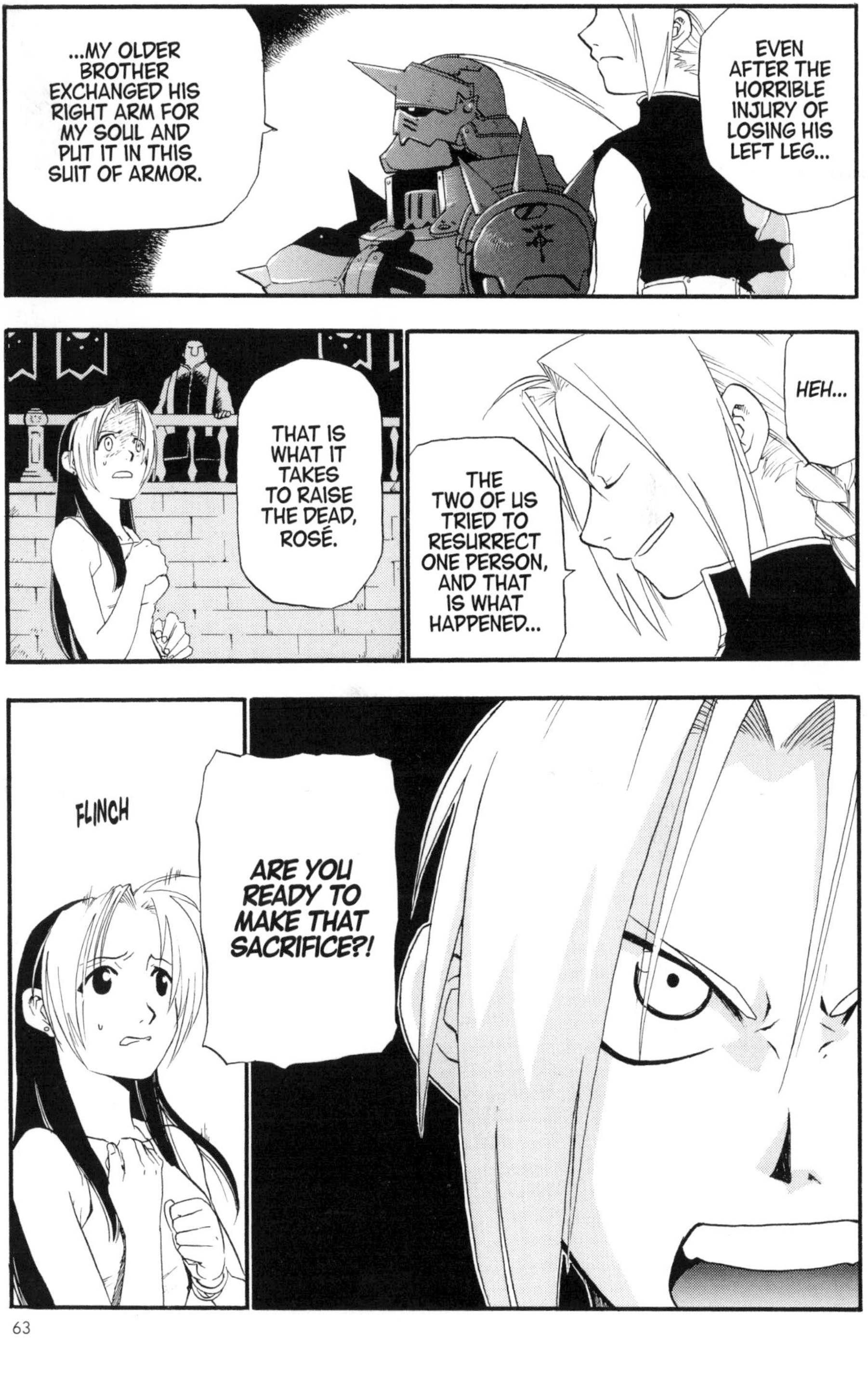
EVEN AFTER THE HORRIBLE INJURY OF LOSING HIS LEFT LEG...
...MY OLDER BROTHER EXCHANGED HIS RIGHT ARM FOR MY SOUL AND PUT IT IN THIS SUIT OF ARMOR.
HEH...
THE TWO OF US TRIED TO RESURRECT ONE PERSON, AND THAT IS WHAT HAPPENED...
THAT IS WHAT IT TAKES TO RAISE THE DEAD, ROSÉ.
ARE YOU READY TO MAKE THAT SACRIFICE?!
FLINCH

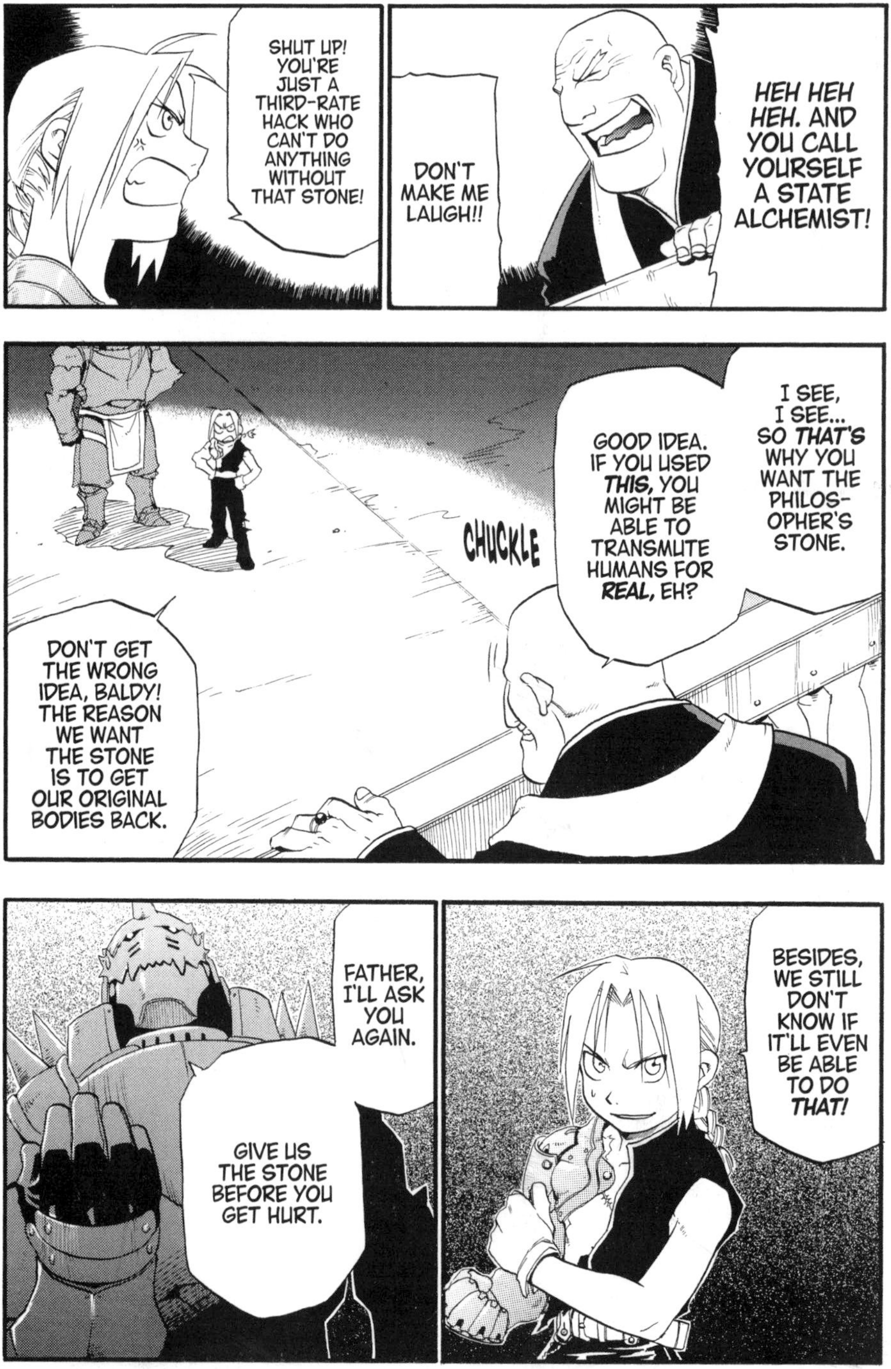
HEH HEH HEH. AND YOU CALL YOURSELF A STATE ALCHEMIST!
DON'T MAKE ME LAUGH!!
SHUT UP! YOU'RE JUST A THIRD-RATE HACK WHO CAN'T DO ANYTHING WITHOUT THAT STONE!
I SEE, I SEE... SO THAT'S WHY YOU WANT THE PHILOS-OPHER'S STONE.
GOOD IDEA. IF YOU USED THIS, YOU MIGHT BE ABLE TO TRANSMUTE HUMANS FOR REAL, EH?
CHUCKLE
DON'T GET THE WRONG IDEA, BALDY! THE REASON WE WANT THE STONE IS TO GET OUR ORIGINAL BODIES BACK.
BESIDES, WE STILL DON'T KNOW IF IT'LL EVEN BE ABLE TO DO THAT!
FATHER, I'LL ASK YOU AGAIN.
GIVE US THE STONE BEFORE YOU GET HURT.

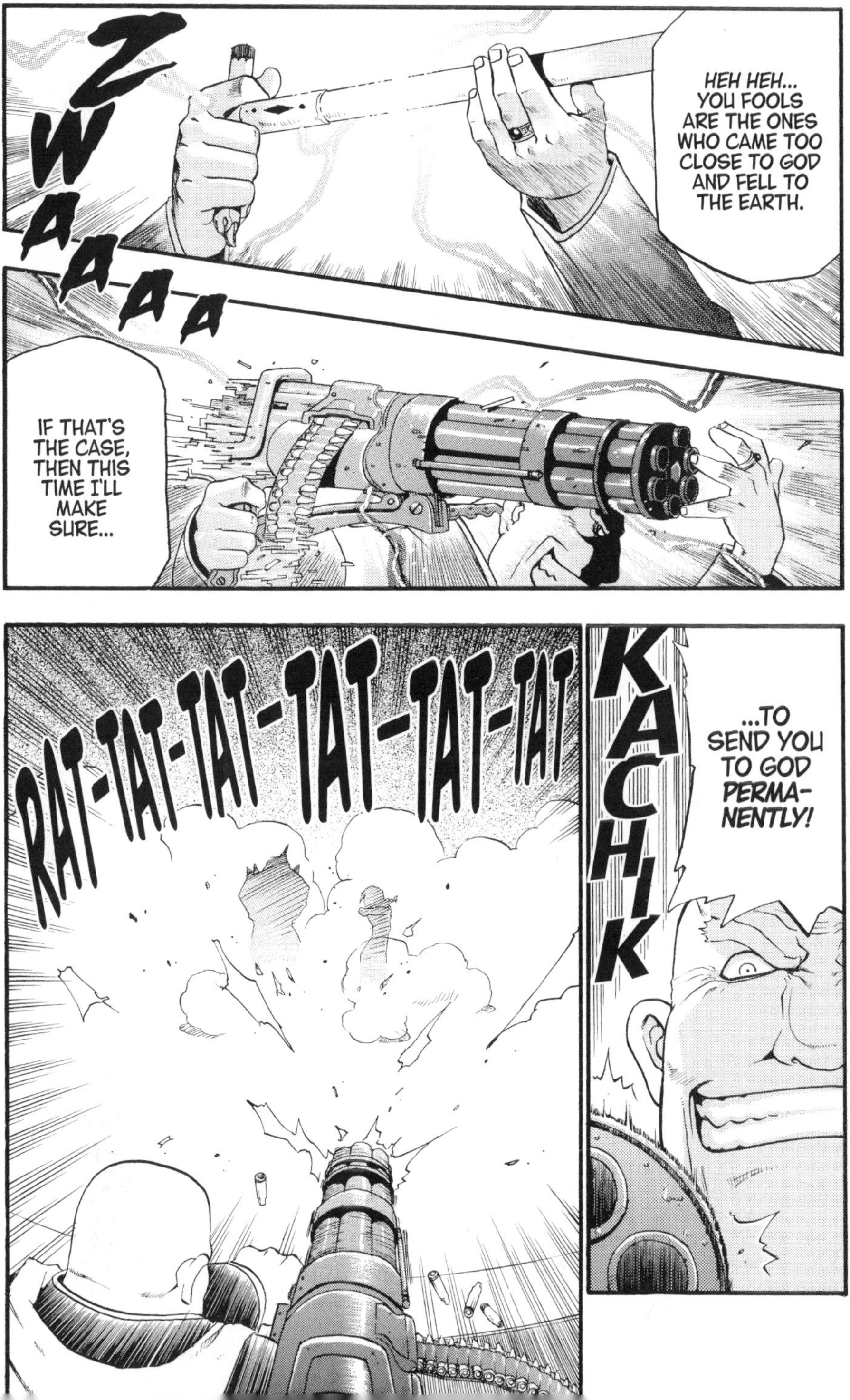
HEH HEH... YOU FOOLS ARE THE ONES WHO CAME TOO CLOSE TO GOD AND FELL TO THE EARTH.
ZWAAAA
IF THAT'S THE CASE, THEN THIS TIME I'LL MAKE SURE...
KACHIK
...TO SEND YOU TO GOD *PERMANENTLY!*
RAT-TAT-TAT-TAT-TAT-TAT-TAT

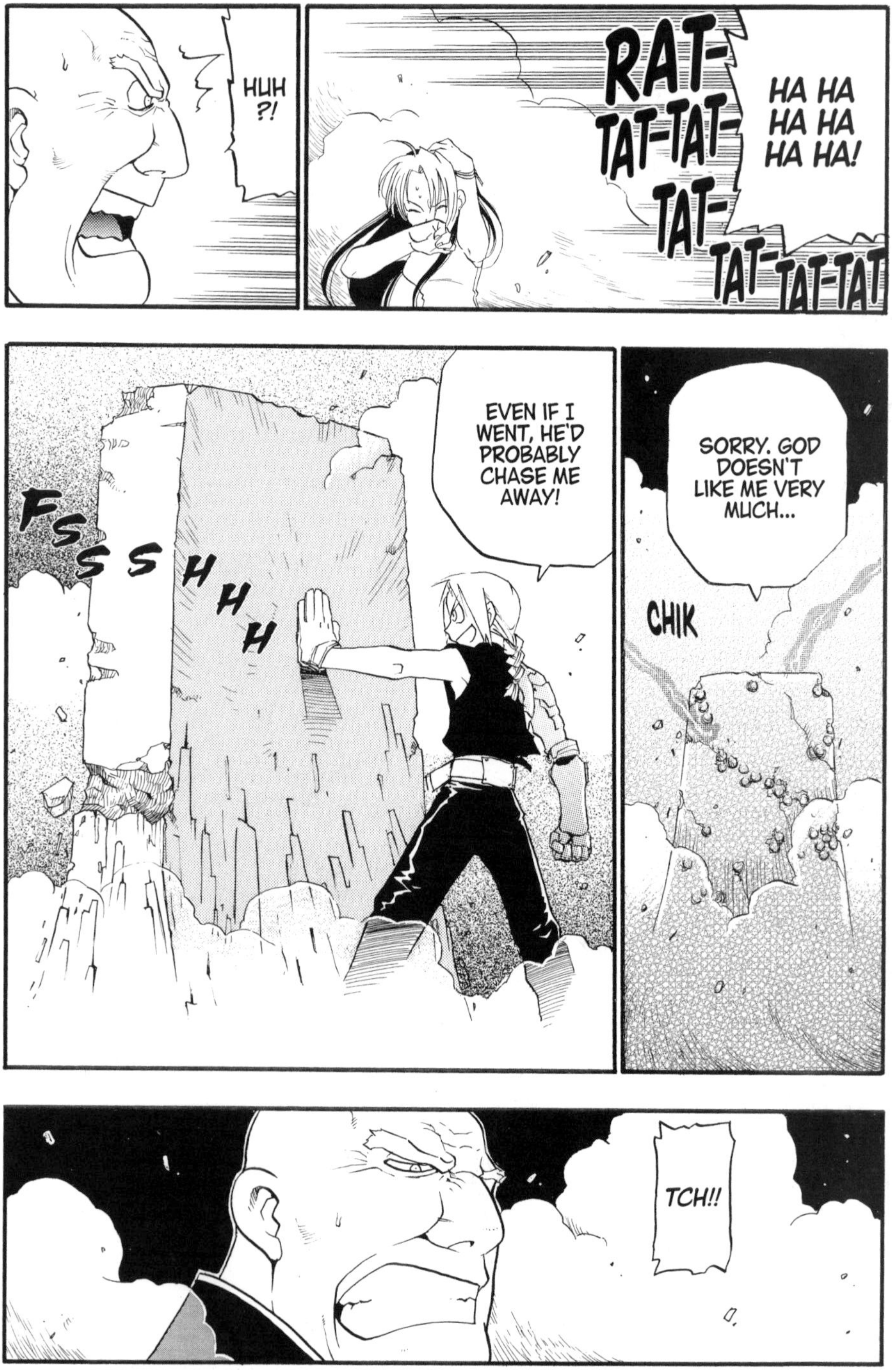
HA HA HA HA HA HA!
RAT-TAT-TAT-TAT-TAT-TAT-TAT
HUH?!
SORRY. GOD DOESN'T LIKE ME VERY MUCH...
CHIK
EVEN IF I WENT, HE'D PROBABLY CHASE ME AWAY!
FSSSHHH
TCH!!

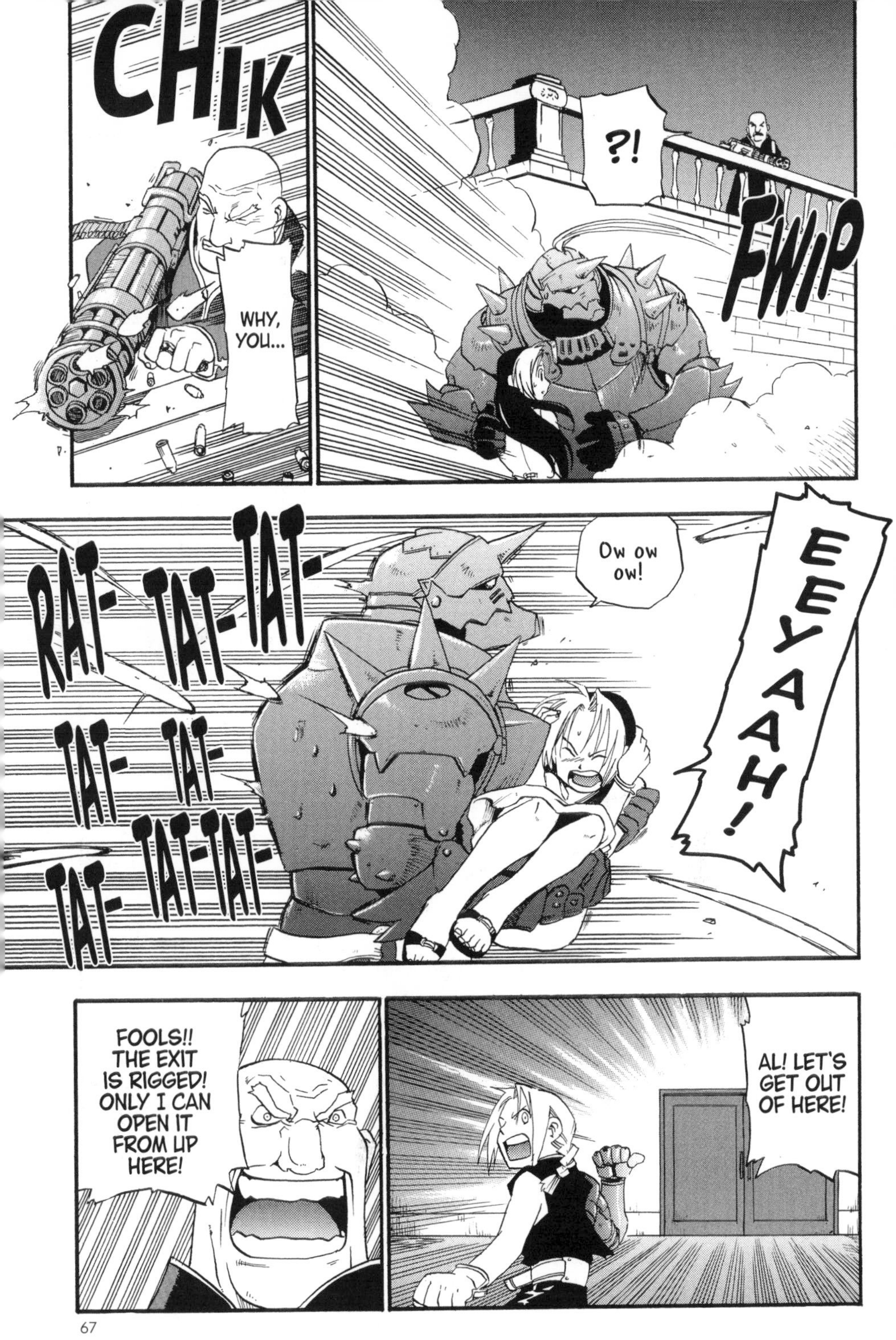
?!
FWIP
CHIK
WHY, YOU...
EEYAAH!
Ow ow ow!
RAT- TAT-TAT-TAT-
TAT- TAT-
TAT- TAT-TAT-
AL! LET'S GET OUT OF HERE!
FOOLS!! THE EXIT IS RIGGED! ONLY I CAN OPEN IT FROM UP HERE!

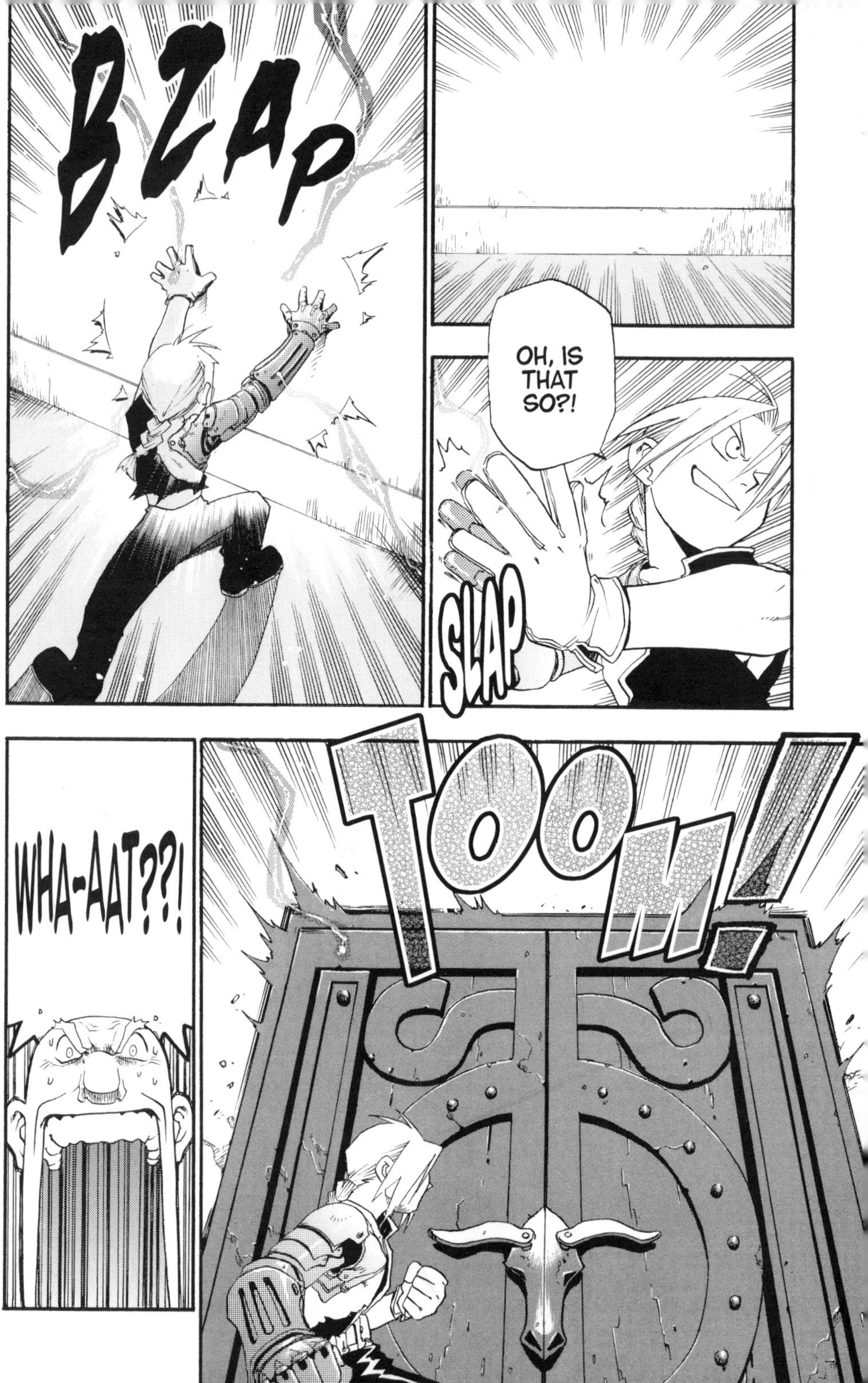
OH, IS THAT SO?!
SLAP
BZAP
TOOM!!
WHA-AAT??!

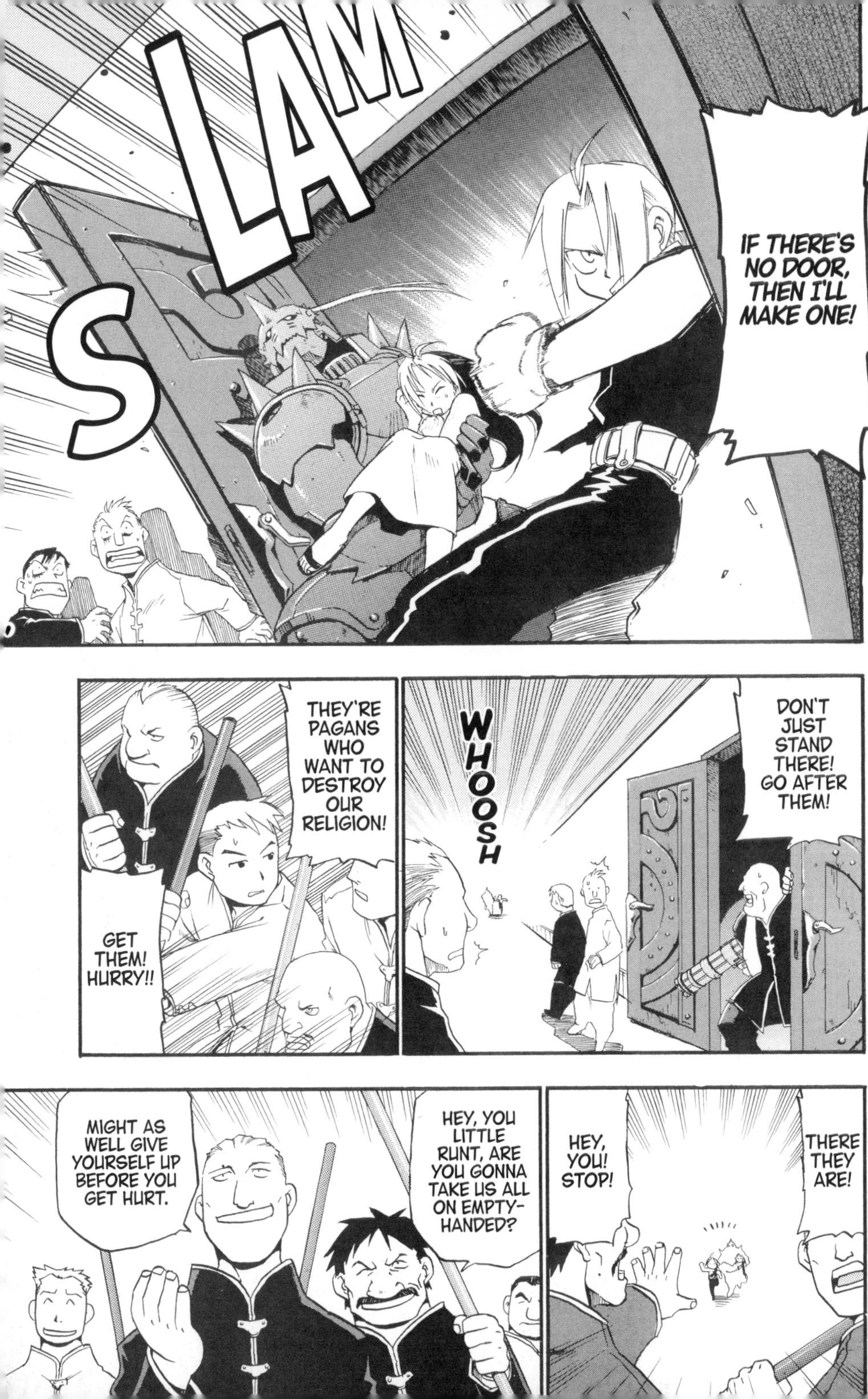
IF THERE'S NO DOOR, THEN I'LL MAKE ONE!
SLAM
DON'T JUST STAND THERE! GO AFTER THEM!
WHOOSH
THEY'RE PAGANS WHO WANT TO DESTROY OUR RELIGION!
GET THEM! HURRY!!
THERE THEY ARE!
HEY, YOU! STOP!
HEY, YOU LITTLE RUNT, ARE YOU GONNA TAKE US ALL ON EMPTY-HANDED?
MIGHT AS WELL GIVE YOURSELF UP BEFORE YOU GET HURT.

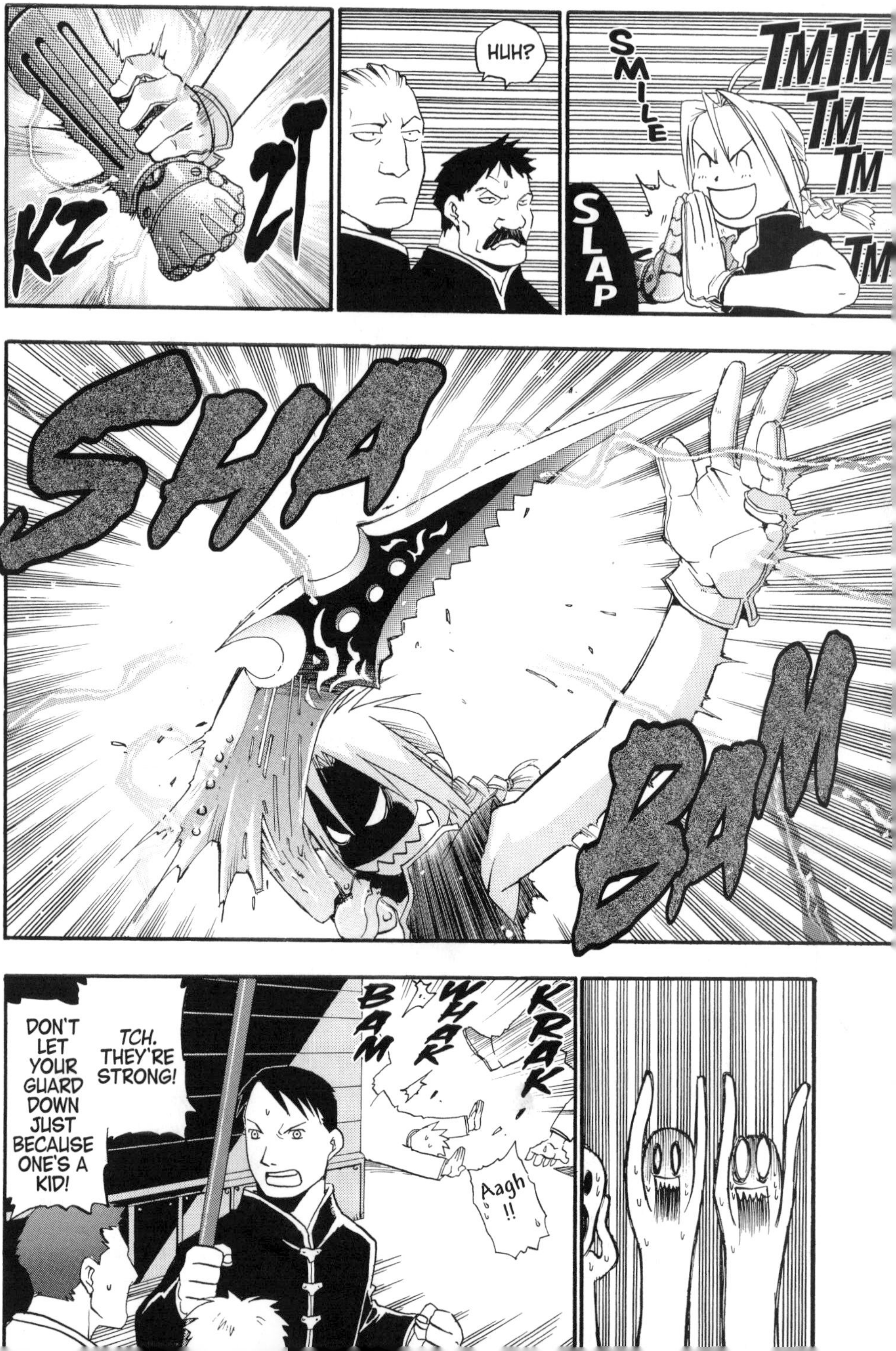
TMTM TM TM TM
SMILE
SLAP
HUH?
KZ ZT
SHA
BAM
KRAK
WHAK
BAM
Aagh !!
TCH. THEY'RE STRONG!
DON'T LET YOUR GUARD DOWN JUST BECAUSE ONE'S A KID!

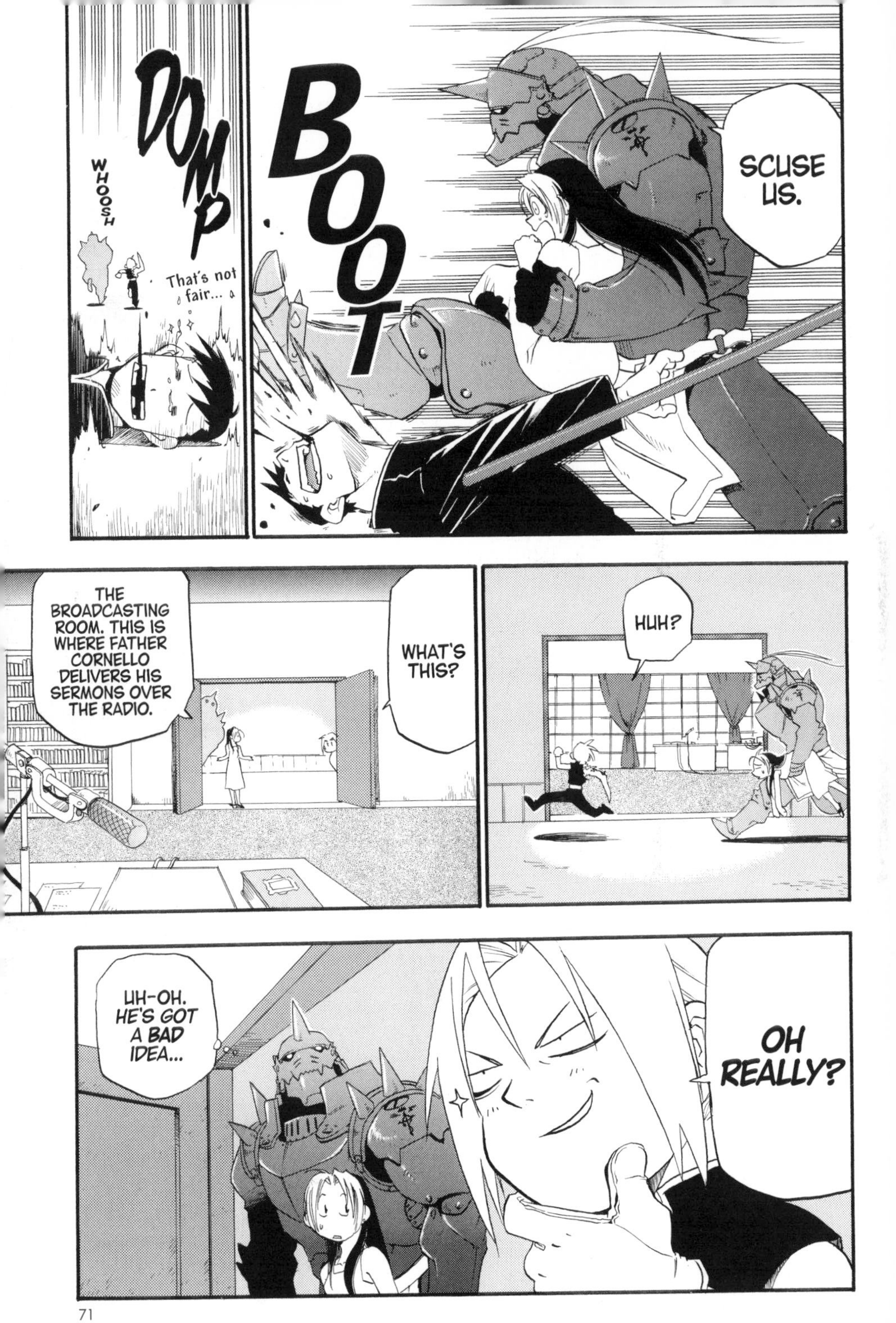

BOOT
SCUSE US.
DOMP
WHOOSH
That's not fair...
HUH?
WHAT'S THIS?
THE BROADCASTING ROOM. THIS IS WHERE FATHER CORNELLO DELIVERS HIS SERMONS OVER THE RADIO.
OH REALLY?
UH-OH. HE'S GOT A BAD IDEA...

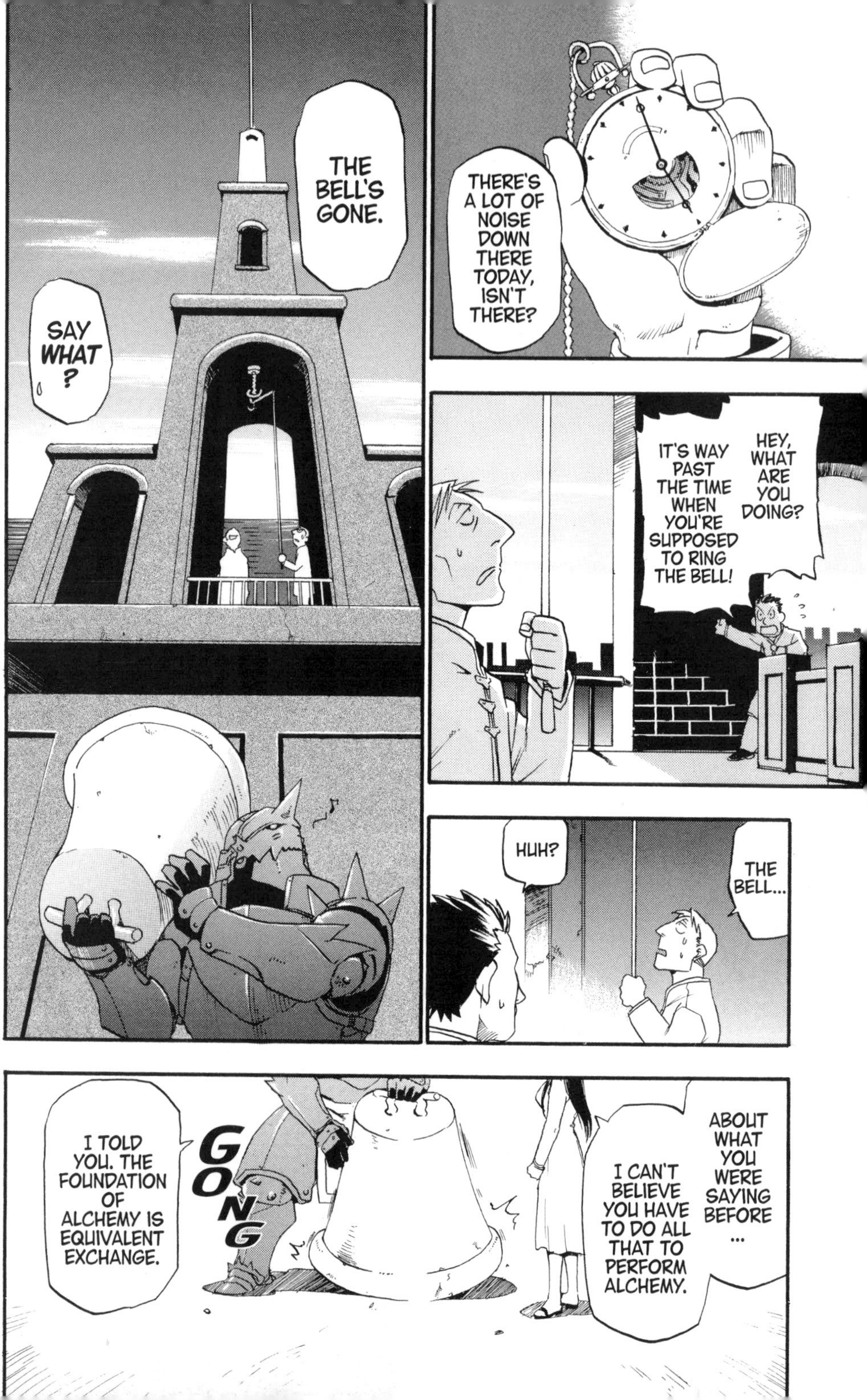
THERE'S A LOT OF NOISE DOWN THERE TODAY, ISN'T THERE?
HEY, WHAT ARE YOU DOING?
IT'S WAY PAST THE TIME WHEN YOU'RE SUPPOSED TO RING THE BELL!
THE BELL...
HUH?
THE BELL'S GONE.
SAY WHAT?
ABOUT WHAT YOU WERE SAYING BEFORE...
I CAN'T BELIEVE YOU HAVE TO DO ALL THAT TO PERFORM ALCHEMY.
GONG
I TOLD YOU. THE FOUNDATION OF ALCHEMY IS EQUIVALENT EXCHANGE.

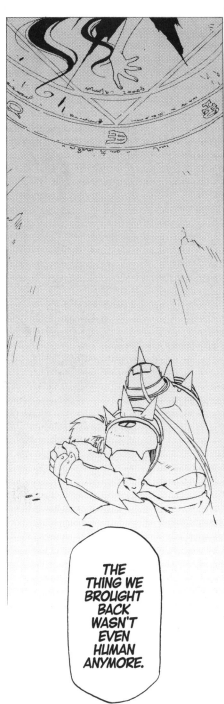

TO OBTAIN SOMETHING, SOMETHING OF EQUAL VALUE MUST BE LOST.

PEOPLE CALL MY BROTHER A GENIUS, BUT THE REASON HE'S SO GOOD AT IT IS BECAUSE HE PAID THE PRICE... AND WORKED SO HARD.

BUT BECAUSE YOU SACRIFICED SO *MUCH*, YOU MUST HAVE BEEN ABLE TO BRING BACK YOUR MOTHER...

THE THING WE BROUGHT BACK WASN'T EVEN HUMAN ANYMORE.

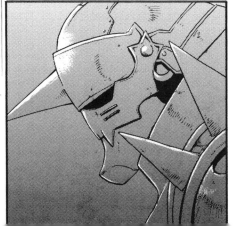

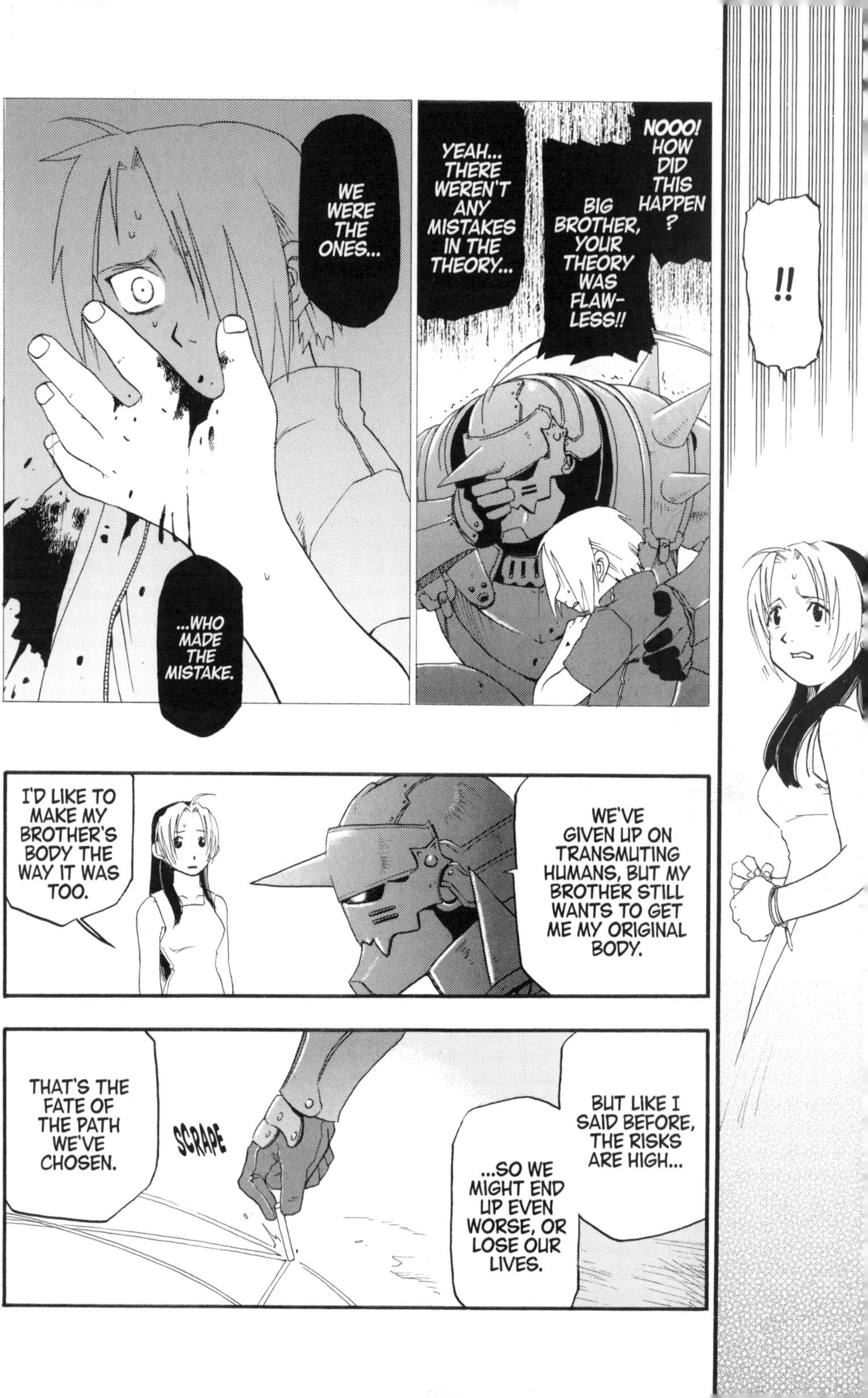
!!
NOOO! HOW DID THIS HAPPEN?
BIG BROTHER, YOUR THEORY WAS FLAW-LESS!!
YEAH... THERE WEREN'T ANY MISTAKES IN THE THEORY...
WE WERE THE ONES...
...WHO MADE THE MISTAKE.
WE'VE GIVEN UP ON TRANSMUTING HUMANS, BUT MY BROTHER STILL WANTS TO GET ME MY ORIGINAL BODY.
I'D LIKE TO MAKE MY BROTHER'S BODY THE WAY IT WAS TOO.
BUT LIKE I SAID BEFORE, THE RISKS ARE HIGH...
...SO WE MIGHT END UP EVEN WORSE, OR LOSE OUR LIVES.
SCRAPE
THAT'S THE FATE OF THE PATH WE'VE CHOSEN.

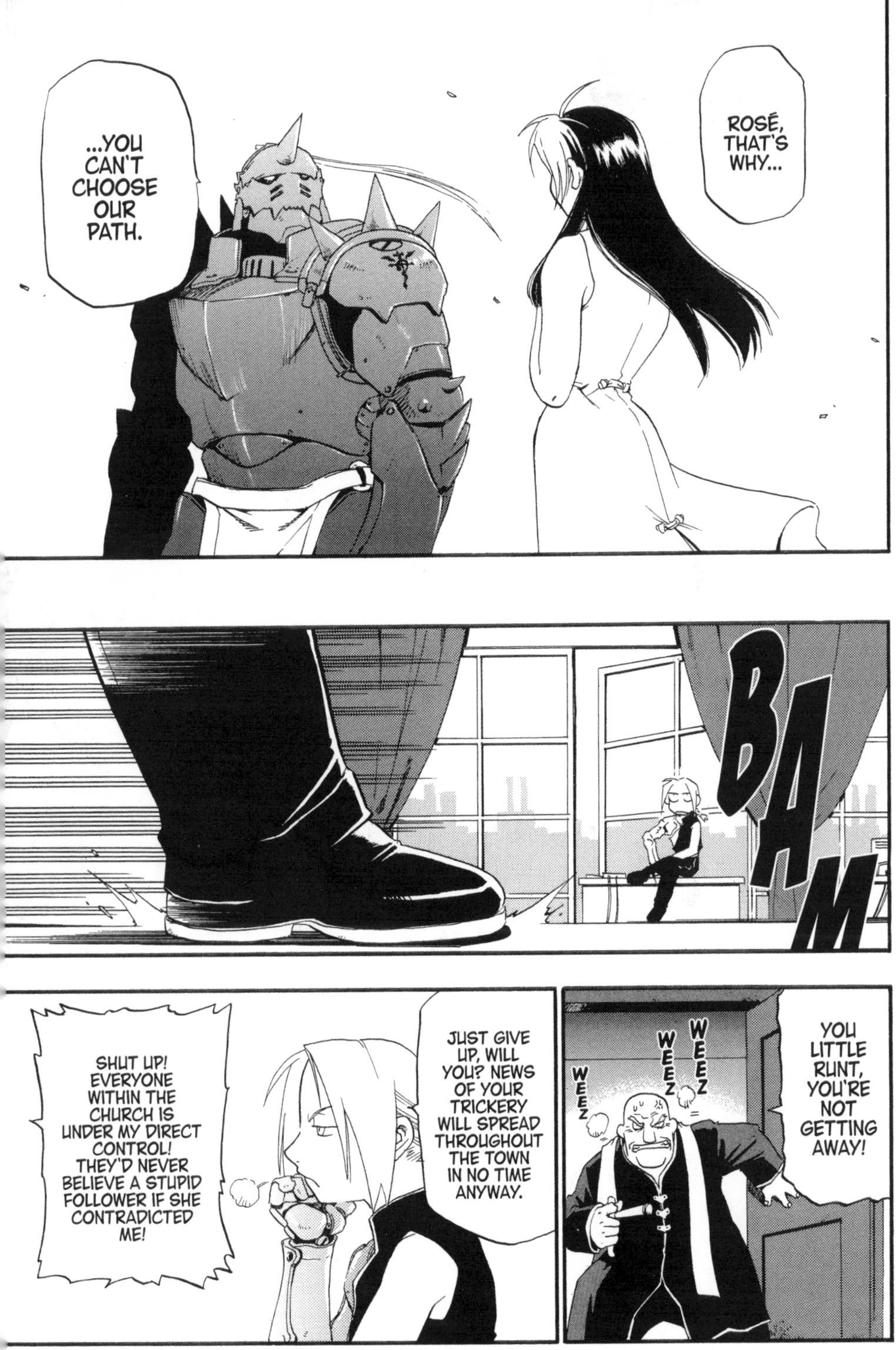
ROSÉ, THAT'S WHY...
...YOU CAN'T CHOOSE OUR PATH.
BAM
YOU LITTLE RUNT, YOU'RE NOT GETTING AWAY!
WEEZ
WEEZ
WEEZ
JUST GIVE UP, WILL YOU? NEWS OF YOUR TRICKERY WILL SPREAD THROUGHOUT THE TOWN IN NO TIME ANYWAY.
SHUT UP! EVERYONE WITHIN THE CHURCH IS UNDER MY DIRECT CONTROL! THEY'D NEVER BELIEVE A STUPID FOLLOWER IF SHE CONTRADICTED ME!

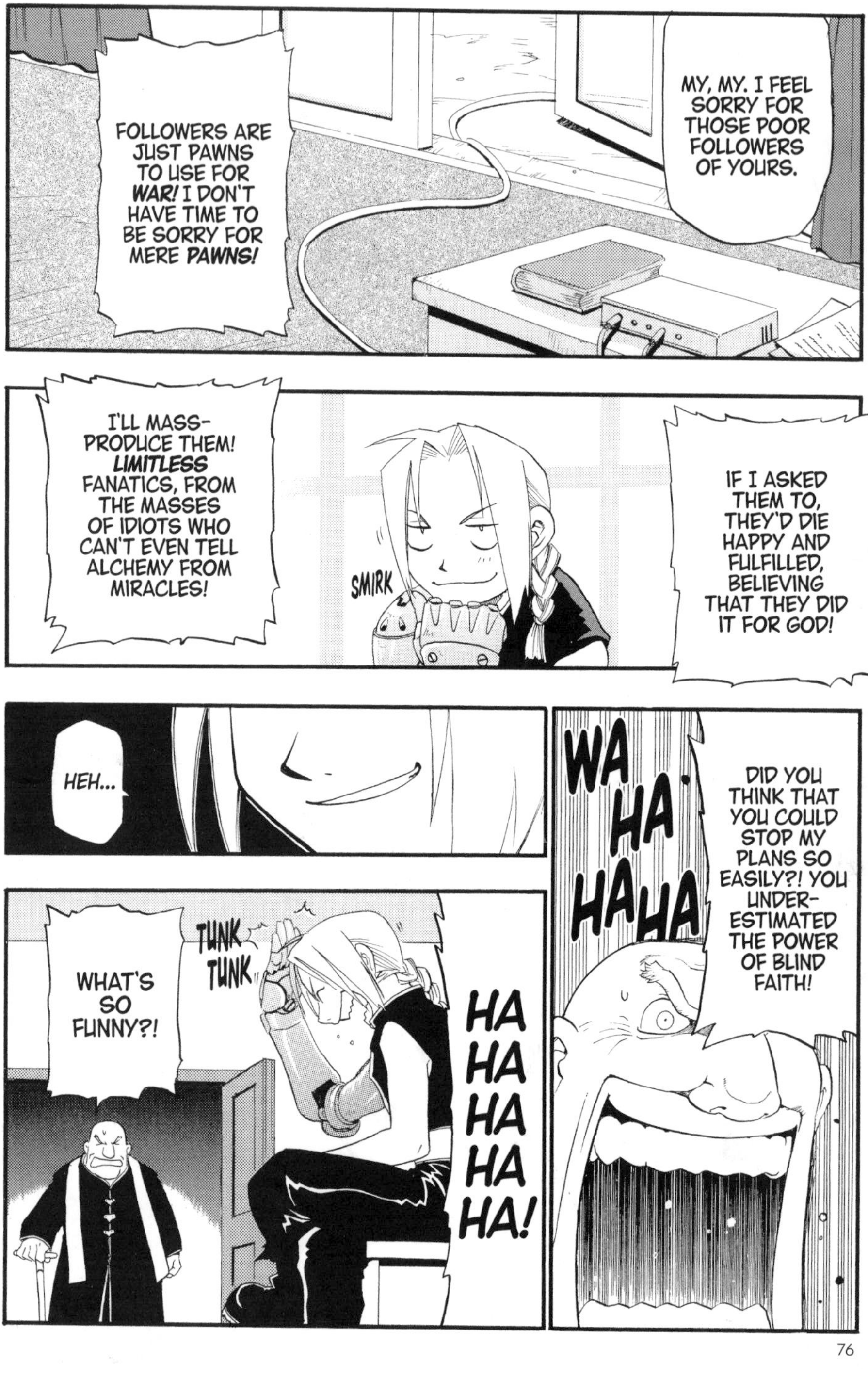
MY, MY. I FEEL SORRY FOR THOSE POOR FOLLOWERS OF YOURS.
FOLLOWERS ARE JUST PAWNS TO USE FOR **WAR!** I DON'T HAVE TIME TO BE SORRY FOR MERE **PAWNS!**
IF I ASKED THEM TO, THEY'D DIE HAPPY AND FULFILLED, BELIEVING THAT THEY DID IT FOR GOD!
SMIRK
I'LL MASS-PRODUCE THEM! **LIMITLESS** FANATICS, FROM THE MASSES OF IDIOTS WHO CAN'T EVEN TELL ALCHEMY FROM MIRACLES!
WA HA HA HA
DID YOU THINK THAT YOU COULD STOP MY PLANS SO EASILY?! YOU UNDER-ESTIMATED THE POWER OF BLIND FAITH!
HEH...
TUNK TUNK
WHAT'S SO FUNNY?!
HA HA HA HA HA!

THAT'S WHY I KEEP SAYING YOU'RE *THIRD-RATE*, BALDY!
HEE HEE
YOU LITTLE BRAT! HOW DARE YOU INSULT ME!!
KNOW WHAT THIS IS? ♪
ON
OFF
ON
ON
OFF
YOU...
BA-BUMP

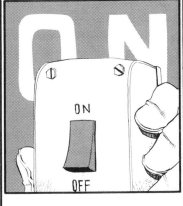

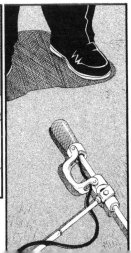

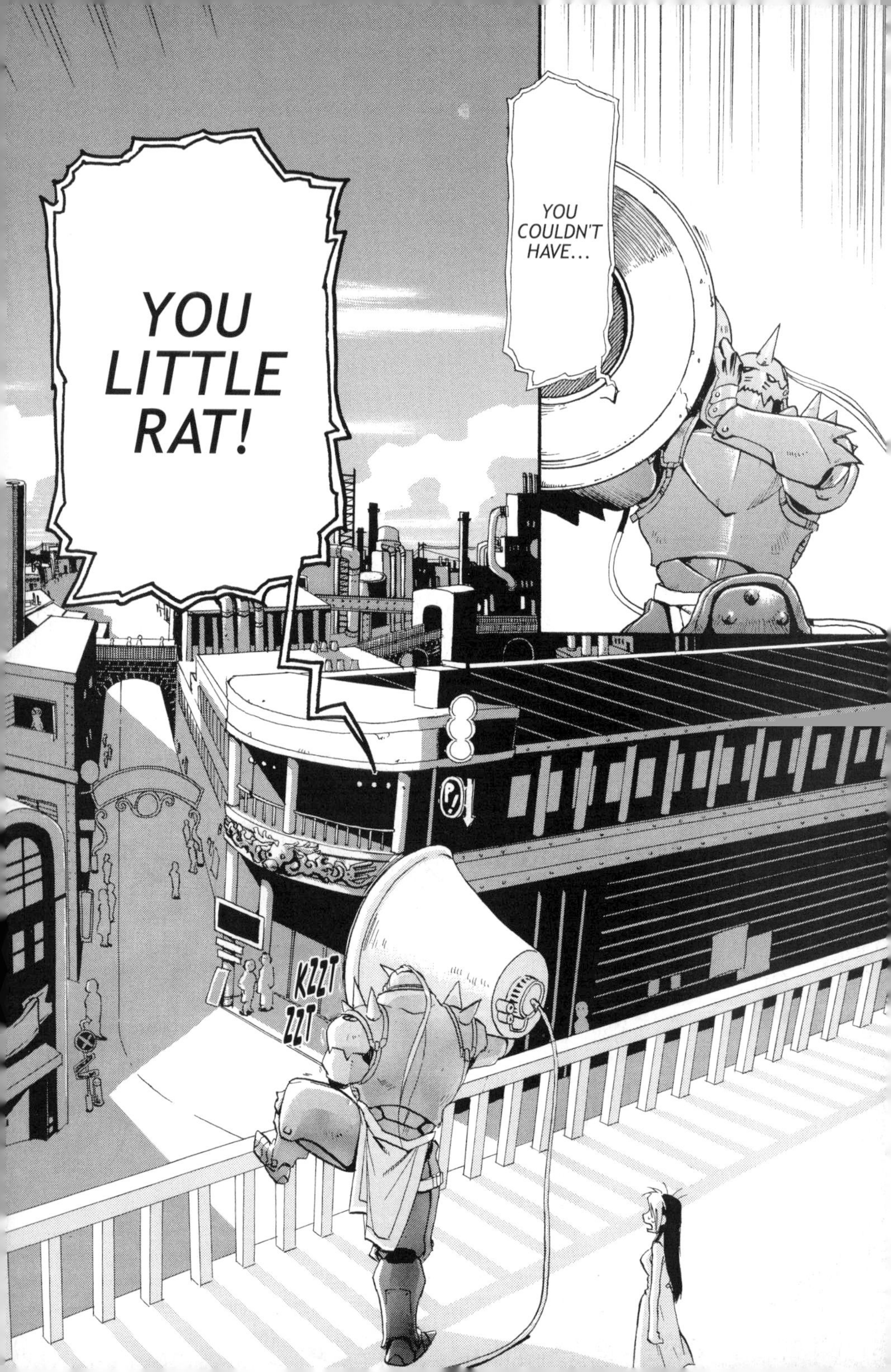

YOU COULDN'T HAVE...
YOU LITTLE RAT!
KZZT ZZT

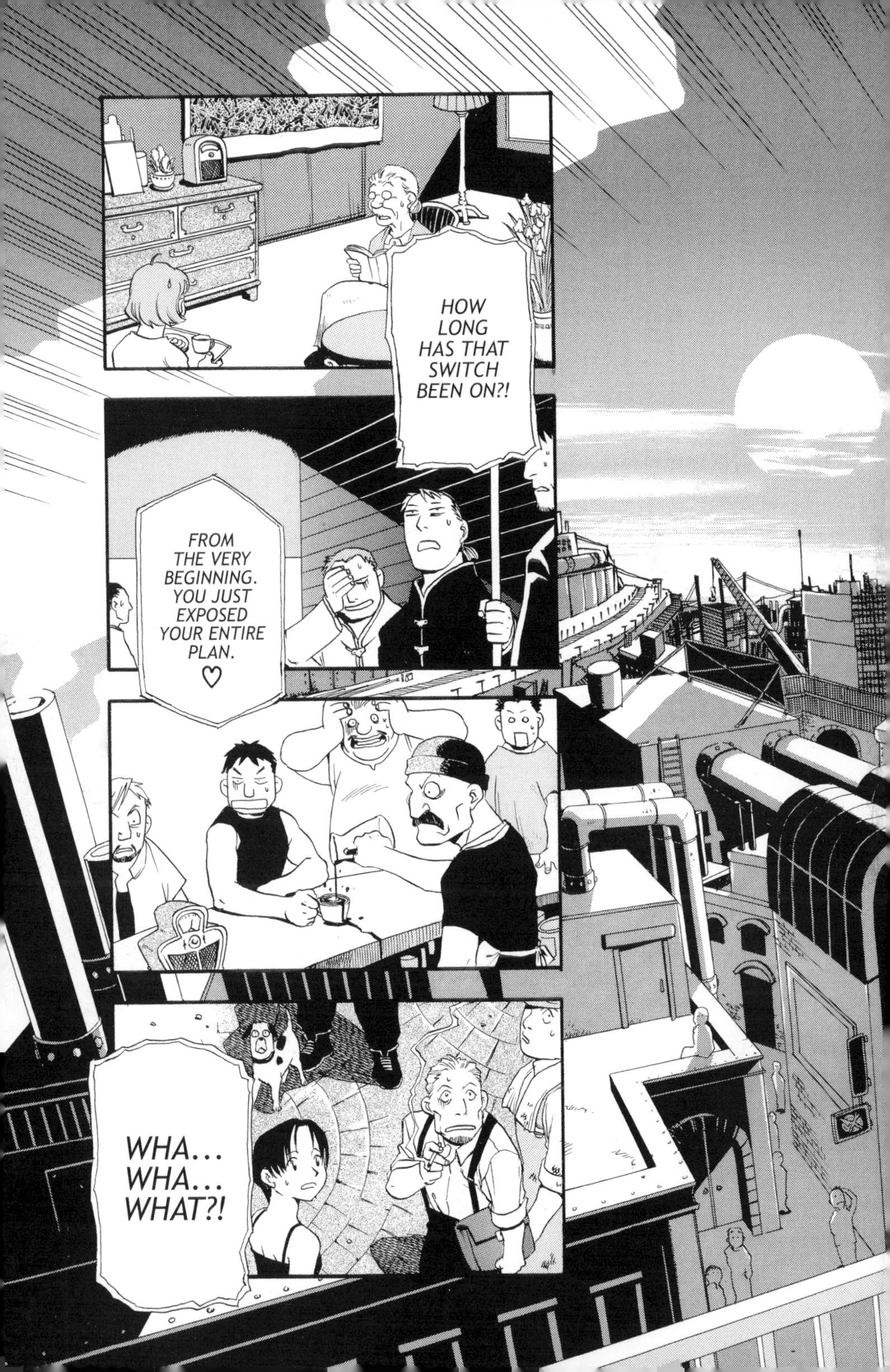
HOW LONG HAS THAT SWITCH BEEN ON?!
FROM THE VERY BEGINNING. YOU JUST EXPOSED YOUR ENTIRE PLAN. ♡
WHA... WHA... WHAT?!

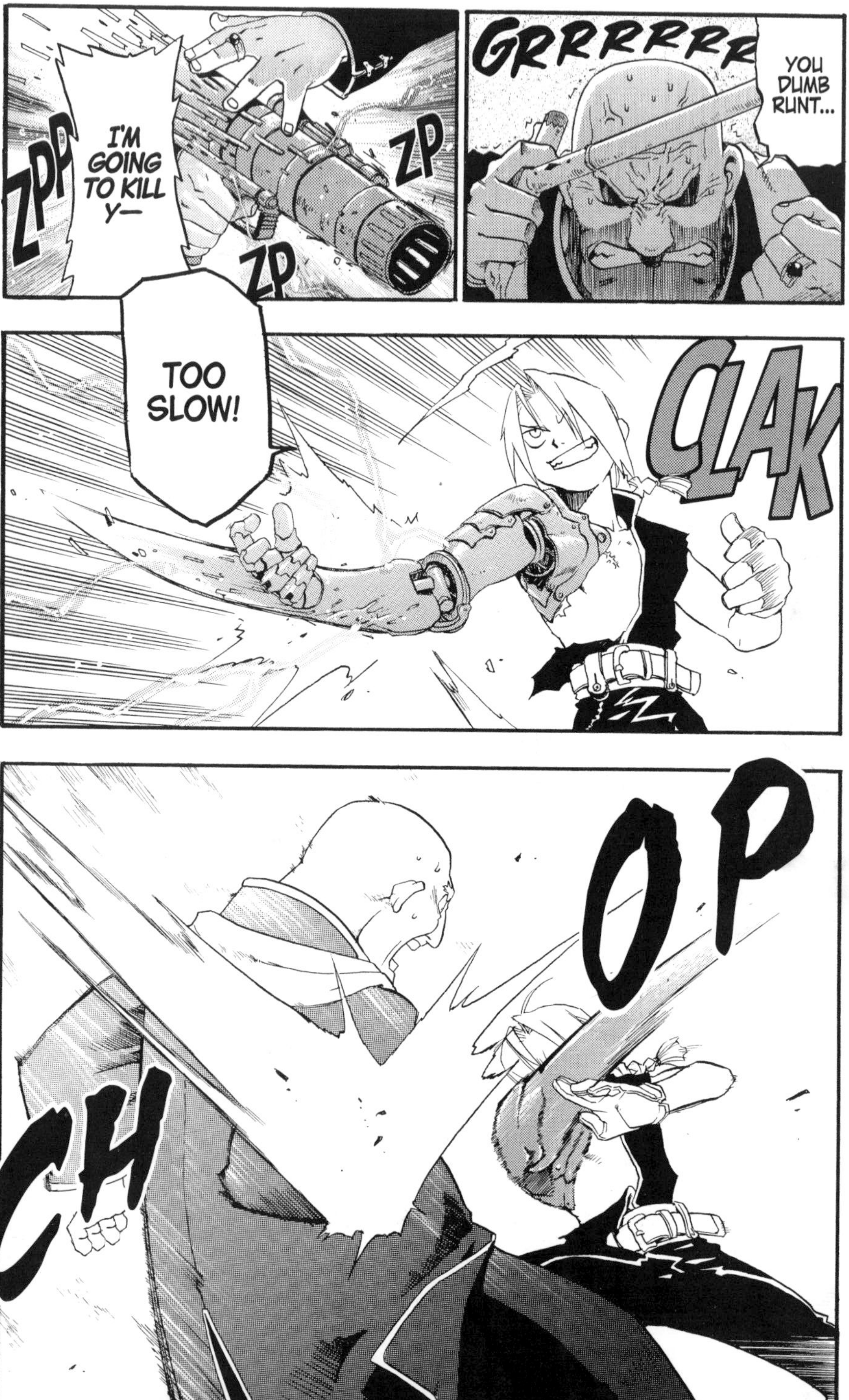

GRRRRRR
YOU DUMB RUNT...
ZPP
I'M GOING TO KILL Y—
ZP
ZP
TOO SLOW!
CLAK
CH
OP

DIDN'T I TELL YOU? THERE'S NO COMPARISON BETWEEN US.

KLANK

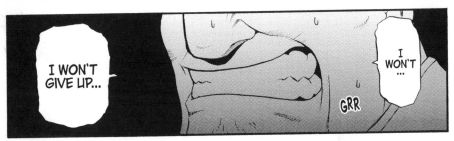

I WON'T GIVE UP...

GRR

I WON'T...

UGH...

AS LONG AS I HAVE THIS STONE, I CAN MAKE MIRACLES AGAIN AND AGAIN!

ZPP

KAZAP

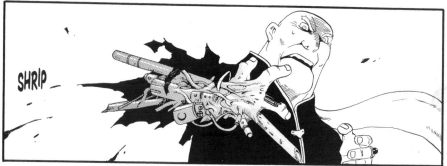

SHRIP

WHY...

WHY DID IT...?

MY ARM! MY ARM!

WH...

AGGHH! IT HURTS! AAGGHH!

GAAAAAHH!

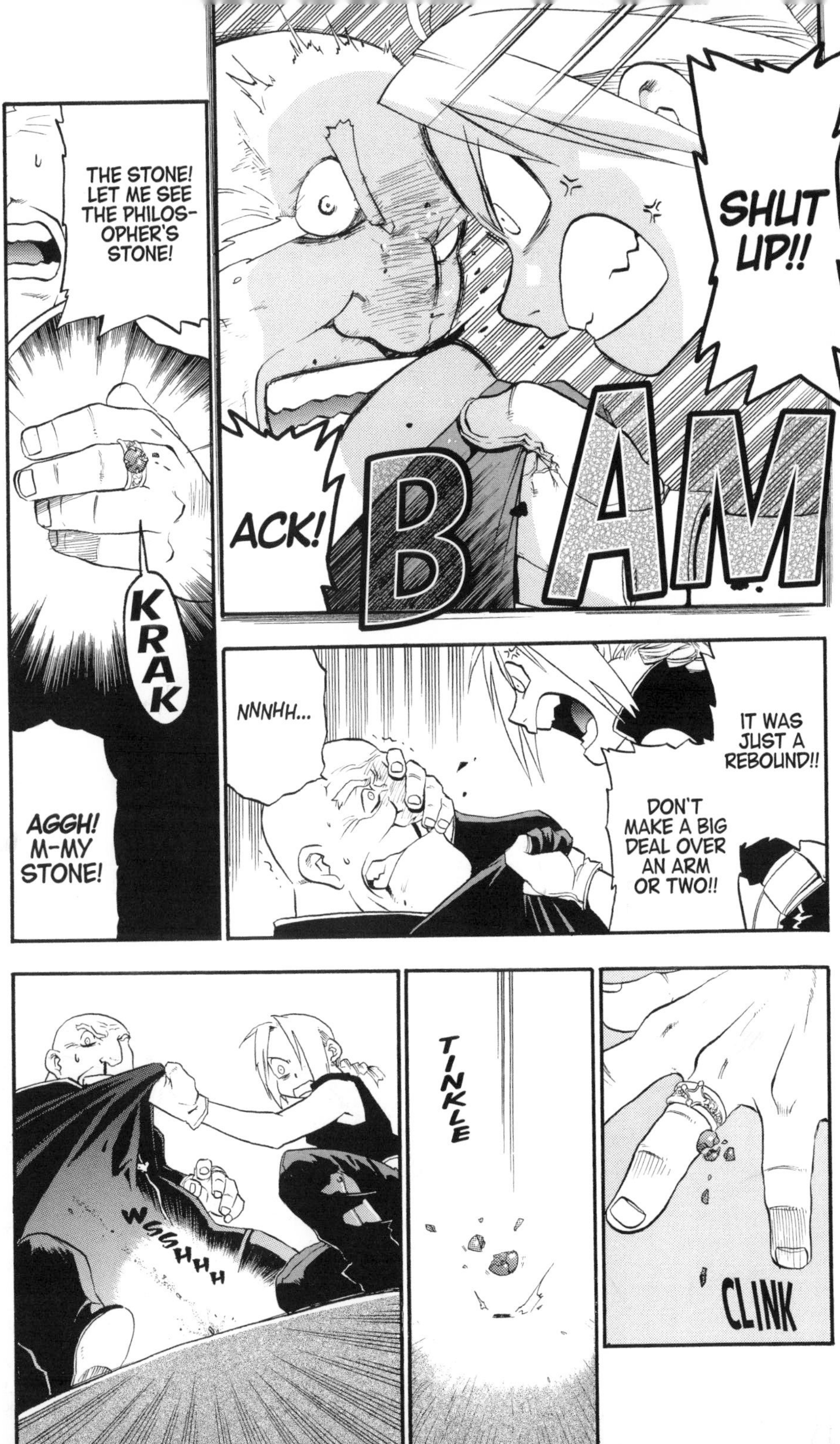
SHUT UP!!
BAM
ACK!
IT WAS JUST A REBOUND!!
DON'T MAKE A BIG DEAL OVER AN ARM OR TWO!!
NNNHH...
THE STONE! LET ME SEE THE PHILOS-OPHER'S STONE!
KRAK
AGGH! M-MY STONE!
CLINK
TINKLE
WSSHHH

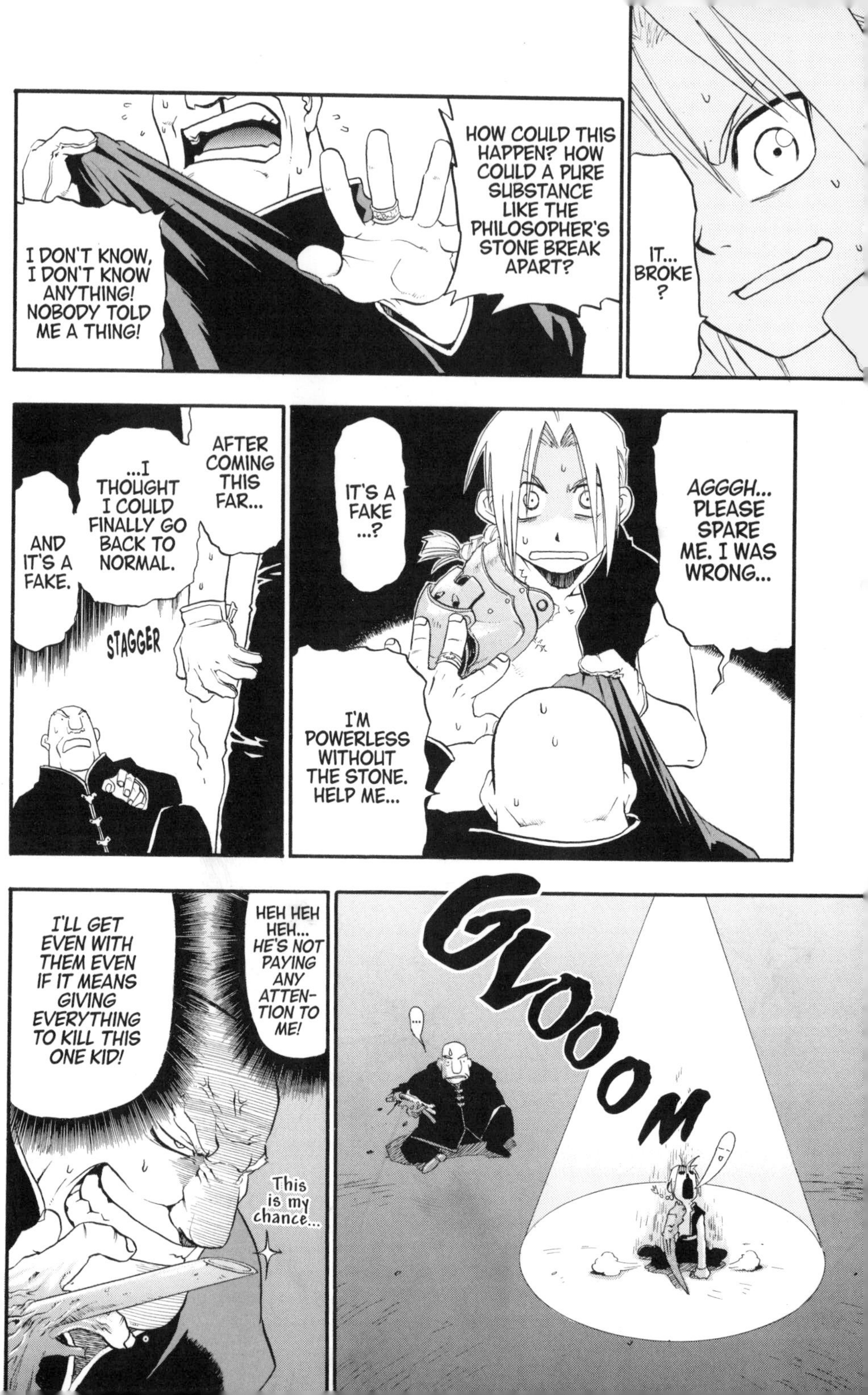
IT... BROKE?
HOW COULD THIS HAPPEN? HOW COULD A PURE SUBSTANCE LIKE THE PHILOSOPHER'S STONE BREAK APART?
I DON'T KNOW, I DON'T KNOW ANYTHING! NOBODY TOLD ME A THING!
AGGGH... PLEASE SPARE ME. I WAS WRONG...
IT'S A FAKE ...?
I'M POWERLESS WITHOUT THE STONE. HELP ME...
AFTER COMING THIS FAR...
...I THOUGHT I COULD FINALLY GO BACK TO NORMAL.
AND IT'S A FAKE.
STAGGER
GVOOOM
...
HEH HEH HEH... HE'S NOT PAYING ANY ATTEN-TION TO ME!
I'LL GET EVEN WITH THEM EVEN IF IT MEANS GIVING EVERYTHING TO KILL THIS ONE KID!
This is my chance...

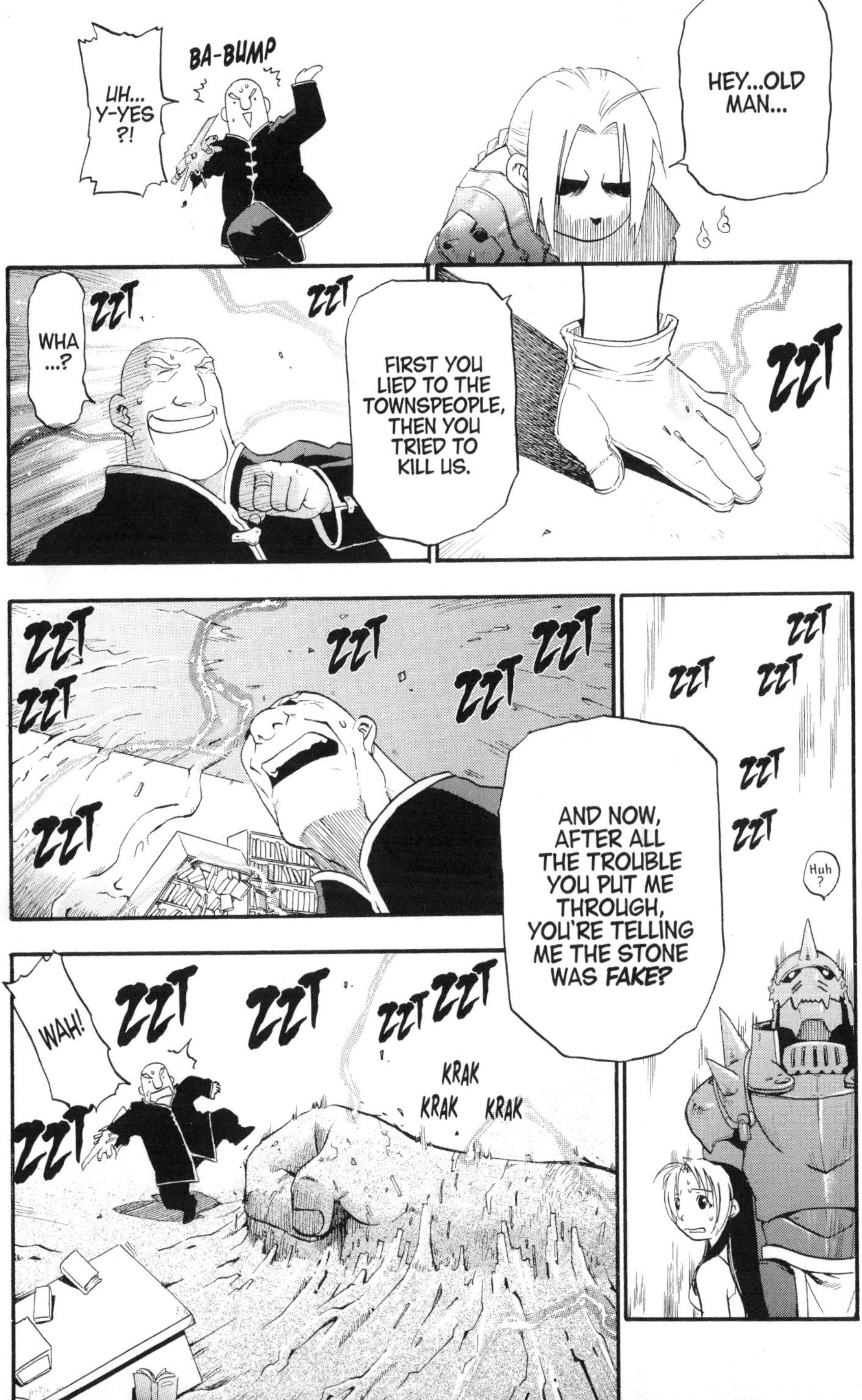
HEY...OLD MAN...
BA-BUMP
UH... Y-YES ?!
ZZT
FIRST YOU LIED TO THE TOWNSPEOPLE, THEN YOU TRIED TO KILL US.
ZZT
ZZT
WHA ...?
ZZT
ZZT
ZZT
ZZT
ZZT
AND NOW, AFTER ALL THE TROUBLE YOU PUT ME THROUGH, YOU'RE TELLING ME THE STONE WAS FAKE?
Huh ?
ZZT
ZZT
ZZT
ZZT
ZZT
ZZT
WAH!
ZZT
ZZT
ZZT
ZZT
ZZT
KRAK
KRAK
KRAK

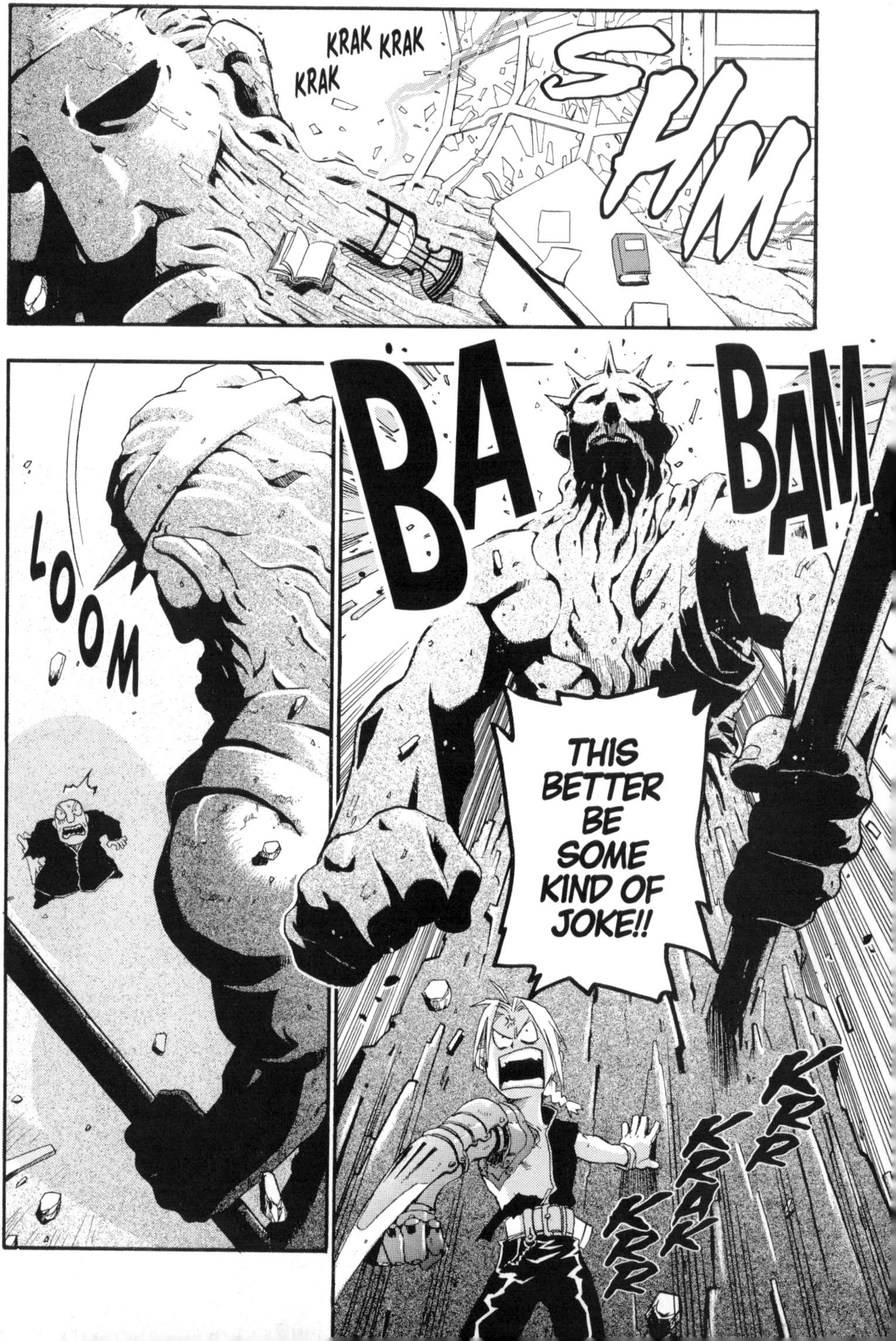
SHM
KRAK KRAK
KRAK
BA BAM
THIS BETTER BE SOME KIND OF JOKE!!
KRR
KRAK
KRR
LOOM

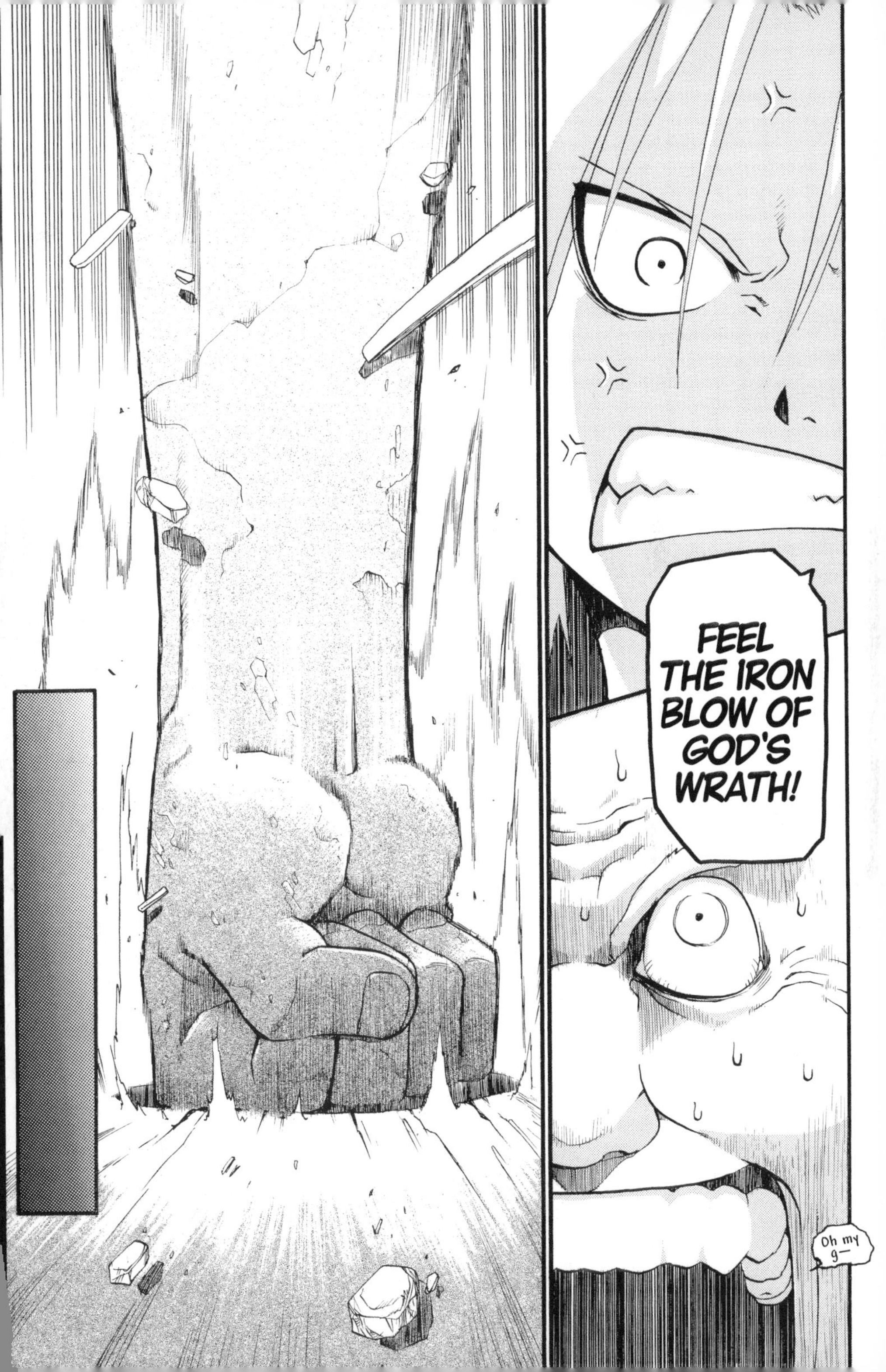
FEEL THE IRON BLOW OF GOD'S WRATH!
Oh my g—

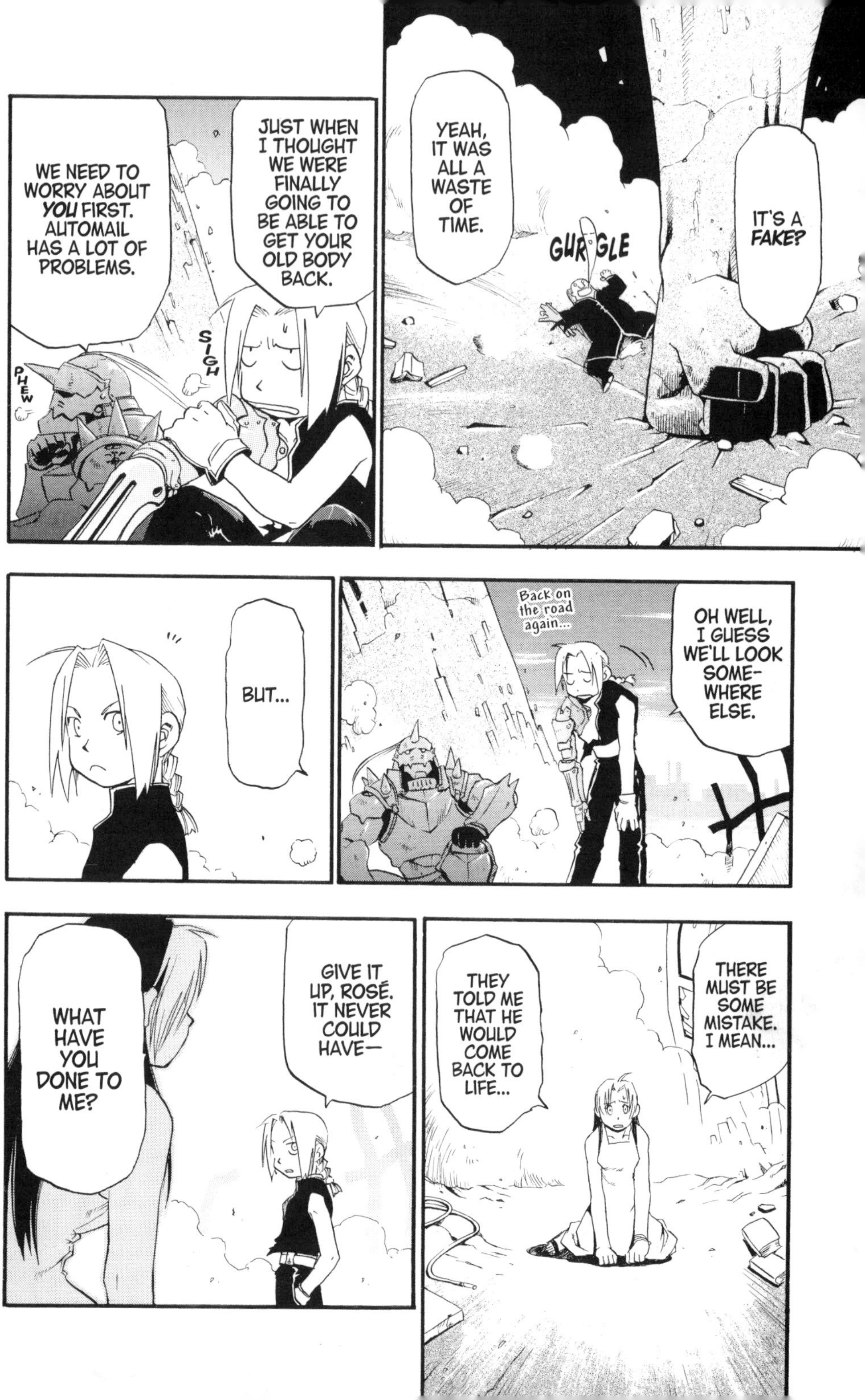
IT'S A FAKE?
GURGLE
YEAH, IT WAS ALL A WASTE OF TIME.
JUST WHEN I THOUGHT WE WERE FINALLY GOING TO BE ABLE TO GET YOUR OLD BODY BACK.
SIGH
WE NEED TO WORRY ABOUT YOU FIRST. AUTOMAIL HAS A LOT OF PROBLEMS.
PHEW
OH WELL, I GUESS WE'LL LOOK SOME-WHERE ELSE.
Back on the road again...
BUT...
THERE MUST BE SOME MISTAKE. I MEAN...
THEY TOLD ME THAT HE WOULD COME BACK TO LIFE...
GIVE IT UP, ROSÉ. IT NEVER COULD HAVE—
WHAT HAVE YOU DONE TO ME?

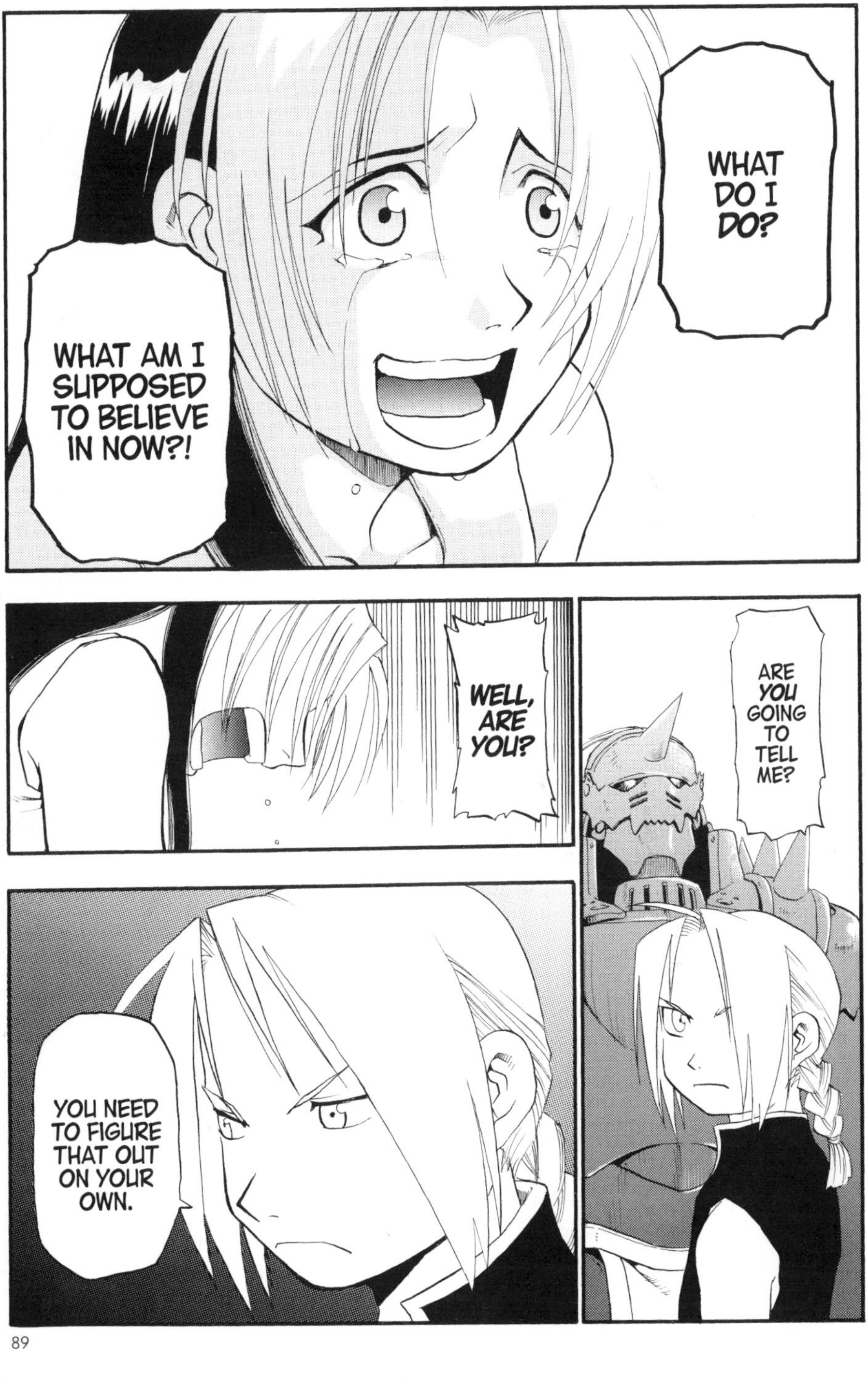
WHAT DO I DO?
WHAT AM I SUPPOSED TO BELIEVE IN NOW?!
ARE YOU GOING TO TELL ME?
WELL, ARE YOU?
YOU NEED TO FIGURE THAT OUT ON YOUR OWN.

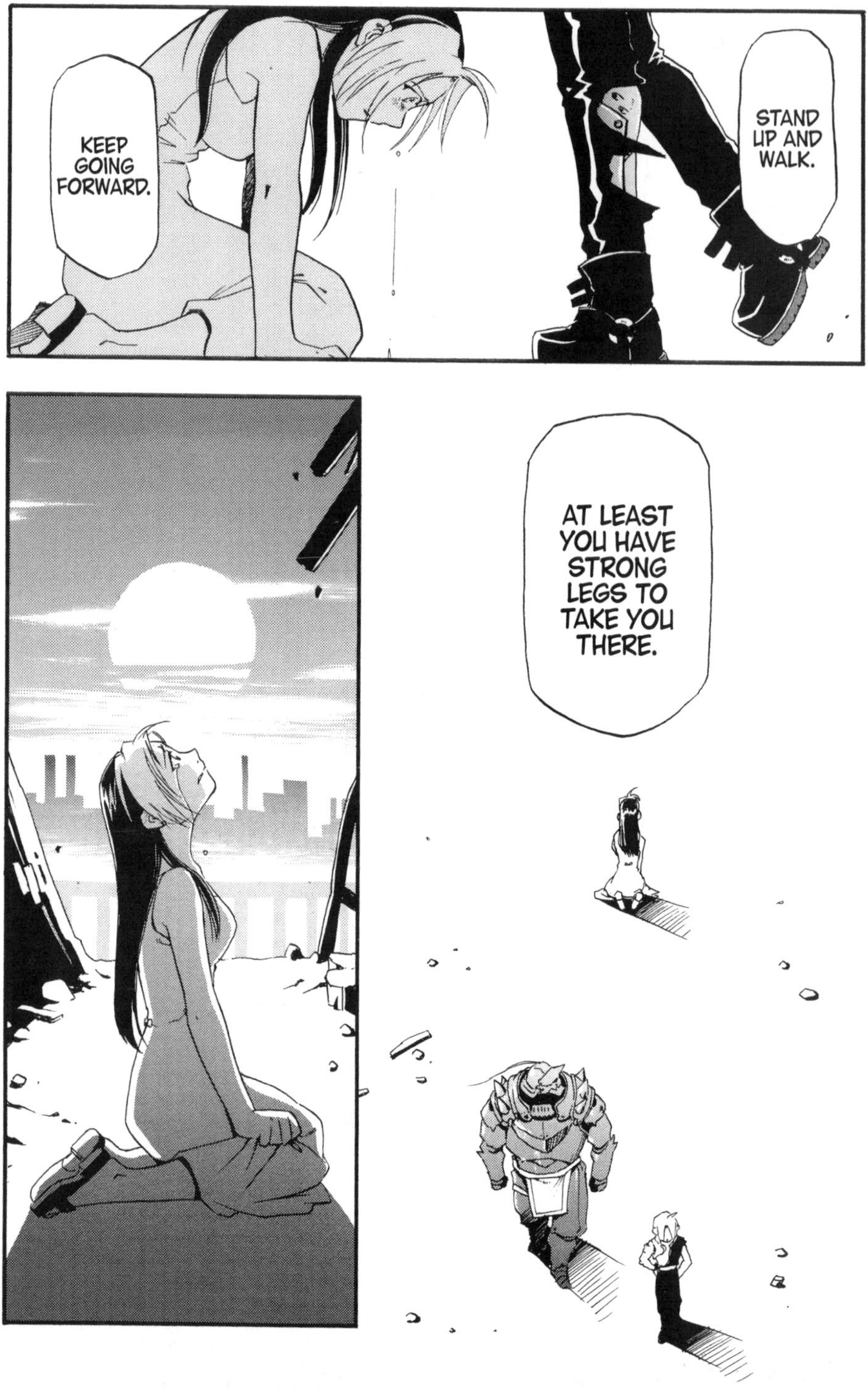
STAND UP AND WALK.
KEEP GOING FORWARD.
AT LEAST YOU HAVE STRONG LEGS TO TAKE YOU THERE.

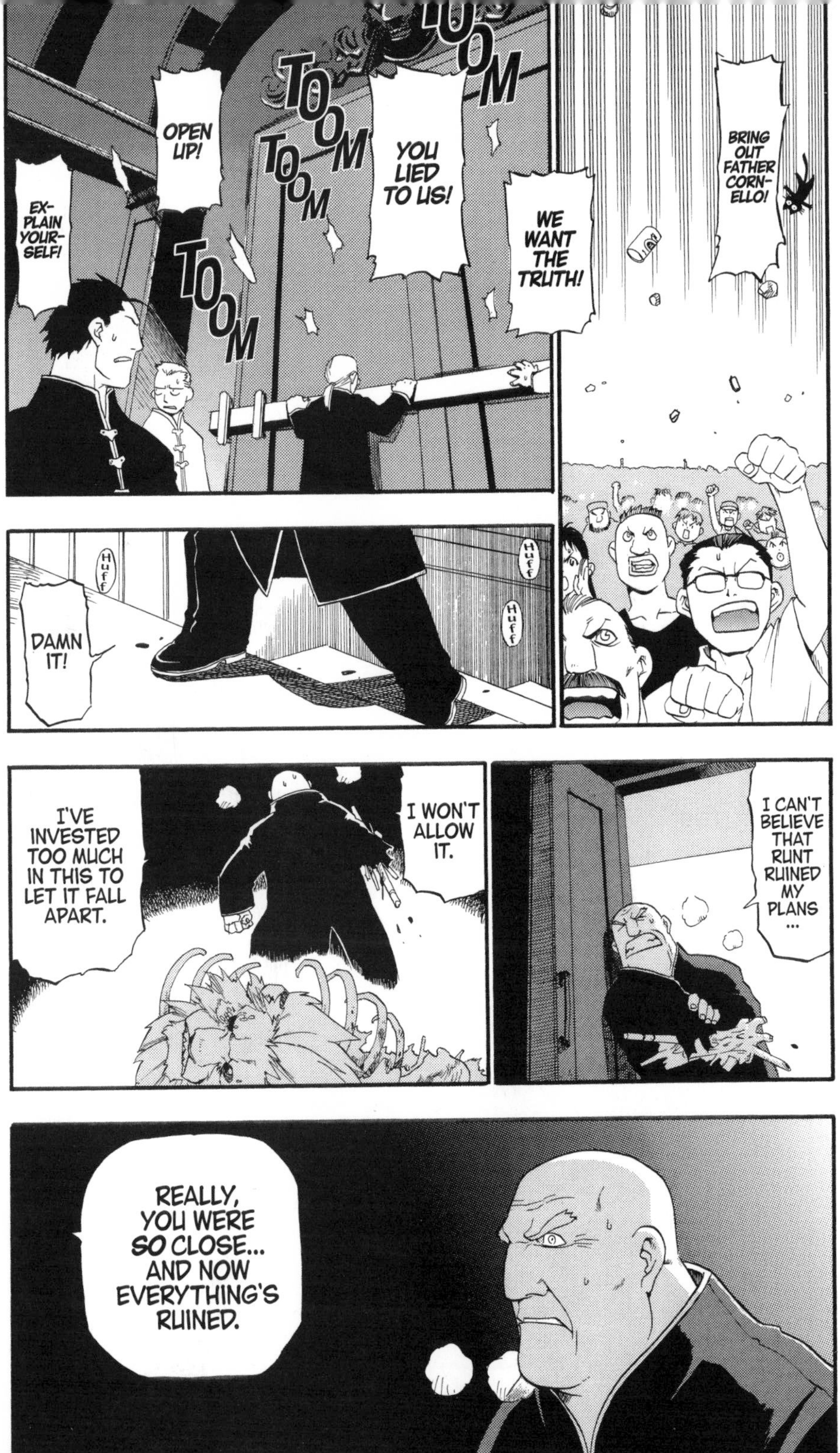
BRING OUT FATHER CORN-ELLO!
TOOM
WE WANT THE TRUTH!
YOU LIED TO US!
TOOM TOOM
OPEN UP!
EX-PLAIN YOUR-SELF!
TOOM
TOOM
Huff
Huff
DAMN IT!
I CAN'T BELIEVE THAT RUNT RUINED MY PLANS...
I WON'T ALLOW IT.
I'VE INVESTED TOO MUCH IN THIS TO LET IT FALL APART.
REALLY, YOU WERE SO CLOSE... AND NOW EVERYTHING'S RUINED.

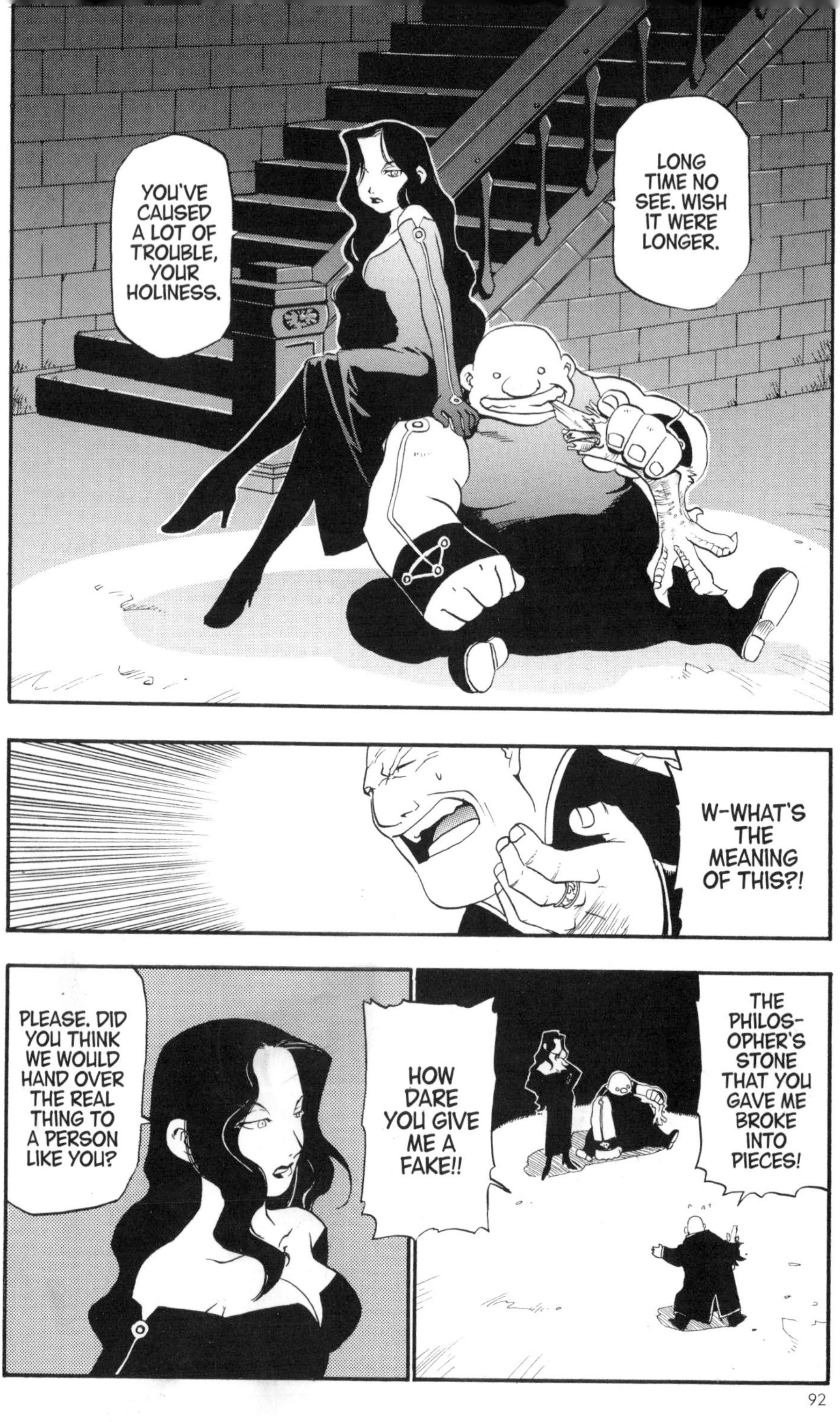
LONG TIME NO SEE. WISH IT WERE LONGER.
YOU'VE CAUSED A LOT OF TROUBLE, YOUR HOLINESS.
W-WHAT'S THE MEANING OF THIS?!
THE PHILOSOPHER'S STONE THAT YOU GAVE ME BROKE INTO PIECES!
HOW DARE YOU GIVE ME A FAKE!!
PLEASE. DID YOU THINK WE WOULD HAND OVER THE REAL THING TO A PERSON LIKE YOU?

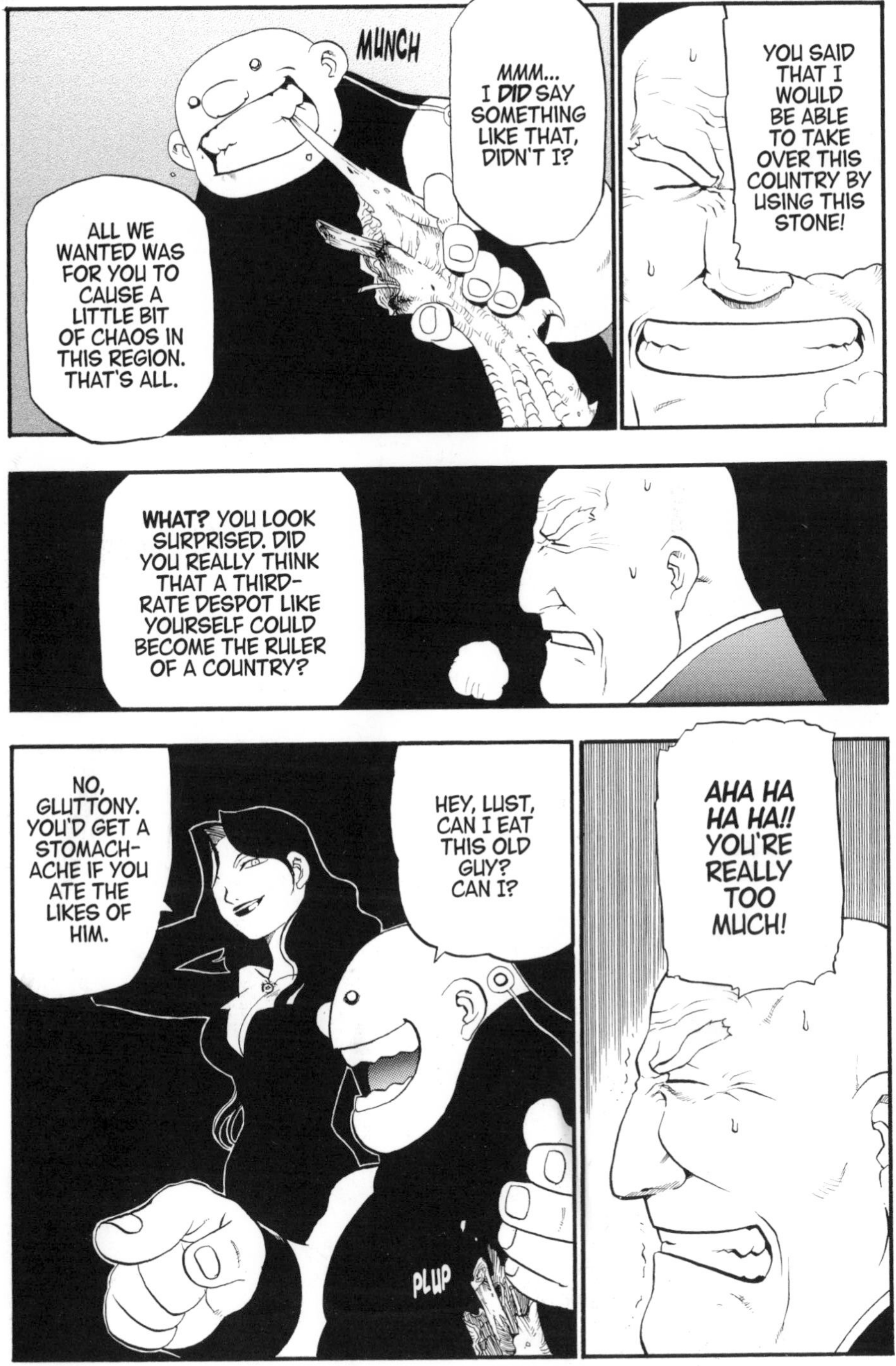
YOU SAID THAT I WOULD BE ABLE TO TAKE OVER THIS COUNTRY BY USING THIS STONE!
MMM... I **DID** SAY SOMETHING LIKE THAT, DIDN'T I?
MUNCH
ALL WE WANTED WAS FOR YOU TO CAUSE A LITTLE BIT OF CHAOS IN THIS REGION. THAT'S ALL.
WHAT? YOU LOOK SURPRISED. DID YOU REALLY THINK THAT A THIRD-RATE DESPOT LIKE YOURSELF COULD BECOME THE RULER OF A COUNTRY?
AHA HA HA HA!! YOU'RE REALLY TOO MUCH!
HEY, LUST, CAN I EAT THIS OLD GUY? CAN I?
NO, GLUTTONY. YOU'D GET A STOMACH-ACHE IF YOU ATE THE LIKES OF HIM.
PLUP

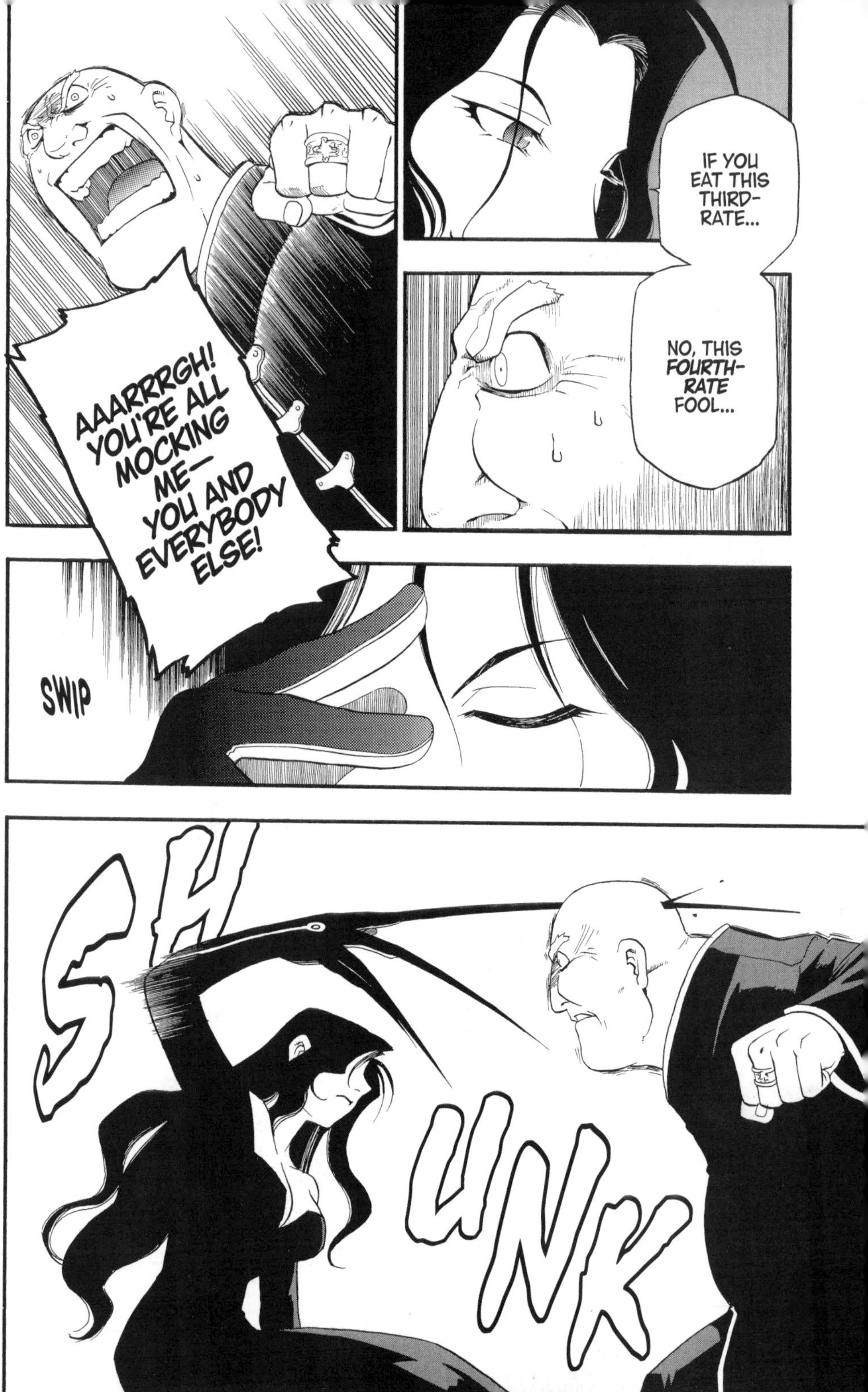
IF YOU EAT THIS THIRD-RATE...
NO, THIS FOURTH-RATE FOOL...
AAARRRGH! YOU'RE ALL MOCKING ME— YOU AND EVERYBODY ELSE!
SWIP
SHUNK

YOU...
...ARE NO LONGER OF ANY USE.
SHAA
SPLUT

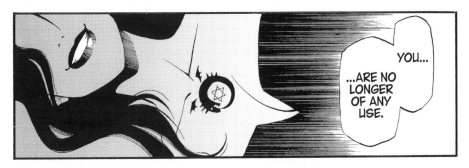

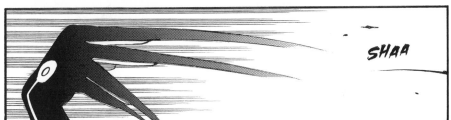

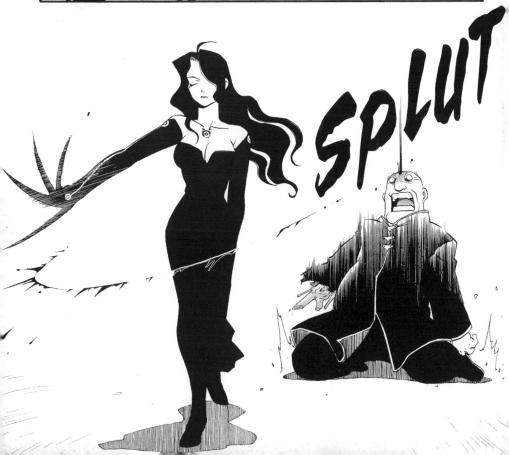

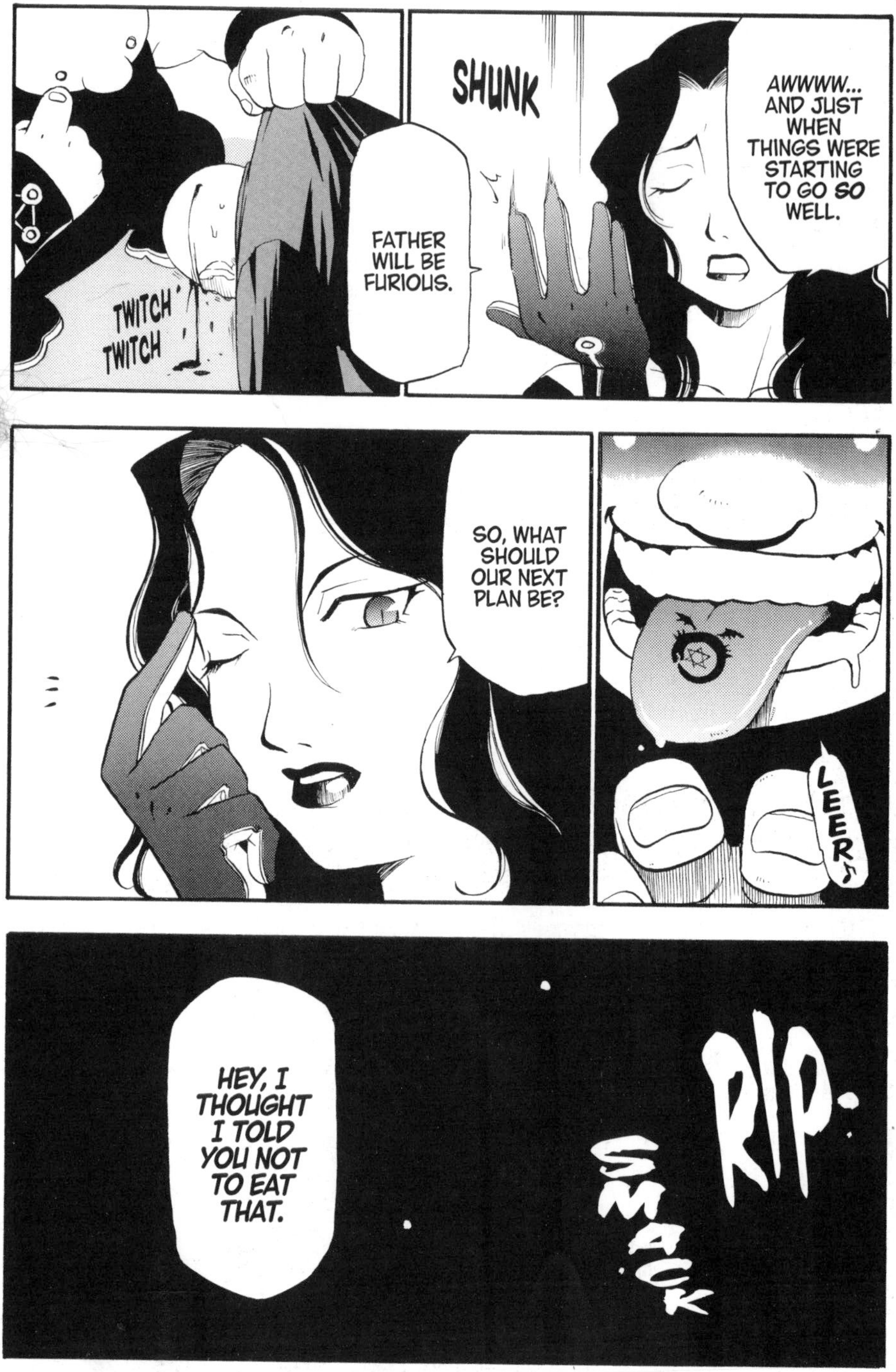
AWWWW... AND JUST WHEN THINGS WERE STARTING TO GO SO WELL.
SHUNK
FATHER WILL BE FURIOUS.
TWITCH TWITCH
LEER♪
SO, WHAT SHOULD OUR NEXT PLAN BE?
RIP
SMACK
HEY, I THOUGHT I TOLD YOU NOT TO EAT THAT.

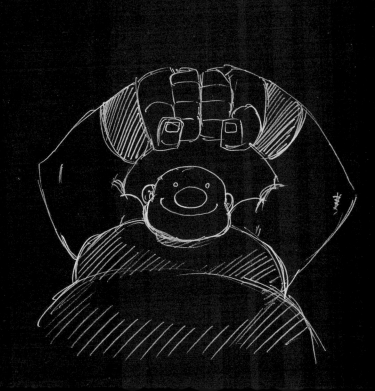

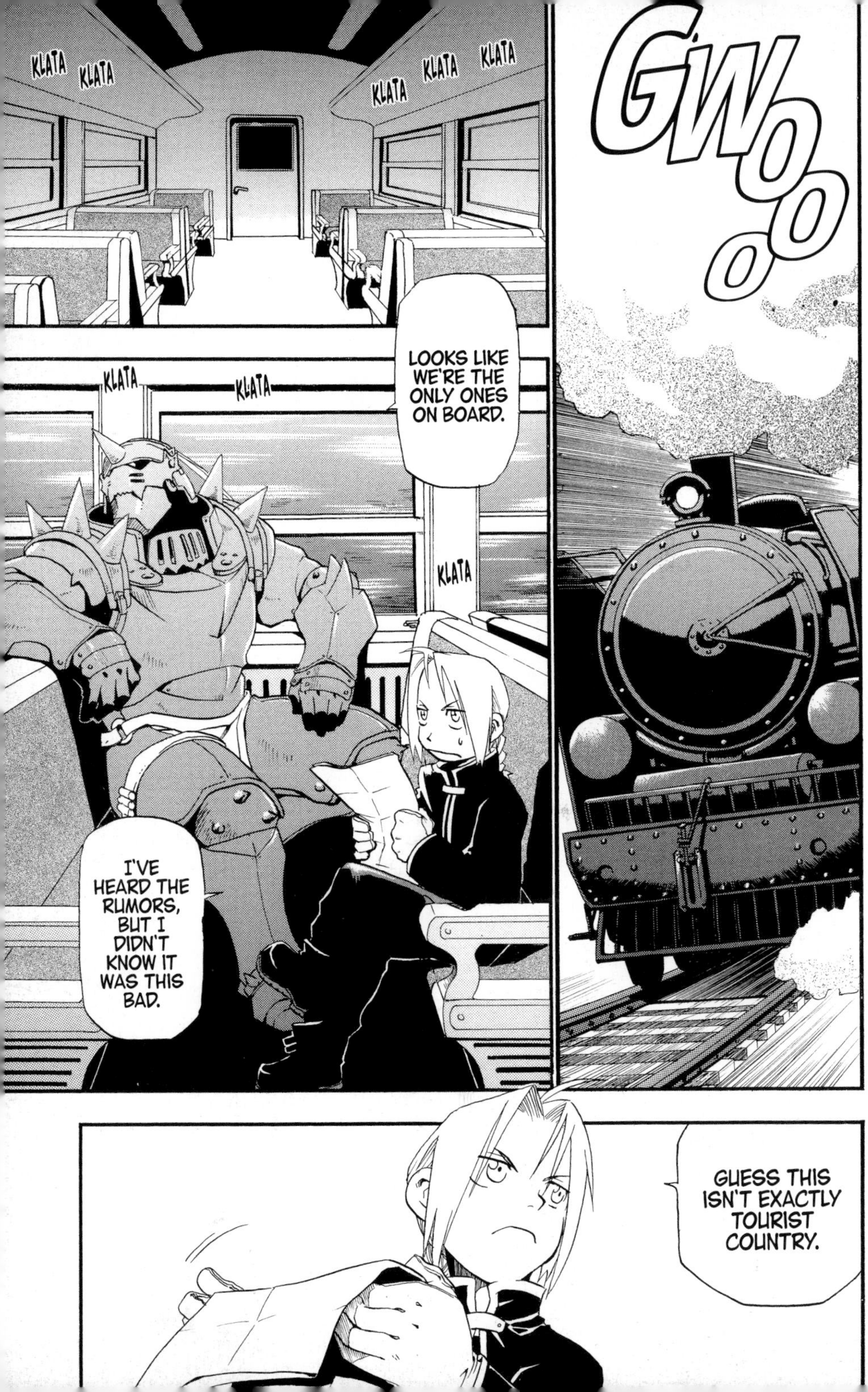
GWOOOO
KLATA KLATA KLATA KLATA KLATA
KLATA KLATA KLATA
LOOKS LIKE WE'RE THE ONLY ONES ON BOARD.
I'VE HEARD THE RUMORS, BUT I DIDN'T KNOW IT WAS THIS BAD.
GUESS THIS ISN'T EXACTLY TOURIST COUNTRY.

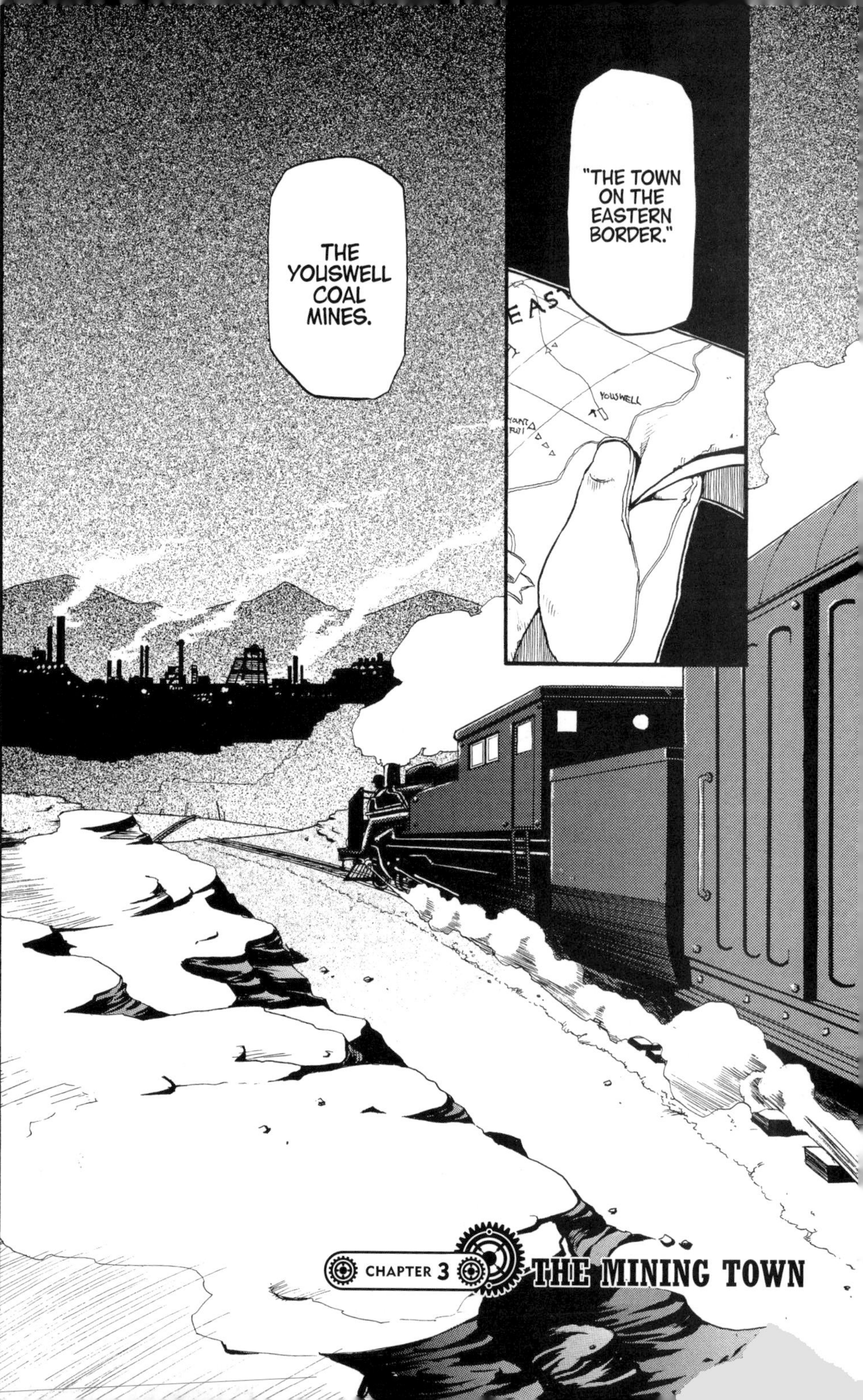
"THE TOWN ON THE EASTERN BORDER."
YOUSWELL
THE YOUSWELL COAL MINES.
CHAPTER 3 THE MINING TOWN

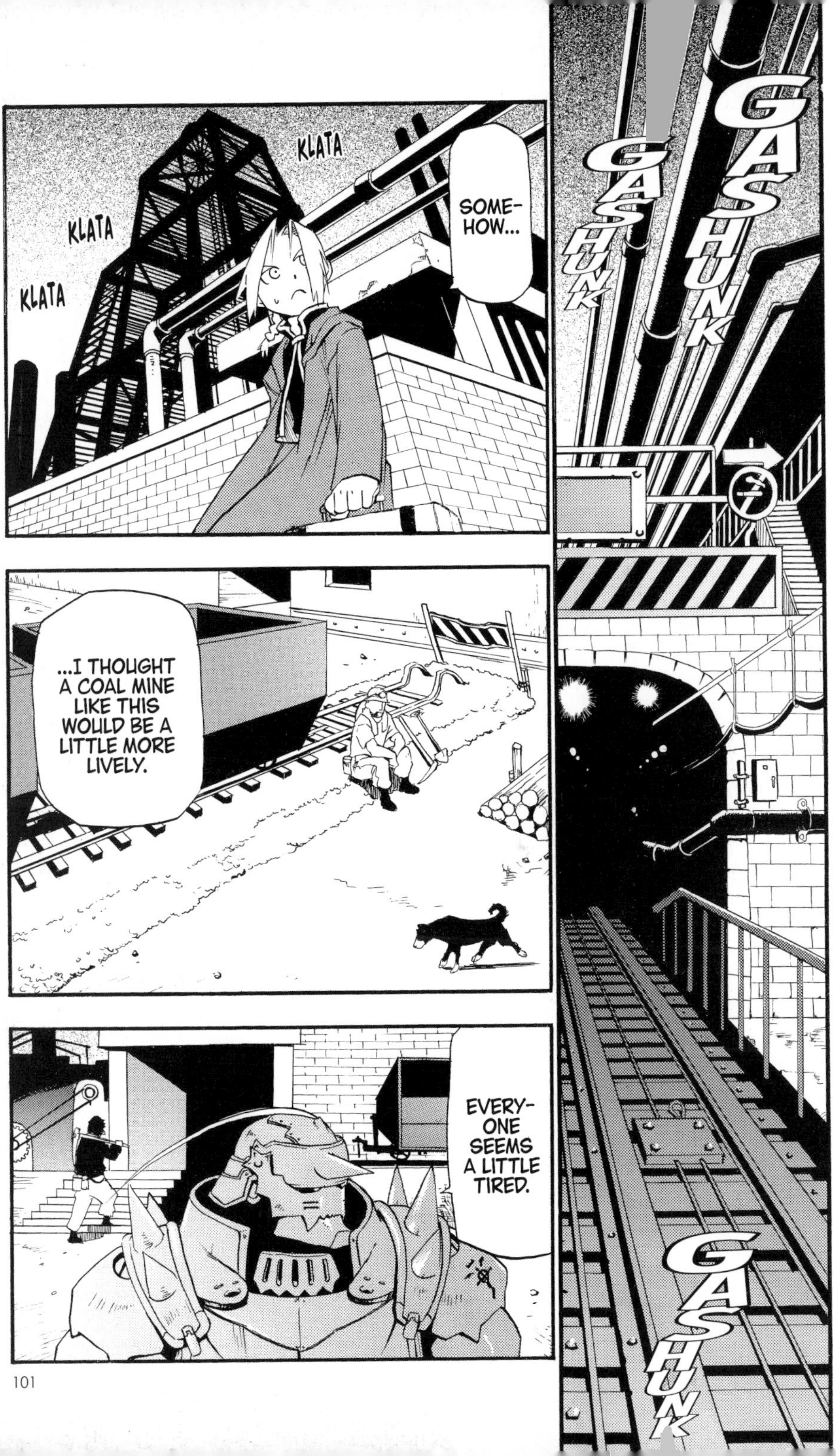
GASHUNK
GASHUNK
GASHUNK
SOME-HOW...
KLATA
KLATA
KLATA
...I THOUGHT A COAL MINE LIKE THIS WOULD BE A LITTLE MORE LIVELY.
EVERY-ONE SEEMS A LITTLE TIRED.

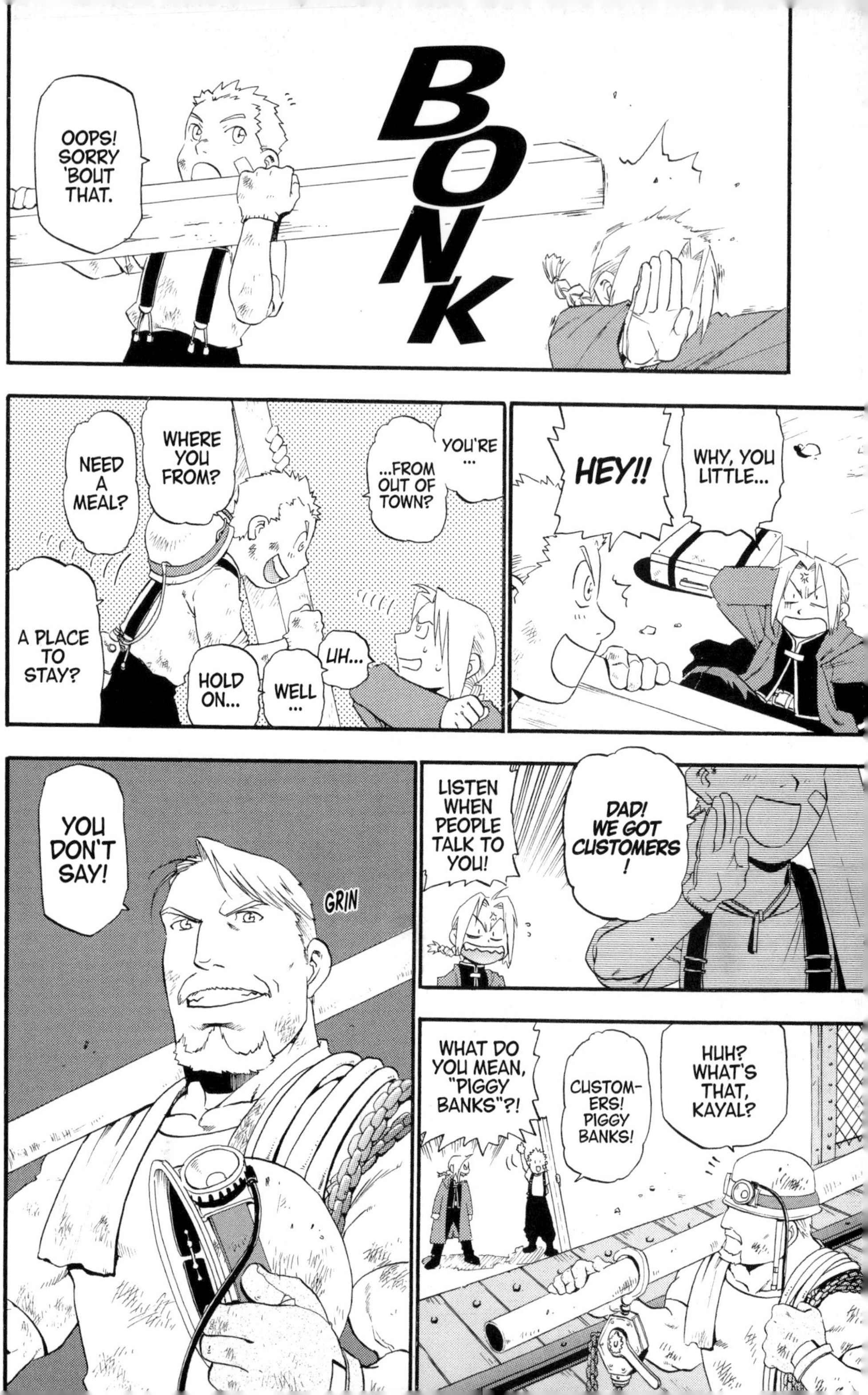
BONK
OOPS! SORRY 'BOUT THAT.
WHY, YOU LITTLE...
HEY!!
YOU'RE ...
...FROM OUT OF TOWN?
WHERE YOU FROM?
NEED A MEAL?
A PLACE TO STAY?
UH...
WELL ...
HOLD ON...
DAD! WE GOT CUSTOMERS !
LISTEN WHEN PEOPLE TALK TO YOU!
HUH? WHAT'S THAT, KAYAL?
CUSTOM-ERS! PIGGY BANKS!
WHAT DO YOU MEAN, "PIGGY BANKS"?!
YOU DON'T SAY!
GRIN

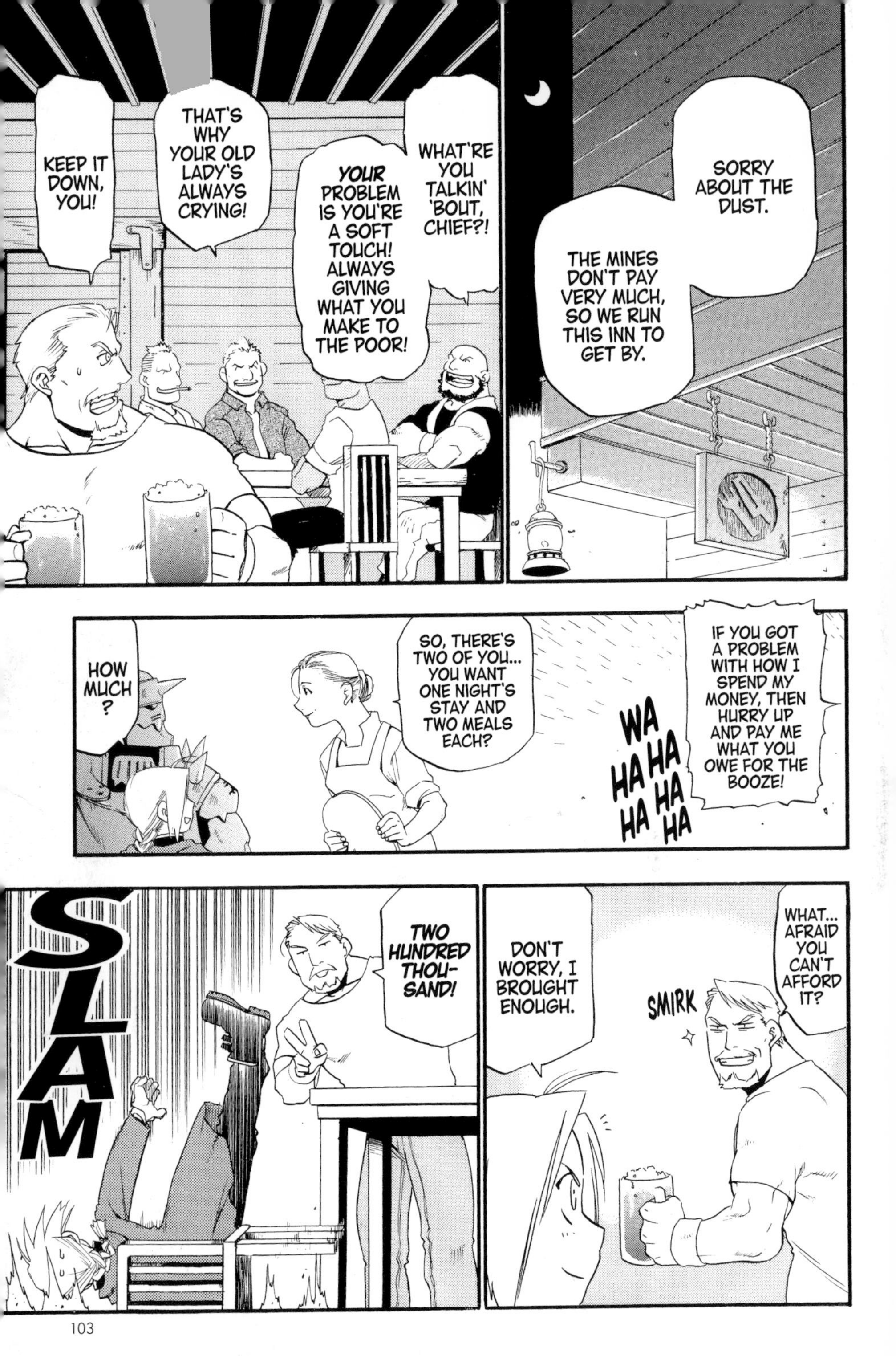
SORRY ABOUT THE DUST.
THE MINES DON'T PAY VERY MUCH, SO WE RUN THIS INN TO GET BY.
WHAT'RE YOU TALKIN' 'BOUT, CHIEF?!
YOUR PROBLEM IS YOU'RE A SOFT TOUCH! ALWAYS GIVING WHAT YOU MAKE TO THE POOR!
THAT'S WHY YOUR OLD LADY'S ALWAYS CRYING!
KEEP IT DOWN, YOU!
IF YOU GOT A PROBLEM WITH HOW I SPEND MY MONEY, THEN HURRY UP AND PAY ME WHAT YOU OWE FOR THE BOOZE!
WA HA HA HA HA HA HA
SO, THERE'S TWO OF YOU... YOU WANT ONE NIGHT'S STAY AND TWO MEALS EACH?
HOW MUCH?
WHAT... AFRAID YOU CAN'T AFFORD IT?
SMIRK
DON'T WORRY, I BROUGHT ENOUGH.
TWO HUNDRED THOU-SAND!
SLAM

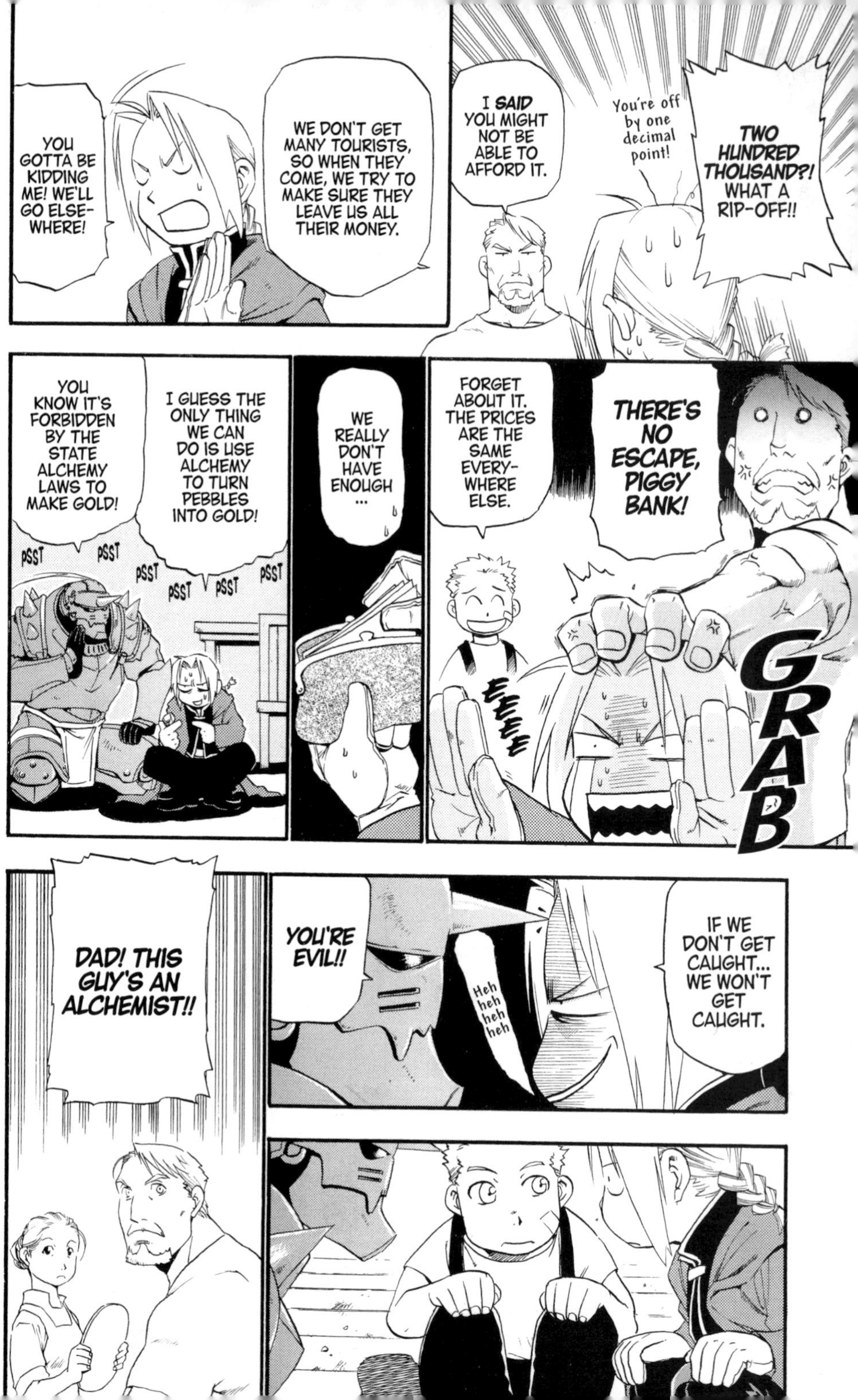
TWO HUNDRED THOUSAND?! WHAT A RIP-OFF!!
You're off by one decimal point!
I SAID YOU MIGHT NOT BE ABLE TO AFFORD IT.
WE DON'T GET MANY TOURISTS, SO WHEN THEY COME, WE TRY TO MAKE SURE THEY LEAVE US ALL THEIR MONEY.
YOU GOTTA BE KIDDING ME! WE'LL GO ELSEWHERE!
THERE'S NO ESCAPE, PIGGY BANK!
FORGET ABOUT IT. THE PRICES ARE THE SAME EVERYWHERE ELSE.
GRAB
EEEE
WE REALLY DON'T HAVE ENOUGH ...
I GUESS THE ONLY THING WE CAN DO IS USE ALCHEMY TO TURN PEBBLES INTO GOLD!
YOU KNOW IT'S FORBIDDEN BY THE STATE ALCHEMY LAWS TO MAKE GOLD!
PSST PSST PSST PSST PSST PSST
IF WE DON'T GET CAUGHT... WE WON'T GET CAUGHT.
Heh heh heh heh
YOU'RE EVIL!!
DAD! THIS GUY'S AN ALCHEMIST!!

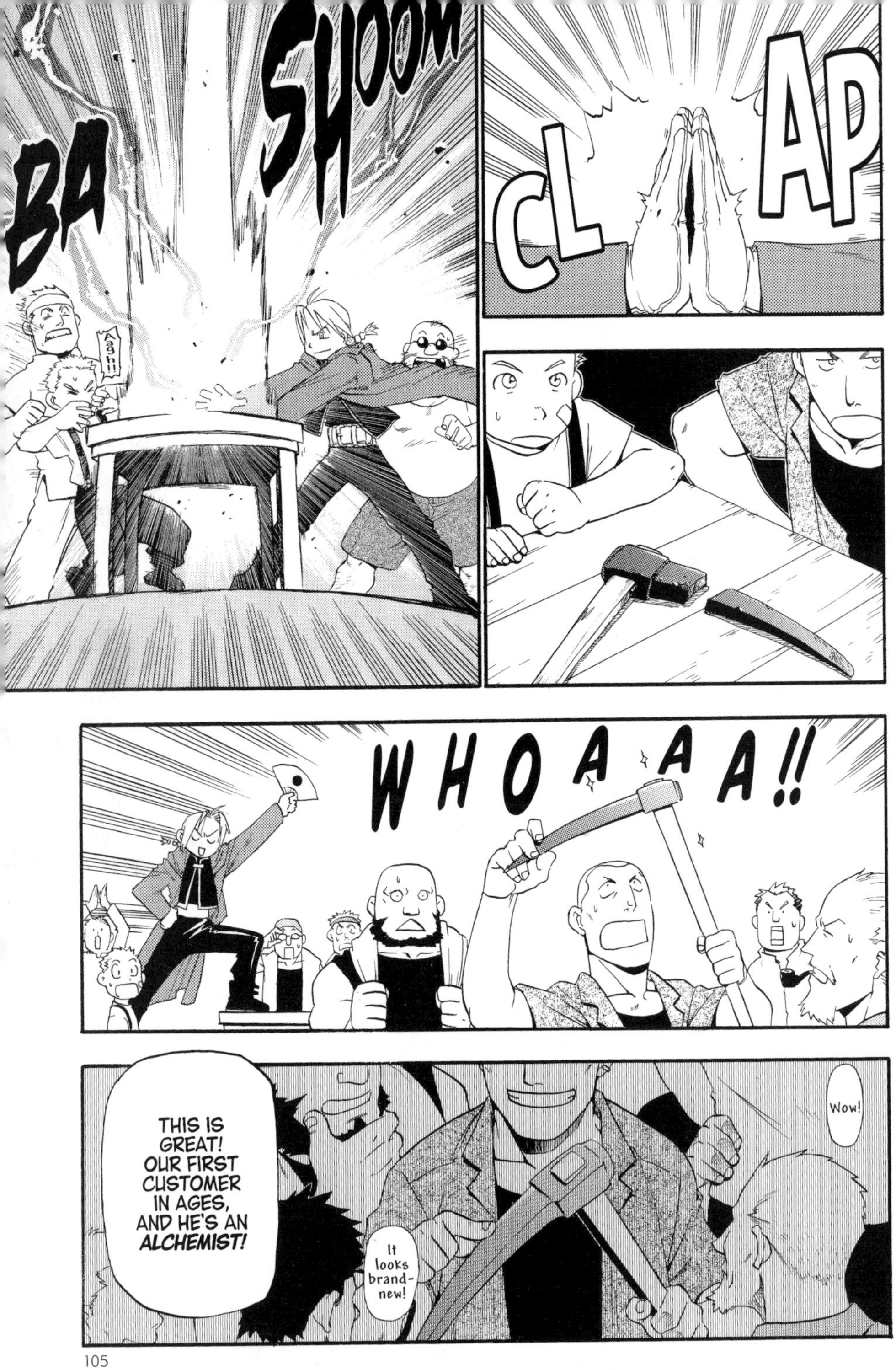
CLAP
BA SHOOM
Aagh!!
WHOAAA!!
Wow!
It looks brand-new!
THIS IS GREAT! OUR FIRST CUSTOMER IN AGES, AND HE'S AN ALCHEMIST!

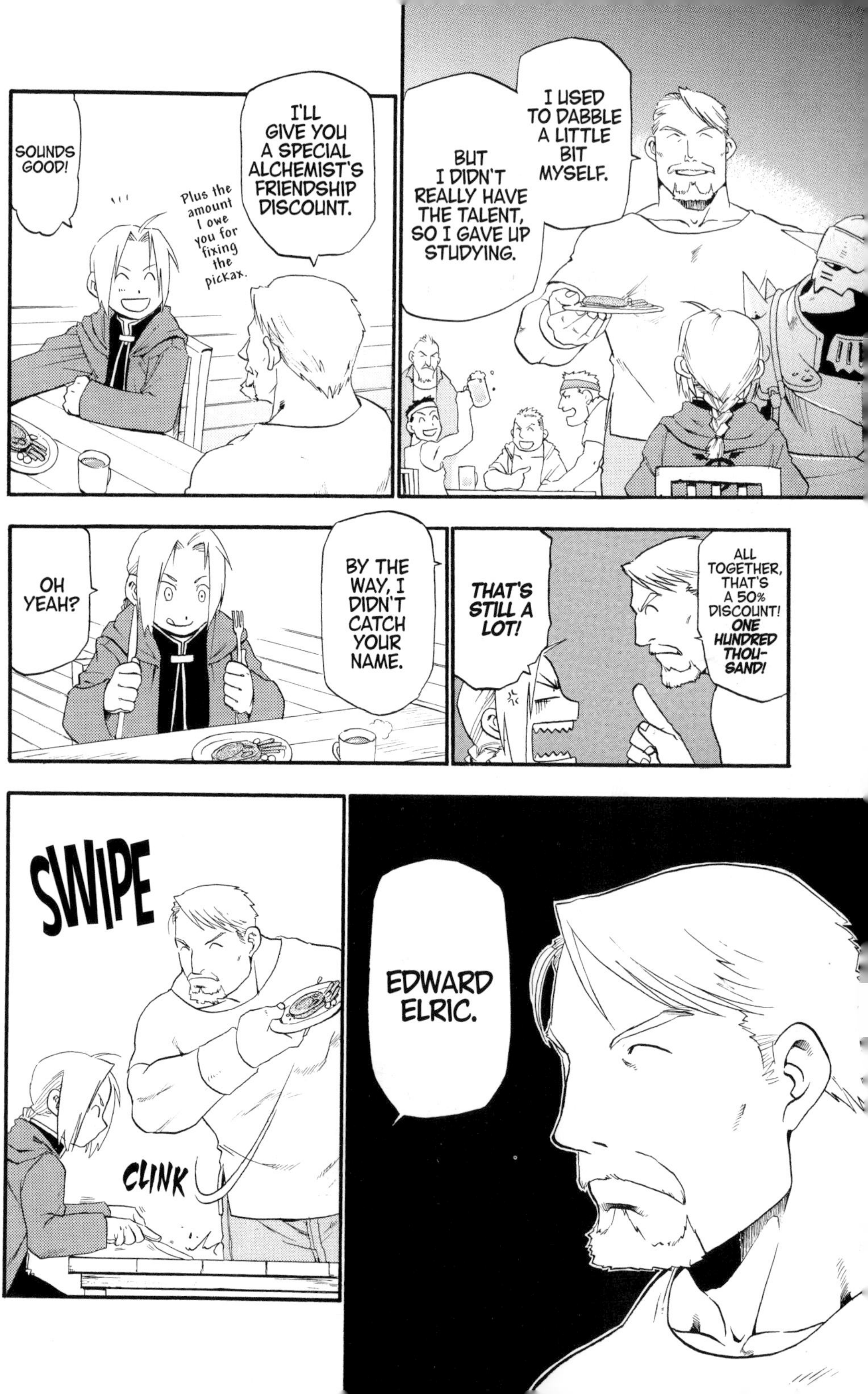
I USED TO DABBLE A LITTLE BIT MYSELF.
BUT I DIDN'T REALLY HAVE THE TALENT, SO I GAVE UP STUDYING.
I'LL GIVE YOU A SPECIAL ALCHEMIST'S FRIENDSHIP DISCOUNT.
Plus the amount I owe you for fixing the pickax.
SOUNDS GOOD!
ALL TOGETHER, THAT'S A 50% DISCOUNT! ONE HUNDRED THOU-SAND!
THAT'S STILL A LOT!
BY THE WAY, I DIDN'T CATCH YOUR NAME.
OH YEAH?
EDWARD ELRIC.
SWIPE
CLINK

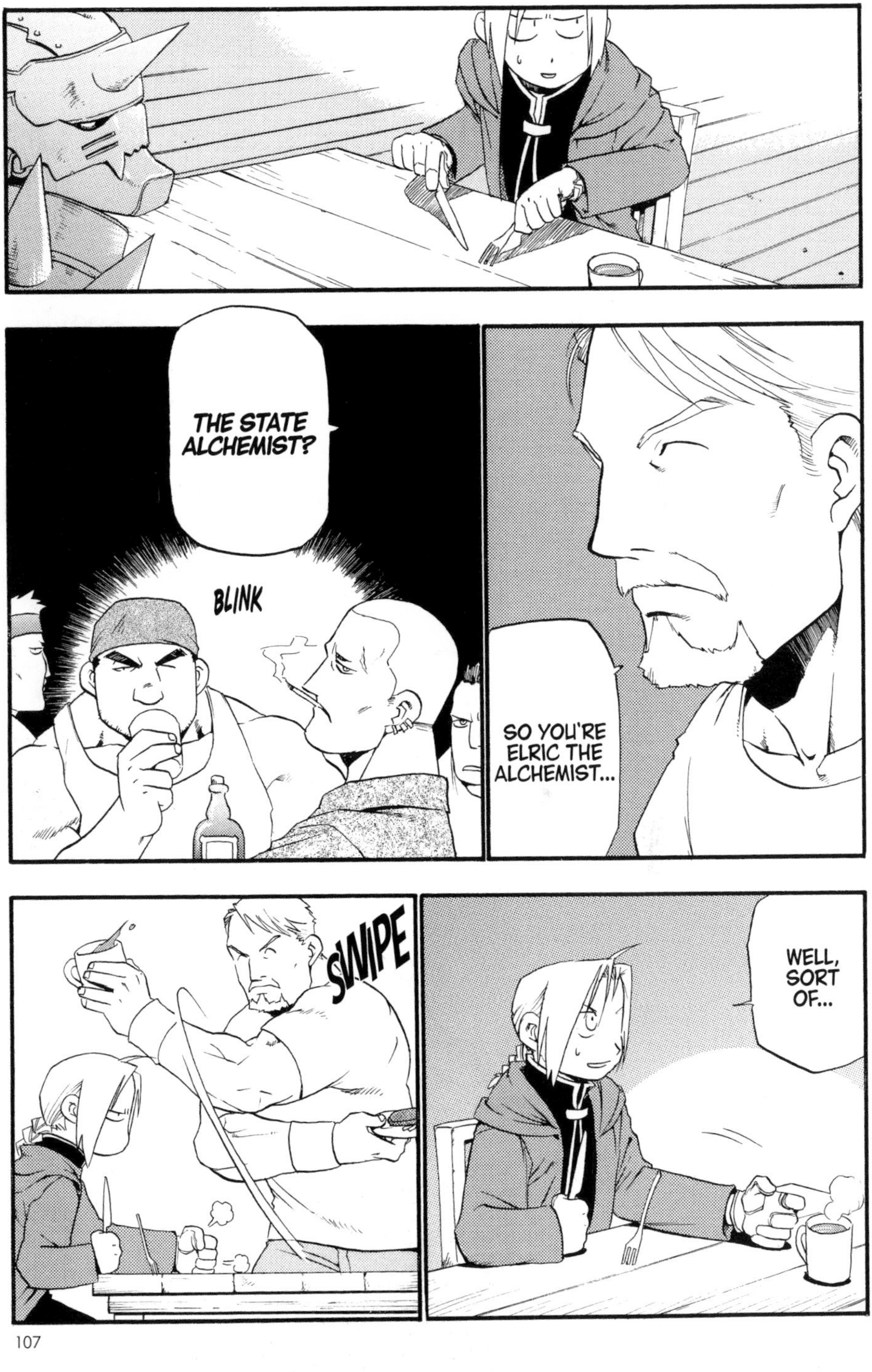
SO YOU'RE ELRIC THE ALCHEMIST...
THE STATE ALCHEMIST?
BLINK
WELL, SORT OF...
SWIPE

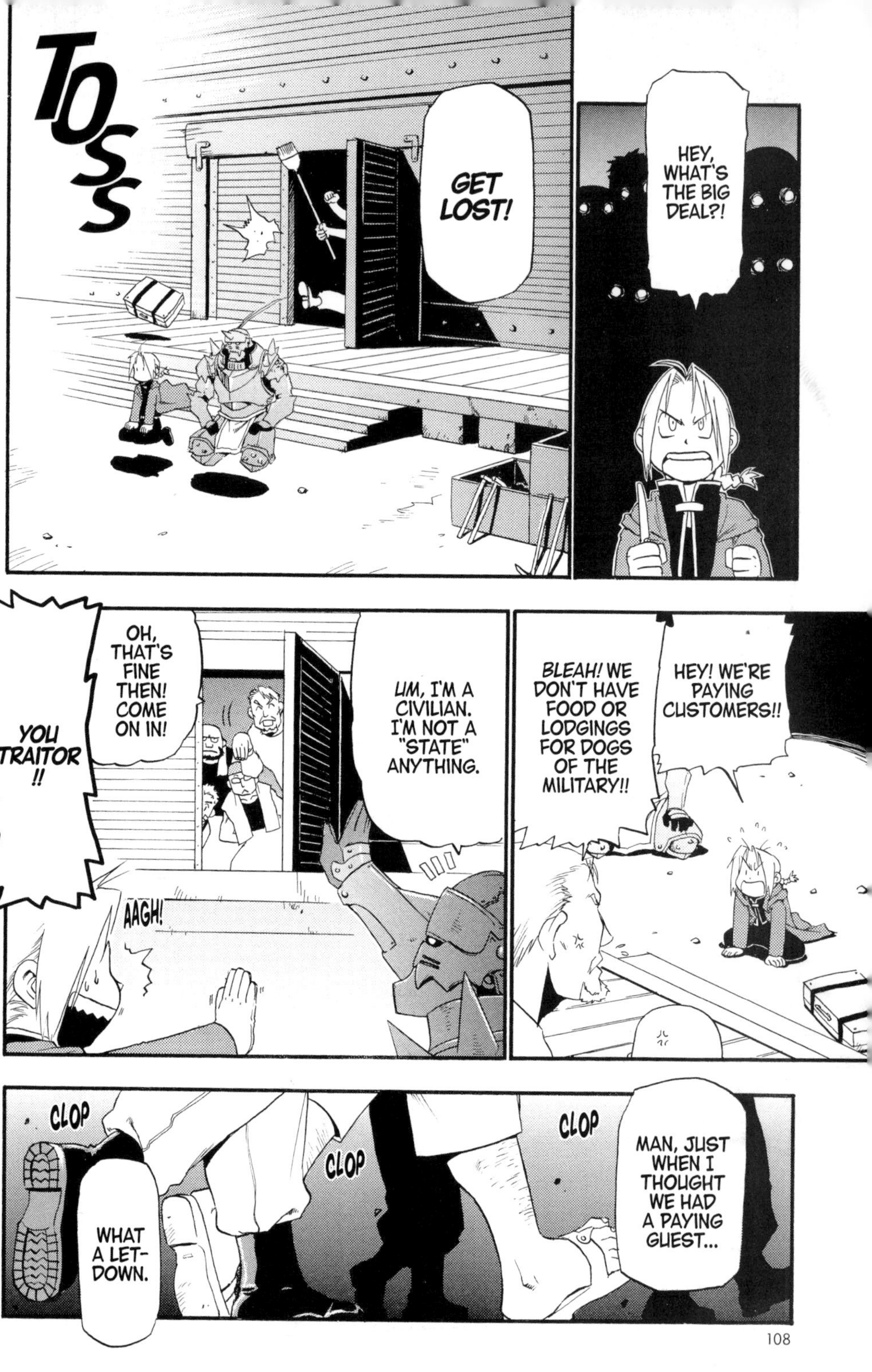
HEY, WHAT'S THE BIG DEAL?!
TOSS
GET LOST!
HEY! WE'RE PAYING CUSTOMERS!!
BLEAH! WE DON'T HAVE FOOD OR LODGINGS FOR DOGS OF THE MILITARY!!
UM, I'M A CIVILIAN. I'M NOT A "STATE" ANYTHING.
OH, THAT'S FINE THEN! COME ON IN!
YOU TRAITOR!!
AAGH!
MAN, JUST WHEN I THOUGHT WE HAD A PAYING GUEST...
CLOP
CLOP
CLOP
WHAT A LET-DOWN.

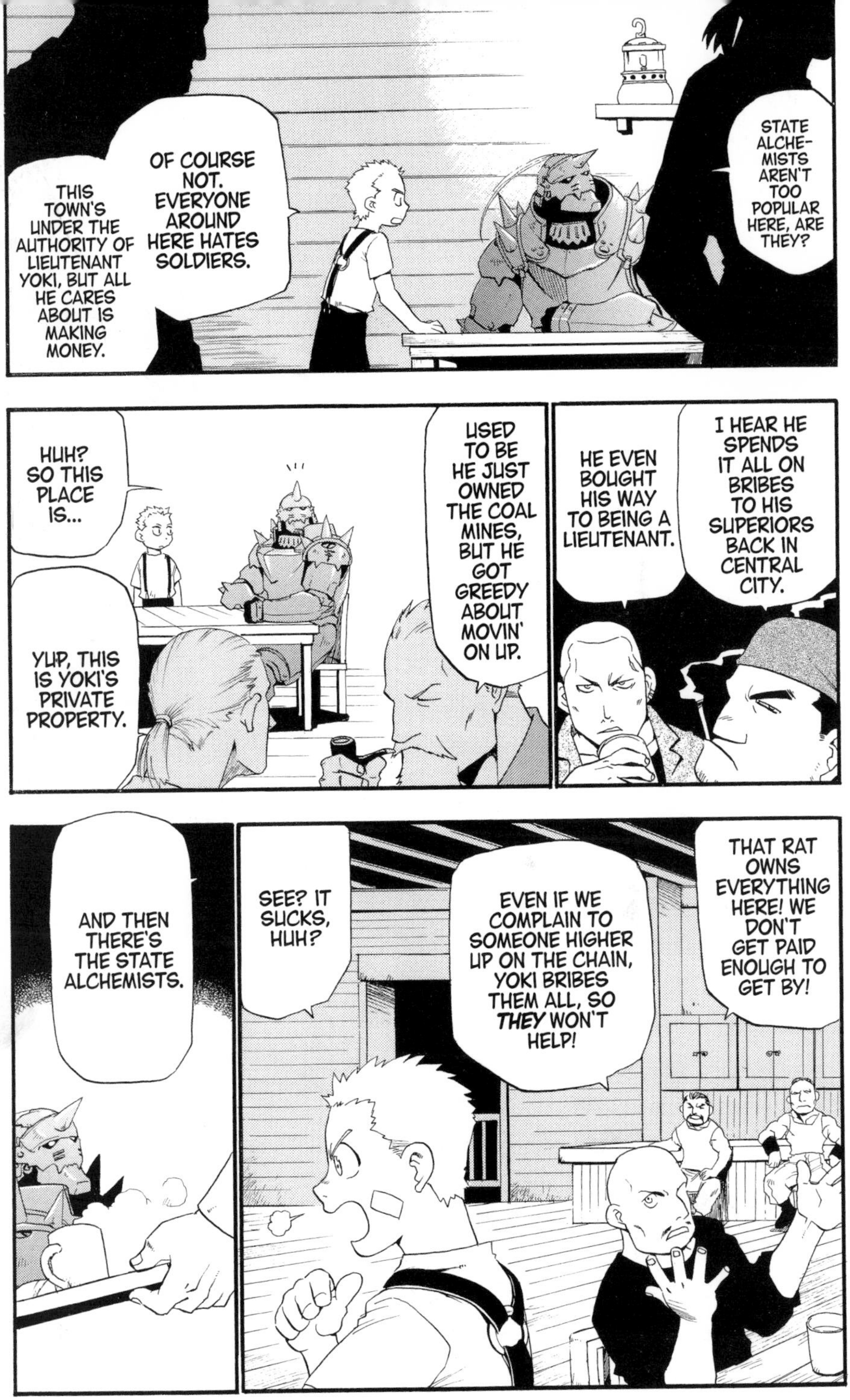
STATE ALCHEMISTS AREN'T TOO POPULAR HERE, ARE THEY?
OF COURSE NOT. EVERYONE AROUND HERE HATES SOLDIERS.
THIS TOWN'S UNDER THE AUTHORITY OF LIEUTENANT YOKI, BUT ALL HE CARES ABOUT IS MAKING MONEY.
I HEAR HE SPENDS IT ALL ON BRIBES TO HIS SUPERIORS BACK IN CENTRAL CITY.
HE EVEN BOUGHT HIS WAY TO BEING A LIEUTENANT.
USED TO BE HE JUST OWNED THE COAL MINES, BUT HE GOT GREEDY ABOUT MOVIN' ON UP.
HUH? SO THIS PLACE IS...
YUP, THIS IS YOKI'S PRIVATE PROPERTY.
THAT RAT OWNS EVERYTHING HERE! WE DON'T GET PAID ENOUGH TO GET BY!
EVEN IF WE COMPLAIN TO SOMEONE HIGHER UP ON THE CHAIN, YOKI BRIBES THEM ALL, SO *THEY* WON'T HELP!
SEE? IT SUCKS, HUH?
AND THEN THERE'S THE STATE ALCHEMISTS.

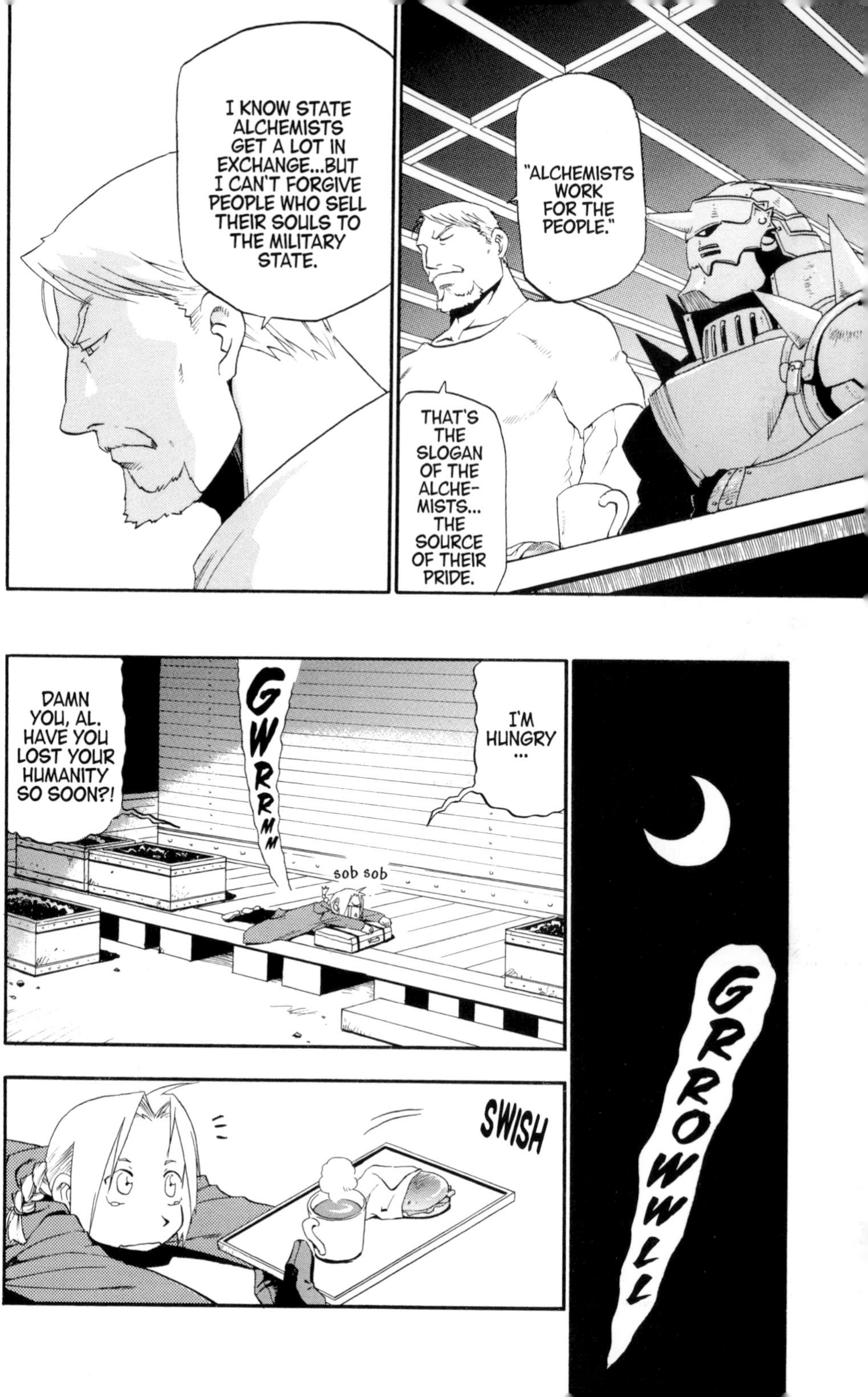
"ALCHEMISTS WORK FOR THE PEOPLE."
THAT'S THE SLOGAN OF THE ALCHEMISTS... THE SOURCE OF THEIR PRIDE.
I KNOW STATE ALCHEMISTS GET A LOT IN EXCHANGE...BUT I CAN'T FORGIVE PEOPLE WHO SELL THEIR SOULS TO THE MILITARY STATE.
GRROWLL
I'M HUNGRY...
GWRRMM
DAMN YOU, AL. HAVE YOU LOST YOUR HUMANITY SO SOON?!
sob sob
SWISH

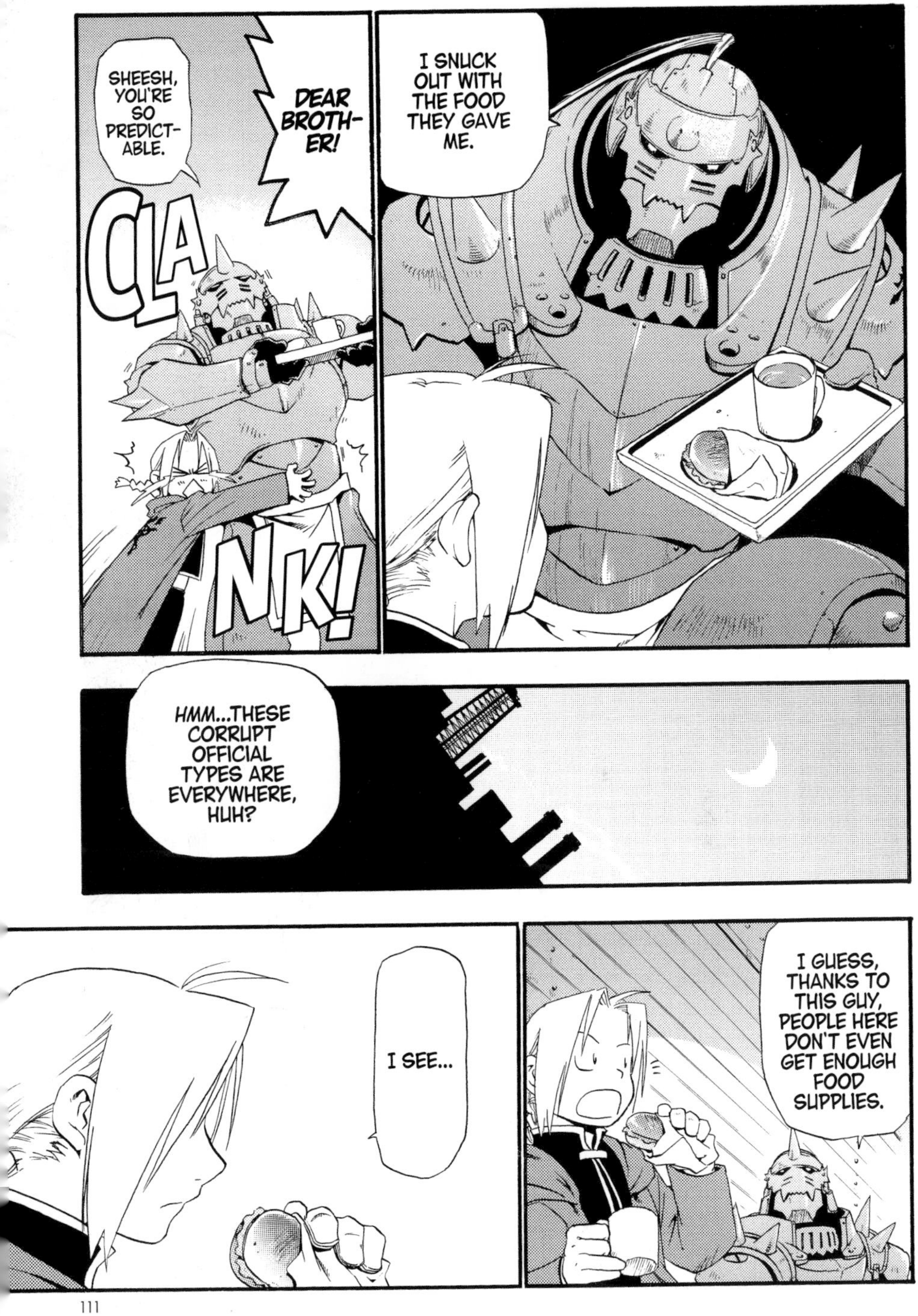
I SNUCK OUT WITH THE FOOD THEY GAVE ME.
DEAR BROTHER!
SHEESH, YOU'RE SO PREDICTABLE.
CLANK!
HMM...THESE CORRUPT OFFICIAL TYPES ARE EVERYWHERE, HUH?
I GUESS, THANKS TO THIS GUY, PEOPLE HERE DON'T EVEN GET ENOUGH FOOD SUPPLIES.
I SEE...

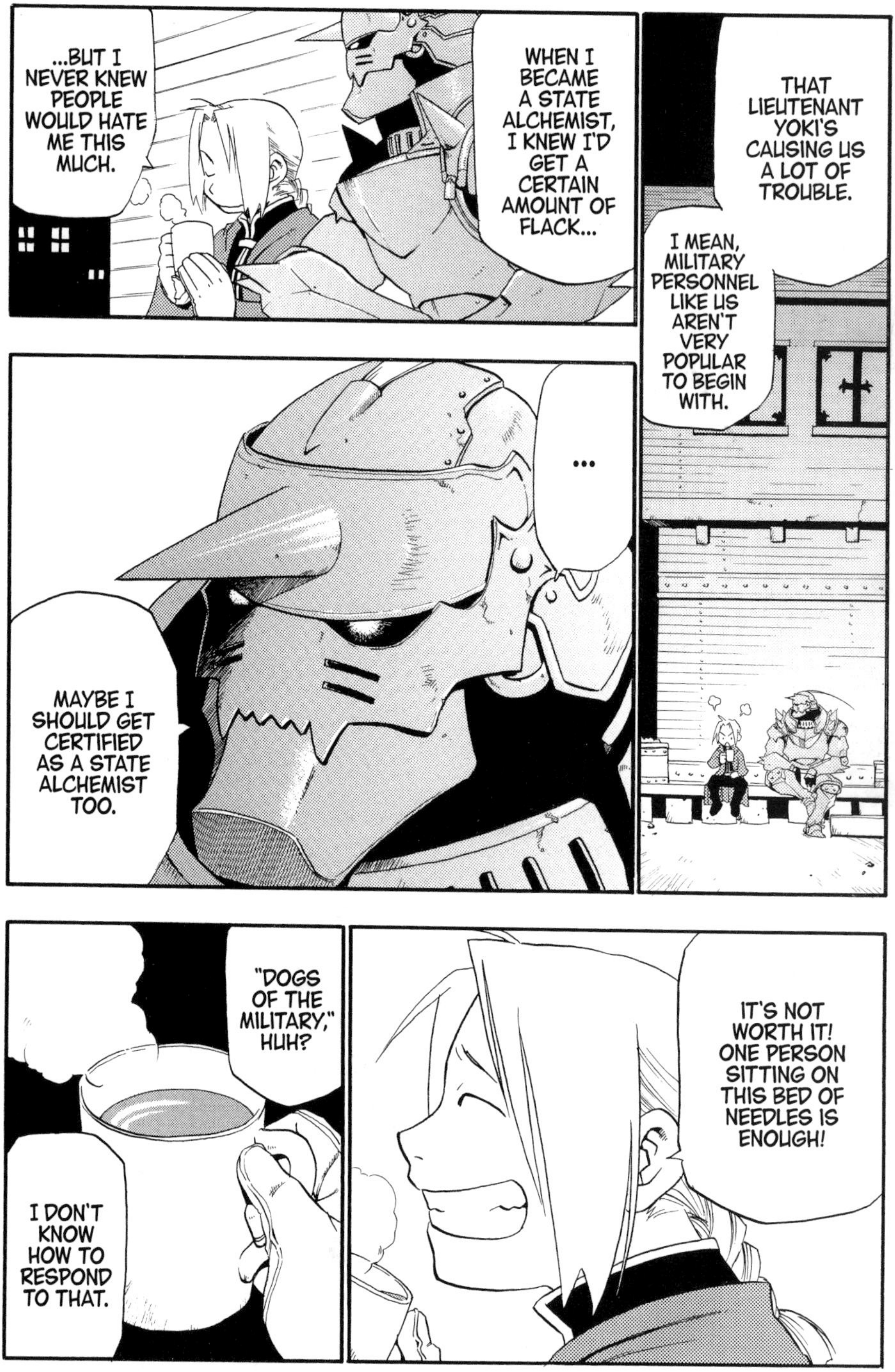
THAT LIEUTENANT YOKI'S CAUSING US A LOT OF TROUBLE.
I MEAN, MILITARY PERSONNEL LIKE US AREN'T VERY POPULAR TO BEGIN WITH.
WHEN I BECAME A STATE ALCHEMIST, I KNEW I'D GET A CERTAIN AMOUNT OF FLACK...
...BUT I NEVER KNEW PEOPLE WOULD HATE ME THIS MUCH.
...
MAYBE I SHOULD GET CERTIFIED AS A STATE ALCHEMIST TOO.
IT'S NOT WORTH IT! ONE PERSON SITTING ON THIS BED OF NEEDLES IS ENOUGH!
"DOGS OF THE MILITARY," HUH?
I DON'T KNOW HOW TO RESPOND TO THAT.

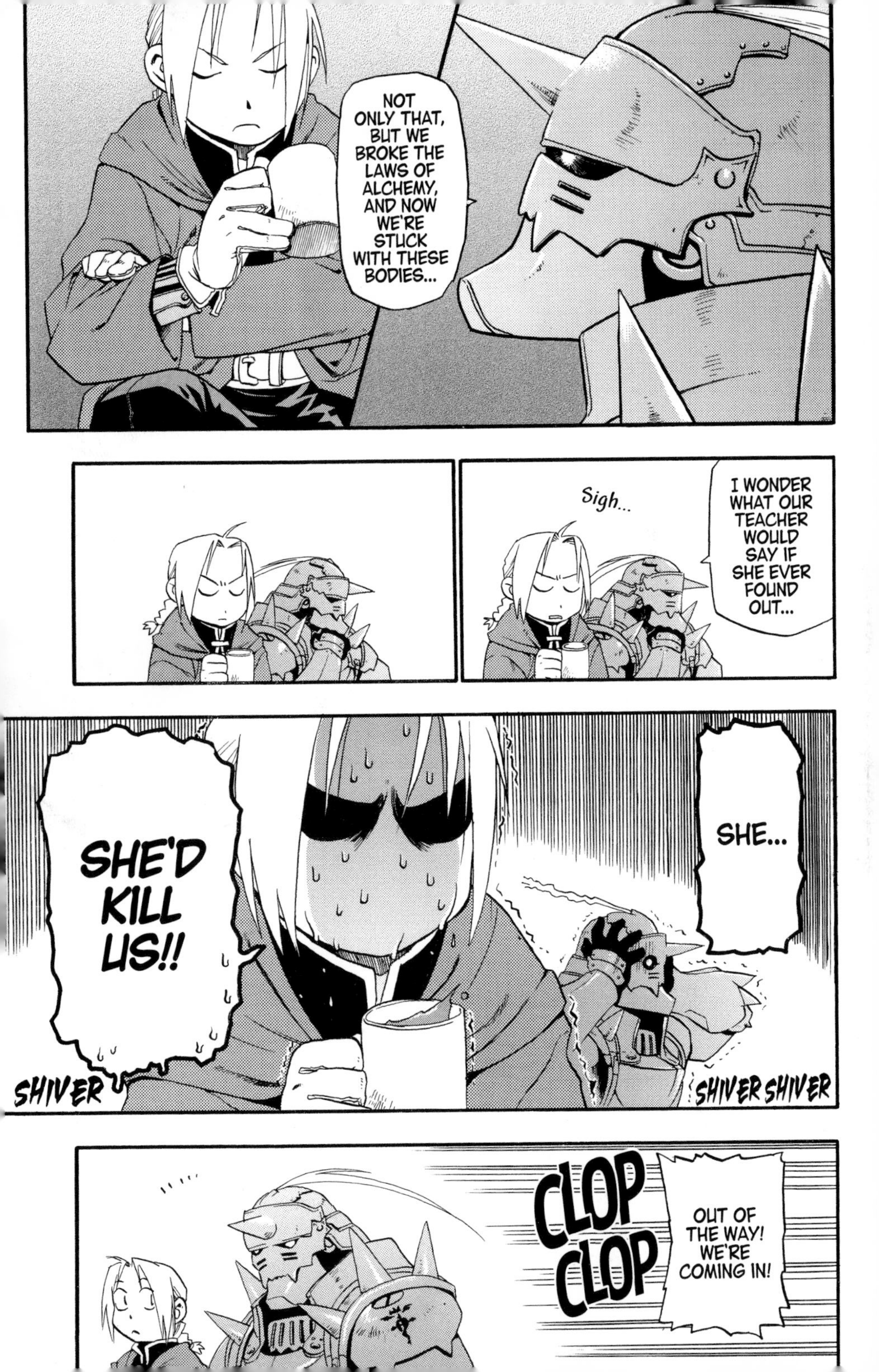
NOT ONLY THAT, BUT WE BROKE THE LAWS OF ALCHEMY, AND NOW WE'RE STUCK WITH THESE BODIES...
I WONDER WHAT OUR TEACHER WOULD SAY IF SHE EVER FOUND OUT...
Sigh...
SHE...
SHIVER SHIVER
SHE'D KILL US!!
SHIVER
OUT OF THE WAY! WE'RE COMING IN!
CLOP CLOP
....

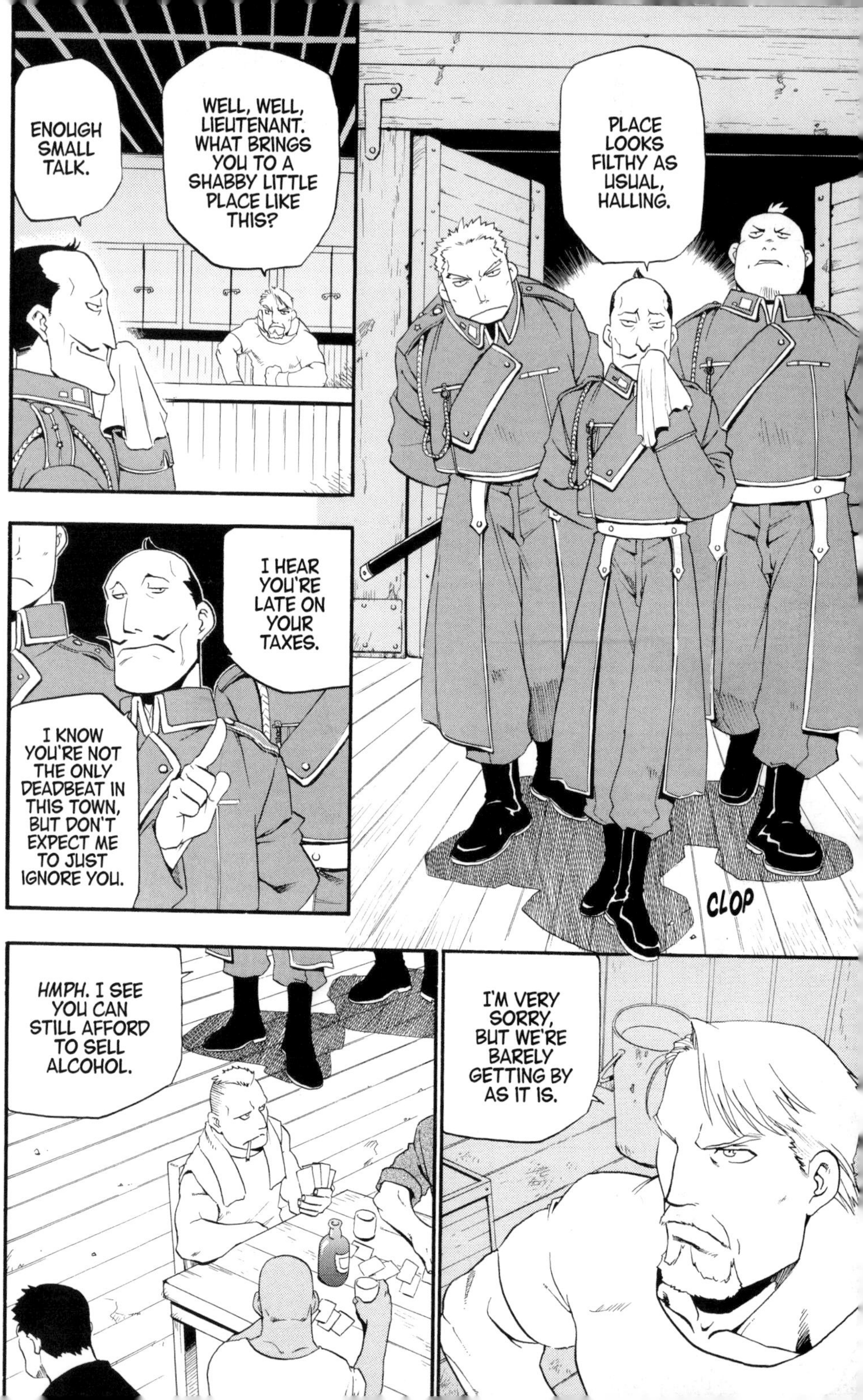
PLACE LOOKS FILTHY AS USUAL, HALLING.
CLOP
WELL, WELL, LIEUTENANT. WHAT BRINGS YOU TO A SHABBY LITTLE PLACE LIKE THIS?
ENOUGH SMALL TALK.
I HEAR YOU'RE LATE ON YOUR TAXES.
I KNOW YOU'RE NOT THE ONLY DEADBEAT IN THIS TOWN, BUT DON'T EXPECT ME TO JUST IGNORE YOU.
I'M VERY SORRY, BUT WE'RE BARELY GETTING BY AS IT IS.
HMPH. I SEE YOU CAN STILL AFFORD TO SELL ALCOHOL.

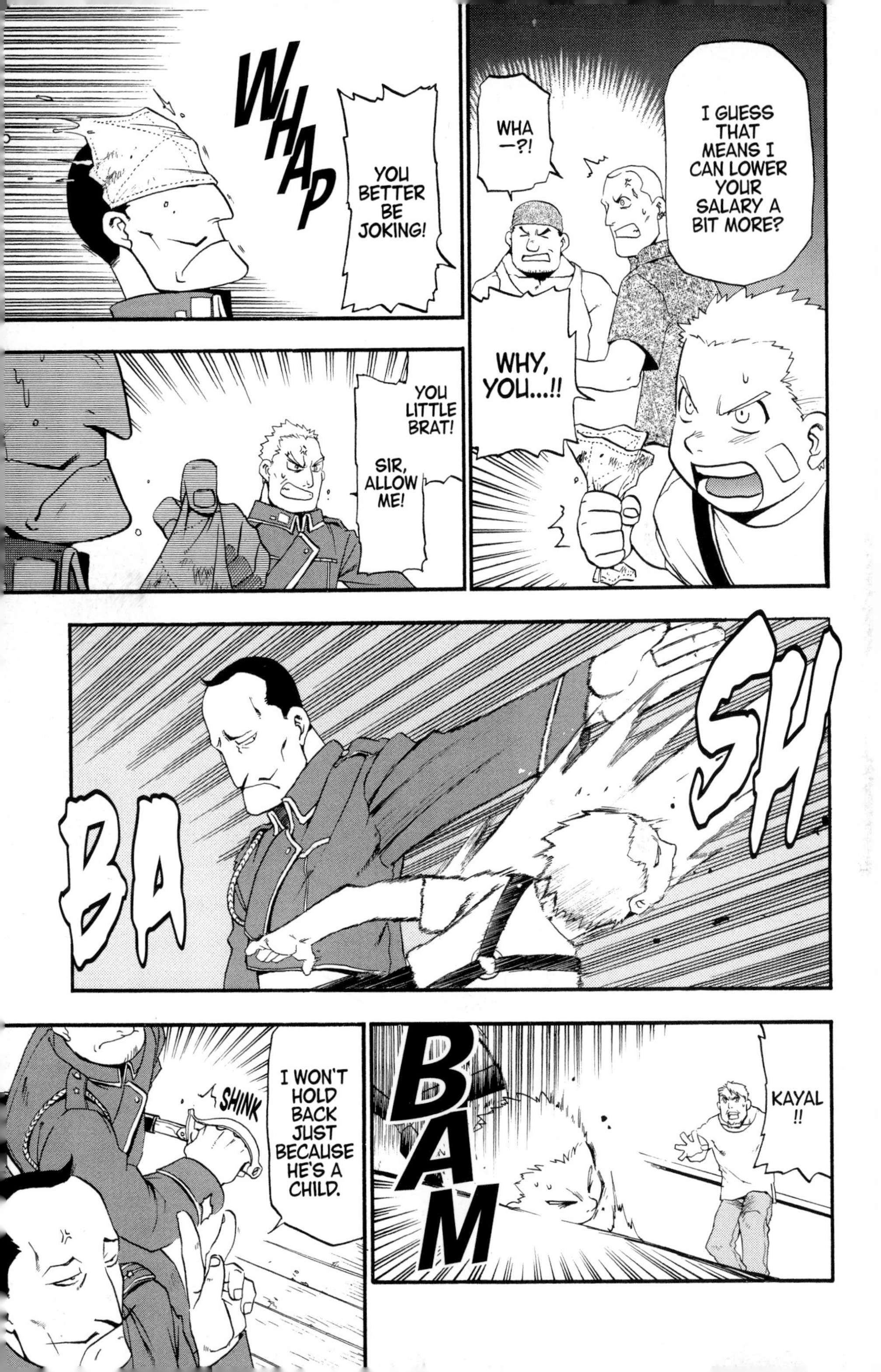
I GUESS THAT MEANS I CAN LOWER YOUR SALARY A BIT MORE?
WHA—?!
WHY, YOU...!!
WHAP
YOU BETTER BE JOKING!
YOU LITTLE BRAT!
SIR, ALLOW ME!
SH
BA
KAYAL!!
BAM
SHINK
I WON'T HOLD BACK JUST BECAUSE HE'S A CHILD.

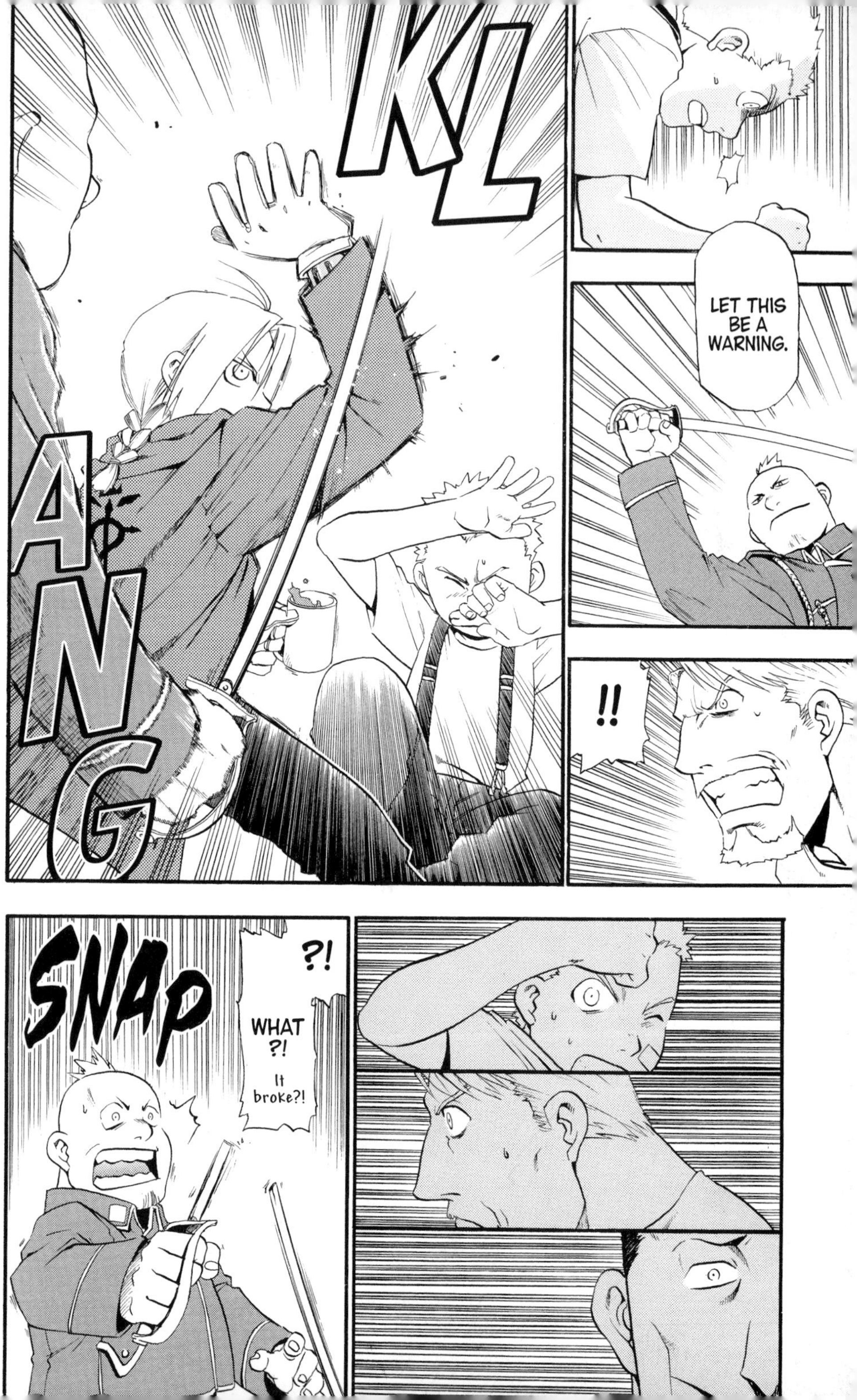
LET THIS BE A WARNING.
!!
KLANG
SNAP
?!
WHAT?!
It broke?!

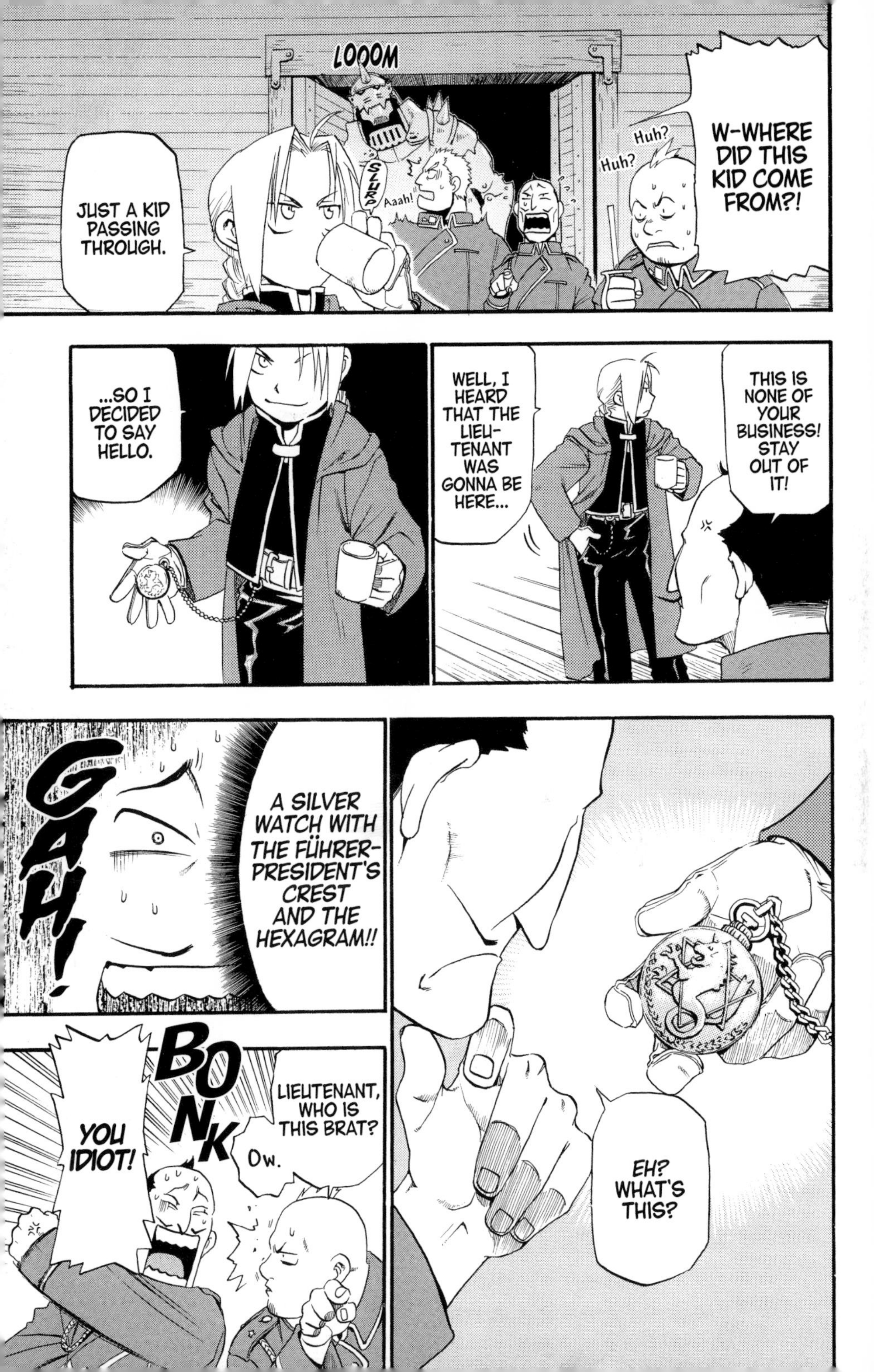
LOOOM
W-WHERE DID THIS KID COME FROM?!
Huh?
Huh?
Aaah!
SLURP
JUST A KID PASSING THROUGH.
THIS IS NONE OF YOUR BUSINESS! STAY OUT OF IT!
WELL, I HEARD THAT THE LIEU-TENANT WAS GONNA BE HERE...
...SO I DECIDED TO SAY HELLO.
EH? WHAT'S THIS?
A SILVER WATCH WITH THE FÜHRER-PRESIDENT'S CREST AND THE HEXAGRAM!!
GAH!
LIEUTENANT, WHO IS THIS BRAT?
BONK
Ow.
YOU IDIOT!

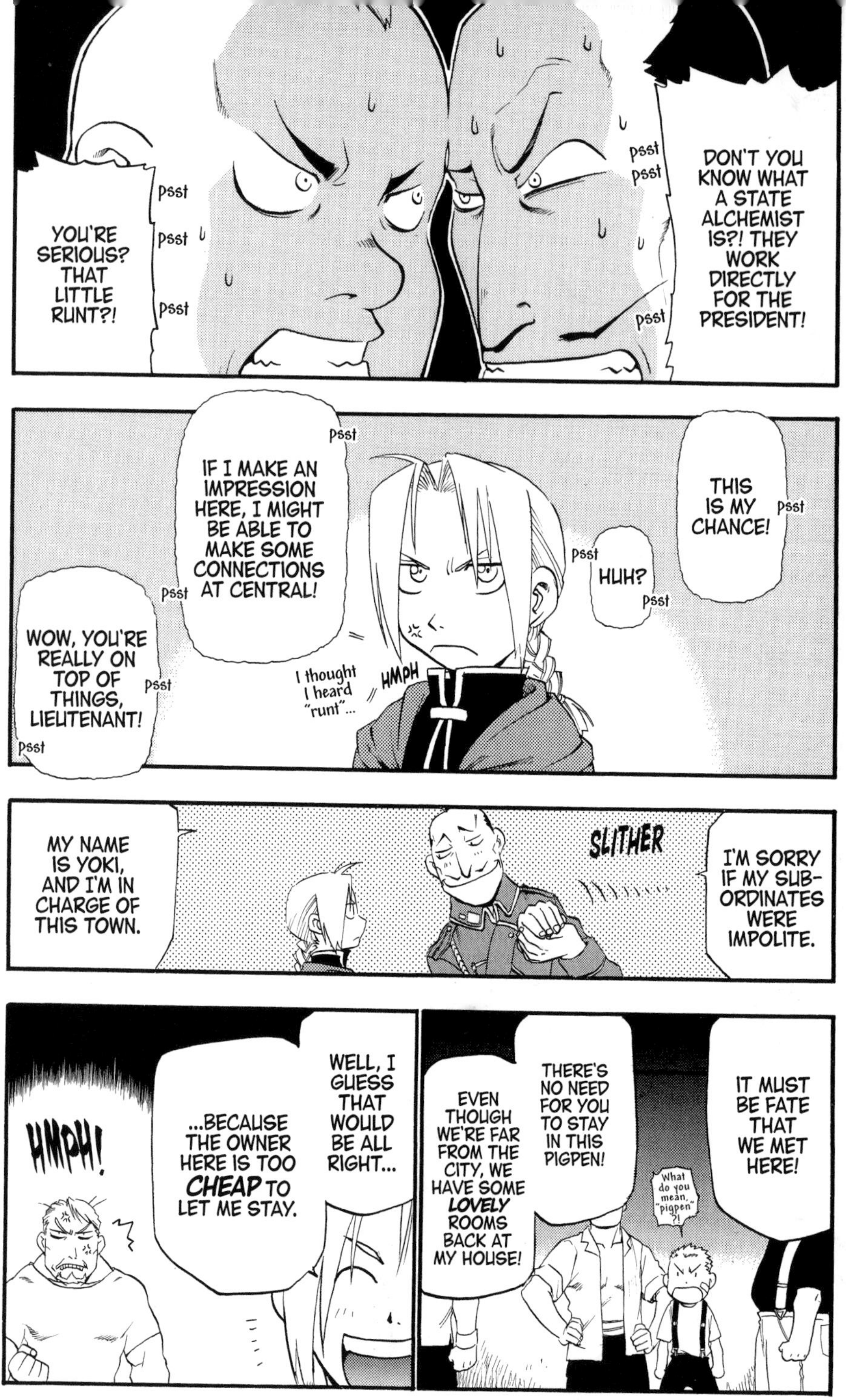

DON'T YOU KNOW WHAT A STATE ALCHEMIST IS?! THEY WORK DIRECTLY FOR THE PRESIDENT!
psst
psst
psst
YOU'RE SERIOUS? THAT LITTLE RUNT?!
psst
psst
psst
THIS IS MY CHANCE!
psst
IF I MAKE AN IMPRESSION HERE, I MIGHT BE ABLE TO MAKE SOME CONNECTIONS AT CENTRAL!
psst
HUH?
psst
psst
WOW, YOU'RE REALLY ON TOP OF THINGS, LIEUTENANT!
psst
psst
psst
HMPH
I thought I heard "runt"...
SLITHER
I'M SORRY IF MY SUBORDINATES WERE IMPOLITE.
MY NAME IS YOKI, AND I'M IN CHARGE OF THIS TOWN.
IT MUST BE FATE THAT WE MET HERE!
THERE'S NO NEED FOR YOU TO STAY IN THIS PIGPEN!
EVEN THOUGH WE'RE FAR FROM THE CITY, WE HAVE SOME LOVELY ROOMS BACK AT MY HOUSE!
What do you mean, "pigpen"?!
WELL, I GUESS THAT WOULD BE ALL RIGHT...
...BECAUSE THE OWNER HERE IS TOO CHEAP TO LET ME STAY.
HMPH!

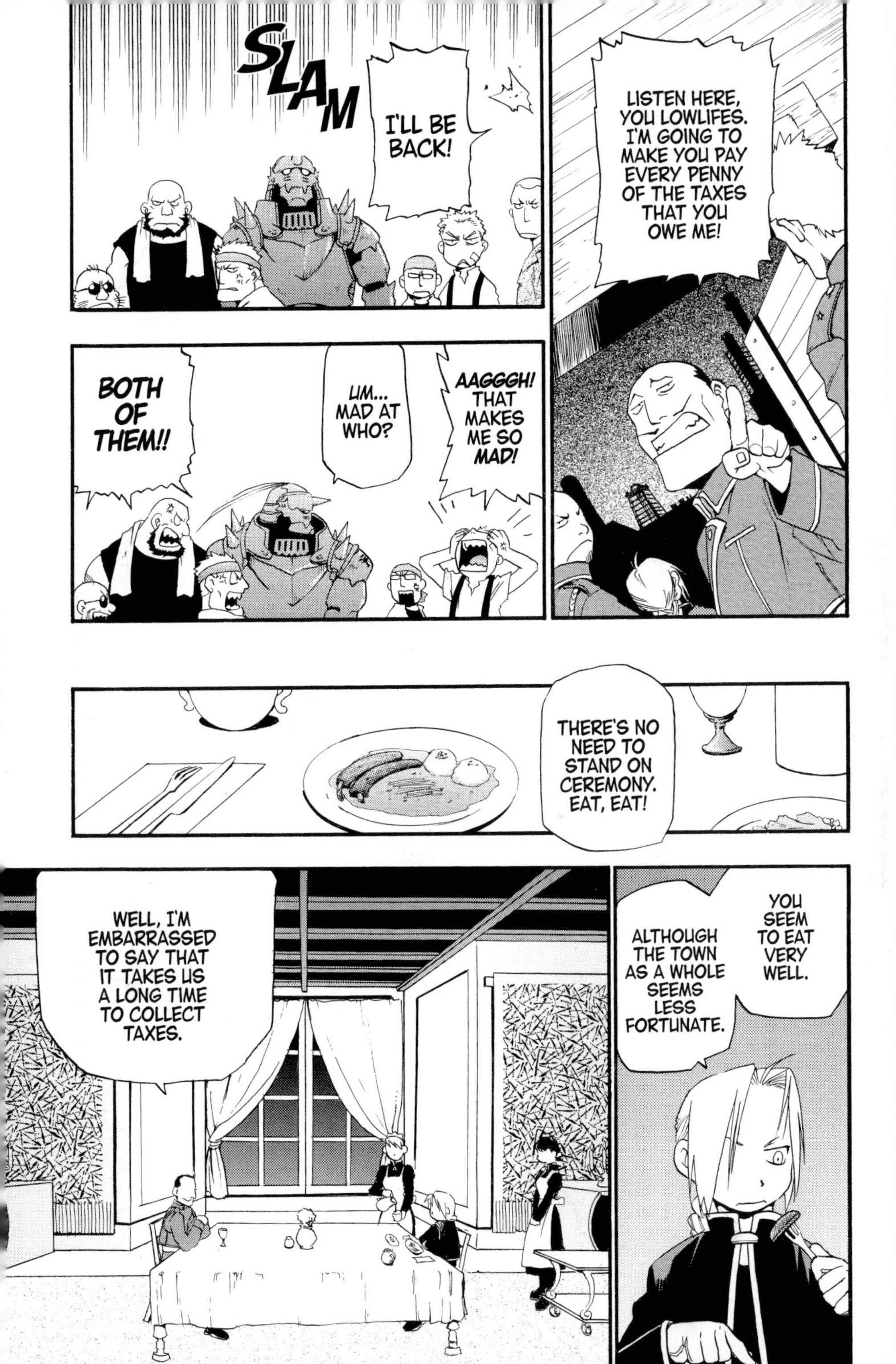
LISTEN HERE, YOU LOWLIFES. I'M GOING TO MAKE YOU PAY EVERY PENNY OF THE TAXES THAT YOU OWE ME!
SLAM
I'LL BE BACK!
AAGGGH! THAT MAKES ME SO MAD!
UM... MAD AT WHO?
BOTH OF THEM!!
THERE'S NO NEED TO STAND ON CEREMONY. EAT, EAT!
YOU SEEM TO EAT VERY WELL.
ALTHOUGH THE TOWN AS A WHOLE SEEMS LESS FORTUNATE.
WELL, I'M EMBARRASSED TO SAY THAT IT TAKES US A LONG TIME TO COLLECT TAXES.

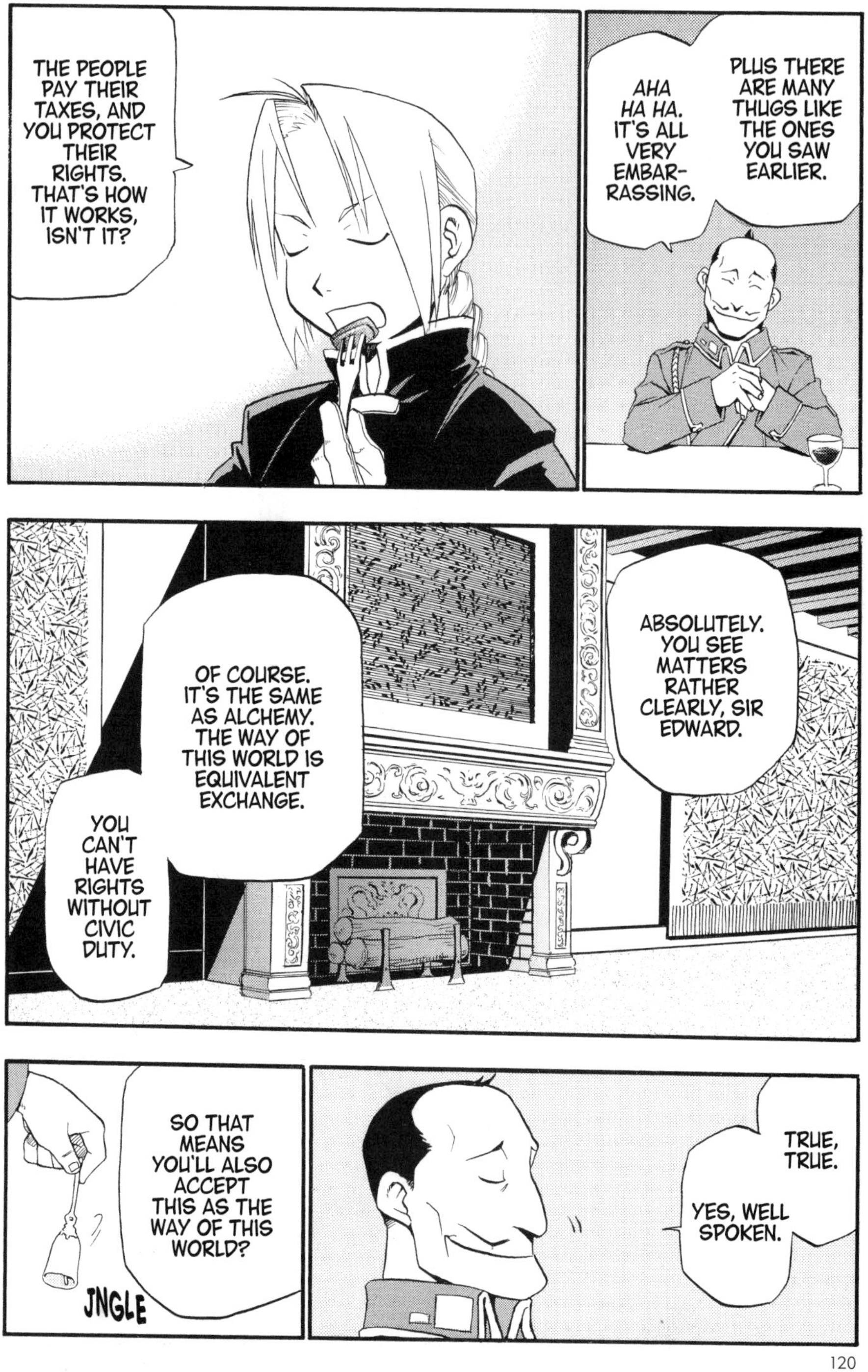
PLUS THERE ARE MANY THUGS LIKE THE ONES YOU SAW EARLIER.
AHA HA HA. IT'S ALL VERY EMBAR-RASSING.
THE PEOPLE PAY THEIR TAXES, AND YOU PROTECT THEIR RIGHTS. THAT'S HOW IT WORKS, ISN'T IT?
ABSOLUTELY. YOU SEE MATTERS RATHER CLEARLY, SIR EDWARD.
OF COURSE. IT'S THE SAME AS ALCHEMY. THE WAY OF THIS WORLD IS EQUIVALENT EXCHANGE.
YOU CAN'T HAVE RIGHTS WITHOUT CIVIC DUTY.
TRUE, TRUE.
YES, WELL SPOKEN.
SO THAT MEANS YOU'LL ALSO ACCEPT THIS AS THE WAY OF THIS WORLD?
JNGLE

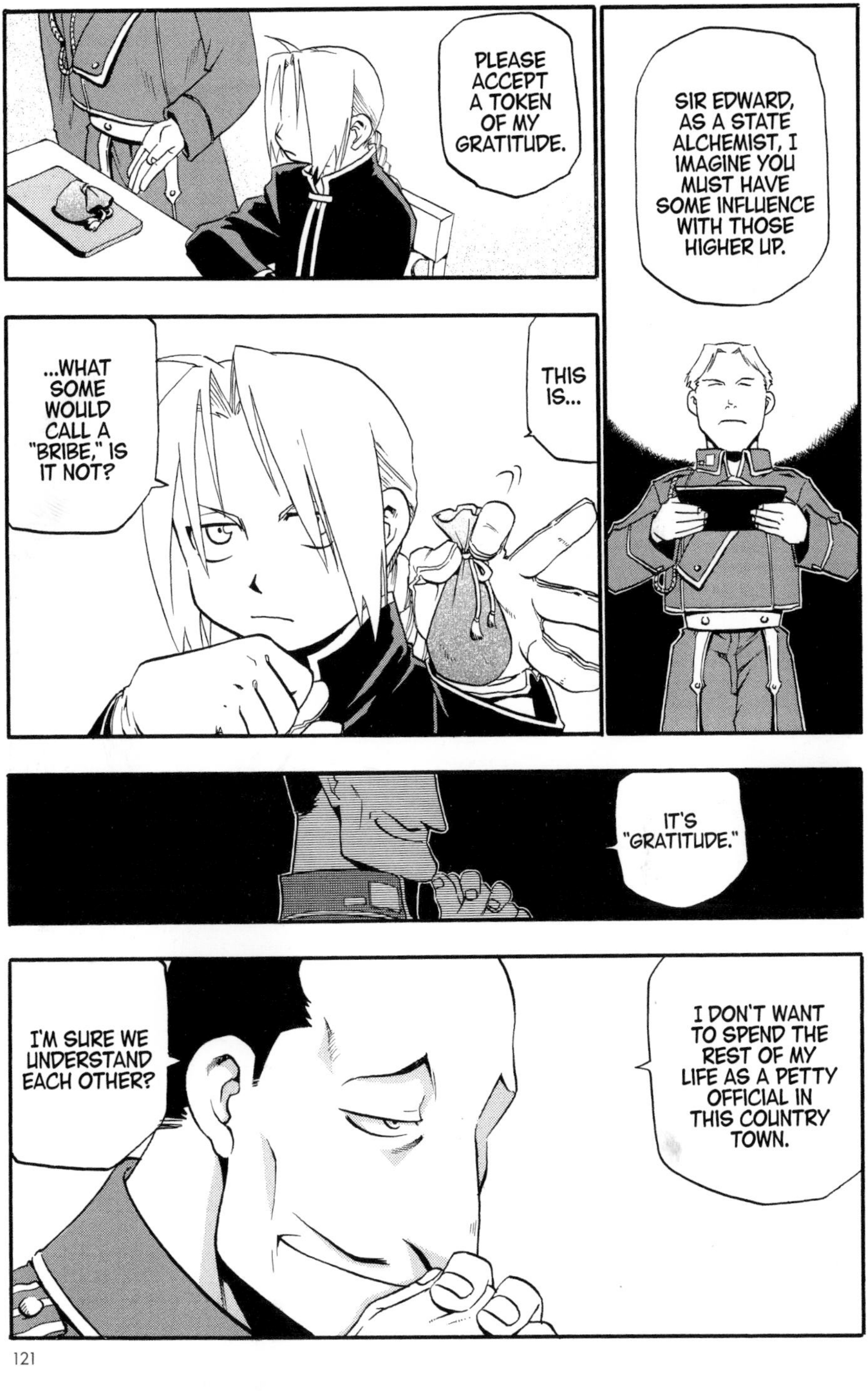
SIR EDWARD, AS A STATE ALCHEMIST, I IMAGINE YOU MUST HAVE SOME INFLUENCE WITH THOSE HIGHER UP.
PLEASE ACCEPT A TOKEN OF MY GRATITUDE.
THIS IS...
...WHAT SOME WOULD CALL A "BRIBE," IS IT NOT?
IT'S "GRATITUDE."
I DON'T WANT TO SPEND THE REST OF MY LIFE AS A PETTY OFFICIAL IN THIS COUNTRY TOWN.
I'M SURE WE UNDERSTAND EACH OTHER?

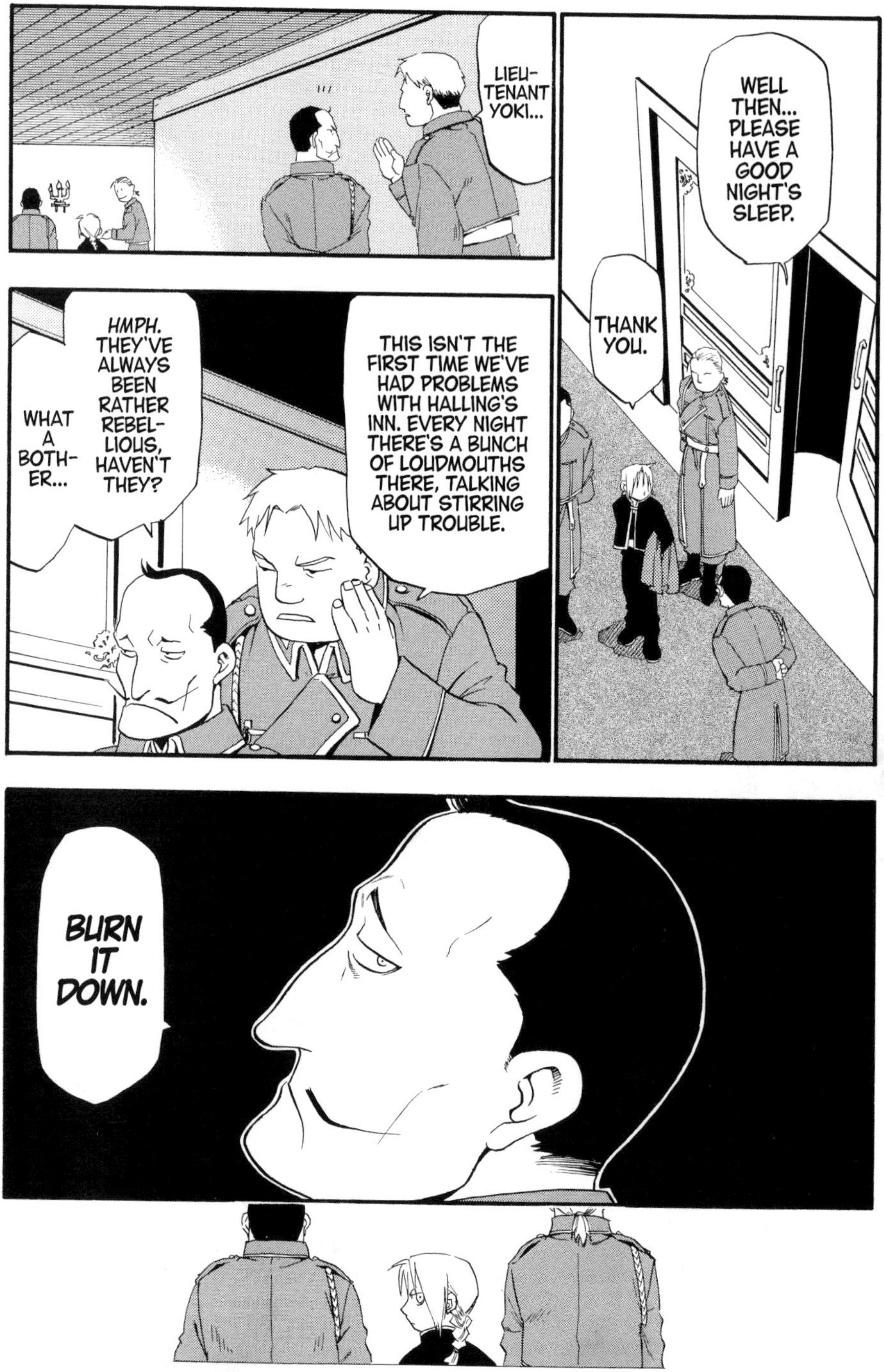
WELL THEN... PLEASE HAVE A GOOD NIGHT'S SLEEP.
THANK YOU.
LIEU-TENANT YOKI...
THIS ISN'T THE FIRST TIME WE'VE HAD PROBLEMS WITH HALLING'S INN. EVERY NIGHT THERE'S A BUNCH OF LOUDMOUTHS THERE, TALKING ABOUT STIRRING UP TROUBLE.
HMPH. THEY'VE ALWAYS BEEN RATHER REBEL-LIOUS, HAVEN'T THEY?
WHAT A BOTH-ER...
BURN IT DOWN.

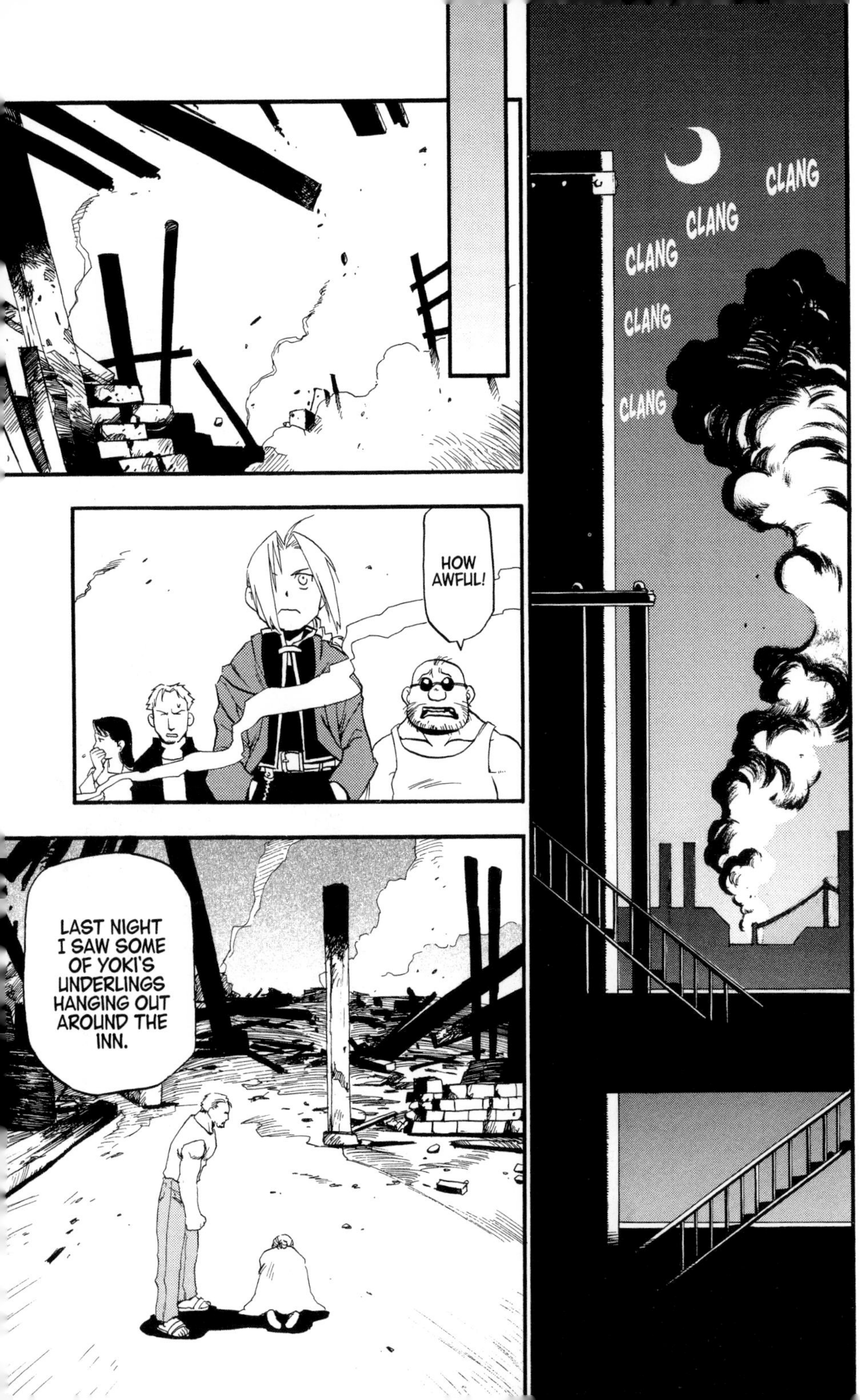
CLANG
CLANG
CLANG
CLANG
CLANG
HOW AWFUL!
LAST NIGHT I SAW SOME OF YOKI'S UNDERLINGS HANGING OUT AROUND THE INN.

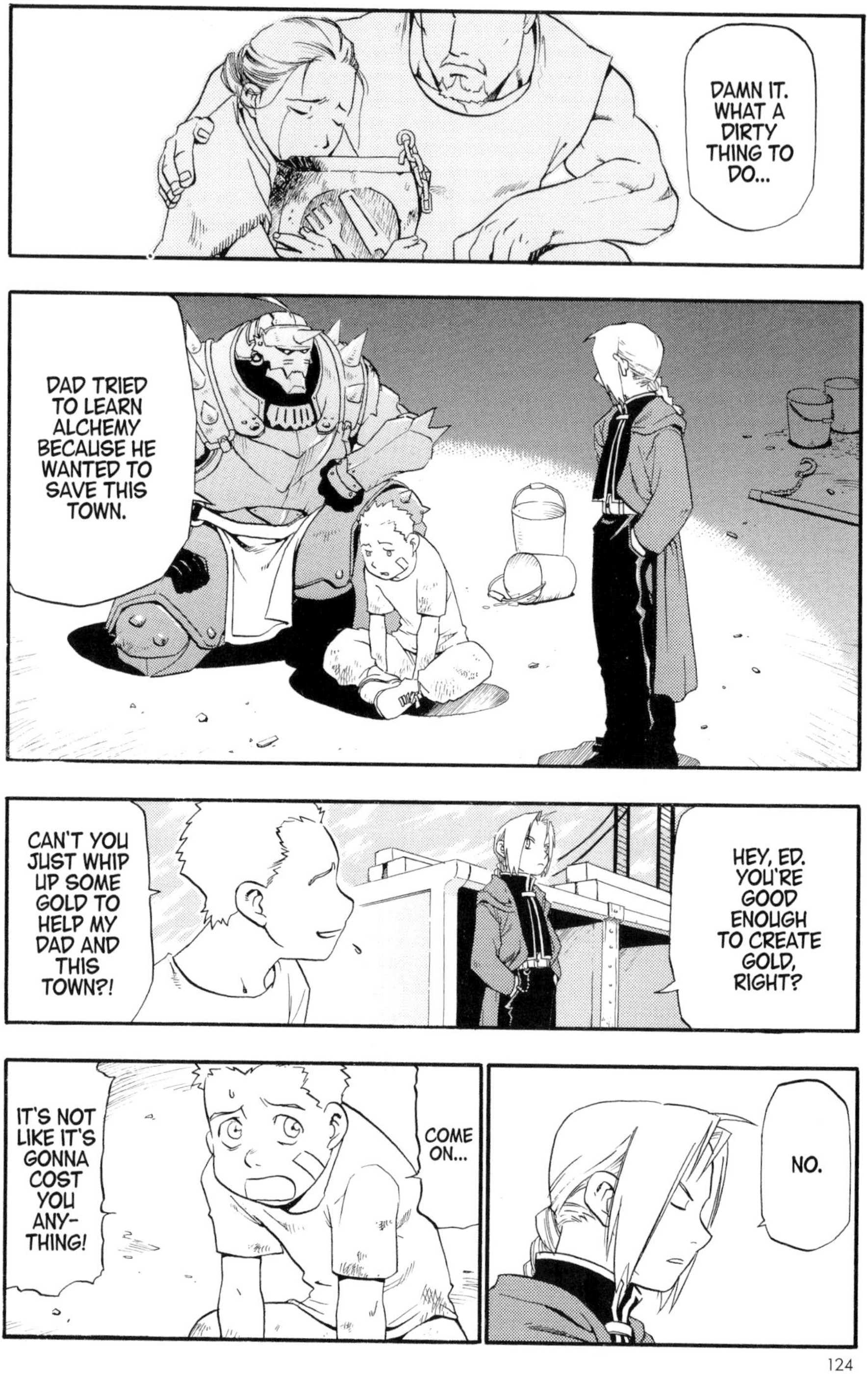
DAMN IT. WHAT A DIRTY THING TO DO...
DAD TRIED TO LEARN ALCHEMY BECAUSE HE WANTED TO SAVE THIS TOWN.
HEY, ED. YOU'RE GOOD ENOUGH TO CREATE GOLD, RIGHT?
CAN'T YOU JUST WHIP UP SOME GOLD TO HELP MY DAD AND THIS TOWN?!
NO.
COME ON...
IT'S NOT LIKE IT'S GONNA COST YOU ANY-THING!

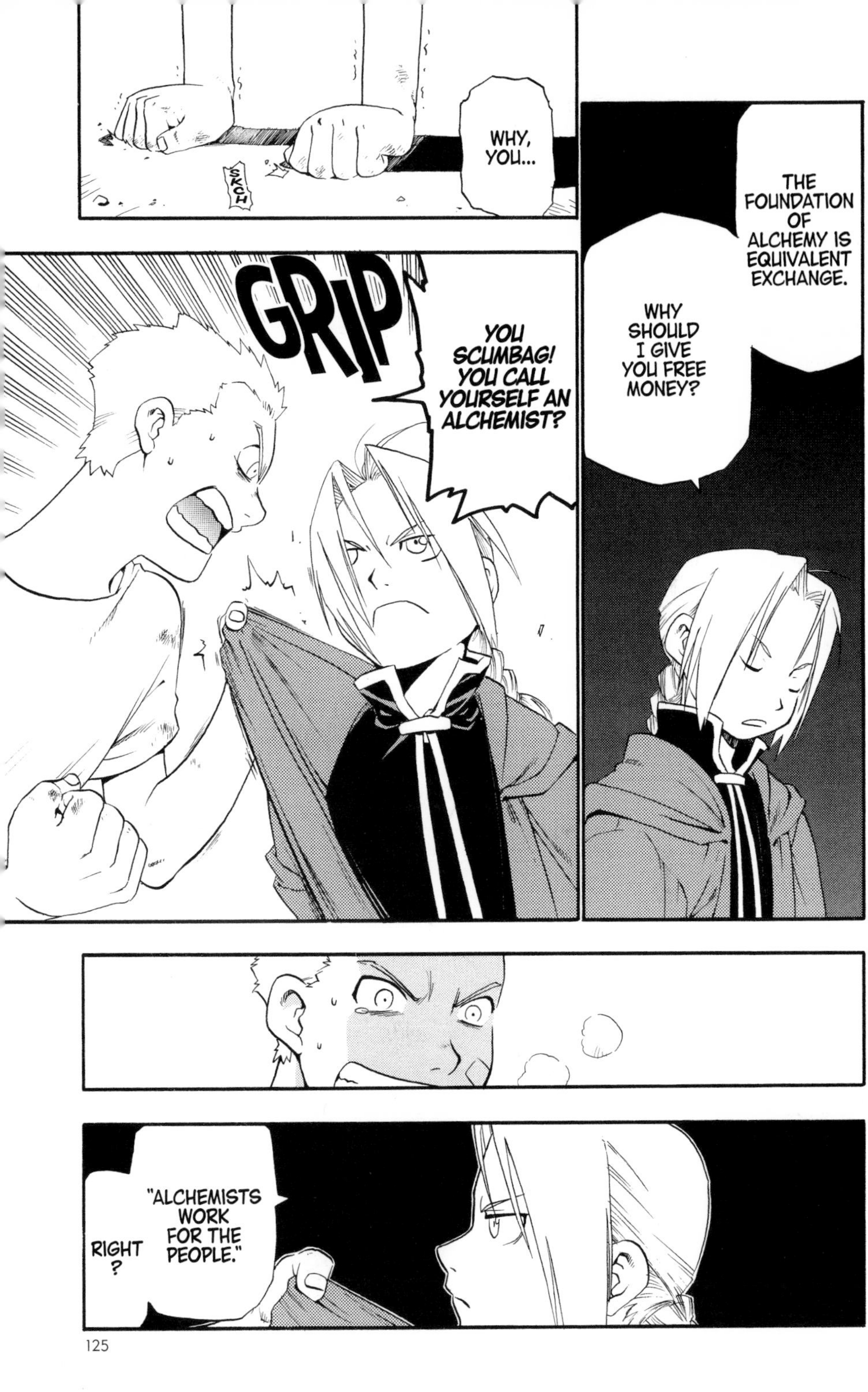
THE FOUNDATION OF ALCHEMY IS EQUIVALENT EXCHANGE.
WHY SHOULD I GIVE YOU FREE MONEY?
WHY, YOU...
SKCH
GRIP
YOU SCUMBAG! YOU CALL YOURSELF AN ALCHEMIST?
"ALCHEMISTS WORK FOR THE PEOPLE."
RIGHT?

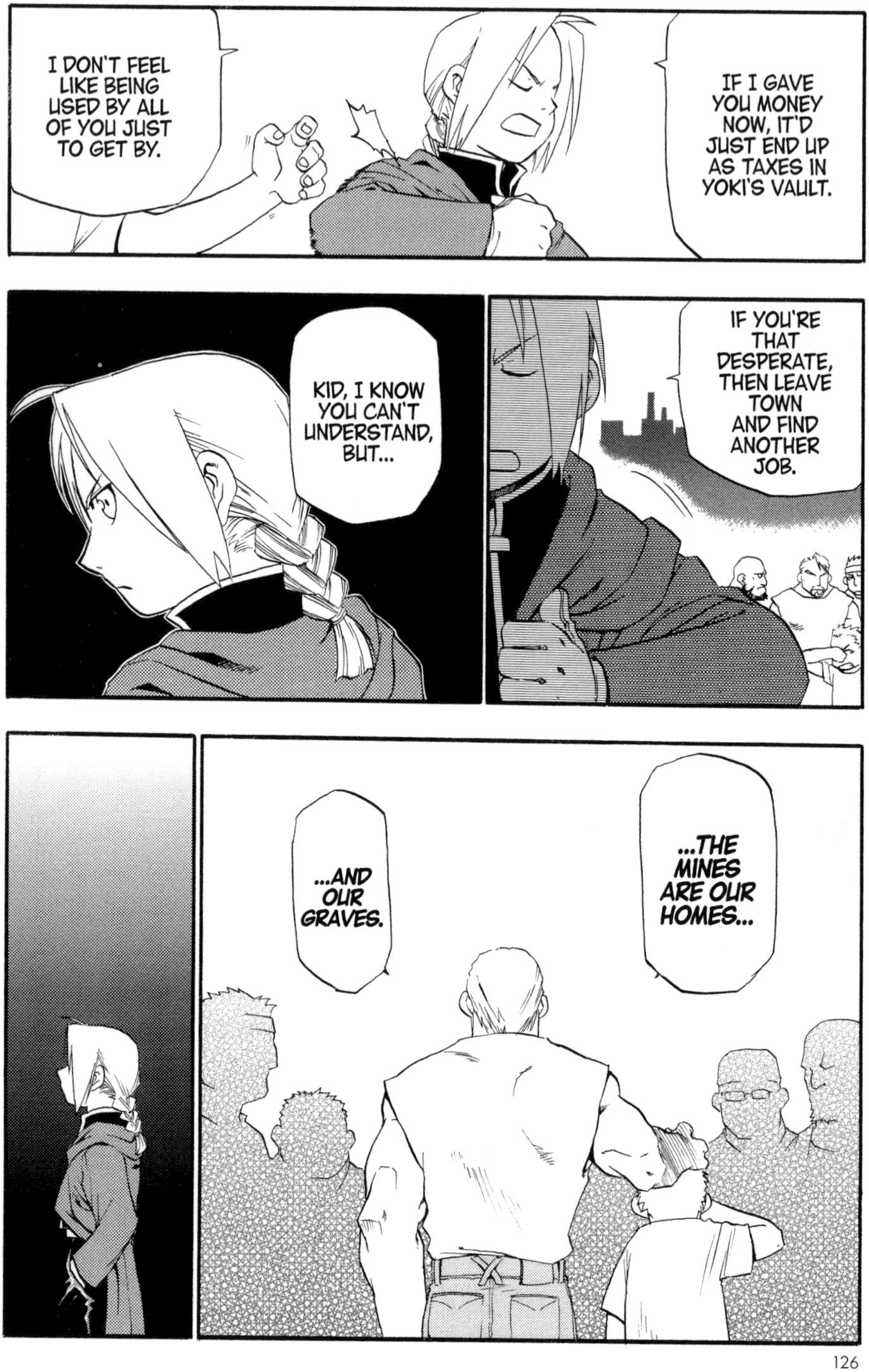
IF I GAVE YOU MONEY NOW, IT'D JUST END UP AS TAXES IN YOKI'S VAULT.
I DON'T FEEL LIKE BEING USED BY ALL OF YOU JUST TO GET BY.
IF YOU'RE THAT DESPERATE, THEN LEAVE TOWN AND FIND ANOTHER JOB.
KID, I KNOW YOU CAN'T UNDERSTAND, BUT...
...THE MINES ARE OUR HOMES...
...AND OUR GRAVES.

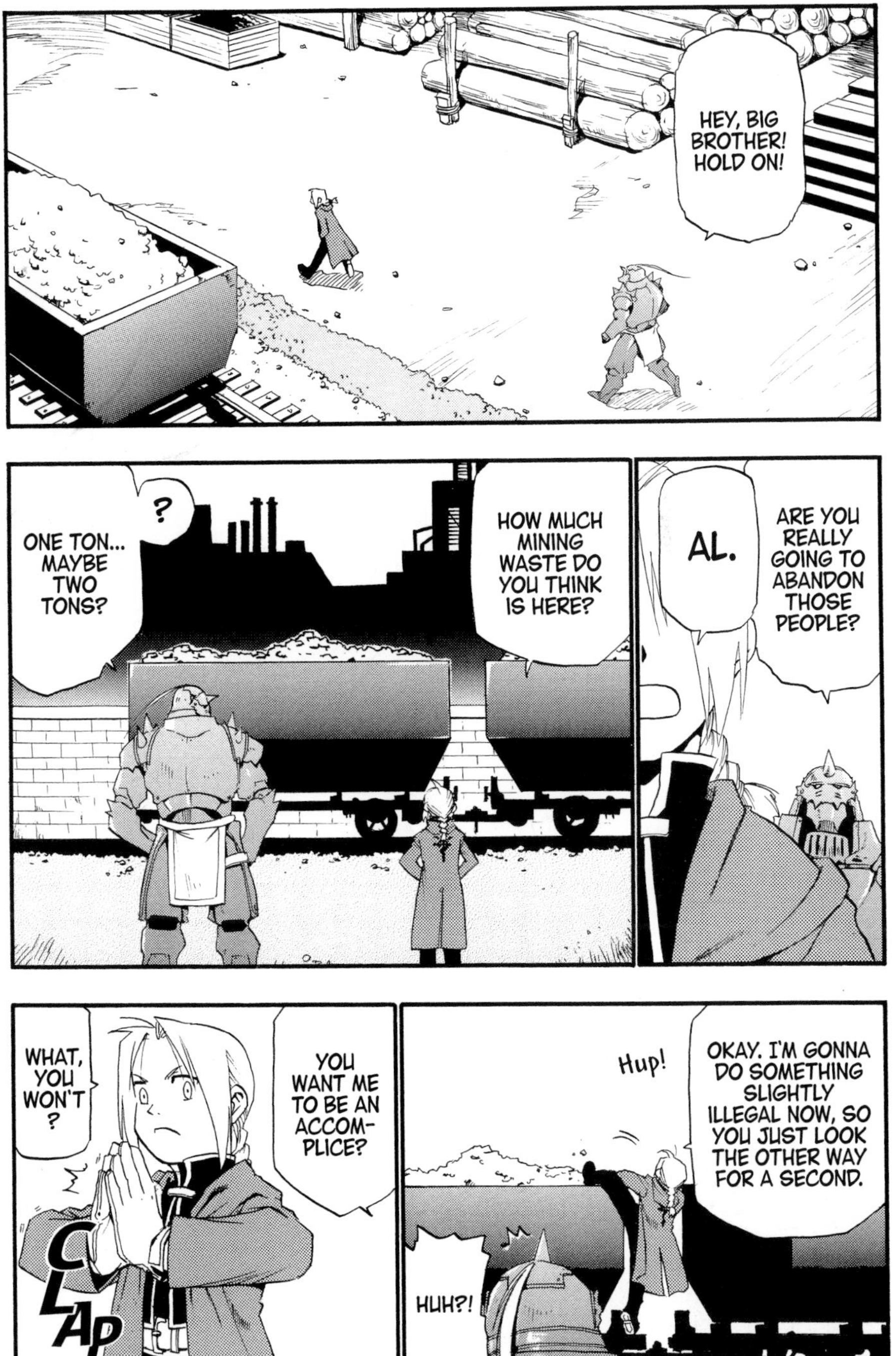
HEY, BIG BROTHER! HOLD ON!
ARE YOU REALLY GOING TO ABANDON THOSE PEOPLE?
AL.
HOW MUCH MINING WASTE DO YOU THINK IS HERE?
?
ONE TON... MAYBE TWO TONS?
OKAY. I'M GONNA DO SOMETHING SLIGHTLY ILLEGAL NOW, SO YOU JUST LOOK THE OTHER WAY FOR A SECOND.
Hup!
HUH?!
YOU WANT ME TO BE AN ACCOMPLICE?
WHAT, YOU WON'T?
CLAP

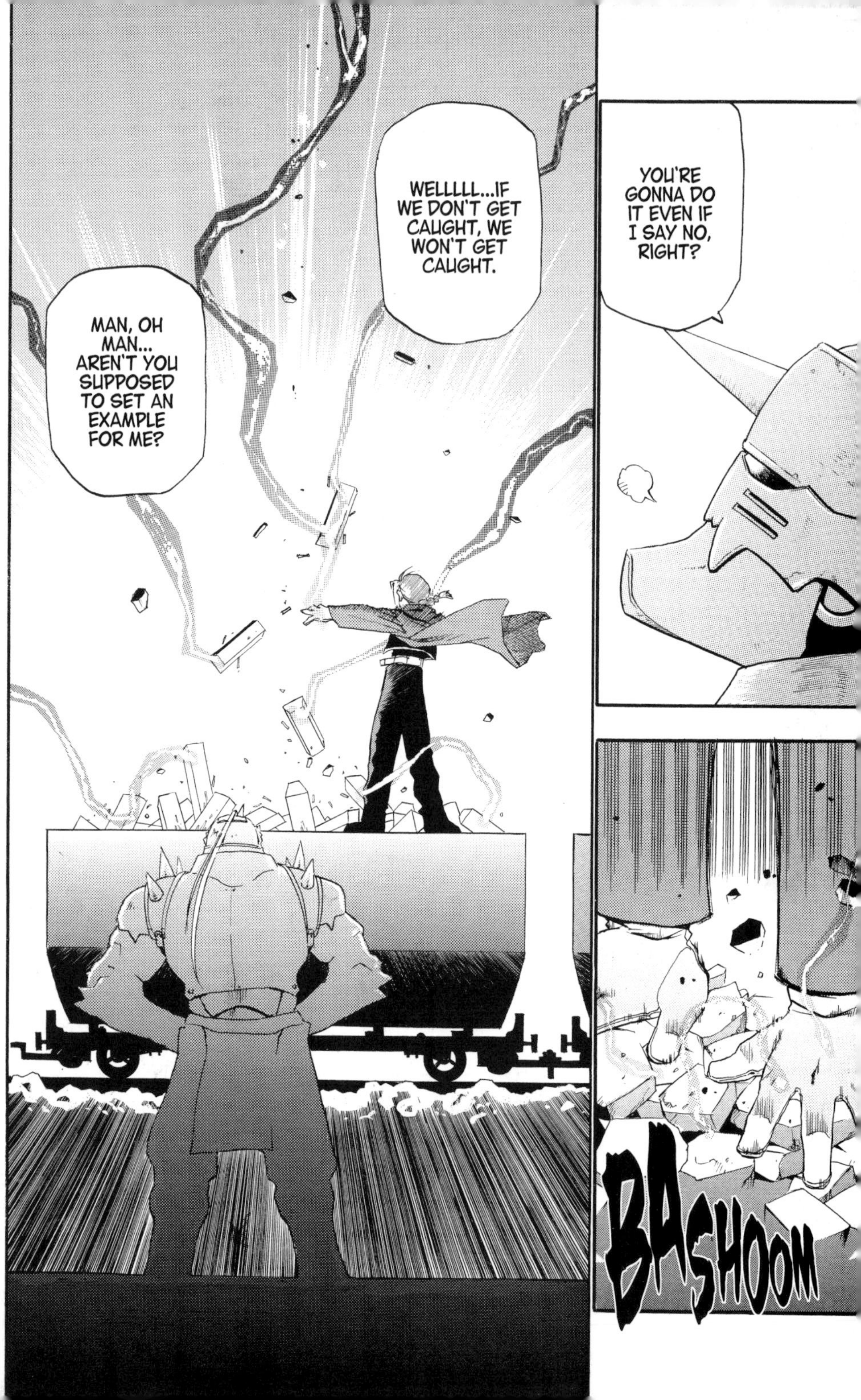
YOU'RE GONNA DO IT EVEN IF I SAY NO, RIGHT?
BASHOOM
WELLLLL...IF WE DON'T GET CAUGHT, WE WON'T GET CAUGHT.
MAN, OH MAN... AREN'T YOU SUPPOSED TO SET AN EXAMPLE FOR ME?

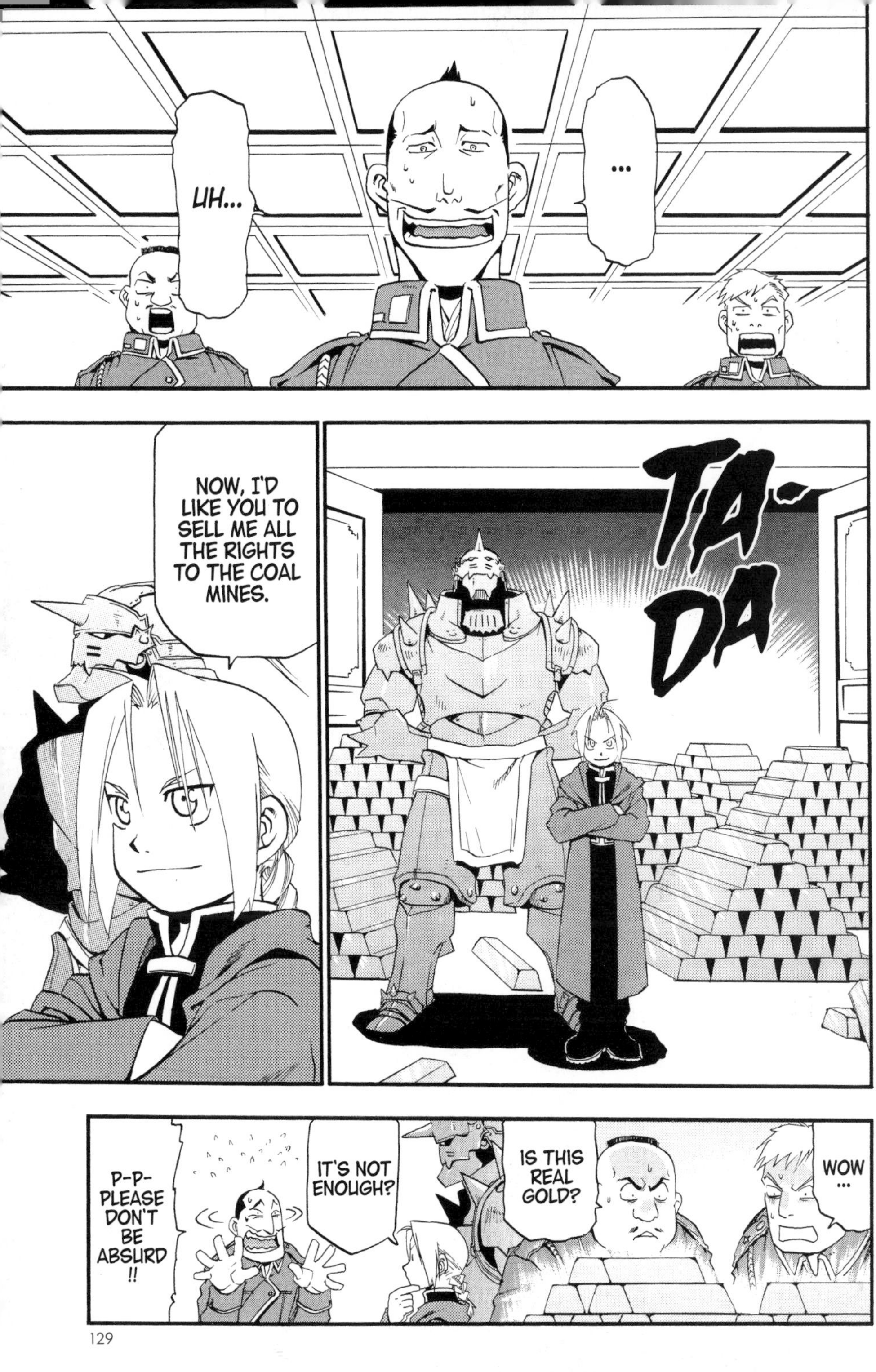
...
UH...
TA-DA
NOW, I'D LIKE YOU TO SELL ME ALL THE RIGHTS TO THE COAL MINES.
WOW ...
IS THIS REAL GOLD?
IT'S NOT ENOUGH?
P-P-PLEASE DON'T BE ABSURD !!

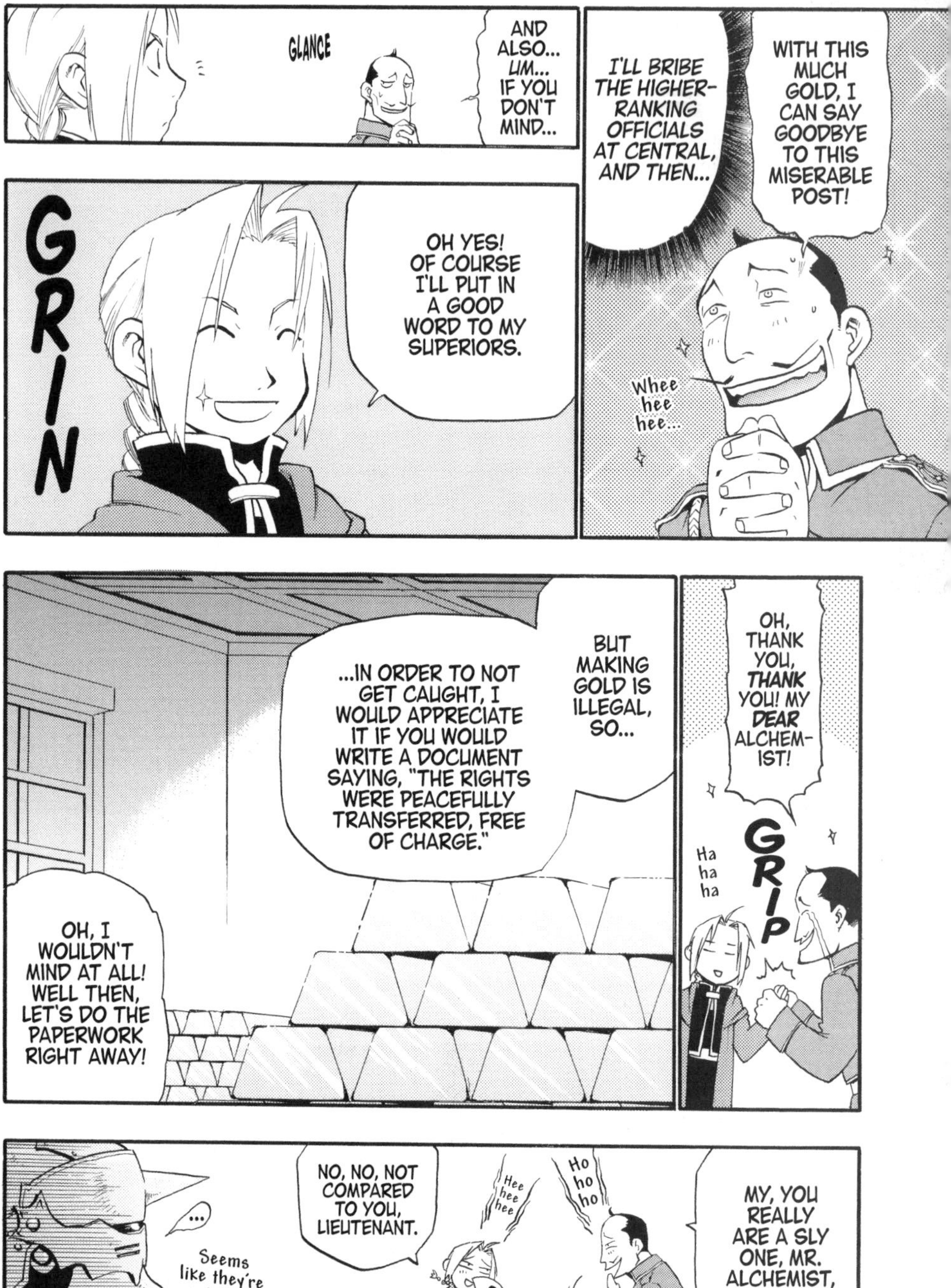
WITH THIS MUCH GOLD, I CAN SAY GOODBYE TO THIS MISERABLE POST!
I'LL BRIBE THE HIGHER-RANKING OFFICIALS AT CENTRAL, AND THEN...
Whee hee hee...
AND ALSO... UM... IF YOU DON'T MIND...
GLANCE
OH YES! OF COURSE I'LL PUT IN A GOOD WORD TO MY SUPERIORS.
GRIN
OH, THANK YOU, ***THANK*** YOU! MY ***DEAR*** ALCHEMIST!
GRIP
Ha ha ha
BUT MAKING GOLD IS ILLEGAL, SO...
...IN ORDER TO NOT GET CAUGHT, I WOULD APPRECIATE IT IF YOU WOULD WRITE A DOCUMENT SAYING, "THE RIGHTS WERE PEACEFULLY TRANSFERRED, FREE OF CHARGE."
OH, I WOULDN'T MIND AT ALL! WELL THEN, LET'S DO THE PAPERWORK RIGHT AWAY!
MY, YOU REALLY ARE A SLY ONE, MR. ALCHEMIST, SIR!
Ho ho ho
Hee hee hee
NO, NO, NOT COMPARED TO YOU, LIEUTENANT.
...
Seems like they're enjoying this...

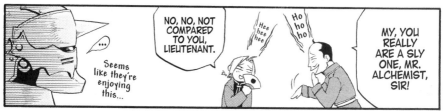

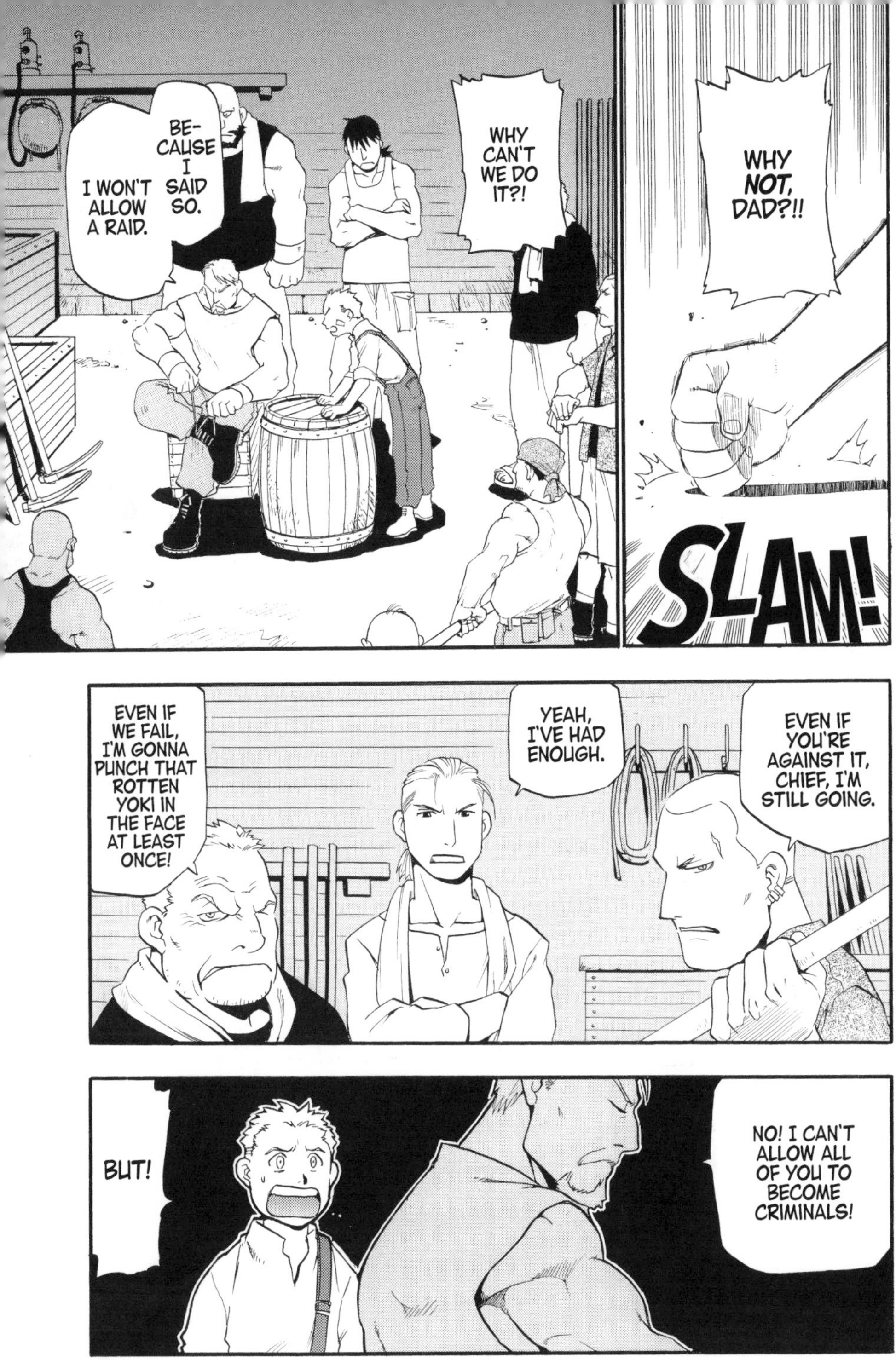
WHY NOT, DAD?!!
SLAM!
WHY CAN'T WE DO IT?!
BE-CAUSE I SAID SO.
I WON'T ALLOW A RAID.
EVEN IF YOU'RE AGAINST IT, CHIEF, I'M STILL GOING.
YEAH, I'VE HAD ENOUGH.
EVEN IF WE FAIL, I'M GONNA PUNCH THAT ROTTEN YOKI IN THE FACE AT LEAST ONCE!
NO! I CAN'T ALLOW ALL OF YOU TO BECOME CRIMINALS!
BUT!

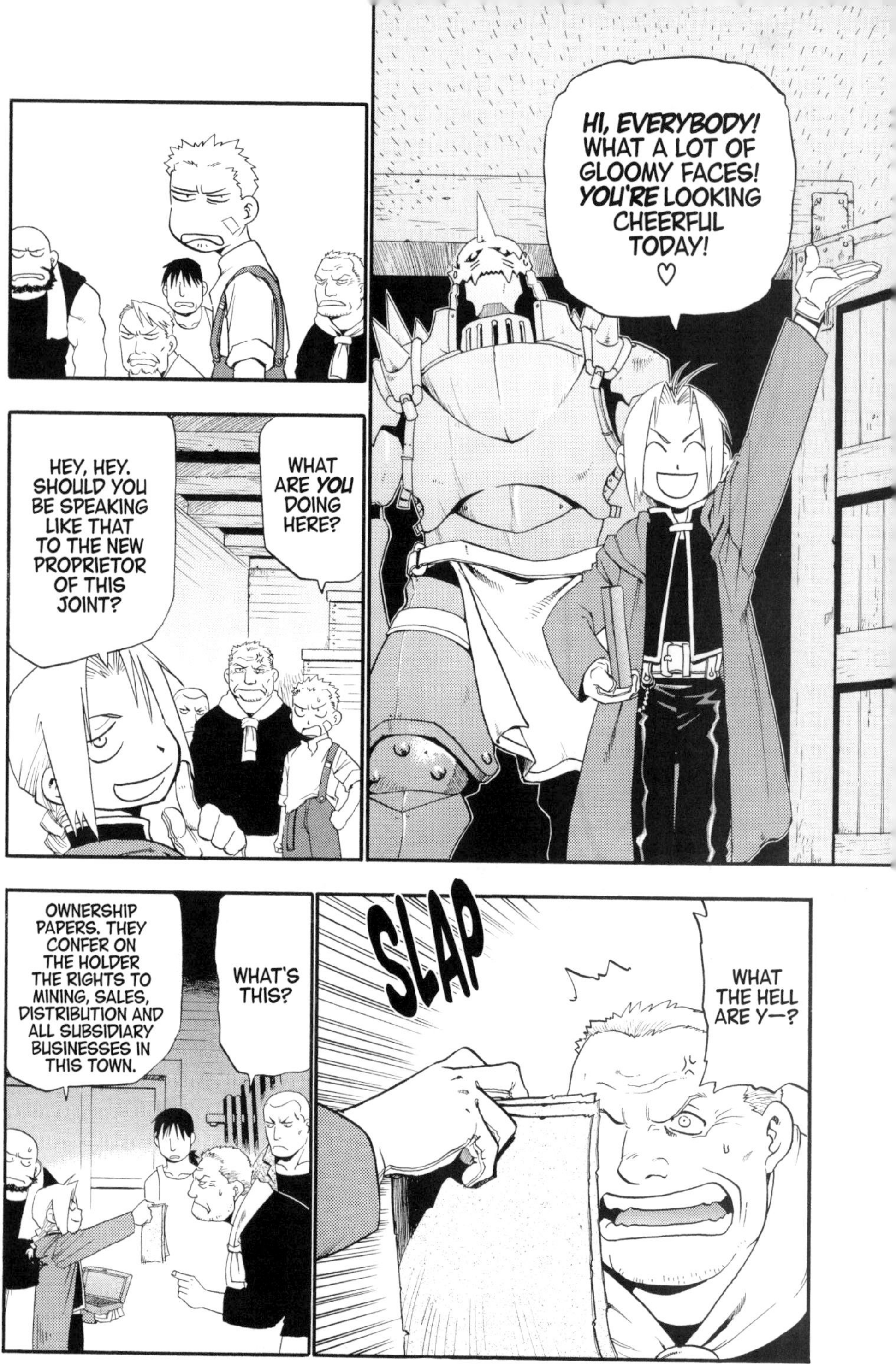
HI, EVERYBODY! WHAT A LOT OF GLOOMY FACES! YOU'RE LOOKING CHEERFUL TODAY! ♡
WHAT ARE YOU DOING HERE?
HEY, HEY. SHOULD YOU BE SPEAKING LIKE THAT TO THE NEW PROPRIETOR OF THIS JOINT?
SLAP
WHAT THE HELL ARE Y—?
WHAT'S THIS?
OWNERSHIP PAPERS. THEY CONFER ON THE HOLDER THE RIGHTS TO MINING, SALES, DISTRIBUTION AND ALL SUBSIDIARY BUSINESSES IN THIS TOWN.

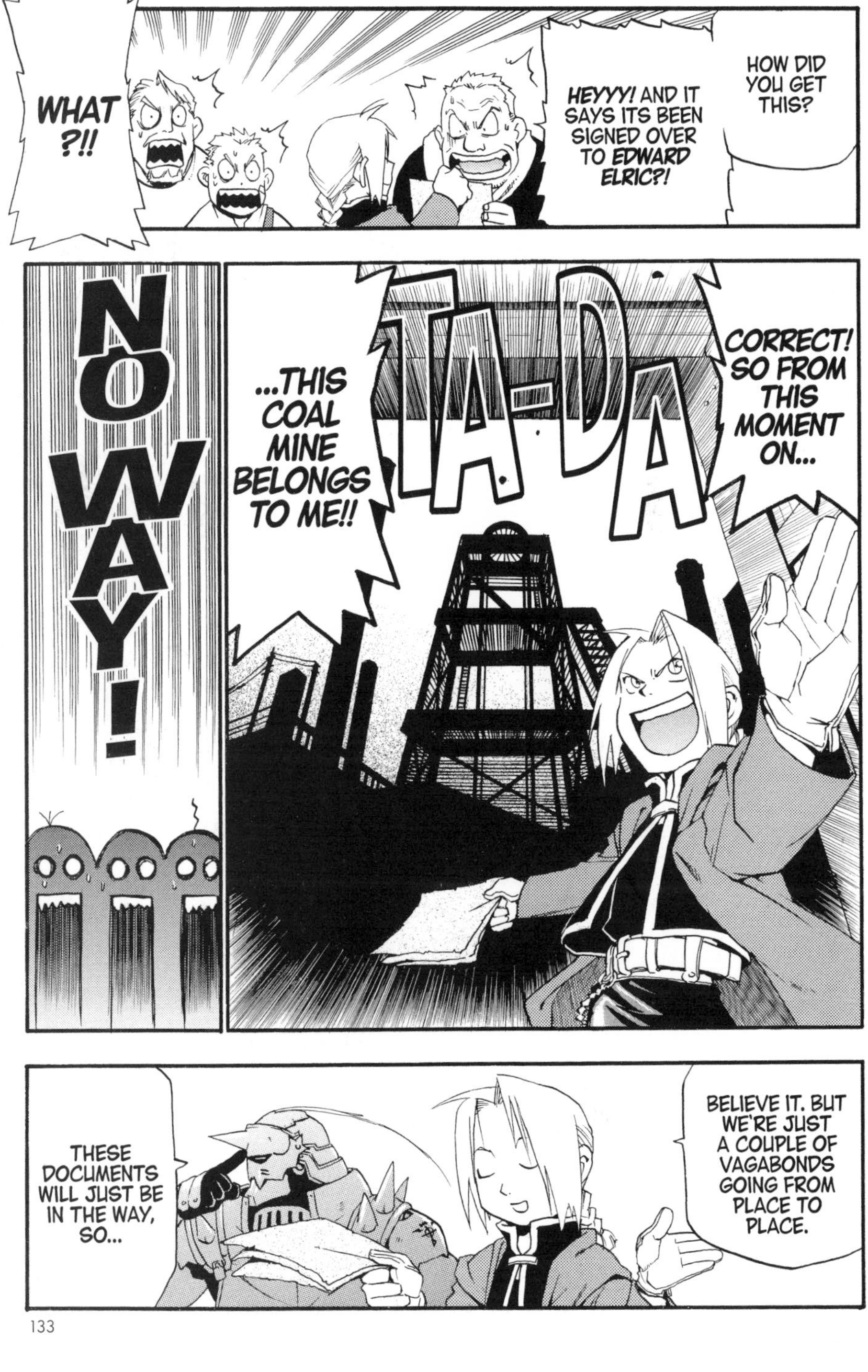
HOW DID YOU GET THIS?
HEYYY! AND IT SAYS ITS BEEN SIGNED OVER TO EDWARD ELRIC?!
WHAT?!!
CORRECT! SO FROM THIS MOMENT ON...
TA-DA
...THIS COAL MINE BELONGS TO ME!!
NO WAY!
BELIEVE IT. BUT WE'RE JUST A COUPLE OF VAGABONDS GOING FROM PLACE TO PLACE.
THESE DOCUMENTS WILL JUST BE IN THE WAY, SO...

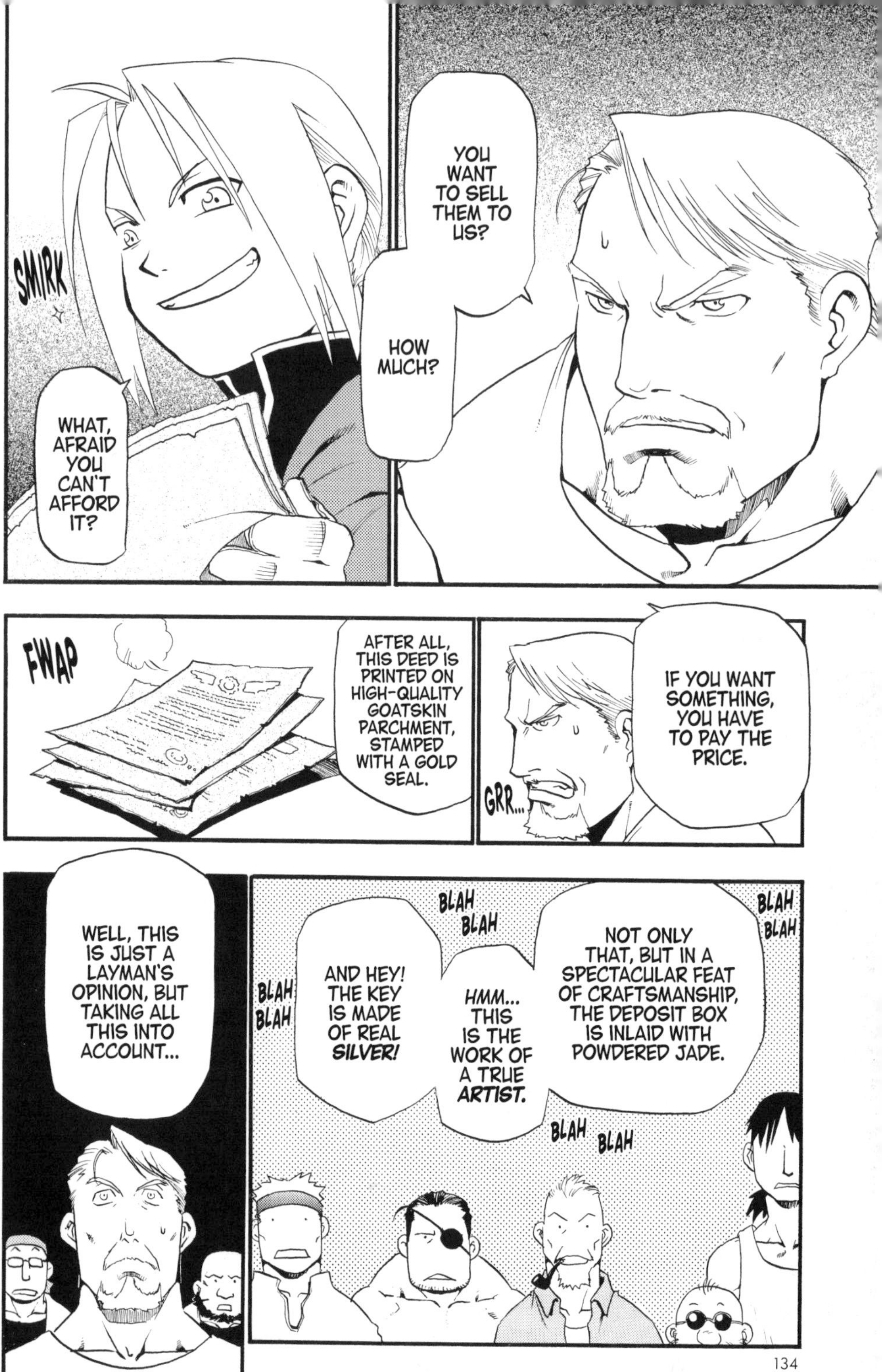
YOU WANT TO SELL THEM TO US?
HOW MUCH?
SMIRK
WHAT, AFRAID YOU CAN'T AFFORD IT?
IF YOU WANT SOMETHING, YOU HAVE TO PAY THE PRICE.
GRR...
AFTER ALL, THIS DEED IS PRINTED ON HIGH-QUALITY GOATSKIN PARCHMENT, STAMPED WITH A GOLD SEAL.
FWAP
BLAH BLAH
NOT ONLY THAT, BUT IN A SPECTACULAR FEAT OF CRAFTSMANSHIP, THE DEPOSIT BOX IS INLAID WITH POWDERED JADE.
BLAH BLAH
HMM... THIS IS THE WORK OF A TRUE **ARTIST.**
AND HEY! THE KEY IS MADE OF REAL ***SILVER!***
BLAH BLAH
BLAH BLAH
WELL, THIS IS JUST A LAYMAN'S OPINION, BUT TAKING ALL THIS INTO ACCOUNT...

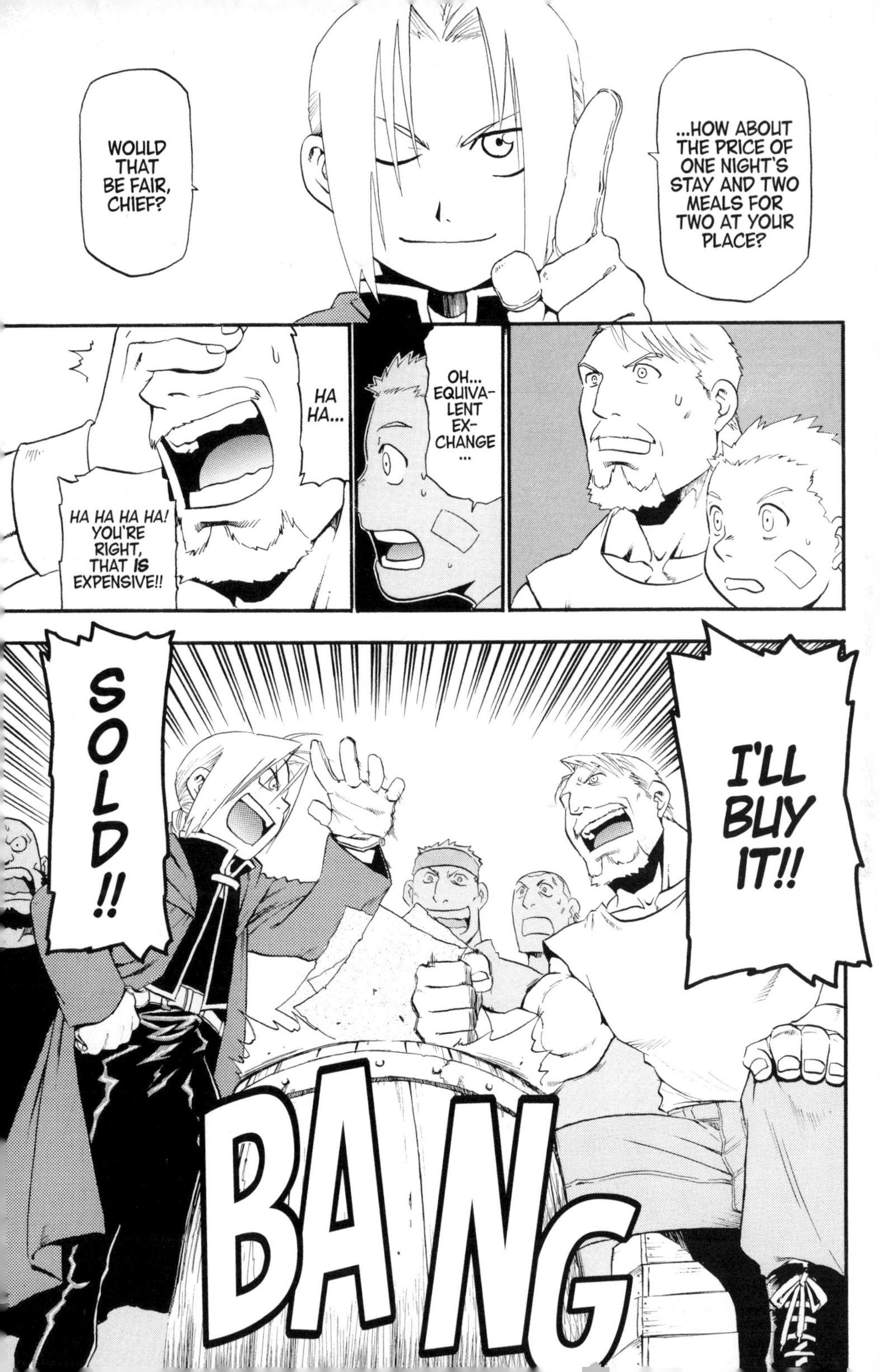
...HOW ABOUT THE PRICE OF ONE NIGHT'S STAY AND TWO MEALS FOR TWO AT YOUR PLACE?
WOULD THAT BE FAIR, CHIEF?
OH... EQUIVALENT EXCHANGE ...
HA HA...
HA HA HA HA! YOU'RE RIGHT, THAT **IS** EXPENSIVE!!
I'LL BUY IT!!
SOLD!!
BANG

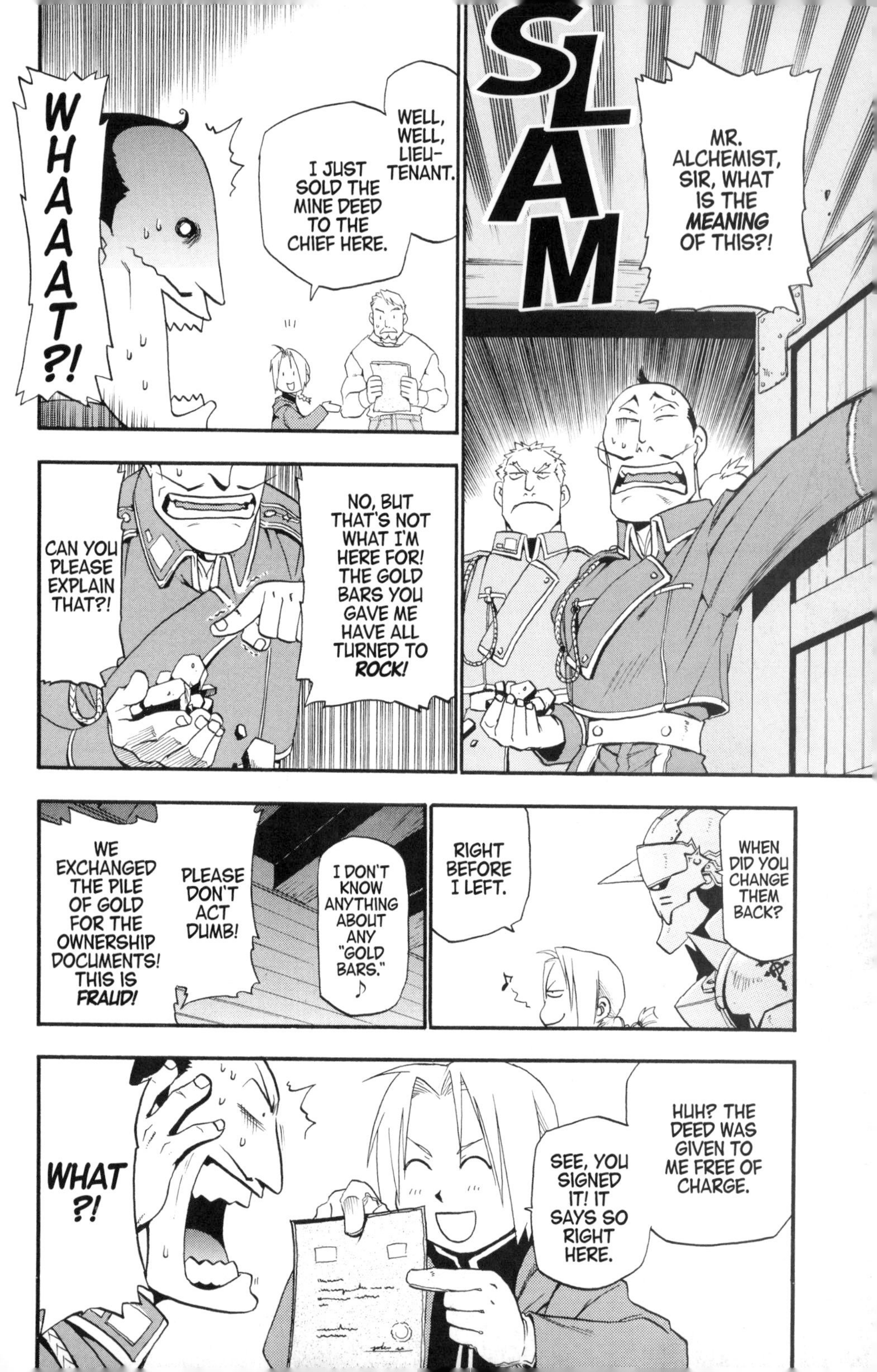
SLAM
MR. ALCHEMIST, SIR, WHAT IS THE *MEANING* OF THIS?!
WELL, WELL, LIEU-TENANT.
I JUST SOLD THE MINE DEED TO THE CHIEF HERE.
WHAAAAT?!
NO, BUT THAT'S NOT WHAT I'M HERE FOR! THE GOLD BARS YOU GAVE ME HAVE ALL TURNED TO *ROCK!*
CAN YOU PLEASE EXPLAIN THAT?!
WHEN DID YOU CHANGE THEM BACK?
RIGHT BEFORE I LEFT.
I DON'T KNOW ANYTHING ABOUT ANY "GOLD BARS." ♪
PLEASE DON'T ACT DUMB!
WE EXCHANGED THE PILE OF GOLD FOR THE OWNERSHIP DOCUMENTS! THIS IS *FRAUD!*
HUH? THE DEED WAS GIVEN TO ME FREE OF CHARGE.
SEE, YOU SIGNED IT! IT SAYS SO RIGHT HERE.
WHAT?!

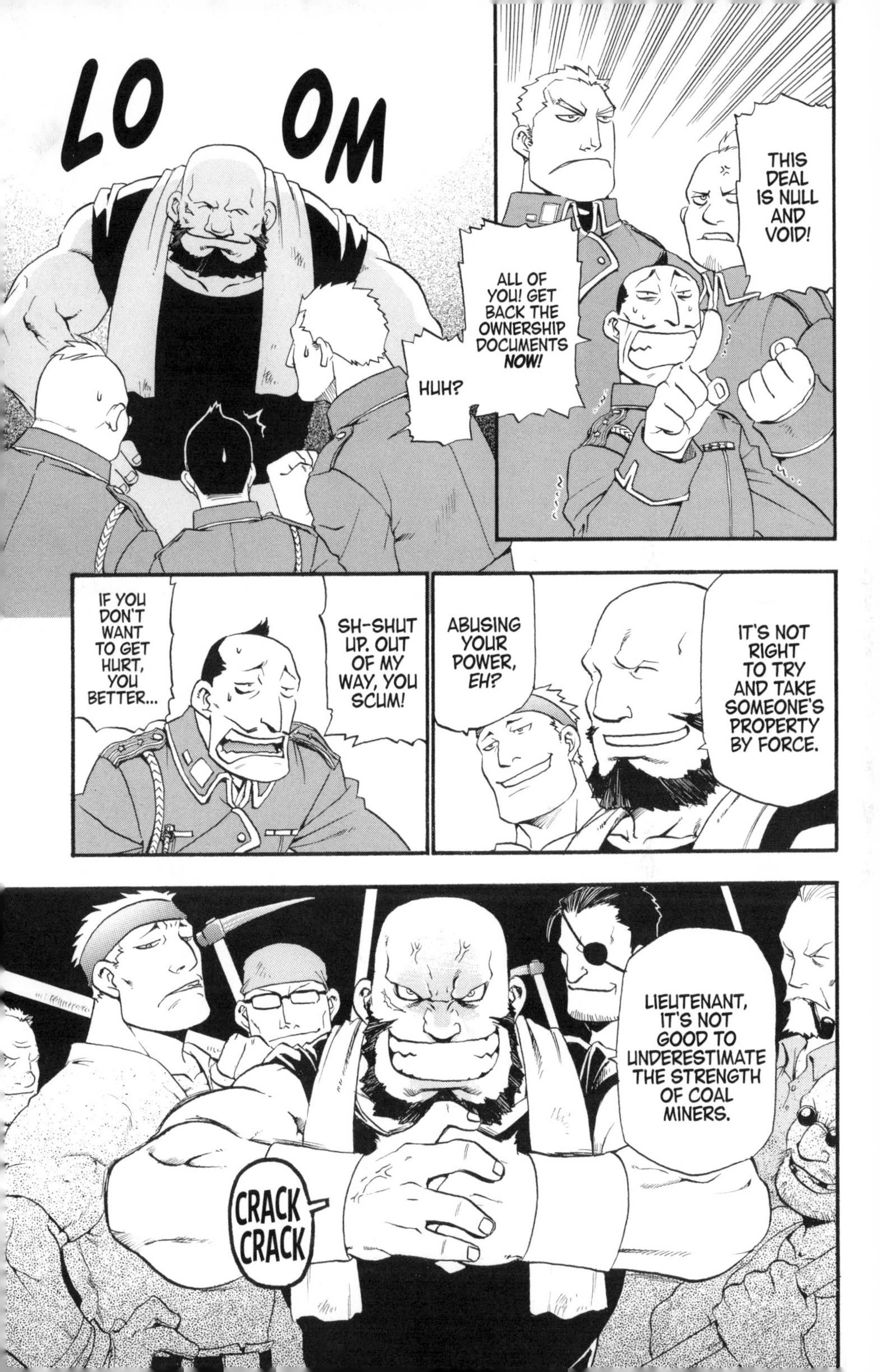
THIS DEAL IS NULL AND VOID!
ALL OF YOU! GET BACK THE OWNERSHIP DOCUMENTS **NOW!**
HUH?
LO OM
IT'S NOT RIGHT TO TRY AND TAKE SOMEONE'S PROPERTY BY FORCE.
ABUSING YOUR POWER, EH?
SH-SHUT UP. OUT OF MY WAY, YOU SCUM!
IF YOU DON'T WANT TO GET HURT, YOU BETTER...
LIEUTENANT, IT'S NOT GOOD TO UNDERESTIMATE THE STRENGTH OF COAL MINERS.
CRACK CRACK

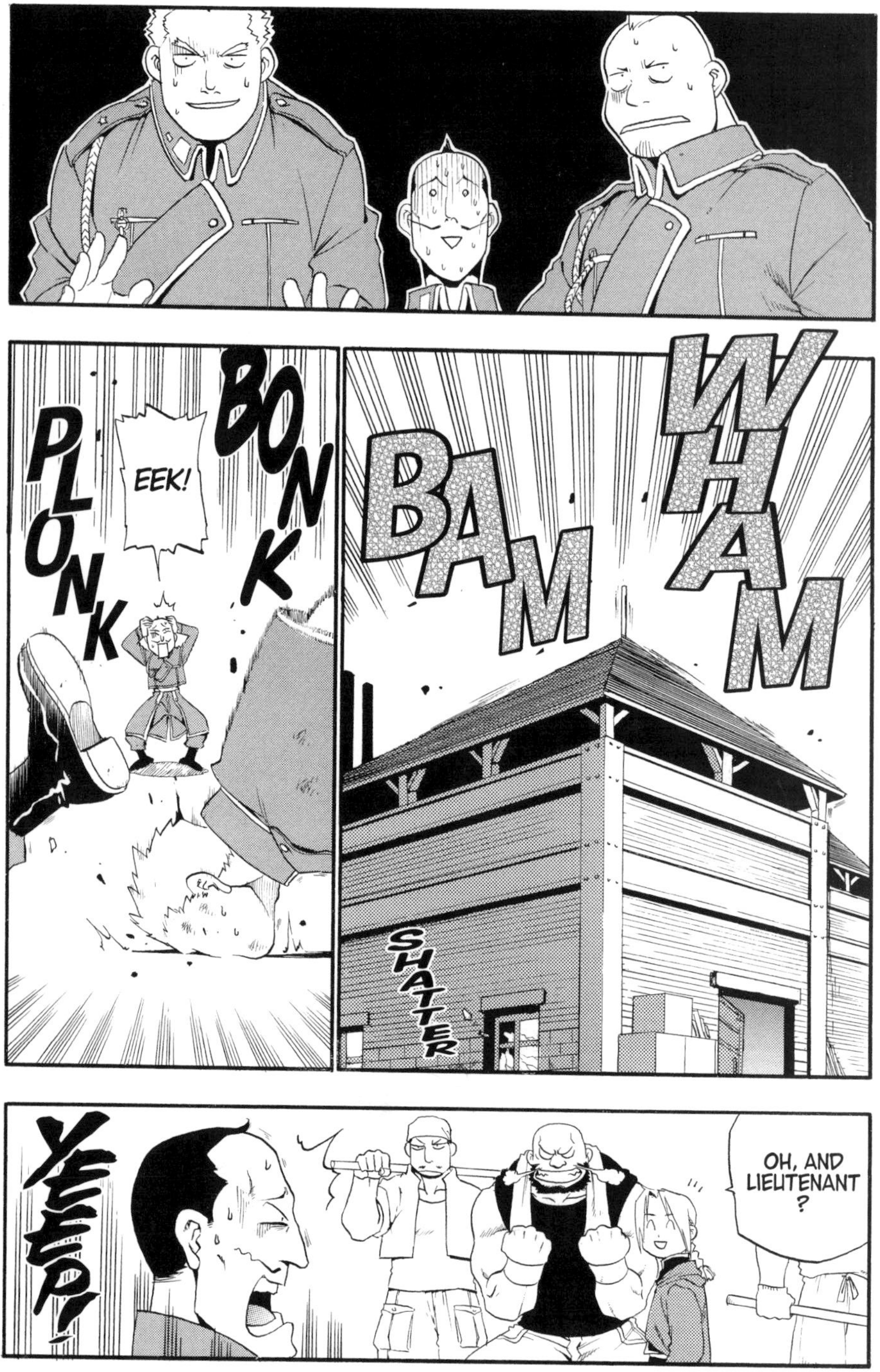
WHAM
BAM
SHATTER
BONK
EEK!
PLONK
OH, AND LIEUTENANT?
YEEEP!

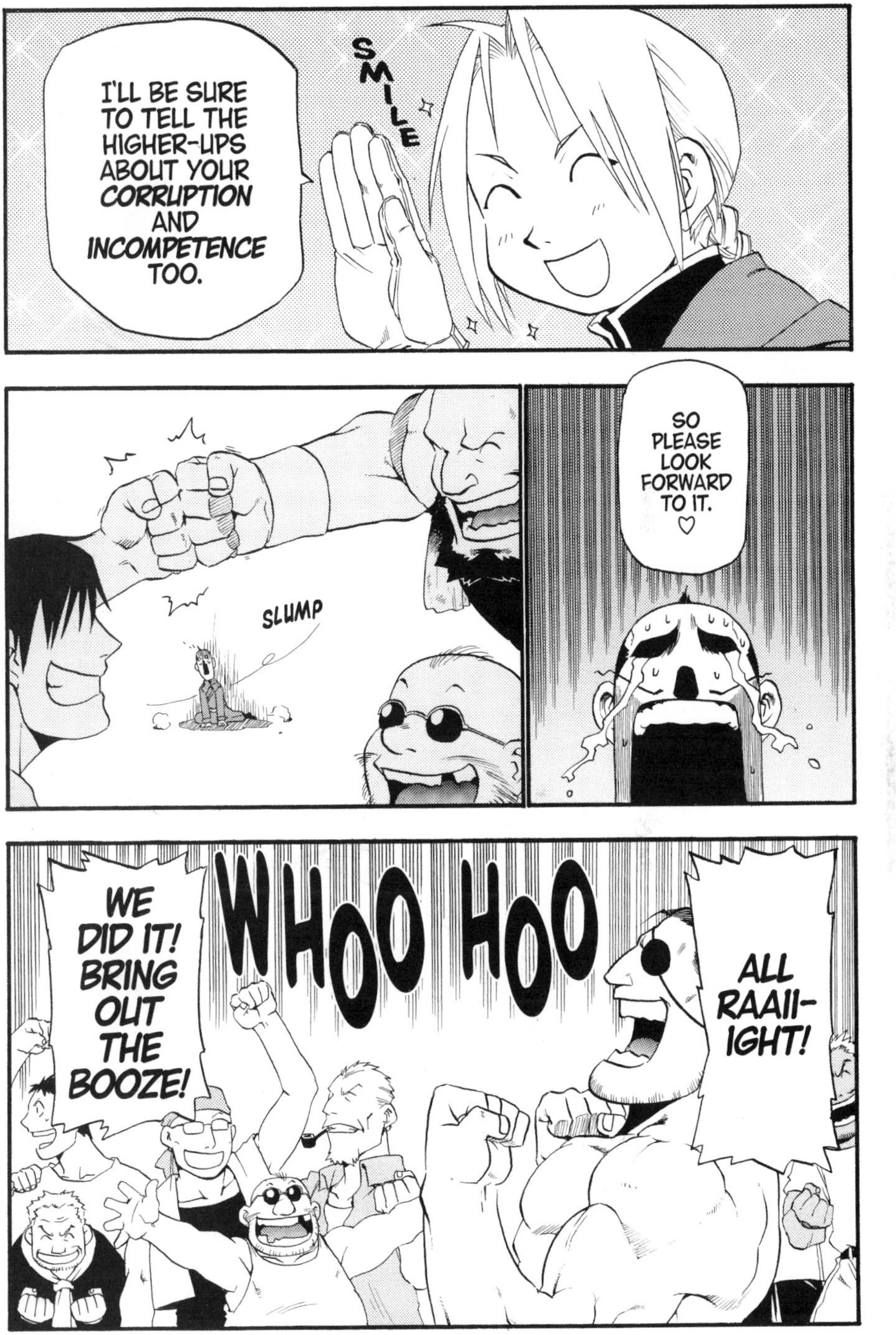
SMILE
I'LL BE SURE TO TELL THE HIGHER-UPS ABOUT YOUR CORRUPTION AND INCOMPETENCE TOO.
SO PLEASE LOOK FORWARD TO IT. ♡
SLUMP
ALL RAAII-IGHT!
WHOO HOO
WE DID IT! BRING OUT THE BOOZE!

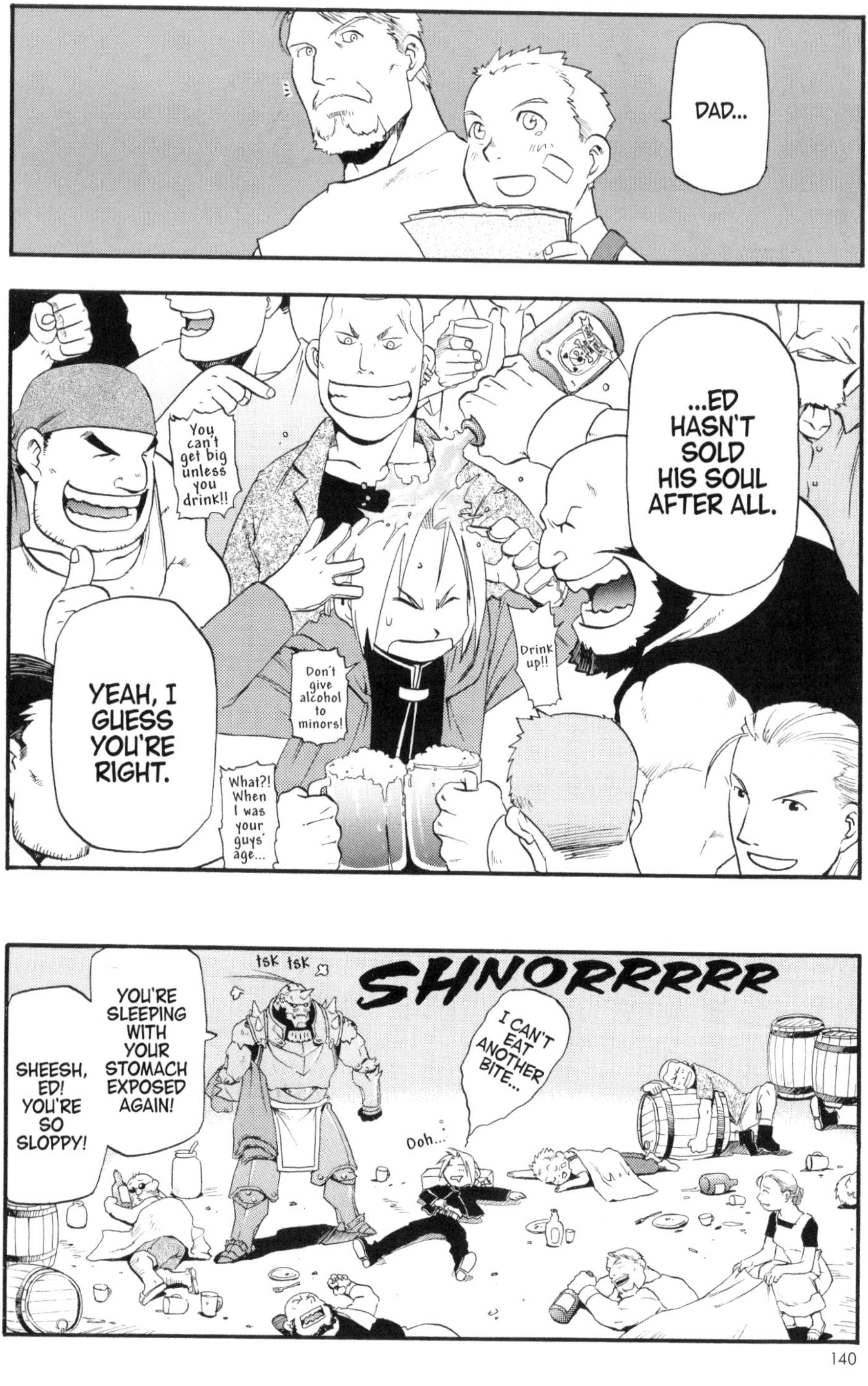
DAD...
...ED HASN'T SOLD HIS SOUL AFTER ALL.
You can't get big unless you drink!!
Drink up!!
Don't give alcohol to minors!
YEAH, I GUESS YOU'RE RIGHT.
What?! When I was your guys' age...
SHNORRRRR
I CAN'T EAT ANOTHER BITE...
Ooh...
tsk tsk
YOU'RE SLEEPING WITH YOUR STOMACH EXPOSED AGAIN!
SHEESH, ED! YOU'RE SO SLOPPY!

CHAPTER 4

BATTLE ON THE TRAIN

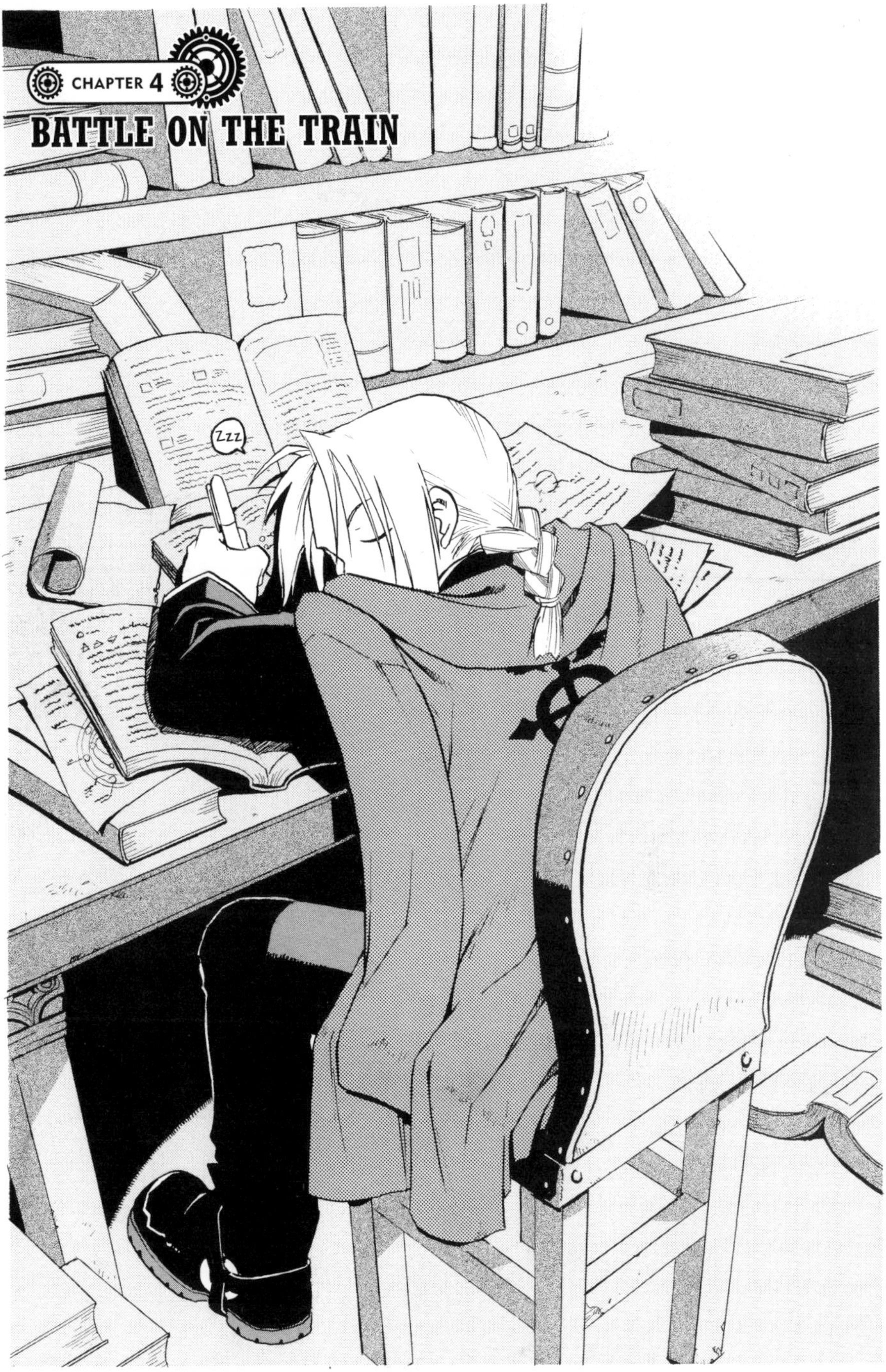
Zzz

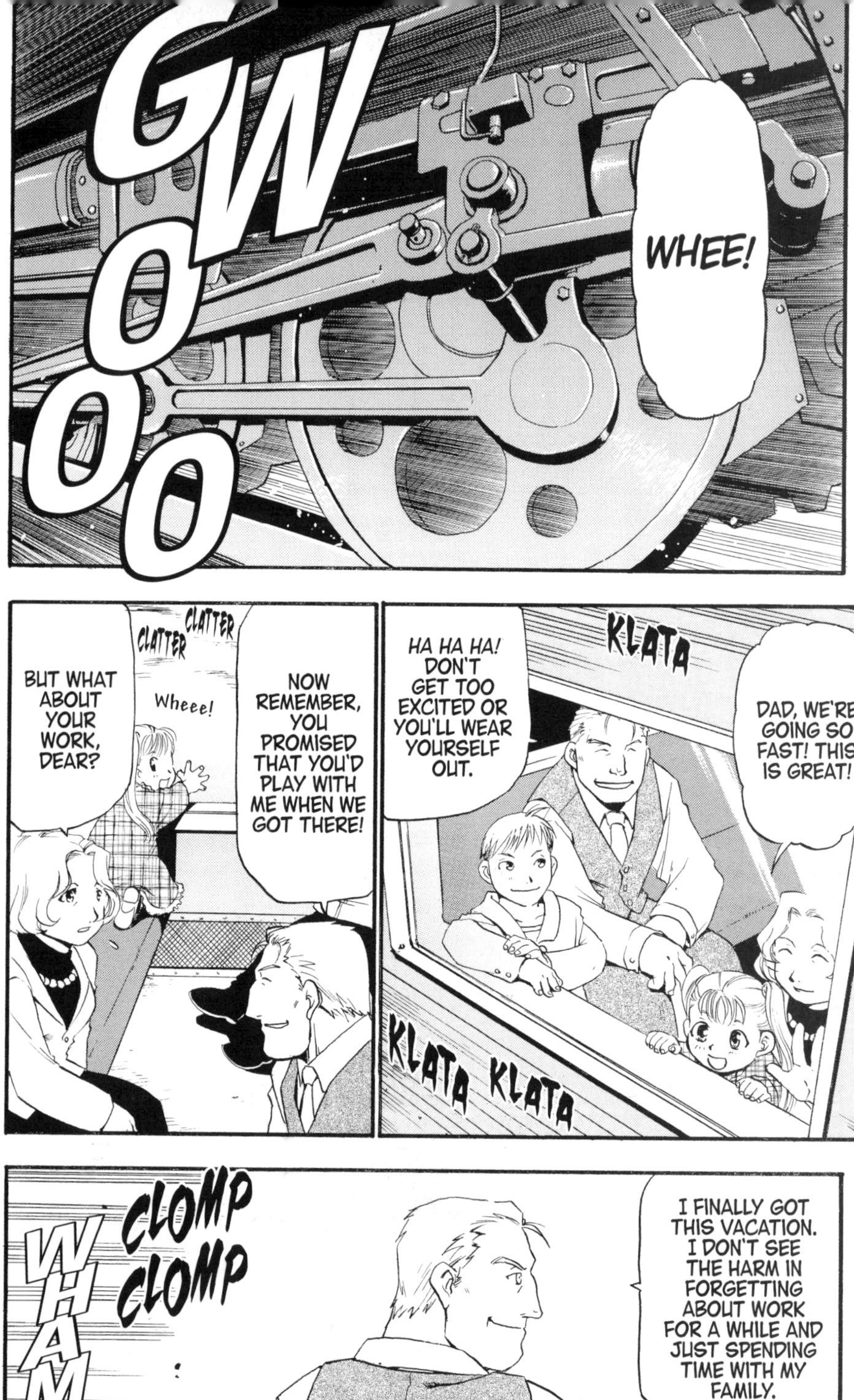
WHEE!
GWOOO
KLATA
DAD, WE'RE GOING SO FAST! THIS IS GREAT!
HA HA HA! DON'T GET TOO EXCITED OR YOU'LL WEAR YOURSELF OUT.
KLATA KLATA
CLATTER CLATTER
NOW REMEMBER, YOU PROMISED THAT YOU'D PLAY WITH ME WHEN WE GOT THERE!
Wheee!
BUT WHAT ABOUT YOUR WORK, DEAR?
I FINALLY GOT THIS VACATION. I DON'T SEE THE HARM IN FORGETTING ABOUT WORK FOR A WHILE AND JUST SPENDING TIME WITH MY FAMILY.
CLOMP CLOMP
WHAM

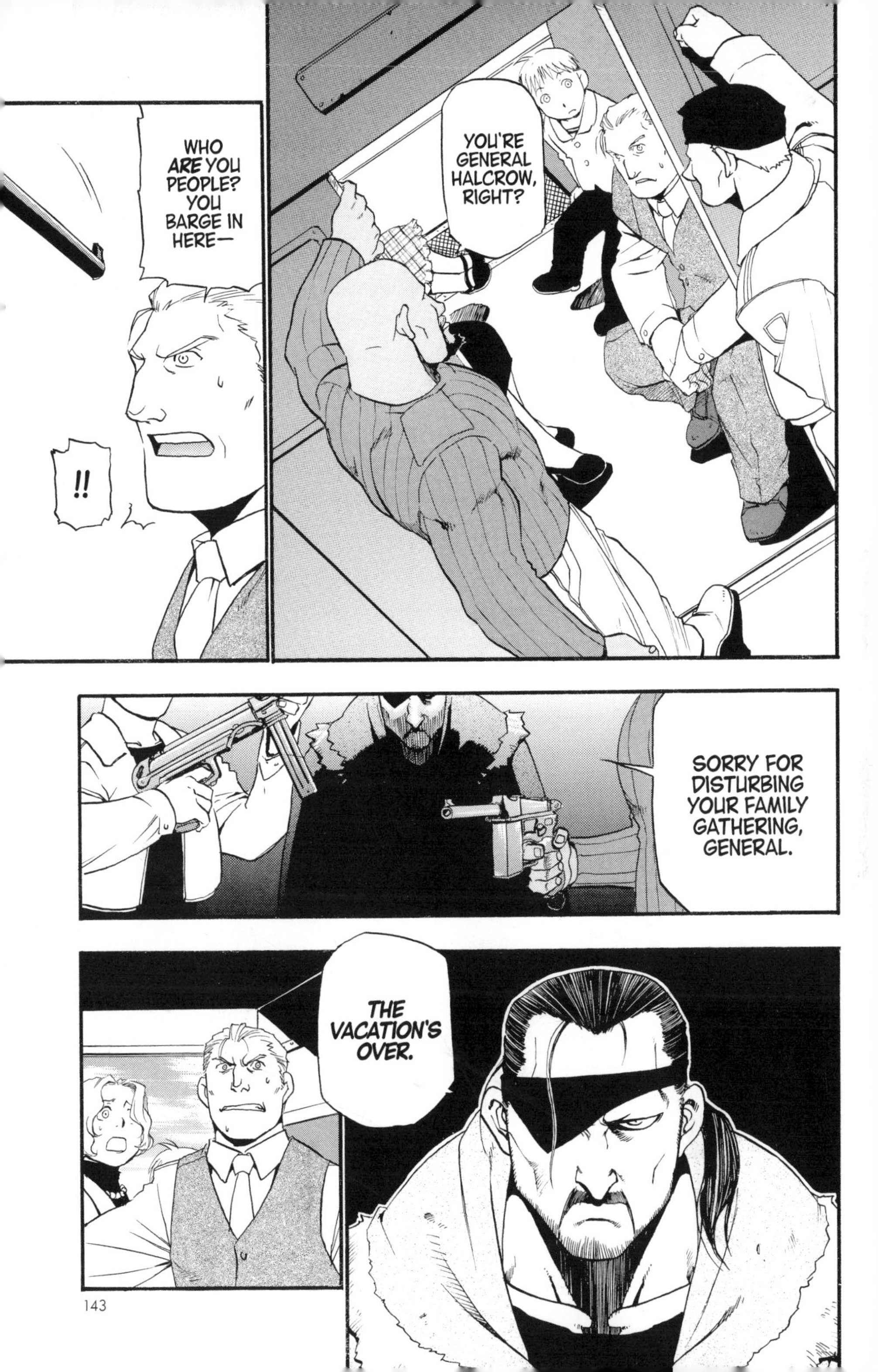

YOU'RE GENERAL HALCROW, RIGHT?
WHO ARE YOU PEOPLE? YOU BARGE IN HERE—
!!
SORRY FOR DISTURBING YOUR FAMILY GATHERING, GENERAL.
THE VACATION'S OVER.

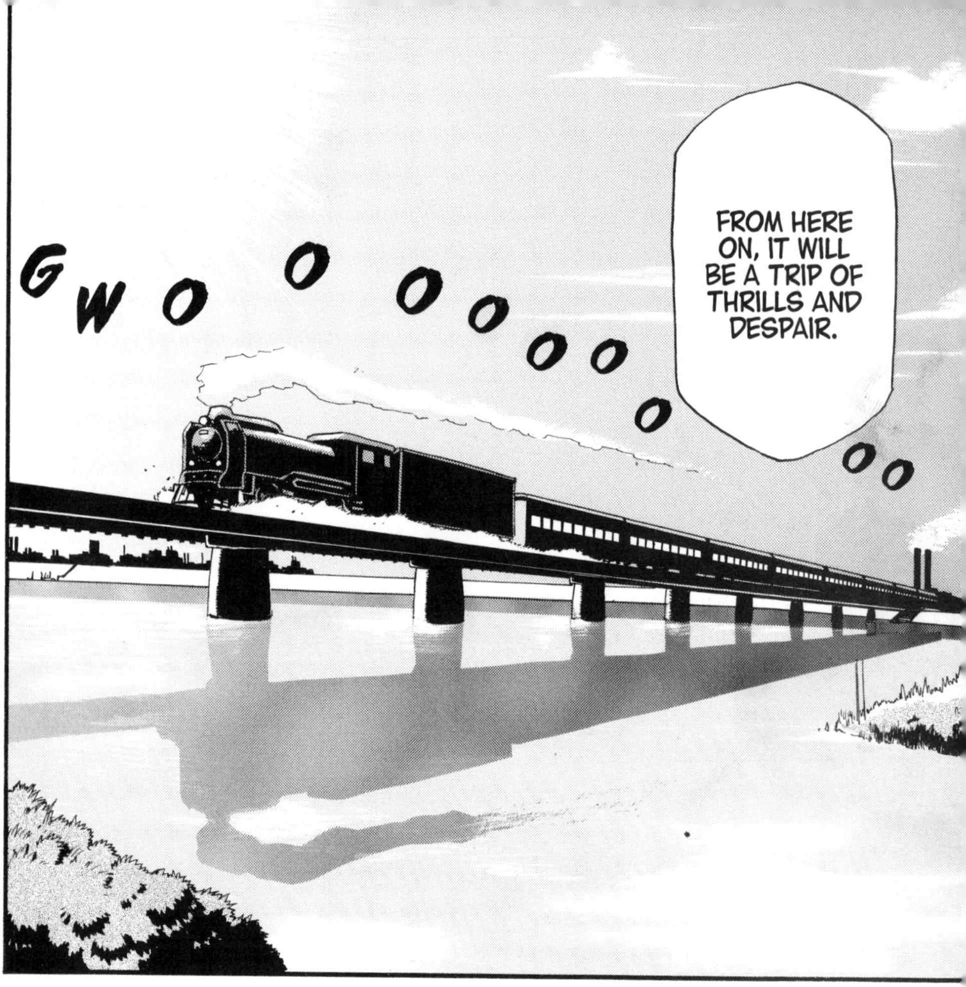
FROM HERE ON, IT WILL BE A TRIP OF THRILLS AND DESPAIR.
GWOOOOOOOOOO

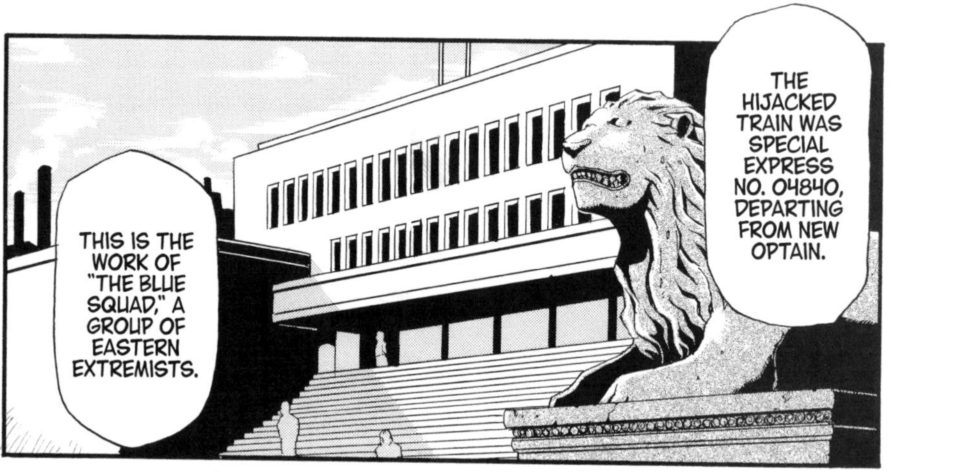
THE HIJACKED TRAIN WAS SPECIAL EXPRESS NO. 04840, DEPARTING FROM NEW OPTAIN.
THIS IS THE WORK OF "THE BLUE SQUAD," A GROUP OF EASTERN EXTREMISTS.

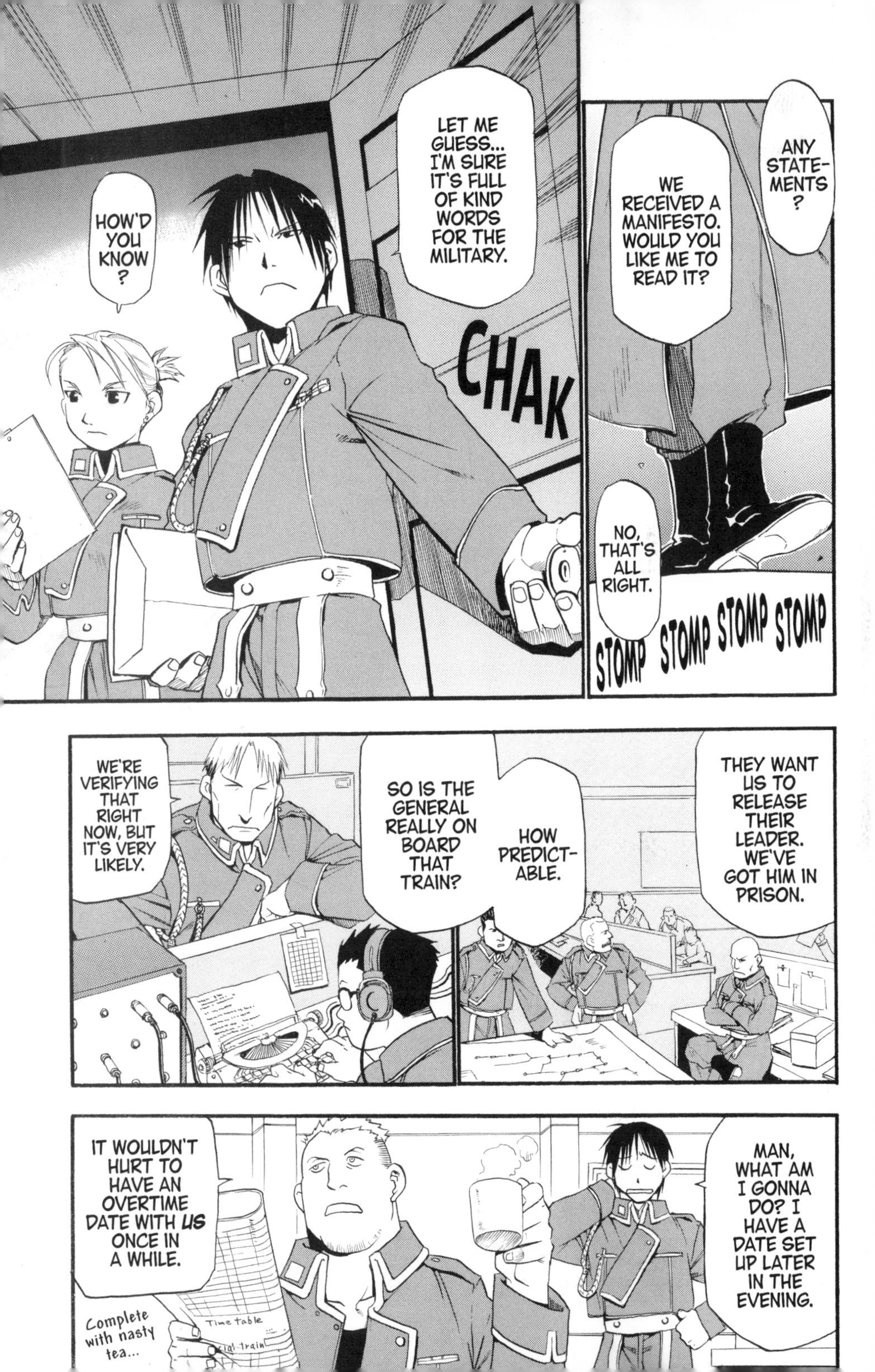
ANY STATEMENTS?
WE RECEIVED A MANIFESTO. WOULD YOU LIKE ME TO READ IT?
NO, THAT'S ALL RIGHT.
STOMP STOMP STOMP STOMP
LET ME GUESS... I'M SURE IT'S FULL OF KIND WORDS FOR THE MILITARY.
HOW'D YOU KNOW?
CHAK
THEY WANT US TO RELEASE THEIR LEADER. WE'VE GOT HIM IN PRISON.
HOW PREDICTABLE.
SO IS THE GENERAL REALLY ON BOARD THAT TRAIN?
WE'RE VERIFYING THAT RIGHT NOW, BUT IT'S VERY LIKELY.
MAN, WHAT AM I GONNA DO? I HAVE A DATE SET UP LATER IN THE EVENING.
IT WOULDN'T HURT TO HAVE AN OVERTIME DATE WITH US ONCE IN A WHILE.
Time table
Complete with nasty tea...

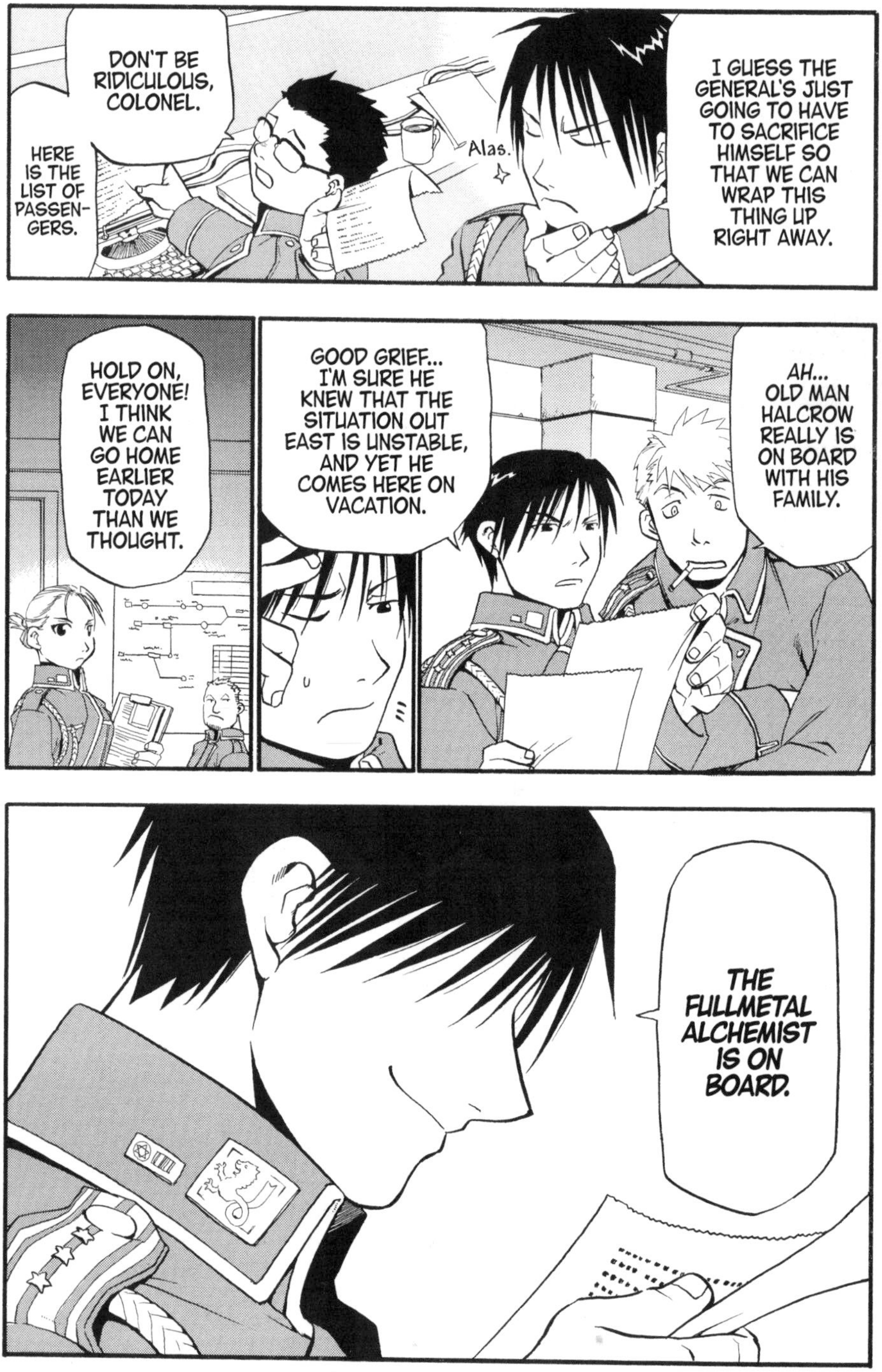
I GUESS THE GENERAL'S JUST GOING TO HAVE TO SACRIFICE HIMSELF SO THAT WE CAN WRAP THIS THING UP RIGHT AWAY.
Alas.
DON'T BE RIDICULOUS, COLONEL.
HERE IS THE LIST OF PASSEN-GERS.
AH... OLD MAN HALCROW REALLY IS ON BOARD WITH HIS FAMILY.
GOOD GRIEF... I'M SURE HE KNEW THAT THE SITUATION OUT EAST IS UNSTABLE, AND YET HE COMES HERE ON VACATION.
HOLD ON, EVERYONE! I THINK WE CAN GO HOME EARLIER TODAY THAN WE THOUGHT.
THE FULLMETAL ALCHEMIST IS ON BOARD.

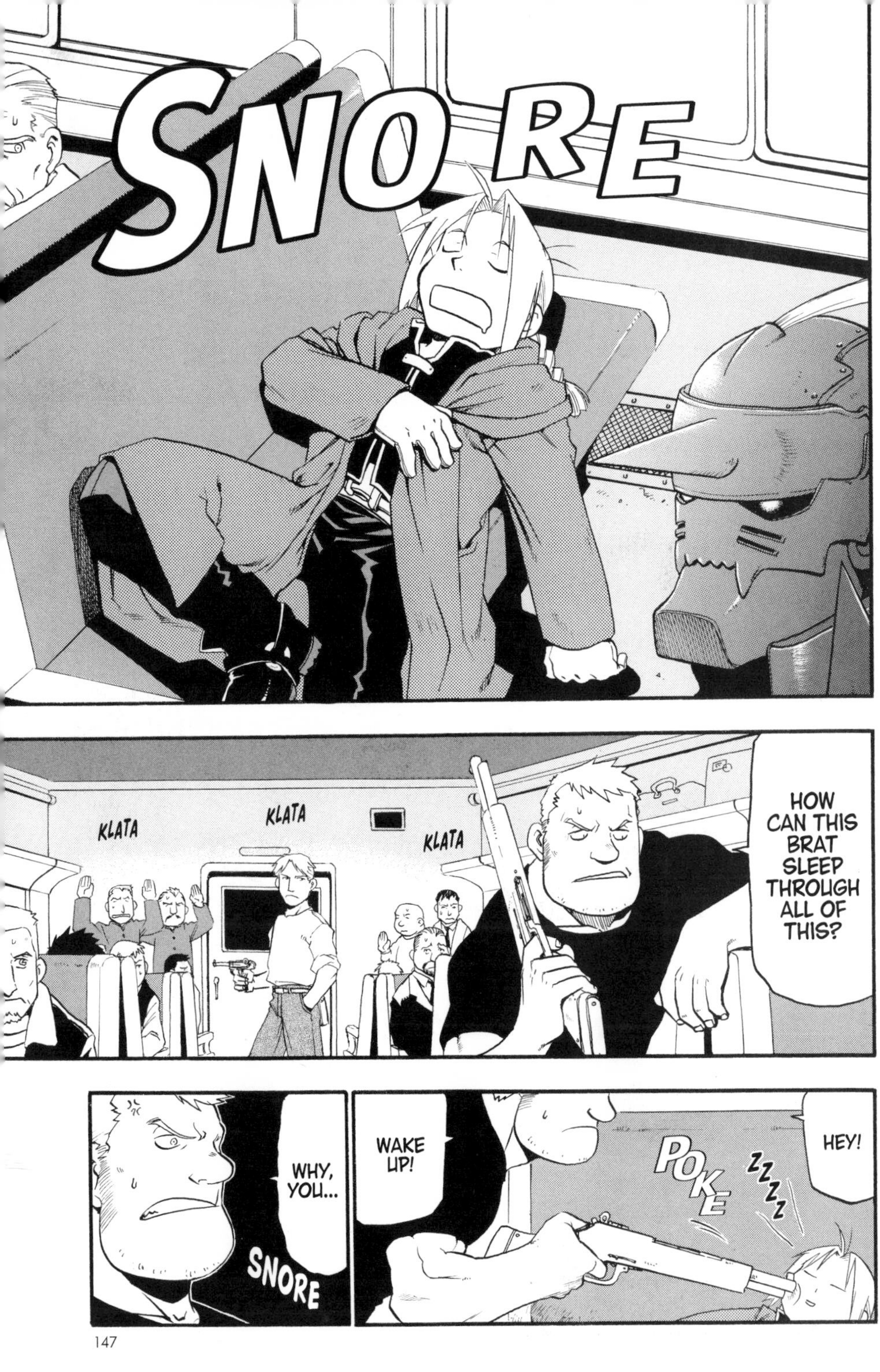
SNORE
HOW CAN THIS BRAT SLEEP THROUGH ALL OF THIS?
KLATA
KLATA
KLATA
HEY!
ZZZZ
POKE
WAKE UP!
WHY, YOU...
SNORE

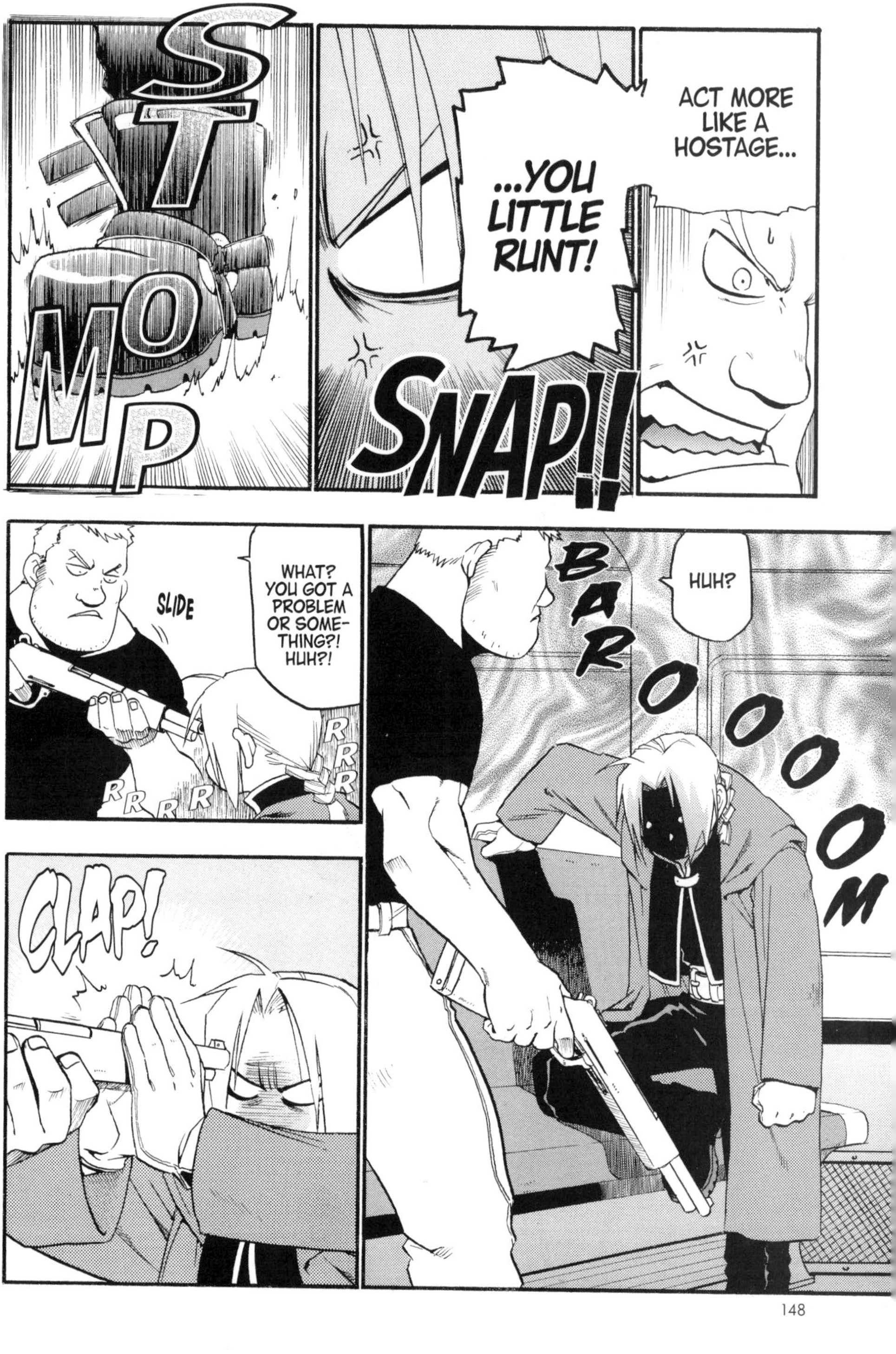
ACT MORE LIKE A HOSTAGE...
...YOU LITTLE RUNT!
SNAP!!
STOMP
HUH?
BAROOOOOM
WHAT? YOU GOT A PROBLEM OR SOME-THING?! HUH?!
SLIDE
RRRRRRRR
CLAP!

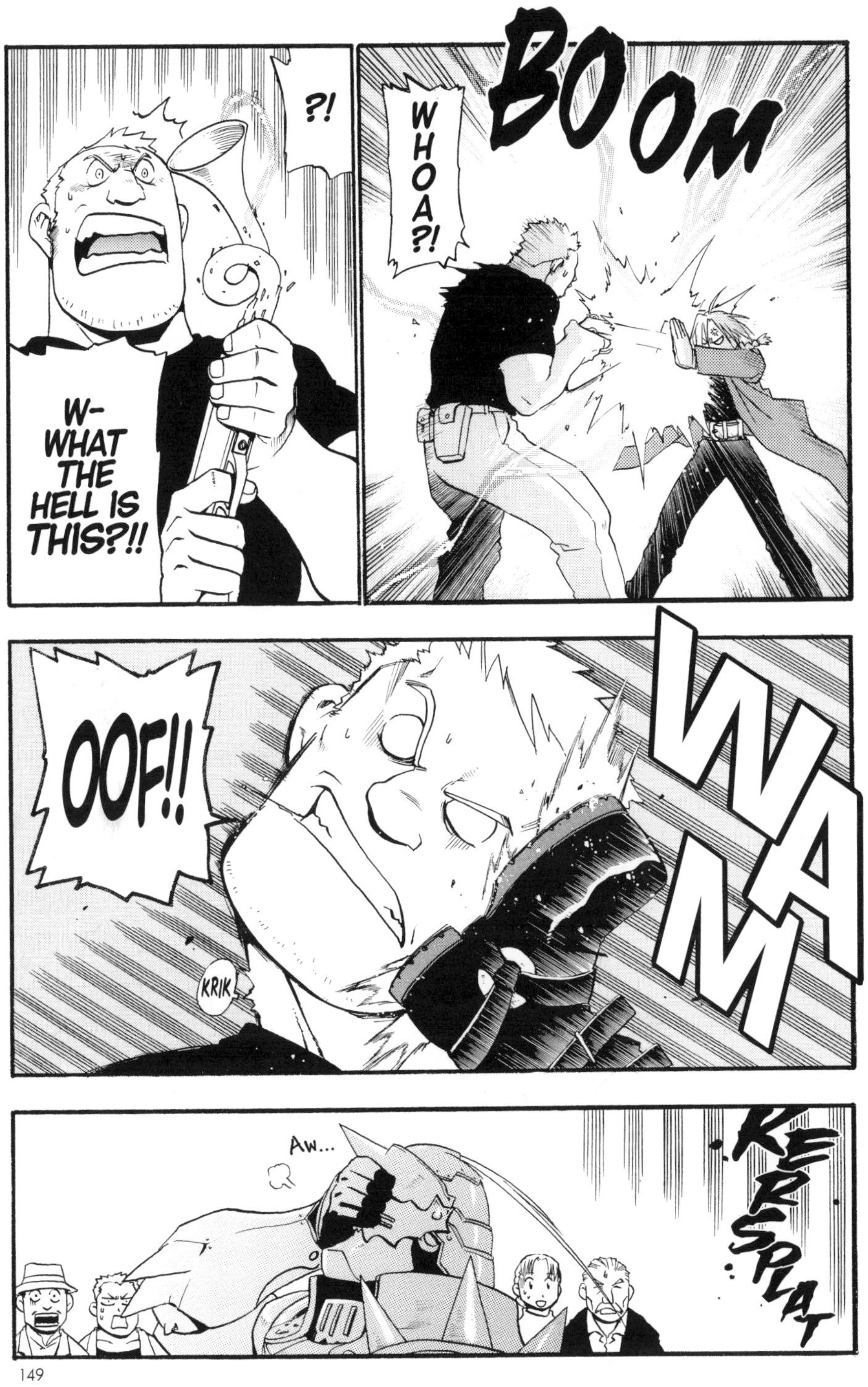
BOOM
WHOA?!
?!
W-WHAT THE HELL IS THIS?!!
WHAM
OOF!!
KRIK
KERSPLAT
Aw...

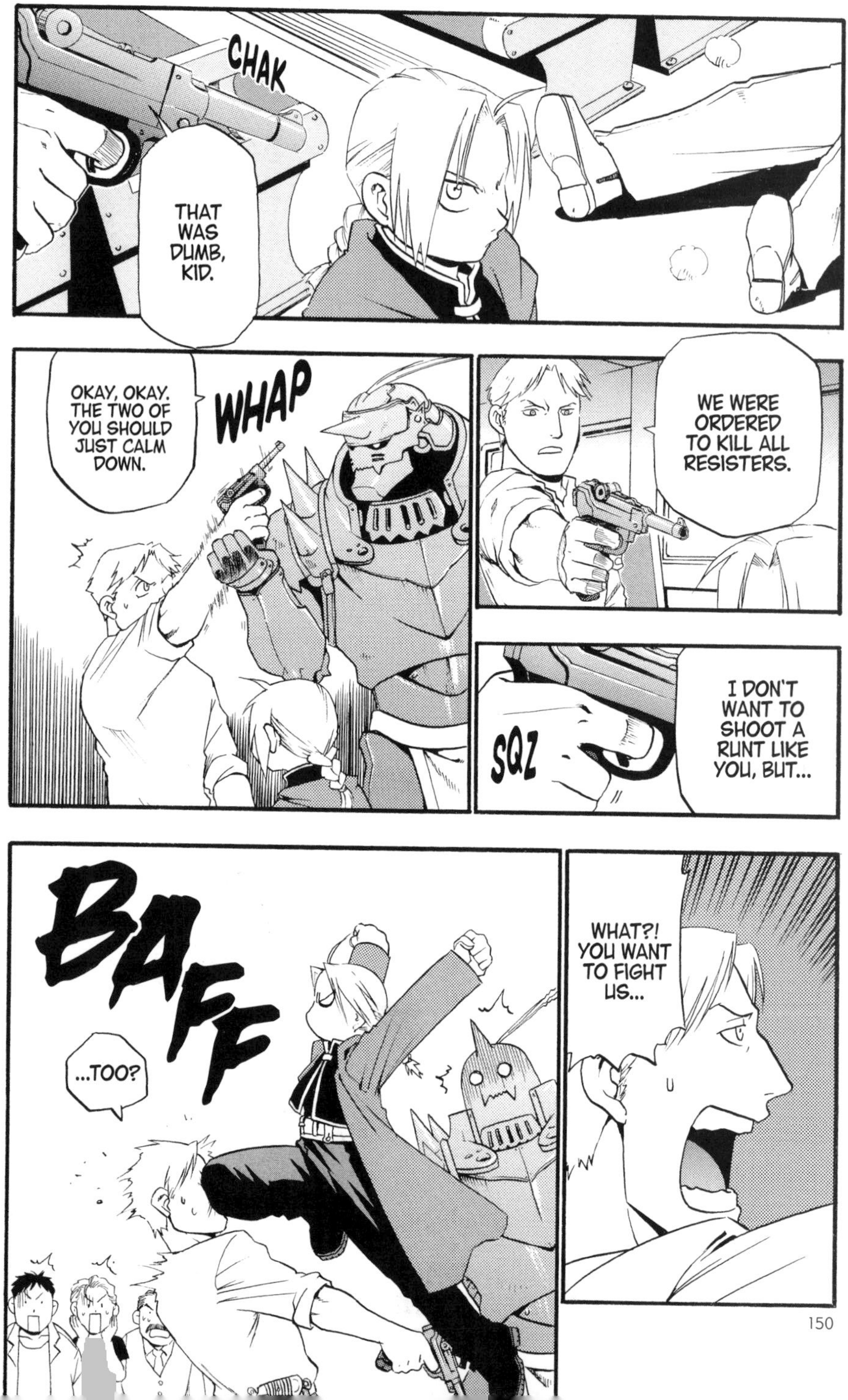
CHAK
THAT WAS DUMB, KID.
WE WERE ORDERED TO KILL ALL RESISTERS.
I DON'T WANT TO SHOOT A RUNT LIKE YOU, BUT...
SQZ
OKAY, OKAY. THE TWO OF YOU SHOULD JUST CALM DOWN.
WHAP
WHAT?! YOU WANT TO FIGHT US...
BAFF
...TOO?

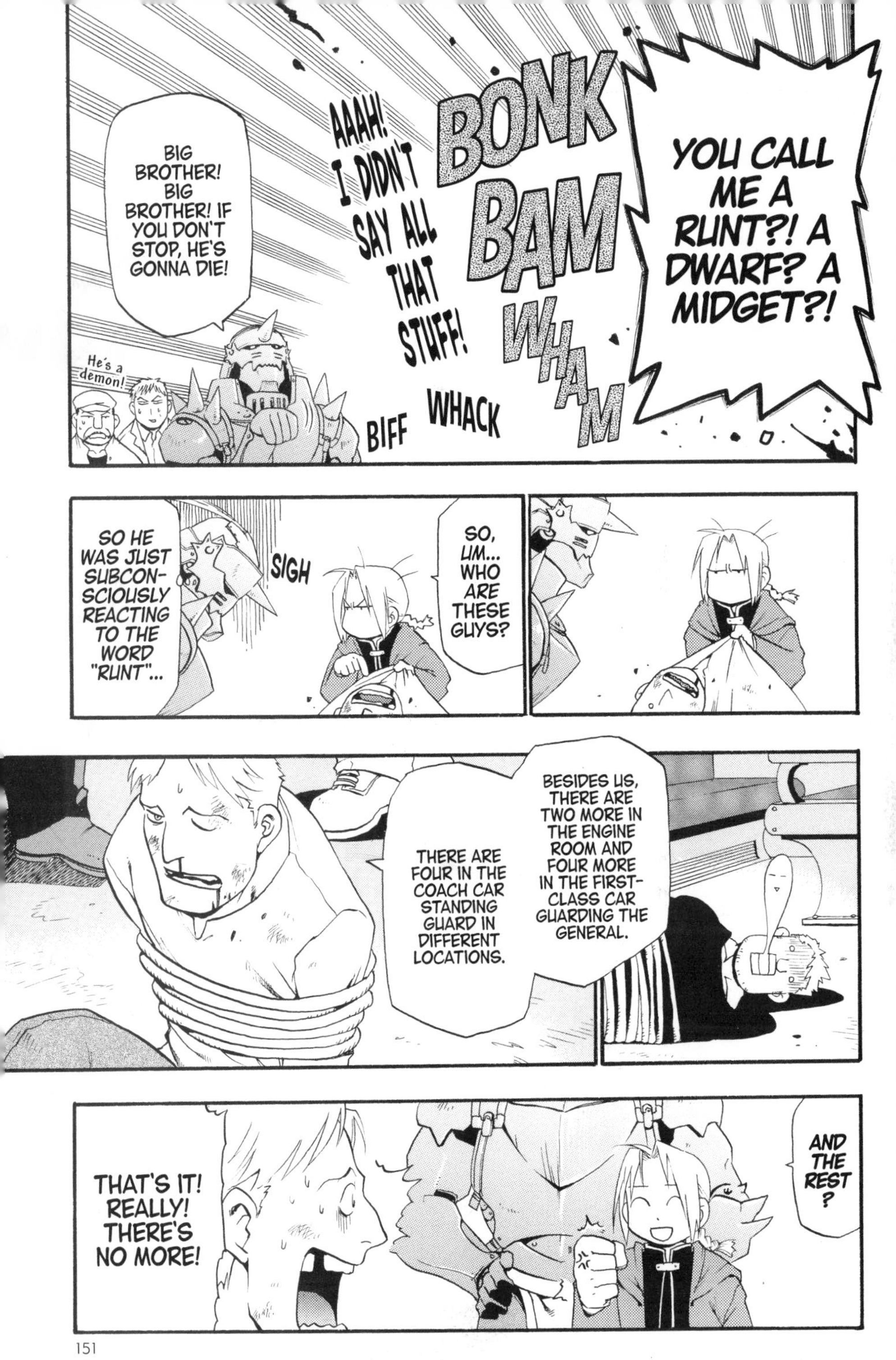
YOU CALL ME A RUNT?! A DWARF? A MIDGET?!
BONK
BAM
WHAM
AAAH! I DIDN'T SAY ALL THAT STUFF!
WHACK
BIFF
BIG BROTHER! BIG BROTHER! IF YOU DON'T STOP, HE'S GONNA DIE!
He's a demon!
SO, UM... WHO ARE THESE GUYS?
SIGH
SO HE WAS JUST SUBCON- SCIOUSLY REACTING TO THE WORD "RUNT"...
BESIDES US, THERE ARE TWO MORE IN THE ENGINE ROOM AND FOUR MORE IN THE FIRST- CLASS CAR GUARDING THE GENERAL.
THERE ARE FOUR IN THE COACH CAR STANDING GUARD IN DIFFERENT LOCATIONS.
AND THE REST?
THAT'S IT! REALLY! THERE'S NO MORE!

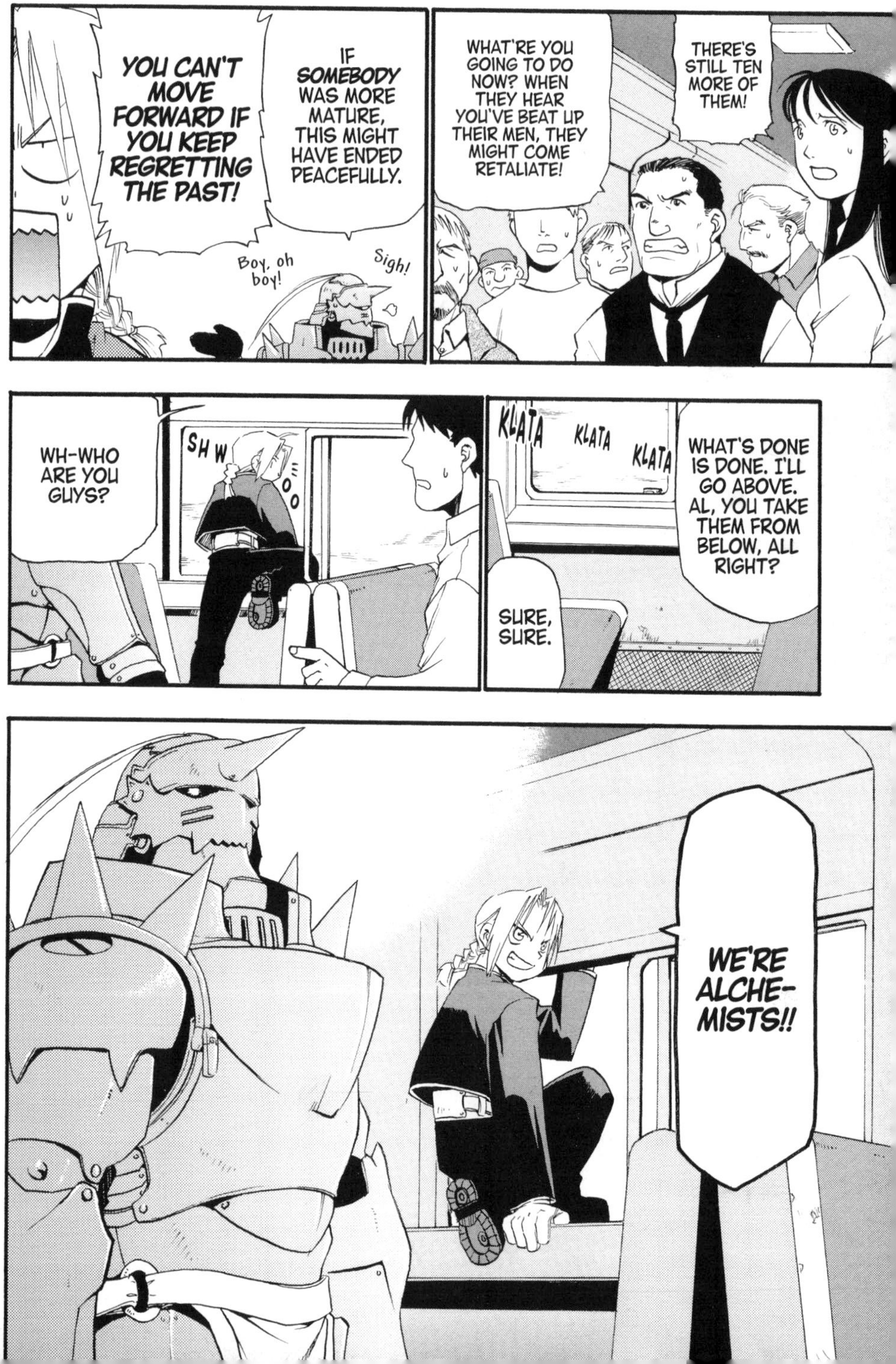
THERE'S STILL TEN MORE OF THEM!
WHAT'RE YOU GOING TO DO NOW? WHEN THEY HEAR YOU'VE BEAT UP THEIR MEN, THEY MIGHT COME RETALIATE!
IF SOMEBODY WAS MORE MATURE, THIS MIGHT HAVE ENDED PEACEFULLY.
Sigh!
Boy, oh boy!
YOU CAN'T MOVE FORWARD IF YOU KEEP REGRETTING THE PAST!
KLATA
KLATA
KLATA
WHAT'S DONE IS DONE. I'LL GO ABOVE. AL, YOU TAKE THEM FROM BELOW, ALL RIGHT?
SURE, SURE.
SHWOO
WH-WHO ARE YOU GUYS?
WE'RE ALCHE-MISTS!!

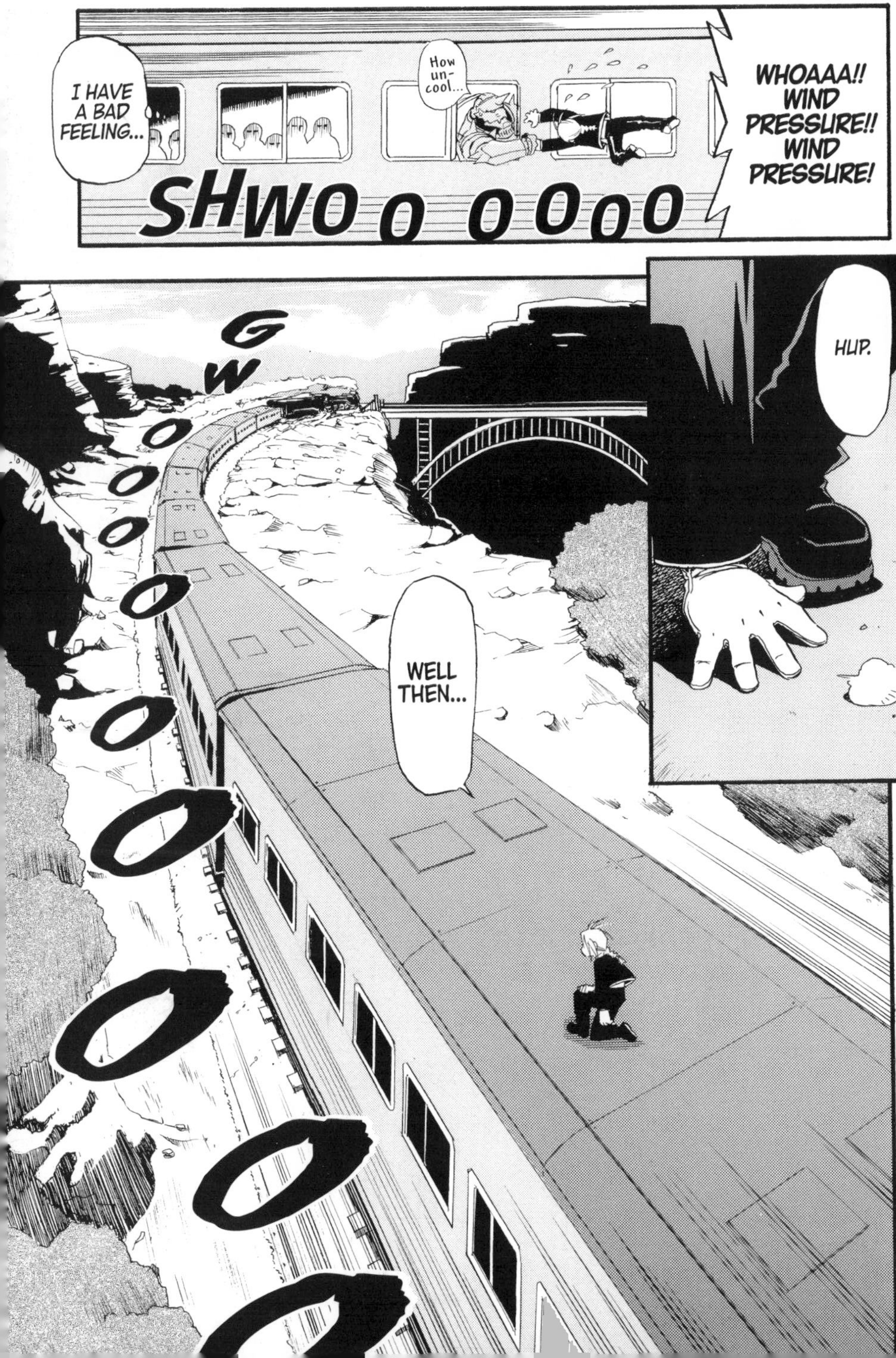
WHOAAA!! WIND PRESSURE!! WIND PRESSURE!
How un-cool...
I HAVE A BAD FEELING...
SHWOOOOOO
HUP.
WELL THEN...
GWOOOOOOOOOO

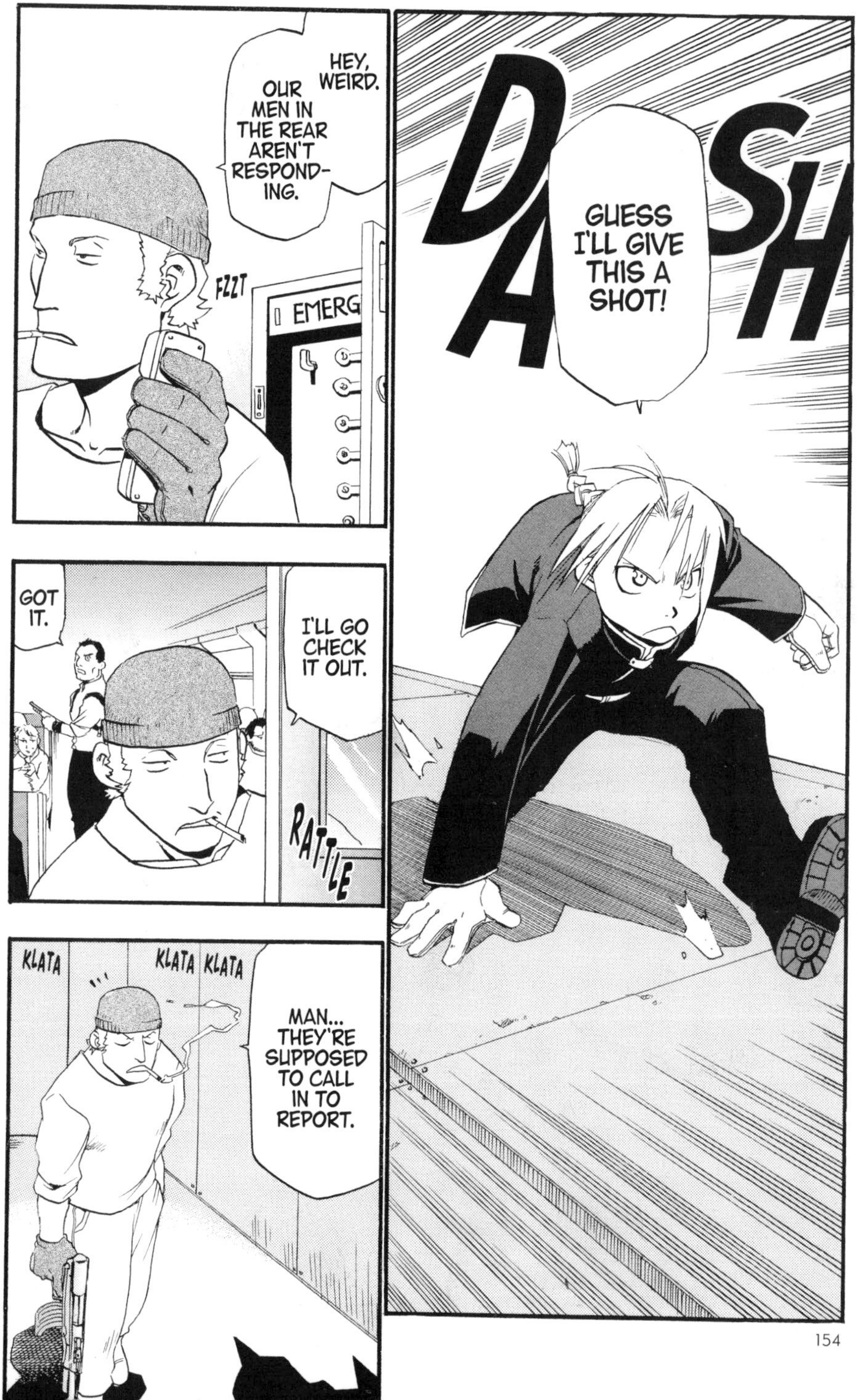
DASH
GUESS I'LL GIVE THIS A SHOT!
HEY, WEIRD.
OUR MEN IN THE REAR AREN'T RESPOND-ING.
FZZT
EMERG
I'LL GO CHECK IT OUT.
GOT IT.
RATTLE
MAN... THEY'RE SUPPOSED TO CALL IN TO REPORT.
KLATA KLATA
KLATA

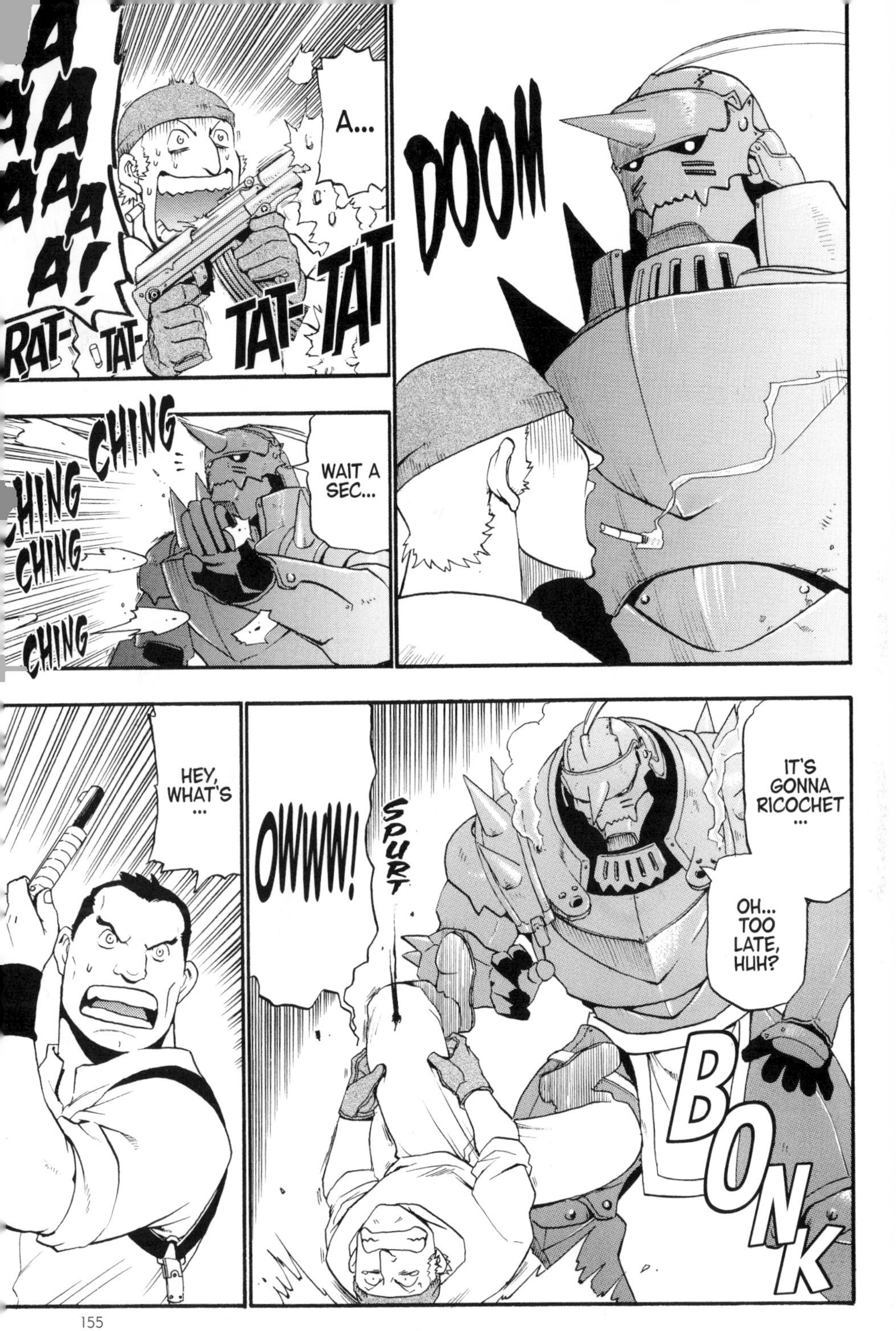
DOOM
A...
AAAAAAA!
RAT-TAT-TAT-TAT
WAIT A SEC...
CHING CHING CHING CHING
IT'S GONNA RICOCHET...
OH... TOO LATE, HUH?
OWWW!
SPURT
BONK
HEY, WHAT'S...

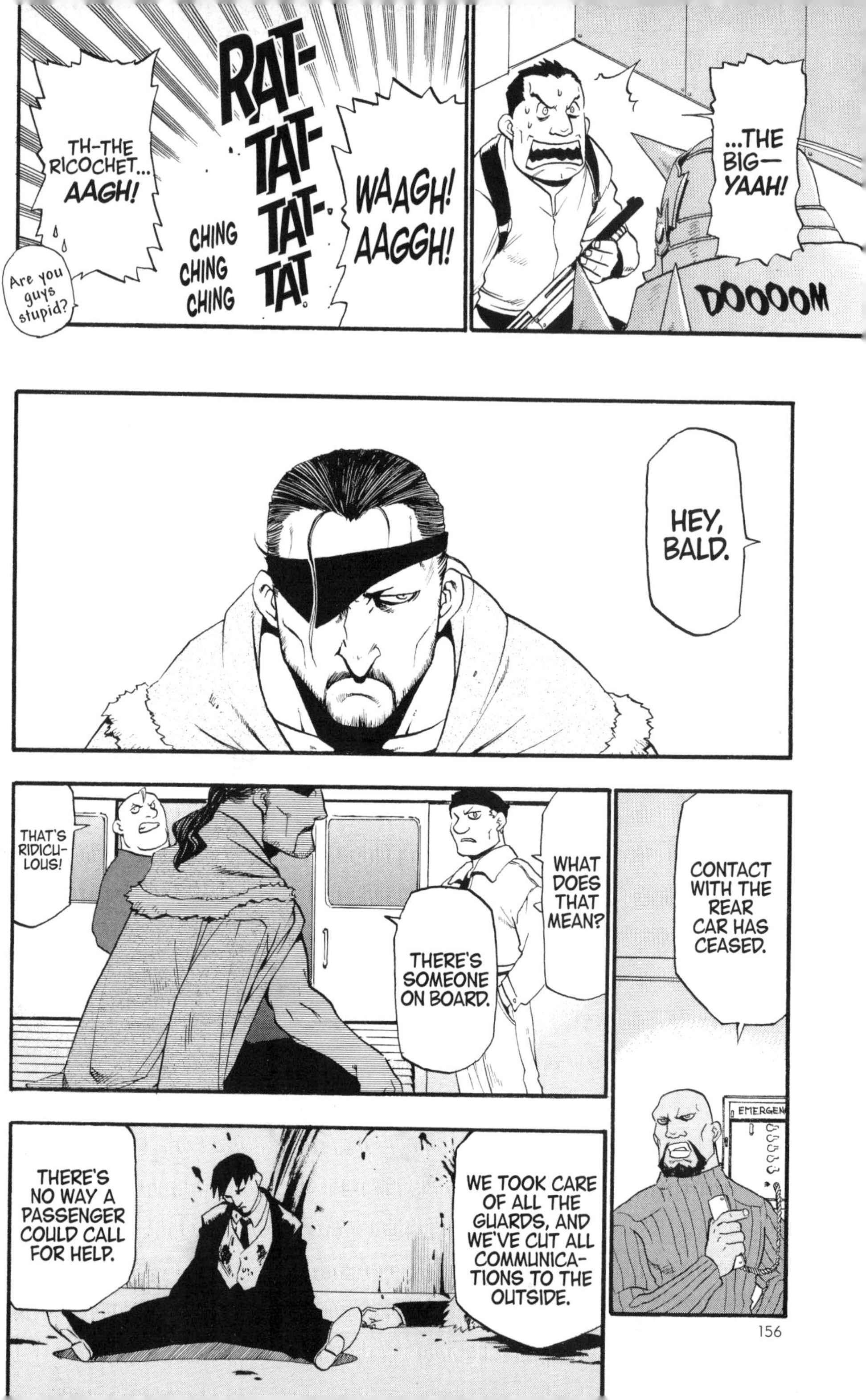
...THE BIG—YAAH!
DOOOOM
WAAGH! AAGGH!
RAT-TAT-TAT-TAT
CHING CHING CHING
TH-THE RICOCHET... AAGH!
Are you guys stupid?
HEY, BALD.
CONTACT WITH THE REAR CAR HAS CEASED.
EMERGEN
WHAT DOES THAT MEAN?
THERE'S SOMEONE ON BOARD.
THAT'S RIDICULOUS!
WE TOOK CARE OF ALL THE GUARDS, AND WE'VE CUT ALL COMMUNICATIONS TO THE OUTSIDE.
THERE'S NO WAY A PASSENGER COULD CALL FOR HELP.

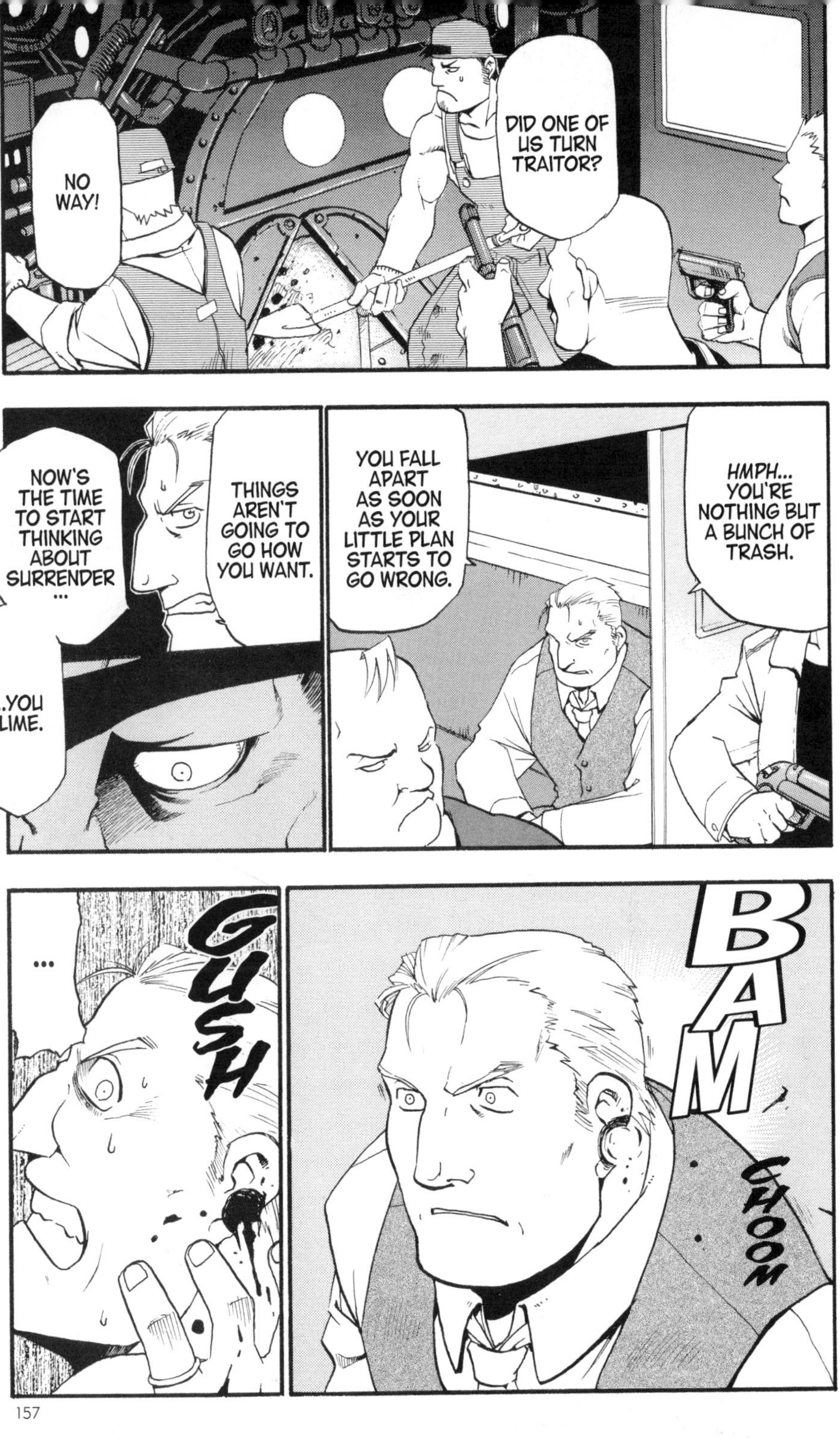
DID ONE OF US TURN TRAITOR?
NO WAY!
HMPH... YOU'RE NOTHING BUT A BUNCH OF TRASH.
YOU FALL APART AS SOON AS YOUR LITTLE PLAN STARTS TO GO WRONG.
THINGS AREN'T GOING TO GO HOW YOU WANT.
NOW'S THE TIME TO START THINKING ABOUT SURRENDER...
...YOU SLIME.
BAM
CHOOM
GUSH
...

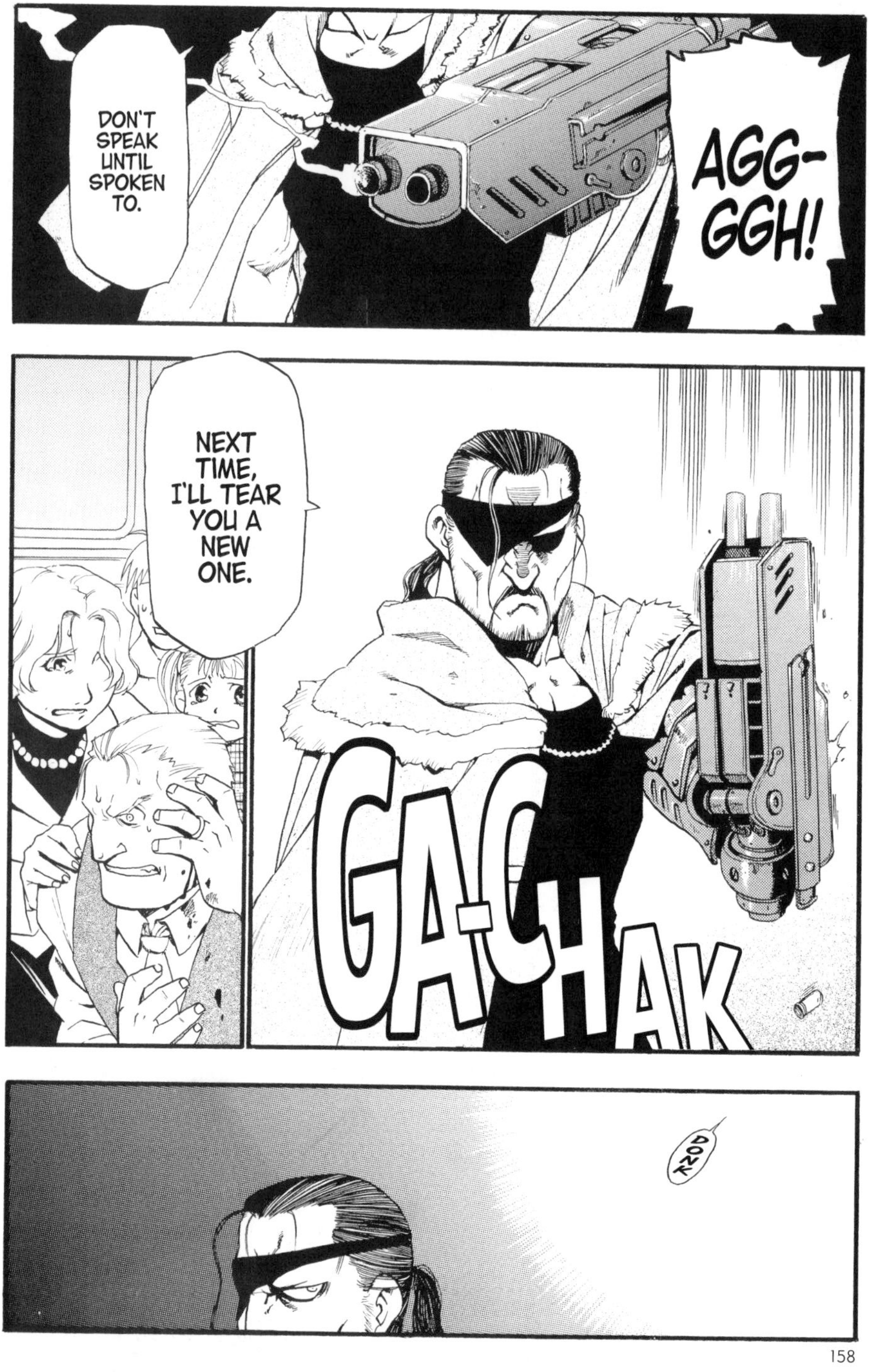
AGG-GGH!
DON'T SPEAK UNTIL SPOKEN TO.
GA-CHAK
NEXT TIME, I'LL TEAR YOU A NEW ONE.
DONK

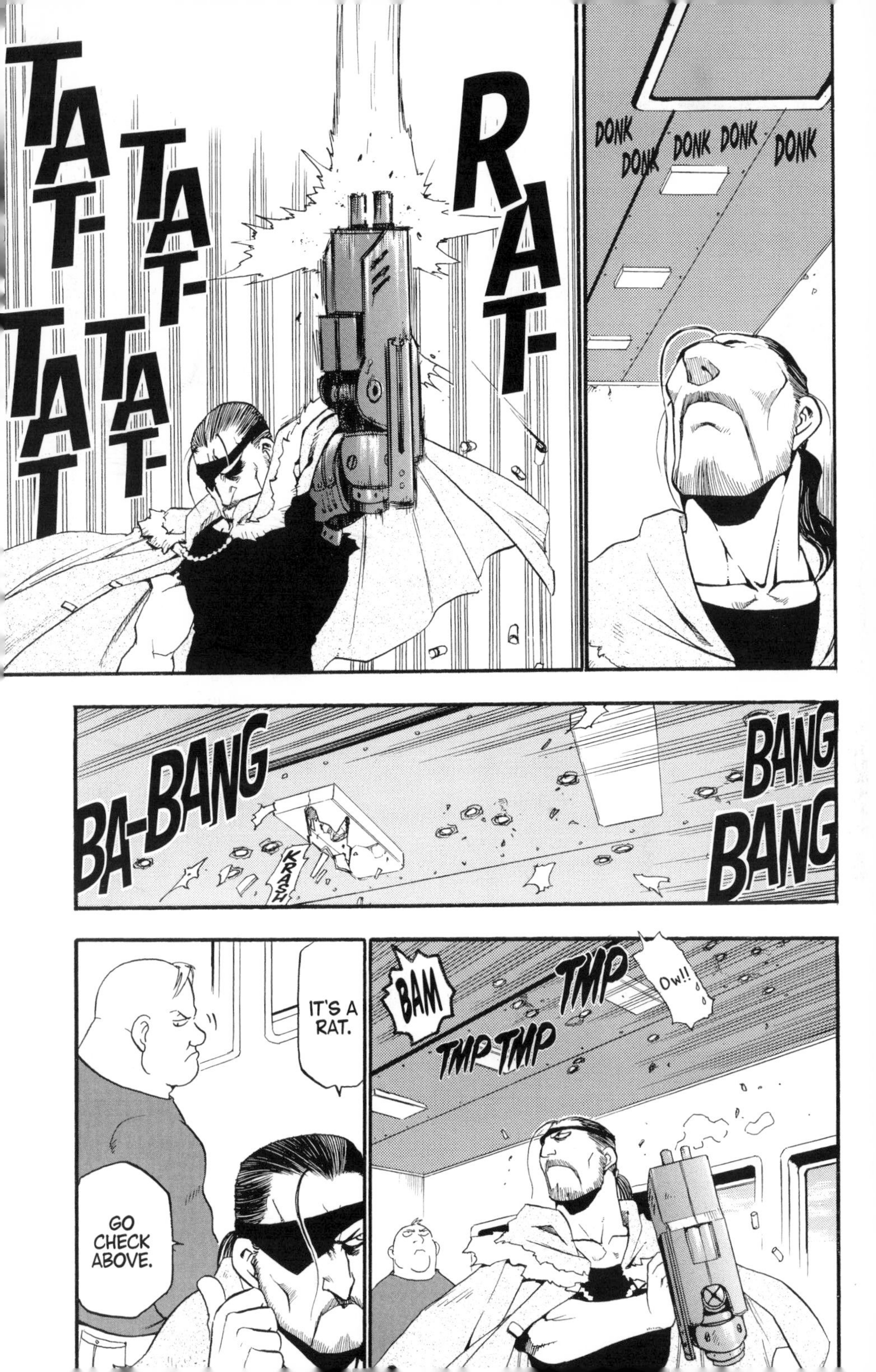

DONK DONK DONK DONK DONK
RAT-
TAT-TAT-
TAT-TAT
BANG BANG
BA-BANG
KRASH
BAM
TMP
Ow!!
TMP TMP
IT'S A RAT.
GO CHECK ABOVE.

WHOA, THAT WAS TOO CLOSE!

KLATA KLATA·KLATA

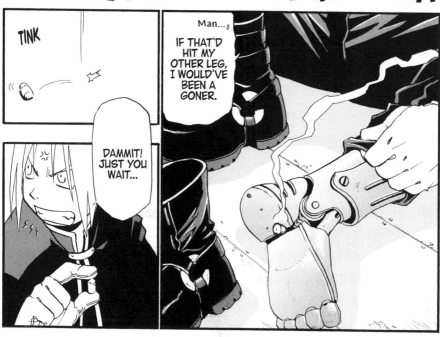

TINK

Man...♪
IF THAT'D HIT MY OTHER LEG, I WOULD'VE BEEN A GONER.

DAMMIT! JUST YOU WAIT...

ROAAA

FIRST, I'LL RECAPTURE THE ENGINE ROOM!!

AARD

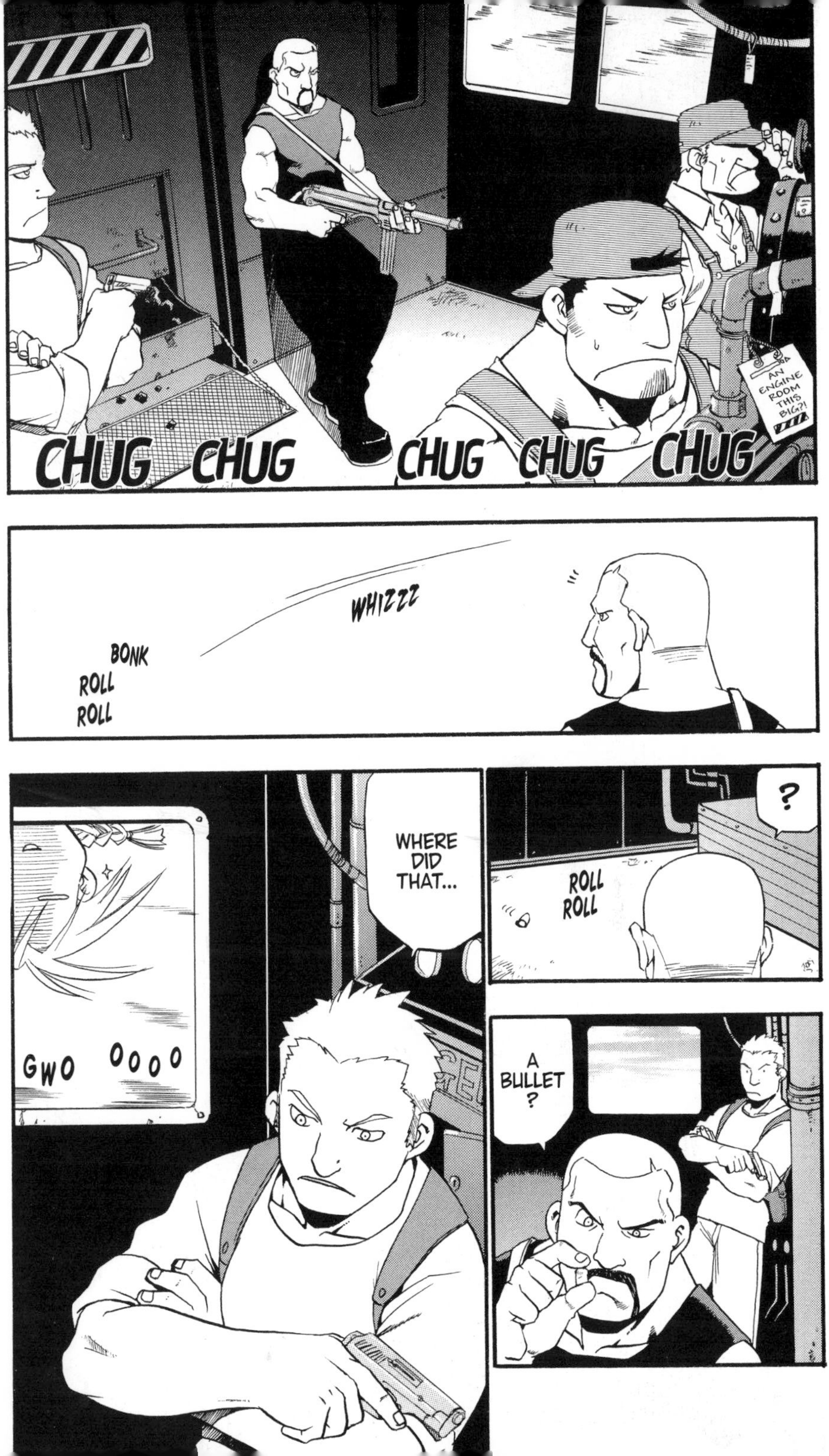

AN ENGINE ROOM THIS BIG?!
CHUG CHUG CHUG CHUG CHUG
WHIZZZ
BONK
ROLL
ROLL
?
ROLL ROLL
A BULLET?
WHERE DID THAT...
GWO OOOO

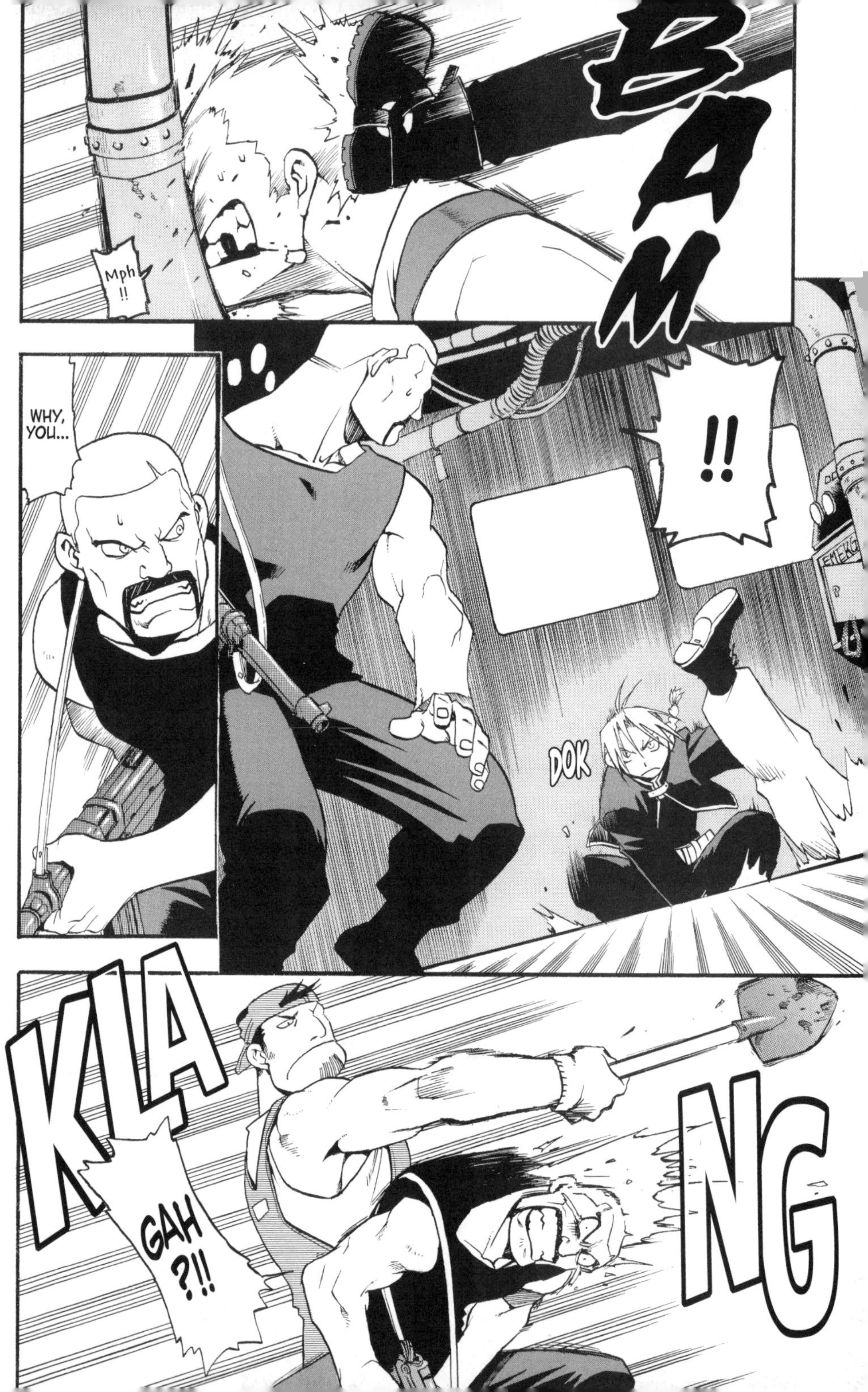
BAM
Mph !!
!!
DOK
WHY, YOU...
KLANG
GAH ?!!

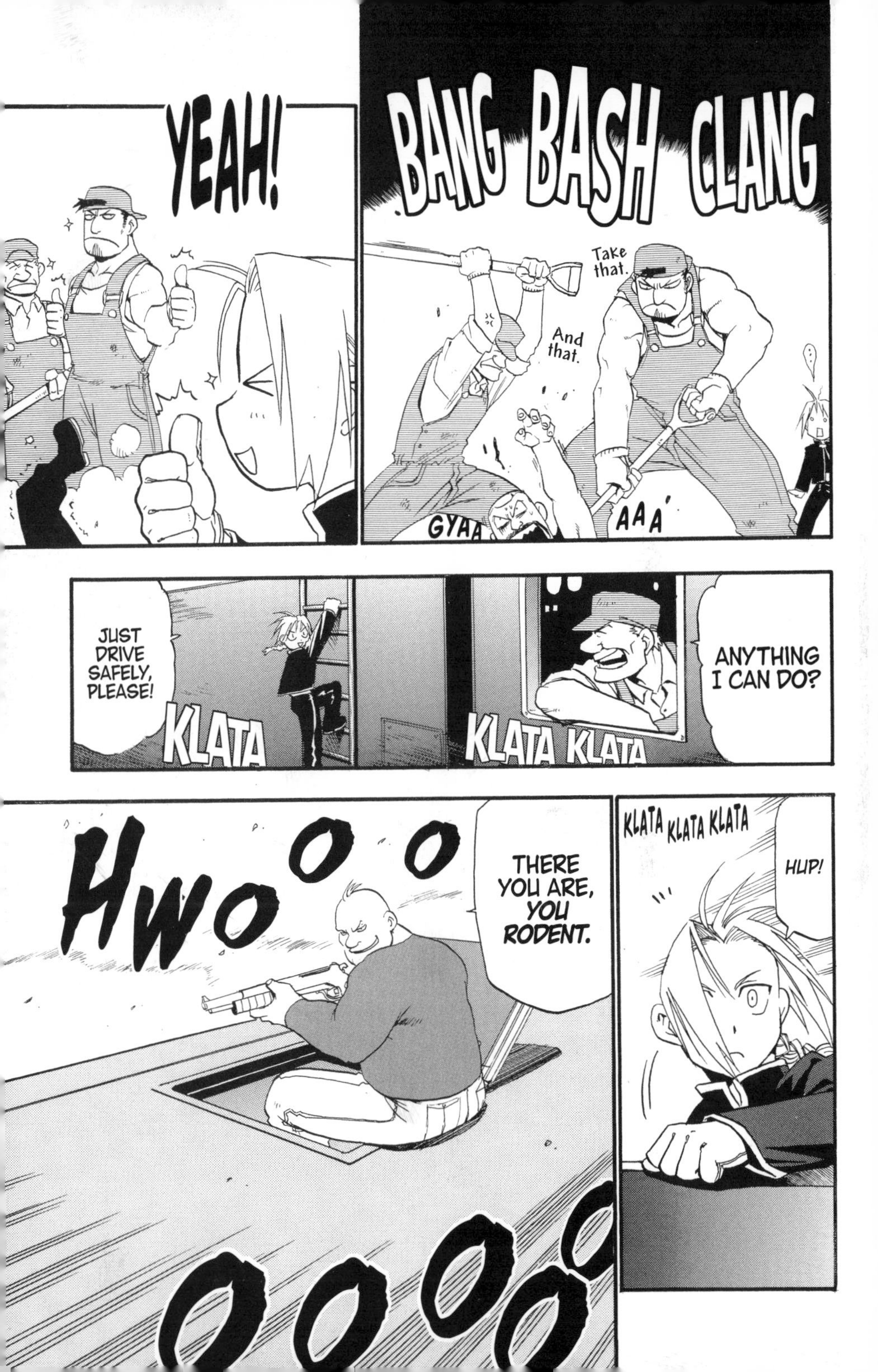
BANG BASH CLANG
Take that.
And that.
GYAA
AAA
YEAH!
ANYTHING I CAN DO?
KLATA KLATA
JUST DRIVE SAFELY, PLEASE!
KLATA
KLATA KLATA KLATA
HUP!
THERE YOU ARE, YOU RODENT.
Hwooo
ooooo

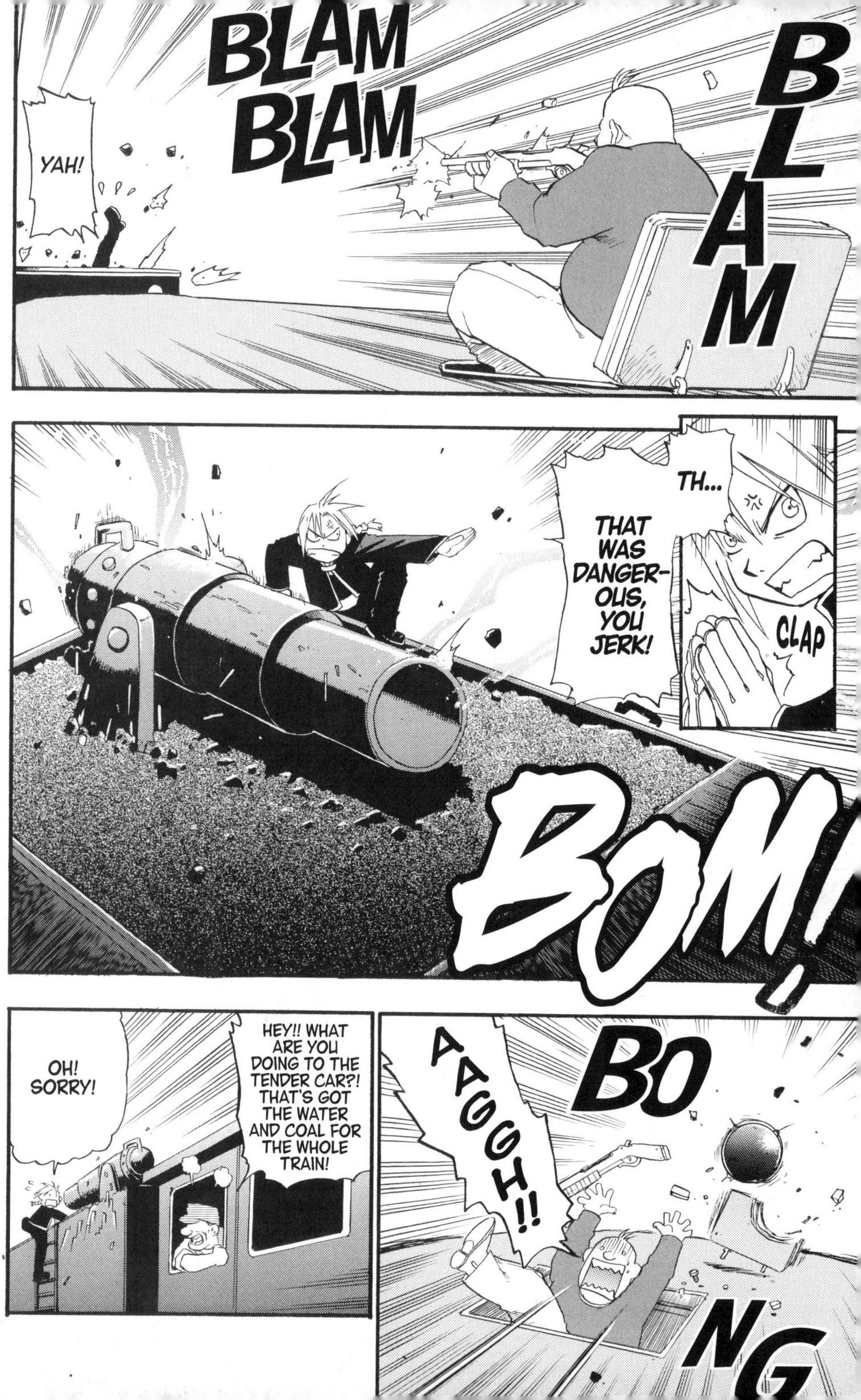
BLAM
BLAM BLAM
YAH!
TH...
THAT WAS DANGER-OUS, YOU JERK!
CLAP
BOM!
BO
AAGGH!!
NG
HEY!! WHAT ARE YOU DOING TO THE TENDER CAR?! THAT'S GOT THE WATER AND COAL FOR THE WHOLE TRAIN!
OH! SORRY!

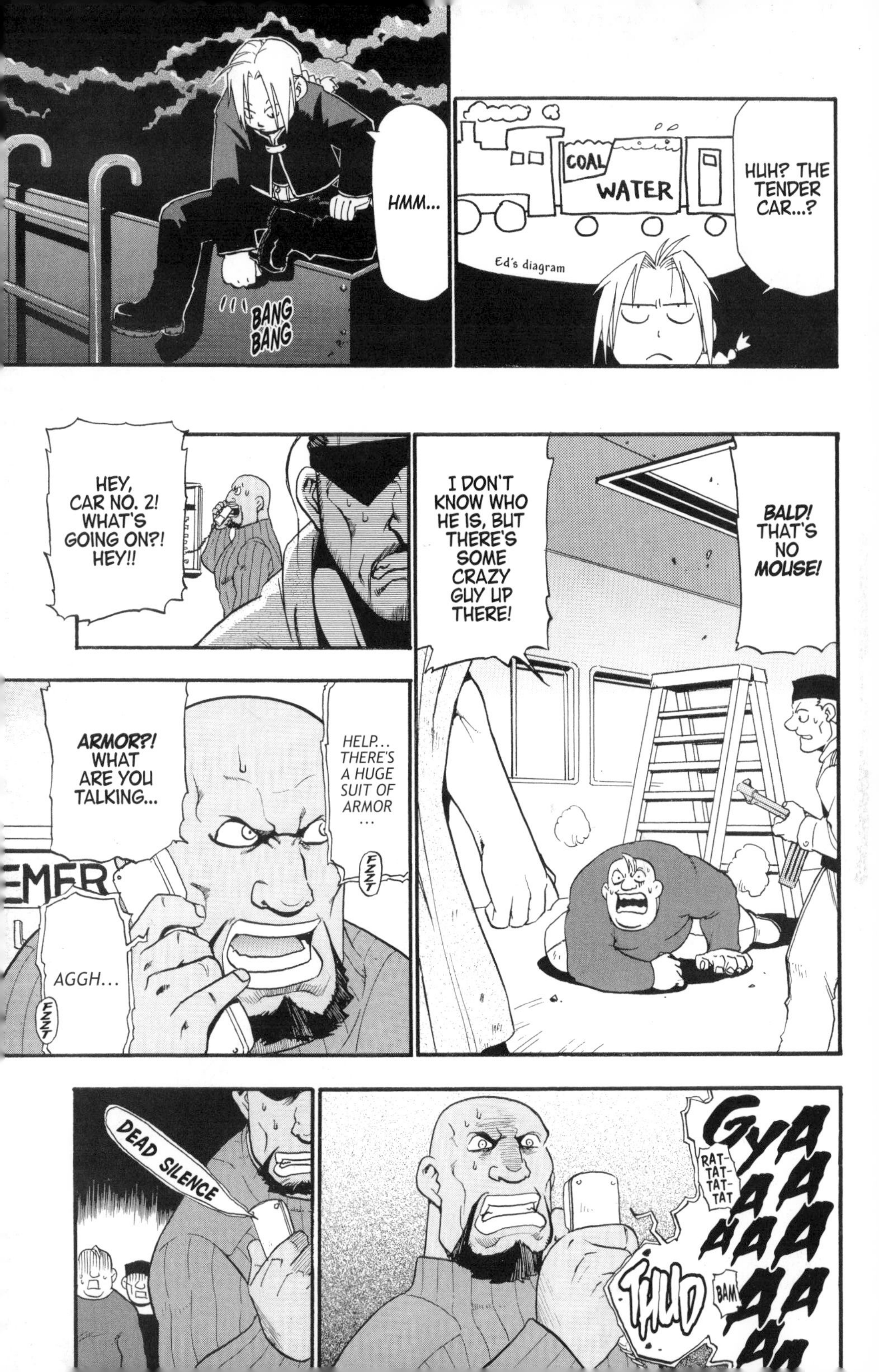
HUH? THE TENDER CAR...?
COAL
WATER
Ed's diagram
HMM...
BANG BANG
BALD! THAT'S NO MOUSE!
I DON'T KNOW WHO HE IS, BUT THERE'S SOME CRAZY GUY UP THERE!
HEY, CAR NO. 2! WHAT'S GOING ON?! HEY!!
HELP... THERE'S A HUGE SUIT OF ARMOR ...
FZZT
ARMOR?! WHAT ARE YOU TALKING...
EMER
AGGH...
FZZT
GYAAAAAAAAAAAAA
RAT-TAT-TAT-TAT
BAM
THUD
DEAD SILENCE

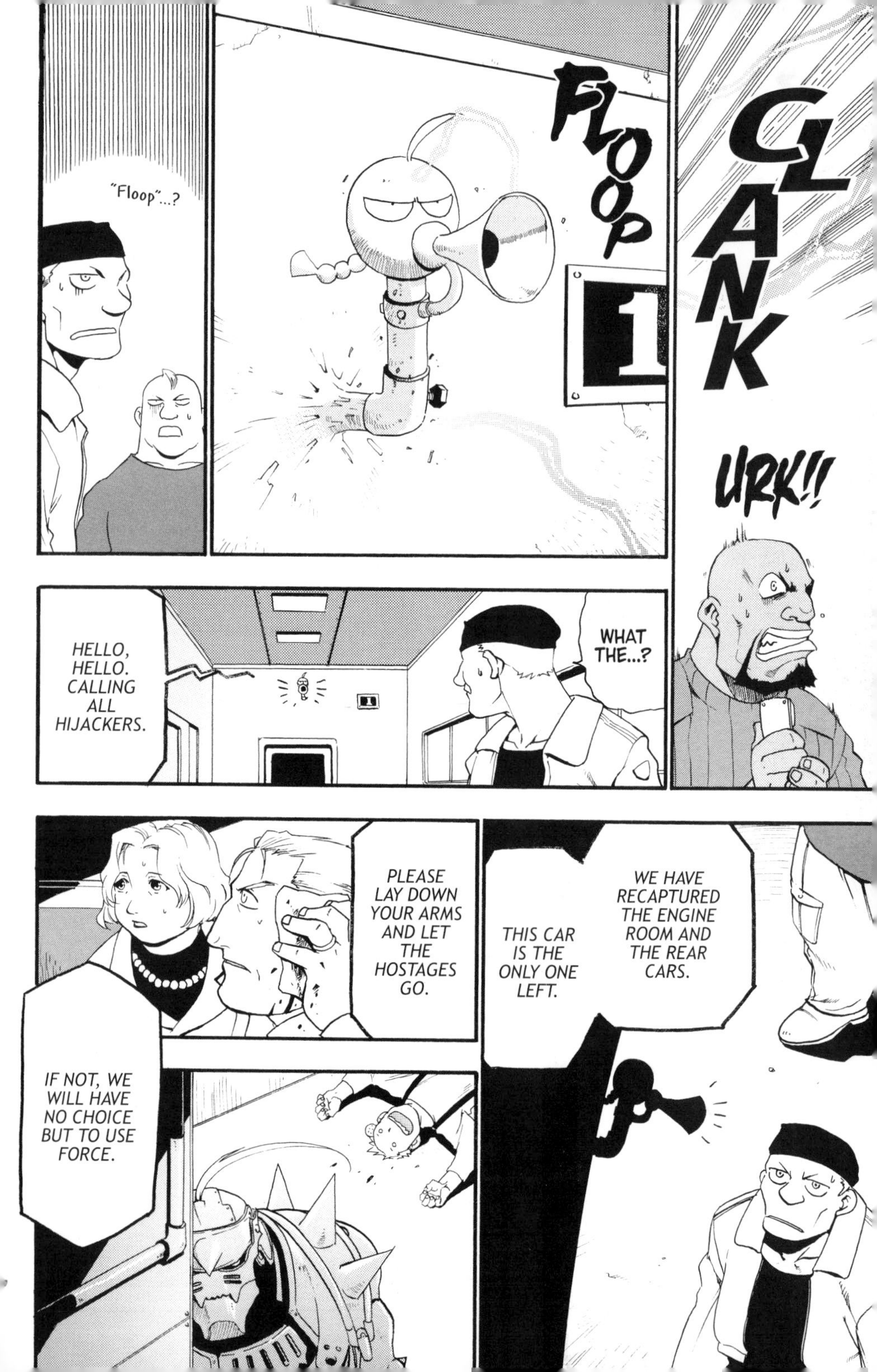
CLANK
URK!!
FLOOP
"Floop"...?
WHAT THE...?
HELLO, HELLO. CALLING ALL HIJACKERS.
WE HAVE RECAPTURED THE ENGINE ROOM AND THE REAR CARS.
THIS CAR IS THE ONLY ONE LEFT.
PLEASE LAY DOWN YOUR ARMS AND LET THE HOSTAGES GO.
IF NOT, WE WILL HAVE NO CHOICE BUT TO USE FORCE.

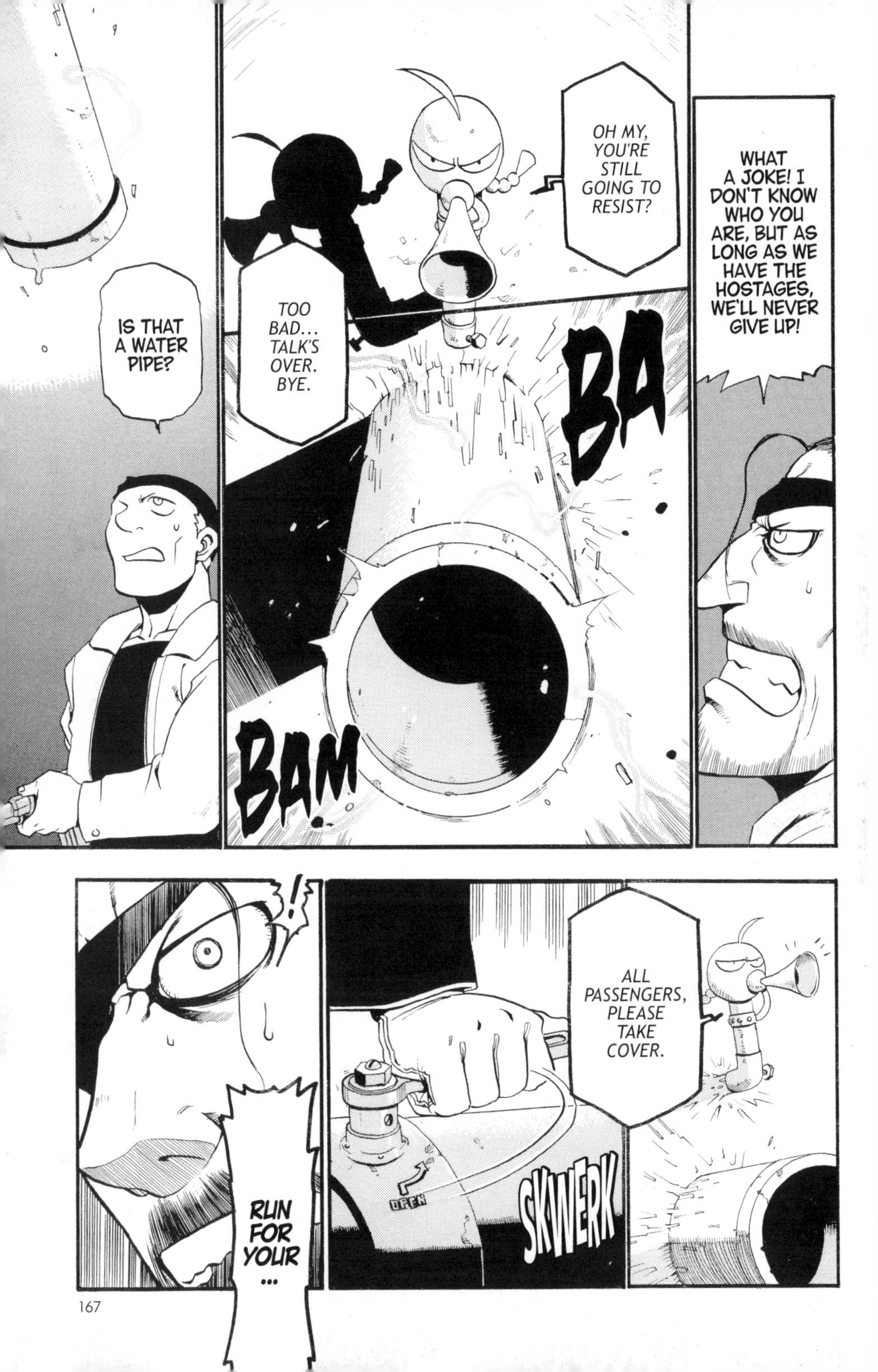
WHAT A JOKE! I DON'T KNOW WHO YOU ARE, BUT AS LONG AS WE HAVE THE HOSTAGES, WE'LL NEVER GIVE UP!
OH MY, YOU'RE STILL GOING TO RESIST?
TOO BAD... TALK'S OVER. BYE.
BA
BAM
IS THAT A WATER PIPE?
ALL PASSENGERS, PLEASE TAKE COVER.
SKWERK
!
RUN FOR YOUR ...

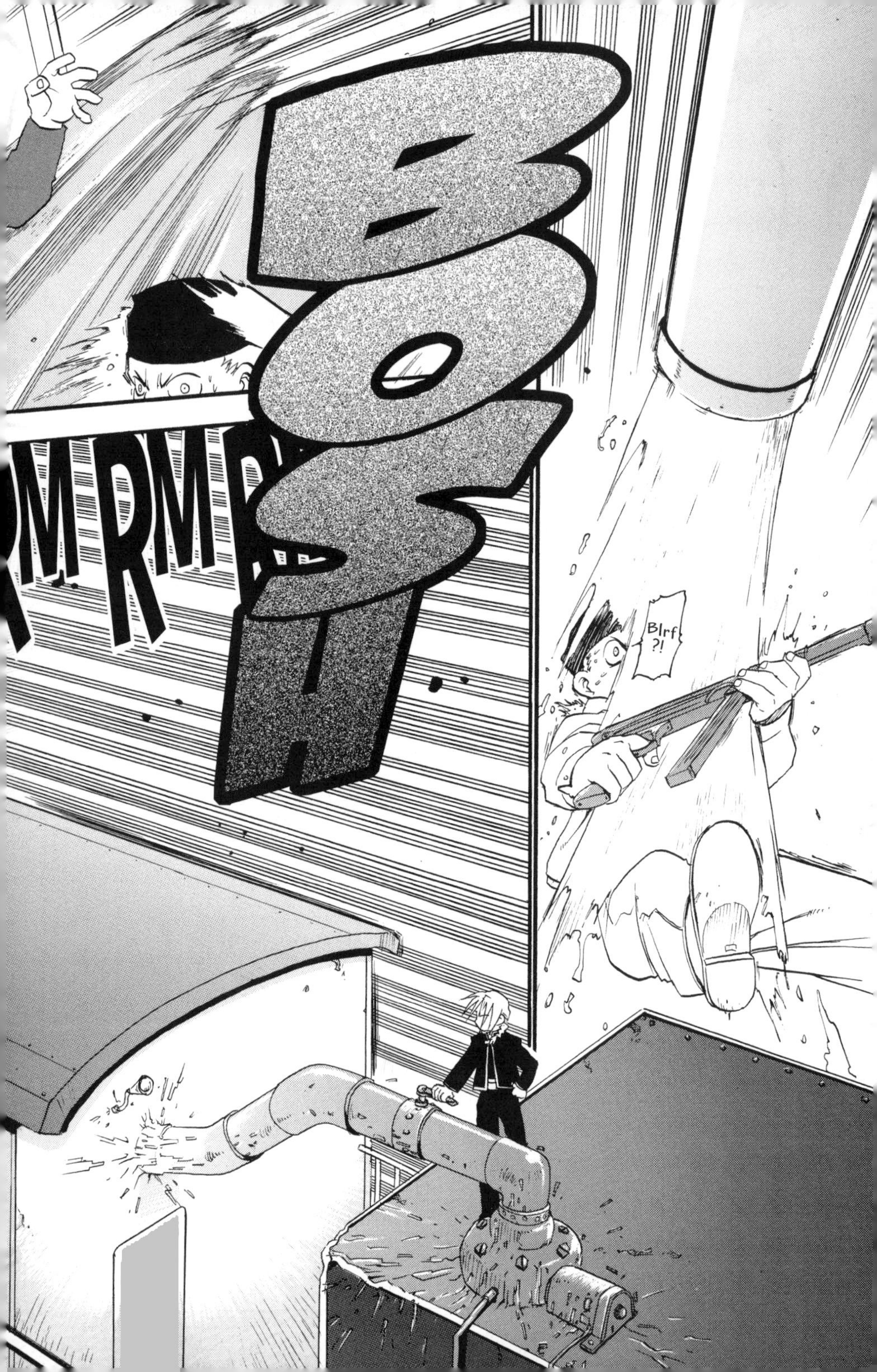
BOSH
Blrf ?!
MRM

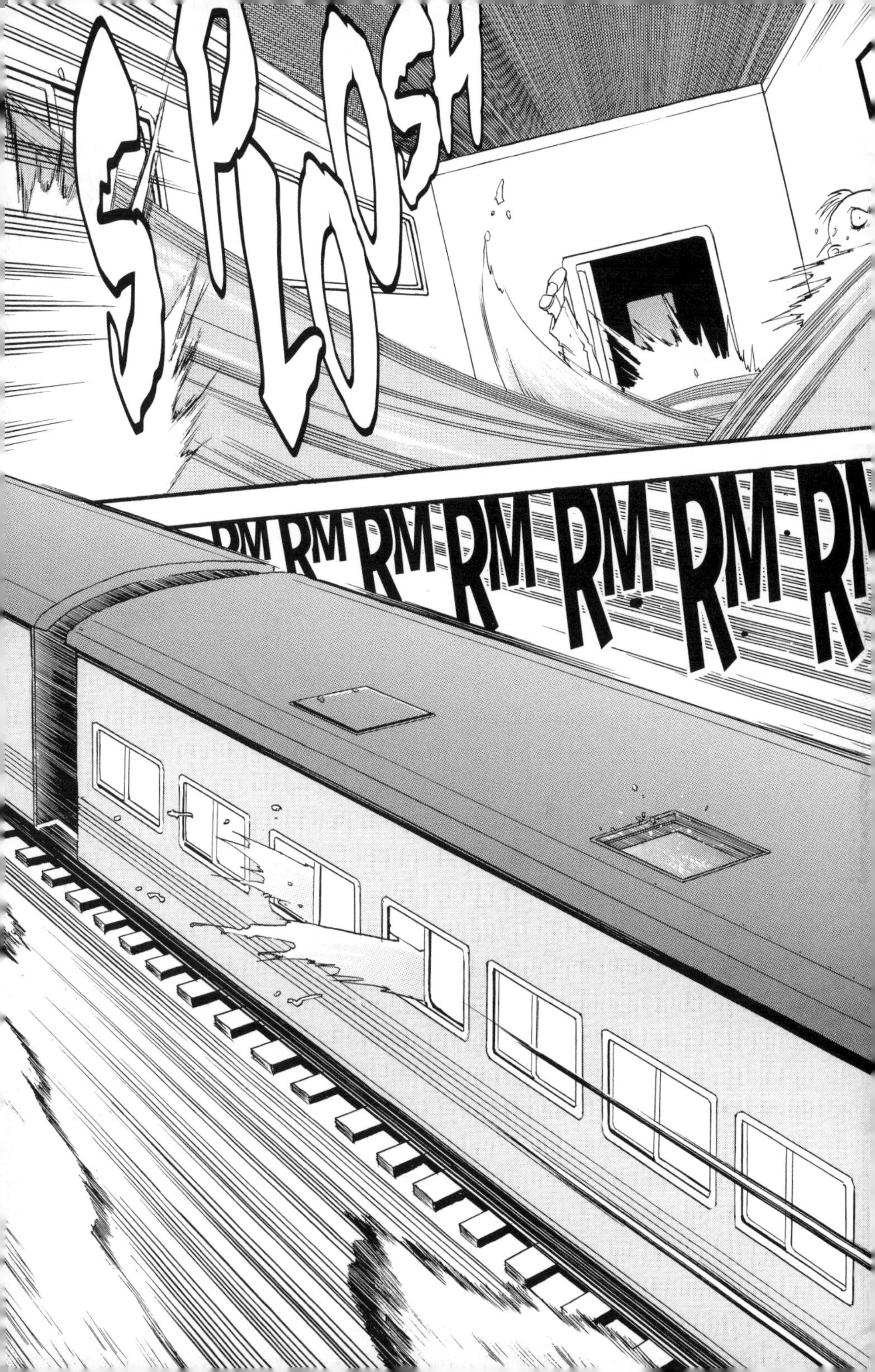
SPLOOSH
RM RM RM RM RM RM RM

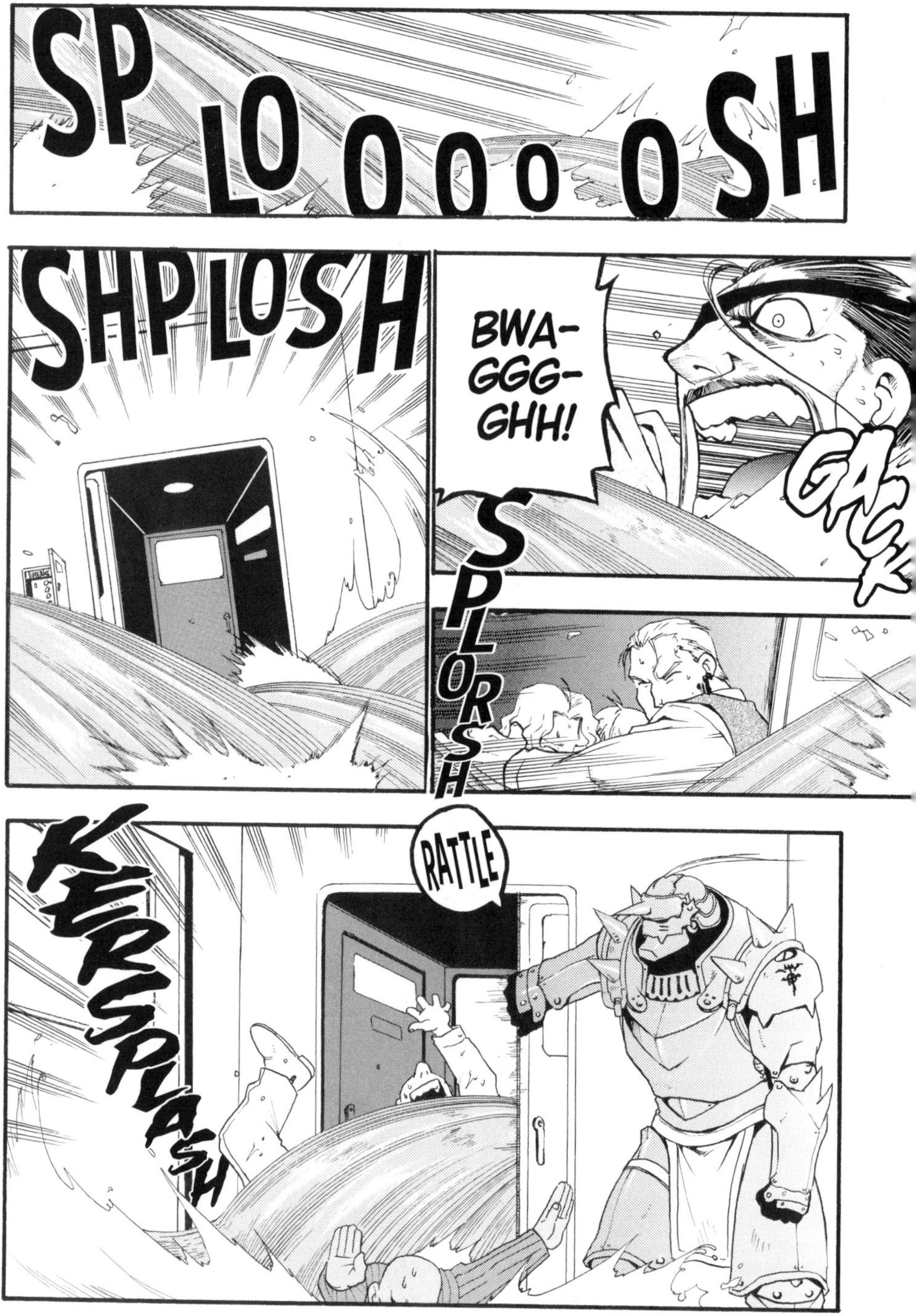
SPLOOOOOSH
BWA-GGG-GHH!
GACK
SPLORSH
SHPLOSH
RATTLE
KERSPLASH

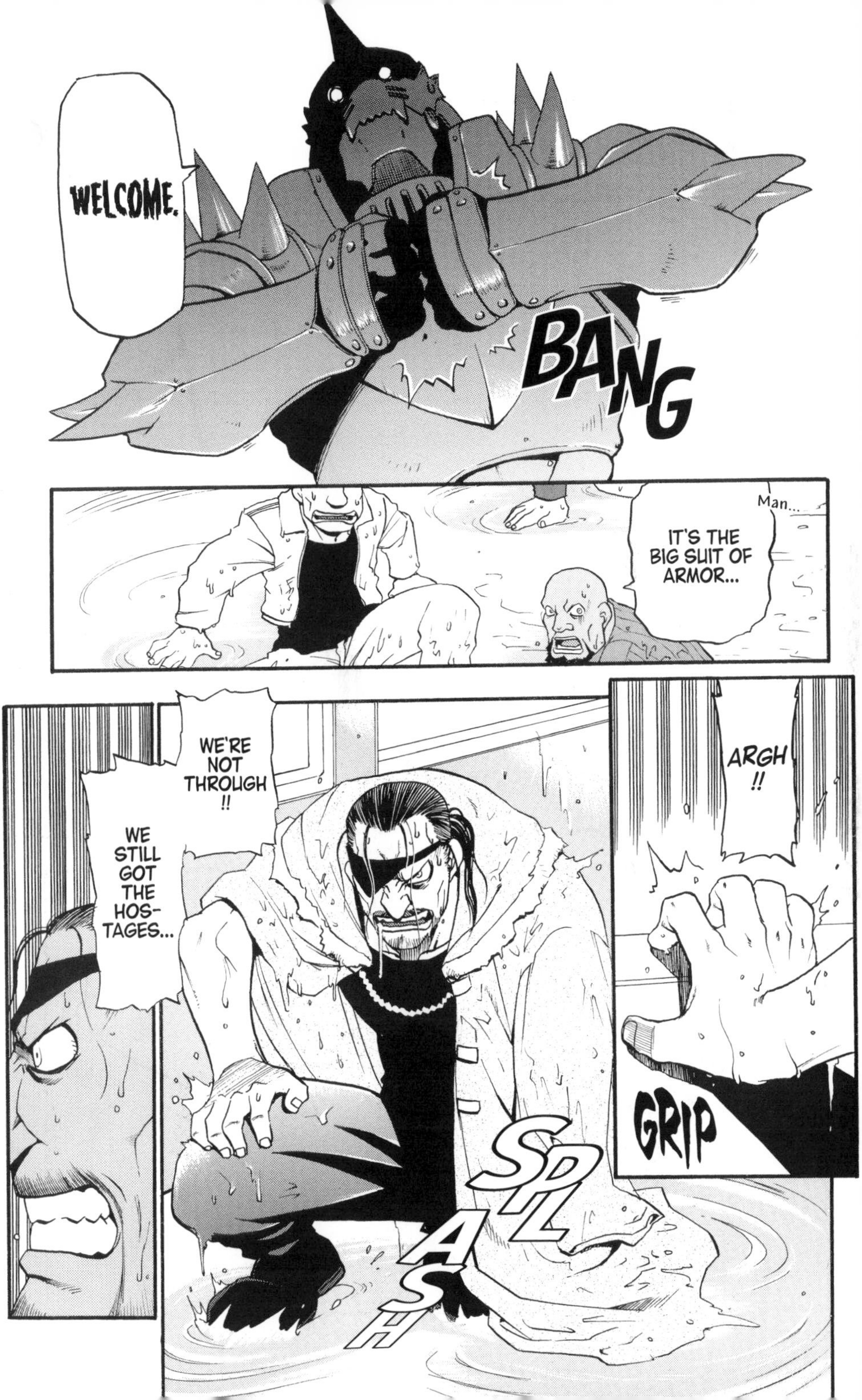
WELCOME.
BANG
Man...
IT'S THE BIG SUIT OF ARMOR...
ARGH!!
GRIP
WE'RE NOT THROUGH!!
WE STILL GOT THE HOS-TAGES...
SPLASH

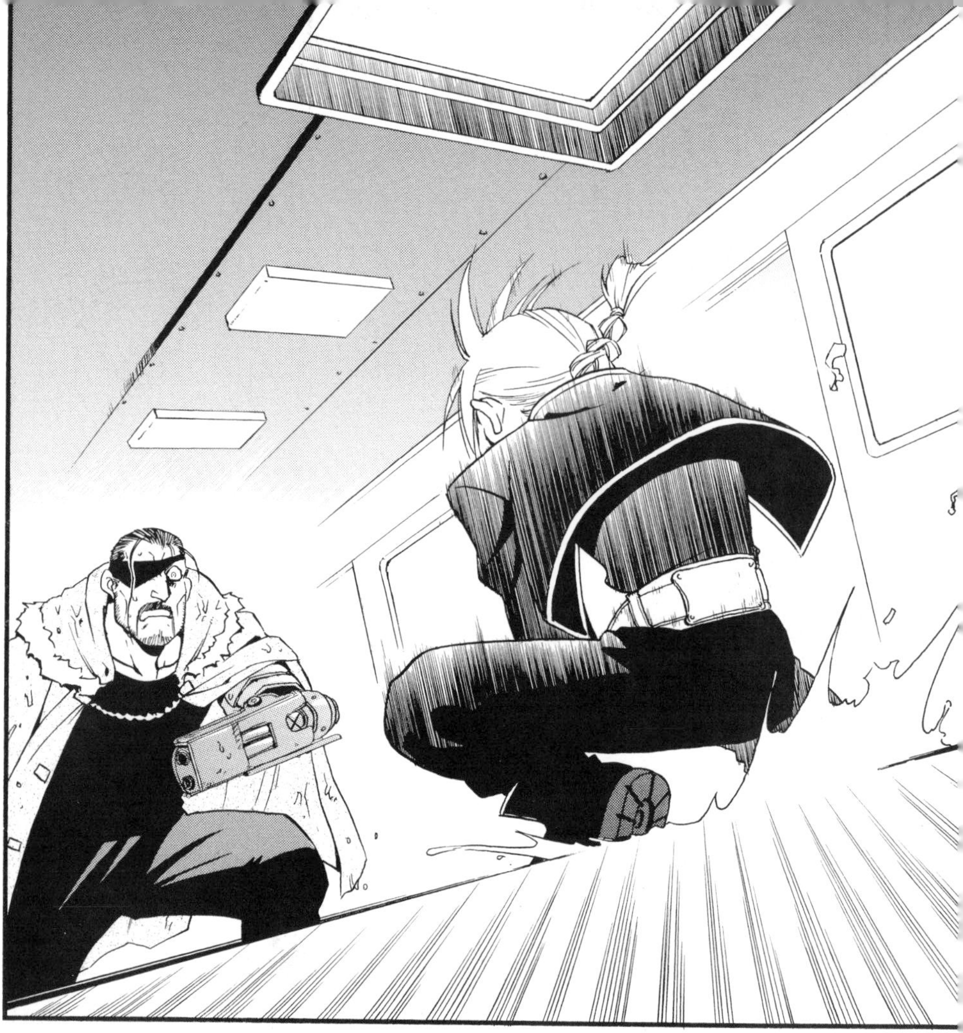

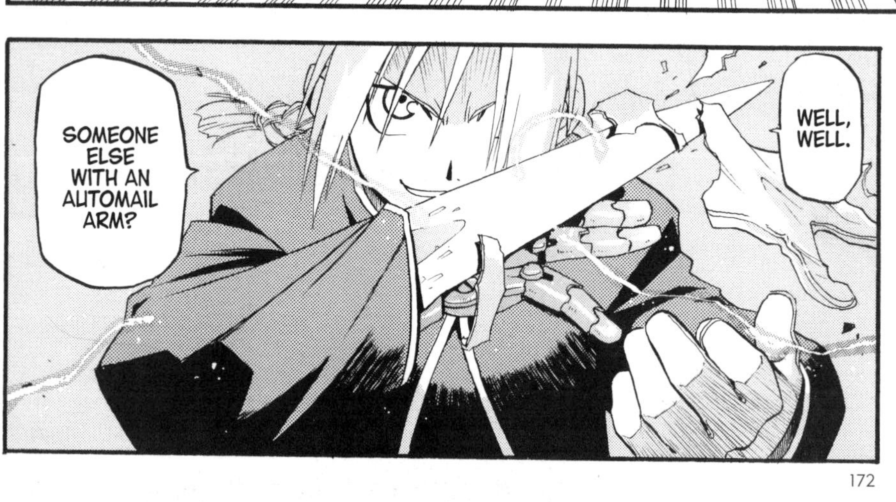
WELL, WELL.
SOMEONE ELSE WITH AN AUTOMAIL ARM?

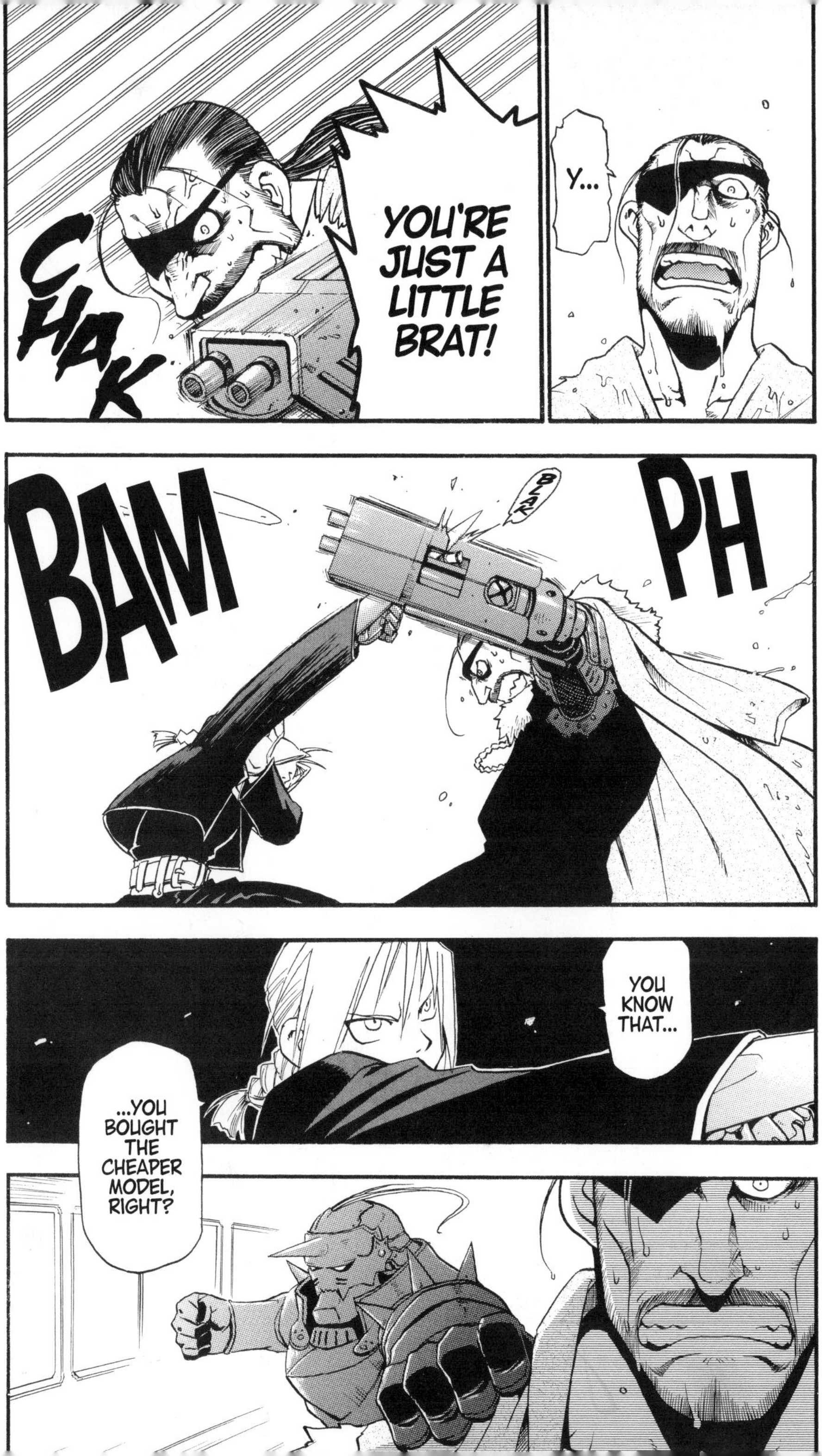
Y...
YOU'RE JUST A LITTLE BRAT!
CHAK
BAMPH
BLAK
YOU KNOW THAT...
...YOU BOUGHT THE CHEAPER MODEL, RIGHT?

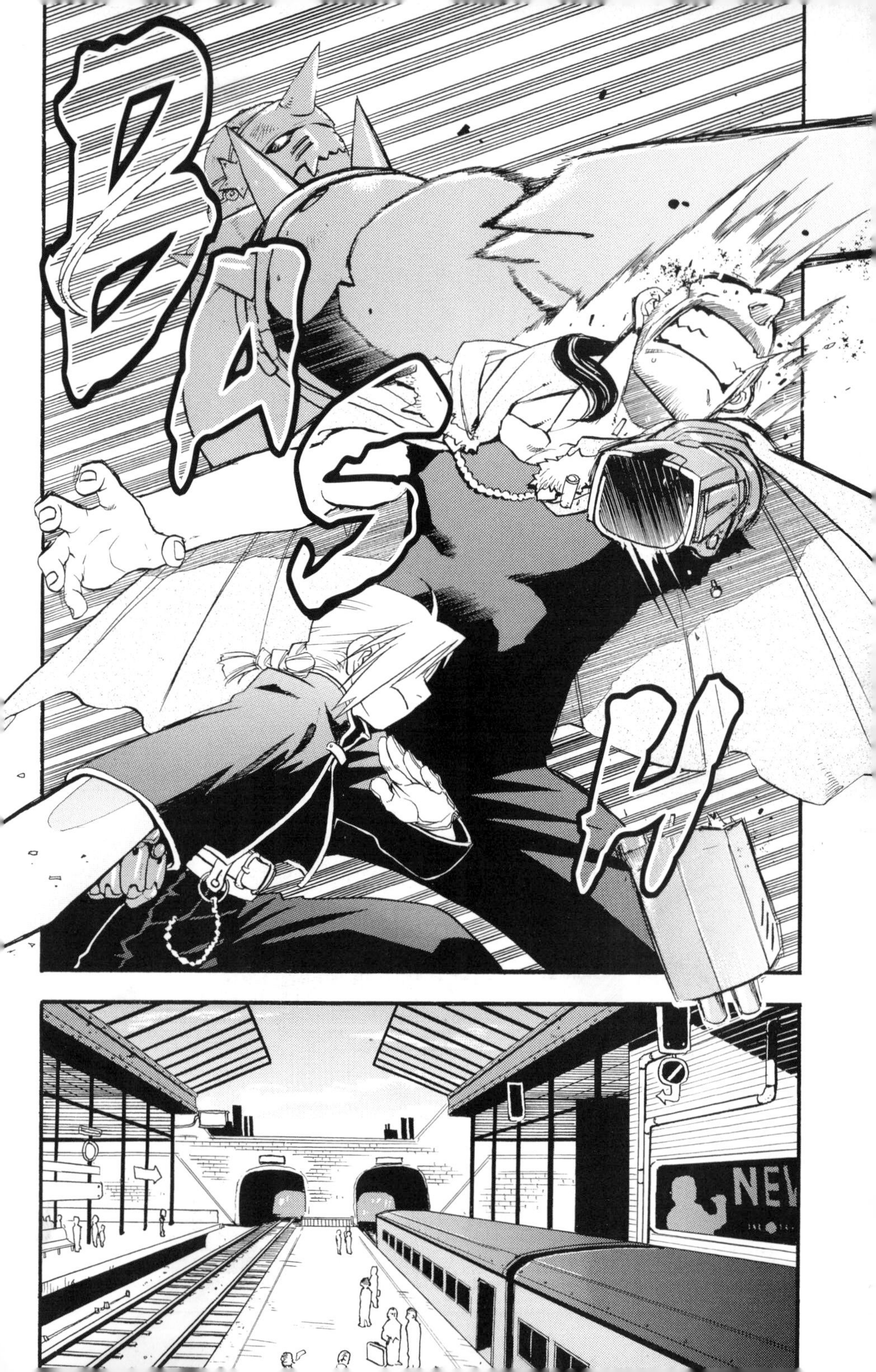
BASH

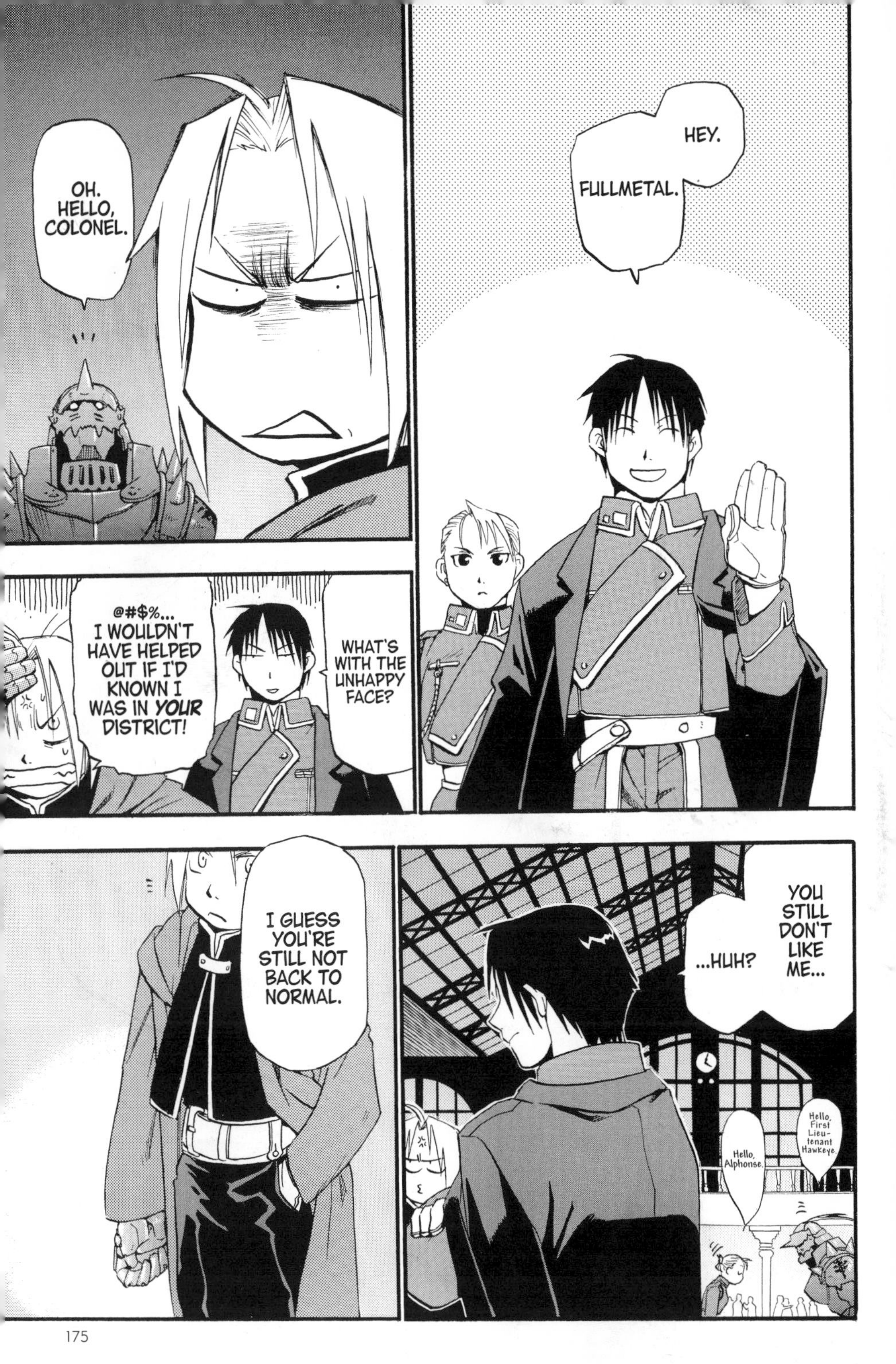
HEY.
FULLMETAL.
OH. HELLO, COLONEL.
WHAT'S WITH THE UNHAPPY FACE?
@#$%... I WOULDN'T HAVE HELPED OUT IF I'D KNOWN I WAS IN *YOUR* DISTRICT!
YOU STILL DON'T LIKE ME...
...HUH?
Hello, First Lieutenant Hawkeye.
Hello, Alphonse.
I GUESS YOU'RE STILL NOT BACK TO NORMAL.

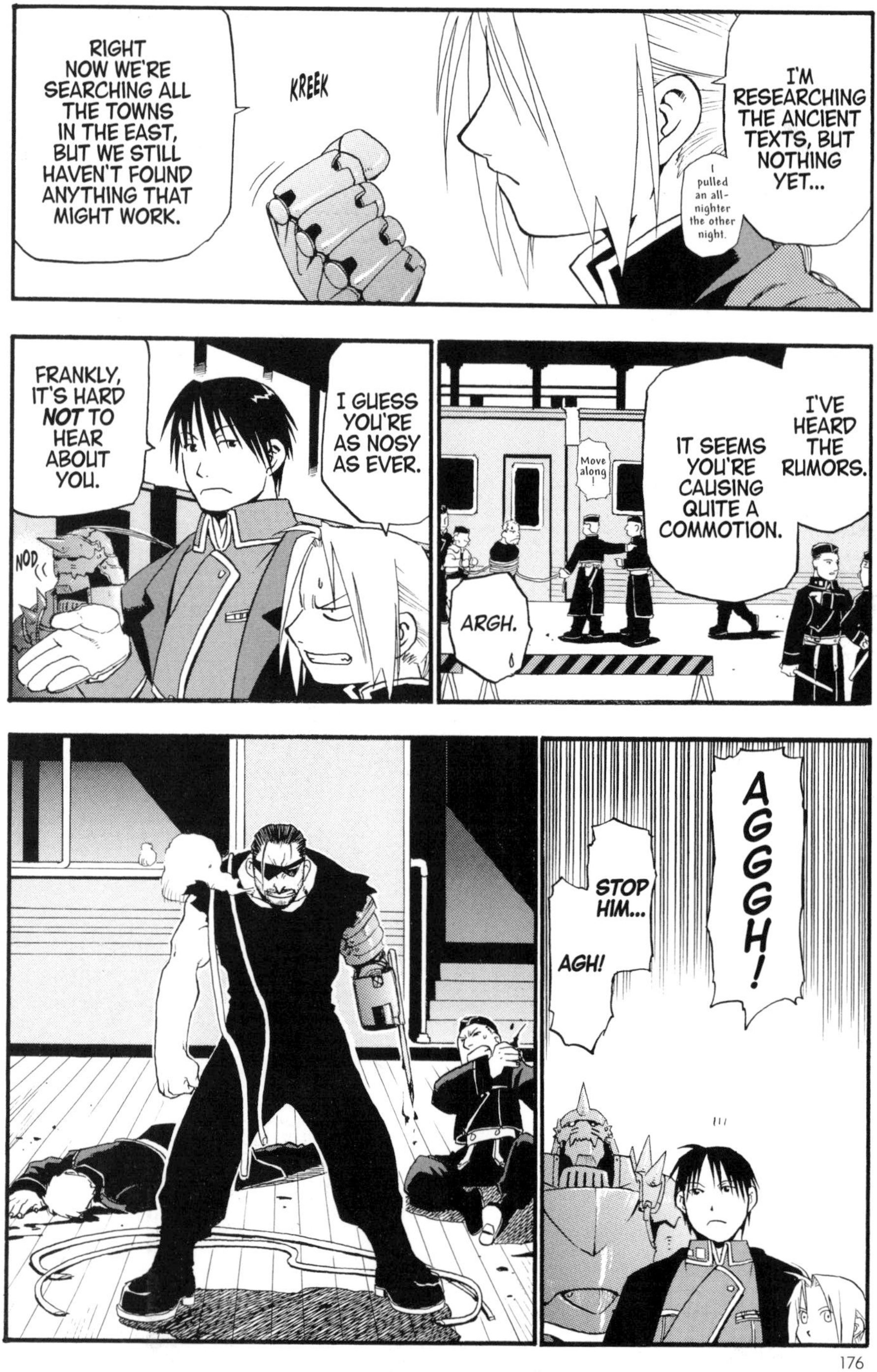
I'M RESEARCHING THE ANCIENT TEXTS, BUT NOTHING YET...
I pulled an all-nighter the other night.
KREEK
RIGHT NOW WE'RE SEARCHING ALL THE TOWNS IN THE EAST, BUT WE STILL HAVEN'T FOUND ANYTHING THAT MIGHT WORK.
I'VE HEARD THE RUMORS.
IT SEEMS YOU'RE CAUSING QUITE A COMMOTION.
Move along!
ARGH.
I GUESS YOU'RE AS NOSY AS EVER.
FRANKLY, IT'S HARD **NOT** TO HEAR ABOUT YOU.
NOD
AGGGH!
STOP HIM...
AGH!

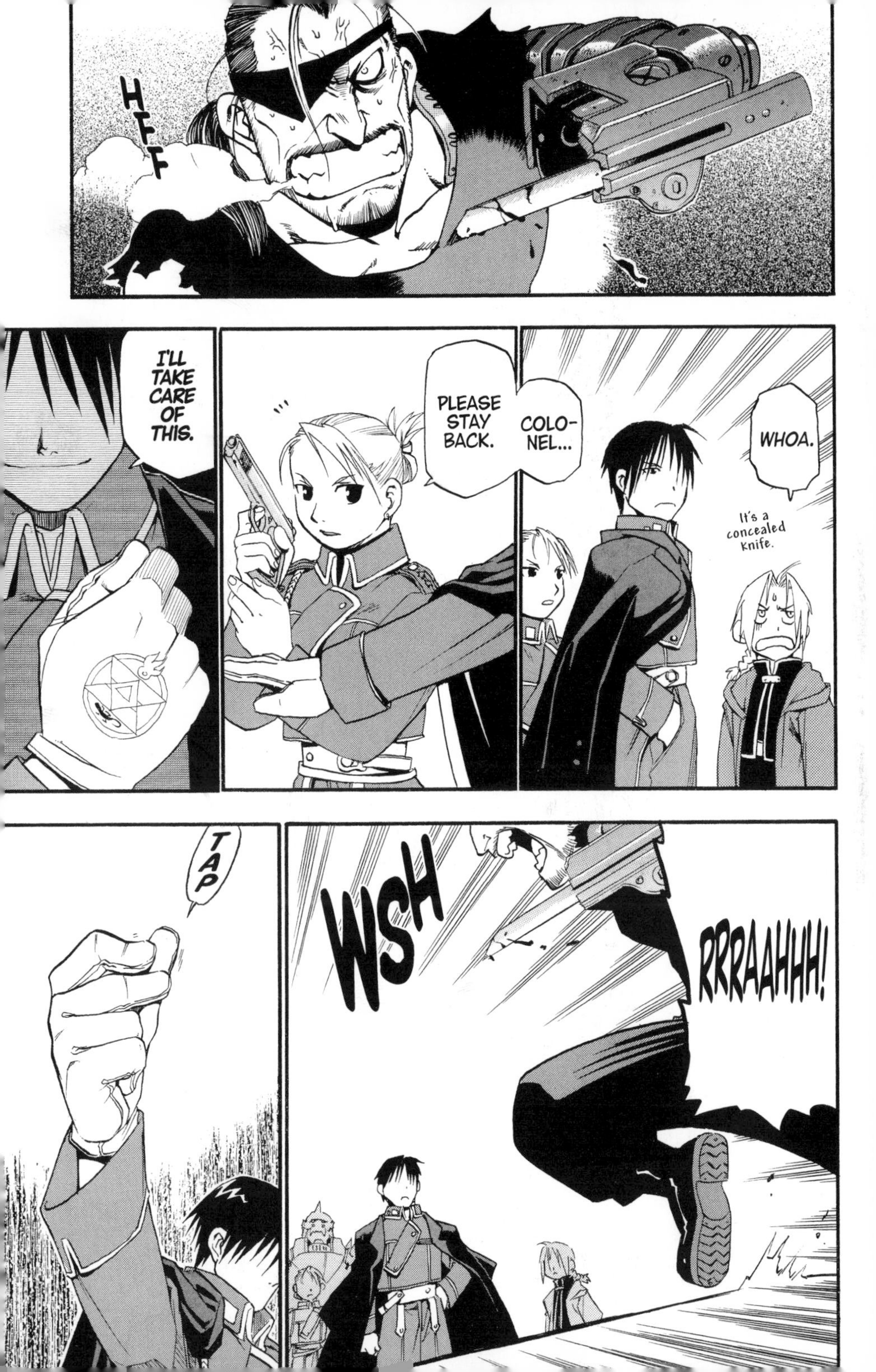
HFF
WHOA.
It's a concealed knife.
COLO-NEL...
PLEASE STAY BACK.
I'LL TAKE CARE OF THIS.
WSH
RRRAAHHH!
TAP

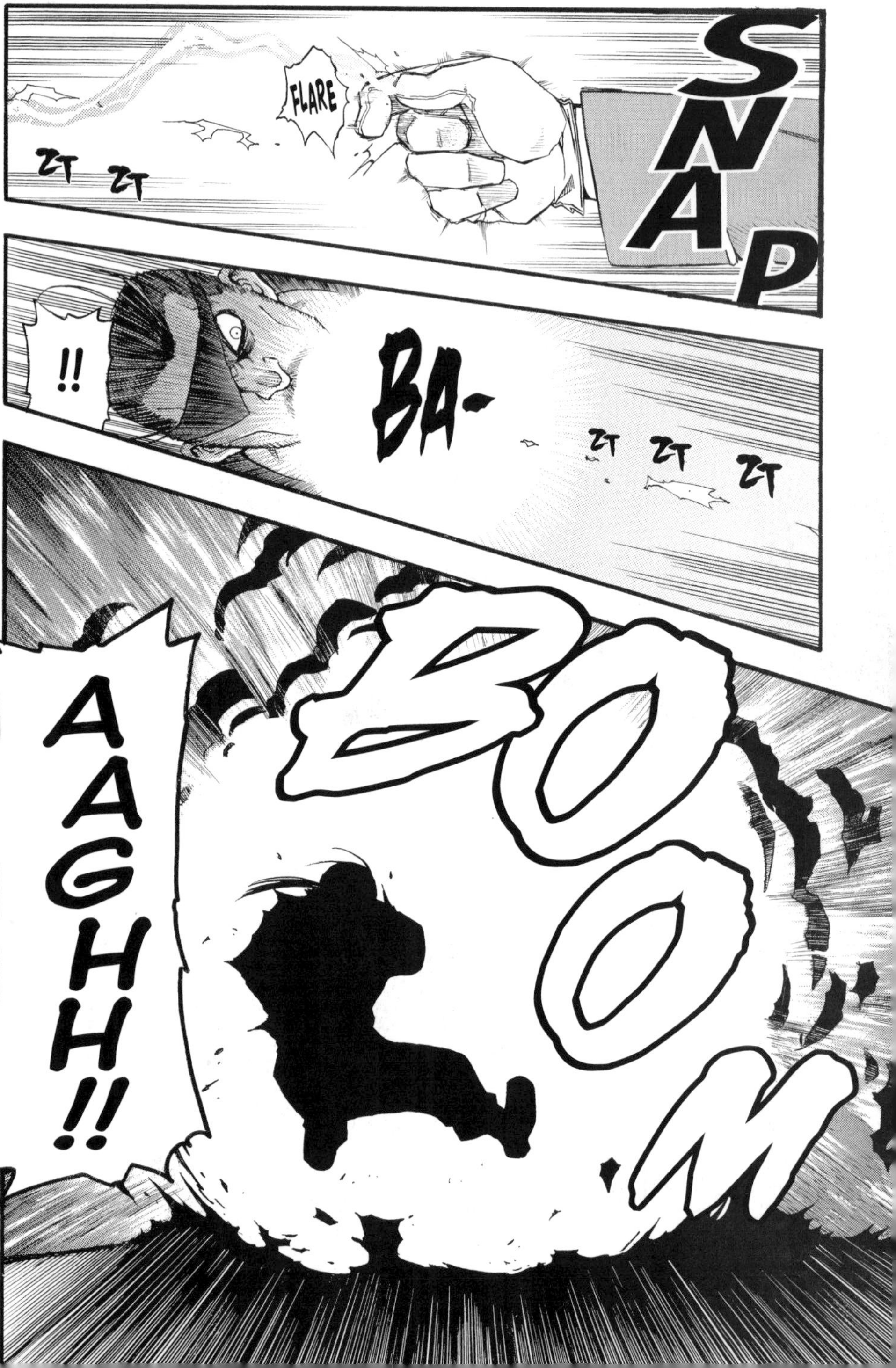
SNAP
FLARE
ZT ZT
BA-
ZT ZT ZT
!!
BOOM
AAGHH!!

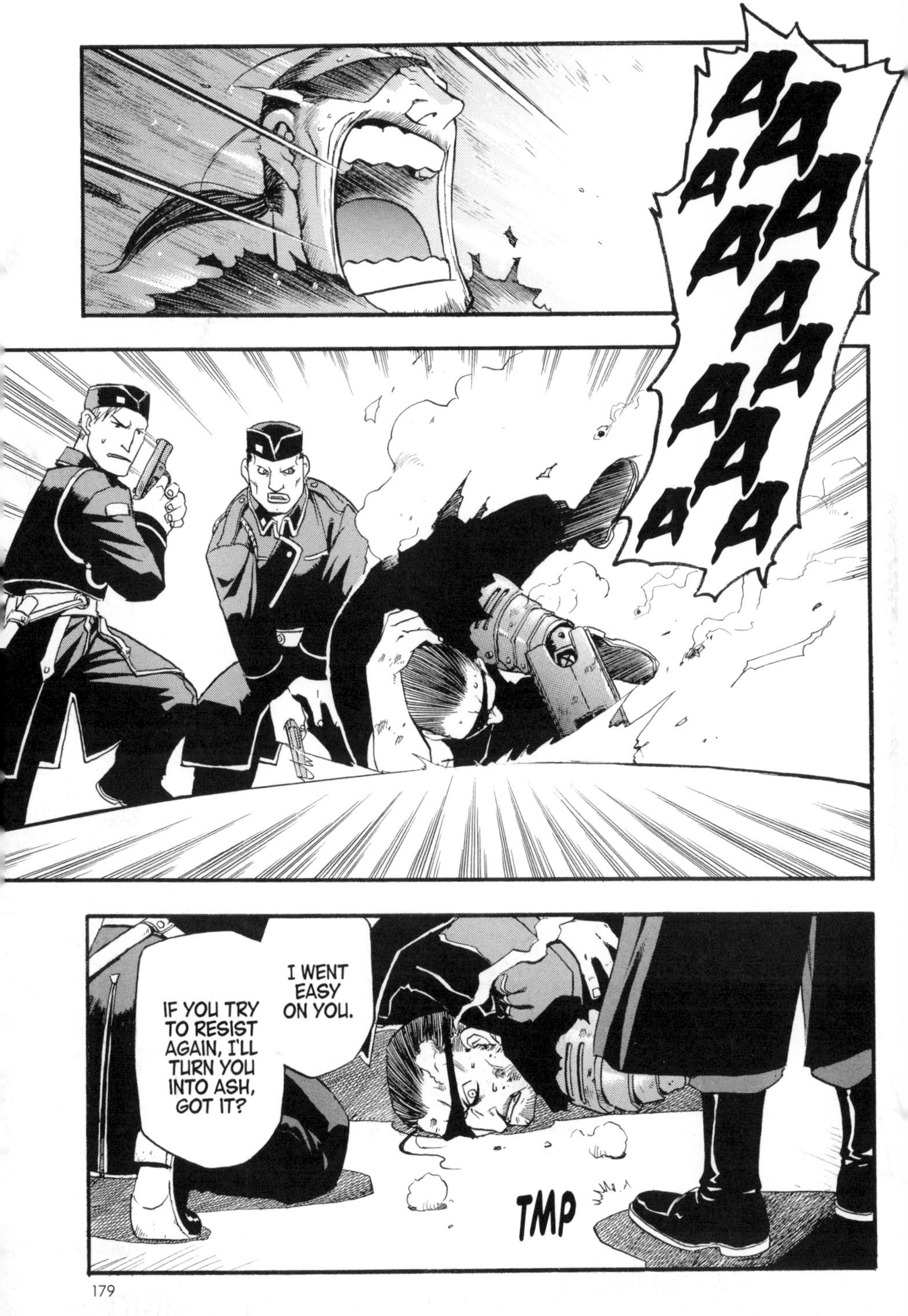
AAAAAAAAAAAAAAAAA
I WENT EASY ON YOU.
IF YOU TRY TO RESIST AGAIN, I'LL TURN YOU INTO ASH, GOT IT?
TMP

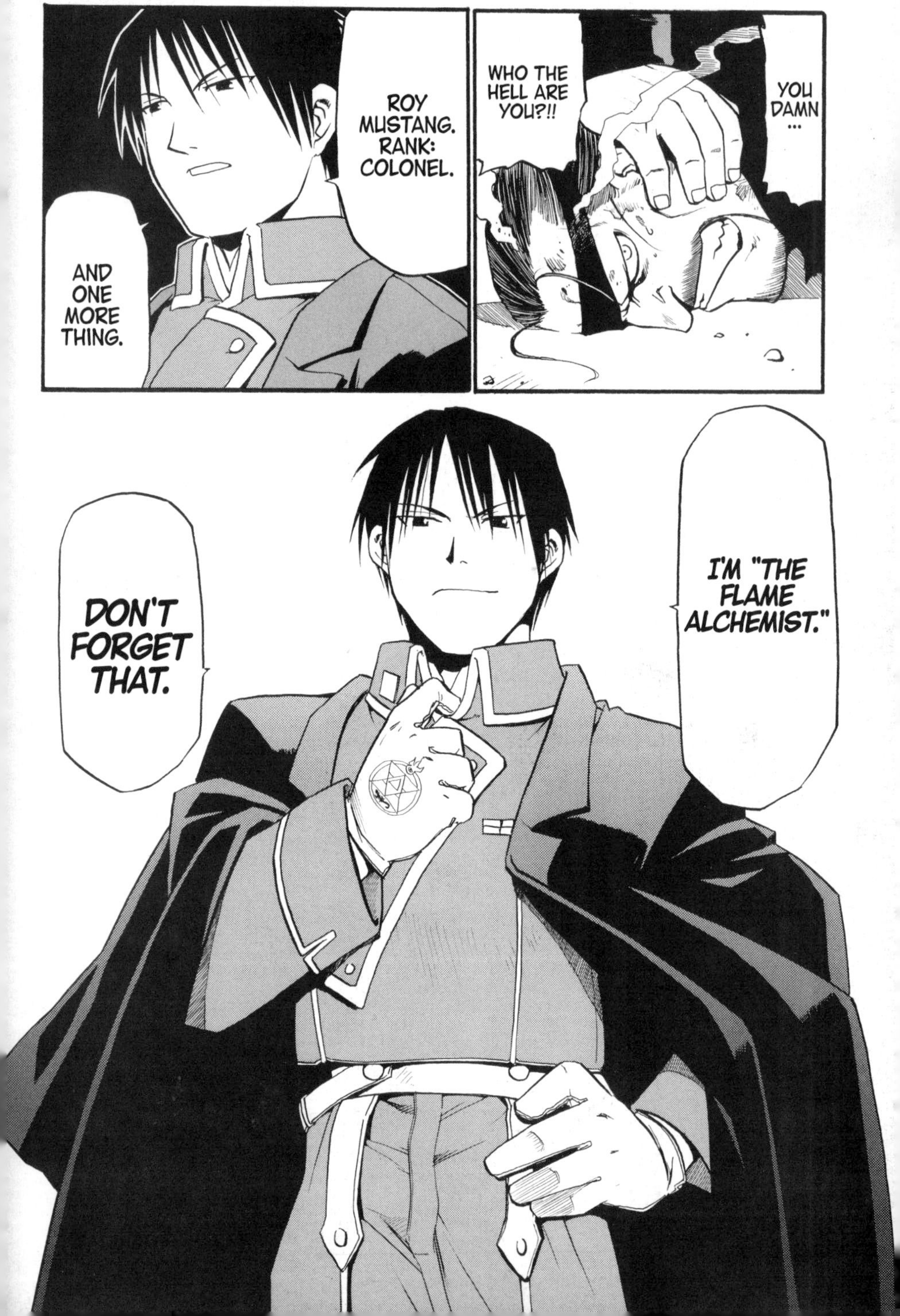
YOU DAMN ...
WHO THE HELL ARE YOU?!!
ROY MUSTANG. RANK: COLONEL.
AND ONE MORE THING.
I'M "THE FLAME ALCHEMIST."
DON'T FORGET THAT.

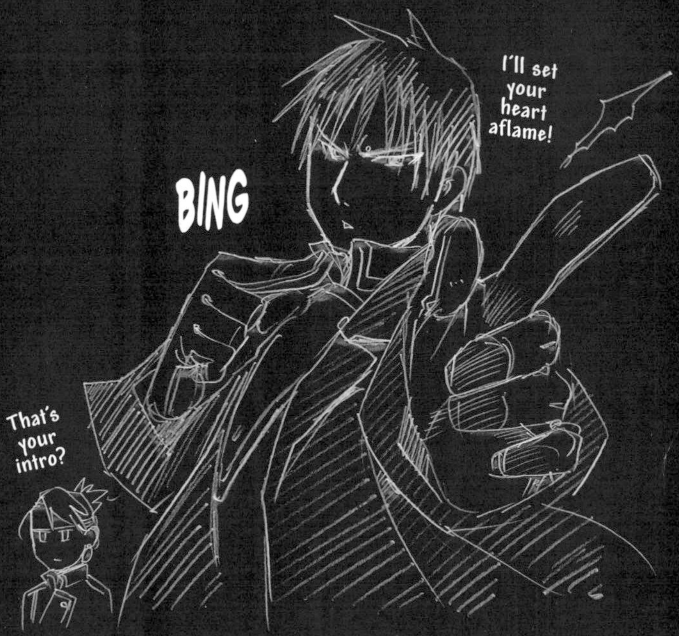
I'll set your heart aflame!
BING
That's your intro?

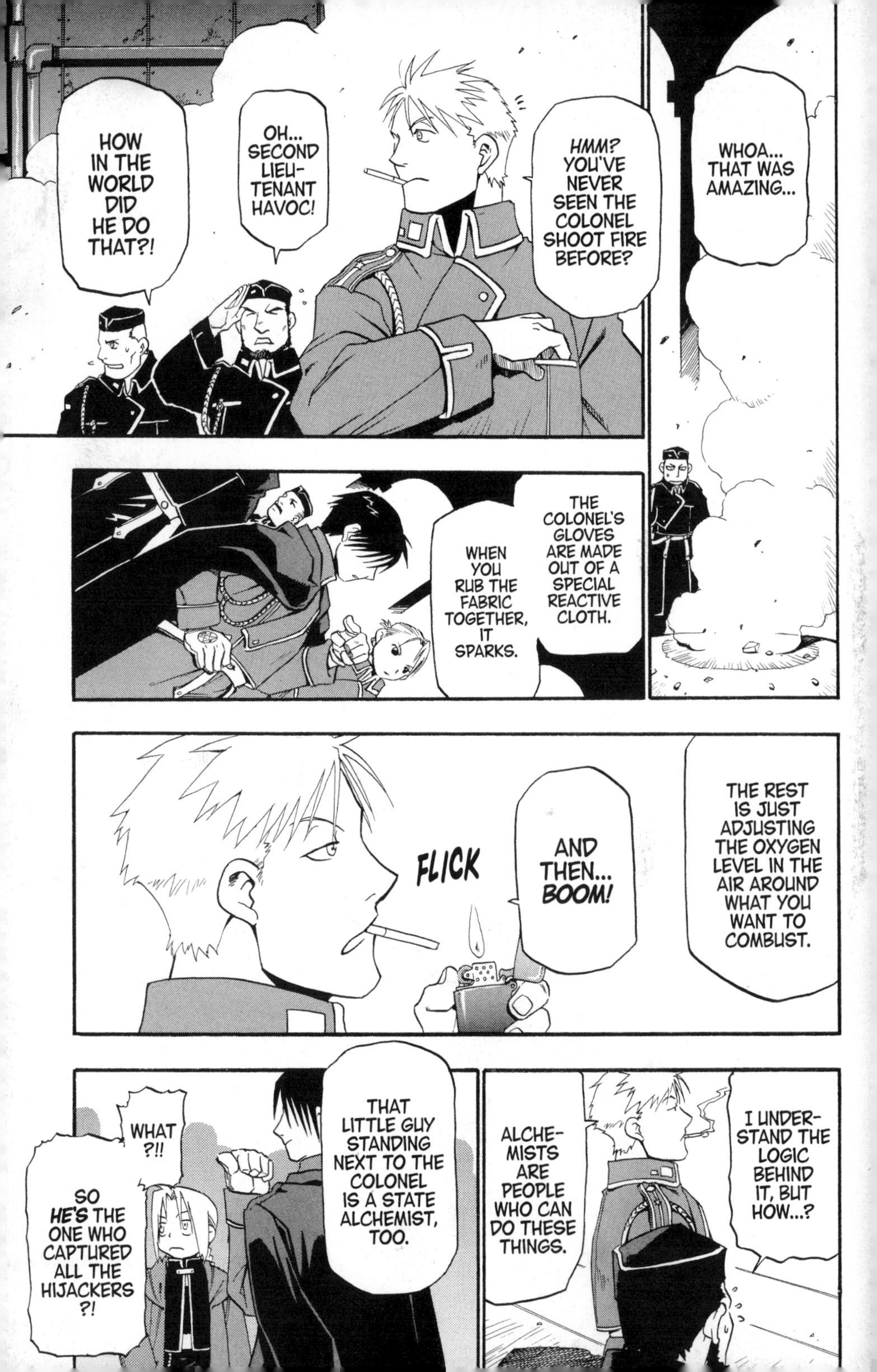
WHOA... THAT WAS AMAZING...
HMM? YOU'VE NEVER SEEN THE COLONEL SHOOT FIRE BEFORE?
OH... SECOND LIEU-TENANT HAVOC!
HOW IN THE WORLD DID HE DO THAT?!
THE COLONEL'S GLOVES ARE MADE OUT OF A SPECIAL REACTIVE CLOTH.
WHEN YOU RUB THE FABRIC TOGETHER, IT SPARKS.
THE REST IS JUST ADJUSTING THE OXYGEN LEVEL IN THE AIR AROUND WHAT YOU WANT TO COMBUST.
AND THEN... BOOM!
FLICK
I UNDER-STAND THE LOGIC BEHIND IT, BUT HOW...?
ALCHE-MISTS ARE PEOPLE WHO CAN DO THESE THINGS.
THAT LITTLE GUY STANDING NEXT TO THE COLONEL IS A STATE ALCHEMIST, TOO.
WHAT?!!
SO HE'S THE ONE WHO CAPTURED ALL THE HIJACKERS?!

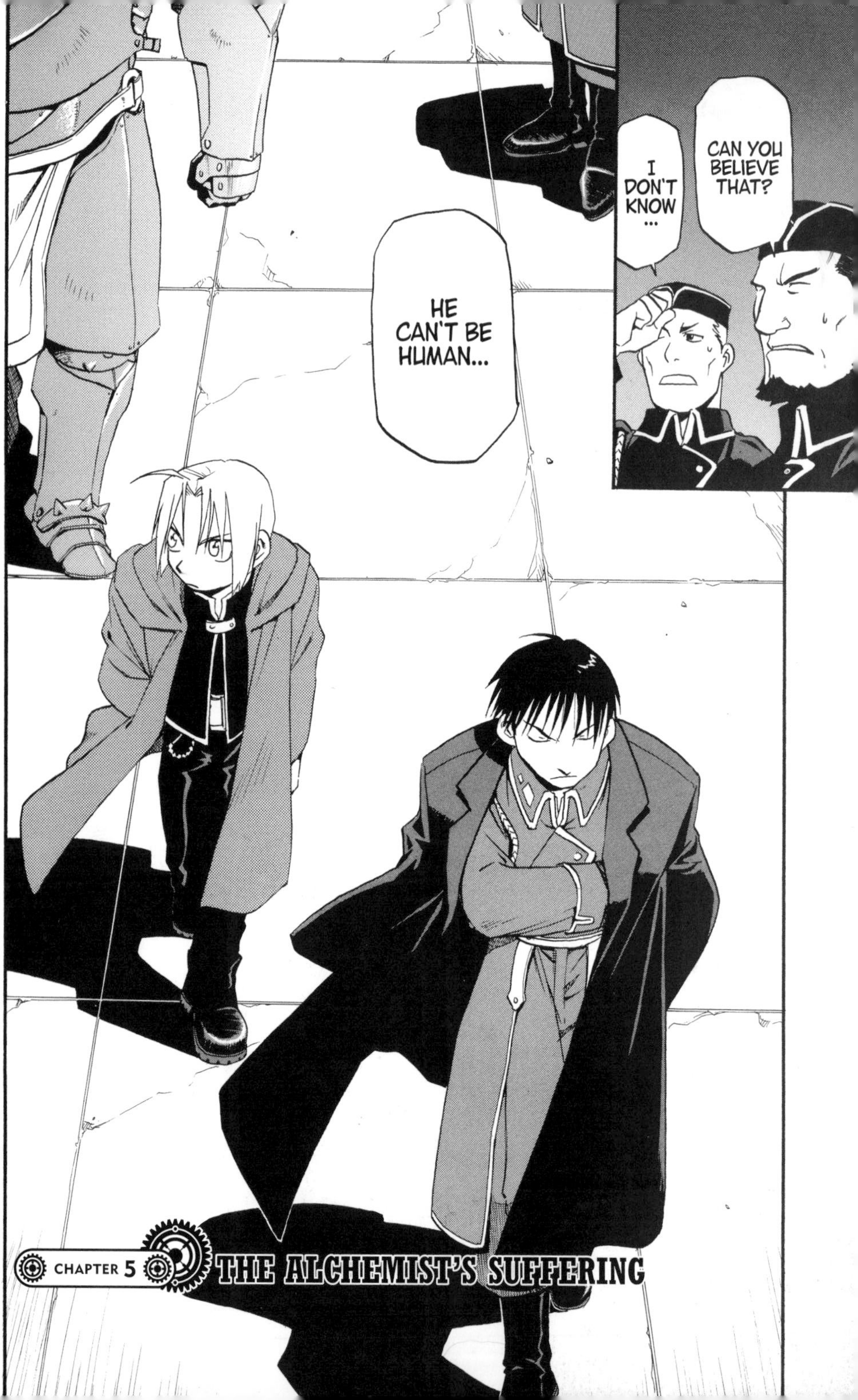
CAN YOU BELIEVE THAT?
I DON'T KNOW...
HE CAN'T BE HUMAN...
CHAPTER 5
THE ALCHEMIST'S SUFFERING

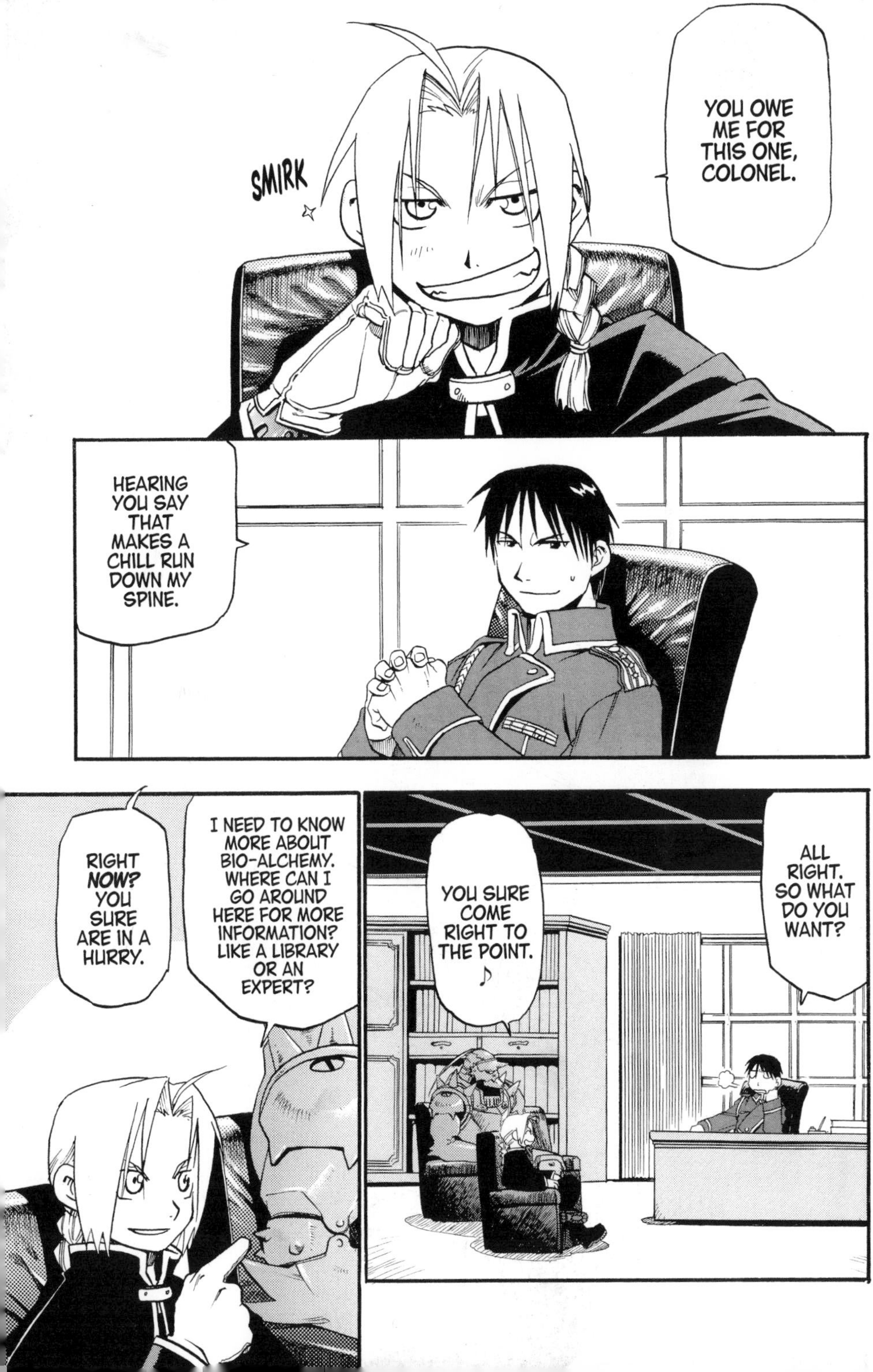
YOU OWE ME FOR THIS ONE, COLONEL.
SMIRK
HEARING YOU SAY THAT MAKES A CHILL RUN DOWN MY SPINE.
ALL RIGHT. SO WHAT DO YOU WANT?
YOU SURE COME RIGHT TO THE POINT. ♪
I NEED TO KNOW MORE ABOUT BIO-ALCHEMY. WHERE CAN I GO AROUND HERE FOR MORE INFORMATION? LIKE A LIBRARY OR AN EXPERT?
RIGHT NOW? YOU SURE ARE IN A HURRY.

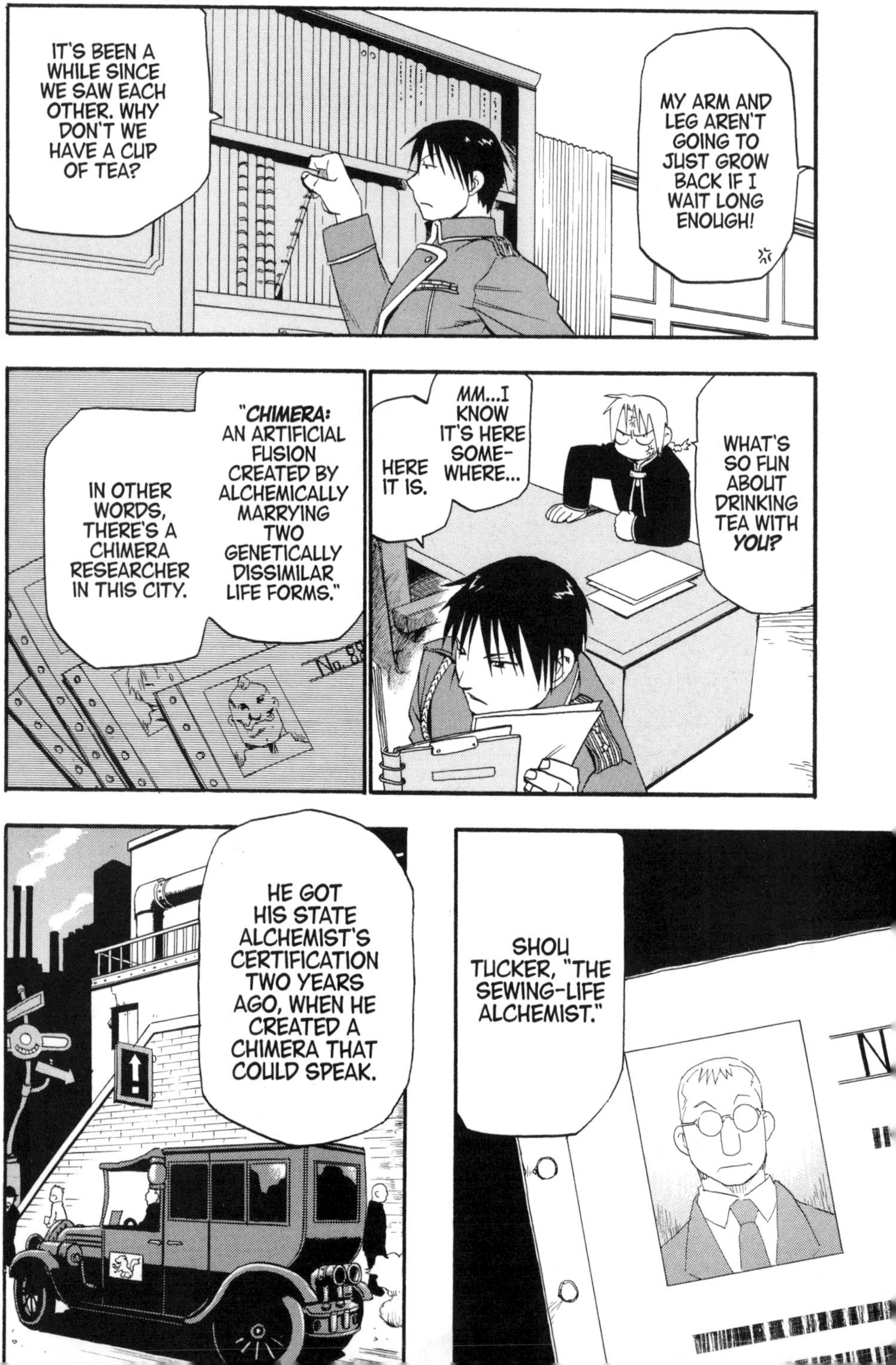
IT'S BEEN A WHILE SINCE WE SAW EACH OTHER. WHY DON'T WE HAVE A CUP OF TEA?
MY ARM AND LEG AREN'T GOING TO JUST GROW BACK IF I WAIT LONG ENOUGH!
WHAT'S SO FUN ABOUT DRINKING TEA WITH *YOU?*
MM...I KNOW IT'S HERE SOME-WHERE...
HERE IT IS.
"*CHIMERA:* AN ARTIFICIAL FUSION CREATED BY ALCHEMICALLY MARRYING TWO GENETICALLY DISSIMILAR LIFE FORMS."
IN OTHER WORDS, THERE'S A CHIMERA RESEARCHER IN THIS CITY.
SHOU TUCKER, "THE SEWING-LIFE ALCHEMIST."
HE GOT HIS STATE ALCHEMIST'S CERTIFICATION TWO YEARS AGO, WHEN HE CREATED A CHIMERA THAT COULD SPEAK.

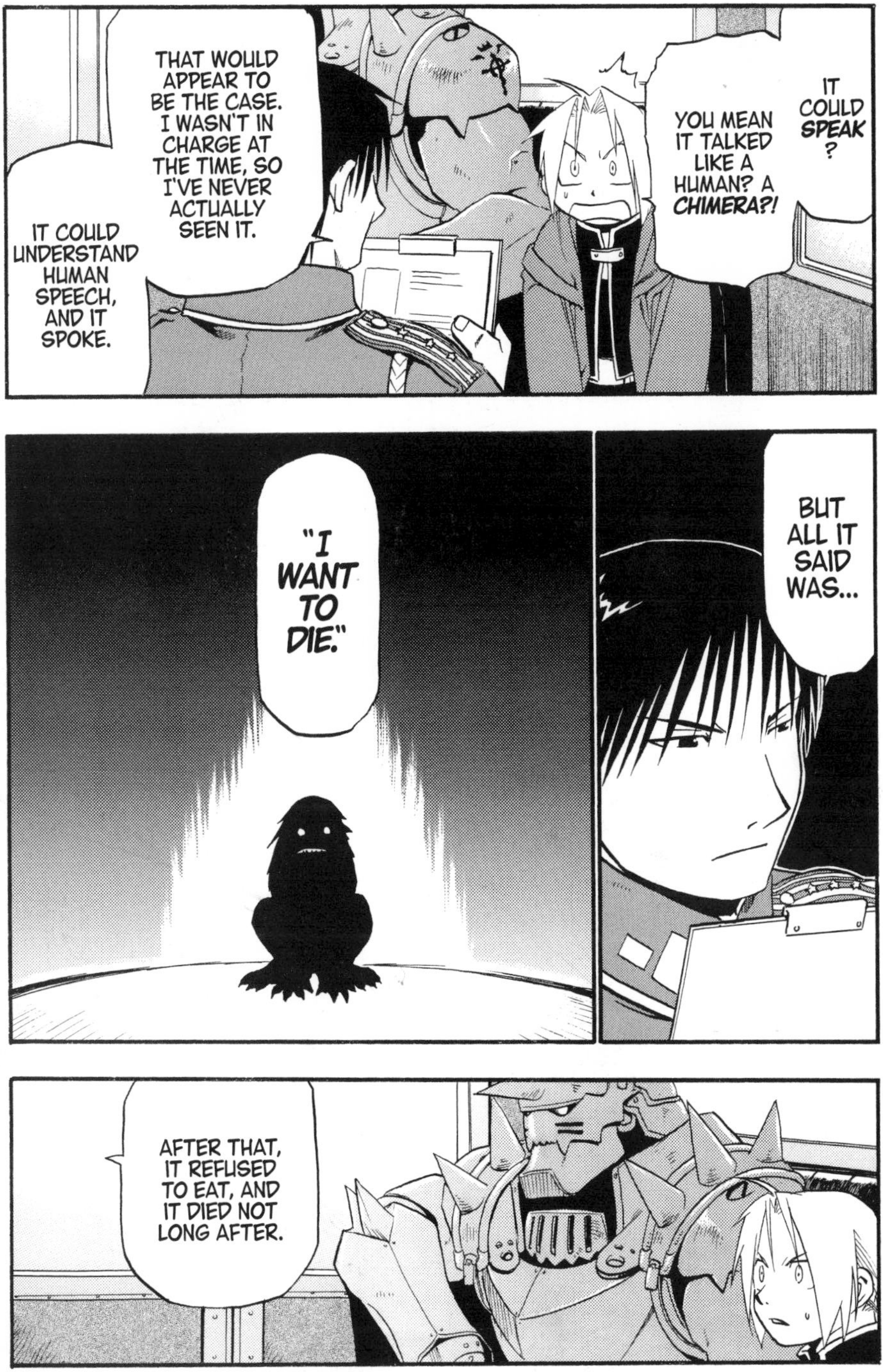
IT COULD SPEAK?
YOU MEAN IT TALKED LIKE A HUMAN? A CHIMERA?!
THAT WOULD APPEAR TO BE THE CASE. I WASN'T IN CHARGE AT THE TIME, SO I'VE NEVER ACTUALLY SEEN IT.
IT COULD UNDERSTAND HUMAN SPEECH, AND IT SPOKE.
BUT ALL IT SAID WAS...
"I WANT TO DIE."
AFTER THAT, IT REFUSED TO EAT, AND IT DIED NOT LONG AFTER.

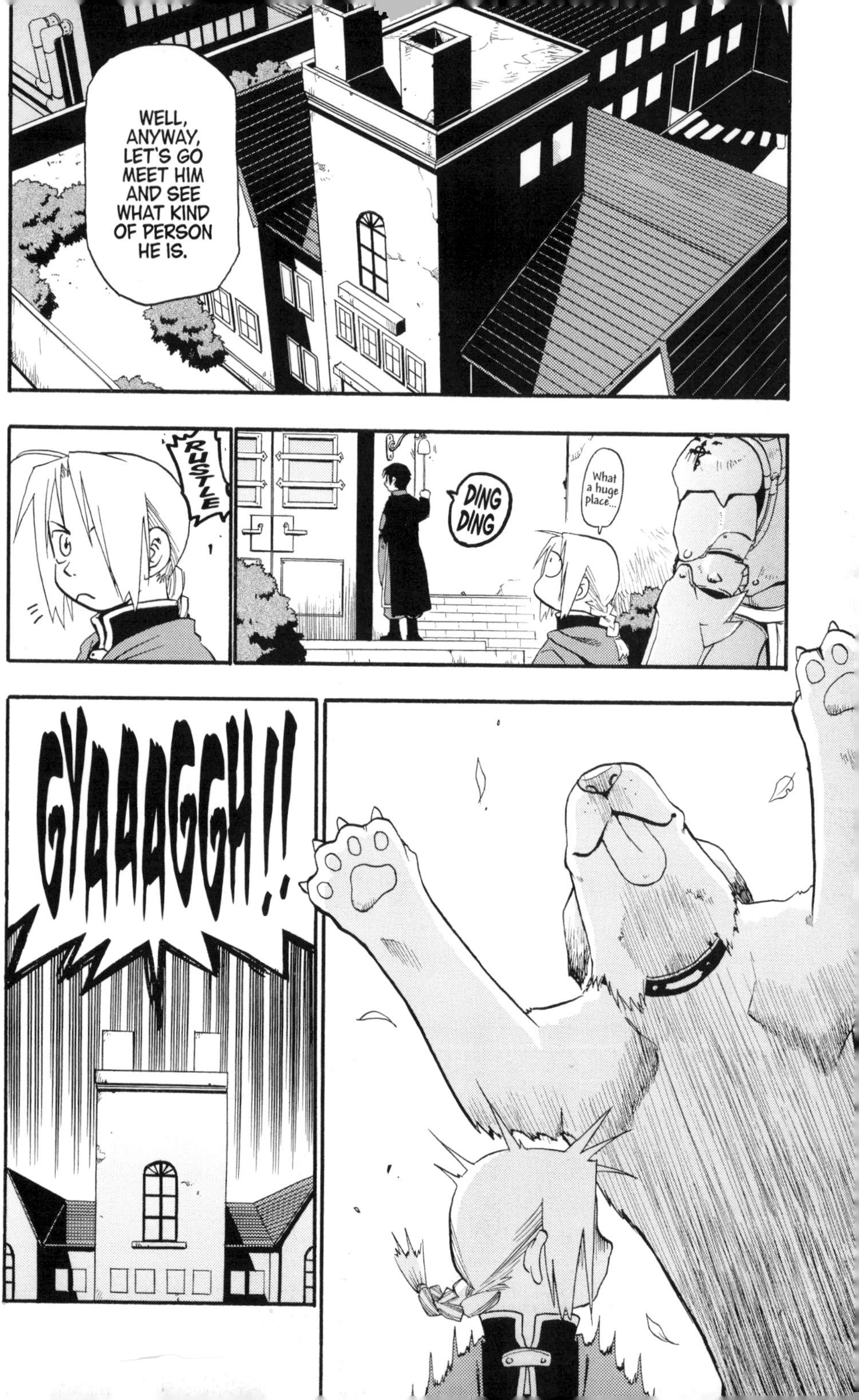
WELL, ANYWAY, LET'S GO MEET HIM AND SEE WHAT KIND OF PERSON HE IS.
What a huge place...
DING DING
RUSTLE
GYAAAGGH!!

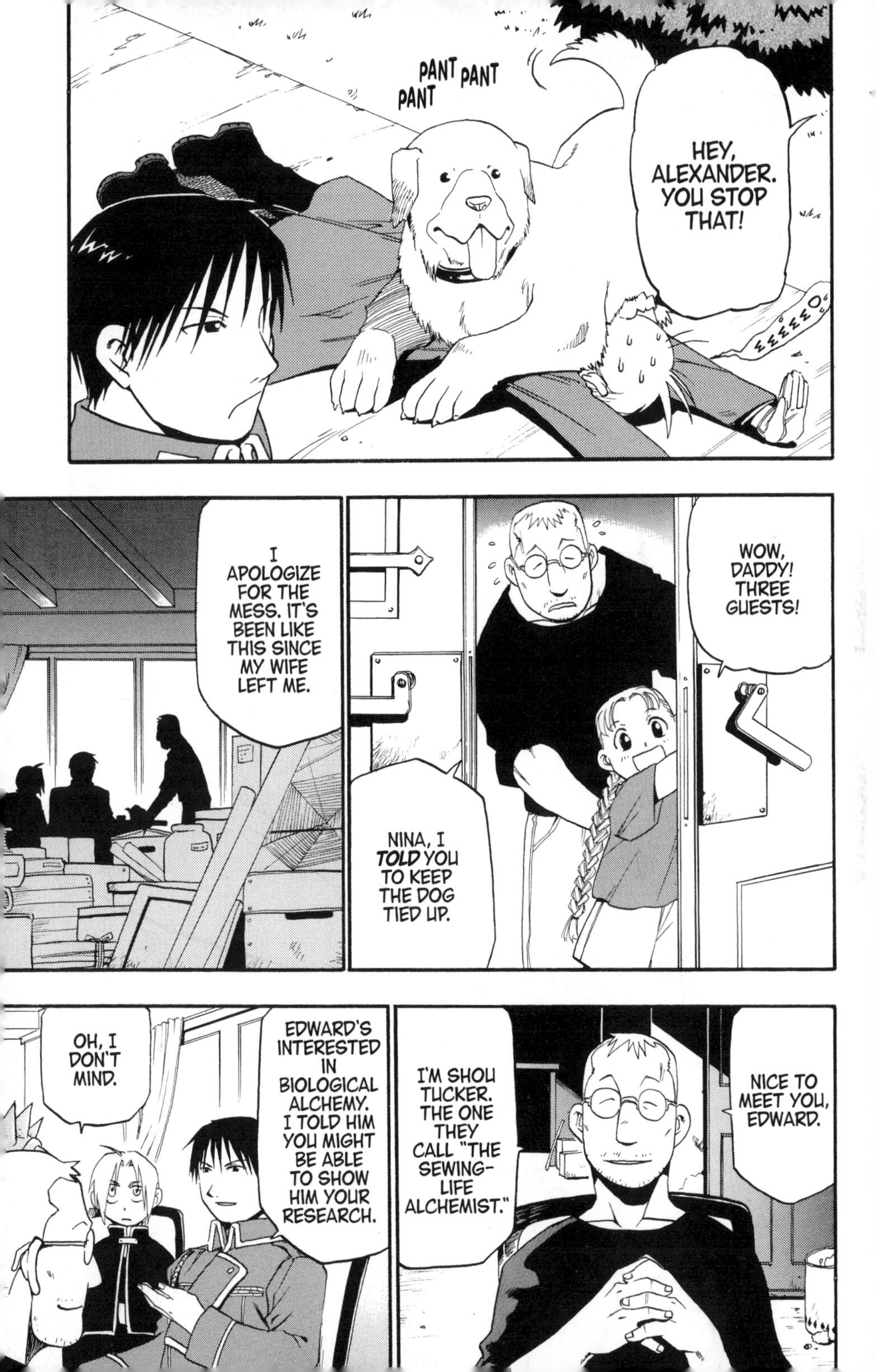
PANT PANT PANT
HEY, ALEXANDER. YOU STOP THAT!
WOW, DADDY! THREE GUESTS!
NINA, I TOLD YOU TO KEEP THE DOG TIED UP.
I APOLOGIZE FOR THE MESS. IT'S BEEN LIKE THIS SINCE MY WIFE LEFT ME.
NICE TO MEET YOU, EDWARD.
I'M SHOU TUCKER. THE ONE THEY CALL "THE SEWING-LIFE ALCHEMIST."
EDWARD'S INTERESTED IN BIOLOGICAL ALCHEMY. I TOLD HIM YOU MIGHT BE ABLE TO SHOW HIM YOUR RESEARCH.
OH, I DON'T MIND.

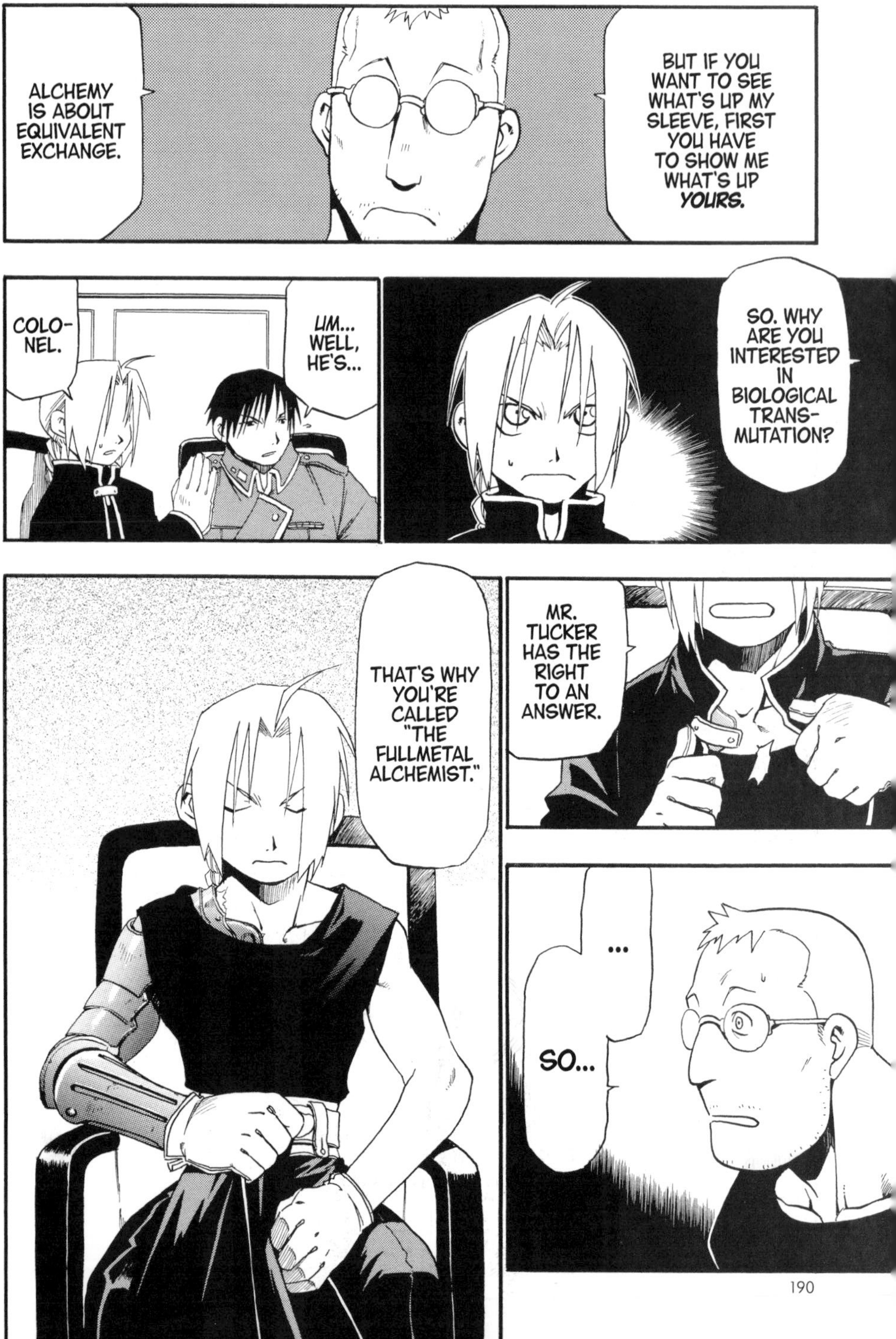
ALCHEMY IS ABOUT EQUIVALENT EXCHANGE.
BUT IF YOU WANT TO SEE WHAT'S UP MY SLEEVE, FIRST YOU HAVE TO SHOW ME WHAT'S UP *YOURS.*
SO. WHY ARE YOU INTERESTED IN BIOLOGICAL TRANS-MUTATION?
COLO-NEL.
UM... WELL, HE'S...
MR. TUCKER HAS THE RIGHT TO AN ANSWER.
...
SO...
THAT'S WHY YOU'RE CALLED "THE FULLMETAL ALCHEMIST."

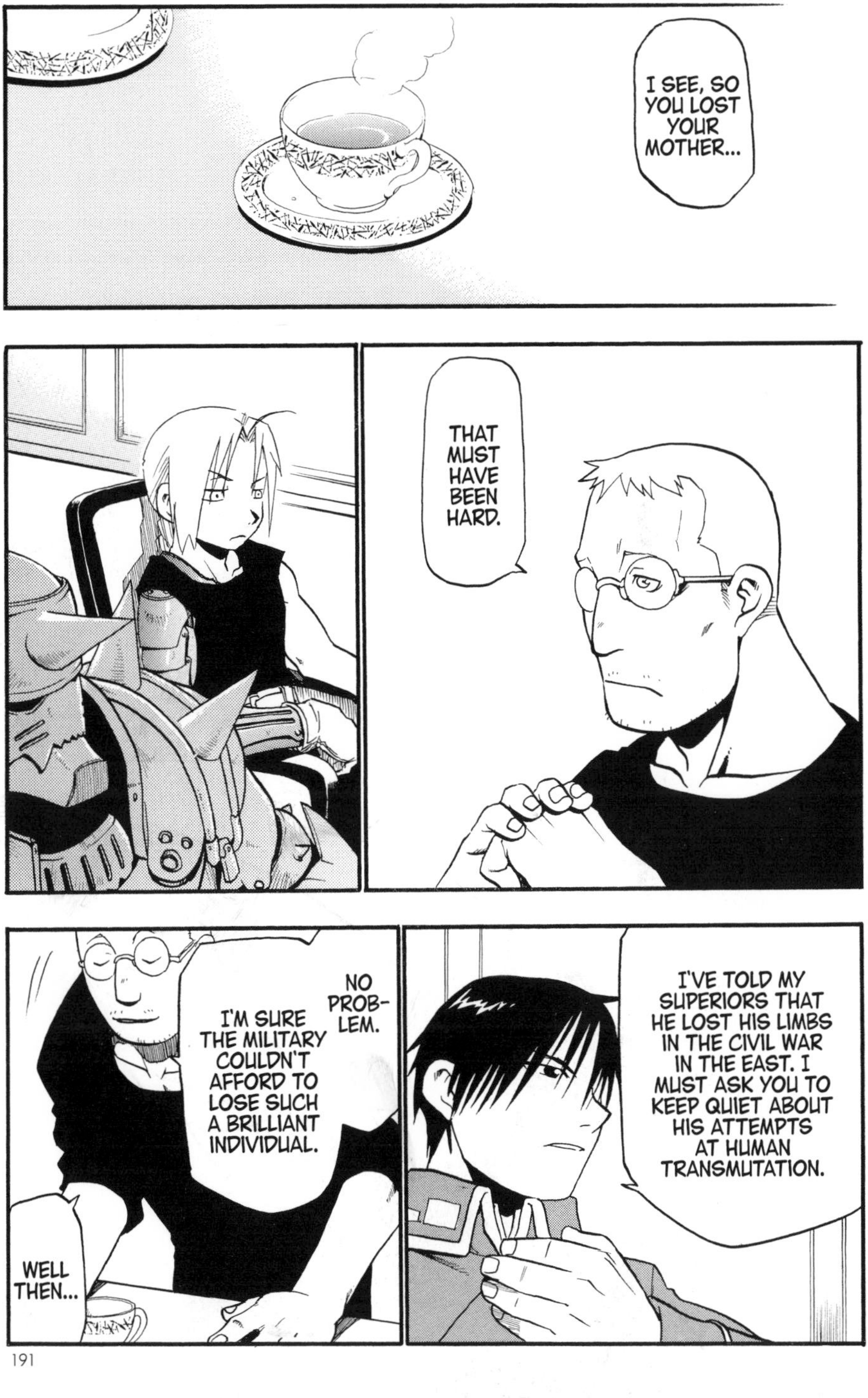
I SEE, SO YOU LOST YOUR MOTHER...
THAT MUST HAVE BEEN HARD.
I'VE TOLD MY SUPERIORS THAT HE LOST HIS LIMBS IN THE CIVIL WAR IN THE EAST. I MUST ASK YOU TO KEEP QUIET ABOUT HIS ATTEMPTS AT HUMAN TRANSMUTATION.
NO PROB-LEM.
I'M SURE THE MILITARY COULDN'T AFFORD TO LOSE SUCH A BRILLIANT INDIVIDUAL.
WELL THEN...

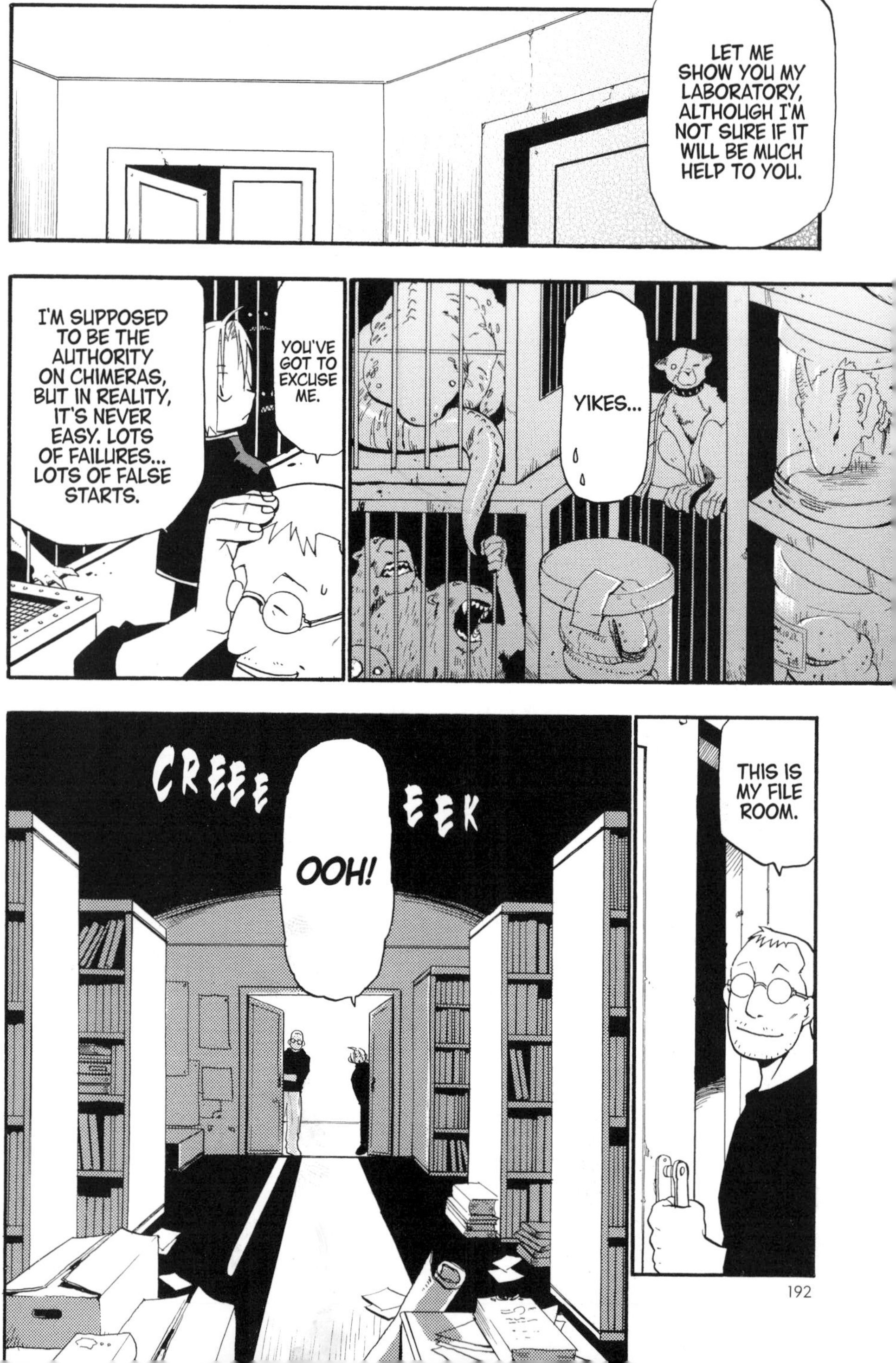
LET ME SHOW YOU MY LABORATORY, ALTHOUGH I'M NOT SURE IF IT WILL BE MUCH HELP TO YOU.
YIKES...
YOU'VE GOT TO EXCUSE ME.
I'M SUPPOSED TO BE THE AUTHORITY ON CHIMERAS, BUT IN REALITY, IT'S NEVER EASY. LOTS OF FAILURES... LOTS OF FALSE STARTS.
THIS IS MY FILE ROOM.
CREEEEEK
OOH!

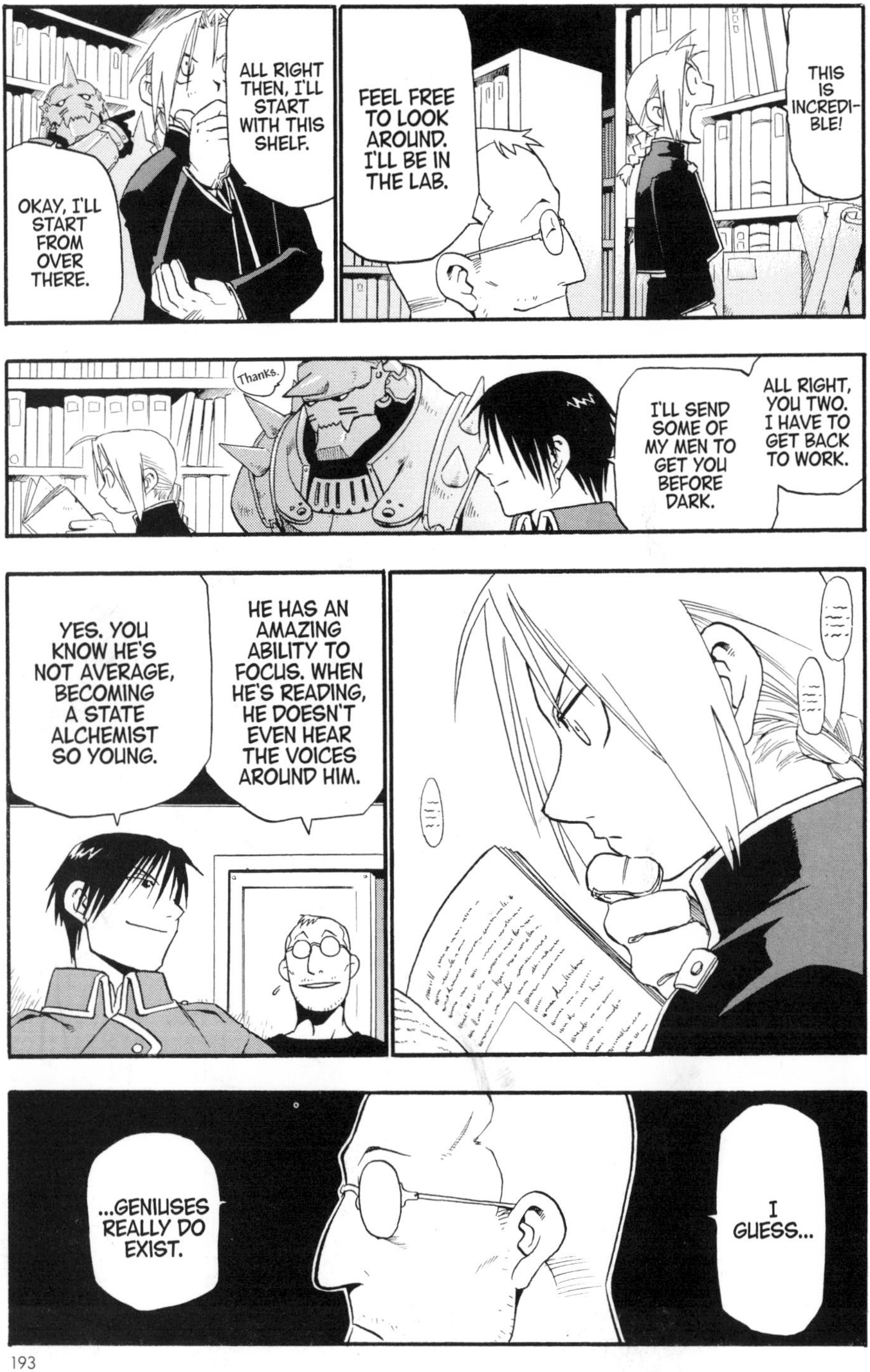
THIS IS INCREDIBLE!
FEEL FREE TO LOOK AROUND. I'LL BE IN THE LAB.
ALL RIGHT THEN, I'LL START WITH THIS SHELF.
OKAY, I'LL START FROM OVER THERE.
ALL RIGHT, YOU TWO. I HAVE TO GET BACK TO WORK.
I'LL SEND SOME OF MY MEN TO GET YOU BEFORE DARK.
Thanks.
HE HAS AN AMAZING ABILITY TO FOCUS. WHEN HE'S READING, HE DOESN'T EVEN HEAR THE VOICES AROUND HIM.
YES. YOU KNOW HE'S NOT AVERAGE, BECOMING A STATE ALCHEMIST SO YOUNG.
I GUESS...
...GENIUSES REALLY DO EXIST.

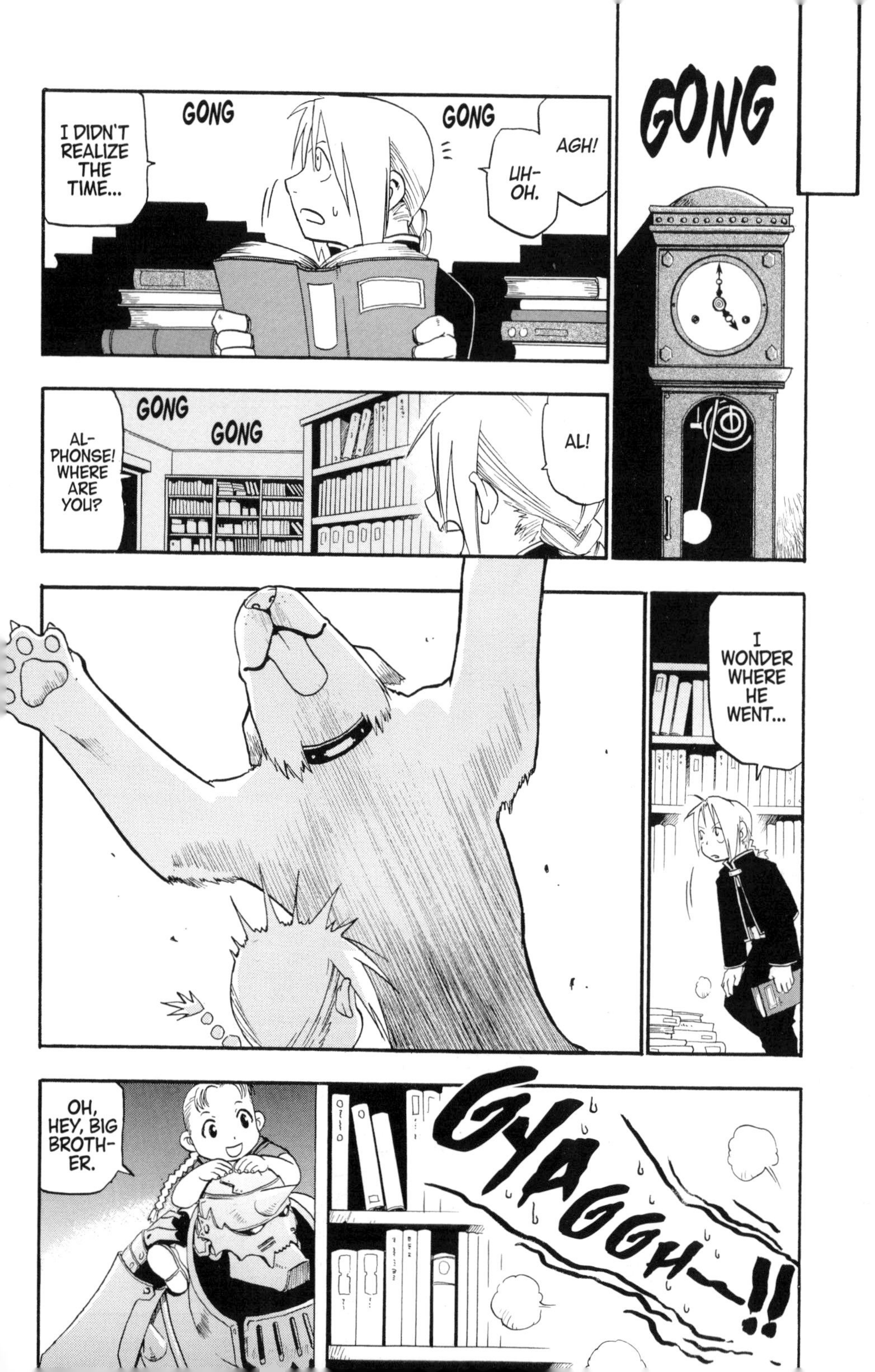
GONG
AGH!
UH-OH.
GONG
GONG
I DIDN'T REALIZE THE TIME...
AL!
GONG
GONG
ALPHONSE! WHERE ARE YOU?
I WONDER WHERE HE WENT...
GYAGGH~!!
OH, HEY, BIG BROTHER.

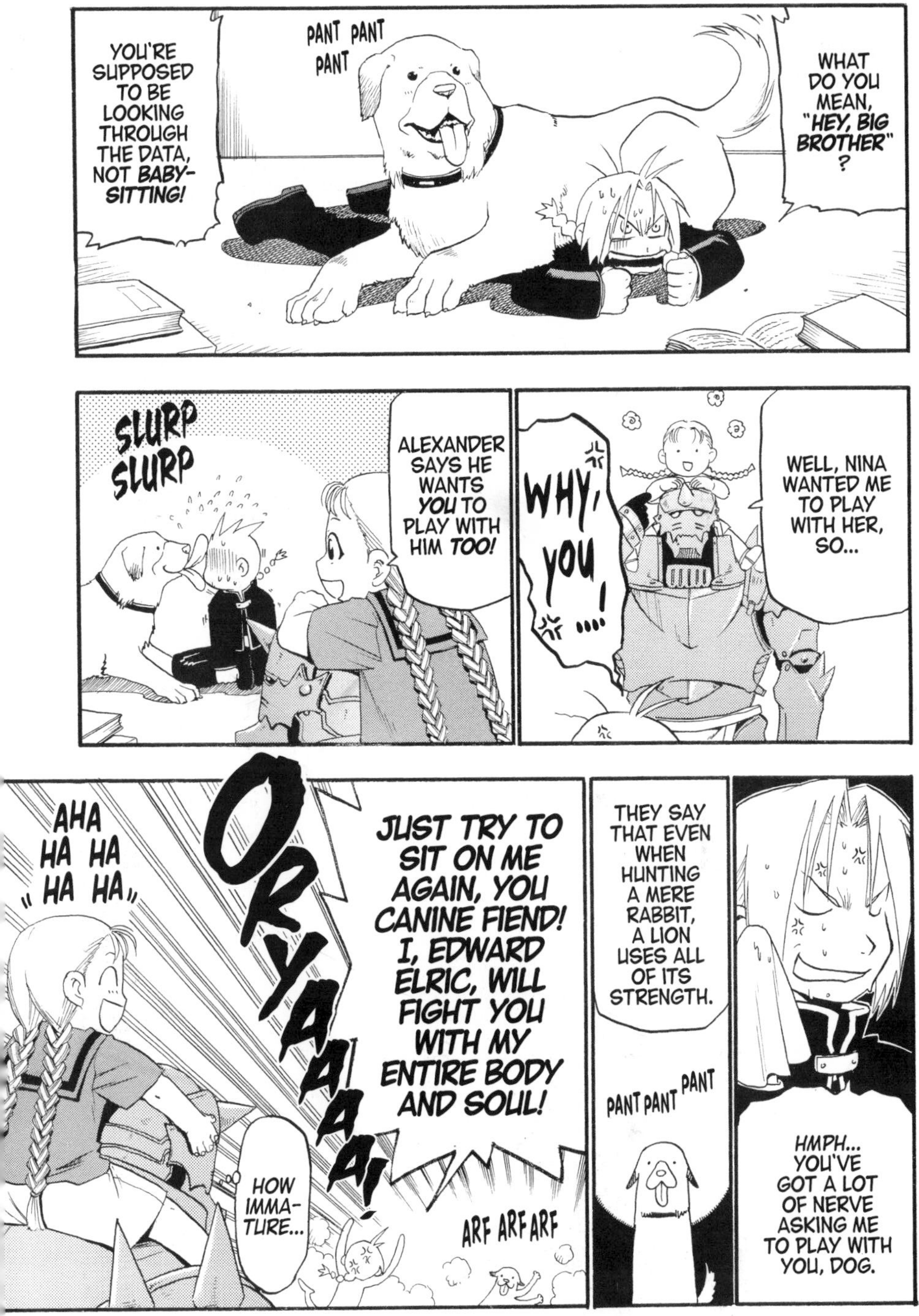
WHAT DO YOU MEAN, "HEY, BIG BROTHER"?
PANT PANT PANT
YOU'RE SUPPOSED TO BE LOOKING THROUGH THE DATA, NOT BABY-SITTING!
WELL, NINA WANTED ME TO PLAY WITH HER, SO...
WHY, YOU ...!
ALEXANDER SAYS HE WANTS YOU TO PLAY WITH HIM TOO!
SLURP SLURP
HMPH... YOU'VE GOT A LOT OF NERVE ASKING ME TO PLAY WITH YOU, DOG.
THEY SAY THAT EVEN WHEN HUNTING A MERE RABBIT, A LION USES ALL OF ITS STRENGTH.
PANT PANT PANT
JUST TRY TO SIT ON ME AGAIN, YOU CANINE FIEND! I, EDWARD ELRIC, WILL FIGHT YOU WITH MY ENTIRE BODY AND SOUL!
ORYAAAAAA!
AHA HA HA HA HA
HOW IMMA-TURE...
ARF ARF ARF

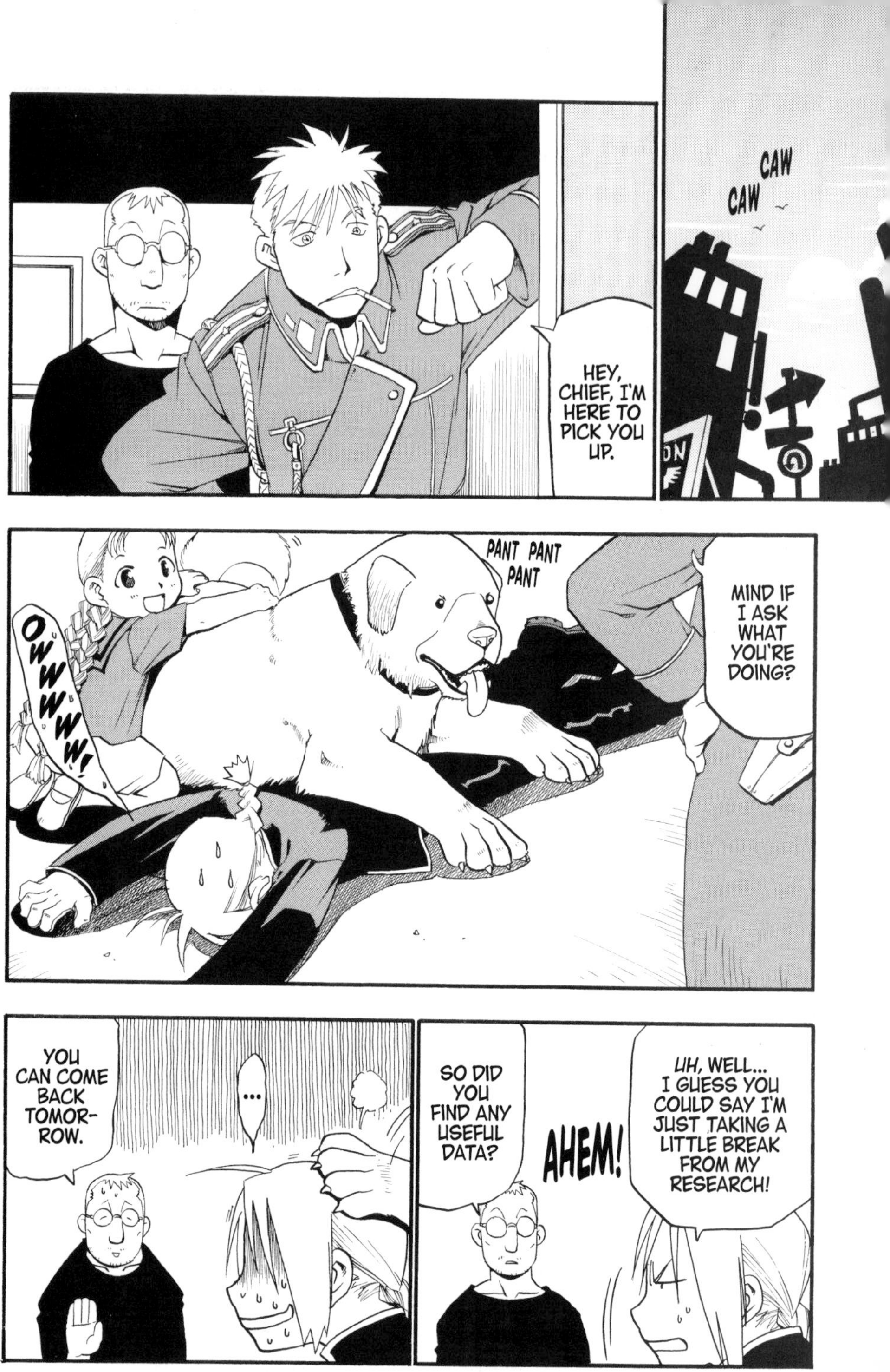
CAW
CAW
HEY, CHIEF, I'M HERE TO PICK YOU UP.
MIND IF I ASK WHAT YOU'RE DOING?
PANT PANT PANT
OWWWWW!
UH, WELL... I GUESS YOU COULD SAY I'M JUST TAKING A LITTLE BREAK FROM MY RESEARCH!
AHEM!
SO DID YOU FIND ANY USEFUL DATA?
...
YOU CAN COME BACK TOMOR-ROW.

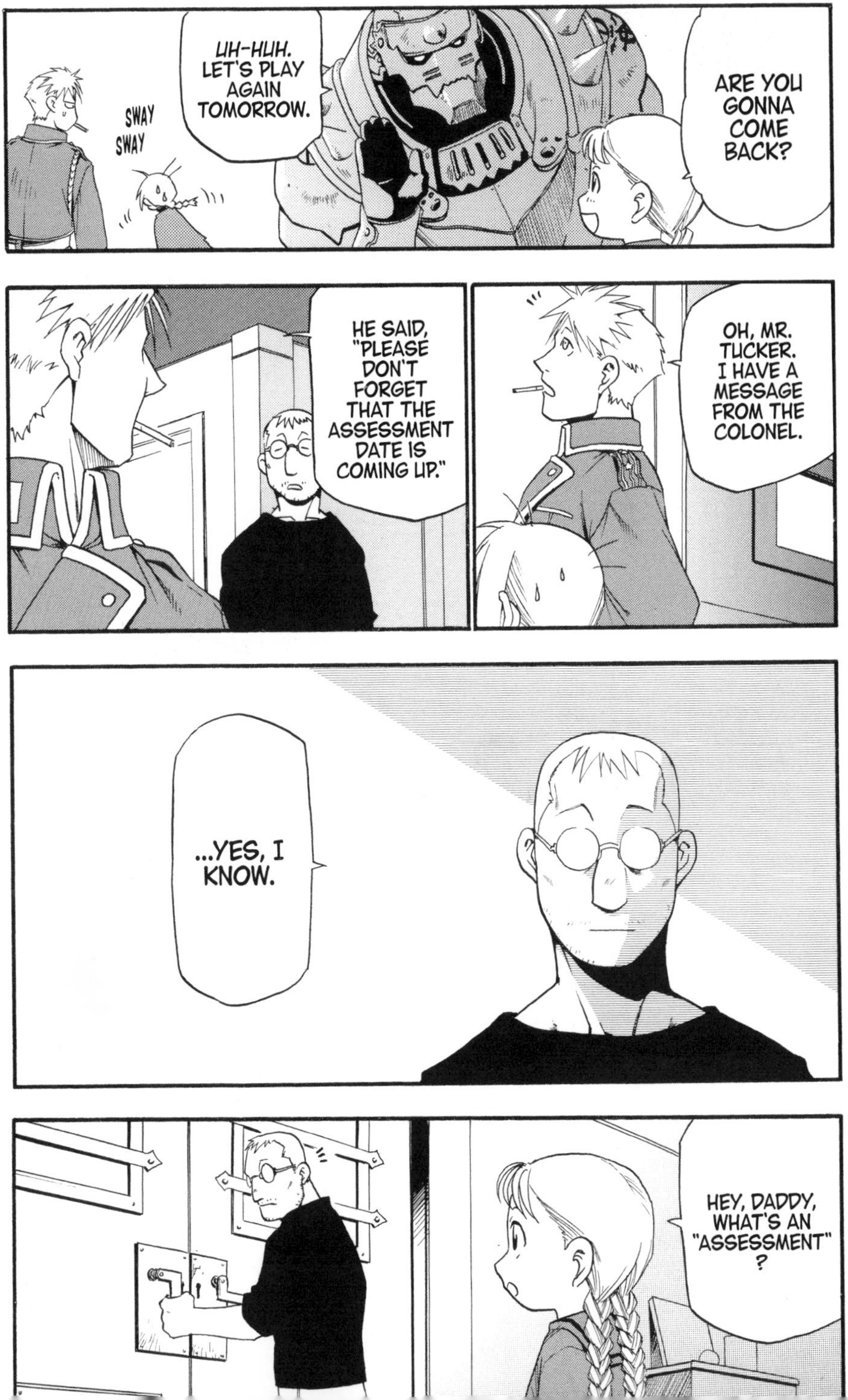
ARE YOU GONNA COME BACK?
UH-HUH. LET'S PLAY AGAIN TOMORROW.
SWAY SWAY
OH, MR. TUCKER. I HAVE A MESSAGE FROM THE COLONEL.
HE SAID, "PLEASE DON'T FORGET THAT THE ASSESSMENT DATE IS COMING UP."
...YES, I KNOW.
HEY, DADDY, WHAT'S AN "ASSESSMENT" ?

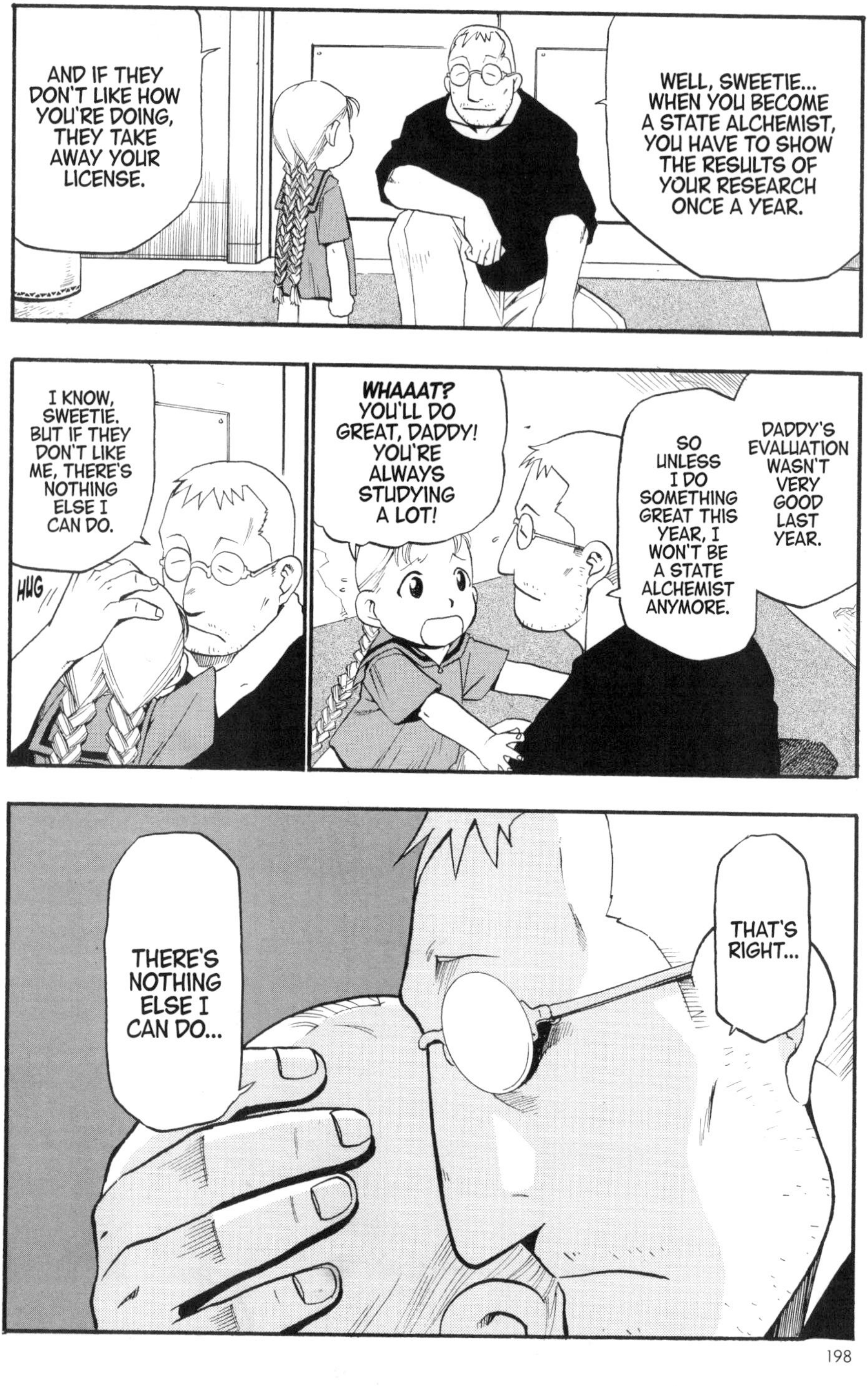
WELL, SWEETIE... WHEN YOU BECOME A STATE ALCHEMIST, YOU HAVE TO SHOW THE RESULTS OF YOUR RESEARCH ONCE A YEAR.
AND IF THEY DON'T LIKE HOW YOU'RE DOING, THEY TAKE AWAY YOUR LICENSE.
DADDY'S EVALUATION WASN'T VERY GOOD LAST YEAR.
SO UNLESS I DO SOMETHING GREAT THIS YEAR, I WON'T BE A STATE ALCHEMIST ANYMORE.
WHAAAT? YOU'LL DO GREAT, DADDY! YOU'RE ALWAYS STUDYING A LOT!
I KNOW, SWEETIE. BUT IF THEY DON'T LIKE ME, THERE'S NOTHING ELSE I CAN DO.
HUG
THAT'S RIGHT...
THERE'S NOTHING ELSE I CAN DO...

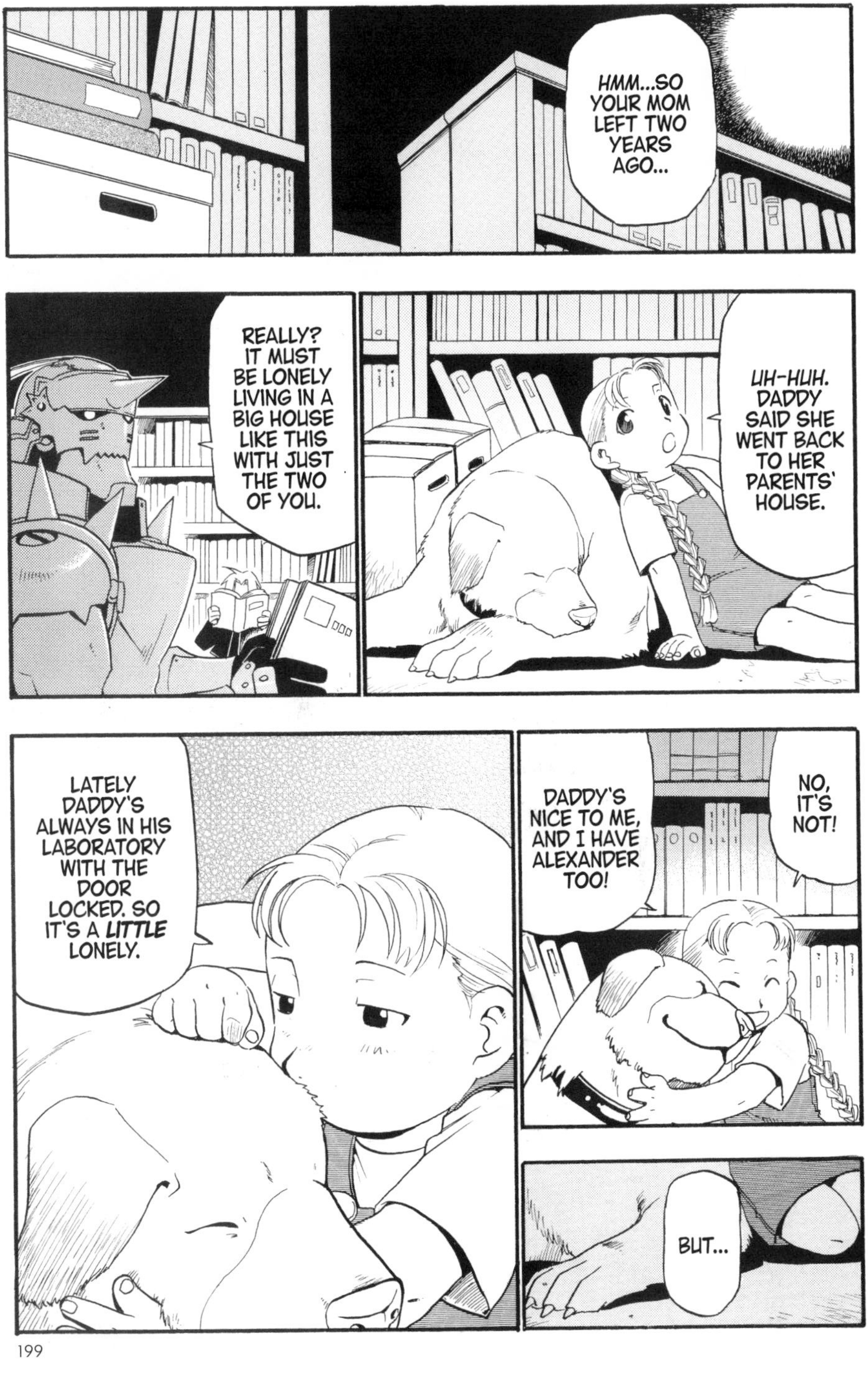
HMM...SO YOUR MOM LEFT TWO YEARS AGO...
UH-HUH. DADDY SAID SHE WENT BACK TO HER PARENTS' HOUSE.
REALLY? IT MUST BE LONELY LIVING IN A BIG HOUSE LIKE THIS WITH JUST THE TWO OF YOU.
NO, IT'S NOT!
DADDY'S NICE TO ME, AND I HAVE ALEXANDER TOO!
BUT...
LATELY DADDY'S ALWAYS IN HIS LABORATORY WITH THE DOOR LOCKED. SO IT'S A *LITTLE* LONELY.

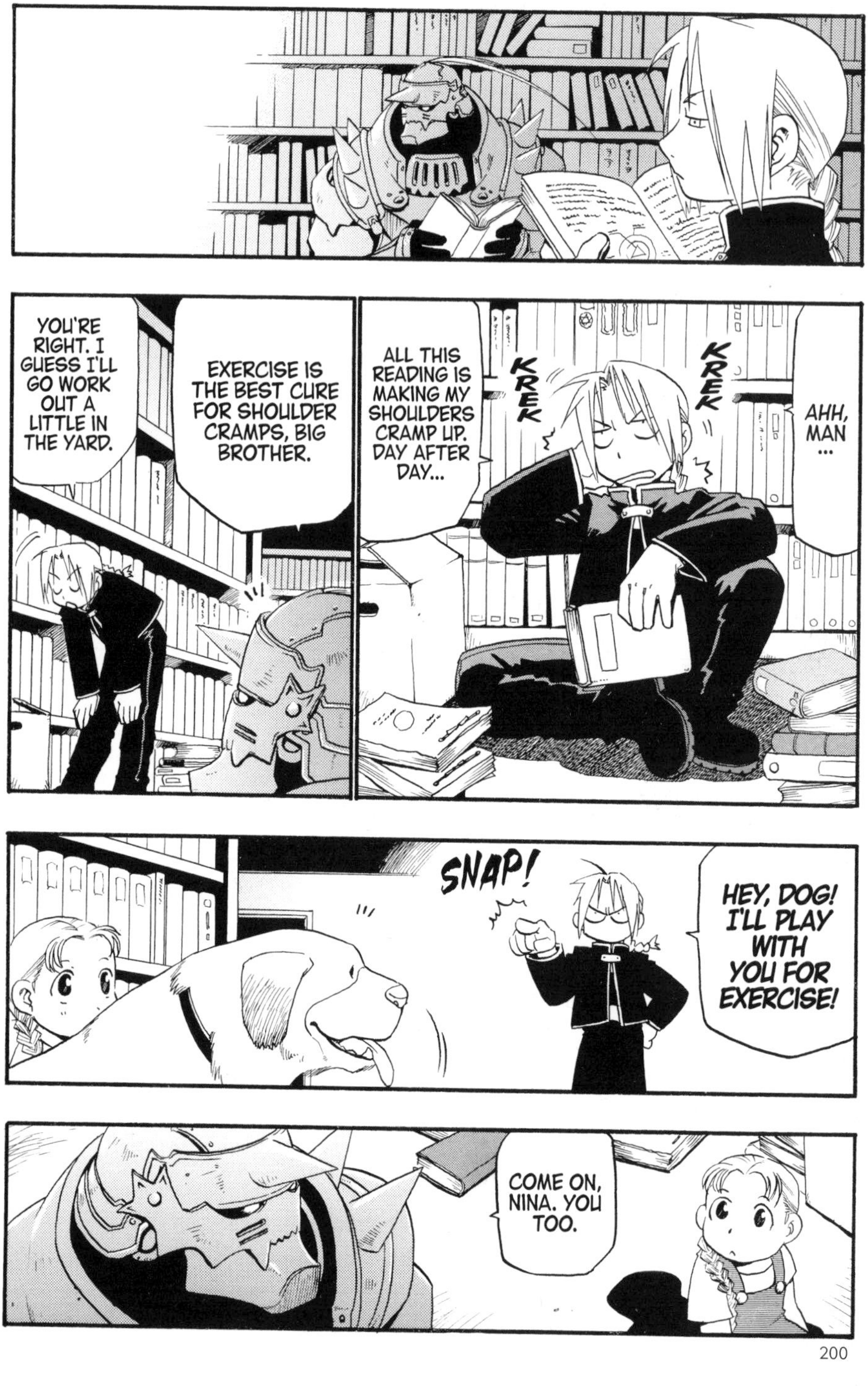
AHH, MAN ...
KREK
KREK
ALL THIS READING IS MAKING MY SHOULDERS CRAMP UP. DAY AFTER DAY...
EXERCISE IS THE BEST CURE FOR SHOULDER CRAMPS, BIG BROTHER.
YOU'RE RIGHT. I GUESS I'LL GO WORK OUT A LITTLE IN THE YARD.
HEY, DOG! I'LL PLAY WITH YOU FOR EXERCISE!
SNAP!
COME ON, NINA. YOU TOO.

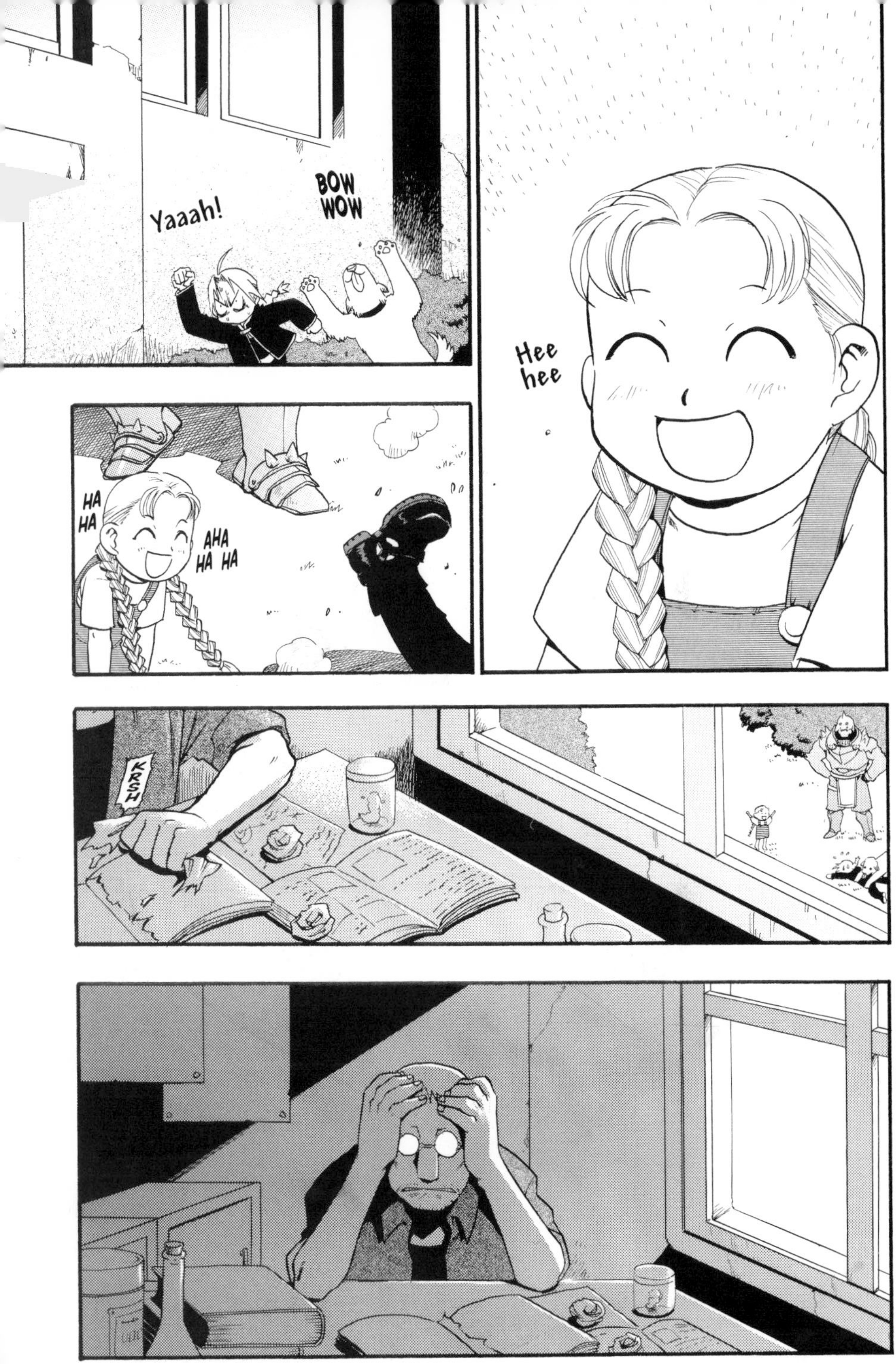
Hee hee
BOW WOW
Yaaah!
AHA HA HA
HA HA
KRSH

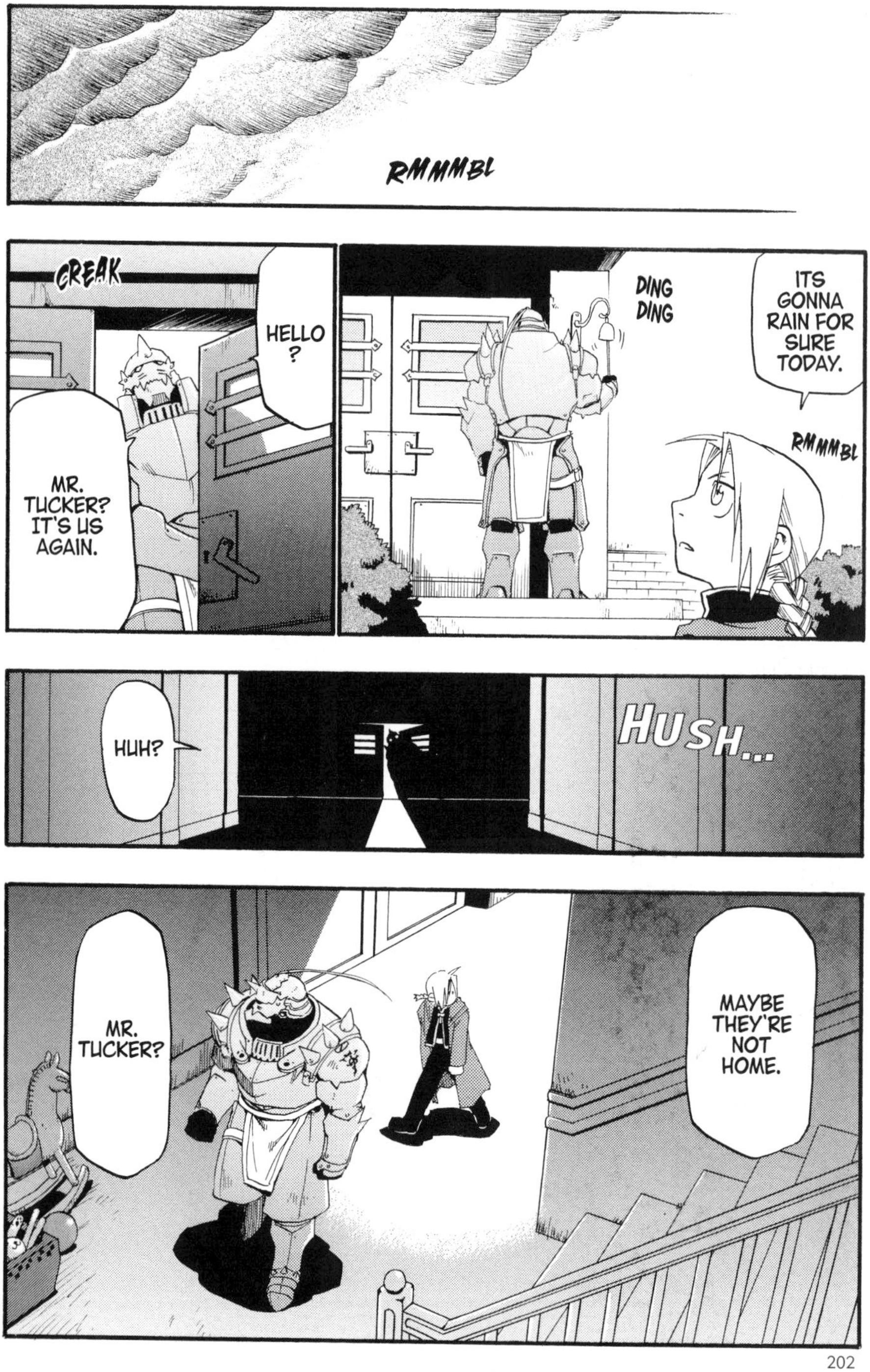
RMMMBL
ITS GONNA RAIN FOR SURE TODAY.
DING DING
RMMMBL
HELLO?
CREAK
MR. TUCKER? IT'S US AGAIN.
HUSH...
HUH?
MAYBE THEY'RE NOT HOME.
MR. TUCKER?

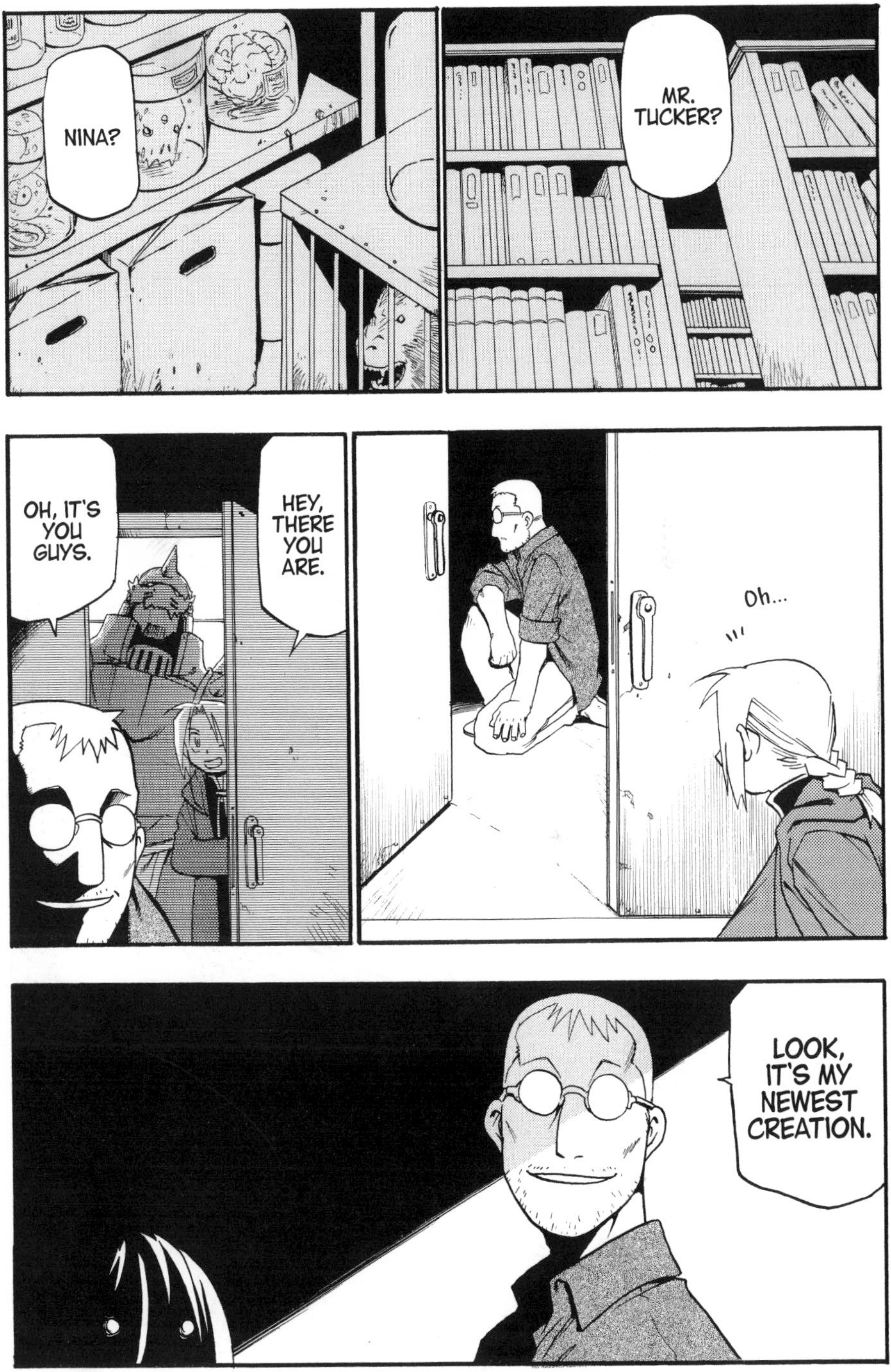
MR. TUCKER?
NINA?
Oh...
HEY, THERE YOU ARE.
OH, IT'S YOU GUYS.
LOOK, IT'S MY NEWEST CREATION.

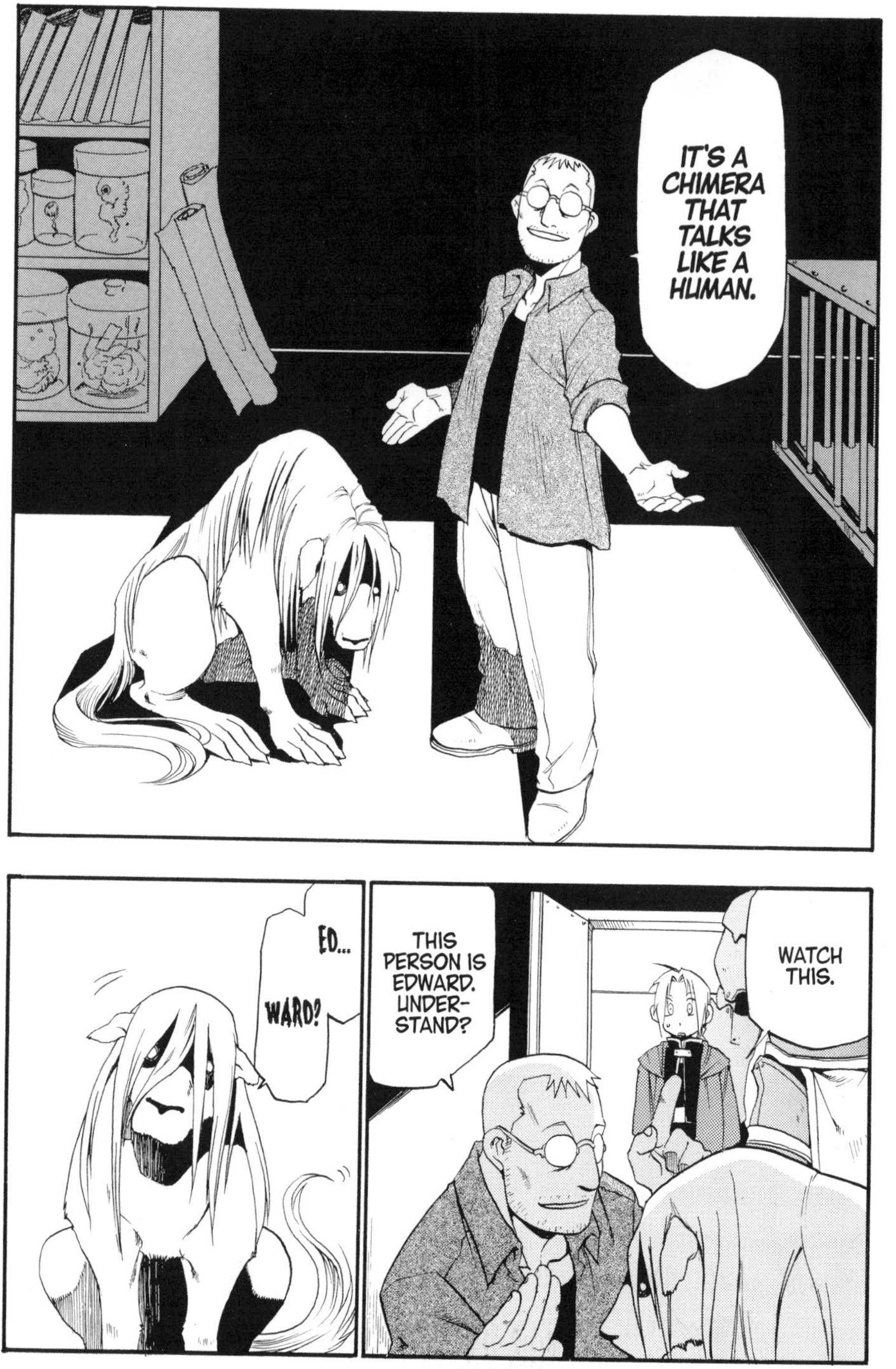
IT'S A CHIMERA THAT TALKS LIKE A HUMAN.
WATCH THIS.
THIS PERSON IS EDWARD. UNDER-STAND?
ED...
WARD?

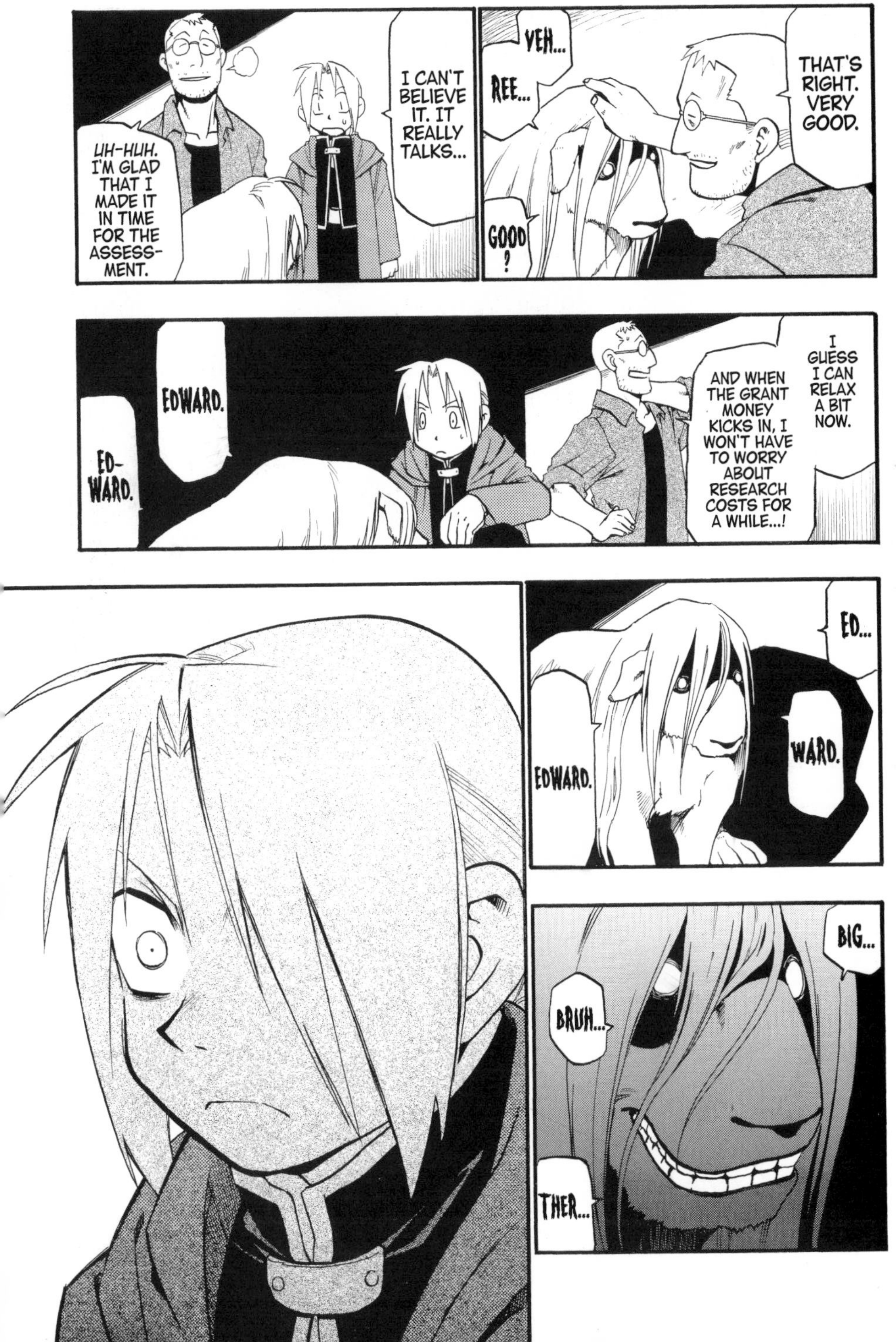
THAT'S RIGHT. VERY GOOD.
YEH...
REE...
GOOD?
I CAN'T BELIEVE IT. IT REALLY TALKS...
UH-HUH. I'M GLAD THAT I MADE IT IN TIME FOR THE ASSESS-MENT.
I GUESS I CAN RELAX A BIT NOW.
AND WHEN THE GRANT MONEY KICKS IN, I WON'T HAVE TO WORRY ABOUT RESEARCH COSTS FOR A WHILE...!
EDWARD.
ED-WARD.
ED...
WARD.
EDWARD.
BIG...
BRUH...
THER...

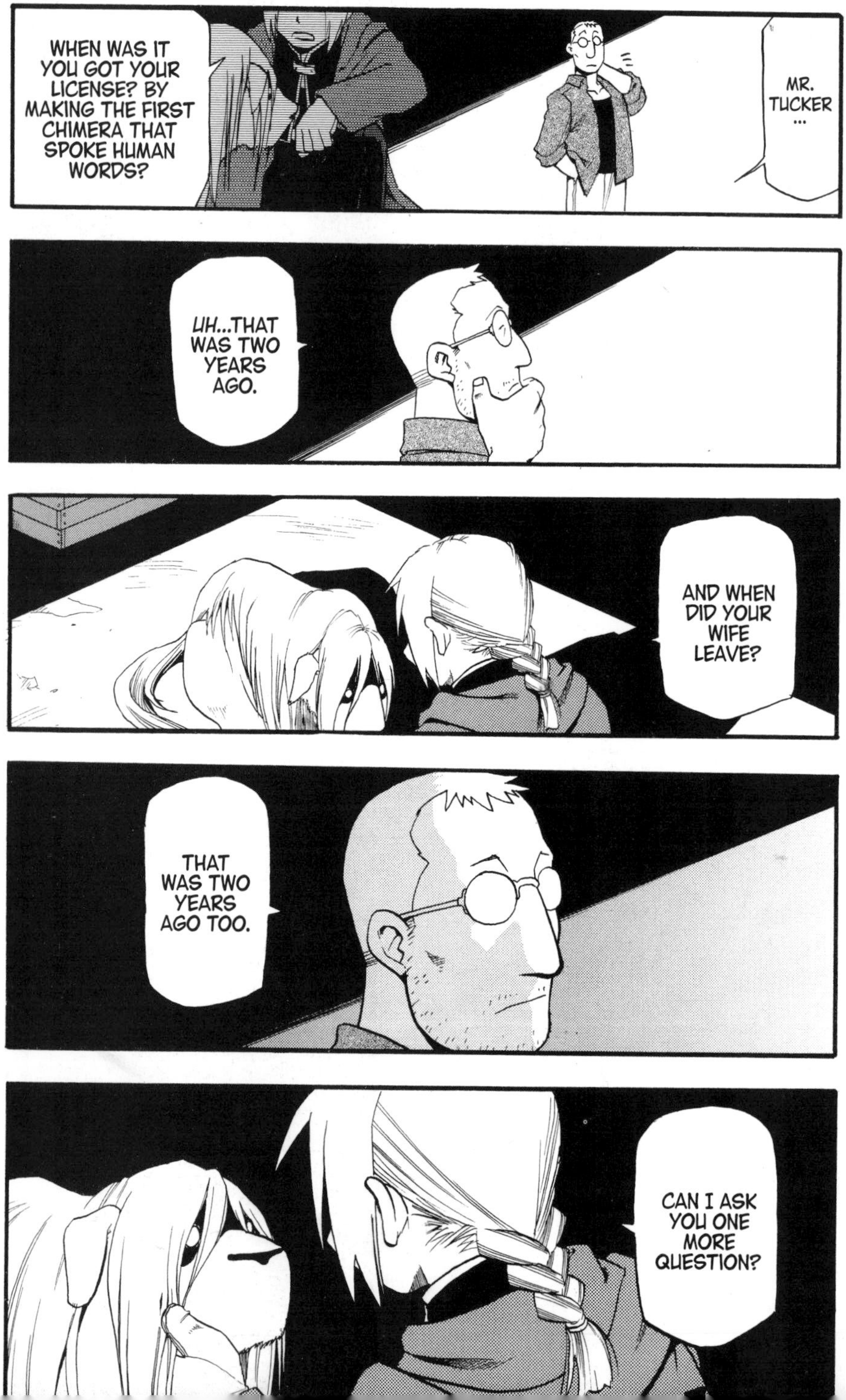
MR. TUCKER ...
WHEN WAS IT YOU GOT YOUR LICENSE? BY MAKING THE FIRST CHIMERA THAT SPOKE HUMAN WORDS?
UH...THAT WAS TWO YEARS AGO.
AND WHEN DID YOUR WIFE LEAVE?
THAT WAS TWO YEARS AGO TOO.
CAN I ASK YOU ONE MORE QUESTION?

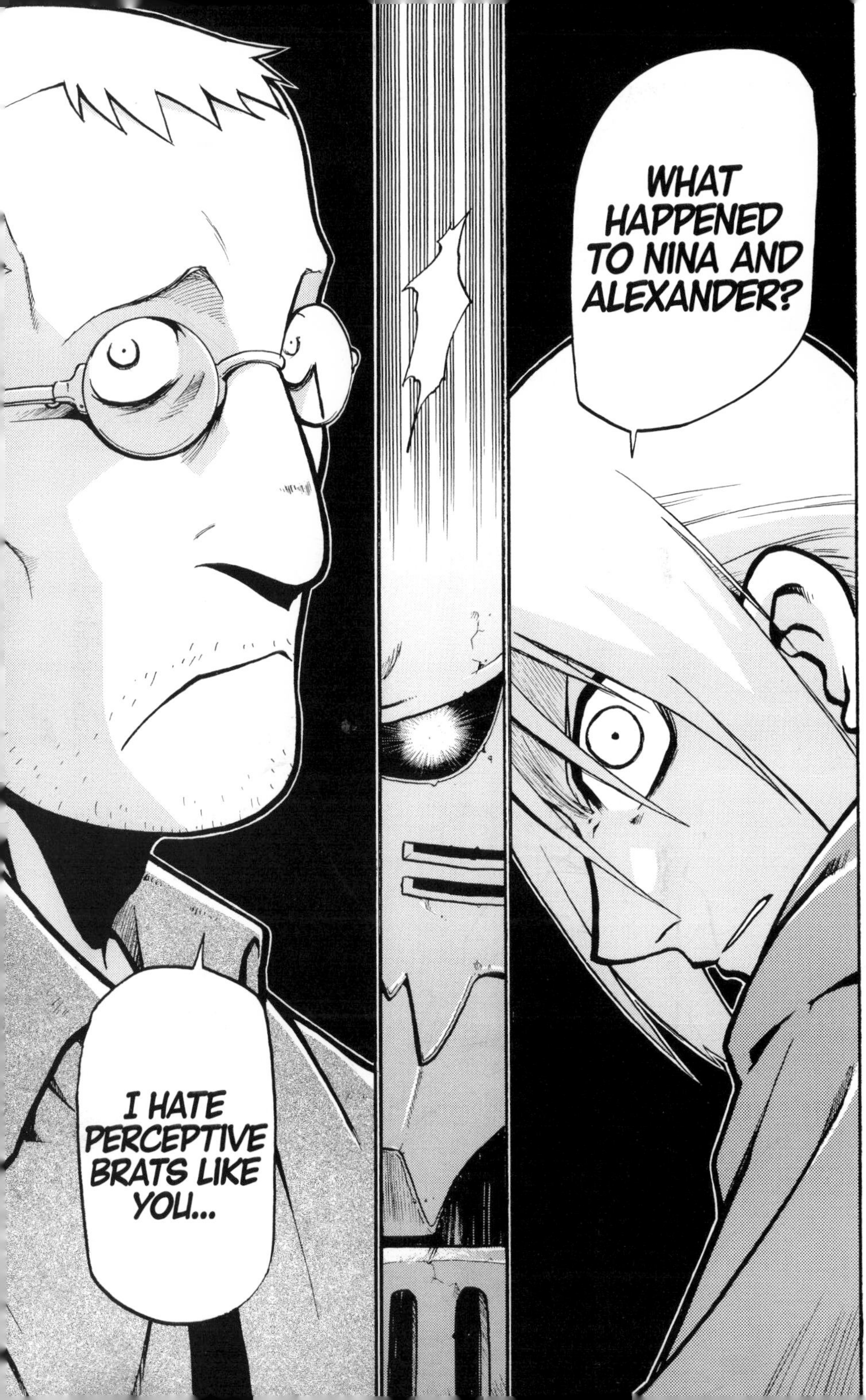
WHAT HAPPENED TO NINA AND ALEXANDER?
I HATE PERCEPTIVE BRATS LIKE YOU...

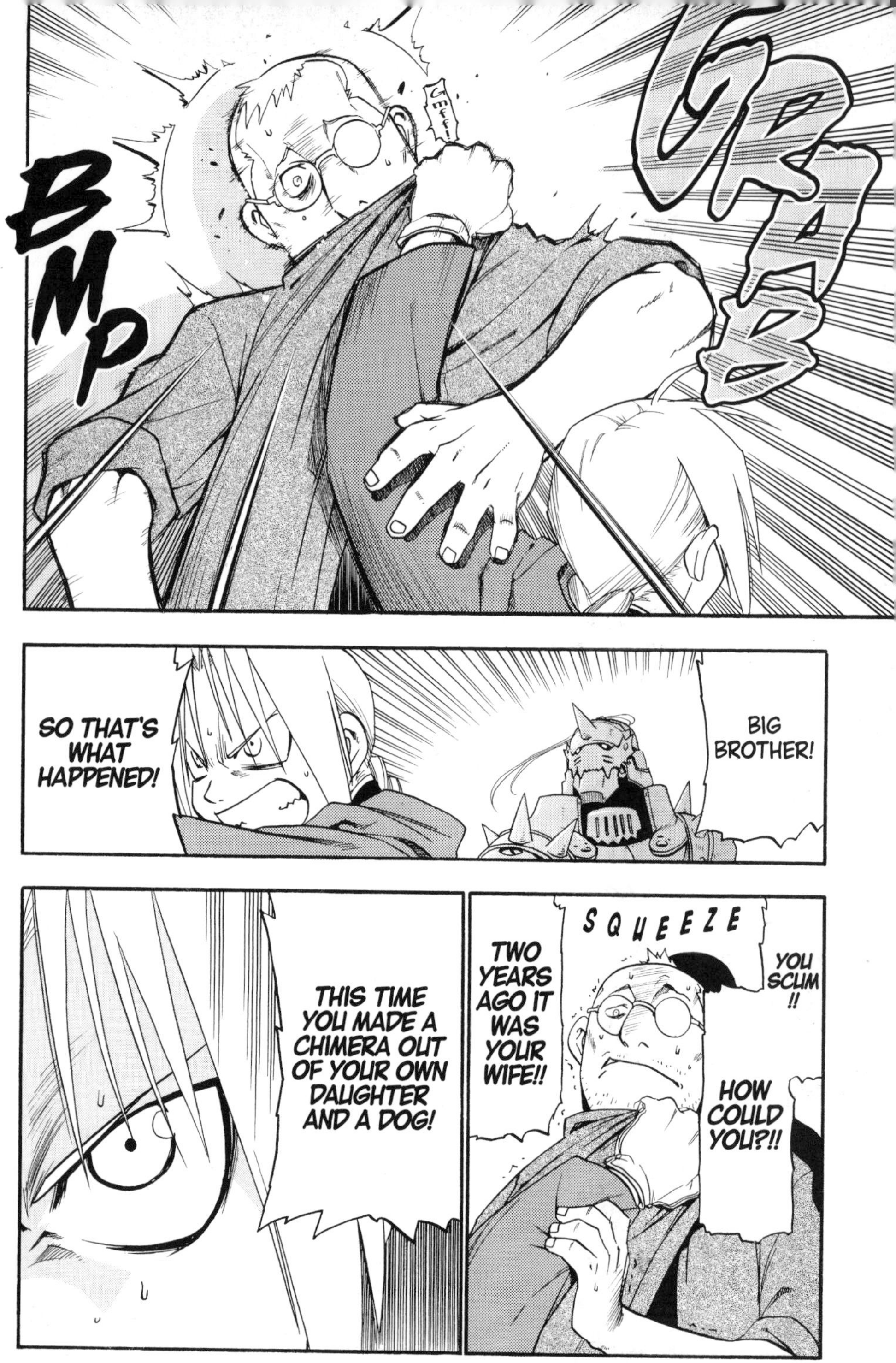
GRAB
Gmff!
BMP
BIG BROTHER!
SO THAT'S WHAT HAPPENED!
SQUEEZE
YOU SCUM!!
TWO YEARS AGO IT WAS YOUR WIFE!!
HOW COULD YOU?!!
THIS TIME YOU MADE A CHIMERA OUT OF YOUR OWN DAUGHTER AND A DOG!

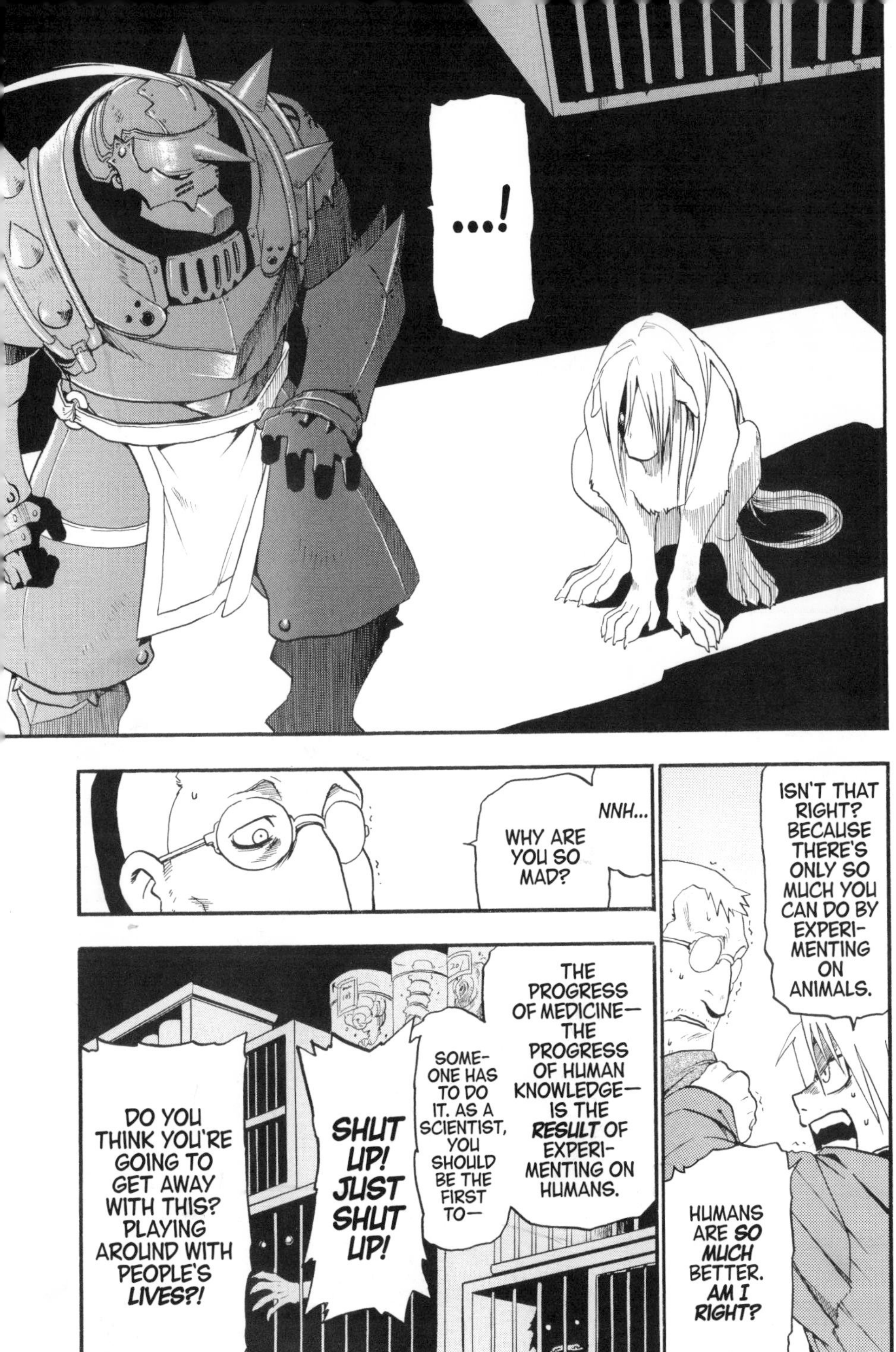
...!
ISN'T THAT RIGHT? BECAUSE THERE'S ONLY SO MUCH YOU CAN DO BY EXPERIMENTING ON ANIMALS.
HUMANS ARE SO MUCH BETTER. AM I RIGHT?
NNH...
WHY ARE YOU SO MAD?
THE PROGRESS OF MEDICINE—THE PROGRESS OF HUMAN KNOWLEDGE—IS THE RESULT OF EXPERIMENTING ON HUMANS.
SOMEONE HAS TO DO IT. AS A SCIENTIST, YOU SHOULD BE THE FIRST TO—
SHUT UP! JUST SHUT UP!
DO YOU THINK YOU'RE GOING TO GET AWAY WITH THIS? PLAYING AROUND WITH PEOPLE'S LIVES?!

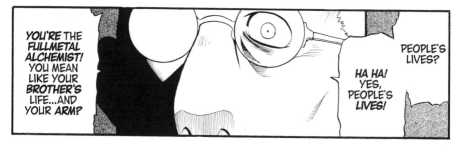

PEOPLE'S LIVES?
HA HA! YES, PEOPLE'S LIVES!
YOU'RE THE FULLMETAL ALCHEMIST! YOU MEAN LIKE YOUR BROTHER'S LIFE...AND YOUR ARM?
THAT'S ALSO THE RESULT OF "PLAYING AROUND WITH PEOPLE'S LIVES," YES?
SNAP
WAM
NHH...
HA HA HA HA!
YOU AND I ARE JUST THE SAME!

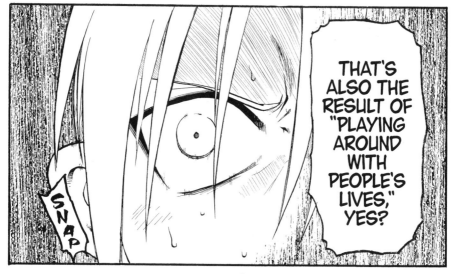

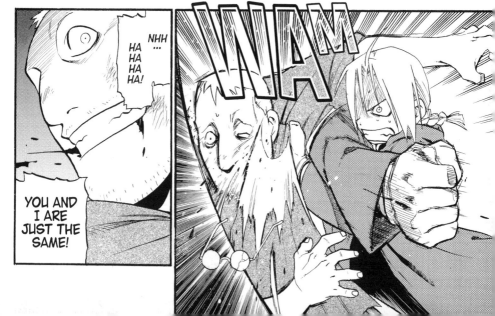

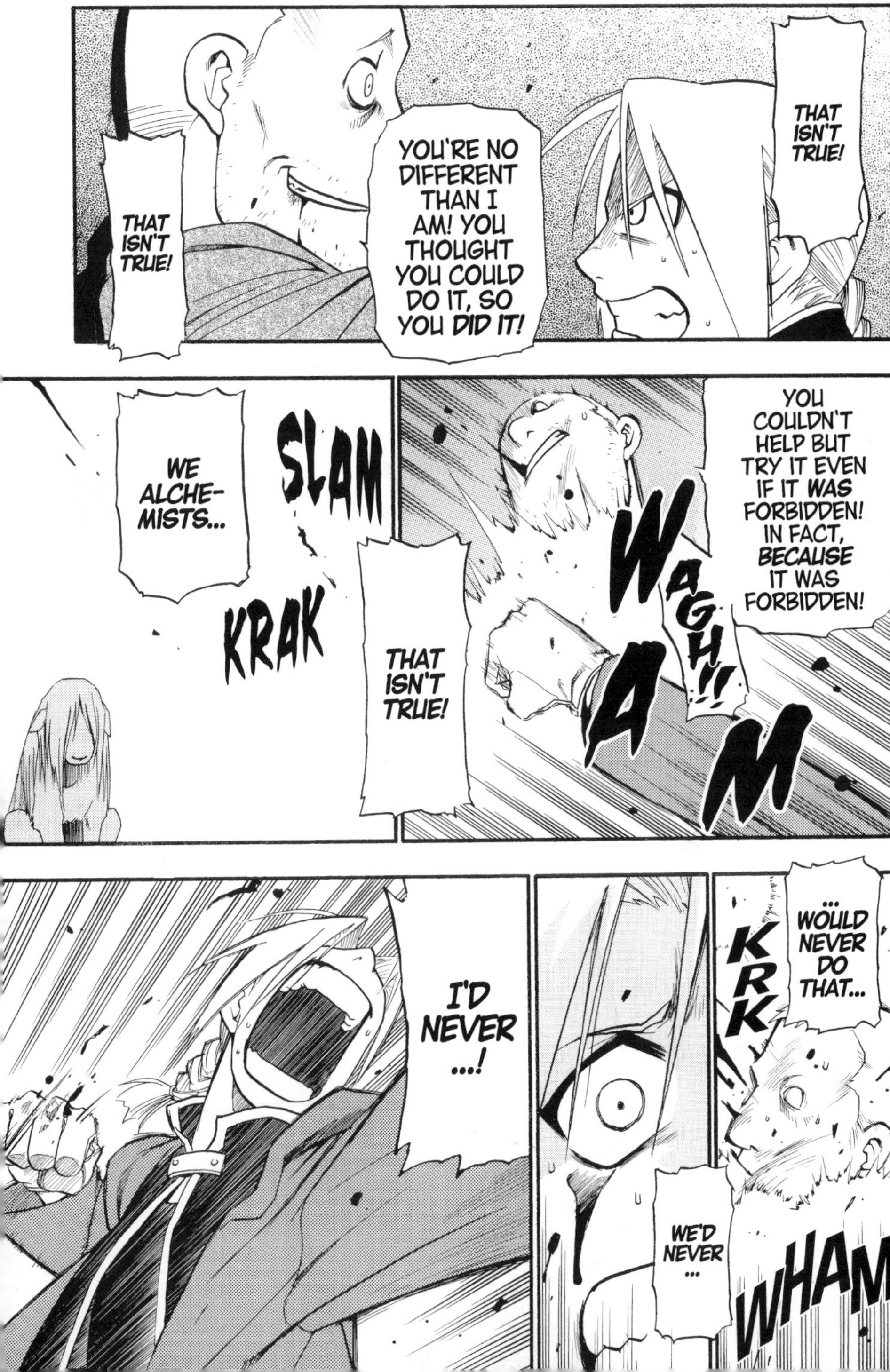
THAT ISN'T TRUE!
YOU'RE NO DIFFERENT THAN I AM! YOU THOUGHT YOU COULD DO IT, SO YOU DID IT!
THAT ISN'T TRUE!
YOU COULDN'T HELP BUT TRY IT EVEN IF IT WAS FORBIDDEN! IN FACT, BECAUSE IT WAS FORBIDDEN!
WAM
AGH!!
THAT ISN'T TRUE!
SLAM
WE ALCHEMISTS...
KRAK
...WOULD NEVER DO THAT...
KRK
WE'D NEVER...
WHAM
I'D NEVER...!

ED-
WARD.

ANY
MORE AND
YOU'LL KILL
HIM.

GRIP

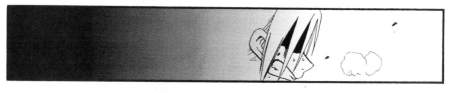

HA
HA...

PRETTY
WORDS
DON'T
GET
ANYTHING
DONE...

SLUMP

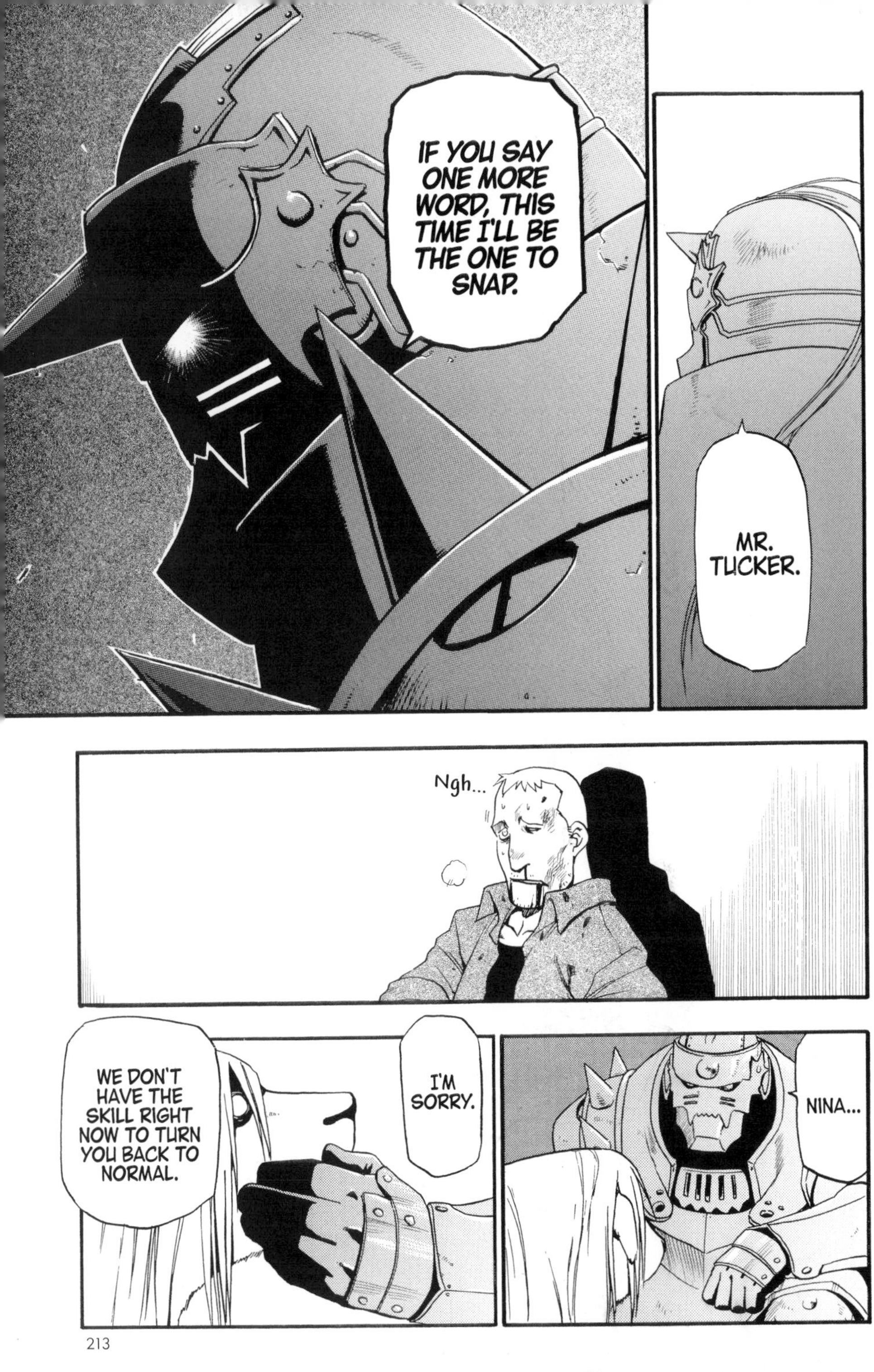
MR. TUCKER.
IF YOU SAY ONE MORE WORD, THIS TIME I'LL BE THE ONE TO SNAP.
Ngh...
NINA...
I'M SORRY.
WE DON'T HAVE THE SKILL RIGHT NOW TO TURN YOU BACK TO NORMAL.

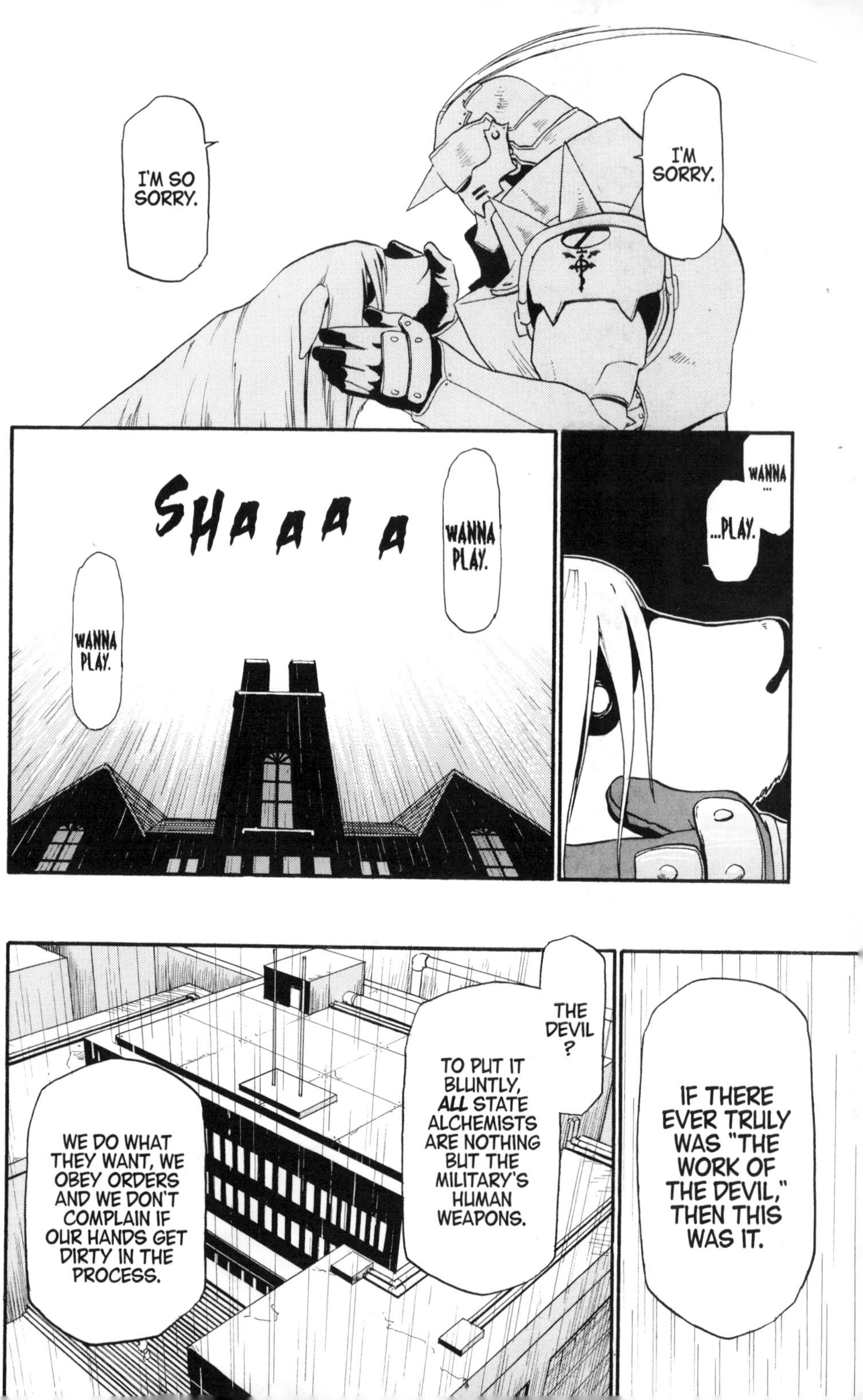
I'M SORRY.
I'M SO SORRY.
WANNA ...
...PLAY.
WANNA PLAY.
SHAAAA
WANNA PLAY.
IF THERE EVER TRULY WAS "THE WORK OF THE DEVIL," THEN THIS WAS IT.
THE DEVIL?
TO PUT IT BLUNTLY, ALL STATE ALCHEMISTS ARE NOTHING BUT THE MILITARY'S HUMAN WEAPONS.
WE DO WHAT THEY WANT, WE OBEY ORDERS AND WE DON'T COMPLAIN IF OUR HANDS GET DIRTY IN THE PROCESS.

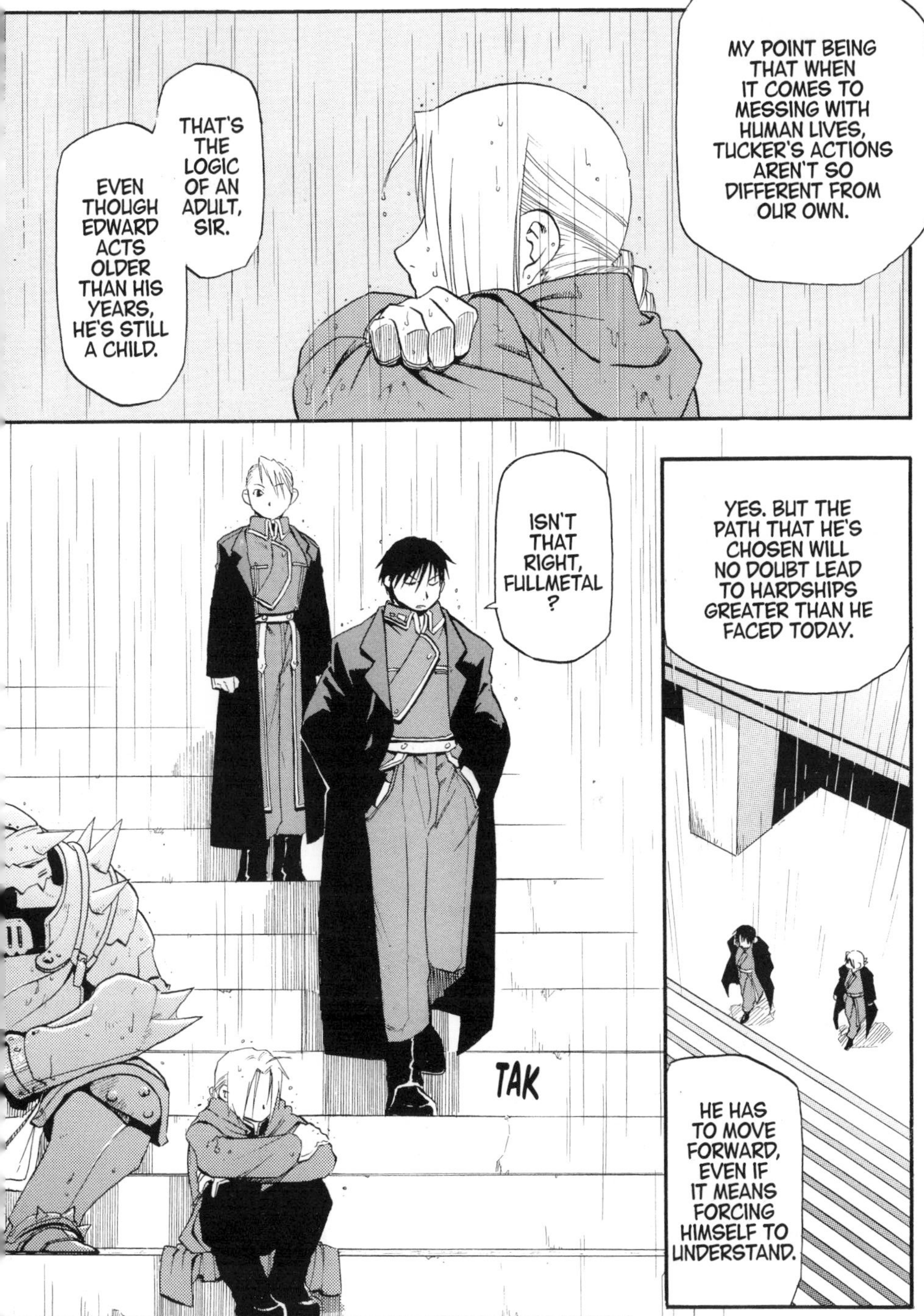
MY POINT BEING THAT WHEN IT COMES TO MESSING WITH HUMAN LIVES, TUCKER'S ACTIONS AREN'T SO DIFFERENT FROM OUR OWN.
THAT'S THE LOGIC OF AN ADULT, SIR.
EVEN THOUGH EDWARD ACTS OLDER THAN HIS YEARS, HE'S STILL A CHILD.
YES. BUT THE PATH THAT HE'S CHOSEN WILL NO DOUBT LEAD TO HARDSHIPS GREATER THAN HE FACED TODAY.
HE HAS TO MOVE FORWARD, EVEN IF IT MEANS FORCING HIMSELF TO UNDERSTAND.
ISN'T THAT RIGHT, FULLMETAL?
TAK

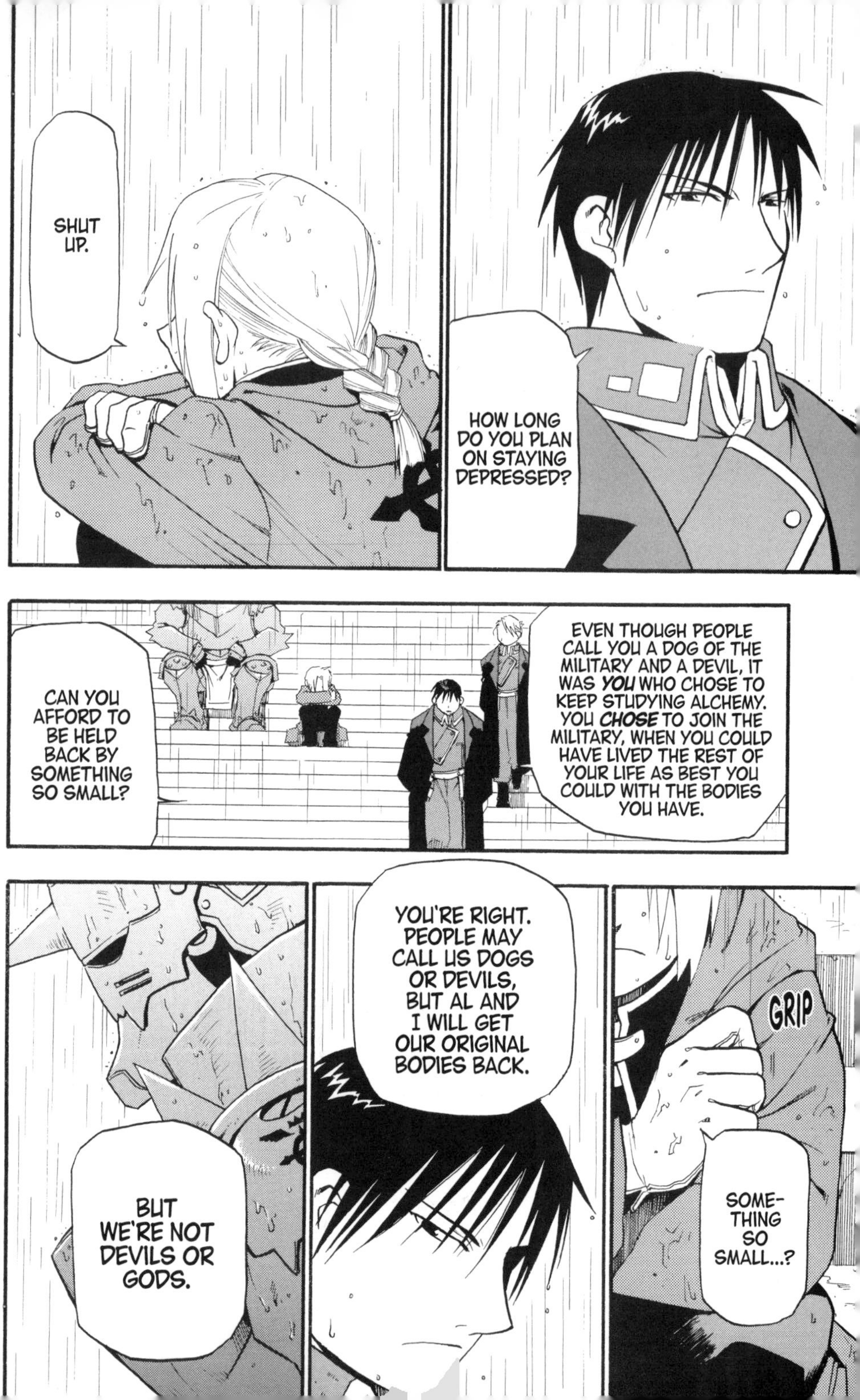
HOW LONG DO YOU PLAN ON STAYING DEPRESSED?
SHUT UP.
EVEN THOUGH PEOPLE CALL YOU A DOG OF THE MILITARY AND A DEVIL, IT WAS *YOU* WHO CHOSE TO KEEP STUDYING ALCHEMY. YOU *CHOSE* TO JOIN THE MILITARY, WHEN YOU COULD HAVE LIVED THE REST OF YOUR LIFE AS BEST YOU COULD WITH THE BODIES YOU HAVE.
CAN YOU AFFORD TO BE HELD BACK BY SOMETHING SO SMALL?
GRIP
SOME-THING SO SMALL...?
YOU'RE RIGHT. PEOPLE MAY CALL US DOGS OR DEVILS, BUT AL AND I WILL GET OUR ORIGINAL BODIES BACK.
BUT WE'RE NOT DEVILS OR GODS.

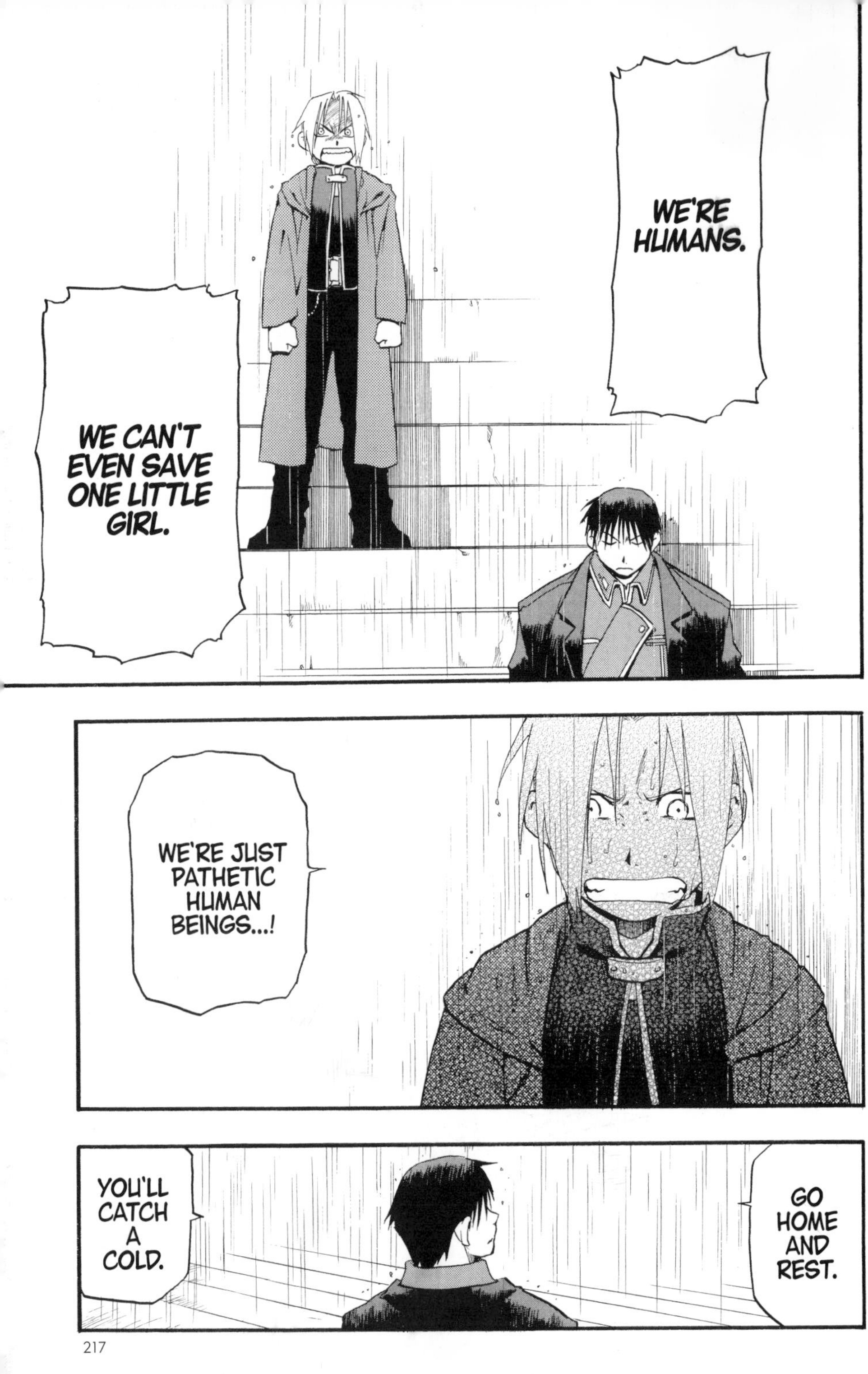
WE'RE HUMANS.
WE CAN'T EVEN SAVE ONE LITTLE GIRL.
WE'RE JUST PATHETIC HUMAN BEINGS...!
GO HOME AND REST.
YOU'LL CATCH A COLD.

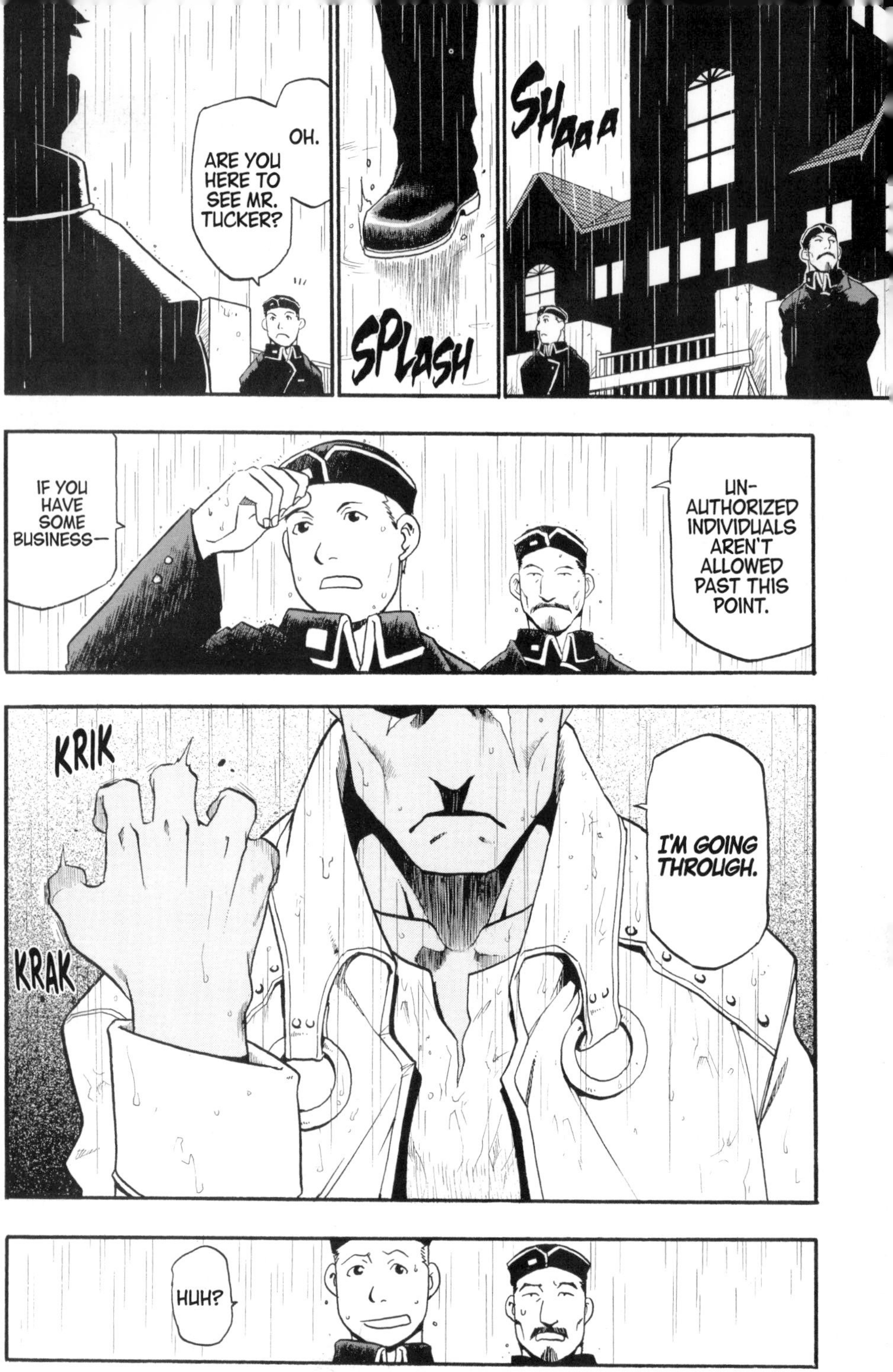
SHAAA
SPLASH
OH.
ARE YOU HERE TO SEE MR. TUCKER?
UN-AUTHORIZED INDIVIDUALS AREN'T ALLOWED PAST THIS POINT.
IF YOU HAVE SOME BUSINESS—
I'M GOING THROUGH.
KRIK
KRAK
HUH?

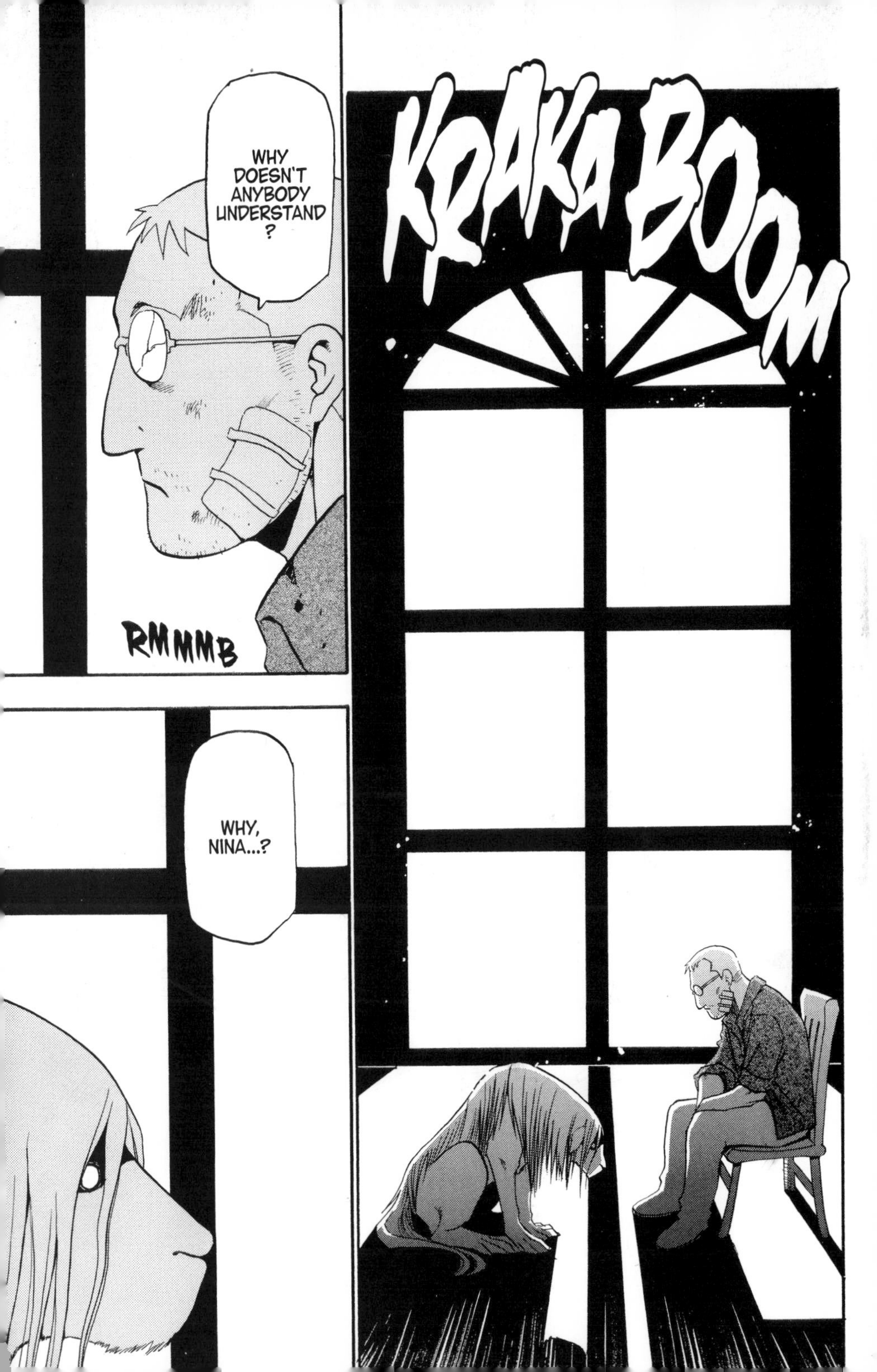
KRAKA BOOM
WHY DOESN'T ANYBODY UNDERSTAND?
RMMMB
WHY, NINA...?

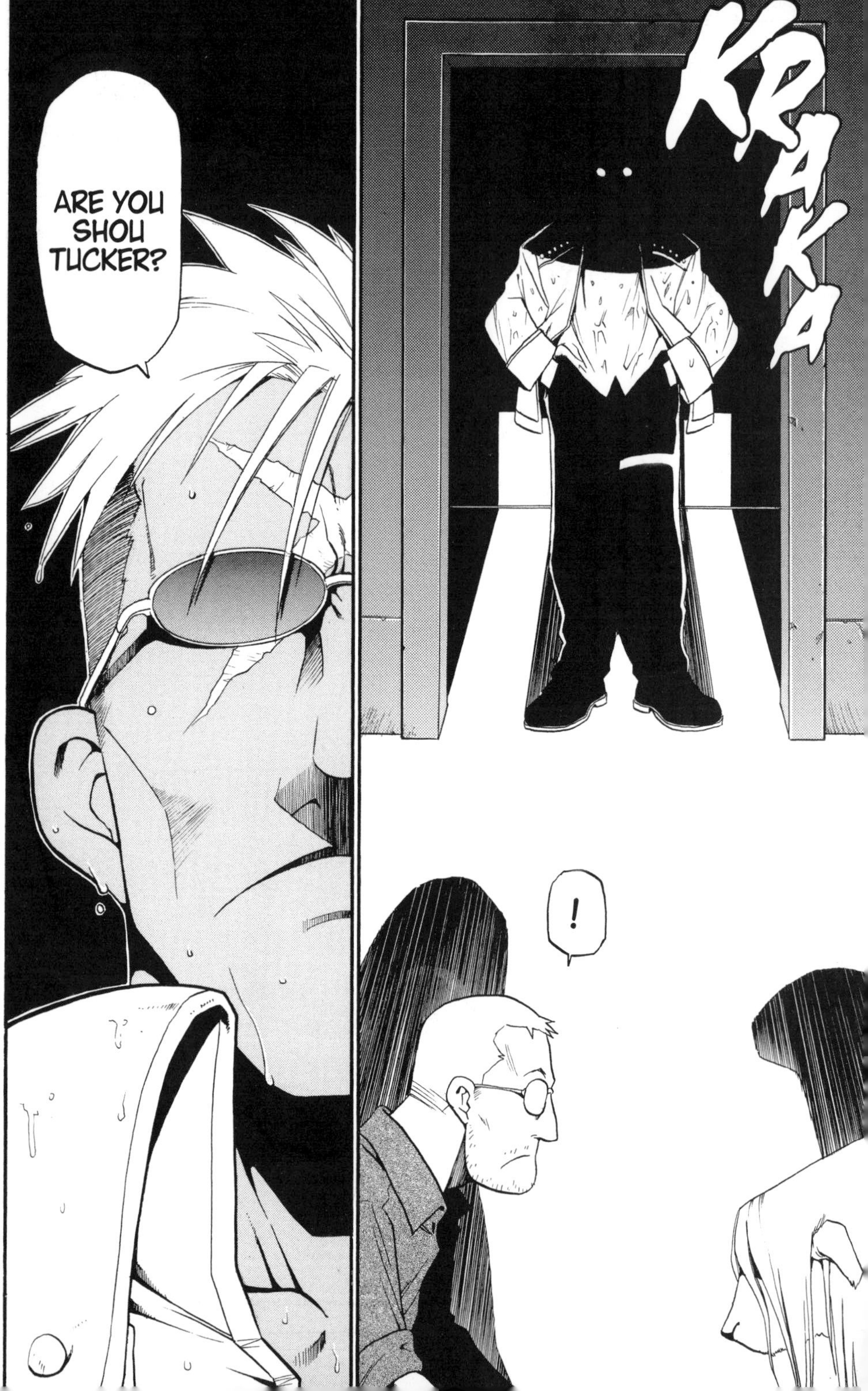
KRAKA
!
ARE YOU SHOU TUCKER?

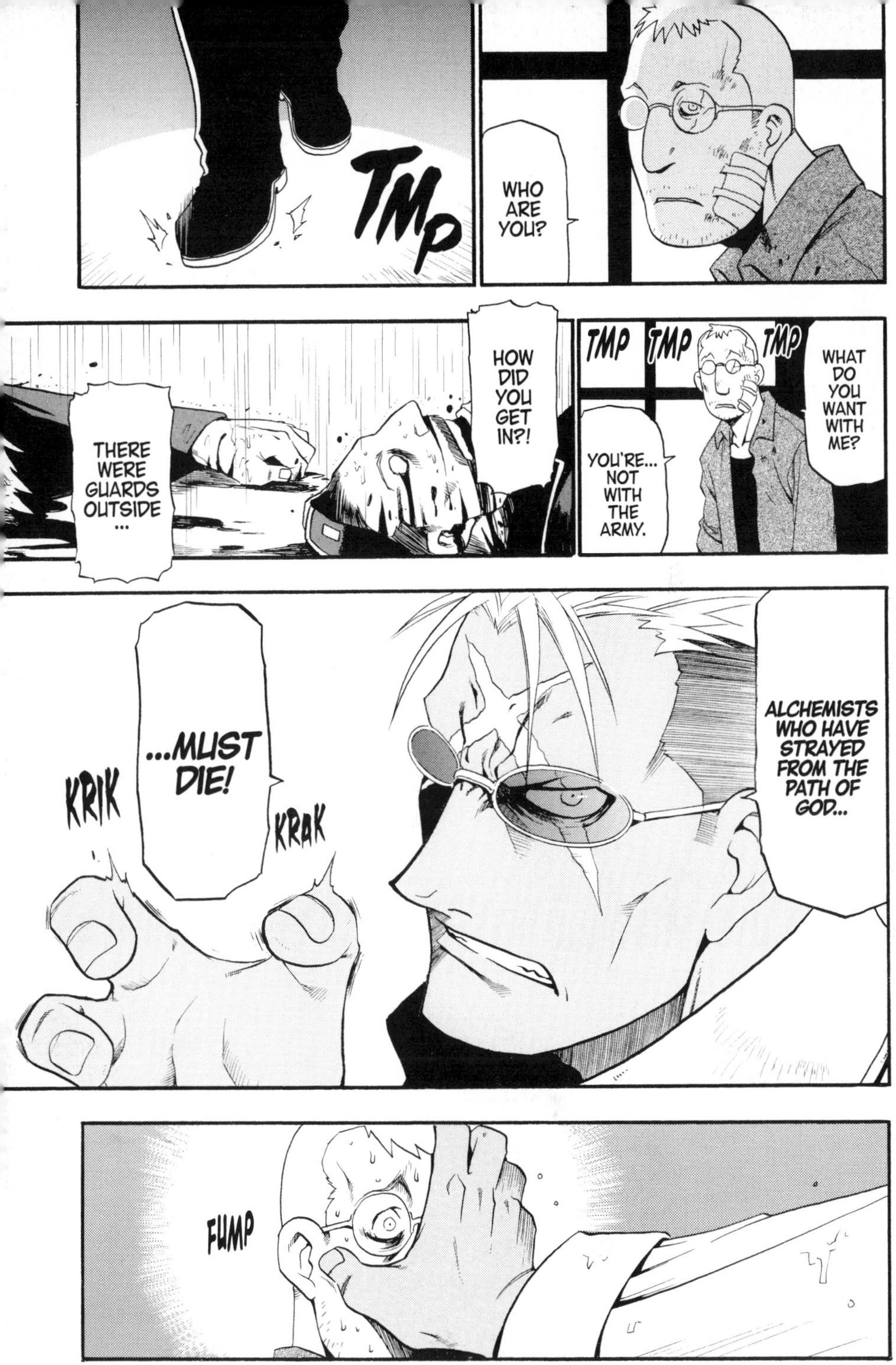
WHO ARE YOU?
TMP
TMP
TMP
TMP
WHAT DO YOU WANT WITH ME?
YOU'RE... NOT WITH THE ARMY.
HOW DID YOU GET IN?!
THERE WERE GUARDS OUTSIDE ...
ALCHEMISTS WHO HAVE STRAYED FROM THE PATH OF GOD...
KRAK
...MUST DIE!
KRIK
FUMP

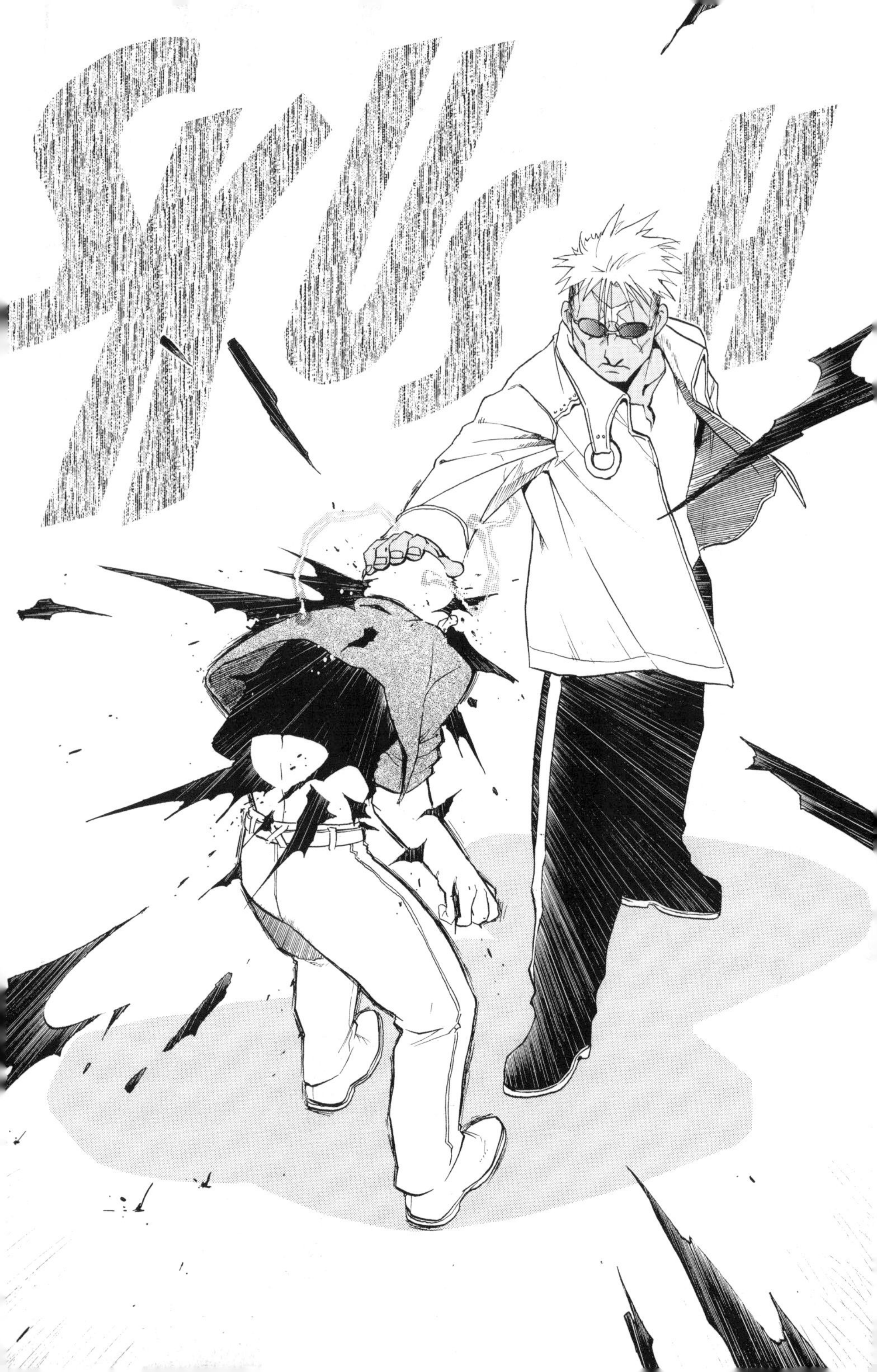
SHUSH

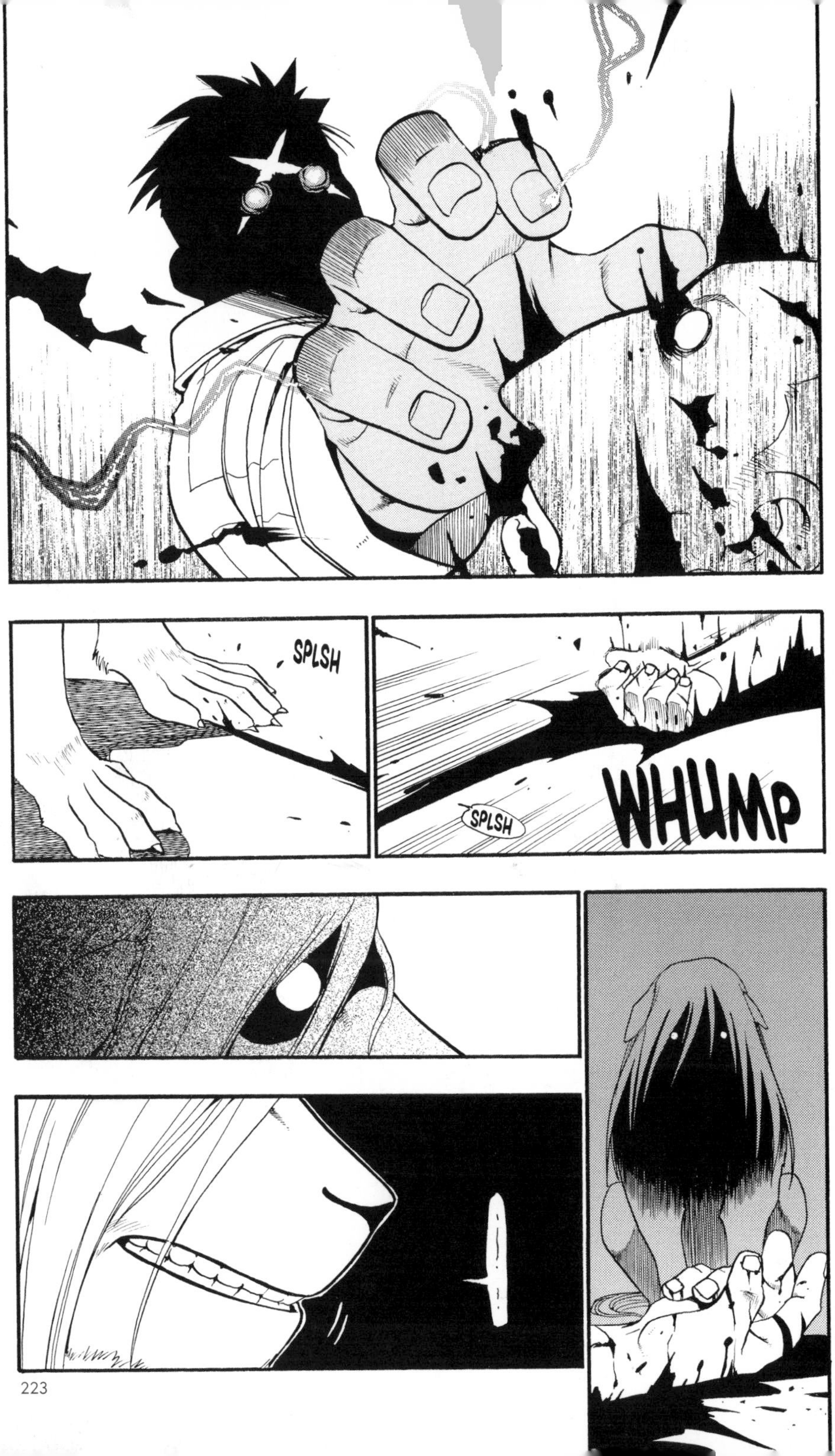
WHUMP
SPLSH
SPLSH
...

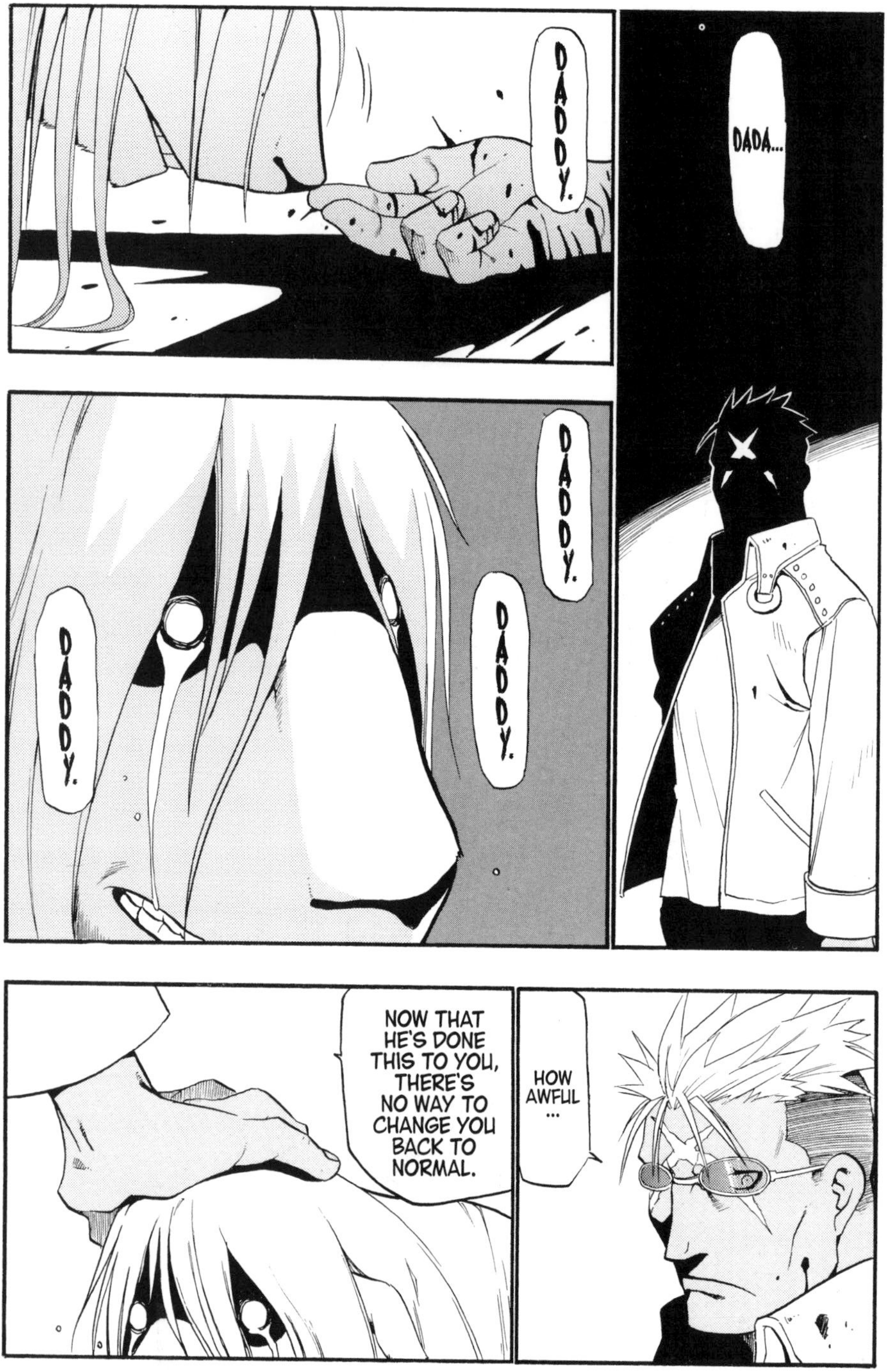

DADA...
DADDY.
DADDY.
DADDY.
DADDY.
HOW AWFUL ...
NOW THAT HE'S DONE THIS TO YOU, THERE'S NO WAY TO CHANGE YOU BACK TO NORMAL.

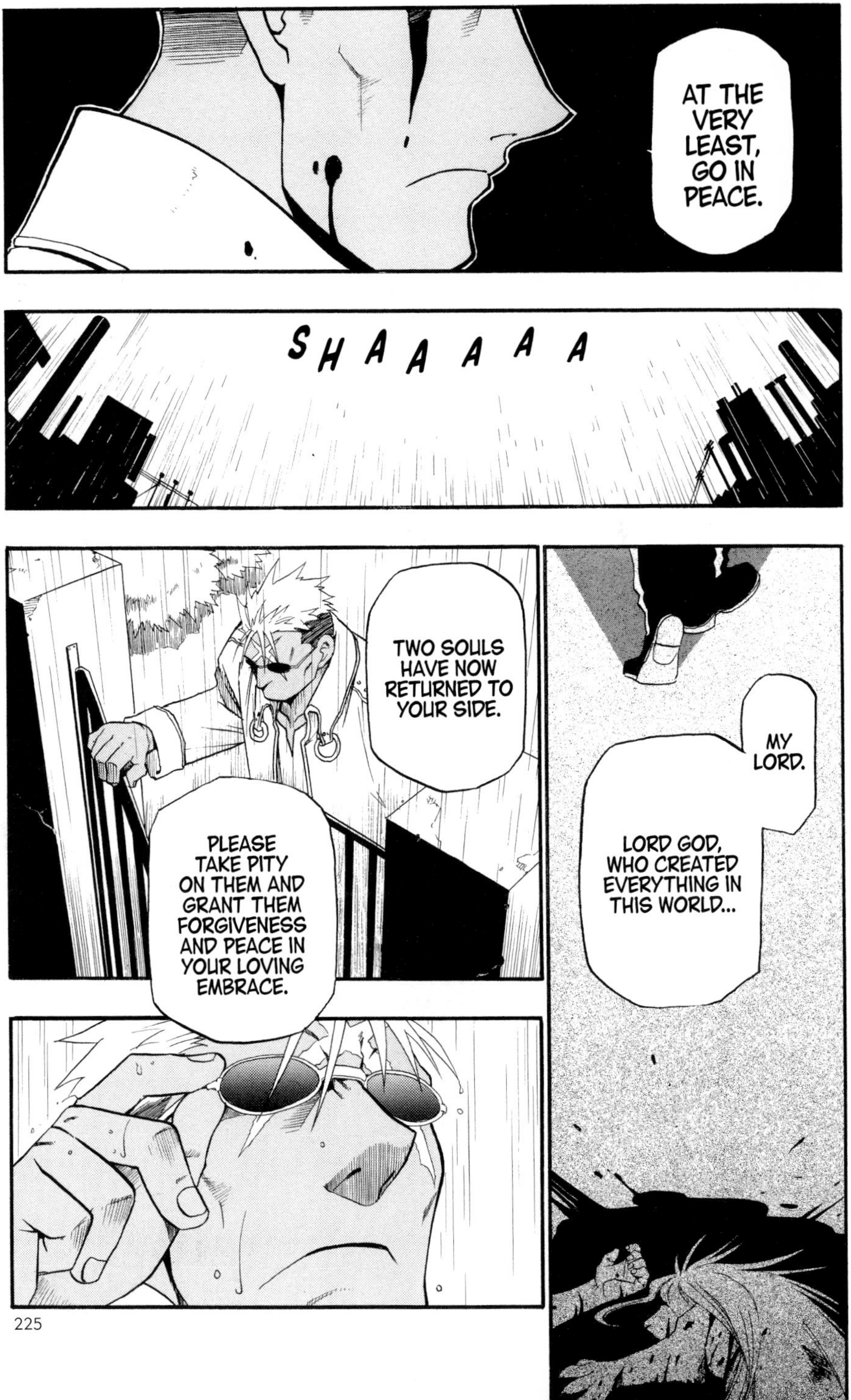
AT THE VERY LEAST, GO IN PEACE.
SHAAAAAA
MY LORD.
LORD GOD, WHO CREATED EVERYTHING IN THIS WORLD...
TWO SOULS HAVE NOW RETURNED TO YOUR SIDE.
PLEASE TAKE PITY ON THEM AND GRANT THEM FORGIVENESS AND PEACE IN YOUR LOVING EMBRACE.

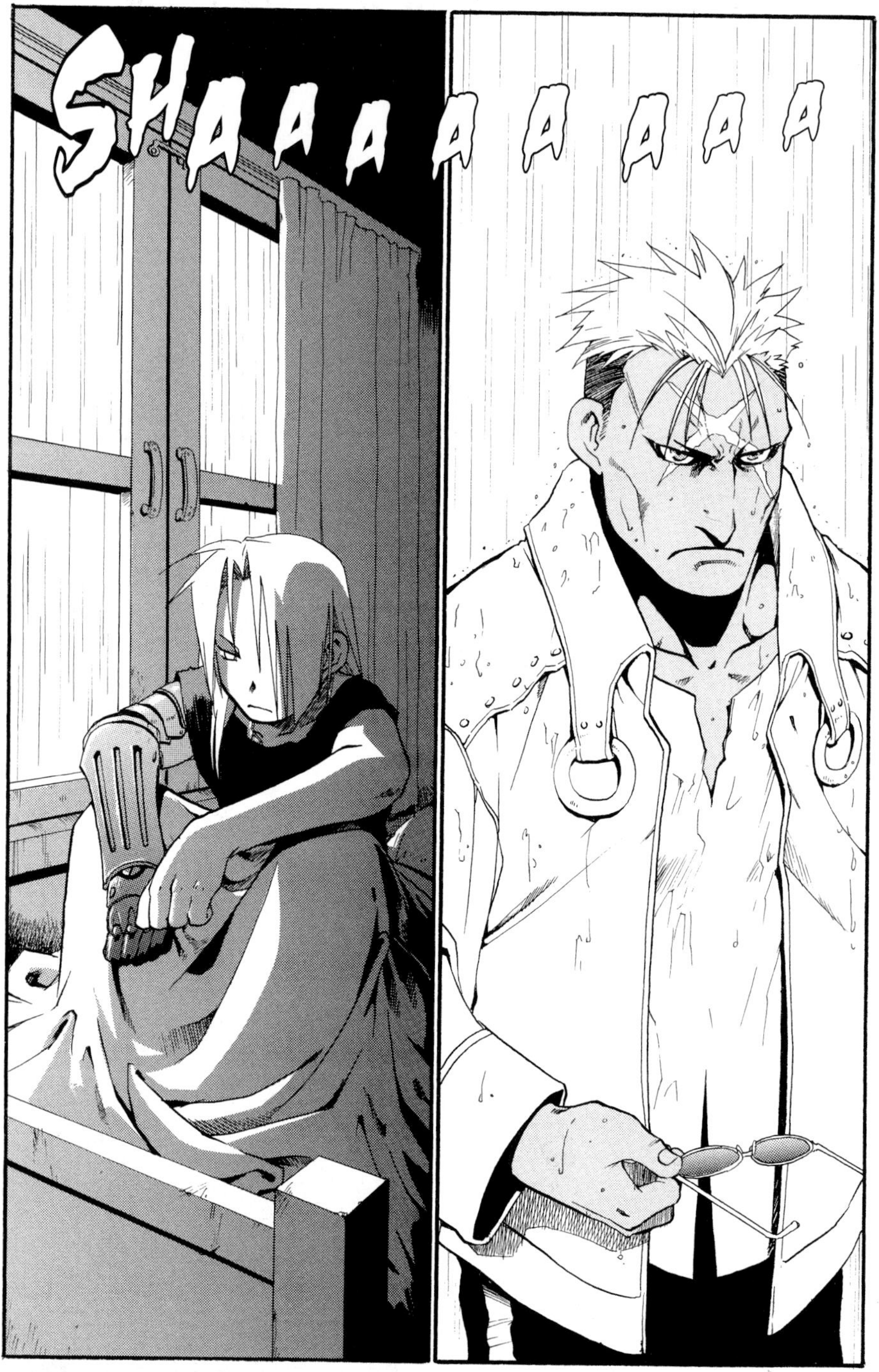
SHAAAAAAAAA

CHAPTER 6

THE RIGHT HAND OF DESTRUCTION

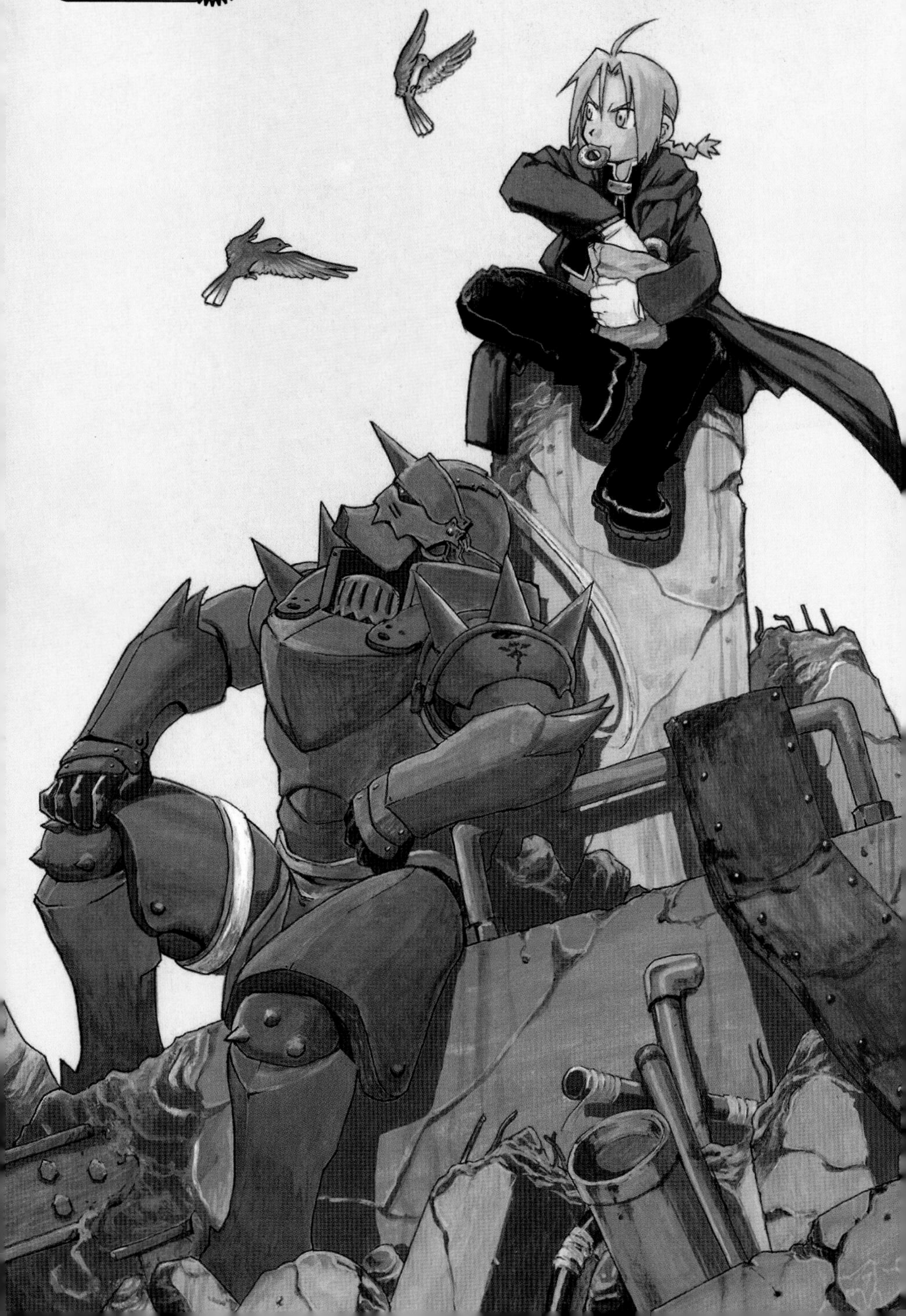

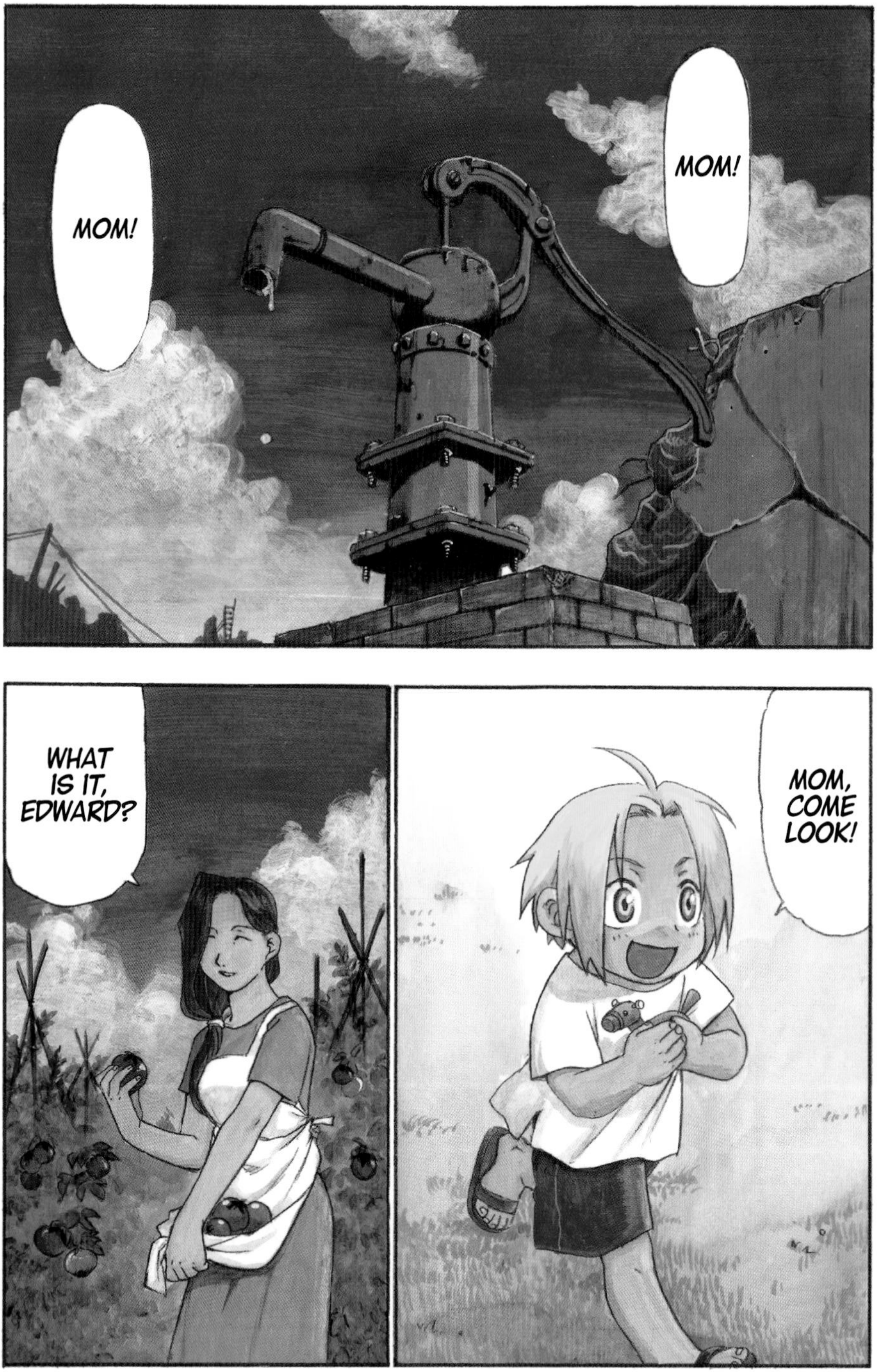
MOM!
MOM!
MOM, COME LOOK!
WHAT IS IT, EDWARD?

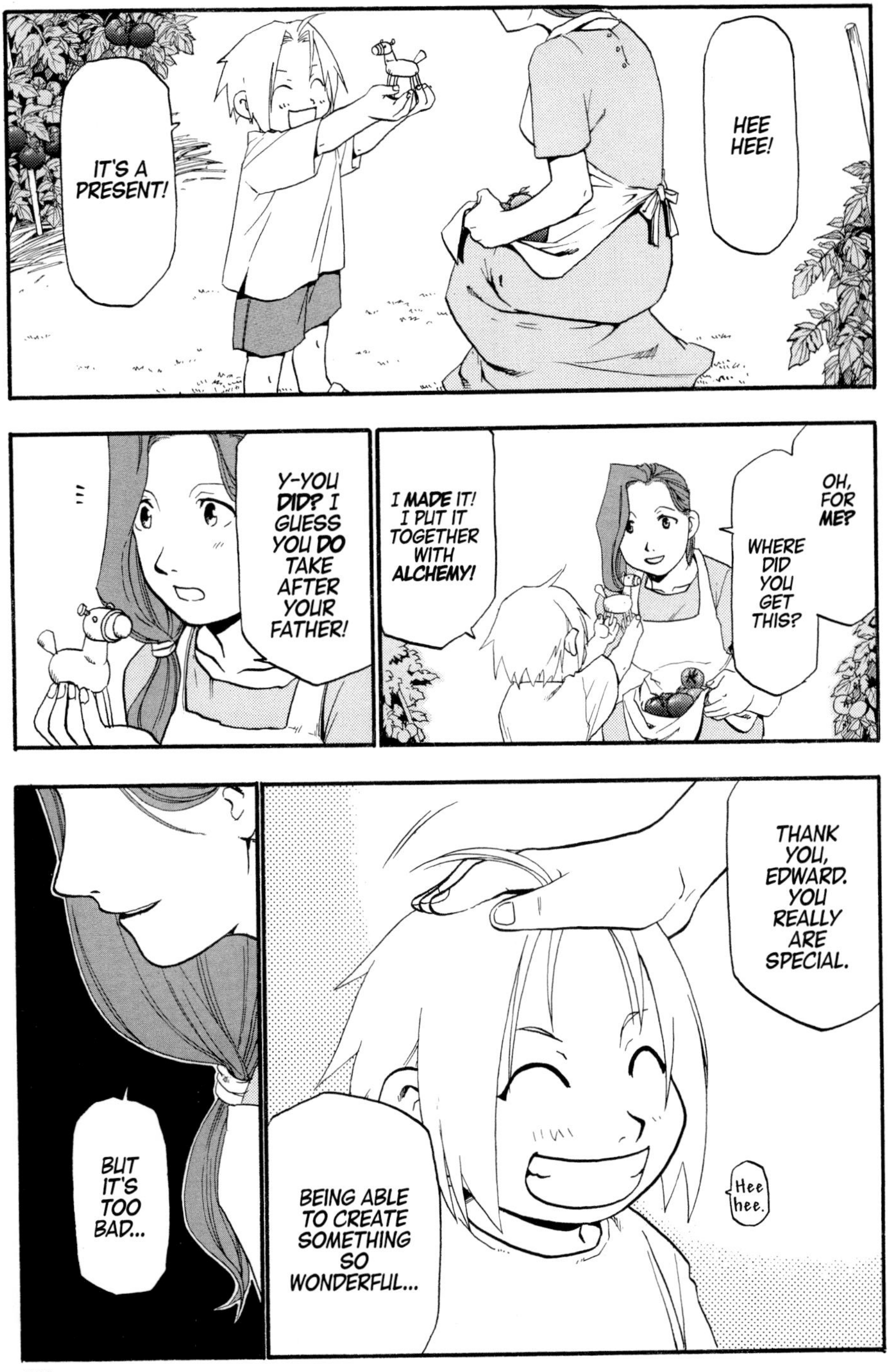
HEE HEE!
IT'S A PRESENT!
OH, FOR ME?
WHERE DID YOU GET THIS?
I MADE IT! I PUT IT TOGETHER WITH ALCHEMY!
Y-YOU DID? I GUESS YOU DO TAKE AFTER YOUR FATHER!
THANK YOU, EDWARD. YOU REALLY ARE SPECIAL.
Hee hee.
BEING ABLE TO CREATE SOMETHING SO WONDERFUL...
BUT IT'S TOO BAD...

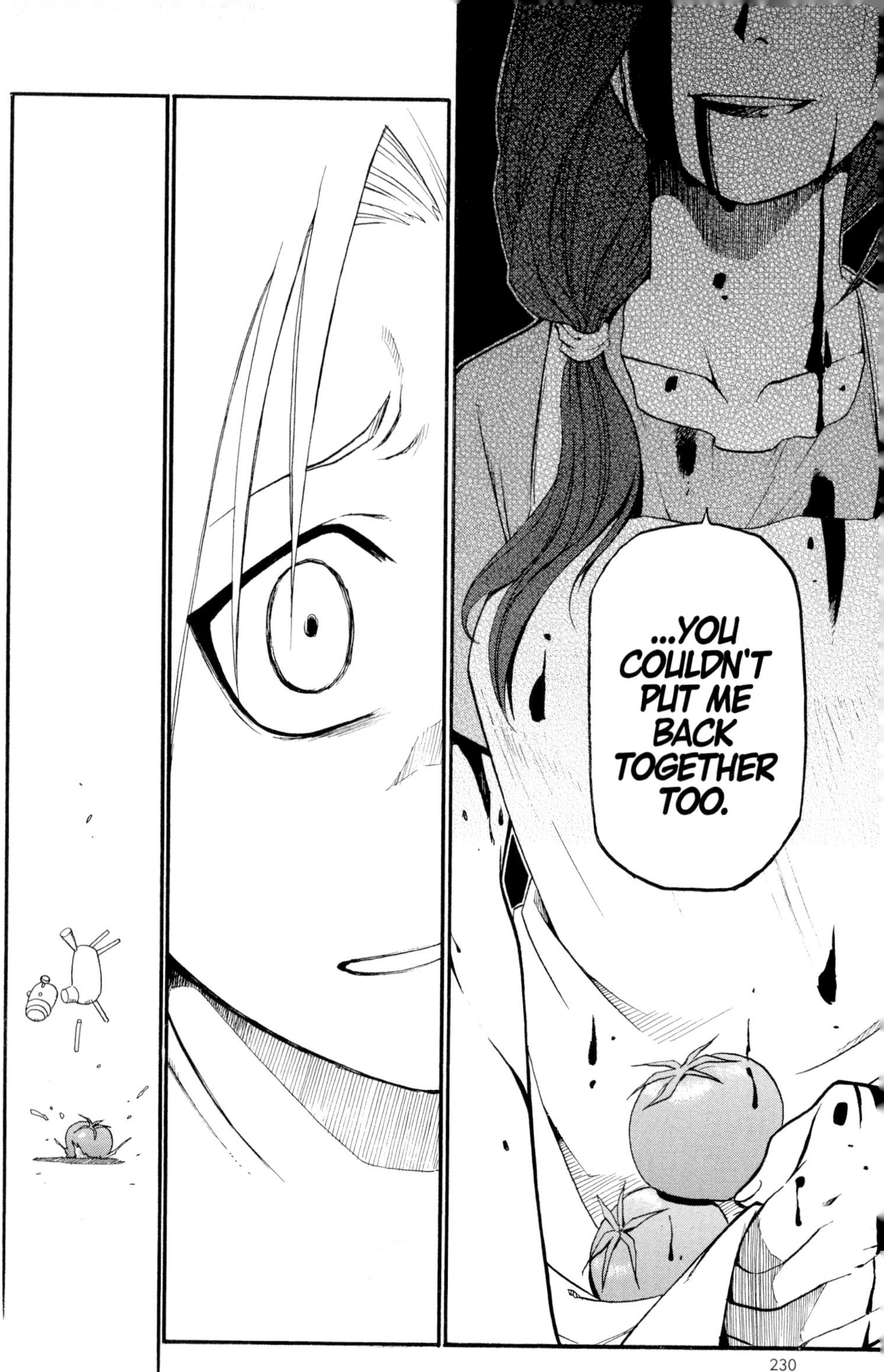
...YOU COULDN'T PUT ME BACK TOGETHER TOO.

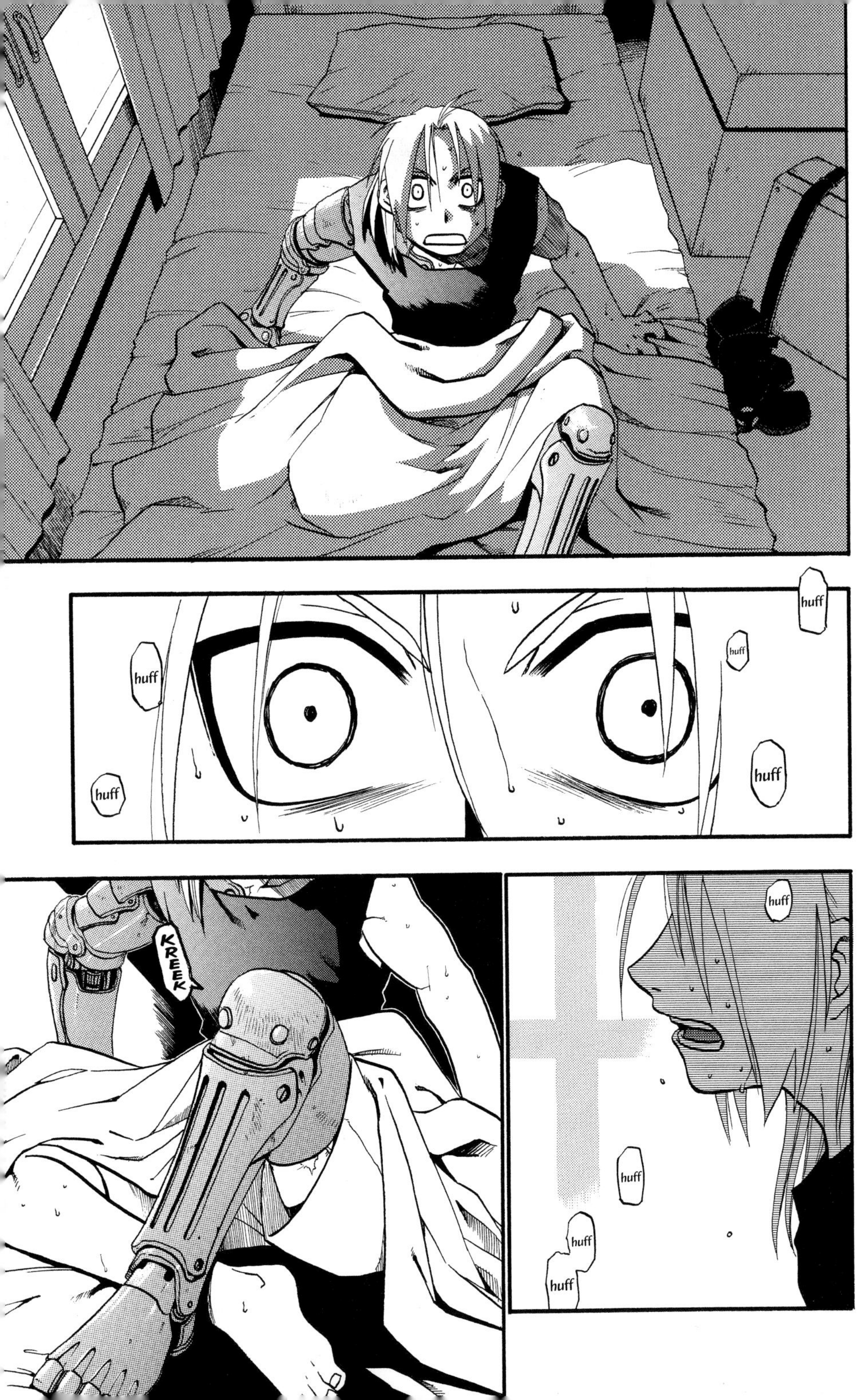
huff
huff
huff
huff
huff
huff
huff
huff
huff
KREEK

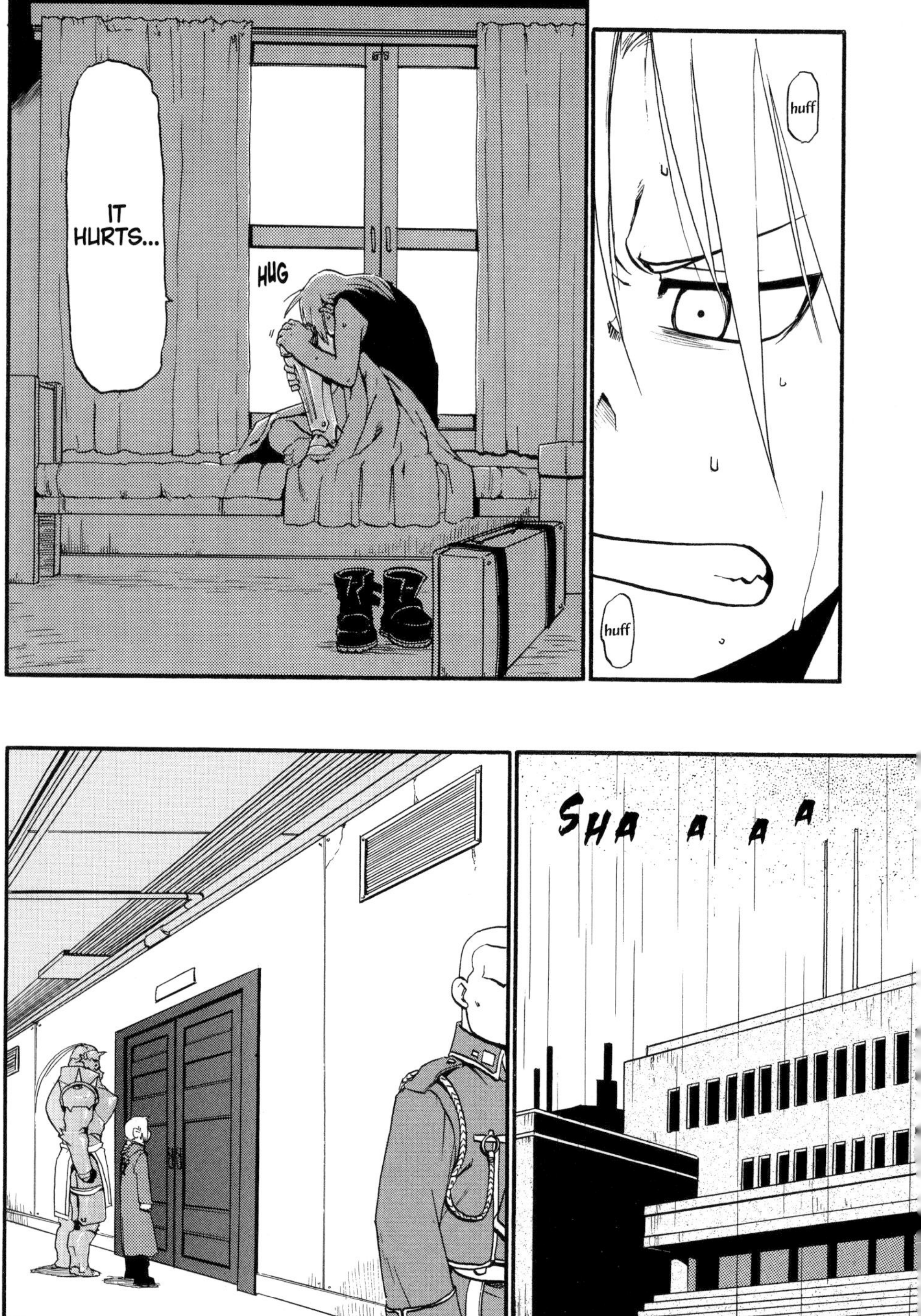
huff
huff
IT HURTS...
HUG
SHA A A A

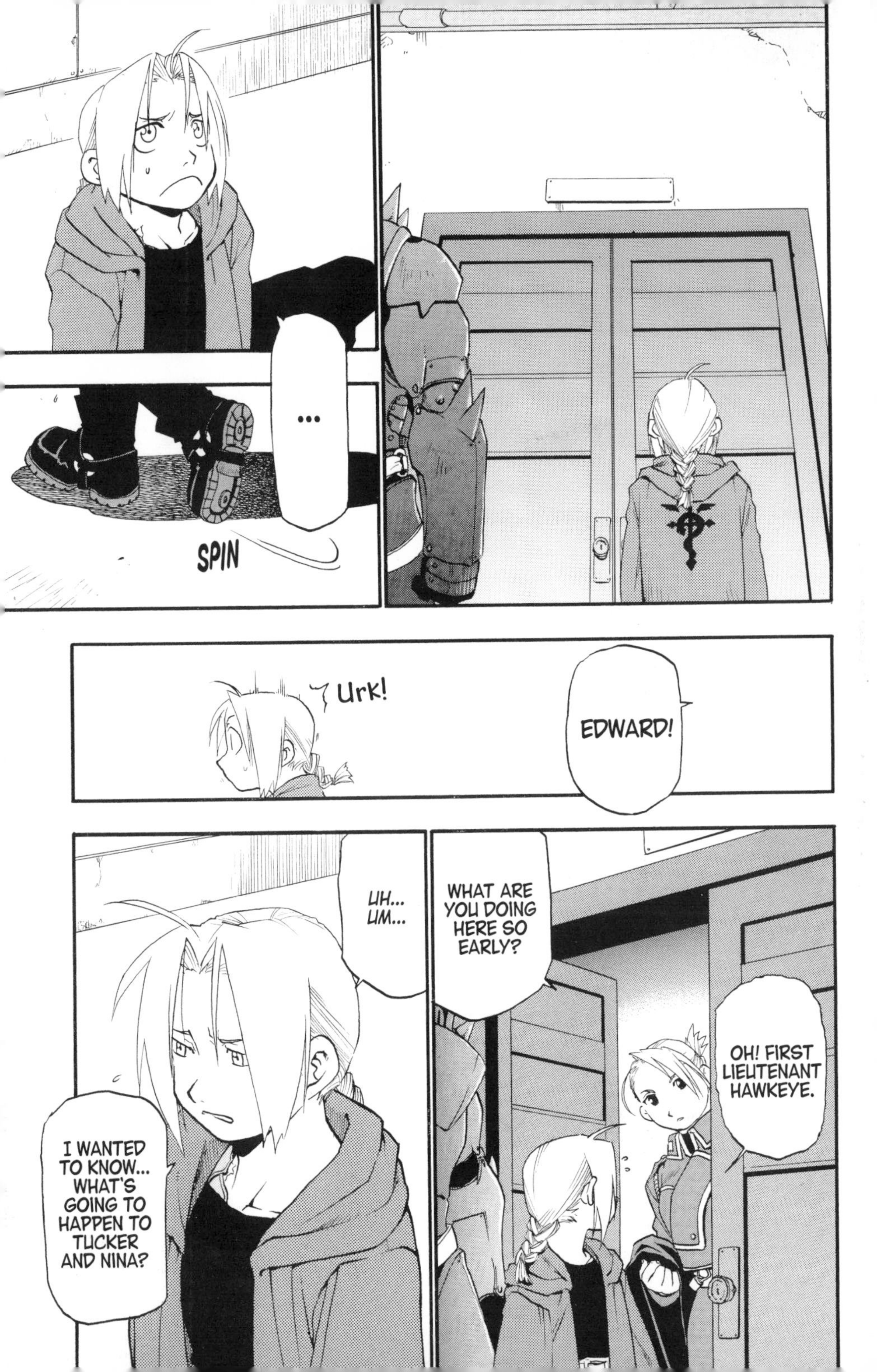
...
SPIN
EDWARD!
Urk!
OH! FIRST LIEUTENANT HAWKEYE.
WHAT ARE YOU DOING HERE SO EARLY?
UH... UM...
I WANTED TO KNOW... WHAT'S GOING TO HAPPEN TO TUCKER AND NINA?

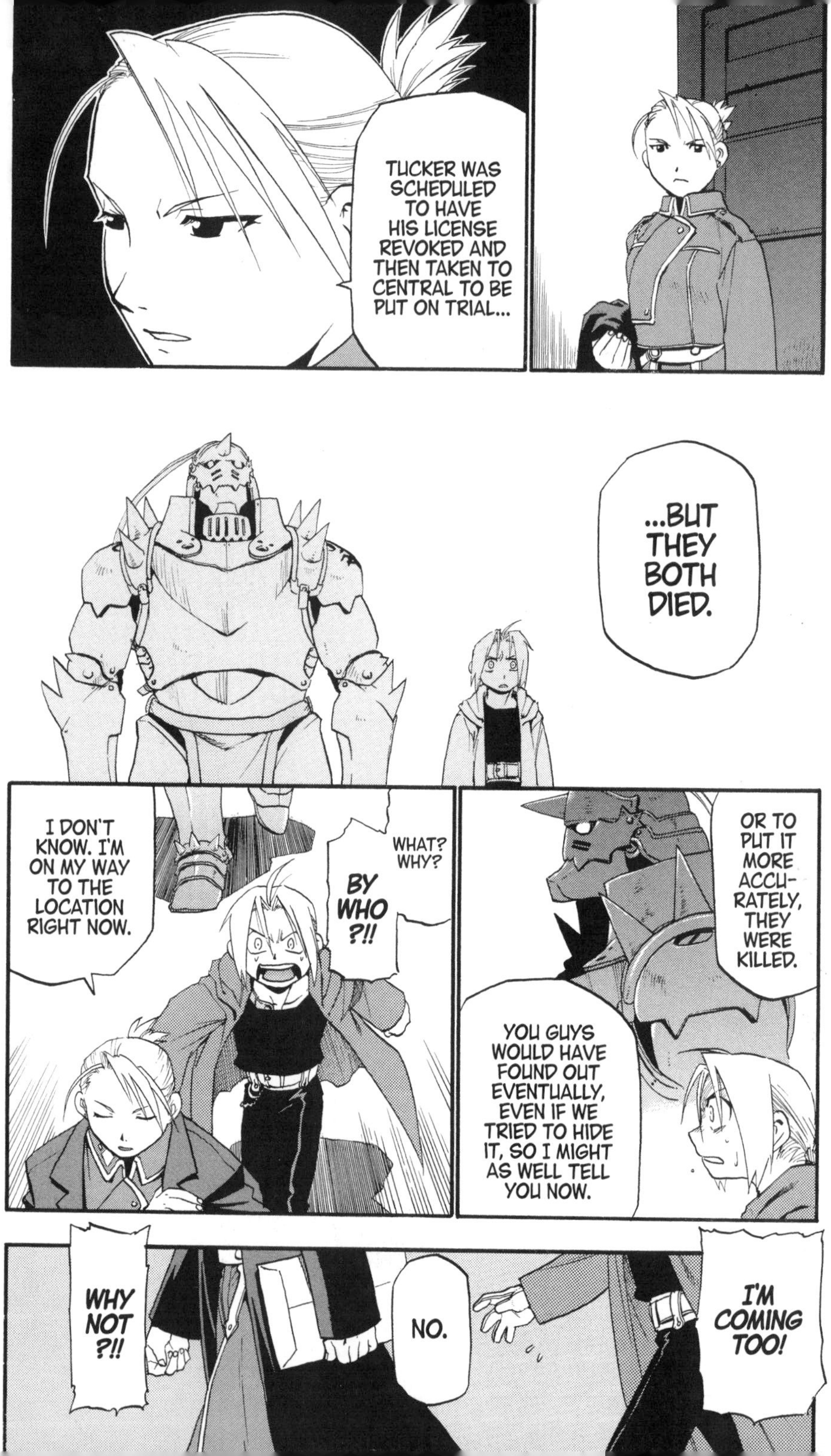
TUCKER WAS SCHEDULED TO HAVE HIS LICENSE REVOKED AND THEN TAKEN TO CENTRAL TO BE PUT ON TRIAL...
...BUT THEY BOTH DIED.
OR TO PUT IT MORE ACCU-RATELY, THEY WERE KILLED.
YOU GUYS WOULD HAVE FOUND OUT EVENTUALLY, EVEN IF WE TRIED TO HIDE IT, SO I MIGHT AS WELL TELL YOU NOW.
WHAT? WHY?
BY WHO?!!
I DON'T KNOW. I'M ON MY WAY TO THE LOCATION RIGHT NOW.
I'M COMING TOO!
NO.
WHY NOT?!!

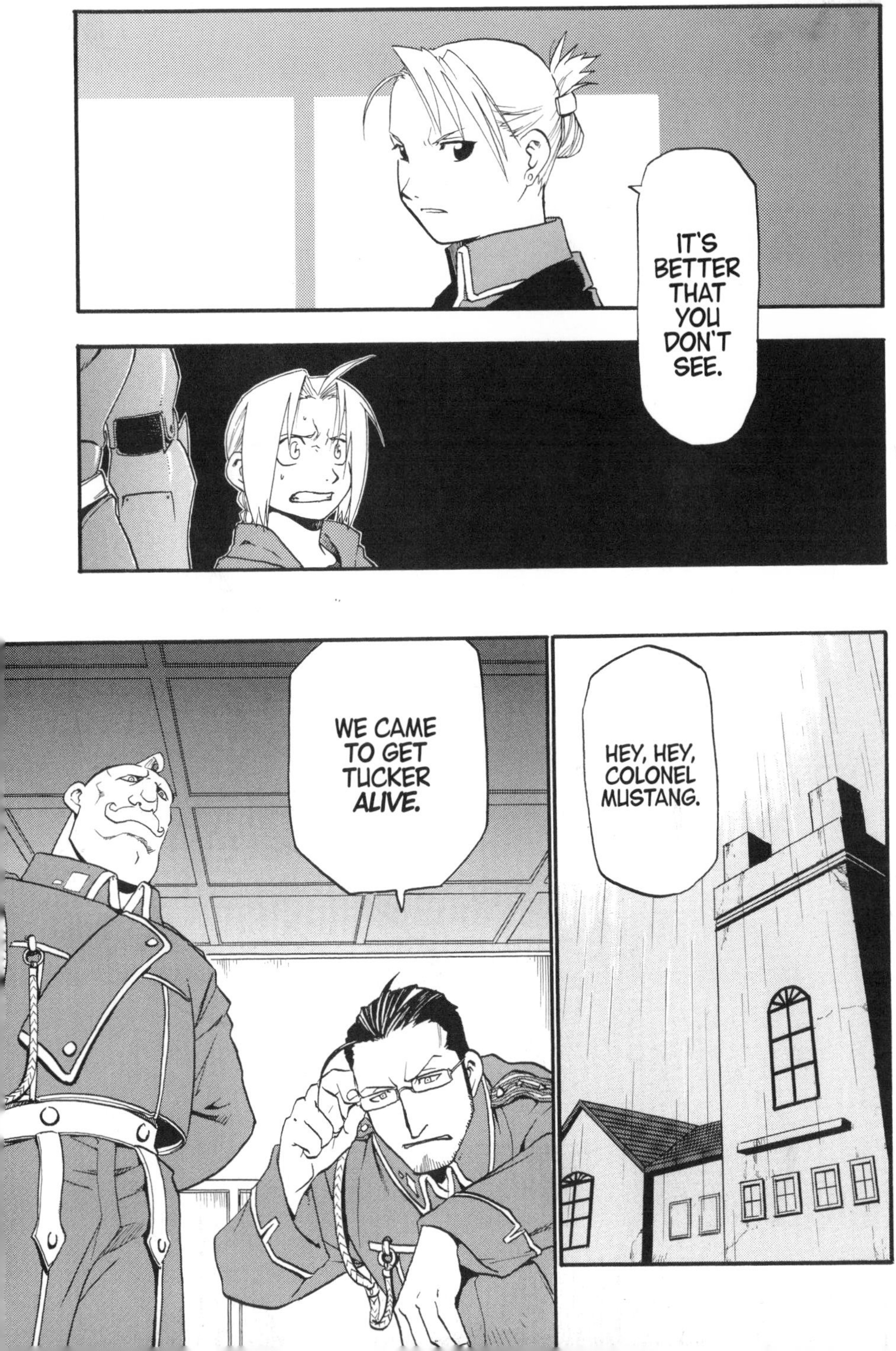
IT'S BETTER THAT YOU DON'T SEE.
HEY, HEY, COLONEL MUSTANG.
WE CAME TO GET TUCKER ALIVE.

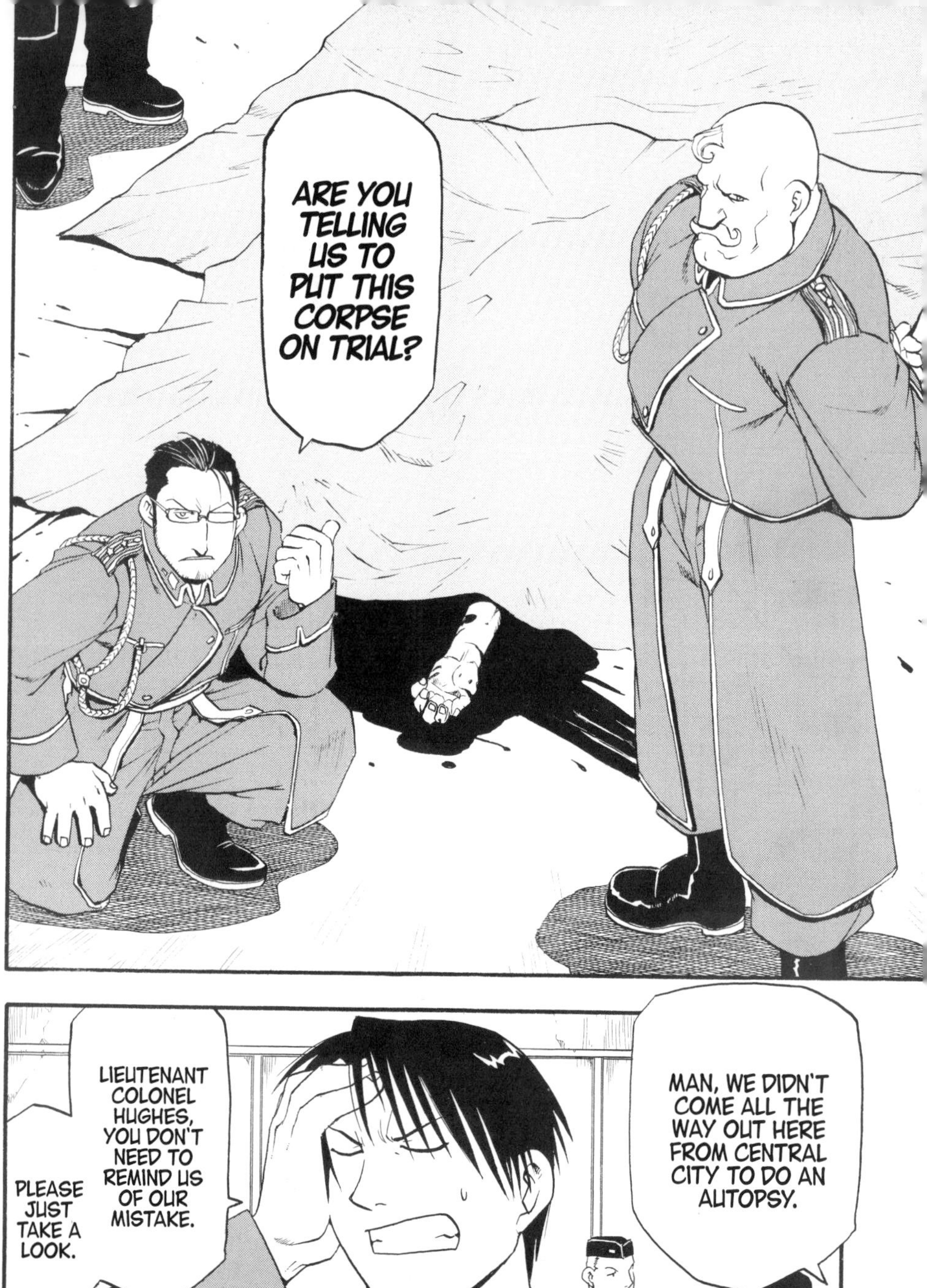
ARE YOU TELLING US TO PUT THIS CORPSE ON TRIAL?
MAN, WE DIDN'T COME ALL THE WAY OUT HERE FROM CENTRAL CITY TO DO AN AUTOPSY.
LIEUTENANT COLONEL HUGHES, YOU DON'T NEED TO REMIND US OF OUR MISTAKE.
PLEASE JUST TAKE A LOOK.

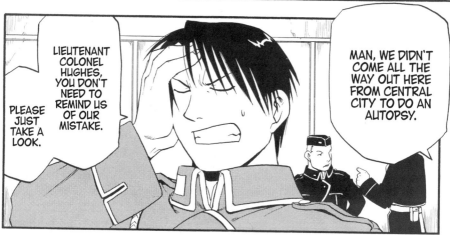

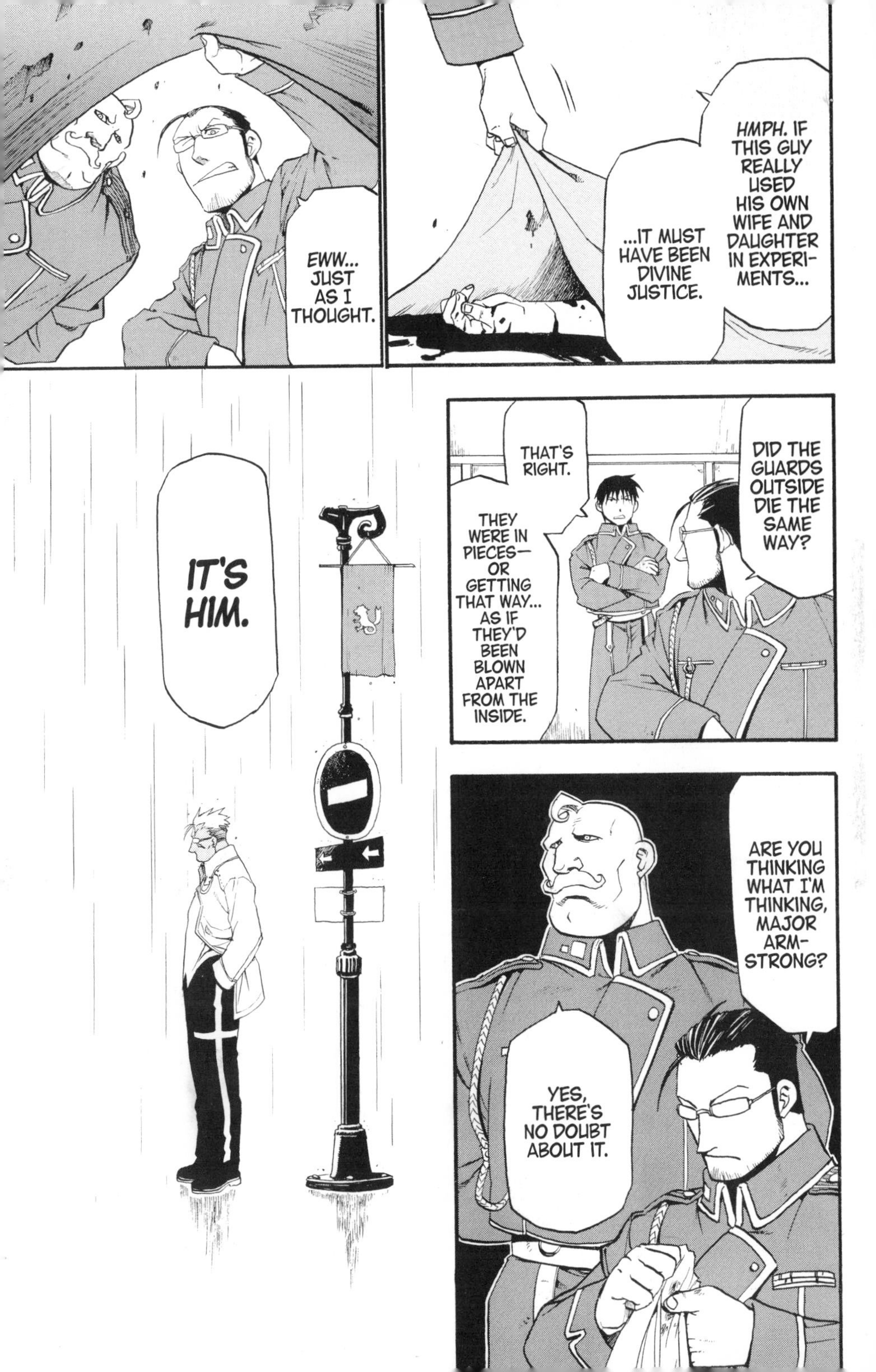
HMPH. IF THIS GUY REALLY USED HIS OWN WIFE AND DAUGHTER IN EXPERIMENTS...
...IT MUST HAVE BEEN DIVINE JUSTICE.
EWW... JUST AS I THOUGHT.
DID THE GUARDS OUTSIDE DIE THE SAME WAY?
THAT'S RIGHT.
THEY WERE IN PIECES— OR GETTING THAT WAY... AS IF THEY'D BEEN BLOWN APART FROM THE INSIDE.
ARE YOU THINKING WHAT I'M THINKING, MAJOR ARM-STRONG?
YES, THERE'S NO DOUBT ABOUT IT.
IT'S HIM.

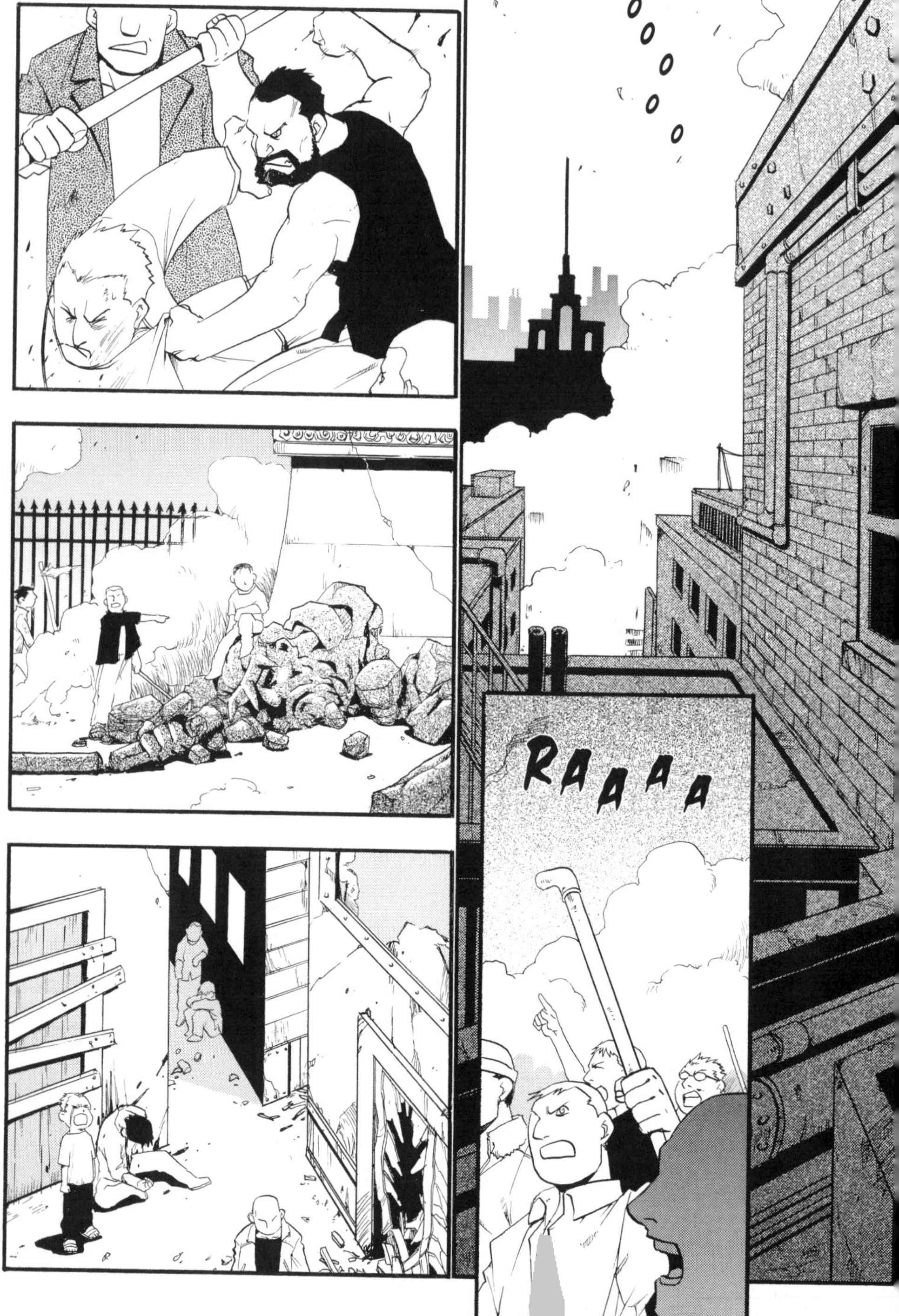
GWOOOOO
RAAAA

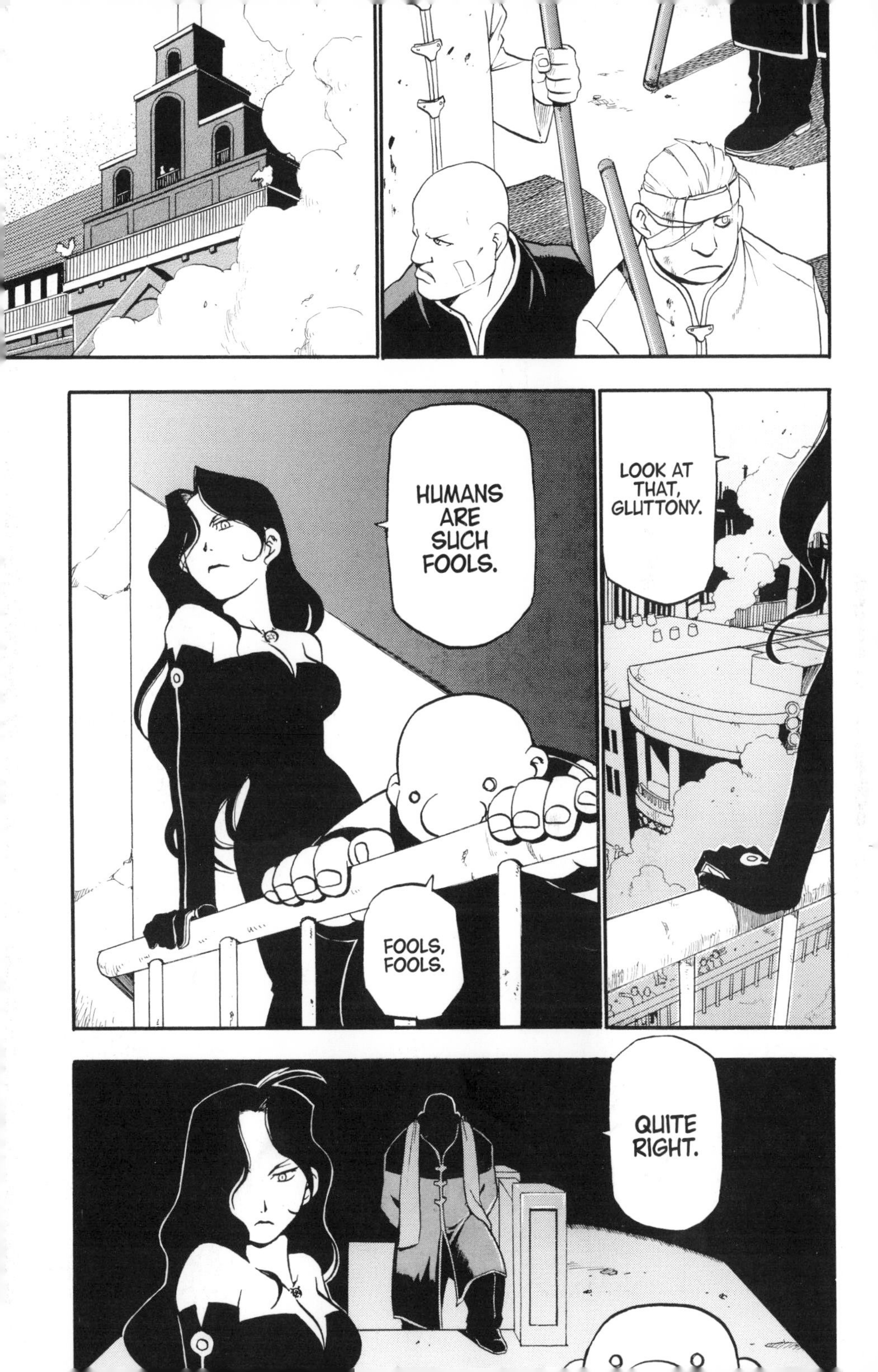
LOOK AT THAT, GLUTTONY.
HUMANS ARE SUCH FOOLS.
FOOLS, FOOLS.
QUITE RIGHT.

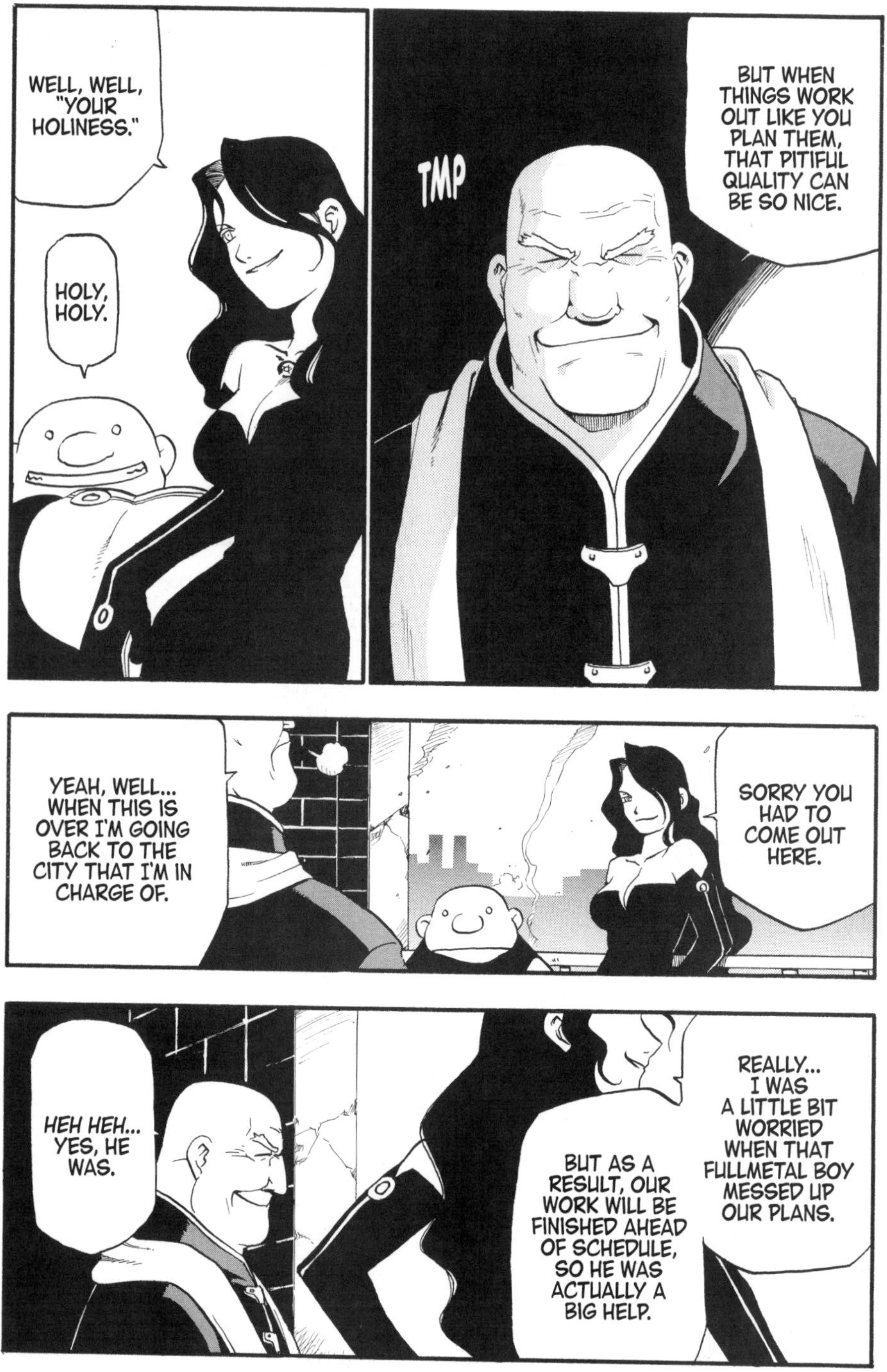

BUT WHEN THINGS WORK OUT LIKE YOU PLAN THEM, THAT PITIFUL QUALITY CAN BE SO NICE.
TMP
WELL, WELL, "YOUR HOLINESS."
HOLY, HOLY.
SORRY YOU HAD TO COME OUT HERE.
YEAH, WELL... WHEN THIS IS OVER I'M GOING BACK TO THE CITY THAT I'M IN CHARGE OF.
REALLY... I WAS A LITTLE BIT WORRIED WHEN THAT FULLMETAL BOY MESSED UP OUR PLANS.
BUT AS A RESULT, OUR WORK WILL BE FINISHED AHEAD OF SCHEDULE, SO HE WAS ACTUALLY A BIG HELP.
HEH HEH... YES, HE WAS.

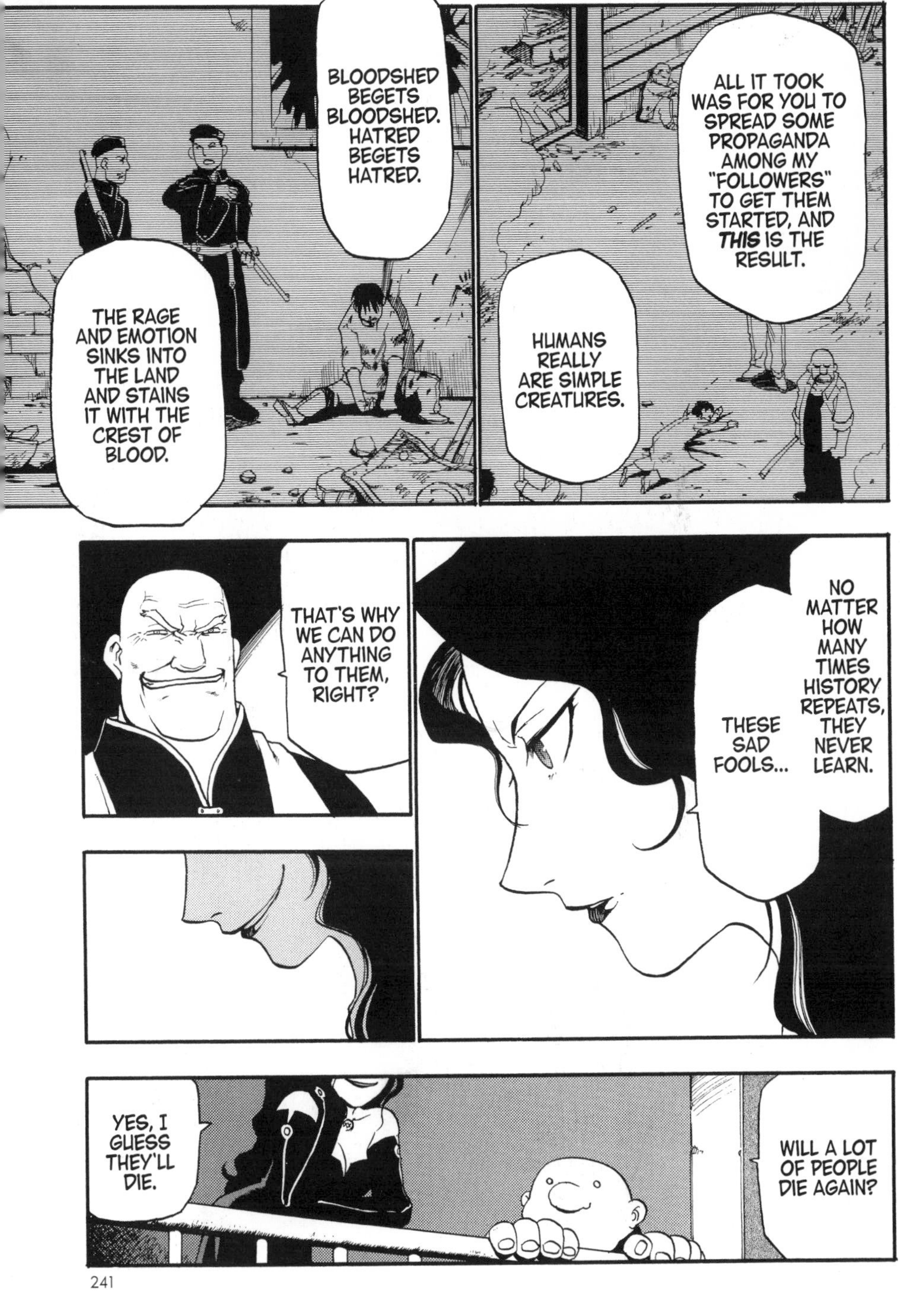
ALL IT TOOK WAS FOR YOU TO SPREAD SOME PROPAGANDA AMONG MY "FOLLOWERS" TO GET THEM STARTED, AND *THIS* IS THE RESULT.
HUMANS REALLY ARE SIMPLE CREATURES.
BLOODSHED BEGETS BLOODSHED. HATRED BEGETS HATRED.
THE RAGE AND EMOTION SINKS INTO THE LAND AND STAINS IT WITH THE CREST OF BLOOD.
NO MATTER HOW MANY TIMES HISTORY REPEATS, THEY NEVER LEARN.
THESE SAD FOOLS...
THAT'S WHY WE CAN DO ANYTHING TO THEM, RIGHT?
WILL A LOT OF PEOPLE DIE AGAIN?
YES, I GUESS THEY'LL DIE.

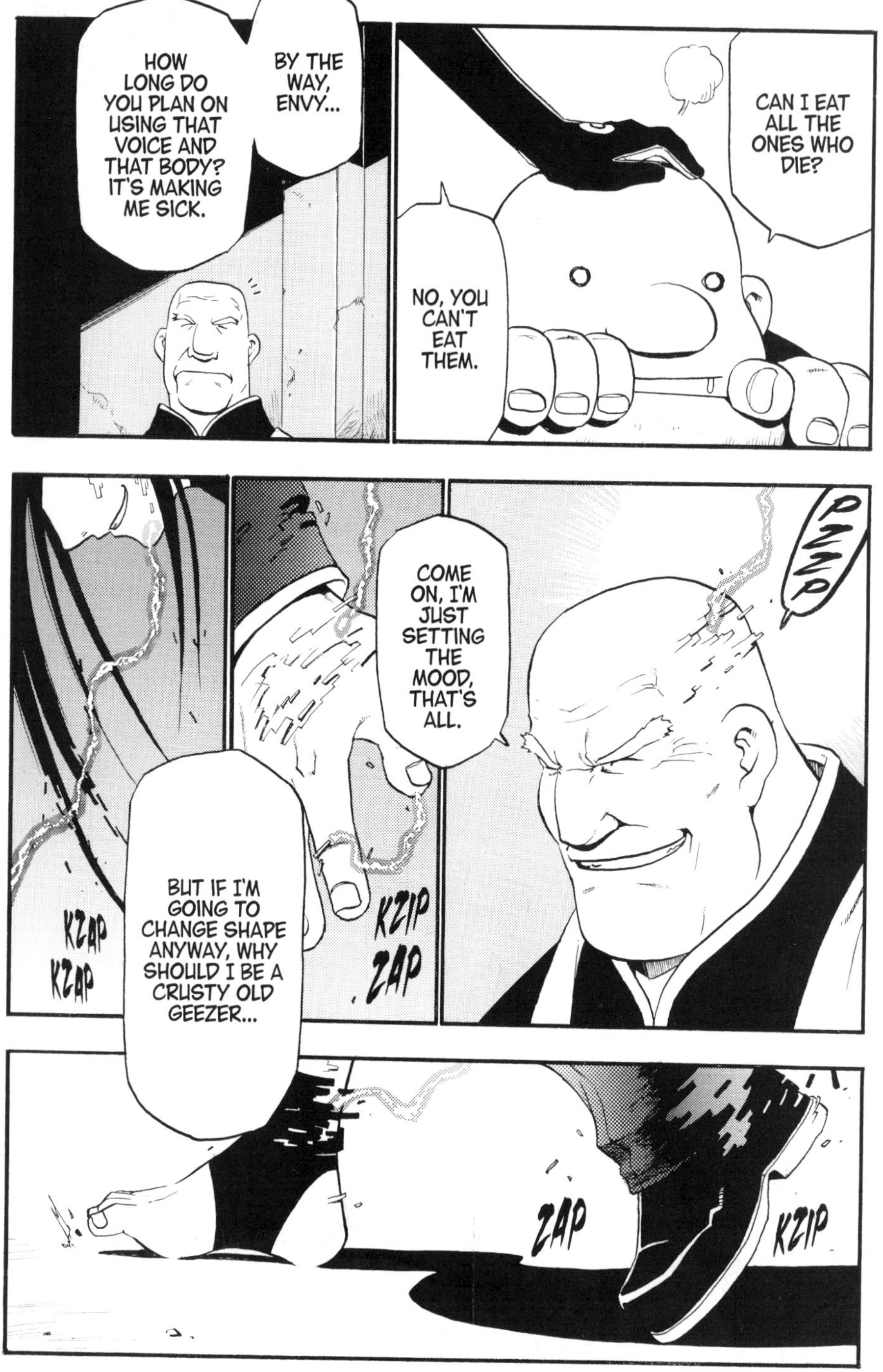
CAN I EAT ALL THE ONES WHO DIE?
NO, YOU CAN'T EAT THEM.
BY THE WAY, ENVY...
HOW LONG DO YOU PLAN ON USING THAT VOICE AND THAT BODY? IT'S MAKING ME SICK.
PZZZP
COME ON, I'M JUST SETTING THE MOOD, THAT'S ALL.
KZIP ZAP
KZAP KZAP
BUT IF I'M GOING TO CHANGE SHAPE ANYWAY, WHY SHOULD I BE A CRUSTY OLD GEEZER...
KZIP
ZAP

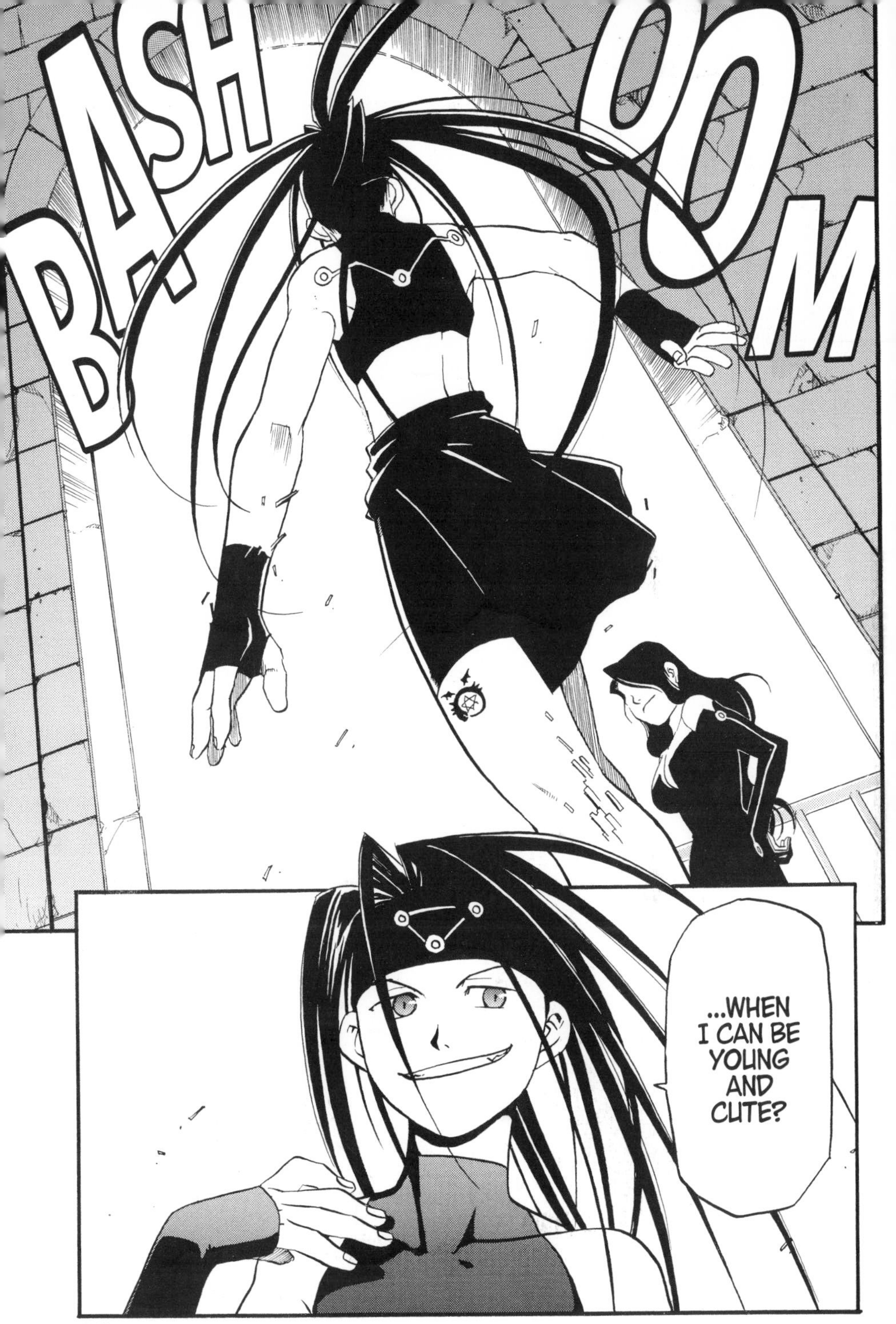
OOM
BASH
...WHEN I CAN BE YOUNG AND CUTE?

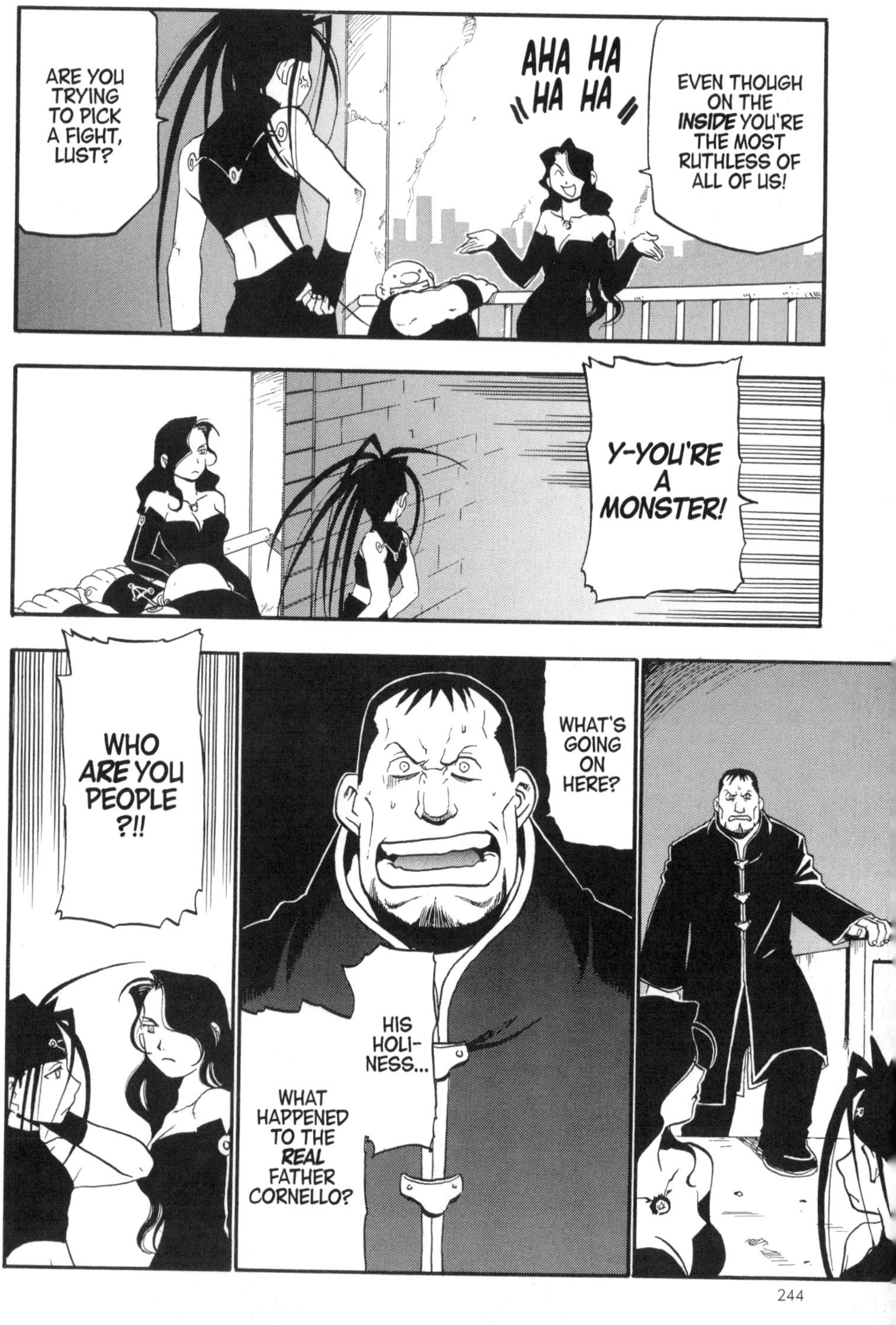
AHA HA HA HA
EVEN THOUGH ON THE INSIDE YOU'RE THE MOST RUTHLESS OF ALL OF US!
ARE YOU TRYING TO PICK A FIGHT, LUST?
Y-YOU'RE A MONSTER!
WHAT'S GOING ON HERE?
HIS HOLINESS...
WHAT HAPPENED TO THE REAL FATHER CORNELLO?
WHO ARE YOU PEOPLE ?!!

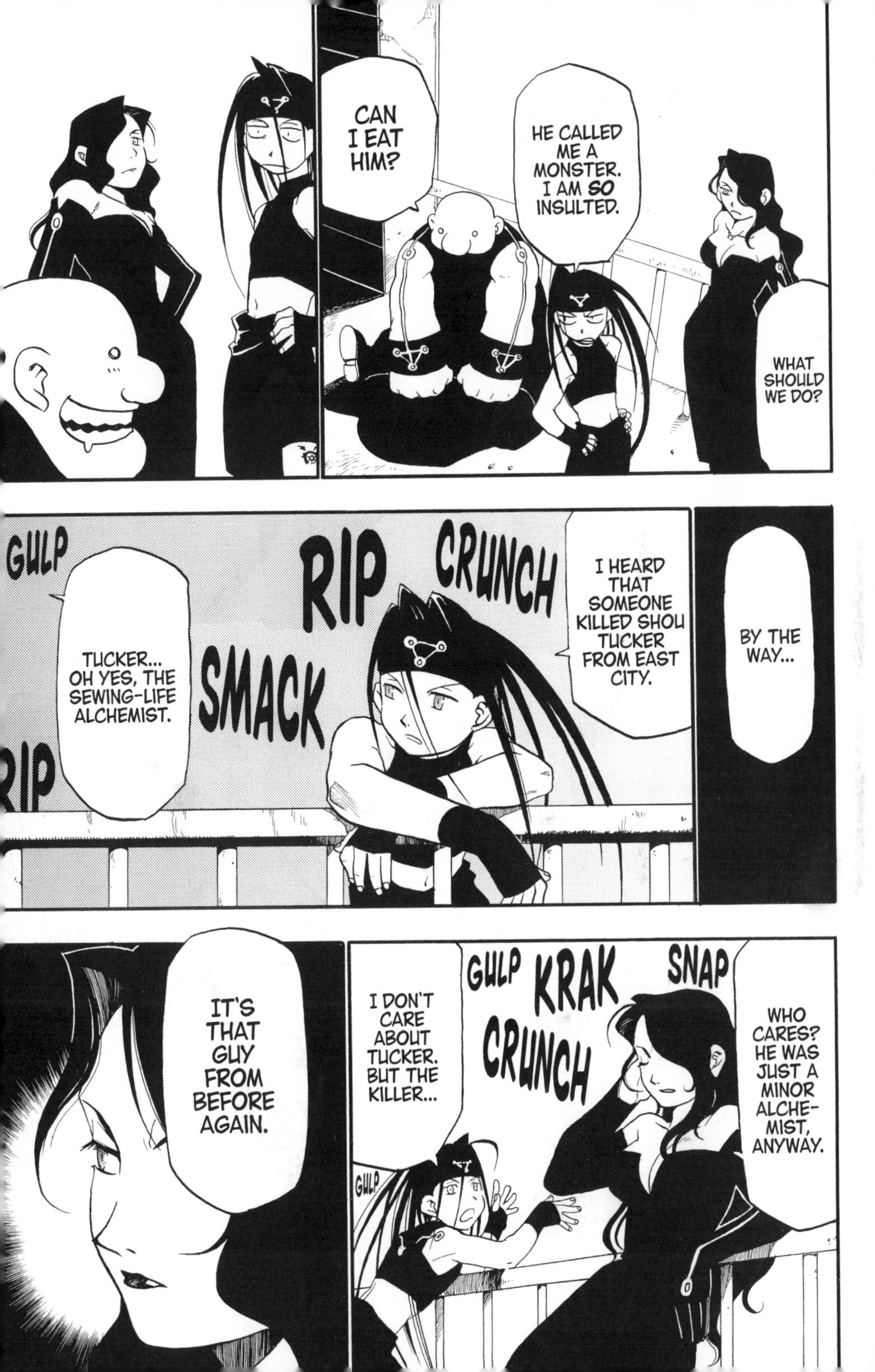
HE CALLED ME A MONSTER. I AM SO INSULTED.
WHAT SHOULD WE DO?
CAN I EAT HIM?
BY THE WAY...
I HEARD THAT SOMEONE KILLED SHOU TUCKER FROM EAST CITY.
CRUNCH
RIP
SMACK
TUCKER... OH YES, THE SEWING-LIFE ALCHEMIST.
GULP
RIP
SNAP
WHO CARES? HE WAS JUST A MINOR ALCHE-MIST, ANYWAY.
KRAK
CRUNCH
GULP
I DON'T CARE ABOUT TUCKER. BUT THE KILLER...
GULP
IT'S THAT GUY FROM BEFORE AGAIN.

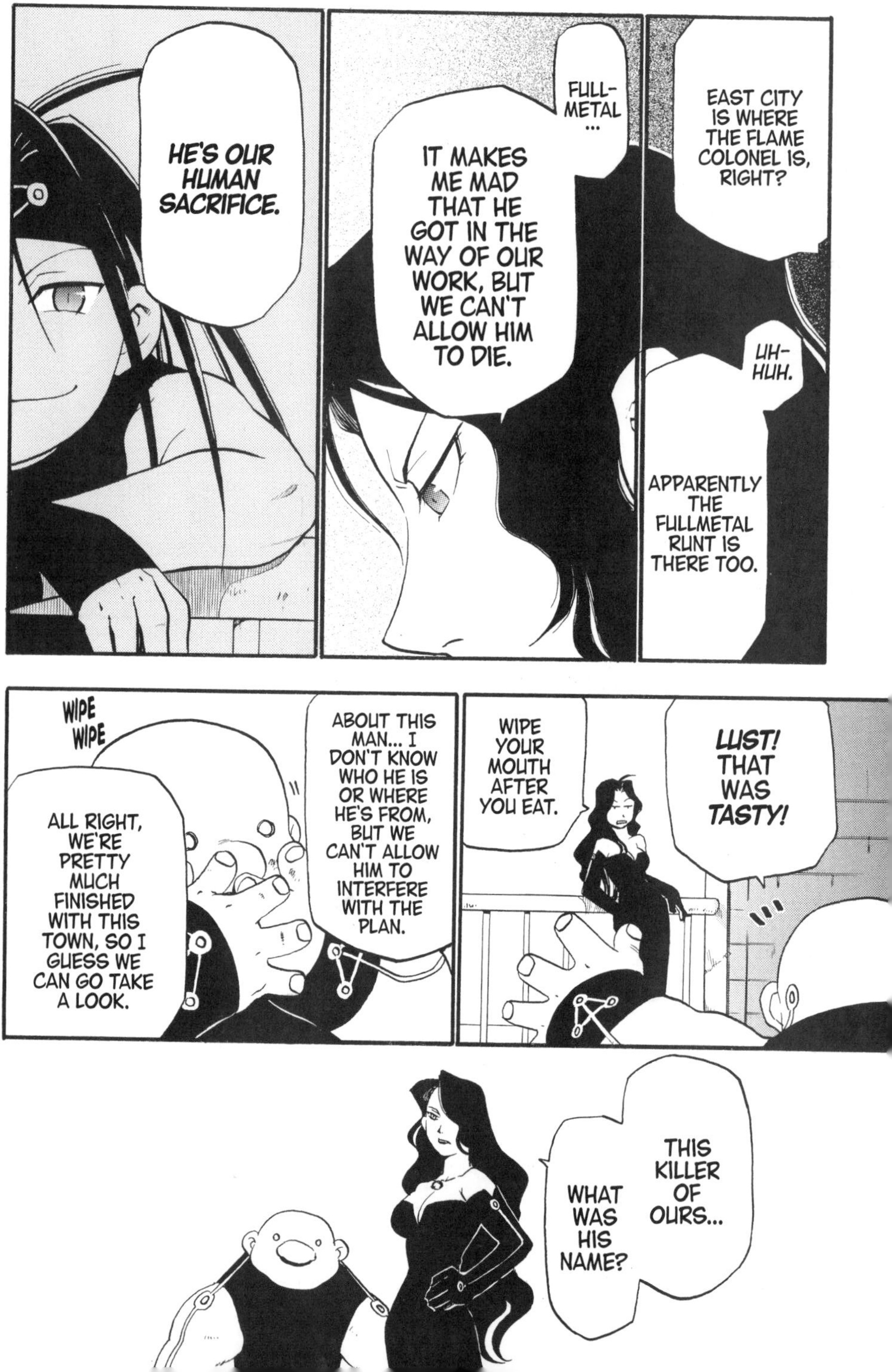
EAST CITY IS WHERE THE FLAME COLONEL IS, RIGHT?
UH-HUH.
APPARENTLY THE FULLMETAL RUNT IS THERE TOO.
FULL-METAL...
IT MAKES ME MAD THAT HE GOT IN THE WAY OF OUR WORK, BUT WE CAN'T ALLOW HIM TO DIE.
HE'S OUR HUMAN SACRIFICE.
LUST! THAT WAS TASTY!
WIPE YOUR MOUTH AFTER YOU EAT.
WIPE WIPE
ABOUT THIS MAN... I DON'T KNOW WHO HE IS OR WHERE HE'S FROM, BUT WE CAN'T ALLOW HIM TO INTERFERE WITH THE PLAN.
ALL RIGHT, WE'RE PRETTY MUCH FINISHED WITH THIS TOWN, SO I GUESS WE CAN GO TAKE A LOOK.
THIS KILLER OF OURS...
WHAT WAS HIS NAME?

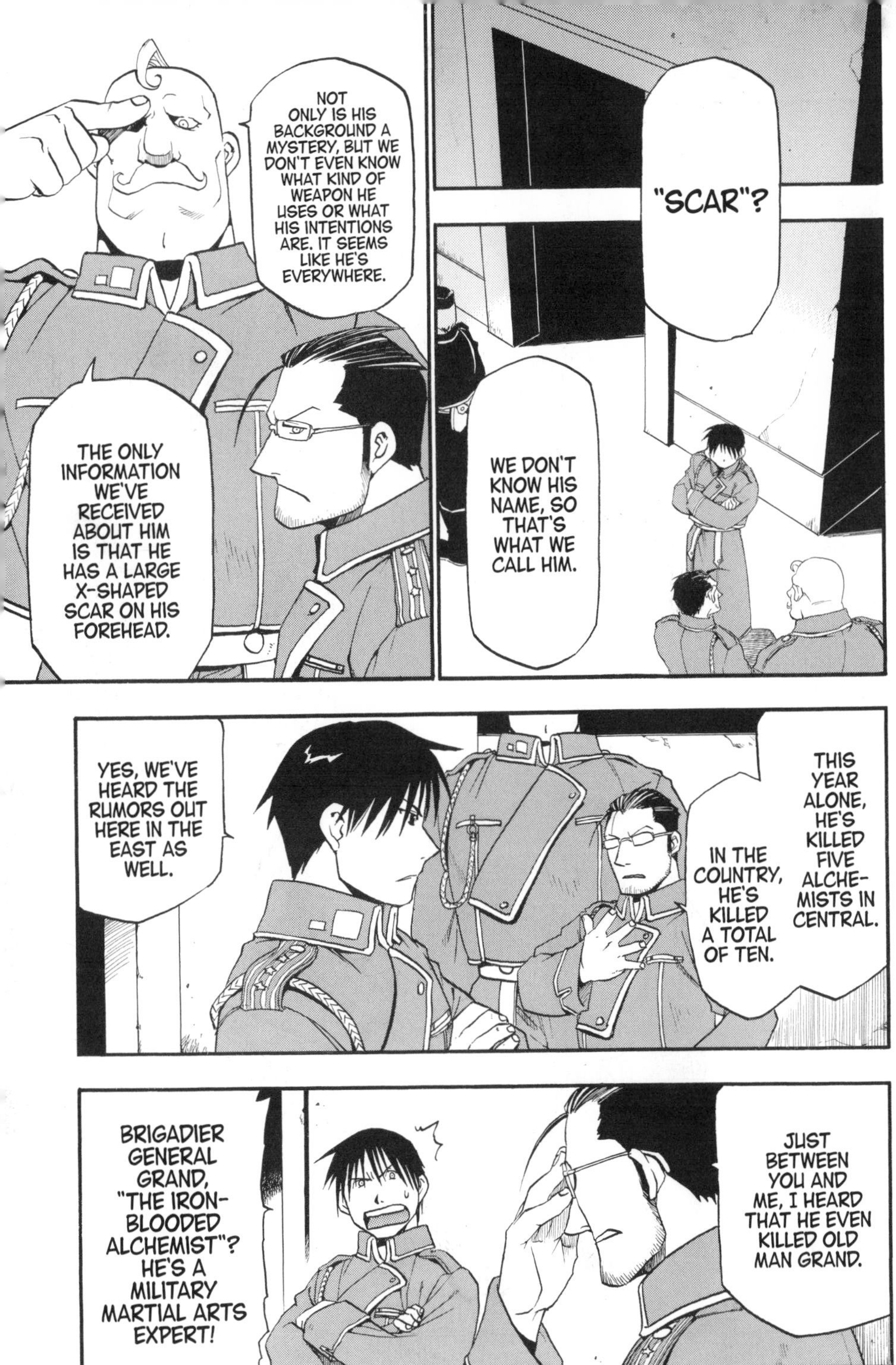
"SCAR"?
WE DON'T KNOW HIS NAME, SO THAT'S WHAT WE CALL HIM.
NOT ONLY IS HIS BACKGROUND A MYSTERY, BUT WE DON'T EVEN KNOW WHAT KIND OF WEAPON HE USES OR WHAT HIS INTENTIONS ARE. IT SEEMS LIKE HE'S EVERYWHERE.
THE ONLY INFORMATION WE'VE RECEIVED ABOUT HIM IS THAT HE HAS A LARGE X-SHAPED SCAR ON HIS FOREHEAD.
THIS YEAR ALONE, HE'S KILLED FIVE ALCHE-MISTS IN CENTRAL.
IN THE COUNTRY, HE'S KILLED A TOTAL OF TEN.
YES, WE'VE HEARD THE RUMORS OUT HERE IN THE EAST AS WELL.
JUST BETWEEN YOU AND ME, I HEARD THAT HE EVEN KILLED OLD MAN GRAND.
BRIGADIER GENERAL GRAND, "THE IRON-BLOODED ALCHEMIST"? HE'S A MILITARY MARTIAL ARTS EXPERT!

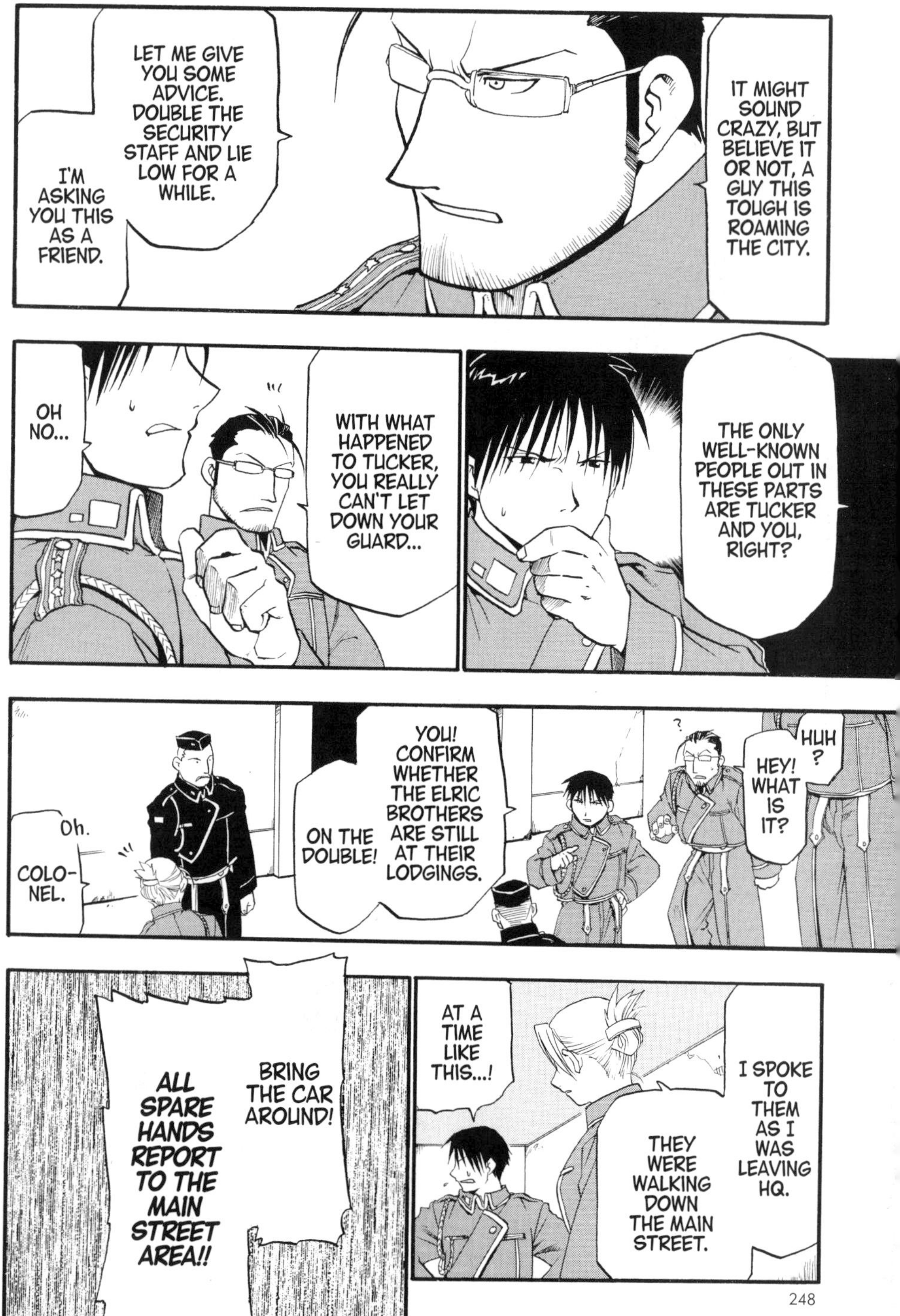
IT MIGHT SOUND CRAZY, BUT BELIEVE IT OR NOT, A GUY THIS TOUGH IS ROAMING THE CITY.
LET ME GIVE YOU SOME ADVICE. DOUBLE THE SECURITY STAFF AND LIE LOW FOR A WHILE.
I'M ASKING YOU THIS AS A FRIEND.
THE ONLY WELL-KNOWN PEOPLE OUT IN THESE PARTS ARE TUCKER AND YOU, RIGHT?
WITH WHAT HAPPENED TO TUCKER, YOU REALLY CAN'T LET DOWN YOUR GUARD...
OH NO...
HUH?
HEY! WHAT IS IT?
YOU! CONFIRM WHETHER THE ELRIC BROTHERS ARE STILL AT THEIR LODGINGS.
ON THE DOUBLE!
Oh.
COLONEL.
I SPOKE TO THEM AS I WAS LEAVING HQ.
THEY WERE WALKING DOWN THE MAIN STREET.
AT A TIME LIKE THIS...!
BRING THE CAR AROUND!
ALL SPARE HANDS REPORT TO THE MAIN STREET AREA!!

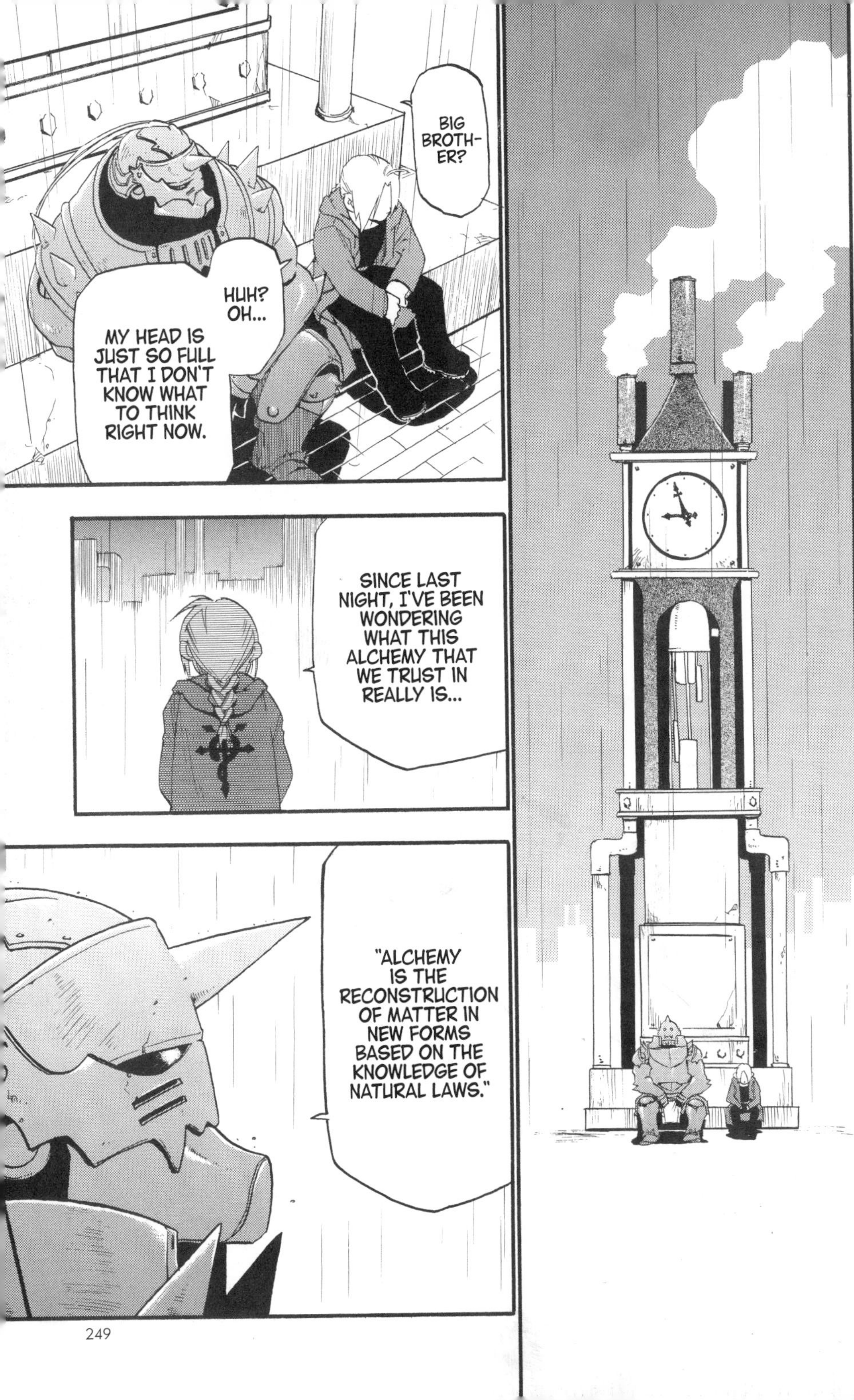
BIG BROTH-ER?
HUH? OH...
MY HEAD IS JUST SO FULL THAT I DON'T KNOW WHAT TO THINK RIGHT NOW.
SINCE LAST NIGHT, I'VE BEEN WONDERING WHAT THIS ALCHEMY THAT WE TRUST IN REALLY IS...
"ALCHEMY IS THE RECONSTRUCTION OF MATTER IN NEW FORMS BASED ON THE KNOWLEDGE OF NATURAL LAWS."

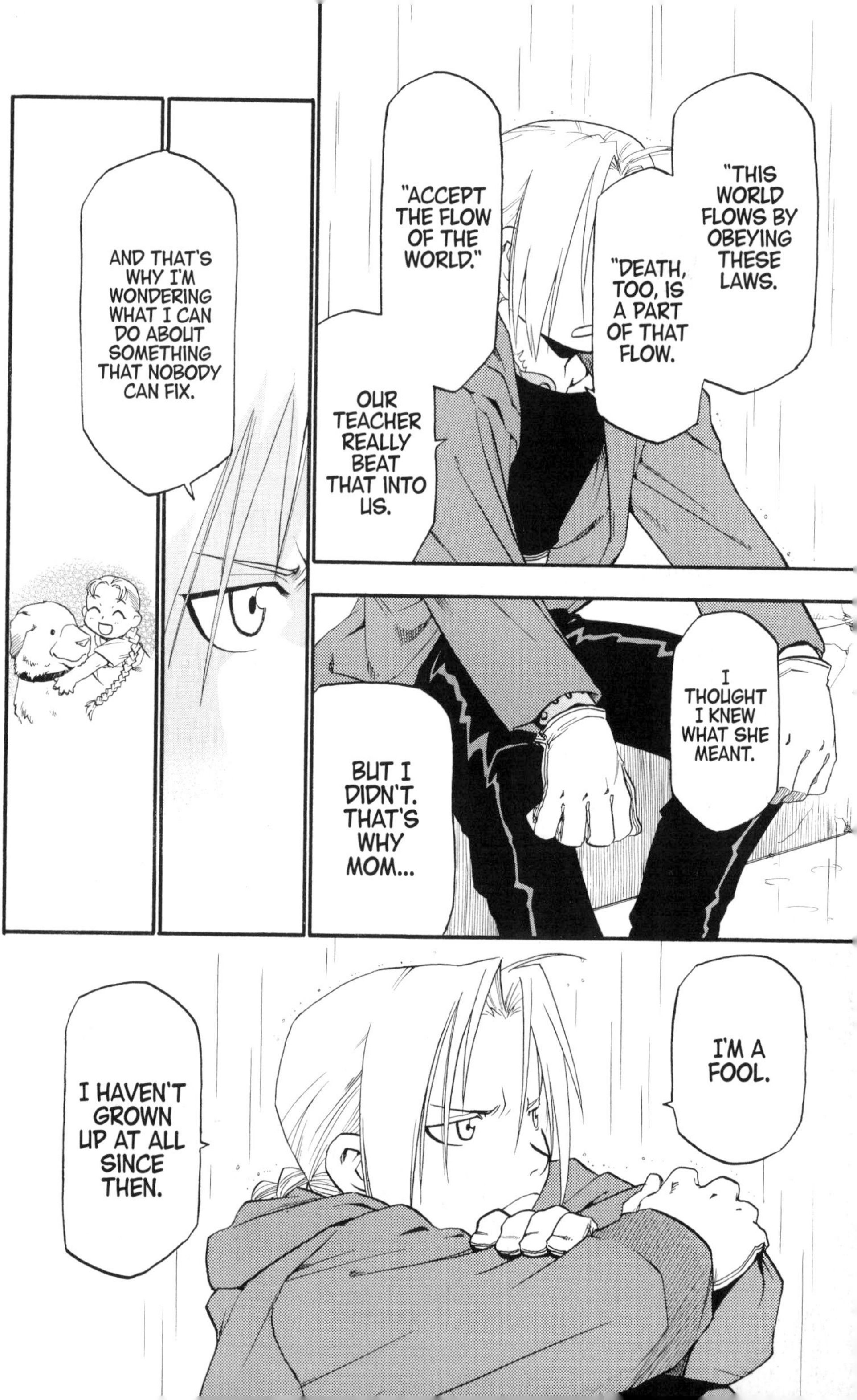
"THIS WORLD FLOWS BY OBEYING THESE LAWS.
"DEATH, TOO, IS A PART OF THAT FLOW.
"ACCEPT THE FLOW OF THE WORLD."
OUR TEACHER REALLY BEAT THAT INTO US.
I THOUGHT I KNEW WHAT SHE MEANT.
BUT I DIDN'T. THAT'S WHY MOM...
AND THAT'S WHY I'M WONDERING WHAT I CAN DO ABOUT SOMETHING THAT NOBODY CAN FIX.
I'M A FOOL.
I HAVEN'T GROWN UP AT ALL SINCE THEN.

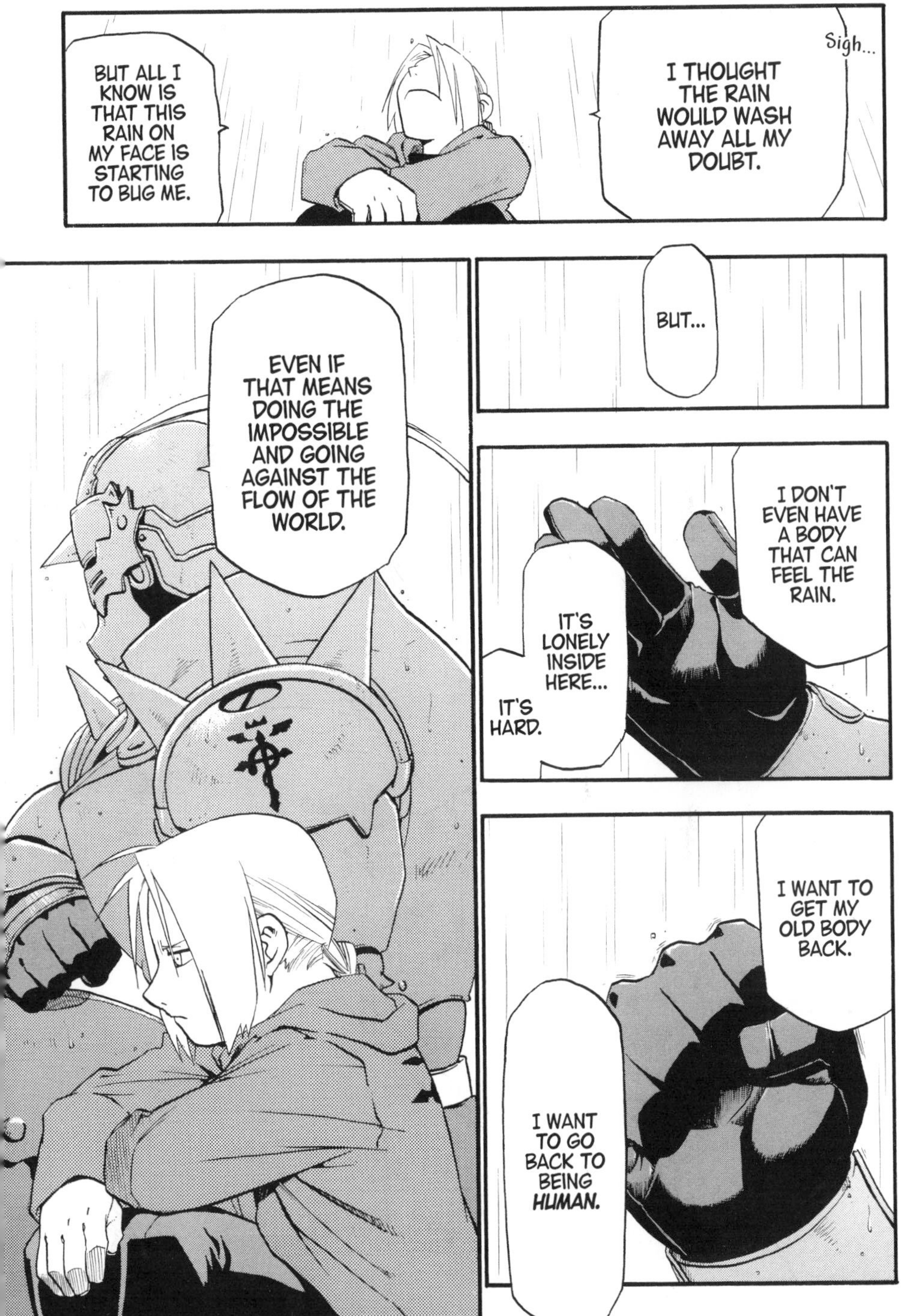
Sigh...
I THOUGHT THE RAIN WOULD WASH AWAY ALL MY DOUBT.
BUT ALL I KNOW IS THAT THIS RAIN ON MY FACE IS STARTING TO BUG ME.
BUT...
I DON'T EVEN HAVE A BODY THAT CAN FEEL THE RAIN.
IT'S LONELY INSIDE HERE...
IT'S HARD.
I WANT TO GET MY OLD BODY BACK.
I WANT TO GO BACK TO BEING *HUMAN.*
EVEN IF THAT MEANS DOING THE IMPOSSIBLE AND GOING AGAINST THE FLOW OF THE WORLD.

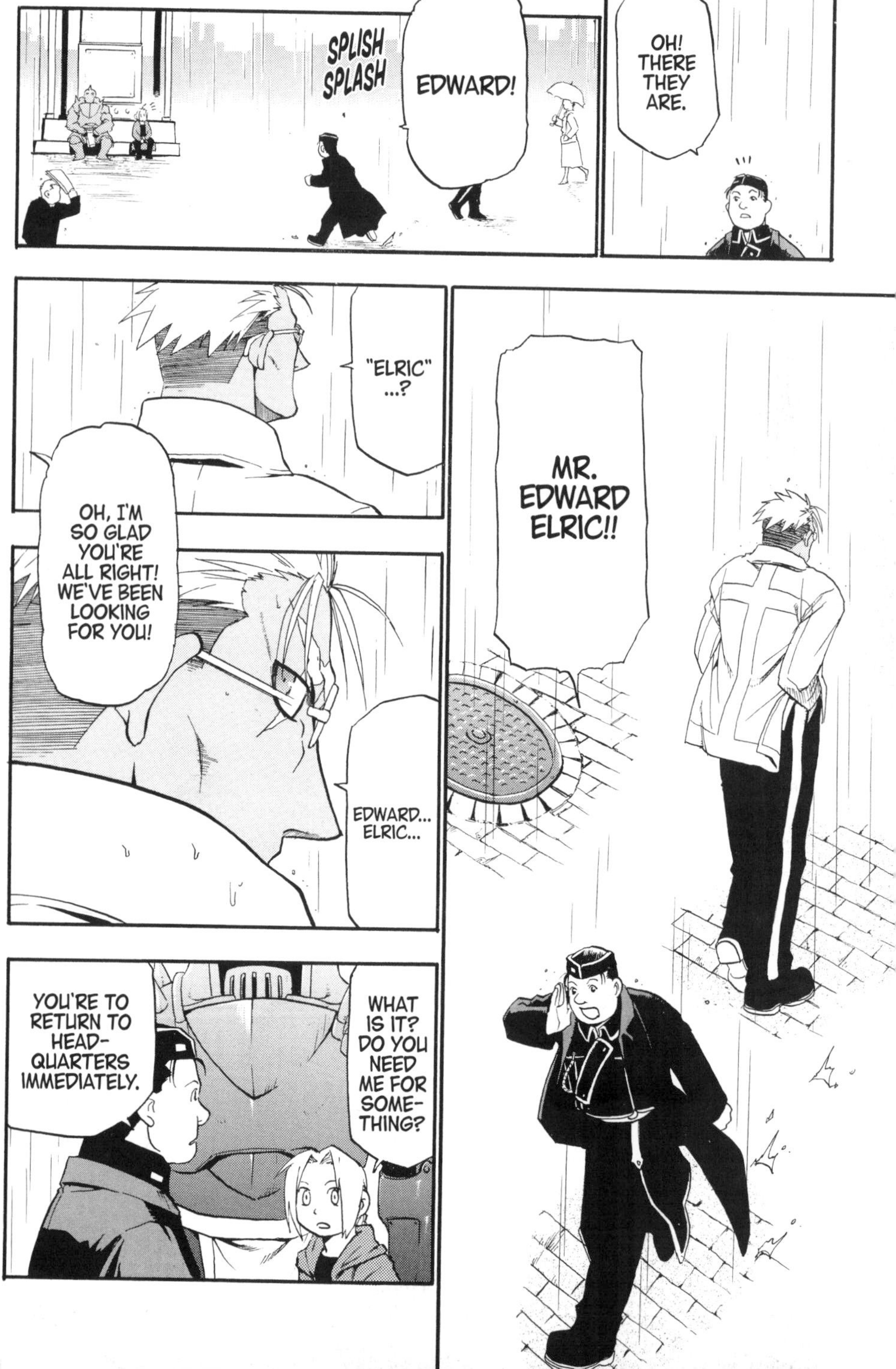
OH! THERE THEY ARE.
EDWARD!
SPLISH SPLASH
MR. EDWARD ELRIC!!
"ELRIC" ...?
OH, I'M SO GLAD YOU'RE ALL RIGHT! WE'VE BEEN LOOKING FOR YOU!
EDWARD... ELRIC...
WHAT IS IT? DO YOU NEED ME FOR SOME-THING?
YOU'RE TO RETURN TO HEAD-QUARTERS IMMEDIATELY.

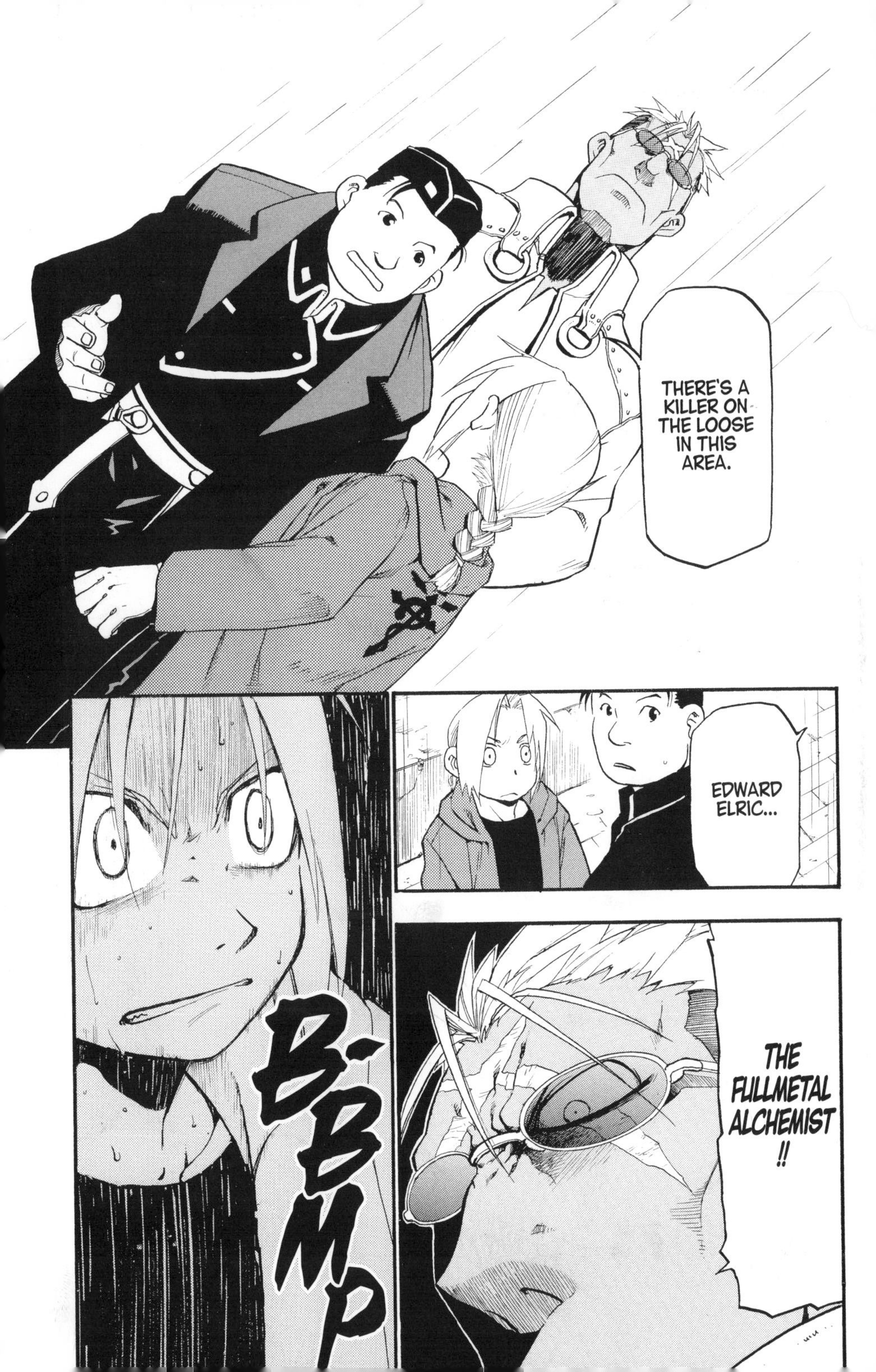
THERE'S A KILLER ON THE LOOSE IN THIS AREA.
EDWARD ELRIC...
THE FULLMETAL ALCHEMIST !!
B-BMP

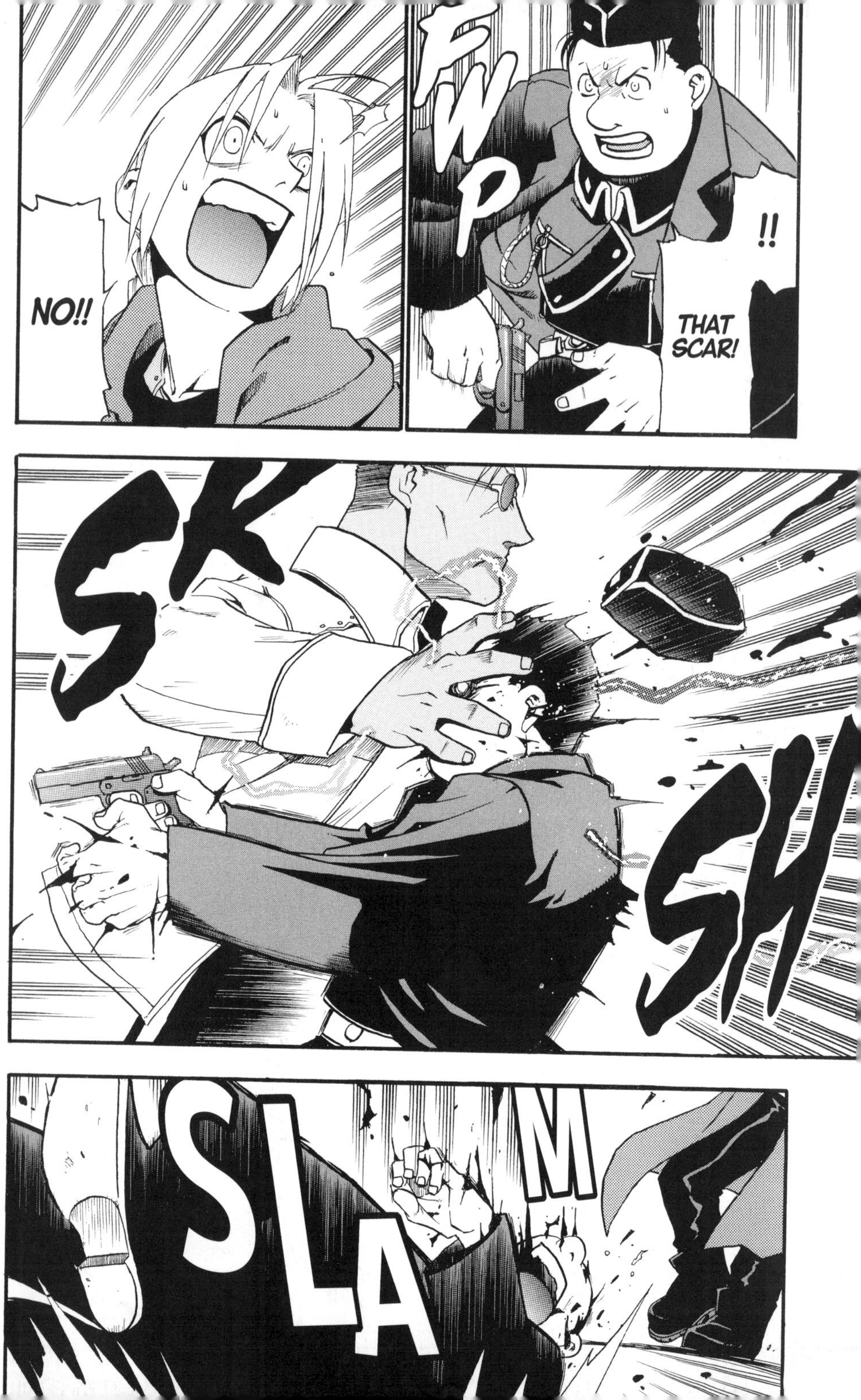
FWP
!!
THAT SCAR!
NO!!
SK
SH
SLAM

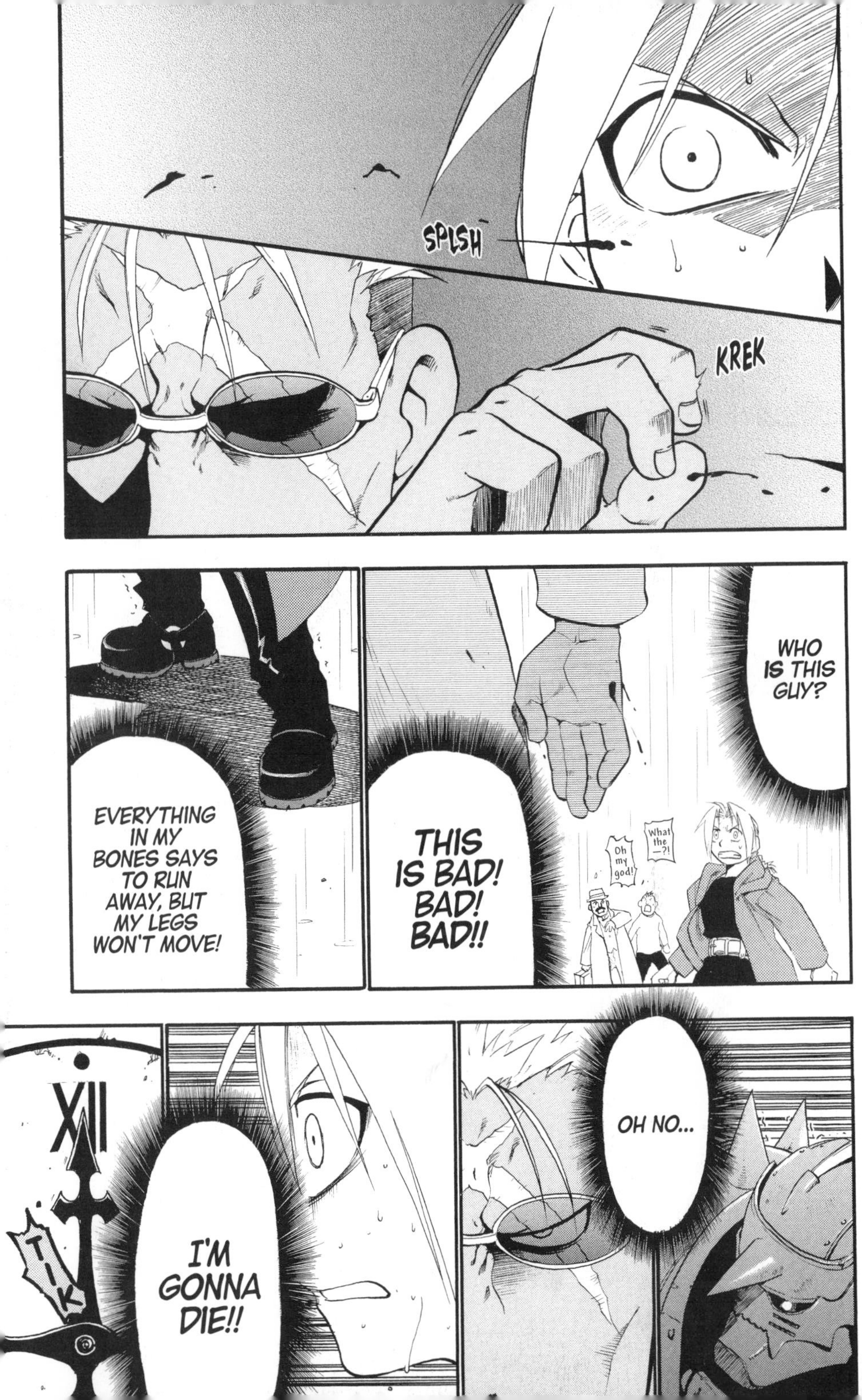
SPLSH
KREK
WHO IS THIS GUY?
THIS IS BAD! BAD! BAD!!
What the—?!
Oh my god!
EVERYTHING IN MY BONES SAYS TO RUN AWAY, BUT MY LEGS WON'T MOVE!
OH NO...
I'M GONNA DIE!!
TIK

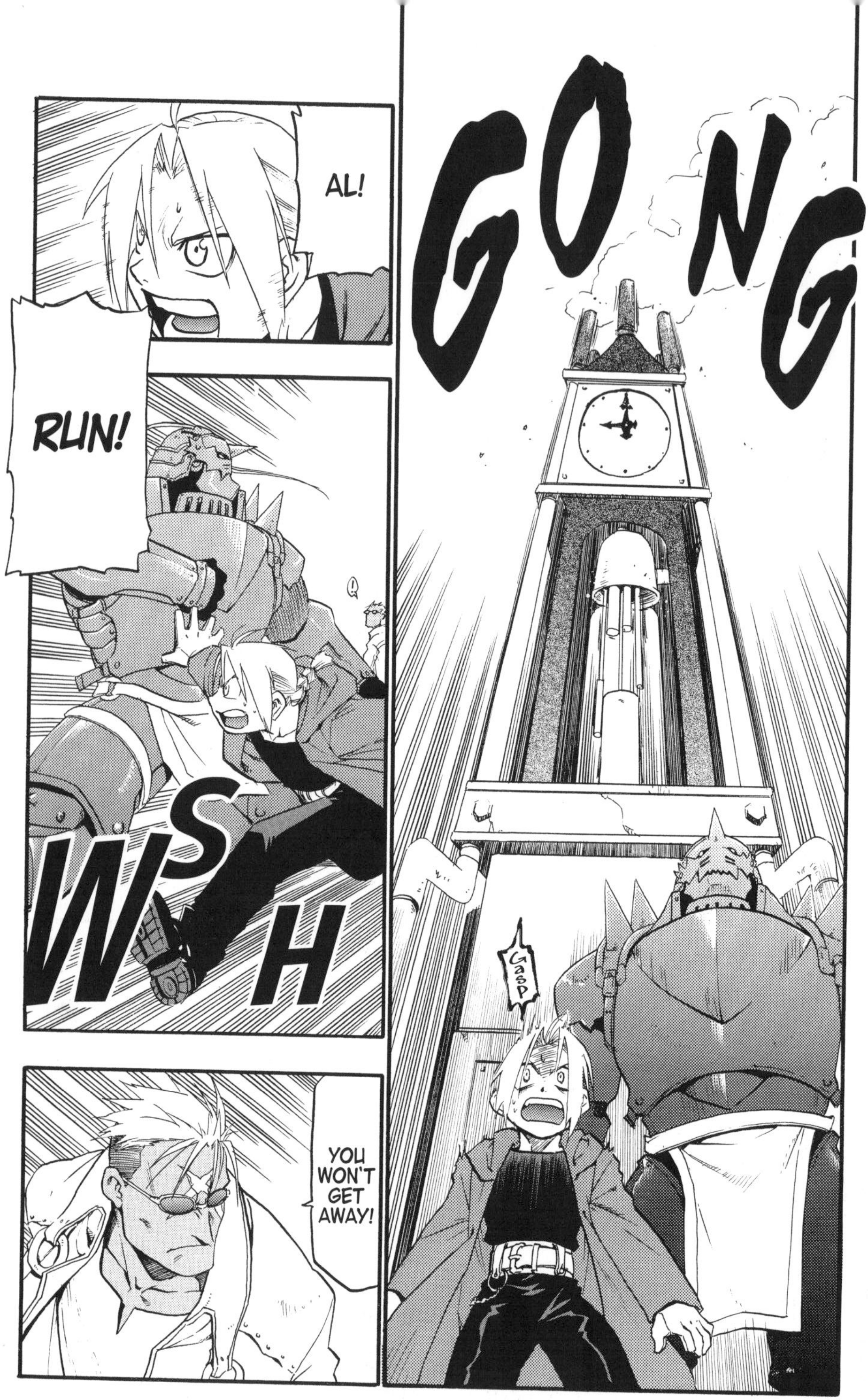
GONG
Gasp
AL!
RUN!
!
WSH
YOU WON'T GET AWAY!

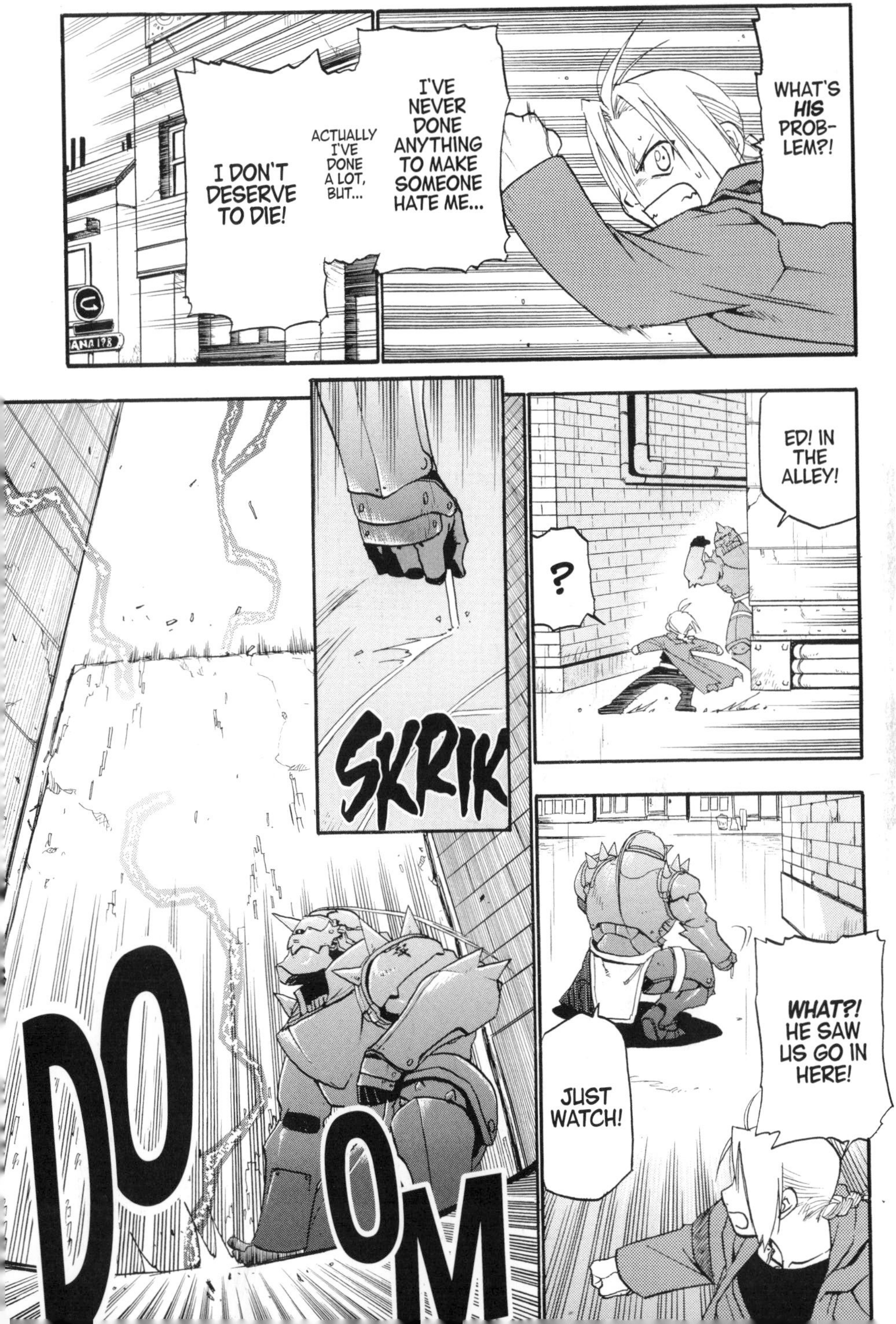
WHAT'S HIS PROBLEM?!
I'VE NEVER DONE ANYTHING TO MAKE SOMEONE HATE ME...
ACTUALLY I'VE DONE A LOT, BUT...
I DON'T DESERVE TO DIE!
ED! IN THE ALLEY!
?
WHAT?! HE SAW US GO IN HERE!
JUST WATCH!
SKRIK
DOOM

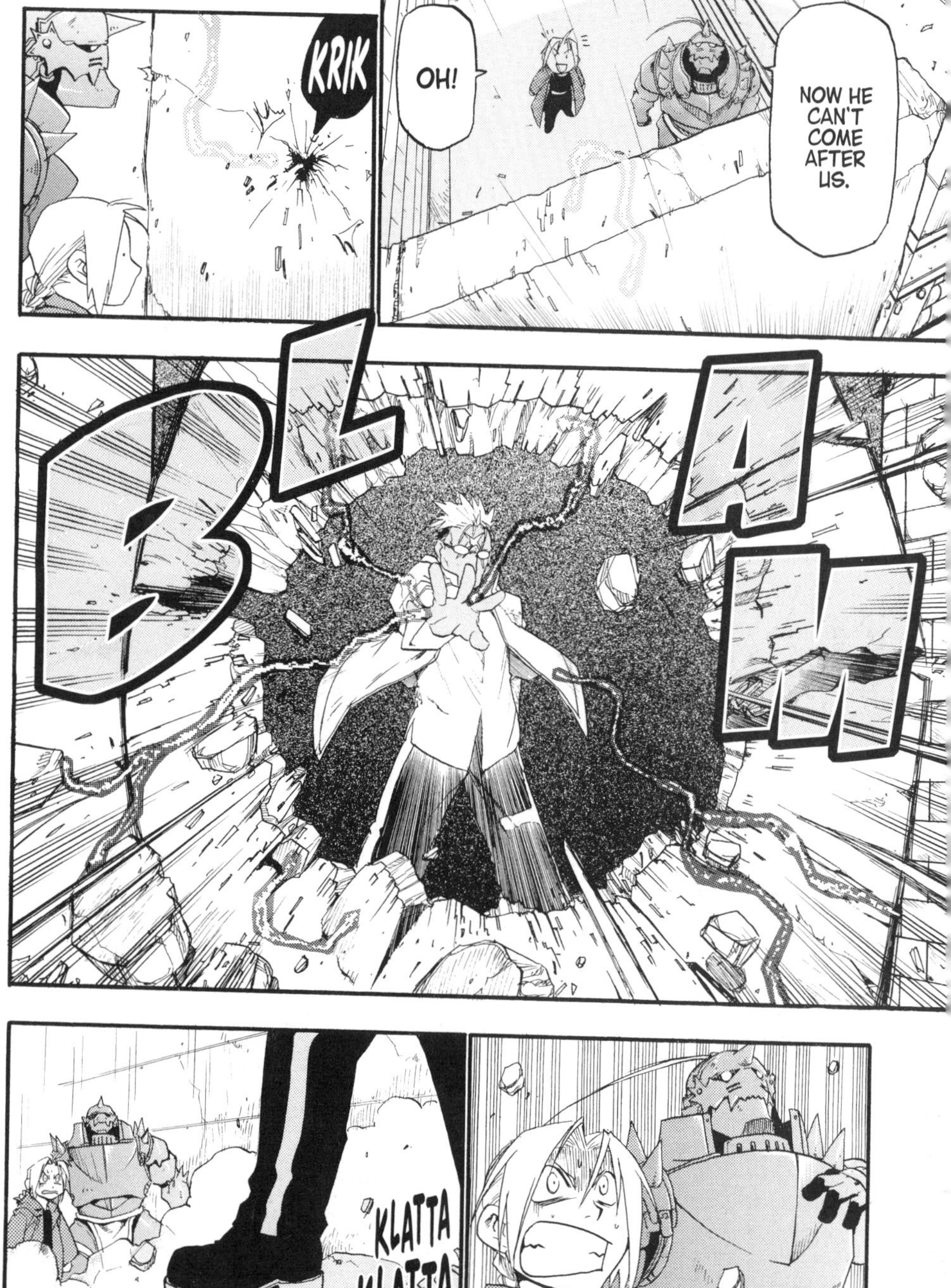
NOW HE CAN'T COME AFTER US.
OH!
KRIK
B-L-A-M
KLATTA KLATTA

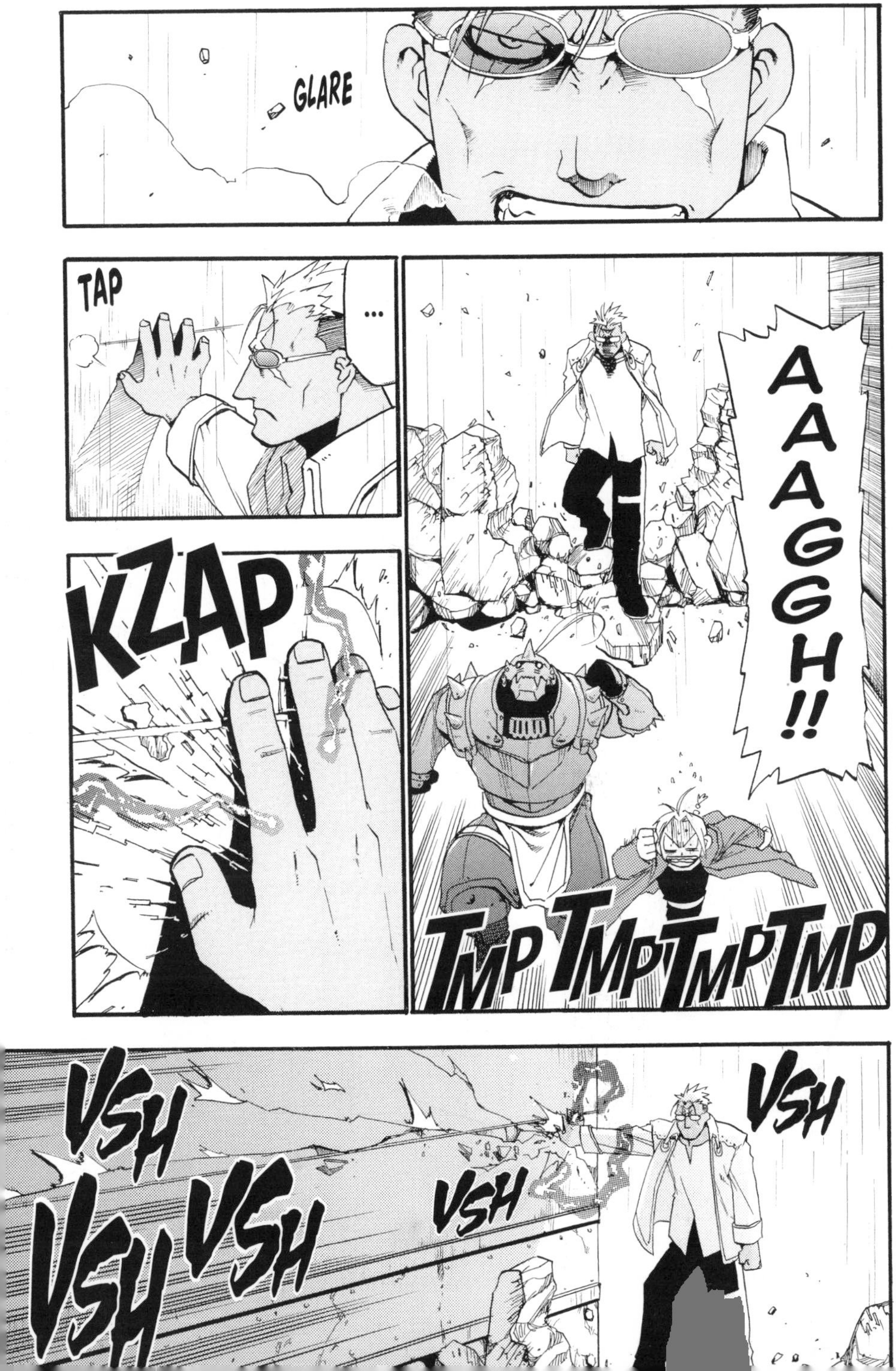
GLARE
AAAGGH!!
TMP TMP TMP TMP
...
TAP
KZAP
VSH
VSH
VSH
VSH
VSH

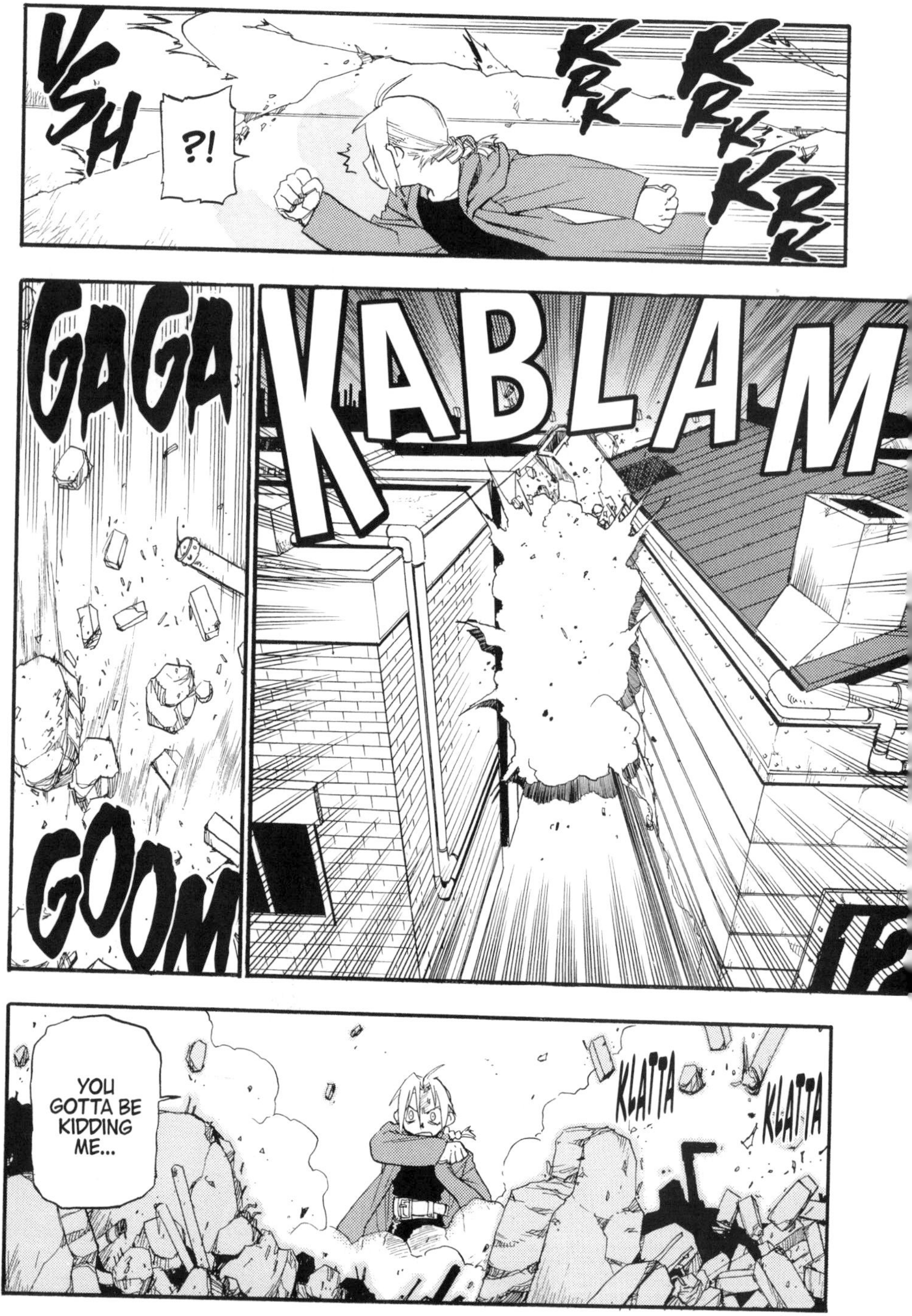
KRK KRK KRK KRR
?!
VSH
KABLAM
GAGA
GOOM
KLATTA KLATTA
YOU GOTTA BE KIDDING ME...

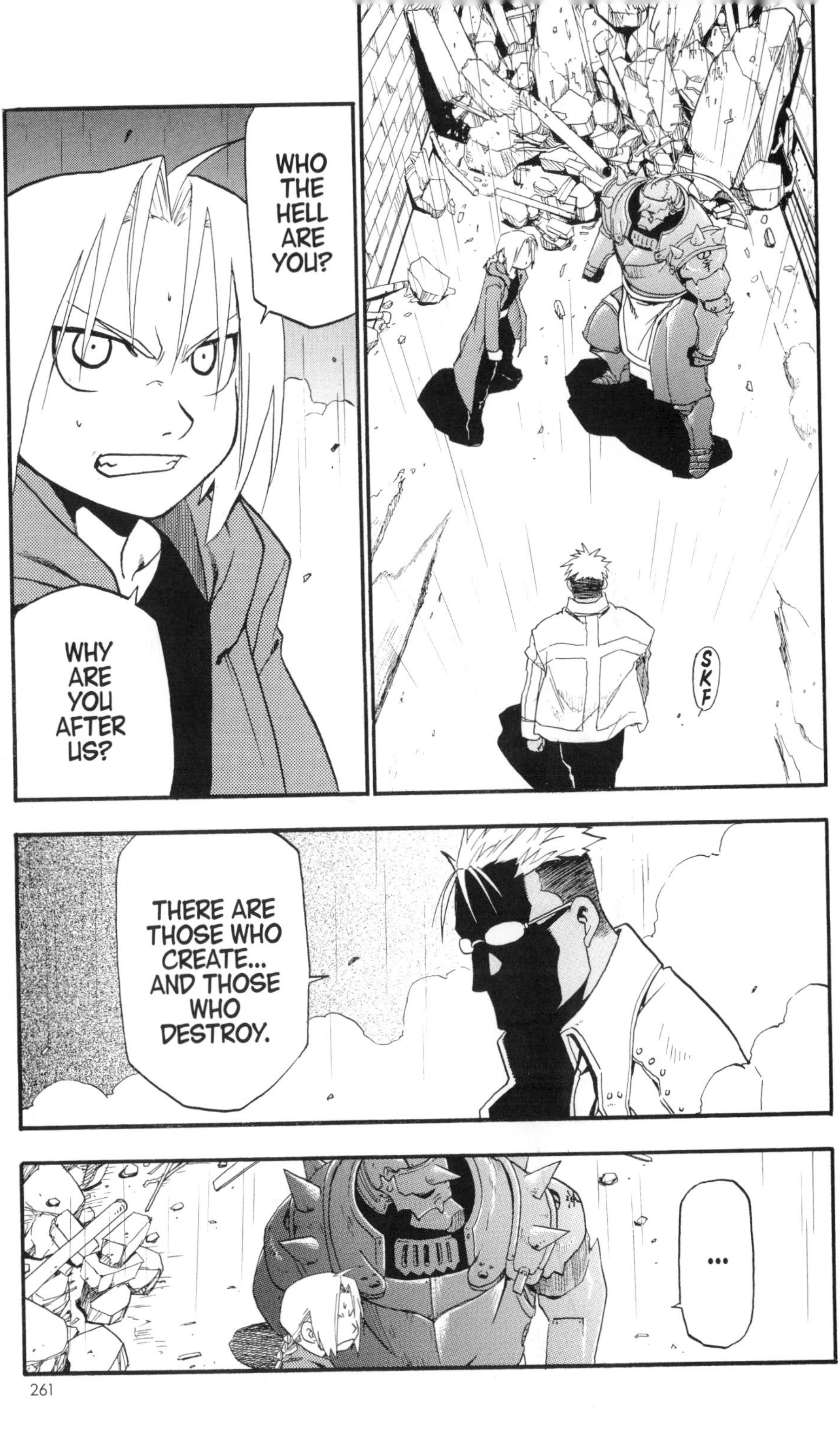
SKF
WHO THE HELL ARE YOU?
WHY ARE YOU AFTER US?
THERE ARE THOSE WHO CREATE... AND THOSE WHO DESTROY.
...

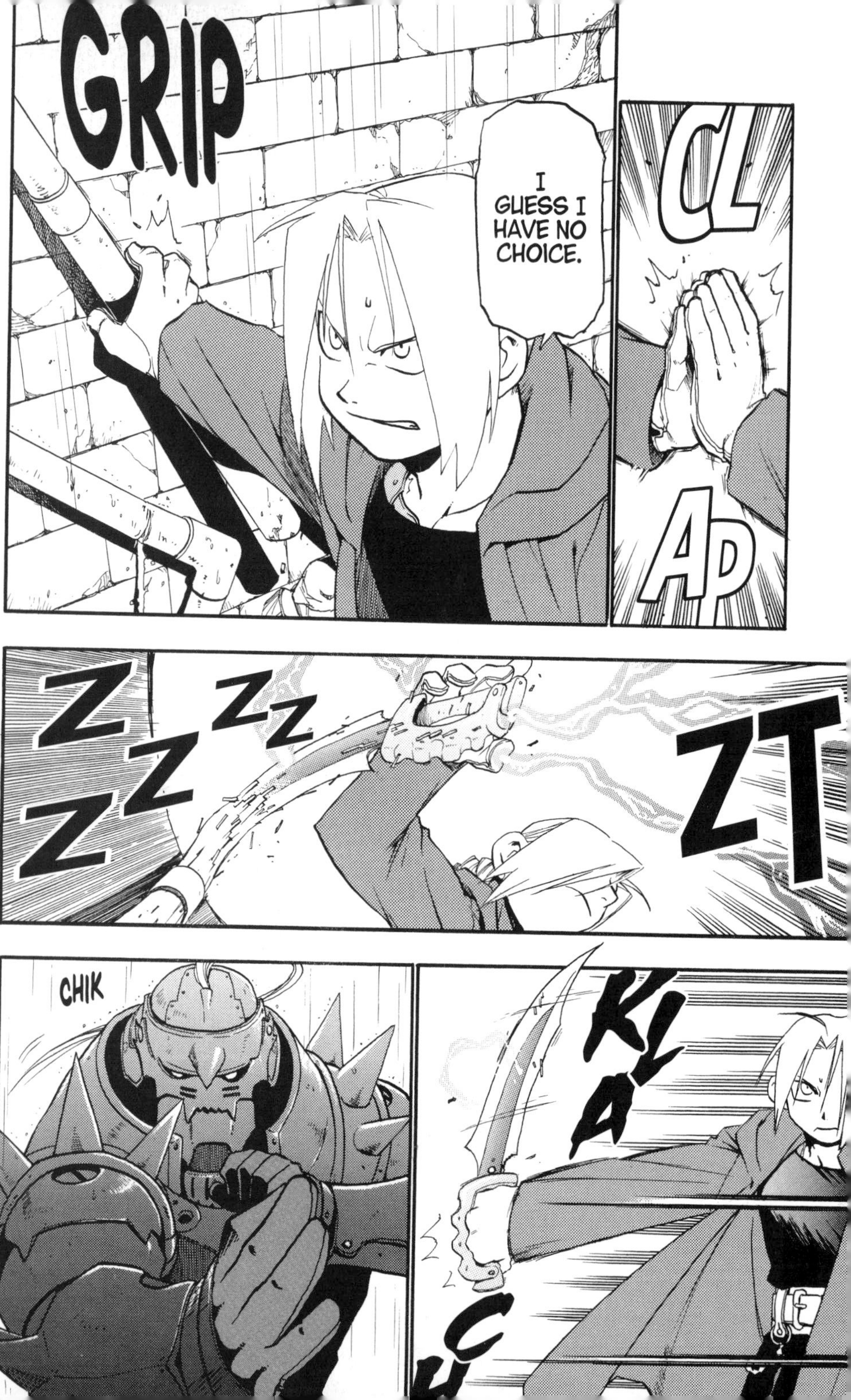
CL
AP
GRIP
I GUESS I HAVE NO CHOICE.
ZZZZZ
ZT
KLA
CK
CHIK

YOU HAVE COURAGE...

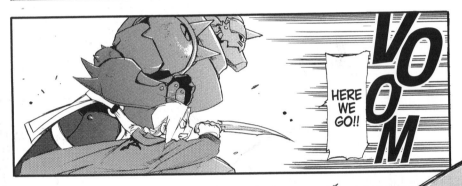

HERE WE GO!!

VOOM

YAH!

WSH

WSH

...BUT YOU'RE SLOW!

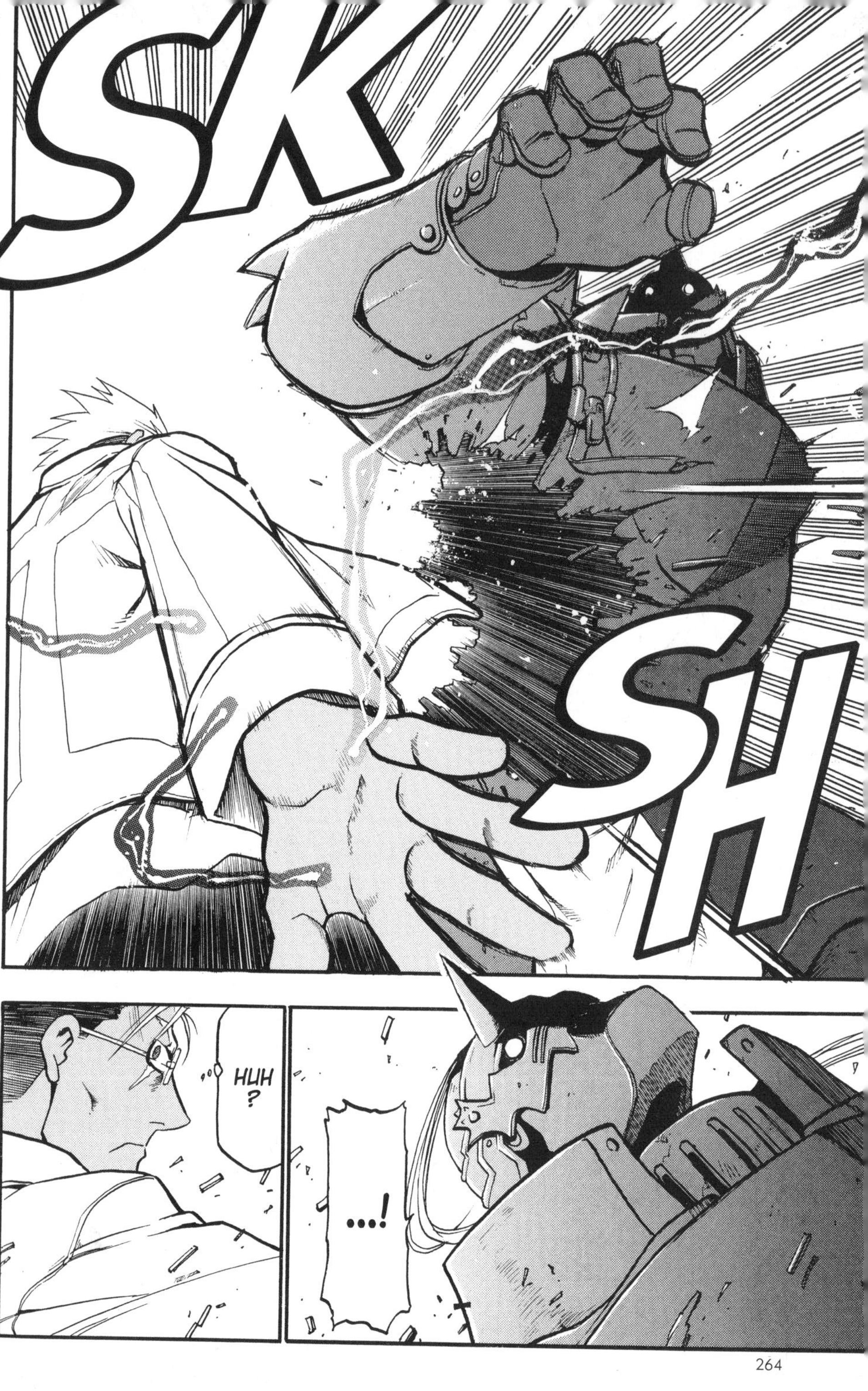
SK
SH
...!
HUH?

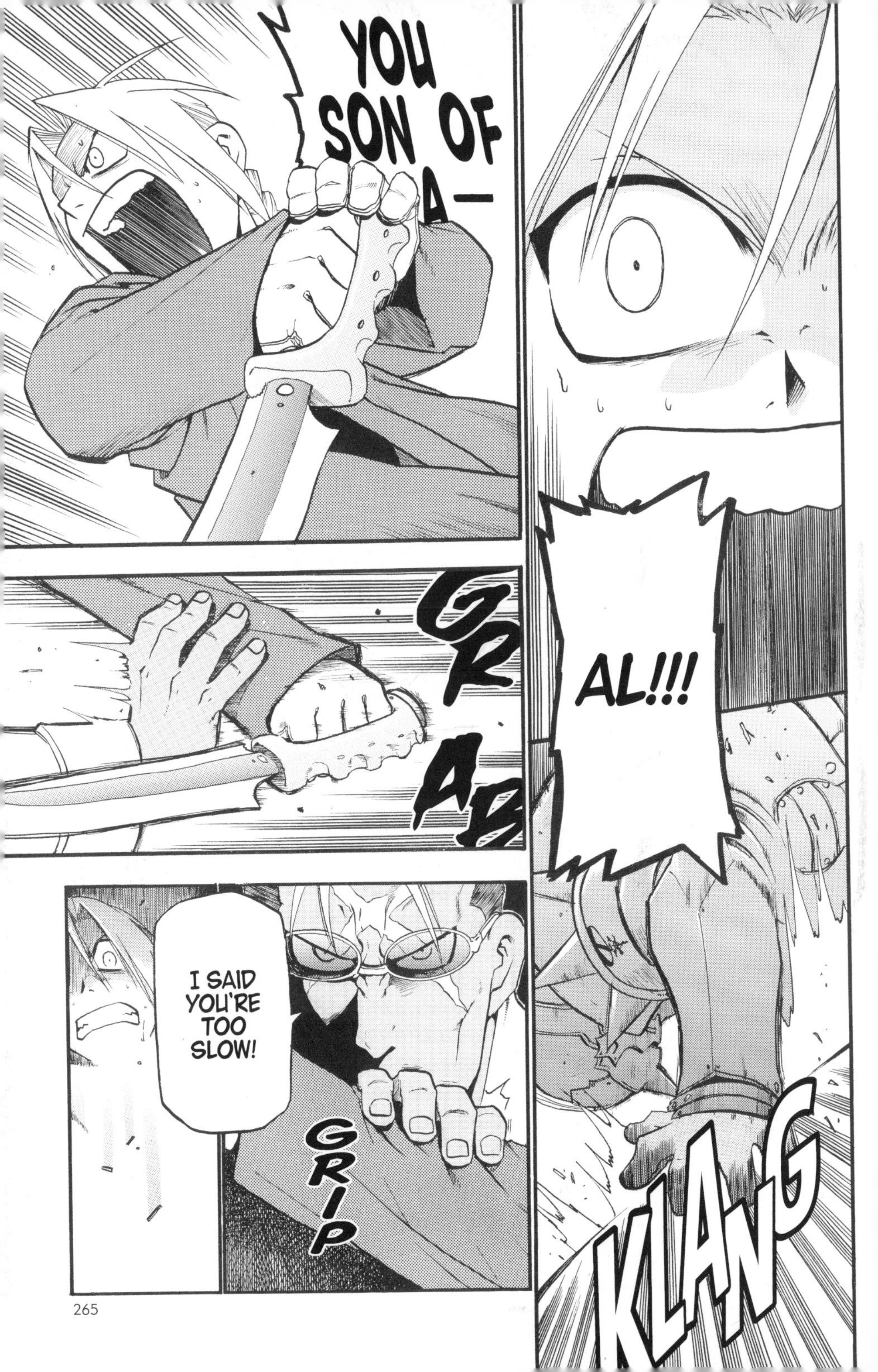
AL!!!
KLANG
YOU SON OF A—
GRAB
I SAID YOU'RE TOO SLOW!
GRIP

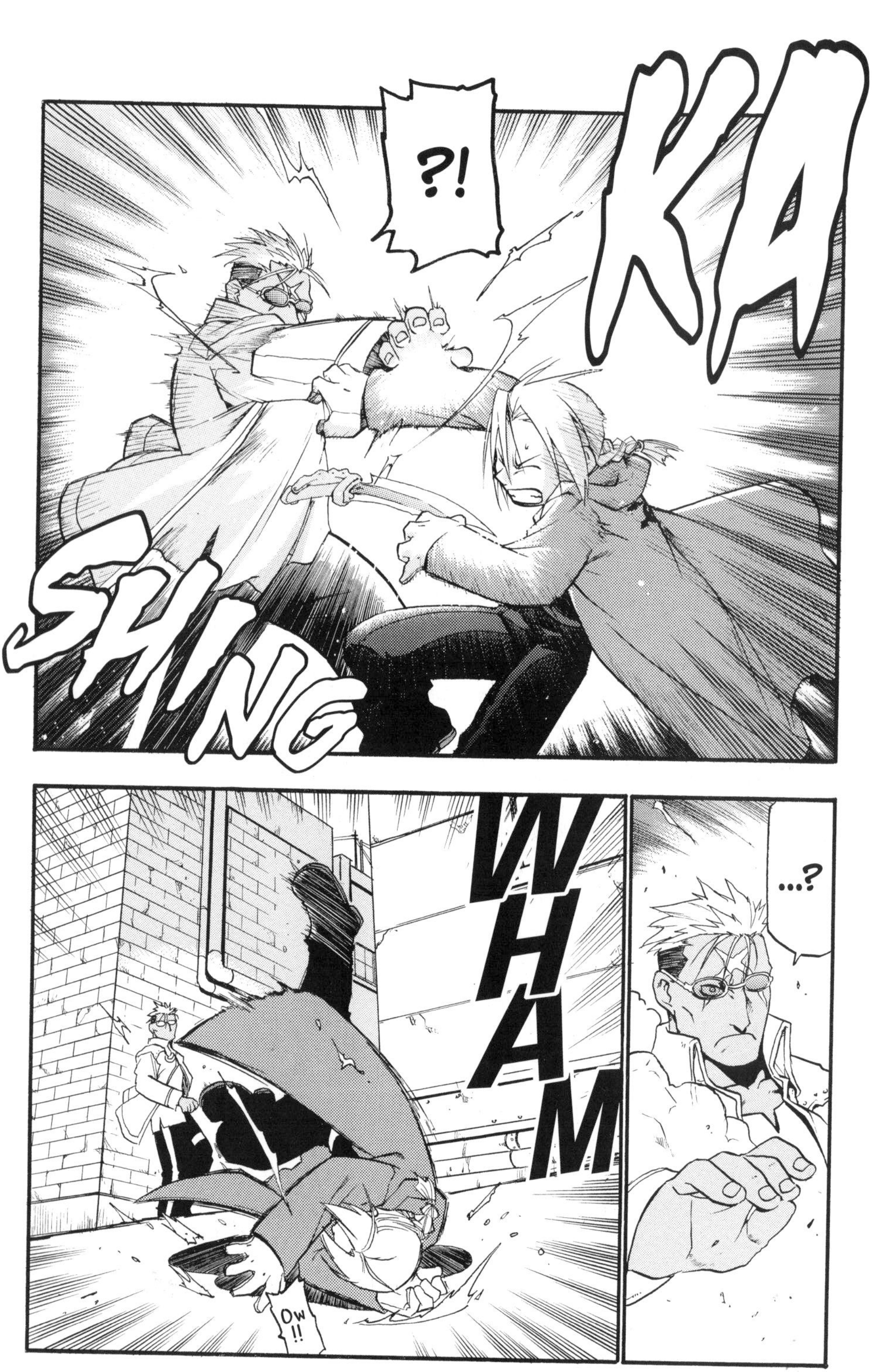
KA
?!
SHING
...?
WHAM
OW !!

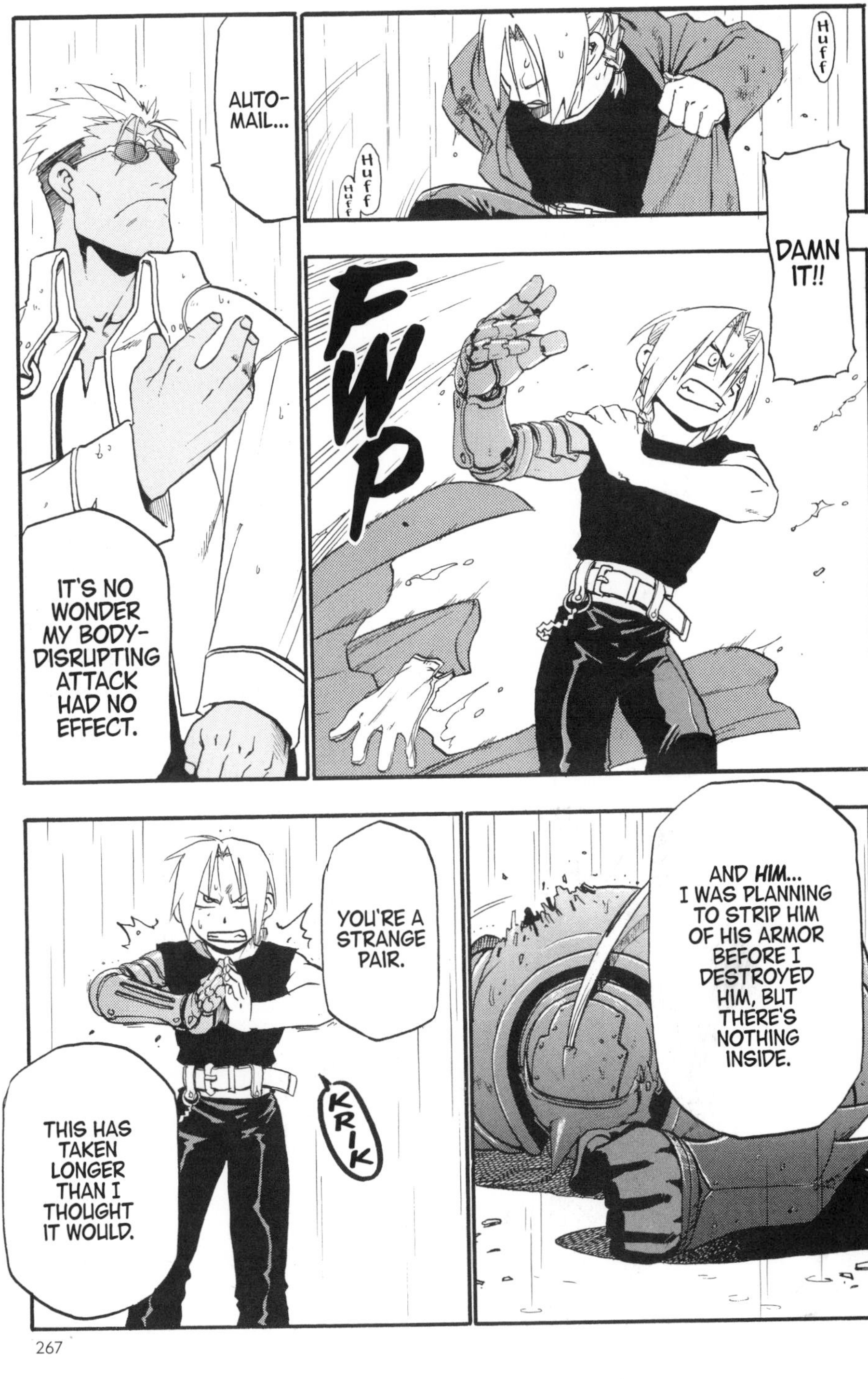
Huff
Huff
Huff
Huff
DAMN IT!!
FWP
AUTO-MAIL...
IT'S NO WONDER MY BODY-DISRUPTING ATTACK HAD NO EFFECT.
AND HIM... I WAS PLANNING TO STRIP HIM OF HIS ARMOR BEFORE I DESTROYED HIM, BUT THERE'S NOTHING INSIDE.
YOU'RE A STRANGE PAIR.
KRIK
THIS HAS TAKEN LONGER THAN I THOUGHT IT WOULD.

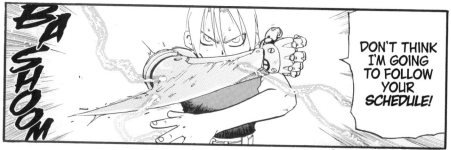

DON'T THINK I'M GOING TO FOLLOW YOUR SCHEDULE!
BASHOOM
NO, EDWARD! YOU HAVE TO RUN...
DON'T BE STUPID! I'M NOT LEAVING WITHOUT YOU!!
HMM...YOU CREATE A TRANSMUTATION CIRCLE BY PUTTING YOUR HANDS TOGETHER AND THEN USE THE POWER THAT FLOWS BETWEEN THEM.
WELL THEN...
KRIK
RRAAAAAAAAAA

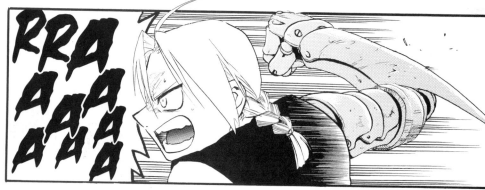

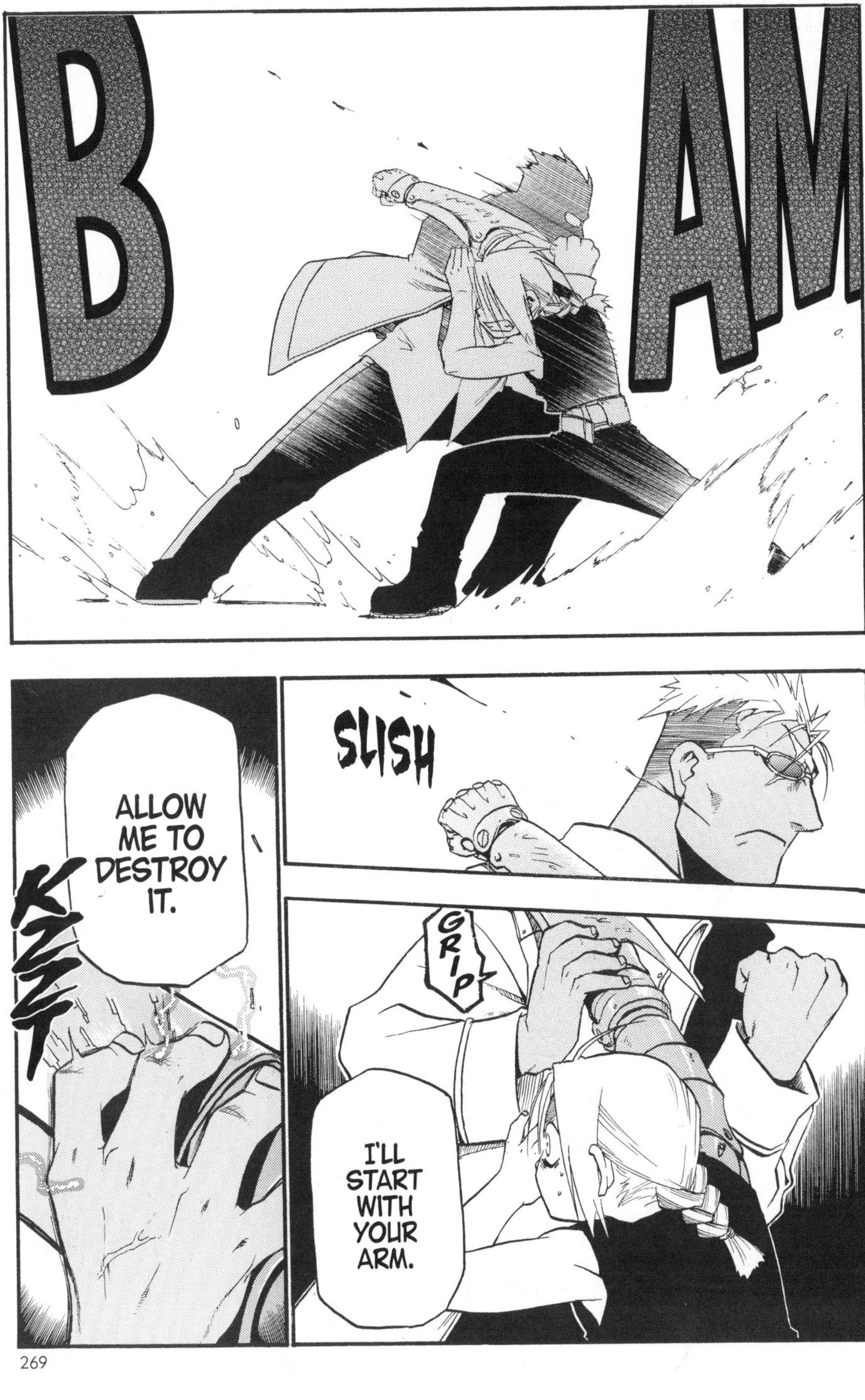
BAM
SLISH
GRIP
I'LL START WITH YOUR ARM.
ALLOW ME TO DESTROY IT.
KZZT

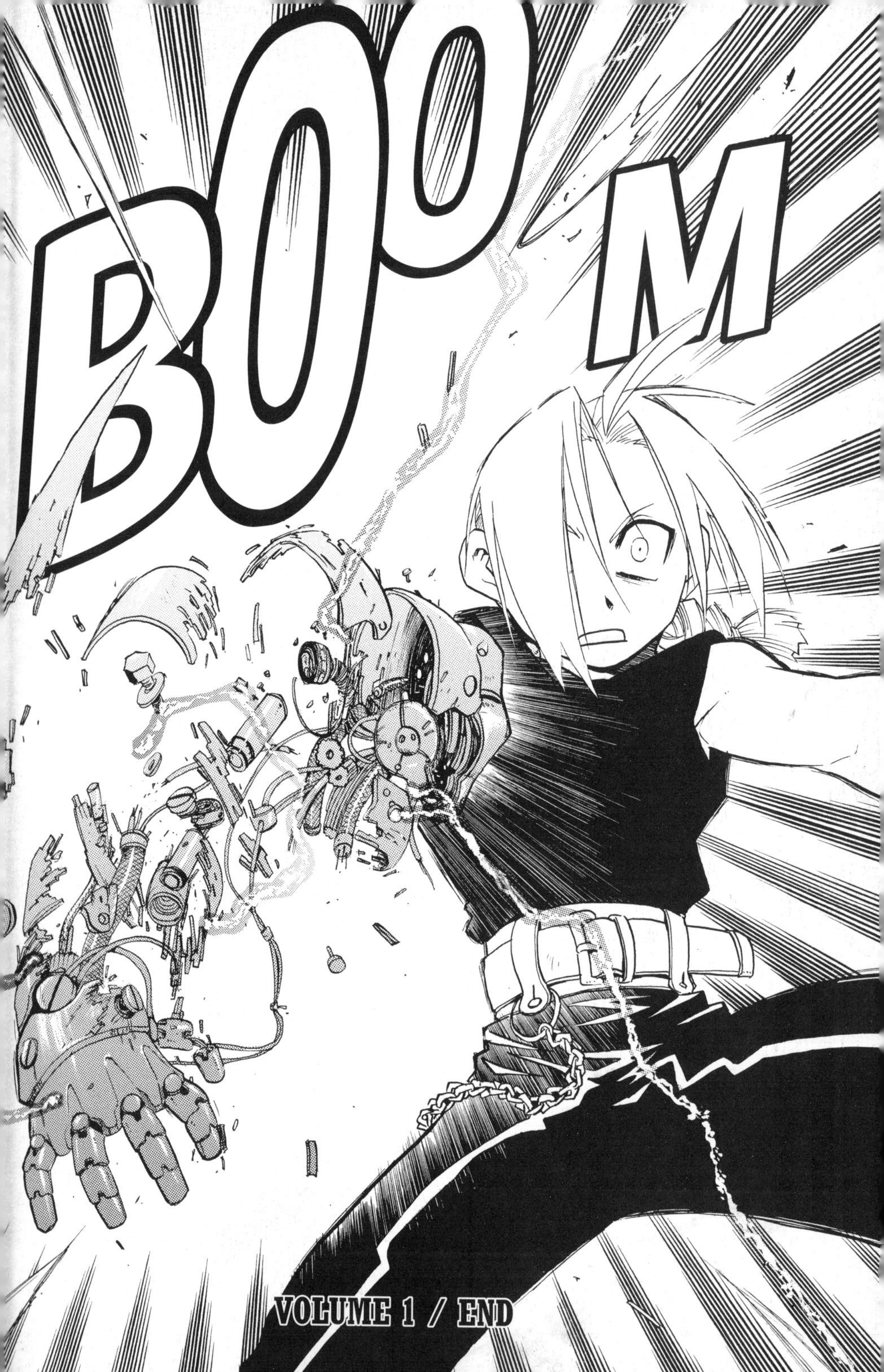
BOOOM

VOLUME 1 / END

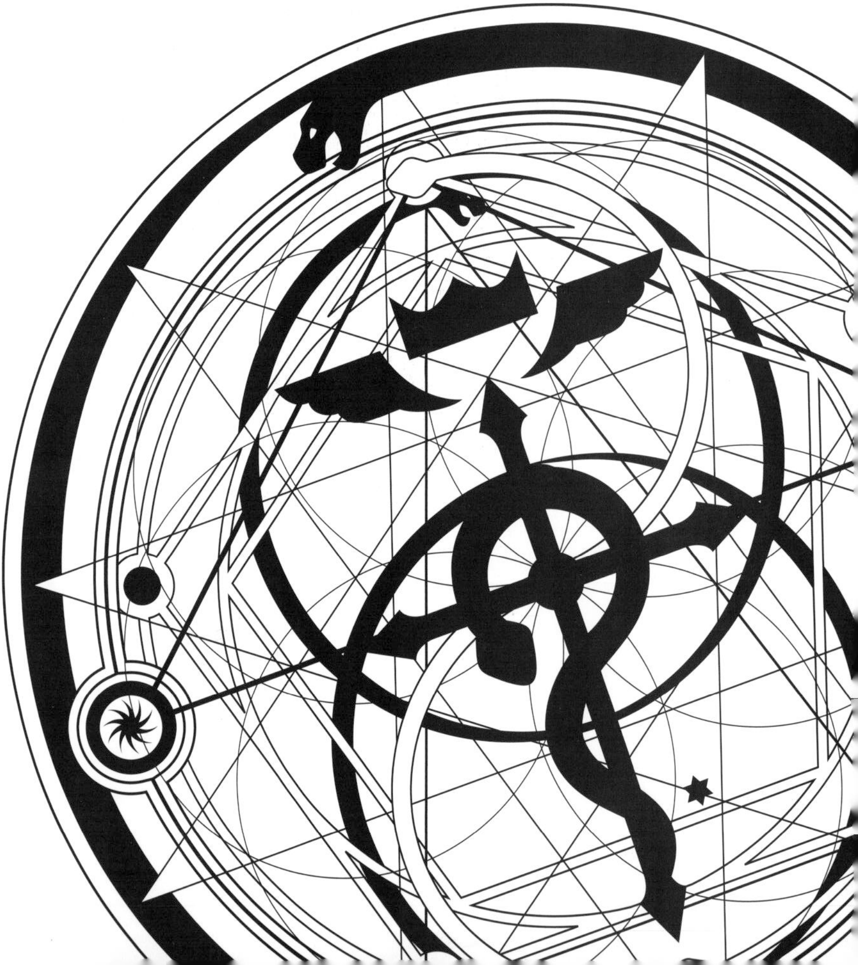

FULLMETAL EDITION

FULLMETAL ALCHEMIST

CONCEPT SKETCHES

01

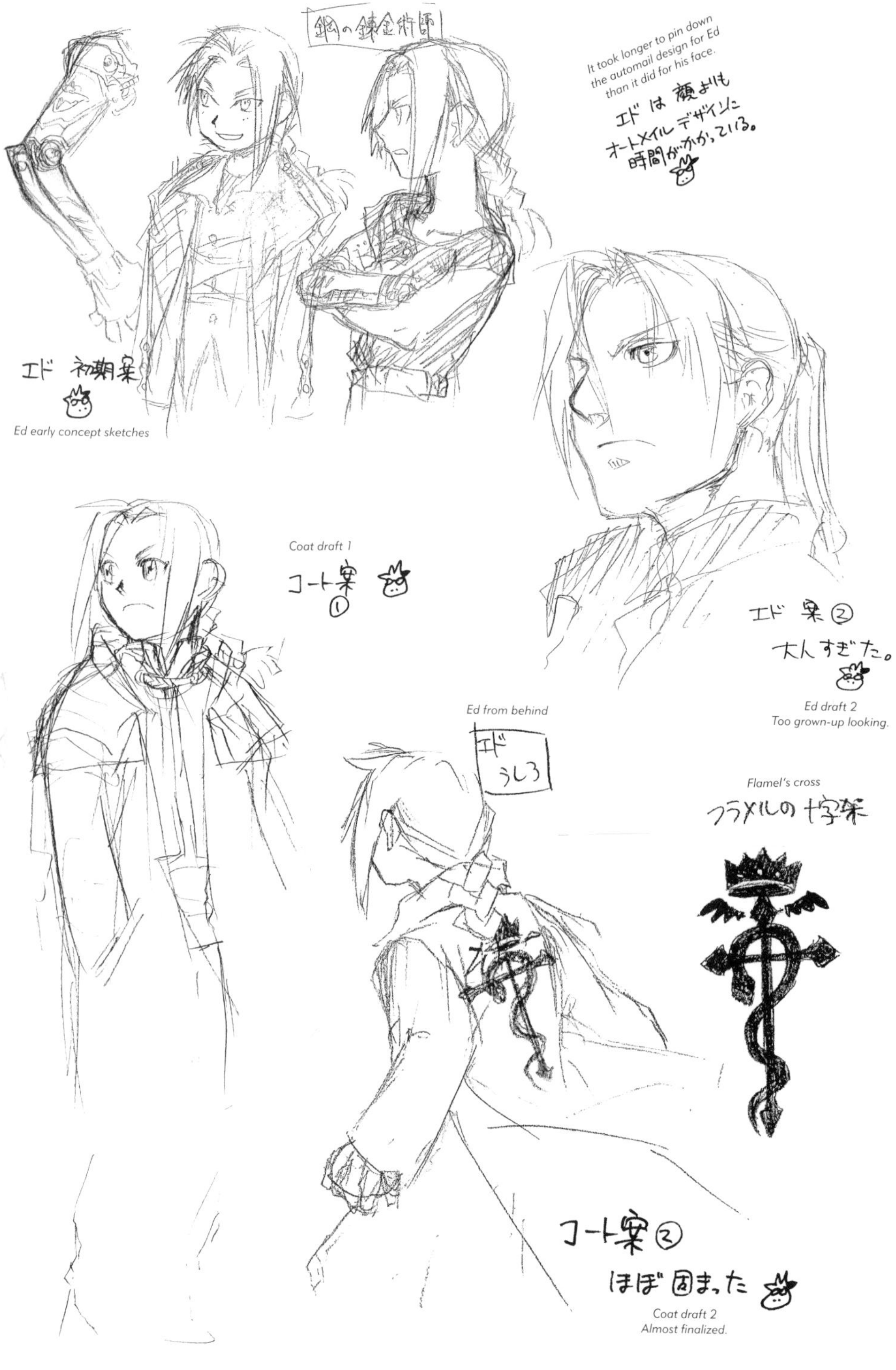
鋼の錬金術師
エドは顔よりも
オートメイルデザインに
時間がかかっている。
エド 初期案
コート案①
エド 案②
大人すぎた。
エド
うしろ
フラメルの十字架
コート案②
ほぼ固まった

Fullmetal Alchemist

It took longer to pin down the automail design for Ed than it did for his face.

Ed early concept sketches

Coat draft 1

Ed draft 2
Too grown-up looking.

Ed from behind

Flamel's cross

Coat draft 2
Almost finalized.

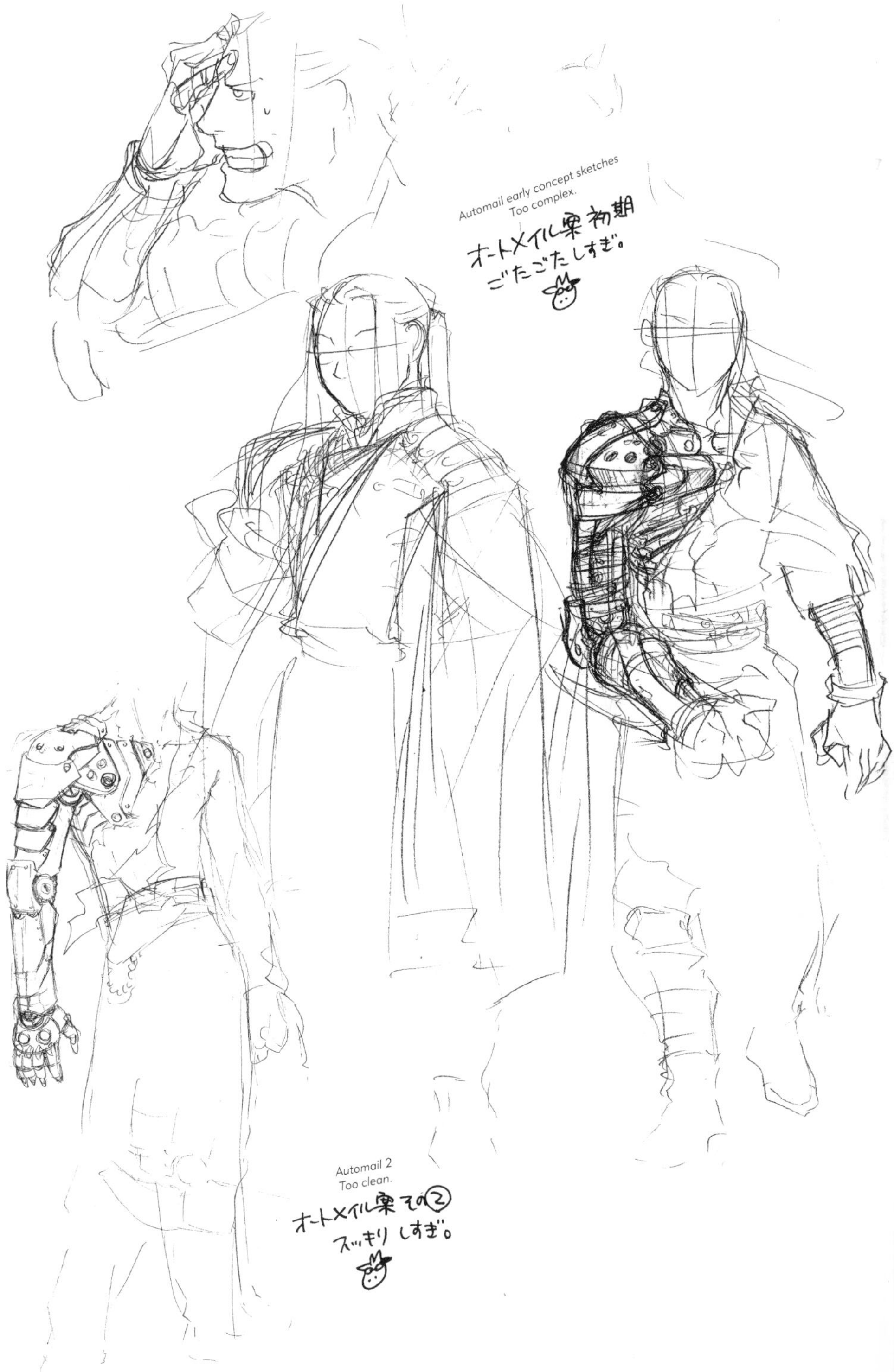
Automail early concept sketches
Too complex.
オートメイル案初期
ごたごたしすぎ。
Automail 2
Too clean.
オートメイル案その②
スッキリしすぎ。

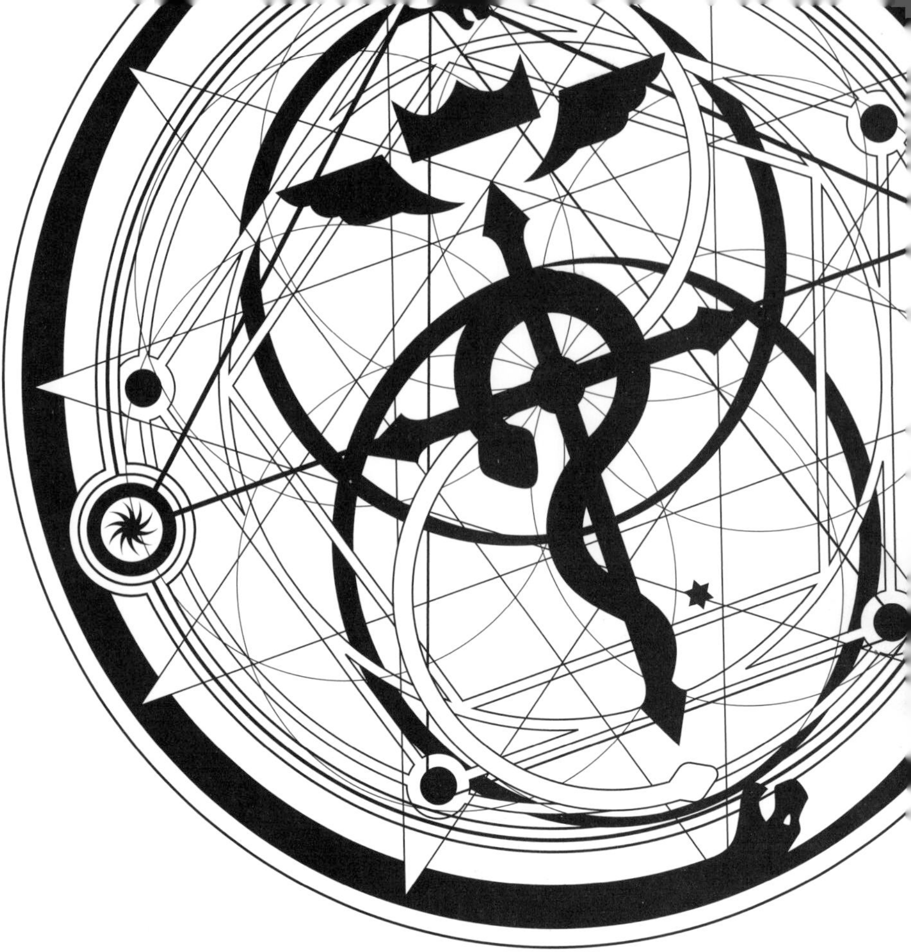

ABOUT THE AUTHOR

Born in Hokkaido, Japan, Hiromu Arakawa first attracted attention in 1999 with her award-winning manga *Stray Dog*. Her series *Fullmetal Alchemist* was serialized from 2001 to 2010 with a story that spanned 27 volumes and became an international critical and commercial success, receiving both the Shogakukan Manga Award and Seiun Award and selling over 70 million copies worldwide. *Fullmetal Alchemist* has been adapted into anime twice, first as *Fullmetal Alchemist* in 2003 and again as *Fullmetal Alchemist: Brotherhood* in 2009. The series has also inspired numerous films, video games and novels.

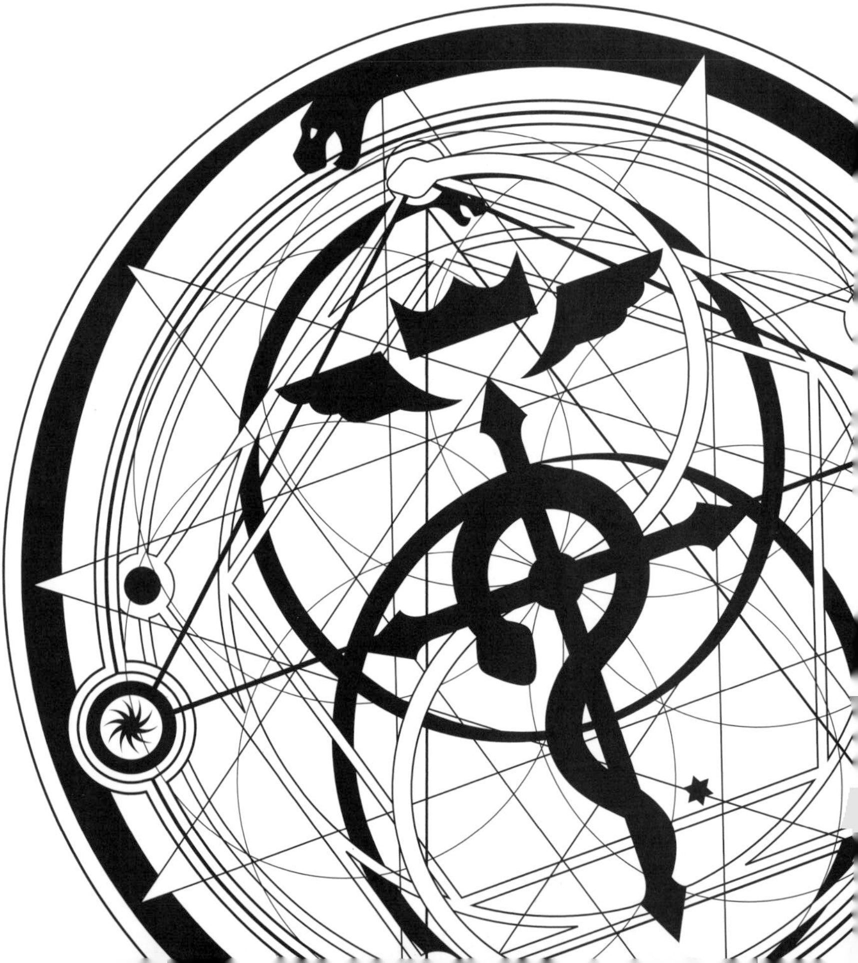

FULLMETAL EDITION

FULLMETAL ALCHEMIST

VOLUME 01

Story and Art by HIROMU ARAKAWA

Translation: AKIRA WATANABE
English Adaptation: JAKE FORBES, EGAN LOO
VIZ Media Edition Editor: JASON THOMPSON
Touch-Up Art & Lettering: STEVE DUTRO
Design: ADAM GRANO
Editor: HOPE DONOVAN

FULLMETAL ALCHEMIST KANZENBAN vol. 1
© 2011 Hiromu Arakawa/SQUARE ENIX CO., LTD.
First published in Japan in 2011 by SQUARE ENIX CO., LTD.
English translation rights arranged with SQUARE ENIX CO.,
LTD. and VIZ Media, LLC

Printed in Canada

Published by VIZ Media, LLC
P.O. Box 77010
San Francisco, CA 94107

10 9 8 7 6 5 4 3 2 1
First printing, May 2018

viz.com

This is the last page.

Fullmetal Alchemist reads right to left.